THE BOOK OF SECRETS

Editor
Marion Buhagiar

BOARDROOM®
CLASSICS

Illustrations: Daniel Pelavin and others.

© 1986, 1987, 1988, 1989, 1990, 1991, 1992, 1993 by Boardroom® Reports, Inc.

Completely Revised Edition
10 9 8 7 6 5 4 3 2

Boardroom Books publishes the advice of expert authorities in many fields. But the use of this material is not a substitute for legal, accounting, or other professional services. Consult a competent professional for answers to your specific questions.

Library of Congress Cataloging in Publication Data Main entry under title:

The Book of Secrets

1. Handbooks, vade-mecums, etc.
2. Life skills—Handbooks, manuals, etc.
I. Buhagiar, Marion.
AG105.G666   1986b   031'.02   86-31050
ISBN 0-88723-059-8

Boardroom® Classics, a division of Boardroom® Reports, Inc.
330 W. 42nd Street, New York, NY 10036

Printed in the United States of America

TABLE OF CONTENTS

The Smart Consumer

In and Around the Home

TABLE OF CONTENTS

You and Your Car

Enjoying Your Leisure

TABLE OF CONTENTS

Your Good Looks

Family Life

TABLE OF CONTENTS

Relationships

Sports and Fitness

TABLE OF CONTENTS

Eating and Dieting

Staying Healthy

Solving Health Problems

TABLE OF CONTENTS

Brain Power

Self Improvement

Communicating Clearly

Kids and College

Career Strategies

Management Skills

Successful Collecting

Smart Investing

TABLE OF CONTENTS

Real Estate Money Makers

Smart Money Management

Financing Retirement

More Insurance for Less

TABLE OF CONTENTS

Tax Strategies

Handling the IRS

Personal Legal Tactics

How to be a bargain shopper

The biggest problem most shoppers have with bargaining is a feeling that nice people don't do it. Before you can negotiate, you have to get over this attitude. Some ammunition:

☐ Bargaining will not turn you into a social outcast. All a shopkeeper sees when you walk in is dollar signs. If you are willing to spend, he will probably be willing to make a deal.

☐ Bargaining is a business transaction. You are not trying to cheat the merchant or get something for nothing. You are trying to agree on a fair price. You expect to negotiate for a house or a car—why not for a refrigerator or a winter coat?

☐ You have a right to bargain, particularly in small stores that don't discount. Department stores, which won't bargain as a rule, mark up prices 100%-150% to cover high overhead costs. Small stores should charge lower prices because their costs are less.

The savvy approach:

☐ Set yourself a price limit for a particular item before you approach the storekeeper.

☐ Be prepared to walk out if he doesn't meet your limit. (You can always change your mind later.)

☐ Make him believe you really won't buy unless he comes down.

☐ Be discreet in your negotiations. If other customers can overhear your dickering, the shop owner must stay firm.

☐ Be respectful of the merchandise. Don't manhandle the goods that you inspect.

☐ Address the salesperson in a polite, friendly manner. Assume that he will want to do his best for you because he is such a nice, helpful person.

☐ Shop at off hours. You will have more luck if business is slow.

☐ Look for unmarked merchandise. If there is no price tag, you are invited to bargain.

Tactics that work:

☐ Negotiate with cash. In a store that takes credit cards, request a discount for paying in cash. (Charging entails overhead costs that the store must absorb.)

☐ Buy in quantity. A customer who is committed to a number of purchases has more bargaining power. When everything is picked out, approach the owner and suggest a total price about 20% less than the actual total.

☐ If you are buying more than one of an item, offer to pay full price on the first one if the owner will give you a break on the other. Or, ask to have an extra, probably small-ticket, item thrown in.

☐ Look for flawed merchandise. This is the only acceptable bargaining point in department stores, but it also can save you money in small shops. If there's a spot, a split seam or a missing button, estimate what it would cost to have the garment fixed commercially, and ask for a discount based on that figure.

☐ Adapt your haggling to the realities of the situation. A true discount house has a low profit margin and depends on volume to make its money. Don't ask for more than 5% off in such a store. A boutique that charges what the traffic will bear has more leeway. Start by asking for 25% off, and dicker from there.

☐ Buy at the end of the season, when new stock is being put out. Offer to buy older goods—at a discount.

☐ Neighborhood stores: Push the local television or appliance dealer to give you a break so you can keep your service business in the community.

Source: Sharon Dunn Greene, co-author of *The Lower East Side Shopping Guide*, Brooklyn, NY.

What goes on sale when

A month-by-month schedule for dedicated bargain hunters:

January

☐ After-Christmas sales.

☐ Appliances.

☐ Baby carriages.

☐ Books.

☐ Carpets and rugs.

☐ China and glassware.

☐ Christmas cards.

☐ Costume jewelry.

☐ Furniture.

☐ Furs.

☐ Lingerie.

☐ Men's overcoats.

- ☐ Pocketbooks.
- ☐ Preinventory sales.
- ☐ Shoes.
- ☐ Toys.
- ☐ White goods (sheets, towels, etc.).

February

- ☐ Air conditioners.
- ☐ Art supplies.
- ☐ Bedding.
- ☐ Cars (used).
- ☐ Curtains.
- ☐ Furniture.
- ☐ Glassware and china.
- ☐ Housewares.
- ☐ Lamps.
- ☐ Men's apparel.
- ☐ Radios, TV sets and phonographs.
- ☐ Silverware.
- ☐ Sportswear and equipment.
- ☐ Storm windows.
- ☐ Toys.

March

- ☐ Boys' and girls' shoes.
- ☐ Garden supplies.
- ☐ Housewares.
- ☐ Ice skates.
- ☐ Infants' clothing.
- ☐ Laundry equipment.
- ☐ Luggage.
- ☐ Ski equipment.

April

- ☐ Fabrics.
- ☐ Hosiery.
- ☐ Lingerie.
- ☐ Painting supplies.
- ☐ Women's shoes.

May

- ☐ Handbags.
- ☐ Housecoats.
- ☐ Household linens.
- ☐ Jewelry.
- ☐ Luggage.
- ☐ Mothers' Day specials.
- ☐ Outdoor furniture.
- ☐ Rugs.
- ☐ Shoes.
- ☐ Sportswear.
- ☐ Tires and auto accessories.
- ☐ TV sets.

June

- ☐ Bedding.
- ☐ Boys' clothing.

- ☐ Fabrics.
- ☐ Fathers' Day specials.
- ☐ Floor coverings.
- ☐ Lingerie, sleepwear and hosiery.
- ☐ Men's clothing.
- ☐ Women's shoes.

July

- ☐ Air conditioners and other appliances.
- ☐ Bathing suits.
- ☐ Children's clothes.
- ☐ Electronic equipment.
- ☐ Fuel.
- ☐ Furniture.
- ☐ Handbags.
- ☐ Lingerie and sleepwear.
- ☐ Luggage.
- ☐ Men's shirts.
- ☐ Men's shoes.
- ☐ Rugs.
- ☐ Sportswear.
- ☐ Summer clothes.
- ☐ Summer sports equipment.

August

- ☐ Back-to-school specials.
- ☐ Bathing suits.
- ☐ Carpeting.
- ☐ Cosmetics.
- ☐ Curtains and drapes.
- ☐ Electric fans and air conditioners.
- ☐ Furniture.
- ☐ Furs.
- ☐ Men's coats.
- ☐ Silver.
- ☐ Tires.
- ☐ White goods.
- ☐ Women's coats.

September

- ☐ Bicycles.
- ☐ Cars (outgoing models).
- ☐ China and glassware.
- ☐ Fabrics.
- ☐ Fall fashions.
- ☐ Garden equipment.
- ☐ Hardware.
- ☐ Lamps.
- ☐ Paints.

October

- ☐ Cars (outgoing models).
- ☐ China and glassware.
- ☐ Fall/winter clothing.
- ☐ Fishing equipment.

- [ ] Furniture.
- [ ] Lingerie and hosiery.
- [ ] Major appliances.
- [ ] School supplies.
- [ ] Silver.
- [ ] Storewide clearances.
- [ ] Women's coats.

November

- [ ] Blankets and quilts.
- [ ] Boys' suits and coats.
- [ ] Cars (used).
- [ ] Lingerie.
- [ ] Major appliances.
- [ ] Men's suits and coats.
- [ ] Shoes.
- [ ] White goods.
- [ ] Winter clothing.

December

- [ ] After-Christmas cards, gifts, toys.
- [ ] Blankets and quilts.
- [ ] Cars (used).
- [ ] Children's clothes.
- [ ] Christmas promotions.
- [ ] Coats and hats.
- [ ] Men's furnishings.
- [ ] Resort and cruise wear.
- [ ] Shoes.

The best factory outlets

Factory outlets are often part of the manufacturer's old warehouse or factory, and furnishings are sparse. Credit and return policies are stricter than in retail stores, and fitting rooms are makeshift at best. However, the money you can save should make up for the lack of customer services.

Guidelines for factory outlets:

- [ ] Go regularly to the outlet store of a manufacturer whose goods you particularly like. If you frequent an outlet, you'll learn the types of goods available and how often they come in.
- [ ] The best buys at a manufacturer's outlet will be its own goods. At a Palm Beach outlet, for example, the resort clothing may be a real bargain—but

other manufacturers' goods on sale there may not be as sharply discounted.

- [ ] Irregulars can be a great buy if the flaw is fixable or unnoticeable. But beware of prepackaged items if you can't open them to check. One pajama leg could be six inches shorter than the other!
- [ ] Always check merchandise for quality. For example, make sure plaids match at seams in skirts and shirts, seam allowances are generous, and the material used in clothing and linens is not flawed.

Top factory outlets:

Clothing

- [ ] *Barbizon Lingerie Factory Outlet,* 20 Enterprise Ave., Secaucus, NJ.
- [ ] *The Company Store,* Factory Outlet Bldg., Rowan St., E. Norwalk, CT.
- [ ] *David Crystal Sales,* 201 N. 13th St., Reading, PA.
- [ ] *Polly Flinders Factory Outlet,* 2700 State Rd. 16, Suite 104, Jacksonville, FL.
- [ ] *Rolane Factory Outlet,* 253 Lee Ave. Extension, Sanford, NC.
- [ ] *Vanity Fair Outlet Store,* 801 Hill Ave., Wyomissing, PA.
- [ ] *Warnaco Outlet Store,* 130 Gregory St., Bridgeport, CT.
- [ ] *The Way Station,* Oak Springs Rd., Rutherfordton, NC.

Home Furnishings & Housewares

- [ ] *Anchor Hocking Kitchen Collection,* 621 N. Memorial Dr., Lancaster, OH.
- [ ] *Dansk Factory Outlets,* 7000 International Dr., Orlando, FL; Route 1, Kittery, ME; junction of routes 202 and 31, Flemington, NJ. There are also other locations. Look in your local telephone book.
- [ ] *Corning Revere Factory Store,* 38 Queshend St., Fall River, MA.
- [ ] *Stonehenge Seconds Shop,* 30 Canfield Rd., Cedar Grove, NJ.

Candy

- [ ] *Russell Stover Candy,* Highway 722, Clarksville, VA.
- [ ] *Wilbur Chocolates' Factory Outlet,* 48 N. Broad St., Lititz, PA.

Shoes

- [ ] *Bally,* 20 Enterprise Ave., Secaucus, NJ.
- [ ] *Bass,* 531 Amherst St., Nashua, NH.

Source: Jean and Jan Bird, authors of *Birds' Guide to Bargain Shopping,* Andrews, McMeel and Parker, Fairway, KS.

Saving at supermarkets

☐ Complete your shopping within half an hour. Why: Customers spend 50 cents a minute after they have been in a supermarket longer than 30 minutes. The almost empty shopping cart invites impulse buying.

Look for:

☐ Generic products. Most popular: Paper goods, canned fruits and vegetables, laundry products and soap, soft drinks, canned soups and canned tuna.

☐ Don't be taken in by advertisements pushing premium paper towels (those that are extra-strong or super-absorbent). For most uses (wiping up small spills or drying your hands), the typical supermarket economy brand probably does the job equally well.

☐ Domestic seltzers. Have no added sodium, and they are less expensive than most imported mineral waters. Insight: Price seldom parallels the taste and quality of various brands of bottled waters. Often the least expensive have the cleanest taste. Basic types: (1) Sparkling mineral water is carbonated water from an underground spring. (2) Seltzer is carbonated tap water. (3) Club soda is also carbonated tap water, usually with mineral salts added.

☐ Buy milk in cardboard containers, not translucent plastic jugs. Reason: When exposed to fluorescent lighting in the supermarket, milk in jugs oxidizes. It develops a flat taste and loses vitamin C.

Source: *Family Practice News.* Tom Grady and Amy Rood, co-authors, *The Household Handbook,* Meadowbrook Press, Deephaven, MN.

How to choose the right checkout line

Successful people play to win. They know the rules, devise plans of attack and follow their plans with discipline, whether it's on the job, in the stock market—or just doing the grocery shopping. To spend less time in the supermarket…

☐ Look for the fastest cashier. Individual speeds can vary by hundreds of rings per hour.

☐ Look for a line with bagger. A checker/bagger team will move a line up to 100% faster than a checker working alone. When the supermarket uses optical scanning equipment, the bagger increases line speed by more than 100%. Note: Two baggers in the same line are barely more helpful than one.

☐ Count the shopping carts in each line. If all else were equal, the line with the fewest carts would be the quickest. But…there are other factors to consider. Look for…

A) Carts that contain many identical items. Two dozen cans of dog food can be checked out faster than a dozen different items. They don't have to be individually scanned or rung into the register.

B) Carts that contain a lot of items. Because each new customer requires a basic amount of set-up time, it's better to stand behind one customer who has 50 items than behind two customers who have 10 items each.

C) Carts that contain a lot of produce. Each item has to be weighed.

D) People with bottles to return. This can take a lot of time.

E) People who look like they're going to cash a check. This too can take a lot of time. Most likely check-cashers: Women who clutch a purse.

Source: David Feldman, author of *How to Win at Just About Everything,* Morrow Quill, William Morrow & Co., 105 Madison Ave., New York 10016.

Shopping for bargains in luxuries

☐ Get to know your neighborhood stores and be known in them. In foodstuffs, ask for what is in season—even for items such as imported cheese.

☐ Visit a new store in the neighborhood promptly. Early customers will be remembered. And new stores generally have the most competitive prices.

☐ Shop at smaller clothing stores where the owner selects merchandise, generally providing better quality fashion at lower prices than department stores.

☐ Select clothing essentials when stock is fresh—even though prices are highest at the start of a season. Fill in with bargains later in the season.

☐ Look into resale shops (better than thrift shops) as a good source for items such as evening gowns, furs, etc.

☐ Look at the fabric, workmanship and country of origin (good ones: Italy, France, West Germany, Ireland, Scandinavian countries) on clothes before trying them on.

☐ When buying appliances, electronic goods or big-ticket items, know exactly what you want when you walk into a store—make, model, options, colors, etc.

☐ Ask the salesperson the price on unmarked goods and then ask for a discount for cash, for travelers checks, for taking the floor model, for carting away the goods right then and there, etc.
Source: *Money,* New York.

If you're thinking of mink

The way to buy the best: Expect to pay $6,000–$12,000 for a top-of-the-line, full length mink coat. You can spend more, but you'll probably be buying a fancy designer label or a prestige store label. If you buy wholesale directly from a furrier, you can find a fine coat for as little as $4,000. Even a long trip to New York City can be justified by the savings. New York City is the wholesale fur capital of the world, and its newspapers are crammed with wholesalers' sale ads during January and February.

☐ A lesser-quality "commercial coat" costs about $2,000. Drawbacks: These coats usually look cheap, hang poorly and wear out within a few years. In the $2,000–$3,500 price range, you're better off with a good mink jacket.

☐ Look for creamy-white skins (inky blue/white skins mean the pelts have been dyed) and dense, silky fur of natural color. (Natural fur is paler on top, while dyed fur is uniform in color throughout.)

☐ Buy a coat roomy enough to accommodate suit jackets or bulky sweaters. A bad fit will stretch the skins and bring on worn spots and rips.
Source: *Personal Investor,* Newport Beach, CA.

How to buy caviar

Tips for getting the best for your money when you buy caviar:

☐ If you want top-of-the-line caviar, buy one of the three grades that come from sturgeon.

☐ Beluga: Biggest grained; black or gray in color; most expensive.

☐ Osetra: Grains almost as big; brown to golden color; somewhat less costly.

☐ Sevruga: Much smaller grains; least expensive of the sturgeon caviars.

☐ The freshest, best caviar is packed with mild salt, labeled Malossol. Also excellent is pressed caviar, which is top-grade but too "ripe" to be packed in whole grains. This kind can be frozen.

☐ Avoid bottom-of-the-line caviar that comes in jars; among other negatives, it is strongly salted.

☐ For good value and flavor, don't overlook red-colored caviar from salmon. Best choice is the smaller-size grains from silver salmon rather than the more common Ketovya or chum salmon caviar, which is often artificially colored.

Buy & enjoy the best cognac

Cognac is a complex liquor from the Cognac region of France. It is made by twice distilling a white-wine base and then placing it in oak casks to age. Different batches are blended to make cognac.

Classification of a cognac is determined by the youngest batch in the blend. (Other parts can be up to 20 years older.) The older the rating, the smoother and better tasting the cognac.

☐ Three Star: Aged 2½ years.

☐ VO (Very Old): Aged 4½ years.

☐ VSOP (Very Superior Old Pale):

This is also aged 4½ years, but the blends are superior to those used in the VO.

☐ XO (Extra Old): Aged 6½ years.

☐ Buy cognac from a reliable producer. This insures quality, since most good producers age their cognacs far beyond what the law requires.

☐ Favorites: Delamain, Hennessy, Remy Martin and Martell.

☐ Drink cognac slowly to appreciate the flavor. Use a medium-sized brandy snifter, and warm the glass in your hand while you sip. Don't warm the glass over a flame, since too much heat will damage the liquor and hide the nuances of its flavor.

Source: Mary Ewing Mulligan, International Wine Center, New York.

Gearing up for auctions

Depending on the kind of auction (country, indoor) and the type of merchandise sought (bric-a-brac, tools, furniture), assemble the appropriate gear. Suggestions:

☐ Cash, travelers checks, credit cards or checkbook. (Be aware that many auctions accept only cash.)

☐ Pens, pencils and notebook.

☐ Pocket calculator.

☐ Rope for tying items to car roof.

☐ Old blankets for cushioning.

☐ Tape measure.

☐ Magnet (for detecting iron and steel under paint or plating).

☐ Folding chair and umbrella (if auction is outdoors).

☐ Picnic lunch (auction food is unpredictable).

How to buy jewelry at auction

Smart jewelry shoppers are buying at auction now. Clearly, "cutting out the middleman" can save shoppers thousands of dollars on just one purchase. Furthermore, many auction diamonds come with Gemological Institute of America (GIA) certificates that show the weight, color and clarity of the stone.

☐ If you're buying contemporary jewelry, where the value of the piece lies almost 100% in the gemstones,

divide the presale estimate by the total weight of the stones.

☐ The size of the stones—separate from their weight—affects prices as well. Example: Two diamond bracelets may have equal total weights, but the bracelet that has fewer and larger stones will be worth more and will sell for more.

☐ In antique jewelry, condition can count far more than design, workmanship or the intrinsic value of the gold and gemstones. Reading the description of the piece in the auction catalog and seeing it are far more important. Words such as repaired, altered, cracked, or later additions can lower the value of the piece drastically.

☐ Buy a 10X jeweler's loupe, which costs less than $25, and carry it with you whenever you're examining jewelry.

☐ Look at the back of the jewelry as well as at the front for alterations. (Example: The front of a brooch may be pink gold, but the pin in back, added later, may be yellow gold. That reduces the value.)

☐ Look for marks of soldering repair. Gold solder, if used carefully, will not alter the value of the piece. Lead solder, which leaves gray marks, can reduce the price by 50%.

☐ Read the catalog carefully for listed imperfections (often printed in italics) such as stone missing, stone cracked, lead solder marks, repaired, enamel worn, later additions, etc.

☐ If the karat of gold is not listed, it's 14K.

Source: Judith H. McQuown writes about antiques and investments and is the author of *Inc. Yourself: How to Profit by Setting Up Your Own Corporation,* Warner Books, New York.

How a Postal Service auction works

A US Postal Service auction is an exciting combination of Las Vegas and a flea market. Anything that can be sent through the mail might turn up at a post office auction. Items typically available: Stereo equipment, TVs, radios, dishes, pots and pans, tools, typewriters, clothing, books, coins.

The Postal Service holds regular auctions of lost, damaged or undeliverable merchandise every two or four months in all major US cities. (The New York City Postal Service has an auction once a month.) Call the main post office in your city for time and date.

Basic ground rules:

☐ Items are sold by "lot." Similar articles are often grouped together, such as a dozen jeans, or four typewriters, or three radios. The items must be purchased together, so bring friends who might want to share a lot with you.

☐ Lots are displayed the day before the auction for viewing. Lots are in compartments or bins that are covered with netting. Nothing (except clothing on hangers) can be handled or tested. Many compartments are badly lighted, so bring a flashlight to get a good look.

☐ All lots are listed by number on a mimeographed sheet given out on the inspection day. They are auctioned off by number, and each has a minimum acceptable bid listed next to it (never less than $10). But the minimum bid is no indication of how much the lot will sell for. Some go for 10 or more times the minimum bid listed.

☐ All lots are sold "as is." There is no guarantee as to quality or quantity. The Postal Service tries to mark items it recognizes as damaged. Remember: All sales are final.

☐ You must pay a nominal fee the day before the auction to obtain a paddle for bidding. Each paddle has a number on it, which the auctioneer recognizes as your bidding number. To bid, hold up your paddle. The cost of the paddle will be refunded if you don't buy anything. Otherwise, it is applied to the purchase price.

☐ You must deposit 50% of the purchase price in cash or certified check 30 minutes after buying a lot. Bring several certified checks in different amounts so you won't have to come up with large sums of cash.

☐ Merchandise must be picked up a day or two after the auction. Bring your own container.

The bidding at Postal Service auctions is extremely unpredictable and quirky. Some lots are overbid, while others go for the minimum bid, often with no obvious relations to actual value. A set of inexpensive plastic dishes may fetch more than the retail price, while a much more valuable and lovely set of china dishes goes for less than the plastic ones.

Sample prices at recent auctions:

☐ Sanyo cassette deck: $100.

☐ Sansui amplifier: $100.

☐ Brother electronic typewriter: $120.

☐ Oriental jewelry chest (very large and ornate): $85.

☐ Hamilton beach blender and hand mixer: $28.

☐ Persian lamb jacket with mink-trimmed sleeves (brand new): $40.

How to bid:

☐ Go through the list of lots carefully while looking at the merchandise, and write down your maximum bids. During the actual auction, bidding is confusingly fast, with prices rapidly increasing by $2 at a time as bidders drop out. Listen carefully to the bidding, and don't exceed your maximum.

☐ Sit in the back of the room so you can see who is bidding against you.

☐ Take someone knowledgeable to the visual inspection, especially if you're planning to bid on something like electronic equipment. Find out how much that particular piece is worth, and calculate your top bid by including the cost of repair.

☐ If you can't find someone who is knowledgeable, stick to bidding on lots that you can see are in good shape. Best bets: Dishes, cutlery, pots and pans, hand tools, furniture, clothing sold by the garment. (Much of the clothing is sold in huge bins and can't be inspected.)

How to track down an out-of-print book

The economics of modern publishing dictate that all but the top best-sellers go out of print very fast, and bookstores cannot afford to stock a full selection of older titles.

To find a book:

☐ Track down the correct title, the author's name and, if possible, the publisher and copyright date. (Your local library can be of assistance.)

☐ Check local used-book or antiquarian booksellers. If you are near New York City, the publishing capital of the country, visit several famous used-book stores: Donan Books, Inc., 253 E. 53rd St., New York 10022; Gotham Book Mart, 41 W. 47th St., New York 10036; Strand Book Store, 828 Broadway, New York 10003.

☐ Contact a book finder. Most of these services do not charge a search fee, but make their profit through the markup on books they do locate and place. Fees can run $5 per book. Most services will quote you the price of a book they have located before they buy it for you. Their ads appear in book review sections of major papers and in other book-related publications. They are listed under "Books, retail" in the *Yellow Pages*. Their success rate in ferreting out old titles is close to 40%.

☐ Tracking down a book can take four to eight weeks because the book finder will check his bookstore sources and then advertise for your title in *A.B. Bookman's Weekly*, a used-book dealers' exchange paper.

☐ Don't approach more than one bookfinder at a time with the same request because several ads for the same book will jack up its price.

A high-tech home

Americans in the 1990s take some pretty startling technology and conveniences for granted. To have a state-of-the-art house, you would already have to have the following:

In the kitchen:
☐ Self-cleaning oven.
☐ Separate turbo (forced air) oven.
☐ Food processor.
☐ Self-defrosting refrigerator/freezer.
☐ Automatic icemaker that keeps the ice bin full.
☐ Family-sized espresso coffee maker.
☐ Microwave oven.

In the family room:
☐ Giant (45-inch, or more, diagonal) television screen.
☐ Cable or satellite dish connection for multiple TV channels.
☐ Video recorders that will tape your favorite shows for a week or even more on a single setting.

☐ Portable video cameras for home movies.
☐ Stereo television.
☐ Audio systems.
☐ Electronic games.

In the bedroom:
☐ Remote-control lights and television controls.
☐ Panic button for alarm system that alerts police.

In the bathroom:
☐ Power shower for neck and shoulder massage.
☐ Water-pressured gum massager.
☐ Towel warmer.
☐ Overhead sun and/or heat lamp.
☐ Wireless telephone that's safe for bathtub use.

Outdoors:
☐ Electric remote-control garage door opener.
☐ Automatic sprinkler system for the lawn.

For the whole house:
☐ Electronic burglar-alarm system.
☐ Touch-tone telephones with optional services (intercom, call forwarding to another number when you are away, automatic dialing, incoming call interrupt feature, etc.).
☐ Automatic timers for turning on lights when you are gone, at different settings each day.
☐ Six-setting automatic thermostat control.
☐ Centralized air conditioning.
☐ Centralized humidifier.
☐ Centralized air purifier.
☐ Fuel-efficient burners for furnaces.
☐ Telephone-answering machine with remote call-in capability.
☐ Home computer for managing family finances, storing information, accessing information, banking by telephone, and word processing and printing.
☐ Solar-powered hot-water heater.

Where to buy a computer

☐ Full-service computer dealers. Generally sell at list price, but offer the most assistance in selecting hardware and software. Help customers set up their systems and give the most attention to post-sale glitches.

☐ Department stores. Moderate discounts and erratic service.

☐ Discount stores and mail-order houses. Best prices but little or no service or support. (You may not need their support, however, if your system's manufacturer provides a toll-free hotline.)

☐ Buy only from an authorized dealer. That guarantees certain standards of sales and service and insures future availability of compatible hardware.

Source: *New York* Magazine, New York.

Extending the life of your personal computer

☐ Better performance, better-looking work, fewer costly visits from $100/hour repairmen and longer life for expensive equipment are the key rewards of conscientious maintenance of computers and their peripherals.

Follow these rules:

☐ Place computer equipment away from open windows and heavy machinery.

☐ Always cover equipment that's not in use.

☐ Don't smoke around your computer.

☐ Forbid snacks and drinks near the computer.

☐ Use antistatic mats or sprays to avoid harmful static charges.

☐ Clean disk drive heads, printer plates and type elements once a week or as frequently as your dealer recommends.

☐ Keep floppy disks in their envelopes and out of sunlight.

☐ Never use a paper clip or staple on a disk.

☐ Never write on the disk jacket with anything but a felt-tip pen.

Source: Lewis A. Whitaker, executive vice president, PerfectData, Inc., Chatsworth, CA.

How to get optimum performance from your videotapes

☐ Do not rewind after use. Wait until just before playing them the next time. This flexes the tape and sweeps away any lingering humidity.

☐ Store tapes in their boxes to keep dust and dirt from reaching them.

☐ Never touch the tape itself. Oil and acid from the fingers do damage.

☐ Avoid abrupt changes in temperature. When bringing a tape into a heated room from the outside, allow half an hour for the tape to adjust to the change before playing it.

☐ Never keep a tape in pause or still frame for more than a minute. The video heads moving back and forth will wear down that section of tape.

Buying a TV monitor (instead of a regular TV)

The next time you go shopping for a new color television set, ask to see the monitor-receivers, as well as standard models. This new generation of video gear can give you a better television picture and make life with video recorders, video players and computers simpler and more effective.

Features to look for in monitors:

☐ Comb filter. This circuit, long a part of professional studio equipment, gives a sharper picture with truer colors.

☐ Separate video inputs for external program sources. By hooking up your VCR or disk player directly, rather than through the antennae terminals, you get a less distorted picture. You can also connect and disconnect outside components more easily.

☐ Separate audio output. This lets you play the sound portion of a video program through your stereo system.

☐ Multiple outlet for a stereo decoder. This will allow you to enjoy stereo-TV broadcasts when they begin in the US.

What to expect in your next TV

The newest wave in home entertainment technology is digital television. A set of five silicon microchips replaces the hundreds of thousands of transistors in conventional televisions, making several new features possible.

☐ Picture within a picture. Watch two images at once, with the second picture inset in a corner of the screen. Sound is switchable from image to image.

☐ Zoom action. Focus on—and "blow up"—a detail of the picture.

☐ Freeze frame. Halt the action to study it (good for sports enthusiasts, but you will miss the continuing action).

☐ Better reception. Broadcast signals will be reproduced unadulterated.

☐ Automatic self-checking system. This makes adjustments for a sharper image as the picture tube ages.

Source: Allan Schlosser, director of public affairs, Electronic Industries Association, Washington, DC.

How to set up a home theater

Today's technology makes it possible to set up your own home theater. All you need is a projection TV, a stereo system…and a room.

The Room

☐ Size. Make sure the electronic equipment you buy fits the room you want to use.

Example: A rear-projection TV* with 50-inch-screen (measured diagonally) is about 28 inches deep. Such sets require large rooms—at least 15 ft. by 15 ft.

☐ Seating. The picture on rear-projection TVs loses brightness and clarity as the angle increases from the *center* of the picture. Best: Sit as close to center as possible.

In a square room, position the TV in the corner. In a long, narrow room—about 1½ times longer than wide—have the set at the short end. This will give you more room for choice seats. Note: Long, narrow rooms also make your audio system sound better.

☐ Lighting. A media room needs lighting that can be adjusted to at least three different levels—*dim* for watching TV, *bright* for reading, *regular* for other times.

Windows will need good blinds or curtains that can be closed during the day.

☐ Acoustics. To prevent echoes, pad the rear wall with sound-absorbing material—drapes or curtains work well.

Designing the rest of the room is really a matter of trial and error. Too *hard* a room (polished wood, no carpets, etc.) or too *soft* a room (wall-to-wall carpeting, lots of upholstered furniture, etc.) will create an unpleasant listening environment.

Equipment

☐ TV. Unlike rear-screen projection TVs, some projection TVs actually project their picture on a screen or a white wall—like a movie projector. The picture size can be adjusted anywhere up to 20 feet (measured diagonally).

The projection unit can be raised off the floor and situated in the back of the room, like in a theater, or hung on the ceiling.

Although all these TVs really need for a screen is a blank white wall, the flat surface will result in distortion around the picture's edges. Better: A curved screen that either stands alone or is mounted on the wall.

These screens are quite ugly and dominate the room. But they can be built into custom-designed furniture that hides the screen when it's not in use.

☐ Speakers. For full, theater-like sound, use two pairs of speakers, one for the front, one for the rear of the room.

☐ Front speakers. Buy a pair with good performance at the low, middle and high frequencies. If the room is extremely large, you may need an additional speaker front and center. Note: Speakers should be placed at least two feet from the wall. Space-saving option: Build the speakers into the wall, with only the front grille showing.

☐ Rear speakers. Because these are used mostly to supply movie sound effects (such as the airplane roar in *Top Gun*), they don't have to be the highest quality. They should, however, offer good performance at the middle frequencies. Exception: High-end audio systems that offer *surround sound* require higher-quality rear speakers.

☐ Bass option. Some speakers, especially smaller models and built-ins, will sound much better if you add a separate bass speaker. The speaker can be placed virtually anywhere in the room. Some look like—and can actually double as—coffee tables.

Source: Architect and designer Ronald Kahn of Kahn Associates, 857 Broadway, New York 10003. He specializes in high-end audio/video installations for executive boardrooms and private residences.

*Rear-projection TVs look *much* like traditional TVs…only everything, including the screen is much larger. They're the most popular type of projection TV sold today. *Recommended:* Models by Pioneer and Mitsubishi.

Where to buy hard-to-find recordings by mail

☐ *Musical Heritage Society*, 1710 Highway 35, Ocean, NJ 07712. The best place to buy rare classical recordings.

☐ *Time-Life Records*, 777 Duke St., Alexandria, VA 22314. Selected masters in the classical and pop fields. Best: A collection of Mozart in 30 boxes and the Giants of Jazz series.

☐ *Smithsonian Records*, 64 Depot Rd., Colchester, VT 05446. Reconstruction of old musical comedies, vintage jazz and other historical treasures.

☐ *Book-of-the-Month Records*, Camp Hill, PA 17012. Everything from great modern classical masters to songs of the Depression taken from old 78-RPM records.

Buying a piano

The best sound comes from a grand piano, but new ones are very costly.

☐ Consider smaller spinet, console, or studio upright. These provide satisfactory sound for most people and are less expensive.

☐ If considering the purchase of a used piano, look for one ten years old or less. Don't buy one more than twenty years old.

☐ Have a piano tuner check out a used piano.

☐ Test a piano before purchasing: Play it by running up and down the scales. High notes should be clean and crisp, low notes should resonate.

☐ Get your piano tuned at least every six months, more frequently if it's new.

☐ Keep it in a cool, dry room, away from direct sunlight and not close to radiators, air conditioners, or vents. Put it at least four inches away from the wall to allow the sound to get out.

☐ Get a professional cleaning every three years. Don't do it yourself.

☐ Avoid getting mothballs or spray inside the piano.

Which dishwasher is right for you?

Today's dishwashers not only save valuable time and energy but they can even conserve water. And—the dishwasher's powerful jet sprays and piping hot water actually clean and sterilize dishes, glassware, even baby bottles, better than you could if you simply washed by hand.

The average dishwasher uses between nine and 12 gallons of water to complete its various washing and rinsing cycles. So, if your dishwashing method involves a tub of sudsy water and a spray rinse, you're probably using close to the same amount to clean a full load.

If, however, you wash under a stream of running water, the dishwasher actually saves on water consumption. Of course, running the dishwasher when it is only half full or rinsing items before loading—a step which really isn't necessary—narrows the margin of savings.

With nearly a dozen brands available, and each brand offering two or more models, finding the right dishwasher is a chore. Before you go shopping, consider all the possible features and group them into categories as follows:

☐ Must have.

☐ Desirable but not essential.

☐ Unnecessary or unsuited to your purposes.

☐ Price range: With dishwashers ranging in price from approximately $300 to $700—and up—you'll need to know just how many of the "desirable but not essential" features you can actually afford.

A basic machine usually includes features such as dial controls to select the cycle: Normal, light or rinse/hold. There are also push-button controls for start, cancel and other basic options.

Separate "rinse" and "dry" options are usually included on the dial and can be accessed manually.

Other basic functions include an energy-saving, "no-heat" dry option and safety interlock system that stops the motor (to prevent water from splashing) when the door is opened.

Most of the lower-priced machines have two-level washing systems. That means that water sprays from two directions within the tank. Slightly higher-priced dishwashers generally have three-level washing action, giving superior cleaning power but reducing available rack space somewhat.

Middle-of-the-line models have specialty cycles, including heavy cleaning (for pots and pans), delicate cleaning (for china and crystal), and/or a sani-cycle, which boosts the water temperature above 140°F during the final rinse for more effective sterilization. It is useful if you keep your home's water heater thermostat set below that level. Some models also come with all push-button controls or electronic touchpad sensors with digital readouts.

Top-of-the-line models usually have superior noise insulation for the quietest possible operation, electronic displays showing everything from the time left in the cycle to the latest warning messages signaling blockages, overfillings or other malfunctions. Some even have a hidden touchpad that locks controls to avoid tampering by children.

Other Features

☐ Energy saver wash—uses lower temperature water—usually 120°F—to save energy.

☐ Drying fan—speeds drying time of dishes and supplements the standard heat element used to dry dishes.

☐ Time delay option lets you preset the machine to run when you're out or in the late evening/early morning hours to take advantage of off-peak electricity rates.

☐ Extra large, multi-position racks, adjustable dividers, extra silverware trays (some located on the door to save space in the rack) and special nylon finishes to protect dishware.

A Word About Portables

If you rent, rather than own, your home, or if your kitchen space is so limited that losing the cabinet space necessary to install the dishwasher would be a major hardship, consider buying a portable dishwasher.

These minis connect to your kitchen faucet and roll away when not in use. Some have practical butcher-block wooden or wood-look top work surfaces with faucet adapters that let you use the faucet while the machine is running. Many are convertible to built-in units if you decide on permanent installation later.

Source: Donna J. Pintek, a home-appliance researcher/writer.

Determining if wooden furniture is well made

Before buying a piece of wooden furniture, answer these questions:

☐ Is the piece stable when you gently push down on a top corner or press against the side?

☐ Is the back panel inset and attached with screws (not nails)?

☐ Do drawers and doors fit well and move smoothly?

☐ Are corners of drawers joined with dovetail joints?

☐ Do long shelves have center braces?

☐ Are table leaves well supported?

☐ Are hinges strong and well secured?

Source: *Better Homes and Gardens,* Des Moines, IA.

A good desk chair

A good desk chair can add as much as 40 minutes to your workday because you won't develop fatigue-induced problems...back strain, leg cramps, etc. Important: Don't sit for longer than 60 minutes at a time or you will tire your body.

What to look for in a chair:

☐ Seat: Made of porous material to let body heat dissipate. Opt for a hard one, slightly contoured to the buttocks (soft cushions roll up around and put pressure on joints).

☐ Front of seat: Rounded or padded so it doesn't cut off circulation in your legs.

☐ Backrest: Extends the width of the chair. Conforms to your spine, and supports the lower and middle back. Straight at the shoulder level to prevent neck strain. Small of the back should fit snugly into the chair back.

☐ Height: Your feet should rest flat on the floor. Otherwise circulation to your feet is slowed. This also takes some of your body weight off your lower back. Be sure height is adjustable.

☐ Arm supports: Firm, softly padded, at least two inches wide.

☐ Swivelability: This enables you to face your work at all times. You'll avoid eyestrain from moving your eyes back and forth.

☐ Look for back- and position-adjustable chairs that let you move forward, tilt backward, sit upright for posture changes that rest and relax you if you're sitting for hours at a time.

Source: *Do It at Your Desk: An Office Worker's Guide to Fitness and Health*, Tilden Press, Washington, DC.

Test of good carpeting

☐ Insist on density. Closely packed surface yarns and tightly woven backing make for carpets that wear and look good longer. Bend a piece of the carpet backward. If a lot of backing is visible through the pile, go for a higher quality.

☐ Avoid soft plush textures when covering moderate-to-heavy traffic areas.

☐ Invest in good padding. It absorbs shocks, lengthens carpet life and creates a more comfortable surface.

☐ If cost is a factor, compromise on the amount or size of carpet, not on the quality. Or choose lesser qualities for low-traffic areas.

Source: *Better Homes and Gardens*, Des Moines, IA.

Caring for down

Down is almost spongelike in its ability to absorb moisture, oils and dirt, its worst enemies. But cleaning is hard on down and even harder on its owner. Some maintenance tips for staving off cleanings:

☐ Sponge off the shell fabric, as soon as possible after spotting, with mild soap and water. Spray clean garments with silicone water repellent (such as Scotchguard or Zepel) yourself. Professional waterproofing is a dip that soaks the down. (Nylon shells will not take silicone spray or dip.)

☐ Enclose comforters in removable sheet casings that can be washed frequently.

☐ Let garments air-dry away from steam pipes, sun or other heat sources before putting them in the closet. (Or put them in a large drier at low heat with a clean sneaker.)

☐ Patch tears, rips or holes in the shell with the pressure-sensitive tapes sold in sporting-goods stores until you can make a permanent repair with a fine needle and thread. Or have a professional make a "hot spot" repair.

☐ Hang vertically channeled coats upside down occasionally to redistribute the down.

☐ Store clean down flat or loosely folded. Wrap it in a breathable covering such as a sheet to protect it from dust, light and rodents.

To wash down:

☐ Care labels frequently recommend washing. (Gore-Tex, for example, is destroyed by dry cleaning.)

☐ Smaller items can be easily washed in a front-loading, tumble-type machine. Empty the pockets and close all the zippers, snaps and Velcro tabs. Run the washer on medium cycle with warm water. Use half the amount of nonphosphorated soap or detergent recommended. Rinse several times to be sure the soap is all out.

☐ Never use a top-loading agitator machine. It will take apart seams, fray internal edges and diminish the life of the garment by 75%.

☐ For larger items, use the bathtub. Dissolve mild soap or detergent in warm water first. Then submerge the jacket or coat completely. Let it soak no more than 15 minutes. Let the water drain out without disturbing the article, and rinse several times until the water runs clear. Do not wring out. Compress the down item to remove the excess water. Then hang the garment over a rack or several lines to dry. Be extra careful with comforters or you will tear the baffling, which is irreplaceable.

To dry down:

☐ Air-drying can take several days even in perfect weather. Be patient, and turn the article often.

☐ Home driers are good only for small items such as vests and children's jackets. Larger items don't have room to fluff properly. Hot driers can melt nylon zippers and even some fabrics.

☐ Best: Commercial dryer with a low heat cycle. Add a couple of clean sneakers (laces removed) or clean tennis balls and a large towel to break up the wet down clumps. Take plenty of change: The process requires several hours.

To dry clean down:

☐ The best solvent for cleaning is a non-chlorinated petroleum product that is banned from most city cleaning establishments because of its flammability. Two companies* specialize in this preferred type of cleaning and take care of customers through United Parcel Service. Both also handle repairs and restylings.

☐ Conventional dry cleaning, which is harder on the product, necessitates careful airing afterward to allow toxic fumes to evaporate.

*Down East, New York; Down Depot, San Francisco.

Recognizing quality in clothes

To take advantage of sales, discount designer stores or consignment shops, look for the details that signal first-class workmanship, label or no label.

☐ Stripes and plaids that are carefully matched at the seams.

☐ Finished seam edges on fabrics that fray easily (linen, etc.).

☐ Generous seams of one-half inch or more.

☐ Buttons made of mother-of-pearl, wood or brass.

☐ Neat, well-spaced buttonholes that fit the buttons tightly.

☐ Felt backing on wool collars to retain the shape.

☐ Ample, even hems.

☐ Straight, even stitching in colors that match the fabric.

☐ Good-quality linings that are not attached all around. (Loose linings wear better.)

Source: Viki Audette, author of *Dress Better for Less,* Meadowbrook Press, Deephaven, MI.

How to care for leather clothes

Leather and suede garments need the same careful treatment as furs. Otherwise, you may lose them.

☐ Buy leather garments a little bigger than you need, because they can never be enlarged. This is particularly important in women's trousers.

☐ Be aware that leather and suede may shrink in cleaning.

☐ Avoid wearing your leather garment in the rain. If the garment does become wet, dry it away from heat.

☐ Use a dry sponge on leather occasionally to remove the surface dust.

☐ Wear a scarf inside your neck to prevent oil stains from your skin.

☐ Don't store the garment in a plastic bag. Put dust covers over the shoulders.

☐ Never put perfume on a suede or leather garment. Even putting it on the lining is risky.

☐ Don't pin jewelry or flowers on leather garments. Pinholes do not come out.

☐ Store leathers as you do furs, in a cool spot. Better yet, store your leathers at the same time you store your furs.

Source: Ralph Sherman, president of Leathercraft Process, New York.

What dry cleaners don't tell you

The dry cleaning process is not mysterious but it is highly technical. After marking and sorting your clothes on the basis of color and material type, the cleaner puts them into a dry cleaning machine. This operates like a washing machine except that it uses special solvents instead of water. After the clothes have gone through the dryer, the operator removes stains from them.

A good dry cleaner will use just the right chemical to remove a stain without damaging the fabric. Pressing correctly is next—also a matter of skill. With some fabrics, the garment is put on a form and steamed from the inside to preserve the finish. After pressing, the clothing is bagged.

What to look for:

☐ Suits should be put on shoulder shapers.

☐ Fancy dresses and gowns should be on torso dummies.

☐ Blouses and shirts should be stuffed with tissue paper at the shoulders.

☐ Except for pants and plain skirts, each piece should be bagged separately.

Taking precautions:

☐ Examine your clothes before leaving them with the cleaner. Point out stains and ask whether or not you can expect their removal. For best results, tell the cleaner what caused the stain.

☐ Don't try to remove stains yourself. You may only make them worse. Bring stained clothing to the cleaner as soon as possible. Old stains are harder to remove.

☐ Bring in together all parts of a suit to be cleaned. Colors may undergo subtle change in the dry cleaning process.

☐ Check all pockets and remove everything. A pen left in a pocket can ruin the garment.

☐ Read care labels carefully. Many clothes cannot be dry cleaned at all. Do not dry clean clothing with printed lettering or with rubber, nylon or plastic parts. If in doubt, ask your dry cleaner.

☐ Make sure your dry cleaner is insured if you intend to store a large amount of clothing during the winter or summer months.

☐ Don't wash clothes and then bring them to the cleaner's for pressing. The saving is minimal.

☐ Ask if the dry cleaner will make minor repairs as part of the cleaning cost. Many cleaners offer such service free.

☐ Don't request same-day service unless absolutely necessary. Rushed cleaners do a sloppy job.

☐ French cleaning means special handling for a fragile garment. The term used to be applied to all dry cleaning, since the process originated in France. Now it indicates shorter dry-cleaning cycles or even hand cleaning. Best: Alert your dry cleaner to the term French cleaning on the label.

35mm SLR camera basics

The 35 mm single-lens reflex (SLR) camera is the most versatile, all-around-useful photo tool ever invented. You can fit virtually any lens to the camera body and through its unique viewing/focusing system, see the exact picture that's going to appear on the film.

Currently on the market: 15 SLR "systems" comprising over 60 camera models. Keep in mind that although you may be buying a camera at the moment, you are investing in a system down the line. Try to anticipate your photographic growth, and consider the overall system in making your choice.

☐ Standard features: Self-timers, exposure information in the viewfinder, exposure compensation ("backlight") switches, "dedicated" autoflash, optional autowinders, autofocus (AF).

☐ More exotic features: Switchable spot or averaging metering systems, super-high shutter speeds, built-in autowinders, and multiple exposure capability.

☐ Shutter speeds in excess of 1/1000 second are of dubious value at best...virtually unnecessary and notoriously inaccurate.

☐ A built-in autowinder saves bulk and weight—if you really want that feature.

☐ Multiple exposure is a function that will go unused by most photographers.

Available AE systems include:

☐ Aperture-priority auto exposure (a-p): You set the aperture (f-stop) and the camera sets the shutter speed. (This is the easiest to manufacture.)

☐ Shutter-priority (s-p) auto exposure: You set the shutter speed and the camera sets the f-stop. (Most photographers feel this is the better system.)

☐ Programmed (prog.) auto exposure: Relatively new. The camera sets an "optimum" combination of speed and f-stop.

☐ Multi-programmed auto exposure: The latest. It's designed to circumvent the problems of a general-purpose program. Consists of two programs...one favoring fast shutter speeds for stopping motion, the other favoring small f-stops for increased depth of field—with or without a "normal" program. (Multi-programming begins to defeat the goal of simplicity, but can certainly be of use.)

☐ Through-the-lens autoflash (TTL flash): Reads light off the film plane and shuts off the flash at just the right instant. This excellent feature greatly simplifies all flash photography.

Hot weather hazards to camera gear

Humidity is the summer photographer's nemesis. Here are some defensive maneuvers:

☐ Don't open new film until you are ready to load and shoot. (It is packed in low-humidity conditions in sealed packets.)

☐ Have exposed film processed as soon as possible. Don't leave it in the camera for long periods—it may stick.

☐ Use slow advance and rewind to avoid moisture static.

☐ Keep equipment dry with towels or warm (not hot) air from a hair dryer.

☐ Store film and gear with silica gel to absorb excess moisture. (Cans of silica gel have an indicator that turns pink when the gel is damp. They can be reused after drying in the oven until the indicator is blue.)

Source: *Modern Photography*, New York.

How to buy sunglasses

☐ Be sure they are large enough.

☐ Make sure no light enters around the edges.

☐ For best performance, select frames that curve back toward the temple.

☐ If you choose plastic lenses, remember that they scratch easily. So clean them with a soft cloth, not a silicone tissue.

☐ If your main concern is preventing glare, buy greenish grays, neutral grays and browns.

☐ Avoid other colors, which absorb wavelengths and can upset color balance.

☐ Always try on sunglasses before buying. The world should appear in true colors, but not as bright.

☐ If you plan to wear sunglasses near water much of the time, get polarized lenses, which block glare reflected off the water. You can have an old pair of prescription lenses tinted to a desired polarized density.

☐ Best all-round sunglass choice: Sunsensor lenses that adjust from dark to light.

Picking the right running shoes

Running shoes do not need to be broken in. They should feel good the moment you try them on. Look for:

☐ A heel counter that holds your heel in place and keeps it from rolling in and out.

☐ Flexibility in the forefoot area so the shoe bends easily with your foot. (If the shoe is stiff, your leg and foot muscles will have to work too hard.)

☐ An arch support to keep the foot stable and minimize rolling inside.

☐ A fairly wide base for stability and balance. The bottom of the heel, for example, should be as wide as the top of the shoe.

☐ Cushioning that compresses easily. (Several different materials are used now.) The midsole area absorbs the most shock and should have the greatest amount of padding. However, the heel (which, particularly for women, should be three-quarters of an inch higher than the sole) needs padding, too. Too much causes fatigue, and too little causes bruising.

☐ Start with the manufacturers' least costly shoes first. Try them on. Then keep trying up the price range until you find the one that feels best. Try on running shoes with the same kind of thick socks you will be wearing with them.

☐ Adequate toe room (at least one-half inch of clearance). Running shoes, particularly in women's sizes, run small, and women often need a half-size or whole-size larger running shoe than street shoe.

Source: Gary Muhrcke, proprietor of the Super Runner's Shop, New York.

How to buy ski boots

First rule: If a boot is not comfortable in the store, it will be worse on the slopes.

☐ Toes should be able to wiggle while the heel, instep and ball of the foot are effectively, but not painfully, immobilized.

☐ Buy in a shop with an experienced shop technician who can expand the shell and modify the footbed and heel wedge.

THE SMART CONSUMER

☐ Check forward flex. When you bend your foot, you should feel no pressure points on your shin or upper ankle.

☐ Look for a high boot with a soft forward flex. Low, stiff boots concentrate loads just above the ankle, which can be painful for the occasional skier.

How to buy the right bike

For city use, make sure the bike has:

☐ Fenders to keep yourself clean. A rack on the back for a newspaper or side racks for your briefcase.

☐ Rubber pedals. (They are less durable than steel, but preserve your leather soles.)

☐ A topnotch lock. (The U-bolt models by Kryptonite and Citadel are among the best ones.)

☐ Touring bikes are right for most people. They have a longer wheel base for a "Cadillac" ride.

☐ With racing bikes, you feel the road more, but you get better handling and efficiency.

☐ Consider a Japanese brand. A European bike of equivalent quality will cost at least 20% more. (Although there are 30 different Japanese makes, they're all produced by one of two corporate families, so they're about the same.)

☐ For more comfort, look for new anatomically designed saddles. These seats, made of leather with foam padding, feature two ridges to support the pelvic bones, with a valley in between to avoid pinching.

☐ Buy a low-impact, plastic shell helmet. In a typical biking accident, this will protect the head better than a high-impact motorcycle helmet.

☐ Padded bike gloves make good shock absorbers. Sheepskin bike shorts provide added comfort. Bike jerseys with rear pockets will keep your keys from digging into your leg with each push of the pedal.

☐ Female bike riders should point the seat slightly downwards to avoid irritating the genital area. Men should point the seat upward, to avoid problems such as irritation of the urinary tract and injury to the testes.

☐ Sizing up a new bike. Straddle the frame with your feet flat on the floor. There should be an inch of clearance between your crotch and the top tube. If you can't find an exact fit: Buy the next smaller size, then adjust seat and handlebar height. A frame that's too big can't be adjusted.

Sources: Charles McCorkell, owner, Bicycle Habitat, New York, *Physicians and Sports Medicine,* and *How to Select and Use Outdoor Equipment,* HP Books, Tucson, AZ.

Best family camping tents

☐ Allow about 25 square feet of floor space for each adult and half that for each child. For a family of four: At least 80 square feet.

☐ Best: An umbrella tent. It folds up neatly to fit into a car trunk. And it weighs only 24-40 pounds. Best material: Nylon.

☐ Make sure tent provides good cross-ventilation. Look for openings with sturdy mesh to keep out insects, windows that close during a storm.

☐ Seams should be double-stitched with 8-10 stitches per inch. Look for lap-felled construction (the material folded back on itself for extra strength and waterproofing). Good tents have extra stitching at points of stress.

☐ Before taking the tent on a trip, set it up in the yard and douse it with a hose. Check for leaks (particularly at the seams).

17

Choosing a sleeping bag: Down vs. polyester

Although waterfowl down still offers the best warmth-to-weight performance as padding, the newer, lightweight, polyester-filled bags are preferred by many campers.

Take into consideration that:

☐ Down is worthless when wet. It takes hours to dry and must be refluffed before re-use.

☐ Polyester keeps two thirds of its insulating capacity when wet. It absorbs very little moisture, and dries much faster.

☐ Down bags must be dry-cleaned.

☐ Polyester bags are machine washable.

☐ Down is a magnet for dust, the real culprit for those who think they are allergic to down.

☐ Polyester is nonallergenic and doesn't collect dust.

☐ Down is much more expensive. Most polyester-filled bags cost about half as much.

The best board games

☐ *Trivial Pursuit*. Still "the" game for trivia buffs, despite the 100-plus copycat games now on the market. It's easy to learn and can be played by almost any number of people. Supplements to the original 6,000 questions are introduced periodically, to keep the game lively and fresh.

☐ *Scrabble*. The ultimate word game. Scrabble (or "Scrabble Brand Cross-word Puzzles," as it is officially known) is a subtly complex game that rewards both knowledge of words and strategic thought. Like many other boardgame classics, it has engendered clubs and tournaments and even a newsletter. Now it's also available in a more congenial *Duplicate Scrabble* version.

☐ *Diplomacy*. Players make and break treaties in an attempt to conquer Europe on the eve of World War I.

☐ *Clue*. The well-known murder-mystery game.

☐ *Big Boggle*. A more challenging version of the original *Boggle*. This is the best word game for large groups.

Whoever comes up with the greatest number of words wins.

☐ *Civilization*. Each player tries to forge a primitive nomadic tribe into the most advanced civilization on earth. Along the way, decisions concerning philosophy, science and other hallmarks of civilization make the difference between success and failure. Requires six or seven players—and up to 10 hours. Best idea: Start at noontime on a rainy Saturday and play all day.

☐ *Ambush!* A single player can enjoy this game, a simulation of World War II army patrols. A little complicated—most war games are—but certainly well worth the effort.

☐ *Cosmic Encounter.* Fast-paced, funny game suitable for family play. Games seldom last more than 90 minutes.

☐ *Blockhead.* One of the few games that can be played almost equally well by adults and children. Tests dexterity, coordination and judgment.

☐ *Shogi.* Unlike chess, draws are virtually impossible. There is also a handicap system that allows experienced players and novices to play exciting games with one another.

☐ *Sherlock Holmes, Consulting Detective.* Really a board game without a board—there's no dice-rolling and no tokens to move about.

☐ *Discretion.* An alternative to the very popular (and overrated) *Monopoly.* To be successful, players are forced to borrow money—from one another or even from dastardly loan sharks. This complicates matters and keeps more players in the thick of things for a longer time than is usually possible with Monopoly.

Source: R. Wayne Schmittberger, senior editor, *Games*, New York.

Choosing a long-distance telephone service

Guidelines to help make the decision easier:

☐ Choose a service that offers the cheapest rates for your calling pattern. (Analyze your last year's telephone bills to see where you called, when you called, and how long you talked to each location.) If you are a heavy long-distance phoner, a company's minimum monthly charge won't hurt you. If you make few long-distance calls, however, the minimum charge might be more than your average telephone bill.

☐ Some companies also have minimum monthly usage requirements and/or volume discounts. Again, choose according to your needs. If you make only a few short calls a month you'll be hard pressed to justify the minimum. If you have high long-distance bills, a volume discount may offer big savings.

☐ Consider whether a company charges by distance or according to its service abilities in the areas you call most frequently. If you tend to call distant or hard-to-reach places, a "cheap" service with fewer connections may end up costing you more.

☐ Rounding off the number of minutes per call can add as much as 10% to your phone bill, especially if you make a lot of shorter calls. Check to see if the company you are considering rounds to the minute or to the tenth of a minute.

☐ Test each long-distance carrier that you consider for line clarity and ease of connection. There is still a big difference among services.

Source: Robert Krughoff, author of *The Complete Guide to Lower Phone Costs*, Consumers' Checkbook, Washington, DC.

Testing your water

If you have your own water from a well or other source, you should check its purity. The old-fashioned tests for biological impurities are not enough.

☐ The basic tests for natural contaminants and for trihalomethanes are a first priority.

☐ The test for trihalomethanes will also pick up common industrial pollutants such as benzine.

☐ If you have a shallow well in a heavily agricultural area, consider tests for pesticides.

☐ If you buy a new house that was recently treated for termites and it has a well, you should test the water for traces of chlorodane.

☐ If untreated sewage is a problem in your area, order tests for biological pollutants.

☐ If you are near an industrial complex, you might want to check out chemical waste products in your water.

☐ If the first analysis shows nothing to be alarmed about, wait a year and test again. If the results are the same, you can rest easy for another 10 years unless, of course, the environment of the house changes radically.

Taking delivery

☐ Before accepting your car from the dealer, allow him enough time to "prepare" the car. Before you buy, find out what the dealer's preparation includes. Engine tune-up? Emission checks? Installation of optional equipment and a test drive? Some automobile dealers charge extra for every step of the preparation.

☐ Inspect the car yourself. Check paint and body moldings. Examine the car in daylight. Look for imperfections and mismatched colors. The car may have been damaged in transit and repainted.

☐ Compare the list of options on your bill of sale with those actually on the car. Be sure they are the options you ordered and not inferior substitutes.

☐ Examine doors, latches and windows to see that they are operating properly. Inspect tires for cuts and bulges. Look at the interior finish. Test the heater, the radio and the air conditioner.

☐ During the first week of ownership, test drive the car under as many conditions as possible. If the car does not perform satisfactorily, then you will have a better chance of getting the car dealer to make adjustments than if you wait a month or two before complaining.

Ways to cut the cost of moving

☐ Schedule the move between October and May, or around the middle of the month, the moving companies' slack periods. Better and faster service can save as much as 10%–15% of cost.

☐ Reduce poundage involved in the move by selling or giving away unneeded items. (Give to charity and keep receipts for later tax deductions).

☐ Collect refunds due from local utilities before leaving.

☐ Arrive at the new location before the van does to avoid charge for waiting time.

☐ Have enough money to pay the exact amount of the estimate plus 10%. That's the maximum customers can be required to pay before goods will be released. Payment must be made in cash, or in certified or traveler's check. A personal check may not be accepted. Get a receipt.

☐ Useful Interstate Commerce Commission publications include: *Household Guides to Accurate Weights; Arranging for Transportation of Small Shipments; People on the Move;* and *Lost or Damaged Household Goods.*

Source: *How to Move Your Family Successfully,* H.P. Books, Tucson.

How to complain effectively

Basic rule when dealing with defective merchandise:

Save receipts, warranties, and all other papers. Then:

☐ Have your facts straight before you act. Be clear about dates, prices, payments and the exact nature of the problem.

☐ Meet with the salesperson or store manager. Describe the problem. Give him copies of the relevant documents. Then ask for a replacement or other compensation. Be polite but firm.

☐ Be specific about what you want done—repair, replacement or refund.

☐ In response to whatever excuse the merchant uses, repeat your demand like a broken record.

☐ Give reasonable deadlines for action you expect to be taken. (A week for store personnel to look into a problem, for example.) Deadlines move the action along.

☐ Write to the manager, going over the points made in the conversation. Include in the letter copies of the sales slips as well as a statement of intention to refer the matter to the Better Business Bureau, a consumer agency, or the manager's superior.

☐ Send copies of receipts. Keep the originals for your records. File copies of all correspondence and notes (with dates) on any telephone dealings. Those records may be the pivotal factor if negotiations are prolonged or you must take your complaint elsewhere.

☐ Be businesslike in your attitude and make it clear you expect a businesslike response.

☐ Find out where you can go if the seller fails to make good, and indicate your intention to follow through. Government agencies, such as a state attorney general's office, may need the very kind of evidence that your case provides to move against chronic offenders. Licensing boards or regulatory bodies are good bets for complaints against banks, insurance companies or professionals.

☐ If that fails, write directly to the president of the company, *not* the customer-relations department. Manufacturers of products are listed in the *Thomas Registry.* Names of executives and addresses of companies are in *Standard & Poor's Register of Corporations.* You can find both these books at the public library.

☐ Recount the facts and the demand for compensation. Include copies of paperwork. Make sure to send a carbon to the store's local manager.

☐ As a last resort, call a consumer agency. State consumer offices are generally in the attorney-general's office. There are 140 Better Business Bureaus in the country and more than 100 consumer hotlines. Complete listings of hot lines are available from Call for Action, Inc., 575 Lexington Avenue, New York 10022.

Additional recourse:

☐ Consumer action centers sponsored by local newspapers and radio and television stations often get swift results.

☐ Small claims court. If you can put a monetary value on your loss, you may get a judgment by suing in small claims court. Collecting can be a problem (you must take the initiative yourself), but the law is on your side and the psychological benefits are enormous.

☐ Trade associations can be effective with their member organizations but not with outside companies.

Source: Nancy Kramer, co-author with Stephen A. Newman of *Getting What You Deserve: A Handbook for the Assertive Consumer,* Doubleday, New York.

How to change your mind after buying from door-to-door salespeople

Impulse buys made from door-to-door salespeople or at houseware parties need not be binding. Under Federal Trade Commission rules, you have three business days to reconsider at-home purchases of $25 or more.

What to do:

☐ When you buy something from a door-to-door salesperson, always ask for two copies of a dated cancellation form that shows the date of sale and a dated contract with the seller's name and address. The contract should specify your right to cancel.

☐ If you wish to cancel, sign and date one copy of the cancellation form and keep the second copy. Send the cancellation to the company by registered mail (receipt requested).

☐ You can expect the seller to act within 10 days. Their obligations: To return any signed papers, down payment and trade-in. To arrange for pickup or shipping of any goods. (Sellers pay shipping.)

☐ You must make the merchandise available for pickup. If no pickup is made within 20 days of your dated cancellation notice, the goods are yours.

☐ If you agree to ship the goods back and then fail to do so, or if you fail to make the goods available for pickup, you may be held to the original contract.

☐ Be aware that the same rules apply at a hotel, restaurant or any other location off the seller's normal business premises. They do not apply to sales by mail or phone, or sales of real estate, insurance, securities or emergency home repairs.

Protect yourself against hospital billing errors

According to the New York Life Insurance Company, which has been auditing hospital bills for the past three years, the average hospital bill contains $600 worth of erroneous charges.

Typical mistake: Because of a clerical error, a $100 electrocardiogram is entered onto your bill as a $1,000 charge. Since you may not know the typical cost of an EKG, the error goes undetected.

Major mistakes:

☐ Respiratory therapy. Equipment, such as oxygen tanks and breathing masks, isn't credited when it's discontinued. Sometimes it's not even removed promptly from the room.

☐ Pharmacy charges. Credit isn't given for drugs that were returned, or unused drugs are not returned.

☐ Lab tests. Cancellations of tests aren't noted.

☐ Central supply items. Hospital staff or nurses may run out of something and borrow it from another patient. They intend to give credit or return the item, but often they don't get around to it.

What to do:

☐ Keep track of the most basic things, such as how many times your blood was drawn. Suggestion: If you're able, jot down what happens daily. Note: If the patient is too sick to keep track of services rendered, a family member should try to keep track of the charges.

☐ Ask questions. Ask the doctor to be specific about tests. If he orders X-rays, ask him what type of X-rays. If he doesn't answer the question to your satisfaction, ask the nurse. The newer generation of doctors is more willing to involve the patient in his own care.

☐ Insist on an itemized bill, not just a summary of charges.

☐ Check room and board charges. Count the days you were in the hospital and in what kind of room. Are you being charged for a private room, even though you were in a semiprivate? Some hospitals have different semiprivate rates for two-bed and four-bed rooms. Check your rate.

☐ Review the charges for TV rental and phone.

☐ Be equally careful with doctor bills. Often these bills are made out by the doctor's assistant, who may not be sure of what was done. Most common errors: Charges for services in the doctor's office, such as a chest X-ray or an injection, that weren't actually performed. Charges for routine hospital physician visits on days that the doctor was not in attendance.

Source: Janice Spillane, manager of cost containment in the group insurance department of New York Life Insurance Co., New York.

How to buy a good man's shirt

When choosing a man's shirt, look for these signs of quality:

☐ Soft tissue-paper packaging (no cardboard).

☐ A well-set collar finished with small, flat stitches.

☐ 16-18 threads per inch in a moderately priced shirt and 22-26 threads per inch in a very good shirt.

☐ Cross-stitched pearl or bone buttons.

☐ Smooth, supple collar fusing (proving that it has not been glued to the material inside and will not flop after laundering.

☐ Removable collar tabs.

Source: *Personal Style* by James Wagenvoord, Holt, Rinehart & Winston, New York.

How to save your fax

Fax copies start to fade after about 20 days and may become completely illegible within two years. If placed near a sunny window, they may fade out in a week. Solution: Always photocopy important fax documents.

How to buy a used computer

When buying a used PC, be particularly wary of:

☐ Keys that stick.

☐ Poor image quality.

☐ Unusual noises from the disk drive.

What you should do before buying the computer:

☐ Get permission to run a continuous 24-hour test. Use everyday software for testing.

☐ Try to copy files.

☐ Test all peripheral devices and ports.

☐ Send a message over the phone lines with a modem.

☐ Send files to a printer.

If the computer has problems, they'll usually show up during these tests.

Source: Alexander Randall, president, Boston Computer Exchange.

What your home says about you

☐ Many people with new money yearn for perfection more than do people with old money.

☐ The biggest giveaway of status anxiety is a place that looks perfect. In the homes of people with new money, everything looks fresh, new, and absolutely, immovably in place. And the newly rich give their children perfect bedrooms with every conceivable toy and gadget, thinking those should keep them content and out of the living room.

☐ The old elite don't look around and get upset about a worn rug or a shabby sofa. Those items are family heirlooms.

☐ People who save the living room for special occasions are terribly conscious of how expensive and irreplaceable everything in it is.

☐ The lower-middle-class woman who keeps her house shiny clean is saying that if she can't have the finest furnishings, at least she can have a clean house. Often her children aren't allowed in her living room.

Are Men Taking More Interest In Decorating These Days?

☐ Older men want a nice home, but they still usually want their wives to handle it. Women still dominate.

☐ Even in the younger generation, decorators say that with their client couples the woman is in charge in 90% of situations.

☐ Men rarely want live plants—nothing that ties them down or needs to be nurtured. And they always want their trophies and paperbacks in the living room, which decorators resist.

☐ Most men's priorities are a comfortable bed and chair, a lamp and a popcorn machine.

☐ Men who do care a lot about their homes get embarrassed because people say to them, "You'd make a great wife," or assume they're gay. When they buy sheets, for instance, they buy stripes, even if they like flowers, because that's what they're expected to buy.

Source: Joan Kron, author of *Home-Psych, the Social Psychology of Home Decoration*, Clarkson Potter, New York.

Instant revenge against obscene phone caller

Keep a referee's whistle handy to respond with a shrill, earsplitting blast right into the speaker of your telephone.

Home appraisal basics

Retain only an appraiser with formal appraisal education and references… pay an appraiser an hourly rate or a contract price—fees based on a percentage of value, or a contingency fee, are unethical…make sure the appraiser will be willing to defend his/her work in court, if necessary…ask for a formal, written report.

Source: Velma J. Miller, Certified Appraiser of Personal Property in Beaverton, Michigan, writing in *AARP Bulletin*, 3200 E. Carson, Lakewood, California 90712.

Better housecleaning

Establish a halfway house for those items (clothing, books, papers, etc.) that you haven't used in years but can't bear to part with. How it works: Pack everything into cartons, marking the boxes with a date two years from now, and store it all away. After two years, review contents.

Source: *365 Ways to Save Time* by time-management consultant Lucy H. Hedrick, Hearst Books, 1350 Avenue of the Americas, New York 10019.

Burglary prevention

Do:

☐ Secure all windows and doors.

☐ Leave drapes open to a normal position.

☐ Engrave your Social Security number on all valuables that can be removed from the house.

☐ Arrange to have the lawn mowed and the newspapers and mail rerouted or stopped when you go on vacation.

☐ Trim shrubbery to eliminate hiding spots for prowlers.

☐ Leave your car lights on until you have opened the garage door.

☐ Have a house key ready when you arrive home.

☐ Instruct family members about these security precautions and procedures.

Don't:

☐ Let the telephone go unanswered or give any inviting information over the phone, such as the fact that you are not at home during the day.

☐ Advertise valuables by making them easily visible through your windows.

☐ Leave a key outside the house.

☐ Leave notes on doors.

☐ Leave a porch or front foyer light on. It advertises that you are probably not home.

☐ Leave a ladder outside.

☐ Enter your home if anything appears suspicious. Call the police from a neighbor's telephone. Don't lose your life trying to save items that can be replaced.

Source: Vertronix, manufacturer of electric burglar-detection systems, Larchmont, NY.

Warning signs burglars fear

If a burglar sees warning signs, no matter how outlandish, on your house, he will think twice before breaking in. These signs should be handwritten, in large, clear print, on six-inch by eight-inch cards posted above each doorknob. Don't put them on the street or in your yard where passersby can see them. You don't want to give a burglar a reason to case your place and find out they are not true. Make up your own wording. Just be sure the signs look fresh and new. Some suggestions:

☐ Danger: Extremely vicious, barkless German Dobermans. In his nervous frame of mind, a burglar probably isn't going to wonder if there is such a thing. He won't want to take the chance.

☐ Knock all you want. We don't answer the door. Most burglars check to see if anyone's home before breaking in. About 95% of those questioned said they'd pass up a house with that sign.

☐ Carpenter: Please do not enter through this door. My son's three rattlesnakes have gotten out of the cage, and we've closed them off in this room until he returns. Sorry for this inconvenience.

☐ Attack dogs trained and sold here. Again, 95% of those questioned said they'd pass up a house with that sign. Have one engraved, and post it on your front door (so it can't be seen from the street).

☐ Leave extremely large bones and two-foot wide dog dishes near all entrances. A person up to no good will think a very large dog lives there.

How burglars say they break in

Some burglar-survey results:

☐ 75% were more likely to go through windows than doors. (Sliding glass doors are easier to open than wooden ones.) Remedy: Storm windows. No one surveyed would bother with them at all.

☐ 85% cased out a house before hitting it. Recommended: If you see a stranger hanging around, call the police.

☐ Only 20% picked locks or tried to pick them. It takes too much skill. There are so many faster ways into a house.

☐ 63% cut the phone lines before entering. Remedy: A sign saying that the police will be notified automatically if the phone lines are cut.

☐ 65% said that a large, unfriendly dog would scare them away. Most frightening: Dobermans.

☐ 80% looked in garage windows to see if a homeowner's car was there. Remedy: Cover your garage windows.

☐ 50% said that neighborhood security guards didn't deter them.

☐ 72% made their entrance from the back.

☐ 56% continued to burglarize if they were already inside when they realized people were home sleeping.

Choosing the right lock

There are two major components to a truly thief-resistant lock system: Strong, tamperproof basic hardware and a key that is impossible to duplicate without your knowledge and permission.

Assuming that the main access door to your house or apartment is structurally sound and hinged on the outside, the standard mechanism for keeping it securely closed is an interlocking deadbolt latch. What makes the latch burglarproof is the outside lock that controls it and the plate that protects the lock.

☐ Current best cylinder and plate: The Abloy disklock. Instead of pins, which can be picked, it has rotating discs like the tumblers on a bank vault door.

☐ Next best locks: The Fichet, Medeco, Bodyguard and Miwa systems.

Add-on security devices:

Steel gates for windows near fire escapes or at ground level (gates must be approved by the fire department).

Source: Neal Geffner, vice president, Abbey Locksmiths, New York.

Choosing a locksmith

☐ Go to the locksmiths' shops to size them up.

☐ Make sure the store is devoted exclusively to the locksmith business and isn't just doing locksmithing on the side.

☐ Ask to see the locksmith's license if it's not displayed. There are a lot of unlicensed people doing business illegally.

☐ Best: Locksmiths who belong to an association. They are keeping up with the latest developments. Look for a sticker in the window indicating membership in a local or national locksmiths' association.

A secure door

☐ If you're buying a door, buy a metal flush door without panels and get an equally strong frame to match it. Cost: About $500. What makes a good frame: A hollow metal construction, same as the door.

☐ On a metal door, use a Segal lock on the inside and a Medeco on the outside with a Medeco Bodyguard cylinder guard plate. If it's a tubular lock, get Medeco's D-11. It gives you the option of a key on the inside, and you don't need a guard plate.

☐ If your door has panels on it, put a piece of sheet steel on it. If the panels are glass, replace them with Lexon, an unbreakable plastic.

☐ If you have a wooden door, get what the industry calls a police lock. This is a brace lock with a bar that goes from the lock into the floor about 30 inches

away from the base of the door. Also, get a police lock if your door frame is weak. It keeps the door from giving because of the brace in the floor. Even the best regular locks won't protect you if the whole frame gives.

☐ Jimmy bars: Don't bother with them. They're psychological protection only. If you have a metal door, a good lock is sufficient protection. Use a jimmy bar on a metal door only if the door has been damaged through a forcible break-in and is separated from the frame. The bar will straighten out the door and hide some of the light shining through. On a wooden door, a jimmy bar can actually help a burglar by giving him leverage. He can put a crowbar up against it, dig into the wood and break through the door.

☐ If your door opens out instead of in, get a double bar lock—one that extends horizontally on each side. With a door that opens out, the hinges are often exposed on the outside, allowing a burglar to remove the door from its hinges. With a double bar lock, he can't pull the door out.

Source: Sal Schillizzi of All-Over Locksmiths, Inc., New York, is a national safecracking champion.

Buying a burglar alarm

Home alarm systems, once mainly for the rich, are coming into widespread use because locks aren't deterring burglars. Recent FBI figures show that 82% of the time, illegal entry is gained through home doors, most often the front door.

Burglars just break open the door with their shoulders. Faced with a deadbolt or double lock, the burglar will use a heavy tool to take out the frame.

☐ What to look for in an alarm: One that sounds off (not a silent alarm), so that the burglar is aware of it and alarm central (a security company office or the local police) is alerted.

☐ Select a system with sensors on vulnerable doors and windows. Good systems need a complex electrical tie-in in the basement, as well as a control panel installed away from prying eyes and little children. Good systems can also switch on lights and TV sets and alert alarm central by automatic telephone dialing or a radio signal.

☐ Have a secondary line of defense. This can be a few thin electronic pressure pads under rugs in high traffic areas or strategically placed photoelectric cells.

☐ Choose a reputable, well-tested system. The brand names are American District Telegraph (ADT), Honeywell, Silent Knight and ADEMCO.

☐ Be aware of the danger of continual false alarms. The police may ticket you if the family is to blame.

☐ Don't forget to test your alarm system regularly.

☐ Don't be lulled into a false sense of security.

☐ Continue to take all necessary precautions with locks and garage doors.

How to buy a security system

To make your home safe from prowlers and thieves, you should have a two-phase security system:

☐ A perimeter system uses different devices to stop an intruder before he gets into your home. It should be applied to all openings—upper and lower windows, for example.

☐ The interior system traps intruders who break through walls, ceilings and floors (often through several inches of concrete) to gain entry. It should protect the alarm system's main controls, areas where your valuables are stored, and halls or stairways to where you sleep.

☐ Secure all openings. This includes air conditioning installations and exterior ducting.

☐ Reinforce the door frames and hinges. A lock does no good if the door can be kicked down.

☐ Don't apply phony decals to windows and doors. These often signal no alarm or easily defeated security measures to a burglar.

☐ Don't depend on timer-activated lights and radios. Burglars call on the telephone or ring the doorbell to see if you are home.

☐ Wire the screens of your windows so that if they are cut or lifted, an alarm sounds.

☐ Wire door panels, as well as the frame. Burglars often break through the door panel to avoid the contact on the door.

☐ Secure your garage. It may provide an excellent location from which an intruder can break unobserved through a wall into your home.

☐ Install exterior automatic lighting around your home. (Exterior motion detectors turn on lighting when people or vehicles approach your home.) Such lighting welcomes guests—and frightens off intruders, who will think they have been detected.

☐ The alarm should be deafening and should continue to sound for 10 minutes. It should then reset automatically, shunting the violated zone of your system but rearming the rest of your home.

☐ The lights it turns on should be bright, illuminating all sides of the house. You want to expose and disorient the burglar, scaring him away.

☐ Connect your entire system to a computerized central station that continuously monitors signals from your security system via your telephone lines. It notifies police, firemen, an ambulance or your designees in the event of an alarm.

☐ It should not be possible for an intruder to play with your keypad until he stumbles upon the proper code or to tamper with its wiring to deactivate the system.

☐ Avoid keypads that have obvious silent-alarm features (red buttons that say Panic or Help or display well-known SOS symbols). If a burglar forces you to turn off your system, you should be able to use a slightly different code—one that turns off the system and notifies police of your predicament without alerting the burglar.

Source: Paul DeMatteis, president, Counterforce Security System.

How to make security devices even safer

☐ Plates: Pulling out the lock cylinder is the burglar's easiest and most effective way of getting in. Most people put a plate over their lock and think that will take care of it. But the bolts on most plates are exposed on the outside. With a hollow metal door, the burglar can pull that plate away from the door with a wedge and simply cut the bolts.

If the head of the bolt is exposed, he can pull it out slightly with pliers and snap it right off. One remedy: A cylinder and plate combination that is drill-resistant, with no exposed bolts, and a sleeve to prevent burglars from chiseling the bolts.

☐ Peepholes: Get one that's as small as possible. Large peepholes use a one-way mirror that doesn't permit you to see around corners. If someone hits that mirror while you're looking through, it could damage your eye. Small peepholes use a double lens, making it possible to see around corners. And if the small peephole is knocked off the door, it won't benefit the burglar. If a big one is knocked off, it creates a weakness in your security. Recommended: If you already have a large peephole, remove it. Have the locksmith bolt two plates on the door, with a smaller hole in one of them.

☐ Window locks: The best window locks use a key, which makes them difficult to manipulate from the outside. Without a key, any window lock is vulnerable. Best: One with a heavy pin that allows you to drill holes for either complete locking or three- or six-inch ventilation.

☐ Window gates: In many cities, fire laws prohibit window gates that lock with a key. Remedy: Gates with keyless locks. They allow you to get out easily, but a burglar can't put his hand through the gate to open it.

☐ Closets: Locking the closet isn't sufficient because most closets open out and have hinges on the outside, making it easy to remove the door. Remedy: A door pin. This involves putting the pin on the hinge side of the door and through a receiving hole in the frame. Anyone who cut the hinges off or removed their pins couldn't lift the door out.

Source: Sal Schillizzi of All-Over Locksmiths, Inc., New York, is a national safecracking champion.

Best places in your house to hide valuables

Even if you have a safe, you still need a good hiding place for the safe key or combination. It should not be hidden anywhere near the safe. And, if you don't have a safe, you should hide your jewelry and other valuables where they won't be found.

☐ Don't hide things in any piece of furniture with drawers. Drawers are the first place burglars ransack.

☐ Don't hide anything in the bedroom. Thieves tend to be most thorough in checking out bedrooms. Find hiding places in the attic, basement or kitchen. In 90% of burglaries, the kitchen is untouched.

☐ Don't be paranoid. If you have thought up a good location, relax. A burglar can't read your mind.

Try hiding things in the following spots:

☐ Inside the phony wall switches and generic label cans sold by mail-order houses.

☐ In a book, if you have a large book collection. So you don't forget which book you chose, use the title to remind you (for example, *The Golden Treasury of Science Fiction*). Or, buy a hollowed-out book for this purpose.

☐ Inside zippered couch cushions.

☐ In the back of a console TV or stereo speakers (thieves usually steal only receivers, not speakers) or in the type of speakers that look like books.

☐ Under the dirt in a plant. Put non-paper valuables in a plastic bag and bury them.

☐ Under the carpet (for small, flat things).

☐ In between stacks of pots in the kitchen, or wrapped up and labeled as food in the refrigerator or freezer.

☐ Inside an old, out-of-order appliance in the basement.

☐ In a pile of scrap wood beneath the workbench.

☐ In the middle of a sack of grass seed.

Source: Linda Cain, author of *How to Hide Your Valuables*, Beehive Communications, Medfield, MA.

What to do if you come home during a burglary

☐ If you walk in on a burglar by accident, ask an innocent question. Example: Oh, you're the guy who's supposed to pick up the package, aren't you? If, at this point, the burglar tries to run away, it's smart to step aside.

☐ Resist the temptation to yell or otherwise bring on a confrontation. Go as quickly and quietly as possible to a neighbor's and call the police from there.

☐ Avoid walking into your home while a thief is there by leaving a $20 bill conspicuously placed, near the door. If the bill is gone when you return home, someone else may be there. Leave at once and call the police.

Sources: Margaret Kenda, *Crime Prevention For Business Owners*, AMACOM, N.Y. and *How to Protect Yourself From Crime*, Avon Books, N.Y.

Home emergencies

Vital information about the house should be known by everyone in the family in case of emergency. Key items:

☐ The location of the fuse box or circuit-breaker panel.

☐ Placement of the main shutoff valves for the water and gas lines.

☐ The location of the septic tank or the line to the main sewer.

☐ Records of the brands, ages and model numbers of the stove, refrigerator, freezer, dishwasher, furnace, washer and dryer.

Source: *Woman's Day*, New York.

House sitting checklist

To decide what kind of sitter you need (to live in or to visit regularly, long term or short term), determine your requirements. Typically, sitters should:

☐ Make the house look lived in, so it won't be burglarized.

☐ Care for plants, pets and grounds.

☐ Make sure the pipes won't freeze.

☐ Guard the house and its possessions against natural disasters.

Where to find help:

☐ Some communities have sitting services or employment agencies that can fill the job.

☐ Better: Someone you know—the teenage child of a friend, a cleaning woman, a retired neighbor.

☐ Placement services at colleges.

☐ When interviewing, test the resourcefulness and intelligence of the candidate.

☐ Check references.

☐ If you find a writer looking for a place to stay or a person from the place you are heading to who would like to exchange houses, you might make a

deal without any money changing hands.

Before you leave:

☐ Walk through every sequence of duties with the sitter.

☐ Put all duties in writing.

☐ List repair, supply and emergency telephone numbers and your own telephone number or instructions on how to reach you.

☐ Make clear that no one is to be admitted to the house or given a key without your prior consent.

What to put in a home improvement contract

Plunging ahead with major improvements or additions to your home without a carefully thought-out contract is asking for trouble.

Here's what to get in writing:

☐ Material specifications, including brand names, and a work completion schedule.

☐ All details of the contractor's guarantees, including the expiration dates. Procedures to be followed if materials or workmanship should prove defective. Trap: Do not confuse manufacturers' guarantees with the contractor's guarantees of proper installation.

☐ An automatic arbitration clause. This provides that an impartial board will mediate if problems of excessive cost overruns arise.

☐ A clause holding the contractor responsible for negligence on the part of subcontractors. Check with your lawyer for specifics.

☐ A clean-up provision, specifying that all debris be removed.

Getting your money's worth from a home improvement contractor

☐ Consult a lawyer before signing a complex contract.

☐ Don't sign a contract with any blank spaces. Write *void* across them.

☐ Don't sign a work completion certificate without proof that the contractor has paid all subcontractors and suppliers of materials.

☐ Don't pay in full until you are completely satisfied.

☐ Don't pay cash.

When serious problems arise with a home improvement contract

☐ Contrary to popular myth, an attorney is not necessary to modify a contract with a home improvement contractor. Just write on a separate sheet "Notwithstanding anything else in the contract to the contrary, we agree as follows…(specify the contract modification)." Then, both parties sign the modification.

☐ The contract should have a clause that describes how changes will be made. Typically, all changes above $100 must be agreed to in writing by both parties to the contract.

☐ If an unforeseen problem crops up (for example, subsurface boulders obstruct the laying of a new foundation), or if the contractor honestly underestimates his costs, renegotiate terms. If you try to hold a contractor to unreasonable terms, he will cut corners, stall, or walk off the job.

☐ It's possible to insert a clause saying what damages you will pay if you cancel a project before work begins. But once work does begin, you should see it through to completion. Courts favor contractors in cases where homeowners want to break off a project halfway through.

Protecting yourself in home improvement contracts

Improving a home has become more attractive than buying a new one for many people.

The key to protecting yourself when hiring a contractor for a major alteration is thoughtful contract negotiation. Even contractors with good reputations sometimes get in over their heads.

☐ Always do your own financing. Terms of lenders working with contractors are usually stiff. Often they give the lender a second mortgage on your house—sometimes without your realizing it. That can leave you without leverage to force correction of bad workmanship.

☐ The contractor should show you the document from his insurance company covering workers' compensation. Standard homeowners' policy does not cover workers (except, in some states, an occasional babysitter).

☐ Fix responsibility for repairing wind, rain, or fire damage, as well as possible vandalism at worksite.

☐ Include a payment schedule in the contract. Typically, a contractor gets 10% of the negotiated fee upon signing a contract, then partial payments at completion of each stage of succeeding work. You should withhold any payment until contractor actually begins work. Then hold down succeeding payments as much as possible, so that contractor does not earn his profit until his work is completed.

☐ Make sure the final payment is contingent upon approval of the work by municipal inspectors.

☐ Make the contractor responsible for abiding by local building codes. If you assume this responsibility, make the contract contingent on your ability to get all necessary building permits.

Be specific about what work you want done, how, and with what materials:

☐ Don't settle for normal contract language about the project's being done in "a workmanlike manner," because homeowners' standards for work they want done is often higher than common trade practice.

☐ To avoid misunderstandings, refer in

the contract to architect's drawings, where possible, and actual specifications.

☐ Include a schedule against which to measure work's progress. Use calendar dates: For example, foundation and framing to be completed by March 1; roughing-in by April 1; sheetrock by May 1; woodwork and finish work by June 1.

☐ Push for a penalty clause if the work is completed unreasonably late. For example, all work to be completed by June 1. If, however, work is not completed by June 1, the contractor will pay the homeowner $100 a day thereafter.

When you need an attorney for a home improvement contract

Consider an attorney when:

☐ The job is very complicated or expensive.

☐ Modifications to an existing house will require a structure to be open to the weather for an extended period.

☐ The nature of the property (swampy, rocky) makes unforeseen difficulties likely.

☐ A thorough check on the contractor's references is impossible.

Source: Birger M. Sween, attorney, Hackensack, NJ.

Cost-cutting steps for construction work

☐ Set up a separate bank account for control of expenditures. This also provides a record of expenses to offset future capital gains.

☐ Check preliminary drawings against all deed requirements. Also check with government authorities that must issue any permits.

☐ Be sure that utilities are available at the site and are adequate for your needs.

☐ Budget for surveys, professional fees, permits, financing costs, bonds and insurance. When possible, include these costs in your long-term loan.

☐ Obtain at least three bids for every area of the job—carpentry, plumbing, etc. Best: Bid and build when others aren't doing so.

☐ Once bids are accepted, never pay in advance.

☐ Be sure no outdated drawings or specifications are left on the job site.

☐ Have the work checked regularly by a knowledgeable person other than the contractor.

☐ Before making final payment to a contractor, be certain all corrections of completed work are made. Set a date for a one-year-after guaranteed inspection.

Source: Werner R. Hashagen, author of *How to Get It Built Better—Faster—For Less*, La Jolla, CA.

The best way to schedule a home remodeling

☐ Complete as much work as possible in summer. At that time, you can send children to camp or to visit relatives. Workers can leave bulky supplies and equipment outside. Don't hold off until winter in the expectation that it will cost less because it's off-season. Interior renovation goes on all year long. And prices seem to go only up.

☐ Get a couple of rooms finished, clean and livable quickly. The best first choice are children's rooms. Children are very adaptable, but they do best when they know where their clothes and toys are.

☐ Keep a spot clear for the children to play in and get out from underfoot while the rest of the work goes on. If the renovation is easy on the children, the parents will have it easier, too.

☐ Make sure supplies and workers are ready at the same time. This is especially important when doing the kitchen. If the job is well coordinated, you will be without a functioning kitchen for only two weeks.

☐ Order kitchen cabinets well ahead. If they are custom-built, plan a six-to-eight-week leadtime.

☐ Don't tear out wiring and plumbing until you know the cabinets are on the way.

☐ Keep the place relatively clean.

Sweep up every evening, even if the workers are coming back the next day to make a new mess. You will feel better.

☐ When bedrooms are being redone, move all your clothes and belongings out. Even if you put your things in drawers, the plaster dust will infiltrate.

☐ Every week or so, invite friends over. If there is no place to sit, spread a tablecloth on the floor and have a picnic. If there is no kitchen, serve takeout food.

Living through a home renovation

Remodeling has become even more important recently because of high purchase prices and mortgage interest rates and the growing trend toward restoring old homes nearer to city centers.

Too many people have an idealized notion of what a renovation entails. To minimize frustration and disappointment:

☐ Budget realistically. Renovations tend to cost more than you expect. You may find that you are paying much more than your neighbor paid to remodel just two years ago. Add 20% to the most conservative estimate.

☐ Assume that everything that can go wrong will.

☐ Be ready to deal with more disruption to family members' lives than you can possibly imagine. Renovating, especially if several rooms are involved, is very messy. And there is no way to make it neat.

☐ Use a professional you can communicate with and trust to get the job done in a reasonable period. This could be an architect, architect-builder, builder-designer, or designer-contractor. The most important qualification is rapport with you. The problem with some architects is over-optimism, which can take the form of not leveling with clients about how time-consuming, costly and messy the project will be.

☐ If you have a competent supervisor, stay away from the house as much as possible.

☐ Be realistic in deciding what to have professionals do and what to do yourself. Almost all the jobs required in a remodeling can be done by an intelligent, reasonably handy amateur. Few are exceptionally difficult. But each task can take an enormous amount of time, in some cases, months, especially if you hold down a full-time job.

☐ Use experienced workers for heavy work such as demolition, basic carpentry, wiring, plumbing and masonry, floor scraping and refinishing.

☐ If you want to cut costs by doing some things yourself, stick to wall-papering, painting, wood-stripping, sanding, tiling (vinyl, asbestos, ceramic), and laying parquet-wood floor squares (messy, but not hard).

☐ Find the best skilled workers by asking for names from the previous owner of the house or apartment, neighbors, realtor, bank.

Source: Richard Rosan, president, Real Estate Board of New York, who has lived through several restorations.

When renovation pays off

Rehabilitating and then renting older buildings in areas undergoing a renaissance can lead to quick profits.

☐ Buy on a block where a third or more of the buildings show some signs of recent renovation or improvement. Don't make the mistake of assuming that one or two efforts, even major ones, indicate a trend.

Signs that an old neighborhood has comeback potential are:

☐ A low crime rate and a declining ratio of low-income families.

☐ Below market rents because of poor property maintenance: If you improve conditions, you can raise rents.

☐ Avoid areas where rents are cheap because tenants don't want to live there.

☐ Parks, lakes, rivers, colleges, shopping areas.

☐ More owner-occupants than absentee landlords.

☐ Neighborhood organizations that actively promote community interests and activities.

☐ Also: Government concern for clean streets, regular trash collection, and visible police protection.

☐ Be sure that banks are willing to lend money for purchase and rehabilitation of buildings.

Source: Jerry Davis, author of *Rehabbing for Profit*, McGraw-Hill, New York.

Building a tennis court

There are four types of tennis courts: Clay, Har-Tru (pulverized clay with a gypsum binder), asphalt and cement. Clay and Har-Tru are soft and need daily maintenance. Asphalt and cement are hard courts that require little upkeep.

Here are the major considerations:

☐ Choosing the right court. Soil and rock conditions can dictate the best type for your yard as much as your playing preference. Sandy soil with good drainage makes an ideal base for any kind of court. Heavy clay soil holds an all-weather court easily but requires additional excavation and filling for a soft court. Rocky areas may need blasting to create a proper base for any kind of court.

☐ Construction time. A tennis court needs time to settle, particularly the hard surfaces (asphalt and cement) that might crack if the base were to heave. In the northern part of the country, where winters are severe, the ideal building schedule for hard courts is to excavate in the fall, let the base settle over the winter and finish the surfacing in the late spring or early summer. With soft courts, settling is less of a problem because cracks can be filled in with more clay or Har-Tru. A soft court can be built in six to eight weeks, with three weeks for settling.

☐ Space requirements. Home tennis courts require much more space than commonly believed. While the actual playing area of a court is relatively small (36 by 78 feet), adding the out-of-bounds areas pushes the total required to 60 by 120 feet, about one-sixth of an acre.

☐ Zoning and permits. Property owners must provide an up-to-date survey of their property and be sure that the proposed court fits within the set-back requirements—or get zoning variances if necessary. Contractors obtain the building permits. Many communities require fencing.

☐ Costs. Prices vary considerably from one part of the country to another.

Special excavating problems create only one of the price variables. In general, however, a clay court with sprinkler system and fencing is less expensive than a similar Har-Tru court. All-weather courts (asphalt in the East, cement in the West) are the least expensive of all.

☐ Maintenance. Soft courts must be swept and relined daily, sprinkled and rolled periodically and refurbished annually (or oftener in climates where they get year-round use). Hard courts must be resurfaced every five to seven years. Many builders offer maintenance-service contracts.

Source: Ray Babij, tennis-court builder, Remsenberg, NY.

Installing a sunroof

If you want the sensation of a cool breeze tousling your hair while you travel along the highway, but you can't spend $6,000 or so to convert your car into a convertible, consider installing a sunroof instead. The procedure (if done right) won't weaken the vehicle in any way nor make it more vulnerable to rust.

You can modify virtually any car, except cars with special ceiling "cockpits," such as Camaros and Firebirds.

Follow these guidelines:

☐ Your best bet is to find a specialist (check the *Yellow Pages* under "Custom Car Work") who installs sunroofs for a living. Although it's a fairly simple job, a novice or a typical all-purpose collision shop may run into problems.

☐ The cost of installation will depend on the value of your car. Costs range from about $200 for an ordinary compact to $500 for a BMW.

☐ The cost of the transparent panel and molding you'll need on cold or rainy days will run less than $100. (The best parts are made by ASC Corp.)

☐ You'll also need an opaque screen for times when you want to avoid the sun.

☐ Have the installer save a piece of the headliner—the cloth covering on the inside roof—to retain a "factory" look.

☐ Expect to be given at least a six-month guarantee against cracks or leakage.

Source: Tony Assenza, associate editor of *Motor Trend*.

How to keep cool without busting your budget

Utility costs continue to rise—so it's more important than ever to keep your air conditioning energy-efficient this summer.

Keys to a cool house and a low electric bill:

☐ Look for an air conditioner with an EER (Energy Efficiency Rating) of at least nine of a possible twelve. Although an efficient unit may cost more, it will save you 3¢–10¢ an hour. Even if you pay an extra $100, you'll get the difference back in as little as two years.

☐ Get the right size. Too small a unit won't cool the room. Too large a unit will cool the room quickly, then go off before removing the humidity, leaving cold clammy air and damp rugs.

☐ Buy an air-conditioner timer. If you will be out all day, set it to switch on an hour before your return.

☐ Keep your air conditioner's temperature control at the lowest comfortable setting. A unit set at 10 won't remove humidity any faster than one set at five.

☐ See if you can remain comfortable at a higher temperature. It costs 25% more to keep a room at 74° than at 78°…39% more to keep it at 72°. People can generally live with higher temperatures when they are sleeping, since their bodies are throwing off less heat.

☐ Be conscientious about maintenance. Keep the filters and outside fins clean (check them every two weeks). Keep outside vents closed when trying to cool a room (but open when it's cooler outside than inside). Direct the cooled air toward the ceiling (it will naturally sink and circulate). Fill the space between top and bottom window sashes with insulation or foam. Seal doorways with weatherstripping. Close fireplace dampers.

☐ Close blinds and drapes in any room facing south or west, to keep the sun's heat out. Direct sun pours up to 4,350 BTUs through a single three-foot by five-foot window every hour—enough to overmatch a room air conditioner. Or, install awnings above windows and doors to reflect the sun.

☐ Install ventilating fans to substitute for air conditioning on all but the most humid days. A fan consumes only 1¢–3¢ worth of energy per hour. An air conditioner swallows 8¢ an hour—and up. The most effective fans have retractable panels that seal the window. They work best when they exhaust hot air through west-facing windows while drawing in cooler air from an open window on the east side of the house.

☐ Make sure you have adequate attic insulation. It keeps summer heat out as well as keeping winter heat in.

Source: Robert Peterson, Con Ed Hotline representative, Conservation Center, New York.

Increasing natural ventilation

Before air conditioning, home builders provided architectural features that promoted natural cooling. Examples: High ceilings (heat rises), indoor and outdoor shutters, floor-to-ceiling double-hung windows. For natural ventilation:

☐ Open windows at night to let in cool air.

☐ Close shutters and draw curtains where sun hits the house during the day.

☐ Use the stack effect: Open a window low on the cool side of the house and another high on the hot side. Cool air will flow in on the low side, and hot air will exit on the high side. If possible, open that window from the top. Transoms between rooms serve the same ventilating function.

☐ Install shutters, and curtain liners tightly sealed to window frames. The liner creates a dead-air space, reducing heat entry.

☐ Old-time canvas awnings, let down during the heat of the day, are very efficient. Bonus: Shading a room from direct sun prevents fading of furniture and fabrics.

☐ Key to super-efficient cooling: A whole-house fan. Needed: An electrical source and a large roof ventilation area.

Air conditioning secrets

Room air conditioners mounted in a window or through the wall are ideal for keeping small, comfortable havens against the worst of summer's hot spells. They can be more economical than central air conditioning because they are flexible—you cool only the rooms you are using. But even a single unit can be expensive.

To keep a room cool with minimum use of the air conditioner:

☐ Limit the use of the air conditioner in the "open vent" setting—it brings in hot outside air that the machine must work hard to keep cooling.

☐ Protect the room from the direct heat of the sun with awnings, drapes or blinds.

☐ Close off rooms that you are air-conditioning.

☐ Turn off unnecessary lights. They add extra heat (fluorescent lights are coolest).

☐ Turn off the unit if you will be out of the room more than 30 minutes.

☐ Service room air conditioners annually to keep them efficient. Replace filters, keep condensers clean and lubricate the moving parts.

☐ Supplement central air conditioning with a room air conditioner in the most-used room.

Source: John D. Constance, licensed engineer specializing in home maintenance, Cliffside Park, NJ.

Using fans to save on air conditioning

Ventilating fans can cool a whole house—or a single room—at a fraction (about 10%) of the cost of air conditioning. The trick is knowing how to use them to move in cooler air and to move hotter air out.

☐ Control the source of the cooler air by manipulating windows. During the day, for example, downstairs windows on the shady northern or eastern side of the house are most likely to provide cool air. All other windows should be closed and shaded from direct sun with blinds and drapes.

☐ At night, shut lower-floor windows for security while upstairs windows provide cool air.

☐ Attic fans are permanent installations above the upper floor. They are powerful enough to cool a whole house. The opening to the outside must be as large as the fan-blade frame in order to handle the air flow properly.

☐ Louvers, bird screening and (particularly) insect screening all reduce the exhaust capacity of a fan.

☐ A doorway or other opening must allow the fan to pull cool air directly up from the rest of the house.

☐ Direct-connected fans are quieter than belt-driven fans.

☐ Some attic fans have thermometers that automatically turn them off and on when the attic temperature reaches a certain degree of heat.

☐ Window fans have adjustable screw-on panels to fit different window sizes. Less powerful than attic fans, they serve more limited spaces.

☐ Box fans are portable and can be moved from room to room to cool smaller areas.

☐ Ventilating fans are rated by the cubic feet per minute (CFM) of air that they can exhaust. For effective cooling, engineers recommend an air-change rate of 20 per hour (the entire volume of air in the area to be cooled is changed 20 times every 60 minutes).

☐ To calculate the required CFM rating for a particular room, calculate its volume in cubic feet. Then multiply this figure by 20/60 ($\frac{1}{3}$). Example: A room 20 feet by 15 feet with an eight-foot ceiling contains 2,400 cubic feet of air. This, multiplied by $\frac{1}{3}$, gives a CFM rating of 800 for a proper-size fan.

☐ The CFM rating of an attic fan is done the same way. Total the cubic feet of the rooms and hallways you want cooled before multiplying by $\frac{1}{3}$.

Source: John Constance, licensed engineer specializing in home maintenance, Cliffside Park, NJ.

How to save water

Whether you live in an area plagued by periodic droughts or simply want to save money on rising water bills:

☐ Install flow restricters in your showers

and take shorter showers. (A normal showerhead sprays up to eight gallons per minute, so even a short, five-minute shower uses up to 40 gallons.)

☐ Get in the habit of turning off the water while shaving, brushing teeth and washing hands, except when you need to rinse.

☐ Put a weighted plastic container into the toilet tank to cut the normal amount of water used in flushing (approximately six gallons per flush) by as much as half. Some people use bricks to displace water in the tank, but this may damage the tank.

☐ Wash only full loads in your dishwasher and clothes washer. Running these machines half empty is a big water waster.

☐ Fix all leaks. Dripping water, even if slow, can cost you a lot of money over the course of several months.

☐ Use buckets of water to do outside chores like washing the car and cleaning the driveway. If you must use a hose, turn it off between rinsings; don't just let it run.

Home energy savers

After you've insulated your home, here are some smaller steps that can trim added amounts from your heating and electricity bills:

☐ Air conditioner covers. Outdoor covers not only block drafts, they also protect the machine from weather damage during the winter. Check the caulking around the outside of the machine, too. Indoor covers can be even more effective draft stoppers than outdoor ones. You can make your own from heavy plastic or buy Styrofoam-insulated ones.

☐ Door and window draft guards. Sand-filled fabric tubes effectively prevent uncomfortable drafts from entering around doors and windows. Easy to install and to remove.

☐ Light dimmers. The newest solid-state dimmers consume little energy themselves but allow reduced lighting levels and lower energy consumption. Some dimmers are installed in the wall in place of conventional switches. Others simply plug into existing sockets or are inserted into lamp cords. A dimmer can save you approximately 50% a year on a single light fixture if you dim it halfway.

☐ Air deflectors. Used in homes heated by forced air, these direct air from the vents away from walls and into the room. Depending on the location of your registers, significant savings can result.

☐ Heat reflectors. Reflectors direct radiator heat into the rooms to save energy. Very inexpensive ones can be made by covering a sheet of plywood or foam board with aluminum foil and placing it between the radiator and the wall.

☐ Storm window kits. You can make your own storm windows with sheets of plastic and tape. Kits are available to install them either inside or outside your existing windows. The cost ranges from as low as 85¢ to $35 per window. Removable rigid plastic storm windows in permanently installed frames are also big energy savers. Some companies will cut them to fit any window at a cost of $4–$5 per square foot. For city dwellers, they also reduce noise levels significantly. Storm windows reduce heat loss by as much as 30%, so an investment in permanent storm windows may pay off in the long run.

☐ Energy audits. Your local utility may offer free home energy audits. For absolutely no cost or obligation, it will inspect your home and suggest ways you can reduce your energy costs. Also, more and more utilities are acting as general contractors in making energy-efficiency changes on houses, ensuring that the work is done properly and on time.

Source: *Bottom Line/Personal*, Springfield, NJ.

Accurate radon testing

Radon testing isn't conclusive the first time unless the reading is very low—below four picocuries per liter. But if you get a reading higher than that, don't panic. It may be a temporary wave of radon, not a permanent condition. You need at least a year of follow-up testing to get a conclusive picture of high radon content. Recommended: If your area is reported to have a high incidence of radon, contact your state environmental protection agency's listing of companies that provide reliable long-term radon testing kits.

Home insulation contract

The best time to negotiate a contract to insulate your home is spring, when contractors are not as busy as in the fall. Your first saving can come on air-conditioning bills. Biggest saving: Heat bills next winter.

The contract and estimate should:

☐ Specify exact areas to be insulated.

☐ Specify type and brand of product to be installed in each area (including the number of packages or bags that will be needed).

☐ Give the R-value (resistance to heat loss) of the products, which is the most important measurement.

☐ Break down the total cost into materials, labor, clean-up, service charges and taxes.

☐ Provide written guarantees of product claims, including inflammability, moisture absorption, shrinkage, settling, odor and sound-proofing.

☐ Provide an adjusted-cost clause that gives you the savings if less than the estimated amount of materials is needed.

☐ Provide a written guarantee of workmanship, including the contractor's responsibility for any future damage caused by the insulation.

Source: John D. Constance, licensed engineer specializing in home maintenance, Cliffside Park, NJ.

New rules on home insulating

Home insulation materials and contractors have taken a nasty beating over the past few years because of the controversy surrounding insulation materials made of urea-formaldehyde foam. So, you may be surprised to learn that adequate insulation is still the most effective way to save money on your coming winter heating bill.

A six- to eight-inch layer of insulation in the attic floor (the easiest place to install insulation) can slash 30%–50% off your fuel bill. Similar savings result from insulation on the attic ceiling. Adding insulation to outside walls, pipes and hot-air ducts will add substantially to your savings, too.

☐ Urea-formaldehyde foams are out, however. It's still legal to sell them, but they're no longer being manufactured in the U.S.

☐ Those inclined to stay with the tried and true can choose among several insulating materials. Cellulose, rock wool, glass fiber, perlite and vermiculite all have withstood the test of time. Their R values (the measure of insulating effectiveness) run 3.8 to 4.2 per inch. (The higher the number, the better the insulating properties. In contrast, urea-formaldehyde foams had a slightly higher R value—about 5.)

☐ For the more adventurous, there are the new polyfoam insulating materials. Based on polystyrene, and containing no urea-formaldehyde, the polyfoams are somewhat more expensive ($1.30–$1.40 per square foot), but they offer a higher R value in return—about 5.

☐ Regardless of your choice of materials, your now cheaper-to-heat home will nonetheless suffer from indoor pollution. Energy experts say that the properly insulated house no longer "breathes." Solution: An air-to-air heat exchanger, a new appliance that looks like an air conditioner. It's installed in a window or wall. Essentially, before the hot air leaves the house, it's used to heat the cooler, fresher air coming in.

Source: *Bottom Line/Personal*, Springfield, NJ.

Making certain insulation is well installed

For attics:

☐ A good contractor will provide proper ventilation above the attic insulation to prevent water condensation and moisture damage.

☐ Never apply attic insulation directly to the underside of the roof.

☐ Apply a vapor barrier on the warm side of the insulation.

For side walls:

☐ Holes for blowing in the insulation should be drilled between all studs and above and below every window.

☐ The contractor should drop a weighted string through each hole to check for obstacles in the wall. (Holes should be drilled below an obstacle as well.)

☐ Require a thermograph (heat picture) to check the finished sidewall insulation. X-rays do not give an accurate picture of total insulation.

Cleaning your chimney without messing up the house

☐ Clean the chimney at least once a year, and more often if the fireplace or airtight stove is used continuously. If your flue contains a buildup of creosote, a tar-like substance created by fire, of more than one-quarter of an inch thick, you run the risk of a chimney fire.

☐ Get the right equipment for the job—a special brush the right diameter for your flue and a set of flexible rods to push the brush up and down the chimney.

☐ Contain the falling soot by sealing off the fireplace with sheets of plastic held by duct tape.

☐ Spread plenty of newspaper around to protect rugs and furniture.

☐ Slit the plastic covering to allow the brush access to the chimney. Run the brush up and down the length of the chimney about six times.

☐ If you really want to avoid a mess, hire a professional chimney sweep.

Woodstove safety

Fire, injuries and deaths are rising rapidly with the increased use of woodburning stoves. Faulty installation, poor maintenance and careless use are to blame.

Installation musts:

☐ Have a professional mason check and repair the chimney before you put in a stove.

☐ Place the stove on a fireproof base that extends 18 inches on all sizes. There should be 36 inches of clearance space between the stove and combustible walls and ceilings. Alternative: Sheet-metal protection for those areas.

☐ Seal off the fireplace where the stove connects to the chimney. Don't use the chimney for other fireplaces.

Maintenance guides:

☐ Check the stove and stovepipe annually for cracks and defects.

☐ Have the chimney professionally cleaned once a year.

☐ Burn only dry, well-seasoned wood.

Apple, red oak, sugar maple, beech and ironwood are the most efficient. (Green wood, aged less than six months, causes creosote buildup in the chimney and stove.)

☐ Never throw trash in the stove.

☐ Never use a starter fluid.

☐ Put ashes in a metal container outdoors.

Burning wood more productively

Heating a home safely and efficiently with wood requires more than a stack of logs and a fireplace. The ground rules:

☐ To be cost-effective, one cord (128 cu. ft.) of wood should cost no more than 150 gallons of fuel oil.

☐ Prices vary widely. Four-foot-long green logs are much cheaper than shorter dry ones. But the latter come ready for the fireplace. (The other must be dried and cut.)

☐ Best bet: Buy green wood in late spring or summer. It will dry in six months, in time for winter use.

☐ Harder woods, such as oak, ash and beech, yield more heat. Less efficient are magnolia, cherry, Douglas fir. The least efficient are poplar, spruce, willow.

☐ The most efficient stoves use baffles, long smoke paths, and heat exchangers to extract as much heat as possible. They are more expensive than simpler types. But, in the long run, they save money.

☐ Make sure to check local restrictions on furnace types. A wide variety of wood-burning (and multifuel) furnaces are available for central heating systems, but not all are permitted everywhere.

☐ Except for emergency use, fireplaces are mainly for aesthetic value, since they are essentially poor heaters. Homeowners who want the best of both worlds should consider efficiency-improving modifications or combination fireplace-stove units.

Source: *Heating with Wood*, U.S. Department of Energy, Washington, D.C.

Keeping street noise out of your home

Noise intrusion is a constant and nagging problem in many buildings because of thin walls and badly insulated floors and ceilings.

How to noise-proof walls:

☐ Hang sound-absorbing materials, such as quilts, decorative rugs, carpets or blankets. Note: Cork board and heavy window draperies absorb sound within a room but do not help much with noise from outside.

☐ If you don't want to hang heavy materials directly on your walls, consider a frame that attaches to the wall. Insulation goes on the wall within the frame, and then a fabric is affixed to the frame.

How to noise-proof ceilings:

☐ Apply acoustical tile directly to the ceiling with adhesive for a quick and inexpensive fix.

☐ If you can undertake more extensive work, put in a dropped ceiling of acoustical tile with about six inches of insulation between the new and existing ceiling.

How to noise-proof floors:

☐ Install a thick plush carpet over a dense sponge rubber padding.

☐ Key: The padding must be dense, at least three-eighths of an inch thick. Your foot should not press down to the floor when you step on the padding.

Appliances and your electric bill

Average costs per year for using some of the most popular household gadgets and conveniences are listed below. In Seattle, where electrical rates are the lowest in the country, the figures will be less. In New York City, where rates are highest, the costs will be much more. However, no matter where you live or what rates you pay per kilowatt hour, the big consumers of electricity will be the same. You must monitor their use to cut your bill.

Electrical Appliance	Avg. Hrs. Used/Yr.	Yearly Cost
☐ Air conditioner, window	750	$88.47
☐ Blanket, electric	831	11.07
☐ Blender	39	1.13
☐ Broiler	70	7.53
☐ Clock, electric	8,760	1.28
☐ Clothes dryer	204	74.77
☐ Coffee maker	119	7.98
☐ Dehumidifier	1,467	28.39
☐ Fan, attic	786	21.91
☐ Fan, window	850	12.80
☐ Freezer (15 cu. ft.)	3,504	89.98
☐ Freezer, frostless (15 cu. ft.)	4,002	132.60
☐ Frying pan	157	14.16
☐ Garbage disposal	67	2.26
☐ Hair Dryer	37	1.05
☐ Heater, portable	133	13.25
☐ Humidifier	921	12.27
☐ Iron	143	10.84
☐ Lights (incandescent)	—	141.00
☐ Mixer	102	.98
☐ Oven, microwave	200	22.59
☐ Oven, self-cleaning	239	86.37
☐ Radio	1,211	6.48
☐ Radio/stereo	1,000	8.21
☐ Range	128	79.07
☐ Refrigerator/freezer (14 cu. ft.)	2,947	136.44
☐ Roaster	154	15.44
☐ Sewing machine	147	.83
☐ Sunlamp	57	1.21
☐ Toaster	34	2.94
☐ TV, black & white	1,500	6.25
☐ TV, color	1,500	22.59
☐ Vacuum cleaner	73	3.46
☐ Washing machine	198	7.76
☐ Water Heater	1,075	362.19

Source: U.S. Department of Energy.

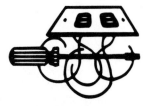

When you need an exterminator and when you don't

Bug problems can usually be solved without an exterminator. Keys: Careful prevention techniques, basic supermarket products and apartment-building cooperation.

Roaches

Roaches are persistent pests that are the bane of apartment dwellers. The problem is not that roaches are so difficult to kill but that the effort has to be made collectively, by every tenant in a particular building. Roaches cannot be exterminated effectively from an individual apartment. If one apartment has them, they'll quickly spread throughout the building.

Most landlords hire exterminating services that visit during daytime hours when most tenants are at work. They wind up spraying just a few apartments, which is totally ineffective.

Recommended:

☐ Apartment dwellers have to get together, contact their landlord and arrange for all apartments to be exterminated at the same time. If the landlord is uncooperative, the Board of Health should be notified. If you live in a co-op, the co-op board should make arrangements for building extermination. Best: A superintendent or member of the building staff should perform regular exterminations, since he can get into apartments at odd hours when the tenants are not home. A professional exterminator should be called only as a backup, in case of a severe problem in a particular apartment.

☐ Incinerators that no longer burn garbage are a major infestation source in large buildings. Many cities, to cut down on air pollution, have ordered the compacting rather than the burning of garbage. Garbage is still thrown down the old brick chutes, which have been cracked from heat, to be compacted in the basement. Roaches breed in these cracks, fed by the wet garbage that comes down the chute, and travel to tenants' apartments. Remedy: Replacement of the brick chutes with smooth metal chutes which don't provide breeding places. Also: Compactors must be cleaned at least once a week.

☐ Rout roaches without poisoning your kitchen. Boric acid or crumbled bay leaves will keep your cupboards pest-free. Another benign repellent: chopped cucumbers.

☐ Homeowners do not need regular extermination for roaches. Since a house is a separate unit, a one-time extermination should do the job. Food stores are the major source of roach infestation in private homes. People bring roaches home with the groceries. Check your paper grocery bags for roaches before you store them.

☐ Ants and silverfish can be controlled by the homeowner himself, unless there is a major infestation. Don't call the exterminator for a half-dozen ants or silverfish. Try a store-bought spray first. Exception: Carpenter ants and grease-eating ants must be exterminated professionally.

☐ Clover mites come from cutting the grass. They look like little red dots. The mites land on windowsills after the lawn is mowed and then travel into the house. Remedy: Spray your grass with miticide before cutting.

☐ Spiders don't require an exterminator. Any aerosol will get rid of them.

☐ Termite control is a major job that needs specialized chemicals and equipment. Call an exterminator.

☐ Bees, wasps and hornets should be dealt with professionally. Their nests must be located and attacked after dusk, when the insects have returned to them. If the nest is not destroyed properly, damage to your home could result. Also: Many people are allergic to stings and don't know it until they are stung.

☐ Clothes moths can be eliminated by hanging a no-pest strip in your closet and keeping the door tightly closed.

☐ Flies can be minimized with an aerosol or sticky strip. An exterminator is of no help getting rid of flies. Best: Screens on all the windows and doors.

☐ Weevils and meal moths can be prevented by storing cereals, rice and grains in sealed containers. Also: Cereals are treated with bromides to repel infestation. The bromides eventually break down. Throw out old cereals.

☐ Wood storage and insects. Firewood kept in the house becomes a refuge and breeding ground for insects. Risky solution: Spraying the logs with insecticides. (When the sprayed wood burns, dangerous fumes could be emitted.) Better: Stack the wood (under plastic) outside and carry in only the amount needed.

Mice

There is no 100% effective solution for exterminating mice. Try these alternatives:

☐ Trapping is effective unless you have small children or pets.

☐ Poison should be placed behind the stove or refrigerator where children and pets can't get at it.

☐ Glue boards (available in supermarkets) placed along the walls can be very effective. Mice tend to run along the walls due to poor eyesight.

Pesticides and Prevention

Many of the residual (long-lasting) sprays have been outlawed because they don't break down and disappear in the environment. The old favorites, DDT and Chlordane, are generally no longer permitted. What to use:

☐ Baygon, Diazanon and Dursban are general-purpose, toxic organo-phosphates meant for residual use in wet areas. They're recommended for all indoor insects, including roaches.

☐ Drione is a nontoxic silica gel, which dries up the membranes in insects. Recommended for indoor use in dry areas only, it is especially effective on roaches.

☐ Malathion is helpful in gardens, but it should not be used indoors.

☐ Pyrethrin is highly recommended, since it is made from flowers and is nontoxic. It has no residual effect, but is good for on-contact spraying of roaches and other insects. If there is a baby in the house, Pyrethrin is especially useful, since children under three months should never be exposed to toxic chemicals. Don't use it around hay-fever or asthma sufferers.

☐ When buying products in the store, look at the label to determine the percentage of active ingredients. Solutions vary from 5% to 15%. The stronger the solution, the better the results.

☐ Prevention is synonymous with sanitation. If you are not scrupulous about cleanliness, you will be wasting your money on sprays or exterminators.

☐ Moisture is the main attractor of insects. If you live in a moist climate, you must be especially vigilant. Coffee spills, plumbing leaks, fish tanks, pet litter and pet food all attract bugs. Clean up after your pets, and take care of leaks and spills immediately. If puddles tend to collect around your house after it rains, improve the drainage.

☐ Word of mouth is the best way to choose a good exterminator. Don't rely on the *Yellow Pages*.

☐ Contracts for regular service, which many exterminators try to promote, are not recommended for private homes. A one-time extermination should do the trick, but apartment dwellers must exterminate buildingwide on a regular basis.

☐ To remove a bat from your house at night, confine it to a single room, open the window and leave the bat alone. Chances are it will fly right out. Otherwise, during the day when the bat is torpid, flick it into a coffee can or other container. (Use gloves if you are squeamish.) Release it outdoors. Bats are really very valuable. A single brown bat can eat 3,000 mosquitos a night. Note: Bats, like other mammals, can carry rabies. If you find a downed bat or you are scratched or bitten by one, call your local animal control agency and keep the animal for testing. However, very few people have contracted rabies directly from bats. More likely source: Skunks.

Source: Tom Heffernan, president of the Ozane Exterminating Co., Bayside, NY, and Clifton Meloan, chemist, Kansas State University, writing in *Science*.

Oil vs. water-based paint

☐ Water-based paint (also known as latex or acrylic) has many distinct advantages over oil-based. It dries in less than an hour, has no paint-like smell, doesn't show brush or roller lap marks as openly and makes for an easy soap-and-water cleanup. It also wears longer, is washable and holds color best.

☐ Latex can be used on all interior surfaces including those with existing oil-based layers. Exception: When there is a water-soluble substance underneath the oil, such as calamines or sizers. The water in latex softens these substances, which leads to peeling. Enough coats of oil-based paint usually shield underlying water-soluble surfaces from the water in the latex. Test: Paint a small area with latex. If there is no peeling within a couple of hours, continue with latex.

☐ Latex exterior paints are ideal for surfaces that have never been painted.

Why: They allow the surface to breathe. And their flexibility during the freeze-thaw cycle enables them to adhere better to the surface. (If you have latex over an oil-based layer that is holding, continue with water-based.)

☐ Stick with oil-based paint if the exterior surface is already painted with an oil-based paint (alkyd resin). Reason: Latex expands and contracts more easily than oil during the freeze-thaw weather cycle. This action may pull off any underlayers of oil-based paint that aren't locked onto the surface.

Source: Neil Janovic, Janovic Plaza, a paint and paper concern founded by his grandfather in 1888, New York.

Painting trouble areas

Often, paint peels in one section of a wall or ceiling. Causes:

☐ A leak making its way through the walls from a plumbing break or an opening to the outside.

☐ The plaster is giving out in that area due to age or wear and tear.

☐ The layers of paint may be so thick that the force of gravity, plus vibrations from outside, make the paint pop and peel in the weakest spots.

How to fix the problem:

☐ If it's a leak, find and correct it first.

☐ Otherwise, remove as much of the existing paint as you can.

☐ Scrape away any loose, damp or crumbling plaster.

☐ Spackle and smooth the area.

☐ Prime and paint it.

For real problem areas:

☐ Spackle, then paste on a thin layer of canvas. Apply it as though it were wallpaper.

☐ Smooth it out so it becomes part of the surface.

☐ Then prime and paint it.

Safe food storage

☐ Yellow bananas can be held at the just-ripe stage in the refrigerator for up to six days. Although the peel might discolor slightly, the fruit retains both its flavor and nutrition. Ripen green bananas at room temperature first. Mashed banana pulp can be frozen.

☐ Nuts in the shell keep at room temperature for only a short time. Put them in a cool, dry place for prolonged storage. Shelled nuts remain fresh for several months when sealed in containers and refrigerated. For storage of up to a year, place either shelled or unshelled nuts in a tightly closed container in the freezer.

Storage times for frozen meats vary significantly. Recommended holding time in months:

☐ Beef roast or steak, 12.
☐ Ground beef, 6.
☐ Lamb, 12.
☐ Pork roasts and chops, 8-12.
☐ Bacon and ham, 1-2.
☐ Veal cutlets and chops, 6.
☐ Veal roasts, 8-10.
☐ Chicken and turkey, 12.
☐ Duck and goose, 6.
☐ Shellfish, not over 6.
☐ Cooked meat and poultry, 1.

Keep an accurate thermometer in your refrigerator or freezer. Optimal refrigerator temperature: 40°F for food to be kept more than three or four days. For the freezer: 0° is necessary for long-term storage. Note: Some parts of the freezer may be colder than other parts. Use the thermometer to determine which areas are safe for keeping foods long term.

Freezing leftovers:

☐ Raw egg whites: Freeze them in ice cube trays.

☐ Hard cheeses: Grate them first.

☐ Soup stock: Divide it into portions.

☐ Stale bread: Turn it into crumbs in the blender.

☐ Pancakes, french toast and waffles: Freeze and reheat in the toaster oven at 375°.

☐ Whipped cream: Drop into small mounds on a cookie sheet to freeze and then store the mounds in a plastic bag.

☐ Citrus juices: Freeze in an ice cube tray.

☐ Freezing fish: Make a protective dip by stirring one tablespoonful of unflavored gelatin into ¼ cup lemon juice and 1¾ cups cold water. Heat over a low flame, stirring constantly, until gelatin dissolves and mixture is clear. Cool to room temperature. Dip the fish into this solution and drain. Wrap individual fish pieces in heavy-duty freezer wrap. Then place them in heavy-duty freezer bags. Use within two months.

☐ If you do your own food canning, preserve only enough food to eat within one year. After that time, quality deteriorates.

Sources: Tom Grady and Amy Rood, coauthors, *The Household Handbook*, Meadowbrook Press, Deephaven, MN, and Joan Cone, author of *Fish and Game Cooking*, EPM Publications, McLean, VA.

Keeping food from becoming tainted

When in doubt, throw it out. This is the general rule concerning food you think may have become spoiled. This includes frozen food that has thawed too long or dishes that haven't been properly handled. Example: Cheesecake left on a counter to cool overnight can easily go bad.

Other tips for storing and handling food:

☐ Keep food at temperatures below 45°F or above 160°F.

☐ Always keep in mind that food left away from heat or cold for two to three hours is probably unsuitable for eating. This is particularly true of foods that are moist, high in protein and low in acid.

☐ Refrigerate leftovers as soon as possible. Don't let them sit at room temperature for more than two hours.

☐ Reheat food in wide, shallow pans rather than deep, narrow ones. Place foods in a preheated oven, not one that's warming up.

☐ When refrigerating large quantities of dishes such as stews, spaghetti sauce or chili, pour them into large, shallow containers. The point is to expose the greatest mass to the preserving effects of the cold refrigerator.

☐ If possible, thaw frozen foods by placing them in the refrigerator. If thawing must be done quickly, immerse the food in cold water or use a microwave oven.

Freezing vegetables from your garden

☐ Tomatoes: Cut out the stems and rotten spots. Squish each tomato as you put it into a big cooking pot. Boil the tomatoes down to about half their original volume. Then put them through an old-fashioned food mill, catching the puree and discarding the skins and seeds. Pour the puree into a large, deep metal baking pan and leave the uncovered pan overnight in the freezer. The next day, run some hot water on the bottom of the pan to remove the puree, place the block of puree on a chopping board and icepick it into small pieces. Bag and freeze the chunks (a few to each bag).

☐ Zucchini: Peel and split it and scrape the seeds out. Grate coarsely. Stir-fry until half-cooked in lots of butter. Follow the same freezing procedure as for tomatoes.

☐ Greens: Boil, drain, squeeze the water out, chop to desired consistency and follow the same freezing process.

Wrapping a package the right way

☐ Seal a sturdy carton with six strips of two-inch-wide plastic tape (not masking or cellophane tape, which tears easily): A strip across the center of top and bottom and across each open edge on flap ends. Don't just go to the ends. Go a few inches around.

☐ Put an address label inside so that if the outside label is lost or defaced, the package can be opened and sent with the second label.

☐ Don't use brown paper or string; they only increase chance of loss if paper tears and label rips off or the string unties and gets caught in a sorting machine.

Things you never thought of doing with plastic bags

Use plastic bags:

☐ As gloves when greasing a cookie sheet, cleaning the oven or changing oil in the car.

☐ To help preserve a plant when you are going away. Spray the leaves with water, then cover the pot with a bag secured at the top with a rubber band.

☐ To protect your camera, film and lenses from moisture.

☐ As storage bags for woolens. Add a few mothballs.

☐ Put meat to be tenderized inside a bag before pounding.

Cleaning jewelry

☐ Gold and platinum: Use a soft brush with a mild, warm water/detergent solution.

☐ Turquoise, ivory, lapis and other porous gems: Mild soap and water only.

☐ Opals: Use barely cool distilled water (they're sensitive to cold).

☐ Pearls: Roll them in a soft cloth moistened with water and soap (not detergent). To rinse: Roll them in a cloth dipped in warm water.

☐ Most other gems: Add a tablespoonful of baking soda to a cup of warm water. Swish the jewelry through or rub it with a soft toothbrush. Rinse well.

Source: *Woman's Day,* New York.

Secrets of a great lawn

You don't have to work harder to get a grassier lawn. In fact, you can work less. Here's how:

☐ Set the mower blades to a height of 2–2½ inches, and cut the grass only once a week. When the weather gets really hot, every other week is fine. Taller grass means less mowing, stronger and healthier plants that spread faster, more shade to discourage weeds.

☐ Let the clippings lie. They will return nutrients to the soil.

☐ Water only when there has been no significant rain for three or four weeks. Then give a one-inch soak. (Use a cup under the sprinkler pattern to measure—it takes longer than you think.) Frequent shallow watering keeps roots close to the surface, where they are vulnerable to drought and fungus disease.

☐ Use herbicides and insecticides only for specific problems. Routine use weakens the grass and kills earthworms.

☐ Sow bare spots with rye grass for a quick fix. Proper reseeding should be done in late August or early September, when the ground is cooler and moister.

☐ Apply fertilizer twice a year, but not in the spring. September and November are the right months.

Home remedies for plant pests

☐ Red spider mites. Four tablespoons of dishwashing liquid or one-half cake of yellow soap dissolved in one gallon of water. Spray weekly until mites are gone, then monthly.

☐ Hardshell scale. One-fourth teaspoon olive oil, two tablespoons baking soda, one teaspoon Dove liquid soap in two gallons of water. Spray or wipe on once a week for three weeks; repeat if necessary.

☐ Mold on soil. One tablespoon of vinegar in two quarts of water. Water weekly with solution until mold disappears.

☐ Mealybugs. Wipe with cotton swabs dipped in alcohol. Spray larger plants weekly with a solution of one part alcohol to three parts water until bugs no longer hatch.

Source: Decora Interior Plantscapes, Greenwich, CT.

Top garden catalogs

Send for these catalogs for the best in mail-order plants and flowers.

☐ *Breck's,* Peoria, IL 61632. Dutch tulips, crocus, etc. Free.

☐ *Brittingham Plant Farms,* Box 2538, Salisbury, MD 21802. Twenty-seven varieties of strawberries. Free.

☐ *W. Atlee Burpee Co.,* 300 Park Ave., Warminster, PA 19874. Many varieties of vegetables and flowers. Free.

☐ *Henry Field's Seed & Nursery,* 415 N. Burnett, Shenandoah, IA 51602. A hundred pages of fruits and vegetables. Free.

☐ *Jackson & Perkins Co.,* 1 Rose Ln., Medford, OR 97501. Bulbs, trees, wide variety of roses. Free.

☐ *J.W. Jung Seed Co.,* 335 South High St., Randolf, WI 53957. Trees, flowers, vegetables. Free.

☐ *Liberty Seed Co.,* Box 806, New Philadelphia, OH 44663. All kinds of garden seeds. Free.

☐ *Lilypons Water Gardens,* 6800 Lilypons Road, P.O. Box 10, Lilypons, MD 21717-0010. Extensive selection of water plants, fish, ponds, pumps, fountains. Free.

☐ *J.E. Miller Nurseries,* 510 West Lake Rd., Canandaigua, NY 14424. Fruit trees, vines, berries. Free.

☐ *Musser Nursery,* Box 340, Indiana, PA 15701. Fine-quality tree seedlings. Free.

☐ *George W. Park Seed Co.,* P.O. Box 31 Greenwood, SC 29648. Complete garden supplies. Free.

☐ *Spring Hill Nurseries,* 6523 N. Galena Rd., Peoria, IL 61632. Widest variety of fruits, vegetables and plants. Free.

☐ *Stokes' Seed Catalog,* Box 548, Buffalo, NY 14240. Everything. Free.

☐ *Van Bourgondien & Sons,* P.O. Box 1000, Babylon, NY 11702. Finest domestic and imported bulbs and plants. Free.

☐ *Vermont Bean Seed Co.,* Garden Lane, Fair Haven, VT 05743. All kinds of vegetables. Free.

☐ *Wayside Gardens,* 1 Garden Lane, Hodges, SC 29695. Over 1,000 varieties of garden plants. Free.

☐ *White Flower Farm,* Litchfield, CT 06759. Everything for the garden. Small charge.

How to make flowers last longer

☐ Cut off the stems half an inch from the bottom. Make the cut at an angle so that the stem will not press against the bottom of the vase, closing off the flow of water.

☐ To slow water buildup (which makes petals droop), make a tiny incision at the base of the bloom.

☐ Fill an absolutely clean vase with fresh water.

☐ Add floral preservative. One recipe: Two squeezes of lemon juice, a quarter teaspoonful of sugar and a few drops of club soda.

☐ Change the water and preservative daily.

☐ Display the flowers out of the sun, and keep them cool at night.

☐ Remove leaves below the water line.

Source: T. Augello and G. Yanker, coauthors, *Shortcuts,* Bantam Books, New York.

Ten foolproof houseplants

These hardy species will survive almost anywhere and are a good choice for timid beginners without a lot of sunny windows.

☐ Aspidistra (cast-iron plant). This Victorian favorite, known as "The Spittoon Plant," survived the implied indignity in many a tavern.

☐ Rubber plant. Likes a dim, cool interior (like a hallway). If given sun, it grows like crazy.

☐ Century (Kentia) palm. A long-lived, slow-growing plant that needs uniform moisture. Give it an occasional shower.

☐ Philodendrons. They like medium to low light and even moisture, but will tolerate dryness and poor light.

☐ Dumb cane. Tolerates a dry interior and low light, but responds to better conditions. Don't let your pet chew the foliage or its tongue will swell.

☐ Bromeliads. Exotic and slow-growing, they like frequent misting, but are practically immune to neglect and will flower even in subdued light.

☐ Corn plant (dracaena). Good for hot, dry apartments.

☐ Snake plant. Will survive almost anything.

☐ Spider plant. A tough, low-light plant that makes a great trailer and endures neglect.

☐ Nephthytis. Will flourish in poor light and survive the forgetful waterer.

Source: Edmond O. Moulin, director of horticulture, Brooklyn Botanical Garden, Brooklyn, NY.

Poison plants

Plant poisoning among adults has increased alarmingly in the last decade. For children under five, plants are second only to medicines as a cause of poisoning. Prime sources: Common houseplants, garden flowers and shrubs, as well as wild mushrooms, weeds and berries.

Among the most common poisonous plants:

☐ Garden flowers: Bleeding heart, daffodils, delphinium, foxglove, hens and chickens, lantana, lily of the valley, lupine, sweet pea.

☐ Houseplants: Caladium, dieffenbachia, philodendron.

☐ Garden shrubs: Azalea, mountain laurel, oleander, privet, rhododendron, yew.

☐ Wildflowers: Autumn crocus, buttercups, jimson weed, mayapple, moonseed berries, poison hemlock, water hemlock, wild mushrooms.

Flowers that are good to eat

Many common flowers also make gourmet dishes. Here are some suggestions:

☐ Calendula (pot marigold): Add minced petals to rice, omelets, chicken soup, clam chowder or stew.

☐ Nasturtium: Serve leaves like watercress on sandwiches, or stuff flowers with basil- and tarragon-seasoned rice, then simmer in chicken stock and sherry.

☐ Squash blossom: Pick blossoms as they are opening, dip in a flour-and-egg mixture seasoned with salt, pepper and tarragon, then deep-fry until golden brown.

☐ Camomile: Dry the flowers on a screen in a dark place to make tea.

☐ Borage: Toss with salad for a cucumberlike taste, or use fresh for tea.
Source: *House & Garden,* New York.

All you need to know about bird feeders

The main thing is to mix your own seed. You can create a mix that will attract a wide variety of birds. What birds like most:

☐ Niger seed (Thistledown).
☐ Sunflower seeds (particularly the thin-shelled oilseed).
☐ White proso millet.
☐ Finely cracked corn.

Avoid:

☐ Milo and red millet, which are used as filler in commercial mixes and are not attractive to birds.
☐ Peanut hearts attract starlings, which you may want to avoid.

Requirements of a good feeder:

☐ It should keep the seed dry (mold by-products are toxic to birds).

☐ Be squirrel resistant (baffles above and below are good protection.

☐ For winter feeding of insect-eating birds (woodpeckers, chickadees, titmice and nuthatches), string up chunks of beef suet.
Source: Aelred D. Geis, Patuxent Wildlife Research Center of the US Fish and Wildlife Service, Laurel, MD.

How to choose a kennel

When you need to board your pet for any length of time, visit the kennel with your dog a week or two before you leave him there. Plan to spend some real time looking for:

☐ Operators who own the kennel. They will have a real stake in your satisfaction.

☐ A staff that shows sincere concern for the pet's welfare, not willingness to do whatever you tell them.

☐ Kennels and runs that are well designed. A combination of two feet of concrete with four feet of fencing above it is desirable so that timid dogs can hide from their neighbors. More important: No dog can urinate into another dog's run. (Urine and feces spread disease.)

☐ A security fence around the entire establishment (in case a dog escapes from its run).

☐ Kennels that are neat and clean. Kennel helpers are picking up waste, hosing down runs, exercising the dogs, etc.

☐ Beds that will not harbor parasites. Fiberglass is good. Wood is bad. Dogs with parasites should be dip-treated before boarding.

☐ A requirement of confirmation of your dog's shots, either by a recent inoculation certificate or contact with your veterinarian.

Questions You Should Ask

☐ What is the kennel owner's background? Ask about his/her experience in breeding and handling. Such experience helps the kennel owner notice when an animal is not feeling or moving well.

☐ What kind of food is used? A good kennel is flexible and serves nearly anything. Some even cook to order.

☐ What will you do if my pet won't eat? If a dog does not eat for two days, the kennel should try a variety of foods until it finds one that works.

☐ What kind of medical and behavioral history is taken? A thorough history includes more than a record of shots and your vet's name and phone number. You should be asked about your pet's temperament, behavior, sociability, likes and dislikes.

☐ Who will administer my dog's medication? Only the owner or the kennel manager should administer medicine, and careful records should be kept.

☐ What happens if my dog gets sick or there's a medical emergency? The kennel owners should call your veterinarian first, then bring your dog to your vet—or, if that's not possible, to a local veterinarian. If it's an emergency, your pet should be taken immediately to the kennel's attending veterinarian. Check the professional credentials of the kennel's attending veterinarian with your own vet.

☐ How often will my dog be walked? Dogs should be walked at least twice a day, in addition to exercising in their kennel runs.

☐ Will my dog be played with, and how often? Your pet should be played with and petted at least twice a day. Some toys should be allowed.

Source: Michael and Phyllis Scharf, owners and operators of Pomona Park Kennels, Pomona, NY.

When to trade in your old furnace

If your fuel bills seem higher than they should be, it may be time to replace your old furnace with a new one.

☐ Calculate whether your old oil furnace is costing you more than the price of a new one:

(1) Estimate your annual fuel bill.

(2) Divide your present furnace's efficiency rating by the efficiency rating of the new model you're considering. (Your local utility will rate your system for a small fee or for free.)

(3) Multiply the result by your annual fuel bill to estimate the savings. A new furnace should pay back its costs in about five to seven years.

Source: *Home*, Des Moines, IA.

Painting guidelines

Follow these simple suggestions for the effect you are looking for:

☐ To make a room look larger, use the same color on walls, floor and ceiling.

☐ Dark colors don't always make a room look smaller, though they can make a large room more intimate.

☐ Dark colors on all surrounding surfaces can highlight furniture and give an illusion of spaciousness.

☐ Cool wall colors make a room seem bigger.

☐ Warm colors make a room seem smaller.

☐ A long, narrow room can be visually widened by painting the long sides a lighter color than those at the ends.

☐ A ceiling slightly lighter in color than the walls appears higher…a darker one, lower.

Source: *Woman's Day*, New York.

The best cars you can buy

For some drivers, no car that comes off a Detroit assembly line is good enough. If you're one of these people, consider a prestige car…and be prepared to pay the price. What you'll get are advanced auto engineering and great luxury.

A sampling:

☐ *Mercedes-Benz 500 SEC.* Less angular lines give this four-door Mercedes a sportier look. New features include heated outside mirrors, theft alarm improvements and better brakes. Seats four to five.

☐ *Ferrari Mondial.* The newest design of the famous Italian sports car. 2.9-liter V-8 engine makes this car very powerful. Quieter and more comfortable to drive than earlier models. Seats four.

☐ *Maserati Quattroporte.* A hefty but very fast Italian four-door sedan. Beautifully finished with leather seats and real wood on the dashboard. Seats four.

☐ *Rolls-Royce Silver Spirit.* The staid, four-door sedan. With upright lines, it resembles a conventional taxicab. Improvements include stainless-steel wheel arches and window frames. Seats four or five.

☐ *Lamborghini Countach.* A very futuristic, exotic-looking Italian car. With retractable headlights and optional wing on the back, one of the most radical car designs on the market at the present time. Seats two.

☐ *Aston Martin Lagonda.* Four-door English sedan has a space-age dashboard with recessed push-button controls that you just touch for electronic digital information. Seats four.

☐ *Rolls-Royce Camargue.* A two-door sedan that's sleeker looking than the Rolls-Royce Silver Spirit. Smoother lines over the roof and above the window give a slightly less boxy appearance. Seats five.

Source: Don Coulter, managing editor, *Car and Driver*, Ann Arbor, MI.

How to win the car-buying game

Car salesmen thrive on confusion. They bombard you with questions and numbers to divert your attention from simple issues.

Tactics:

☐ Go shopping armed with specific information. Remember that you're not there to fall in love with a car or to make a friend of the salesman. Get answers you can understand.

☐ Buy the latest edition of *Edmund's New Car Prices.* It lists the base costs of each car and accessories, such as air conditioning and automatic transmission.

☐ When you find the car you like, copy down all pricing information from the manufacturer's sticker on the window. Compare the sticker prices with those in *Edmund's* to determine the dealer's profit. This gives you real bargaining ammunition.

☐ Be indecisive. The salesman will think there's a car you like better down the road. That means he must give you his best shot.

☐ Best times to shop: The last day of the month, when dealers close their books and want good sales figures, and very late in the day, when the sales staff is exhausted.

☐ Beware of red tag sales. Dealers' profits are higher than at any other time. Customers mistakenly assume they will save money during special sales. Really, they are fantasies that draw you away from reality. Stay with black-and-white issues you can control.

☐ Stick with what you can afford. This is determined by two things: How much cash your trade-in gives you towards the down payment and how much you can pay each month.

☐ Tell dealers you are interested in selling your car for cash. Their figures will give you a better idea of what your car is worth than a blue book. It's best to sell your car privately.

Source: Remar Sutton, car dealer and author of *Don't Get Taken Every Time: The Insider's Guide to Buying Your Next Car,* Penguin Books, New York.

What to look for when you test-drive a car

Before you buy a new car, take full advantage of your test drive. Make sure the dealer lets you drive the vehicle where you can give it a thorough workout…on bumpy roads…in stop-and-go traffic…and on highways, especially the entrance and exit ramps. Pay special attention to how the car matches up to your expectations for comfort, drivability, interior layout and power.

Comfort

☐ Engineers call the science of fitting the car to the person ergonomics. You'll soon see how well they did when you climb in behind the driver's seat.

☐ You probably won't be the only one driving the new car regularly. Don't forget that the "feel" of the car should suit your co-drivers and frequent passengers.

☐ Clearance: Can you get in and out without hitting your head?

☐ Headroom: Your hair shouldn't touch the ceiling. If it does, and you love the vehicle, consider ordering it with a sunroof. This will give you another inch or two.

☐ Seat height: Does it give you good road visibility?

☐ Headrest: Will your head, neck and back be comfortable after driving for a while?

☐ Leg room: Does the seat move far enough forward and back not only for you but for all drivers?

Drivability

☐ Test-drive the car at night to make sure that the headlights are powerful enough for your comfort.

☐ Power: Does the car run smoothly and accelerate adequately? Hint: Make sure the car you test has the engine size, transmission type, or gear ratios that you want.

☐ Rear visibility: Can you see adequately with the exterior rear-view mirrors? If they're too small, be aware that replacements don't exist.

☐ Noise: Does engine exhaust or wind noise bother you?

☐ Fuel type: Does the car need expensive high-test gas? High-performance, multi-valve, super- and turbo-charged models all do.

Interior

☐ Instrumentation: Can you read the gauges easily?

☐ Controls: Do you hit the wiper switch and put the radio on?

☐ Door handles: Can you find them in the dark?

Bottom line

☐ If you're satisfied with your test drive, don't assume the car that the dealer delivers to you will be as good.

☐ Check out the finish of the car you want to buy to make sure you haven't been sold a vehicle that already has been driven…or damaged in transit. Look for tell-tale signs of repainting…like paint traces on the rubber stripping or trim, mismatched colors and misfit panels. And take a good look at the undercoating. It should look slightly weathered—not sparkling clean and still soft.

☐ Insist on a test drive of your new car before you accept delivery. Also: Never take delivery at night. You want to examine your car carefully in broad daylight. You may also want to have the car looked over by a good mechanic.

Source: Dré Brungardt, editor, *Nutz and Boltz*, Box 123, Butler, Maryland 21023.

Understanding car terms

☐ Rack-and-pinion steering: This compact system has fewer moving parts than older systems and therefore is cheaper to make. But it is not necessarily better than the standard system.

☐ Unibody construction: Everything fastens onto the body, reducing the car's weight and increasing mileage. But a minor fender-bender can create hidden damage in another part of the structure.

☐ Automatic overdrive transmission: This is a fuel-economy measure. An extra high gear slows the engine when the car is cruising at a constant speed. Disadvantage: The car has reduced acceleration and hill-climbing ability when in this gear.

☐ Overhead camshaft engine: This slightly improves efficiency at high speeds, which is why some race cars use it. But this difference is not significant in normal driving.

Source: Automobile Club of New York.

Making the right choice of options on a new car

The value of an optional feature depends on how, when, and where most of the driving will be done.

Important for everyone: Options that make the car safer.

☐ Air bags.

☐ Steel-belted radial tires. They hold the road better, provide better fuel economy and longer life.

☐ Buy accessories that relate to the character of the automobile. A very lightweight car does not require power steering or power brakes.

Important but not essential:

☐ Cruise control. This is a great advantage for driving long distances on a regular basis. It sets the pace and helps the driver avoid speeding tickets.

☐ Air conditioning. This is very important for comfort and for the subsequent resale value of the car.

☐ Heavy-duty suspension system. It makes the car feel taut and firm and hold the road better. There is little initial cost and little value on resale. It is important for car owners who are either going to carry heavy loads or who love to drive and are extra sensitive to the performance of the car. It's not an important feature for those whose car use is limited mainly to trips to the supermarket.

☐ Power seats. Extremely useful feature for drivers who go long distances regularly. Permits moving the seat back. Allows arm position to be manipulated and fine-tuned in relation to steering wheel. In some ways a safety factor because it helps ward off driver fatigue. Power seats are quite expensive.

☐ Adjustable seat back. Some form of this is highly recommended and should be considered because it wards off driver fatigue and thus is a safety element.

☐ Tilt steering wheel. This is another aid in fine-tuning the driver's relation to the car and is therefore recommended as a safety factor. It is an important feature especially for large or short people.

☐ Electric door locks. Key unlocks all doors simultaneously. Button locks all doors at once, including the trunk lid. It is a convenience because it makes it unnecessary to open each door from the outside in bad weather. When driving through dangerous neighborhoods, the electric lock provides immediate security with the touch of a button.

Some options have disadvantages:

☐ Sunroof. Redundant if the car has air conditioning. Noise and the problem of water leakage are constant irritations.

☐ Power windows. They are recommended for drivers who use toll highways on a regular basis. Power windows can be dangerous to both small children and pets.

Fixing your present car vs. buying a new one

Most older cars can be refurbished— and in fact be made as good as new— for far less than the cost of a brand new car. The key: The break-even point of the deal.

To figure fix-up costs: Have a competent mechanic give you a detailed list of everything that's wrong and costs to fix it up. With that kind of renovation, a car should be good for another five years with no major repair expenses.

☐ Even if the car needed a completely new engine, it would still be cheaper to repair the old car than to buy a brand new one.

☐ Gas mileage is not a key consideration. Assume that a new car would get 50% better gas mileage than the older car. It would still take at least 10 years to break even on mileage alone. Example: Your present car gets 15 MPG, and a new car would get 30 MPG. You buy 1,000 gallons of fuel per year (15,000 miles of driving) and it costs $1.40 per gallon. Your present gas bill is $1,400 per year. The 30 MPG car would cost you $700 per year. At that rate, disregarding all the other expenses of the new car, it would take 14 years for a payback on the improved mileage.

☐ On the other hand, if your car is worth less than $1,000 and is rusting, rebuilding is not recommended. Severe rusting can't be fixed.

Source: Tony Assenza, editor of *Motor Trend*.

Shop for a used car

Before looking for a used car, decide the exact make, model and price you want (just as you would if you were buying a new car).

☐ Determine whether you want to use the car for extensive traveling, for weekends and summer travel, or just for getting to the train station and back. This helps you decide whether you want a 3- to 5-year-old car (extensive travel) or one 5 to 7 years old (suitable for weekend use and summer travel). For trips to the train station in the morning, or for equivalent use, a car that is 7 to 10 years old will do.

☐ Choose a popular make in its most successful and long-lasting model. Repair parts are also easier to find.

☐ Get the local paper with the most advertising for used merchandise. Privately owned cars are often very well maintained and are generally available at prices much lower than those being offered by dealers.

☐ Look for the deluxe model of the popular make you've chosen. Since it cost a lot more when it was new, there's a better chance it was well cared for.

☐ Establish (by shopping) the going price of your desired make and model. Then select only those cars offered at above the average price. Owners of the better-cared-for cars usually demand a premium, and it's usually worth it.

How to check out a used car

You don't have to be an expert to decide whether a used car is worth paying a mechanic to check out. The key steps:

☐ Get the name and telephone number of the previous owner if you buy the car from a dealer. If the dealer won't give you this information from the title, pass up the car. (It could be stolen.)

☐ Call the former owner and ask what the car's major problems were (not if it had any problems). Also, get the mileage on the car when it was sold. If the speedometer now reads less, it has

been tampered with. Go elsewhere.

☐ Inspect the car yourself. Even a superficial look can reveal some signs that will warn you off or will be worth getting repair estimates for before you settle on a price.

☐ Check the car for signs of fresh undercoating. There is only one incentive for a dealer to undercoat an old car—to hide rust. Check this with a knife or screwdriver (with the dealer's permission). If you find rust, forget the car.

☐ Rub your finger inside the tailpipe. If it comes out oily, the car is burning oil. Your mechanic should find out why.

☐ Kneel down by each front fender and look down the length of the car. Ripples in the metal or patches of slightly mismatched paint can indicate bodywork. If a rippled or unmatched area is more than a foot square, ask the mechanic to look at the frame carefully. (Ask the former owner how bad the wreck was.)

☐ Open and close all the doors. A door that has to be forced is another sign of a possible wreck.

☐ Check for rust around moldings, under the bumper, at the bottom of doors, in the trunk, under floor mats, and around windows. Lumps in vinyl tops are usually a sign of rust. Rust and corrosion on the radiator mean leaks.

☐ Check the tires. Are they all the same type? Does the spare match? If there is excessive wear on the edges of any single tire, the car is probably out of alignment.

☐ Check the brakes by applying strong pressure to the pedal and holding it for 30 seconds. If it continues to the floor, it needs work.

☐ Test-drive the car, and note anything that doesn't work, from the air conditioner to the windshield wipers. Listen for knocks in the engine and grinding or humming in the gears. Check the brakes and the steering. Drive over bumpy terrain to check the shock absorbers.

Source: Remar Sutton, author of *Don't Get Taken Every Time: The Insider's Guide to Buying Your Next Car,* Penguin Books, New York.

Buy a car at police auctions

Big-city police departments, in the course of their work, collect abandoned cars, evidence vehicles (those used in crimes) and towed-away cars that haven't been picked up. Buying a car at auctions of these vehicles can be a good deal, especially for a teenager who can do repair work.

Rules to follow:

☐ Inspect the autos the day before the auction. Each is listed by its make and year and is given an auction number that also appears on the windshield of the car. (You can make notes on the list of the cars that interest you and then check prevailing prices for such cars in the local newspaper want ads or in publications at the library.)

☐ Usually there is no ignition key, and in most cities you're not allowed to hotwire a start, either. What you can do: Inspect the car by opening the doors and hood and working the windows. Inspect the engine compartment for quality of maintenance and check the wires, hoses, motor oil level, transmission and brake fluid levels. Find out the mileage and determine the condition of the interior and tires.

☐ At the auction, fill out a form with your name and address to get a bidding number. All transactions are cash. You must pay the full price, plus tax, during the auction, not afterward. All sales are final.

☐ Set limits to your bidding and stick to them. No more than one-half the Blue Book value is recommended, and no more than one-third is safer. This way you'll come out ahead even if major repairs prove necessary.

☐ Collect a bill of sale acceptable to the local state motor vehicle department for registering the car when you pay. If you live out of state, check with your state automotive agency to see what other documents might be necessary to register the car in your state.

☐ Arrange to have the car towed away within a day or two of the auction. Even if you replace the ignition or jump start it, the car has no license plate or insurance. It also may not run.

Auto lemonaid

If that new car you just bought has been in the shop more than on the road, don't despair. Under state "lemon laws" you may be able to get most of

your money back, or at least a more reliable car...and without the risk of heavy court costs.

☐ The law: The car is usually covered for one year or the written warranty period, whichever is shorter.

☐ If a defect isn't repaired in four tries, the manufacturer must replace the car or give a refund (less depreciation). The same goes if the car is out of commission for 30 days or more for any combination of defects.

☐ If the manufacturer has a federally approved arbitration program, you must first submit your complaint to the arbitrators. But if you aren't satisfied with their decision, you can still take the company to court.

Strategy:

☐ Check the state attorney general's office for details of the law. Key point: Whether the manufacturer (as well as the dealer) must be given a chance to solve the problem.

☐ Submit a list of repairs to the dealer each time you bring the car in. Keep a copy for yourself.

☐ Keep a detailed record of car-repair dates and of periods when the car was unavailable to you.

☐ If the company agrees to settle but offers too little money or a car with too many miles, don't be afraid to dicker. The company doesn't want to go to court any more than you do.

Source: *Medical Economics*, Oradell, NJ.

Buying a car in Europe

Frequently, you can save hundreds or even thousands of dollars by buying a car straight from the factory in Europe.*

The saving varies according to the price of the car, but the best deals are on expensive cars. After shipping and other incidental expenses are paid, purchasing a car abroad should save you about 10%. And, because you'll have your own car to drive, you'll avoid transportation costs when traveling abroad.

☐ Almost a dozen European manufacturers offer special overseas delivery programs through their American dealers. Typical procedure:

*Overseas delivery programs are offered only by European auto makers. Japanese manufacturers, restricted by US importation quotas, cannot afford to offer such programs.

The customer orders and pays for his car in this country. Then he travels abroad to take delivery and arranges to have it shipped back home.

☐ It's possible to deal directly with European dealers and save even more (30%–35%), but this strategy has one fatal flaw: Although cars sold through European dealerships may look like their American counterparts, they generally lack the crucial safety and pollution-control equipment required by US law. Result: The cars must not be driven in this country without extensive—and often exceedingly costly—modifications.

☐ If you are considering purchasing a car overseas, be sure to make arrangements far in advance. Most auto makers need two to three months to process an order. Consult your dealer to be safe.

☐ American dealers require a deposit of $250 to $1,000 to place an order through an overseas delivery program. Settle all financial arrangements (including financing plans) before leaving this country.

☐ It generally does not pay to shop around in this country for the best price. European delivery prices are established by the manufacturer, not by individual dealers.

☐ Keep an eye on currency exchange rates. A devaluation of foreign currency can shave hundreds of dollars off the purchase price—if you buy at the right time.

☐ Ideally, begin your European trip in the city where the factory is located and end at a major European port. If such arrangements are impractical, however, you can arrange to have your car transported between cities—at a modest cost.

☐ Find out beforehand what will be expected of you once you arrive at the factory. Some companies favor a "casual" approach. This means you will have to take care of many of the final details for shipping. BMW and Mercedes-Benz, among others, take care of everything for the customer. Your dealer will fill you in on the details.

☐ Shipping costs vary, depending upon what distance your car must be transported. Factory representatives should be able to suggest a reputable shipping firm.

☐ Insurance should be purchased both for the time you'll spend driving in Europe and for the return trip on the freighter.

☐ Vehicle preparation, when not included in the purchase price of the automobile, is an additional expense. However, some gasoline-powered cars must be fitted with a catalytic converter after your European drive is over, which can increase costs.

☐ Registration: You must register the car for European driving and reregister the car for American driving (once you return home).

☐ Customs duties usually are 2.7% of the purchase price. This amount must be paid when your car arrives in the US.

Source: J. Bruce McWilliams, president, Galamander, Ltd.

Recreational vehicles

Design improvements have made recreational vehicles (RVs) cheaper, better built and more fuel-efficient. Miles-per-gallon have doubled. Weight has been reduced by the use of plastics, aluminum, and other lightweight materials.

Motorized RVs

☐ Motor homes: These provide all the conveniences of home (bathroom, air conditioning, etc.) and sleep 6 to 10 people. They come in three types of size.

☐ Van conversions: Conventional vans are turned into campers by installing beds and stoves. They sleep up to six people.

Towable RVs

☐ Travel trailers: Considered mobile bunk rooms that sleep eight. The conventional trailer is attached to a car. The fifth-wheel trailer attaches to a pick-up truck by means of a special plate (the "fifth wheel").

☐ Park trailers: Meant for long stays in one place. These little houses attach to the facilities of a trailer park for power and water. They sleep eight.

☐ Folding camper trailers: Collapsible sides that fold into a boxlike shape make these small enough to be towed by compact cars. They can sleep up to eight.

☐ Truck campers: Similar to van conversions in features, these units fit on the flatbed of a pick-up truck. They can sleep up to eight.

☐ Maintenance: The RV is a combination home and car…and requires the maintenance of both. You have to be alert to car-related upkeep as well as the emergencies you would encounter at home, such as frozen pipes or faulty wiring. Before you start on a trip, make sure everything in both the car and the RV is in good working order. Recommended: A checkup by your local service center.

☐ RV appliances are fueled by liquid propane. Some tunnels and urban areas do not allow RVs to enter with propane aboard. Check ahead for regulations in areas where you plan to drive.

☐ Driving an RV or the car that tows one requires special skills. Upon request, the Recreation Vehicle Industry Association will send you a list of its booklets that can help you learn the new skills.

Source: Bill Garpow, vice president, Recreation Vehicle Industry Association, Chantilly, VA.

Best car burglar alarms

Most insurance companies will give you a discount if your car is equipped with a burglar alarm system. Generally it's 10% off the premium—each year.

Don't put stickers in the car window announcing to the world what type of burglar alarm system you have. Most experts feel that this removes the element of surprise and can even help the thief.

Cheap alarms provide little more than a false sense of security for a car owner. A good thief can foil them easily. The features of a good alarm system:

☐ Passively armed. That is, it should require nothing more of the driver than shutting off the motor and removing the ignition key, without complicated setup procedures.

☐ Instant "on" at all openings. That means the alarm should trigger as soon as any door, the hood, or the trunk is opened.

☐ Remotely disarmed by a code, instead of by means of a switch or a key. A lock can be picked. A code is impossible to break.

☐ Hood lock. Denying a thief access to your engine, battery, and siren is a major deterrent.

☐ Backup battery to prevent a thief from crawling under your car, cutting the car's main battery and killing the entire electrical system, and, therefore the alarm system.

☐ Motion detector. The best kinds are the electronic motion detectors that sense a car's spatial attitude at the time the alarm is armed whether it's on a hill, on uneven ground, etc. (Also least prone to false alarms.)

☐ Extras: Pressure-sensitive pads in the seats and under carpeting. Glass-breakage detectors. Paging systems and air horns.

☐ Wheel locks if you own expensive optional wheels.

Make your car hard to steal

☐ Lock your car.

☐ Take your keys.

☐ Park in well-lighted areas.

☐ Park in attended lots. Leave ignition key only (not trunk key) with attendant.

☐ Install a burglar alarm.

☐ Activate burglar alarm or antitheft device when parking.

☐ Don't put the alarm decal on your car.

☐ Install a secondary ignition switch.

☐ Park with wheels turned toward the curb.

☐ Remove rotor from distributor.

☐ Install a fuel-shut-off device.

☐ Remove coil wire from distributor cap. (Especially useful for long-term parking at airports.)

☐ Close car windows when parking.

☐ Replace T-shaped window locks with straight ones.

☐ Install a steering-wheel lock, and use it.

☐ Install an armored collar around the steering column to cover the ignition.

☐ Don't hide a second set of keys in car.

☐ Never leave your car running when no one is in it.

☐ Don't let a potential buyer "test drive" alone.

☐ For front-wheel-drive cars, put on emergency brake and put in park.

□ Back your car into your driveway. A potential thief will then be forced to tinker with ignition system in full view of neighbors.

□ Lock your garage door.

□ Lock your car in your garage.

□ Be sure inspection sticker and license tag are current and were issued by the same state.

Source: Aetna Life and Casualty.

Sensible car maintenance

□ Average life expectancy for some vital parts of your car. Suspension system: 15,000 miles. Ignition wires: 25,000 miles. Water pump: 30,000 miles. Starter: 40,000 miles. Brake master cylinder, carburetor and steering mechanism (ball joints): 50,000 miles. Fuel pump: 75,000 miles. Clutch, timing gear chain/belt, universal joints: Up to 100,000 miles.

□ Replace brake fluid at least once a year. This isn't a common practice, and few owner's manuals mention it, but brake fluid attracts water (from condensation and humidity in the air), often causing corrosion in the master and wheel cylinders, shortening their lives. Replacing brake fluid regularly saves the more costly replacement of cylinders.

□ Cold weather probably means your tires need more air. A tire which may have lost a few pounds of pressure during the summer and fall driving season could easily become 8–10 pounds underinflated on a freezing day. This is enough to cut tire life by 25%. Rule of thumb: For every 10-degree drop in the ambient temperature, the air pressure in a tire decreases by one-half to one pound.

□ The oil-pressure warning light on the dashboard is not a foolproof system. By the time the light flashes, the engine has been without oil long enough to harm the machinery.

□ Car-scratch repair. When the scratch hasn't penetrated to the metal: Sand with fine sandpaper (400–600 grit) until the scratch disappears. Wipe the area clean with a soft cloth. Paint it carefully, and let the paint dry for a few days. Then apply rubbing compound according to the directions in the package. When the scratch has penetrated to the metal: After sanding with fine paper, apply a primer. After the primer dries, sand again with 320–400 grit sandpaper. Paint and let dry. Apply rubbing compound. Buy materials at an auto-supply store.

□ Use vinegar to clean dirt from chipped exterior car surfaces. Then, when the spot is dry, restore with touch-up paint.

□ Essential warmup. Idling the car doesn't warm up all the car's systems, such as lubricants, steering fluid or even all the drive train. Better: Keep speeds under 30 mph for the first quarter mile and not much over that for the next several miles.

□ Replace radials whenever the tread is worn down to 1/16 inch from the bottom of the tire groove. At that point, the grooves are too shallow to take water away, and hydroplaning may occur at higher speeds.

□ Do not "cross-switch" radials. Always exchange the left front with the left rear and right front with the right rear. Radials should never be remounted in a manner that will change the direction of rotation.

□ If your car is shaking and vibrating, wheels may need aligning. Improper alignment causes excessive tire wear and increases fuel consumption.

□ Wax your car at least twice a year…more often if it is exposed to salt air, road salt or industrial air or if it's parked outside. Clue: If water doesn't bead up on the car's surface after rain, waxing is needed.

Source: *National Association of Fleet Administrators' Bulletin* and *The Durability Factor*, edited by Roger B. Yepsen, Jr., Rodale Press, Emmaus, PA.

Auto service intervals

Average recommended service intervals (in miles) under both normal and severe driving conditions, from a survey of mechanics:

□ Oil & oil filter change. Normal: 4,155, Severe: 2,880.

□ Replace air filter. Normal: 10,363, Severe: 5,927.

□ Replace fuel filter. Normal: 11,597, Severe: 8,591.

□ Replace spark plugs. Normal: 14,185, Severe: 11,298.

□ Tune-up. Normal: 14,254, Severe: 11,245.

□ Replace PCV valve. Normal: 16,202, Severe: 14,288.

Flush & change coolant. Normal: 22,848, Severe: 18,049.

Replace V-belts. Normal: 24,853 or when necessary, Severe: 20,610 or when necessary.

Replace radiator and heater hoses. Normal: 29,031 or when necessary. Severe: 24,679 or when necessary.

Change auto-transmission fluid. Normal: 25,862, Severe: 18,994.

Adjust auto-transmission bands. Normal: 26,591, Severe: 19,141.

Chassis lubrication. Normal: 5,550, Severe: 4,701.

Repack wheel bearings. Normal: 21,580, Severe: 16,414.

Rotate tires. Normal: 9,003, Severe: 7,929.

Replace windshield wiper blades. Normal: 15,534 or when necessary, Severe: 11,750 or when necessary.

Source: *National Association of Fleet Administrators' Bulletin.*

Car battery rules

Car batteries give off explosive hydrogen gas and contain sulfuric acid. When cleaning or working around a battery, take the following precautions:

Never smoke or light a match.

Remove rings and other jewelry. The metal could cause a spark if it touches a battery terminal.

Wear goggles to prevent acid from splashing into your eyes.

If acid spills on your skin or on the car, flush the area with water immediately.

Work in a well-ventilated area.

Source: *The Family Handyman,* New York.

Buying the right size tire

With the exception of high-performance sports cars, the tires manufacturers install as original equipment are too narrow and too small. While they're perfectly adequate for the kind of day-to-day driving most people do, they don't offer the same performance offered by aftermarket tires. Finding the right tire depends on your needs.

If you're a very aggressive driver, you'll want a wider, low-profile tire that puts more rubber on the road.

If you're an average driver, who makes modest demands on his car, switching the original tires may not be a worthwhile expense. However, even an average, non-high-performance driver can gain some safety advantages in braking and wet weather adhesion by investing in uprated (wider, lower) tires.

The key to determining tire size for any car: The ratio of the width of the tire to its height (called "aspect ratio").

Most compacts these days are fitted with a 14-inch wheel and a 70 series (aspect ratio) tire.

Some small cars still come equipped with a 13-inch wheel.

To increase performance and traction, a driver with a 14-inch wheel and 70 series tire could move up to a 60 series tire with little or no compromise in ride.

Rule of thumb: Virtually any original equipment tire could be replaced by one size larger.

Source: Tony Assenza, editor of *Motor Trend.*

New-tire do's and don'ts

First check your owner's manual for the correct tire size. It may also list an optional size, but tires must be the same size and construction on each axle.

If you must mix tire constructions, the radial pair should be on the rear axle.

If you're buying only a pair of replacement tires, put the new ones on the rear wheels for better handling.

Buy tires according to your needs. If you are planning to sell your car soon, don't buy long-lasting radials—get a shorter-term tire, such as a bias ply or bias belted.

Consider the new all-season tires, especially if you live in a colder climate. These radial tires combine the traction of snow tires with the quiet ride and longer tread wear of a highway tire. And twice-a-year changing is not necessary, as it is for conventional snow tires.

Radial tires are expected to last for 40,000 miles; bias-belted tires for 30,000; and bias-ply tires for 20,000.

☐ Spring and fall are best for good discounts on tire prices.

☐ All tires sold in the US must meet Department of Transportation standards. You should always look for the DOT symbol on the sidewall of any tire sold in the US, whether foreign or domestic.

☐ Any tires, old or new, must be properly inflated if you expect good performance and long wear.

Source: Ed Lewis, deputy director, Tire Industry Safety Council, Washington, D.C.

Cutting down on gas usage

☐ Tuning. Poor engine tuning adds 5%–20% to fuel usage.

☐ Acceleration. The best mileage is at cruising speed (usually 35–45 mph). Recommended: A brisk, smooth acceleration to the highest gear.

☐ Stopping. A red light ahead? Slow down. If you can avoid stopping altogether, you will save gas. Don't follow others closely, or you'll pay for their stops in your fuel bill.

☐ Luggage. Every 100 pounds of needless weight costs up to .5 mpg.

☐ Remove ski or luggage racks (which create wind drag) when not in use.

☐ Speed. Driving an eight-mile commute each day at 70 mph instead of 55 mph will add more than $100 a year to fuel costs.

☐ Tire pressure. Inflate to the maximum listed on the sidewall.

☐ Radials. Cut 3–4% off the average gasoline bill.

☐ Hill driving. A 3% grade will add 33% to fuel usage. On the downward slope, build up momentum to carry you through the base of the next hill. Let up on the accelerator as you climb.

☐ Gas usage increases 2%–6% with automatic transmission; 1%–2% for each 10°F drop in temperature; 10% with heavy rain or head winds.

Source: California Energy Commission.

How to winterize your car

To make your winter driving easier:

☐ Put snow tires on all four wheels for maximum traction. If this isn't possible, make sure to put them on the drive wheels.

☐ Drain and flush the cooling system on any car more than two years old. C newer cars, add antifreeze if necessary.

☐ Use a concentrated windshield-washing solution: One quart rubbing alcohol, one cup water and one tablespoonful of liquid dishwashing detergent.

☐ Keep your gas tank at least half full prevent condensation that might freez and block the fuel line.

☐ For better traction on rear-wheel-drive cars, place sandbags in the forward part of the trunk.

☐ Keep these winter supplies where you can get at them easily: A scraper/brush, a shovel, and a bag of sand or kitty litter.

Source: Parents, New York.

Car emergency equipment

☐ Flashlight with fresh batteries.

☐ Flares or warning reflectors.

☐ Extra washer fluid.

☐ First-aid kit.

☐ Drinking water and high-energy foo

☐ Booster cables.

☐ Extra fan belt and alternator belt.

☐ Fully inflated spare tire.

☐ Tool kit (including jack, lug wrench, screwdrivers, pliers, adjustable wrenc and electrical tape).

Extras for winter driving:

☐ Tire chains and traction mats.

☐ Ice scraper.

☐ Warm clothing or blankets.

☐ Square-bladed shovel.

☐ Extra antifreeze.

A flashlight isn't enough

An old-fashioned flashlight is helpful, but it's not enough for all driving contingencies. Your car should have:

☐ A spotlight to pick out street signs and house numbers at night.

☐ A floodlight for broad illumination (under the hood, around a flat tire).

☐ A map-reading light that can be used without bothering the driver.

☐ A signal light to alert other cars to a breakdown.

☐ Most convenient: Two multipurpose

lights—one that plugs into your cigarette lighter and one that operates on flashlight batteries.

Flat tire do's and don'ts

☐ Avoid use of instant tire sealants. They camouflage the slow loss of air that signals a punctured tire.

Repair a tire (rather than replace it) only when the puncture in the tread area is ¼ inch in diameter or smaller. This puncture must be at least 15 inches away from a prior one, and tire tread depth must be more than ¹⁄₁₆ inch.

☐ Remove the tire from the wheel. A permanent repair can be made only from inside the tire. An internal inspection is a must. Driving on a flat (even a short distance at low speeds) can damage the crucial inner surface.

☐ After repair, have the tire and wheel assembly rebalanced. This will more than pay for itself in a smoother ride and longer tire life.

Coping with car trouble on the highway

Unexpected breakdowns on the open road are frustrating and can be very dangerous.

How to avoid them:

☐ Practice preventive maintenance. Have your car checked before you set out on a long trip.

☐ Likeliest sources of trouble: Battery, tires, belts and engine hoses.

☐ Be sure you have emergency supplies, such as flashlights, flares, and basic tools, and that your spare tire is inflated.

☐ At the first hint of trouble, move off the road, activate your emergency flashers and only then assess the problem.

☐ Fix the things you can yourself.

☐ If your car is overheating, you may be able to let it cool down and then proceed slowly to a gas station if you know one is nearby.

☐ If you are really stuck, wait for help.

Major highways are regularly patrolled by troopers. Less traveled roads may require a Good Samaritan.

☐ Don't leave your car. An abandoned car is vulnerable to theft and vandalism. And in winter, you are vulnerable to the elements.

☐ To signal for help, raise your hood or your trunk lid as a distress signal. Hang a white handerchief or colored scarf from it. If you have flares or reflectors, set them out (in those states where they are legal).

☐ Run the motor (and heater or air conditioner) only 15 minutes out of every hour, keeping a window slightly open to guard against carbon monoxide poisoning.

☐ If you are a woman alone, keep the car doors locked and the windows rolled up while waiting. This gives you a protected vantage point for sizing up strangers who approach the car.

☐ When help arrives, describe your car problem clearly so a service station can send the proper equipment. Beware of helpful strangers who are not mechanically inclined. Using battery jump cables incorrectly can cause an explosion or ruin your alternator. Improperly hitched tows can ruin your automatic transmission.

☐ You must stay calm and be patient. If this is too upsetting a proposition for you, consider investing in a car phone or CB radio so that you can get help sooner.

Source: Francis C. Kenel, Ph.D., director of traffic safety, American Automobile Association, Falls Church, VA.

Your car radio

☐ Don't turn on your car stereo during the first five minutes of your drive. Use that time to listen for noises that could signal car trouble.

☐ Organize your stereo tapes before you leave, so you can pick them out without taking your eyes off the road.

☐ Keep all tapes within easy reach.

☐ Don't wear headphones while you drive. A safe driver must be able to hear the traffic as well as watch it.

☐ Wait for a straight patch of road before glancing at the stereo to adjust it.

☐ Read your tape cassette titles at eye level so you can see the road at the same time.

Source: *High Fidelity*, New York.

Top-of-the-line car stereos

For the serious music lover who spends a lot of time in a car, first-rate radio and tape systems are available—at a price. Although most factory-installed stereos are mediocre, a number of audio companies make good sound systems for cars.

Like home stereo systems, car stereos are bought in components:

☐ Radio/tape decks: Alpine, Kenwood, and Sony.

☐ Speakers: Sound to rival home units…B and W and ADS.

☐ Amplifiers: High-powered units with low distortion and good reliability are made by ADS and Alpine.

☐ Essential: Professional installation with a warranty. Proper mounting and wiring of the components affects not only the sound but also the system's longevity.

Buying a cellular phone

Before you buy a cellular phone, be aware that:

☐ They are now connected to brain cancer in some studies.

☐ Phone bills are expensive because you're billed for incoming as well as outgoing calls. And—an access charge is tacked on to your monthly bill.

☐ Insurance costs may go up because few basic auto policies now cover the theft of cellular phones from cars. Figure on $50 a year per vehicle for additional insurance.

☐ Some equipment is being marketed by companies that may not be in business in the future as the competition gets tougher.

☐ The phone is worth the expense whenever (1) Making calls from your car actually frees you for more productive activities at the office, or (2) You can prove that the calls really result in an increase in company business.

What to look for today when you buy a cellular phone:

☐ A speaker-phone model so you can talk without holding the handset, a valuable feature because it lets you keep both hands on the wheel except when you're dialing.

☐ A system that hooks into the company switchboard. Then office calls can be forwarded directly to you by the switchboard operator.

☐ An electronic lock that lets you dial a code number to stop calls from being made to or from the phone.

☐ A switch that enables you to talk on both frequencies that cellular transmitters use in cities when they're available. Phones with only one frequency occasionally lose quality when the car passes through an area where there's interference with the radio waves that carry the conversation.

☐ A manufacturer that's been in existence for several years and isn't known to have financial problems.

Source: Fritz Ringling, vice president of communications research, Gartner Group, Stamford, CT.

Driving small cars safely

In a severe crash between a large car and a small one, those in the small car are eight times more likely to be killed. Defensive strategies:

☐ Wear seat belts. A belted occupant of a small car has the same chance of surviving as the unbelted occupant of a big car in a crash between the two.

☐ Keep your lights on at low beam full time to increase visibility.

☐ Be aware that light poles and signs along the road may not break away as designed when hit by a lightweight compact car.

☐ Respect the inability of larger vehicles to maneuver or stop as quickly to escape a collision.

Dealing with trucks on a highway

To pass a truck:

☐ Blow your horn or blink the headlights to indicate your intentions.

☐ If it's raining, pass as quickly as possible to reduce road spray.

☐ After passing, speed up to avoid tailgating.

When following:

☐ Maintain a distance of 20–25 feet so the truck driver has a complete view of your vehicle.

☐ Be prepared for a possible truck shift to the left (even when it's signaling a right turn) as the driver makes sure he clears the right curb.

☐ Stay at least one or two car lengths back so as to remain in the truck driver's line of vision. This is especially important on an upgrade, where the truck may roll back a few feet.

Source: Canadian Vehicle Leasing's *Safe Driving Bulletin,* as reported in the *National Association Fleet Administrators Bulletin,* 295 Madison Ave., New York.

Driving in hot weather

☐ Inspect the auto radiator for leaks, and check the fluid level.

☐ Check all hoses for possible cracks or sponginess. Make sure all connections are tight and leak free.

☐ Test the thermostat for proper operation. If it does not operate at the proper temperature, overheating could occur.

☐ Inspect the fan belt for cracks and proper tension. Belt slippage is a common cause of boilovers. It also drains electrical power.

☐ If loss of coolant has been a problem, check for water seepage on the water pump around the engine block.

☐ Don't turn off the engine when the temperature warning light goes on. If stuck in traffic, shift to neutral, and race the engine moderately for 30 seconds at two-minute intervals.

☐ Shut off the air conditioner to avoid further overtaxing of the cooling system.

☐ Turn on the heater for a few minutes. It may help.

☐ If the radiator continues to overheat, drive the car off the road, turn off the engine and raise the hood.

☐ Wait at least half an hour before removing the radiator cap. Then do it very slowly and carefully, with the help of a towel or thick rag. Keep your face turned away from the radiator.

☐ If your car has the see-through overflow catch tank, replace any loss of coolant. Don't touch the radiator.

☐ If the fluid level is low, restart the engine while adding cool or warm water as the engine idles.

Source: Automobile Association of America.

Preparing for cold weather driving

☐ Radiator coolant: Read the label on your antifreeze to be sure you make the right blend of water and antifreeze. The antifreeze keeps your radiator from freezing and cracking; the water, even in winter, keeps your car from overheating.

☐ Battery condition: Your car needs three to four times more starting power in winter than in summer. Have a mechanic do a complete battery draw and load test. If your battery fails, a recharge may save it for another year. Otherwise, invest in a new one.

☐ Windshield washer fluid: Frozen fluid in the washer tank is dangerous. Use a premixed commercial fluid. Check that the hoses are clear, and clean the washer nozzles out with a thin piece of wire.

☐ Electrical system: Make sure the distributor cap, points, condenser, ignition coil, spark plugs, and spark-plug cables are in good shape. Borderline components that still function in summer will give out in cold weather.

☐ Hoses and belts: If they are cracking or fraying, replace them.

☐ Tires: If you have all-season tires, be sure the tread is still good enough to give you traction on slippery roads. Otherwise, put on snow tires. Important: If you have a front-wheel drive car, the snow tires go on the front. Store summer tires on their sides, not on the tread. (Storing on the tread causes a flat spot and an unbalanced tire.) Inflate stored tires to only 50% of their operating pressure.

☐ Windshield: Apply antifogging compound to the inside.

☐ Cleaning: Clear dead bugs off the radiator by hosing it from the inside of the engine compartment. Pick out dead leaves and debris from the fresh-air intake box of the ventilation system.

☐ Stock up: Buy flares, an aerosol wire-drying agent, a scraper and brush, chains and a military-style collapsible trench tool for emergencies. Keep a lock de-icer at home and/or at the office.

How to brake on ice

☐ Start early.

☐ Squeeze the brakes with a steady pressure until just before you feel them begin to lock.

☐ Ease up, and slowly repeat the pressure.

☐ Disc brakes do not respond well to pumping (the old recommendation for drum brakes). They will lock, causing you to lose control of the car.

Source: National Safety Council, Chicago, IL.

How to get out of a snow drift

To get unstuck:

☐ Turn your wheels from side to side to push away the snow.

☐ Check to be sure that your tailpipe is clear (so carbon monoxide won't be forced into the car).

☐ Start the motor.

☐ Put the car in gear, and apply slow, steady pressure to the accelerator to allow the tires to get a grip.

☐ Don't spin the wheels (this just digs you in further).

☐ Let the car pull out straight ahead if possible.

☐ Extra help: Sprinkle kitty litter in front of the wheels for traction.

Source: National Safety Council, Chicago, IL.

Auto dealer ripoff

☐ Car-purchase padding: A prep fee of $100 or more (whatever the dealership thinks it can get away with). The cost of preparing your car for delivery is already included in the manufacturer's sticker price.

Source: *Consumer Guide to Successful Car Shopping* by Peter Sessler, TAB Books, Blue Ridge Summit, PA.

Accidents with aggressive drivers

Violent and aggressive drivers are dangerous when they get into an accident. If you're in an accident with one, stay calm.

☐ Don't escalate any argument.

☐ Copy down the other driver's license number immediately.

☐ If you are threatened, leave at once.

☐ Call the police so that you won't be charged with leaving the scene of an accident…but do it from a safe distance.

☐ If your car is disabled, lock the doors and wait for the police to arrive.

All about speeding tickets

The best way to avoid speeding tickets is, of course, to avoid speeding. But all of us drive over the limit occasionally.

Here are some suggestions to help you avoid tickets:

☐ Know the limits. It's no illusion that police officers generally ignore cars driving just slightly over the posted speed. In fact, many departments set threshold speeds (six miles an hours above the limit in one state, for example) at which officers are to take no action. You might be able to slip by at 65 mph in a 55 mph zone, but you're unlikely to do the same at 70 mph.

☐ Be selective. Most speeding tickets are written during the morning and evening rush hours, when there are more motorists and more police officers on the road. Late night and very early morning are not watched nearly as carefully.

☐ Drive unobtrusively. Flashy cars attract attention, something to keep in mind if you drive a red Maserati. The same applies to flashy driving styles. Don't tailgate slower cars to force them aside. Don't weave in and out of traffic.

☐ Be vigilant. The likeliest spot to get nabbed on the highway is just beyond a blind curve or the crest of a hill, the best hiding places for patrol cars. Learn to recognize likely traps, and reduce your speed whenever appropriate.

☐ Remember that police officers can nab speeders from virtually any position—the rear, the front, the side, or even from aircraft. Be on the lookout at all times. An unmarked car on the side of the road with its trunk open is especially suspect (A radar device may be inside.)

☐ Fight back. Radar guns can be foiled occasionally. What to do: Position your car close to other cars whenever possible. Police officers generally cannot match you with the speed indicated on their guns unless they have an unobstructed view of your car. In most states, motorists also can make use of radar detectors, devices designed to alert drivers to radar early enough to slow down before police officers can get a good reading. If you do a lot of driving, a detector is a sensible investment if it is legal in your area.

☐ Use psychology. All is not lost even if you are pulled over. Police officers feel vulnerable when stopping speeders— you could be speeding away from a murder for all they know, and consequently they are usually nervous. Put them at ease. Sit still, keep your hands in plain view (on the steering wheel is a good place). Be courteous and respectful. Above all, be honest. If you have a good excuse for going over the limit, state it. Otherwise, admit guilt and apologize. Police officers can be surprisingly lenient if you're cordial.

How to ease long-distance driving

For a safe, healthy trip when you're driving a long distance:

☐ Do most of your driving during daytime hours. Visual acuity is lessened at night.

☐ Be particularly careful to check out your car's exhaust system before leaving—a leak can send odorless but deadly gases into the car.

☐ To insure sufficient fresh air inside the car, leave both a front and a back window open. Tailgate windows should be kept closed. Use your air conditioner. It provides fresh air and quiet inside the car. Although it reduces gas mileage, the loss is not much more than the loss from open windows' drag.

☐ Use seat belts and shoulder harnesses to relieve fatigue, as well as to boost safety.

☐ Take 20- to 30-minute rest breaks after every one-and-a-half or two hours of driving.

☐ Exercise during your breaks.

☐ Eat frequent high-protein snacks for improved driving performance.

☐ Don't stare straight ahead, even if you're the only car on the road. Keep your eyes moving.

Eating on the road

☐ Don't simply follow the truck drivers. Their first priority is a huge parking lot, not the best food.

☐ Avoid restaurants on or very near major highways and shopping centers. You're likely to do better downtown. Good bets: College or university towns.

☐ Best authorities: Bookstore managers, fancy kitchenware and gourmet food store's personnel. Worst: Tollbooth or gas-station attendants.

☐ Beware of large signs and quaint spellings.

☐ Check out the parking lot. Too many out-of-state license plates suggest a tourist trap. Good sign: A high proportion of foreign cars (especially European ones).

Source: *Travel & Leisure.*

Car games

To make the ride less tedious, here are some games to play:

Educational Games

☐ Spelling Bee. Take along a dictionary.

☐ Discover America. As someone keeps score, riders name the states of the union and their capitals.

☐ Add a Letter. Start with a single letter and go around building a word.

☐ I'm a Famous Person (also known as Botticelli). Pretend to be a celebrity— living or dead. Give clues to your personality as others try to guess who you are.

☐ Quiz Kids. Before the trip, collect an assortment of difficult questions and answers. (You can use Trivial Pursuit cards.)

☐ Words. Select a long word, such as *separation*, and then see how many words can be made from its letters. Have pencil and paper handy.

Silly Games

☐ Famous Pairs. Within a given period of time, perhaps half an hour, reel off the first names of famous couples. Examples: George and Martha, Ron and Nancy, Jimmy and Rosalynn.

☐ Don't Say That Word. Prohibit certain words from the conversation, such as *it, no, yes.* Try to maintain a dialog without using them.

☐ What Time Do We Arrive? Each person guesses the time of arrival at various places along the route—the next big city on the map, when you stop for lunch or gasoline.

☐ Animals. See who can spot the most cows, horses, etc. in the fields by the side of the road.

☐ Name That License Plate. Look for funny personal license plates that have names, initials or unusual numerical combinations.

☐ Plates and States. Keep lists of cars from different states. The person who gets the most states within a set period wins.

☐ Sign Games. Think up lines to rhyme with interesting billboards or signs.

☐ Let's Find It. Agree to look for one special thing—a covered bridge, a bright red automobile. The first one to spot it wins and then selects the next thing to look for.

☐ If I Were a Millionaire. Ask what people would want if they were millionaires. Then ask them for second wishes.

☐ Favorite Books and Movies. Review the books and movies you have liked best. Tell what makes them enjoyable.

☐ Sports Favorites. Prepare a series of questions about sports events and stars before you depart. Then quiz sports fans while on the trip.

☐ Where Am I Going? Mentally select a place where you are headed. Give hints about your imaginary destination, and let the other passengers guess where you are going.

Song Games

☐ Sing-Along. See how many songs you can sing by different composers—Cole Porter, Irving Berlin, Billy Joel, The Beatles.

☐ Sing Along With Me. Bring a book of popular songs and lead the car in an old-fashioned sing-along.

☐ Tap-a-Song. Tap out the rhythm of a famous song. Give each person three guesses.

Semi-serious Games

☐ Personal History. Spin tales of family remembrances—a time spent with grandparents, a favorite birthday, a lovely trip taken in the past. Give each person a chance to share an experience.

☐ Play Psychiatrist. Ask everyone what bothers them most about their lives. Try to help them resolve their problems.

How never to get lost on interstate highways

The system to the numbering:

☐ One- or two-digit even-numbered highways: Major East-West routes.

☐ One- or two-digit odd-numbered highways: Major North-South routes.

☐ Three-digit figure starting with an even number: Loop route around a city.

☐ Three-digit figure starting with an odd number: Road that is heading to or from center city.

Collect full auto insurance benefits

Expedite your insurance claim—and increase your chances of a fair settlement—by keeping careful records of the accident.

Guidelines:

☐ Immediately set up an orderly file containing police records, repair estimates, hospital bills, and copies of claims submitted.

☐ Document everything in writing. Write a follow-up letter confirming any telephone conversations with insurance company representatives. Include the date and the names of the persons with whom you spoke. File a copy.

☐ If the insurance company stalls, check your policy to see whether your coverage includes use of a rental car during the settlement period. If so, rent one. By spending the company's money, you may speed up the claim.

Source: The National Insurance Consumer Organization, Alexandria, VA.

Leaving the office at the office

It's important to learn to separate your professional from your private life. Particularly today, when the business world seems more fast-paced than ever, this can be hard to do. In the now famous quote of a hard-driving executive: "Nobody ever said on his deathbed, 'I wish I had spent more time at the office.'" Bear in mind that work has its busy seasons and its peak periods. Then, and during ambitious times such as a business start-up, it may not be appropriate to think of leaving the office behind every day. But that shouldn't always be the case. Balance is the goal to work toward.

☐ Make a conscious effort to change your mind-set when you are not at work. Clues that your head is still at the office: You chafe because the host is slow in moving you and other guests to the dining table...You make an agenda before going out to spend the afternoon with your child and stick to the agenda even when something more interesting intrudes. These are business mind-sets inappropriate to nonoffice activities.

☐ Give yourself a steady stream of physical cues to help you separate your office from your private world. Don't wear a watch on weekends. If you feel time pressures even when you're at home, don't use digital clocks in the car or home. They pace off the seconds and minutes too relentlessly for many people.

☐ Change your clothes as soon as you get home. And if you feel naked without your dictating machine or your briefcase with you at home, experiment with feeling naked!

☐ Use your physical setting to help you keep work in its place. Tell yourself that you can work only at a particular place at home if you must work. Don't take papers to bed with you. Don't spread them out over the couch, the dining table and the floor.

☐ Relax before plunging into housework or domestic activities. Working women especially have trouble giving themselves a 10-minute break when they get home because they're inclined to feel anxious about talking with the children or starting dinner. Take the break. It can make all the difference between experiencing the rest of the evening as a pleasure or as yet another pressure.

☐ Rituals are a useful device for making the switch. Secretaries do this by tidying up the desk or covering the typewriter. Lyndon Johnson symbolically turned off the lights in the Oval Office when he left. For managers, some useful rituals are loosening ties or other constricting clothing, turning a calendar page or making a list of things to do for the next day. They all help make the break. The to-do list also helps curb the desire to catch up on tomorrow's tasks while you're at home.

☐ Resist the growing tendency to abuse the whole winding-down process by taking up activities that create problems of their own...compulsive sex...addictive exercise...overeating or overdrinking...recreational drugs. Better: Use the transition time as a period of discovery. Walk or drive home along a different route. Pick up something new at the newsstand instead of the usual evening paper.

☐ The other side of leaving the office at the office is to leave home at home. It may be productive to use lunchtimes to buy paint, but that's not helpful in keeping the two worlds separate.

Source: Dr. Marilyn Machlowitz, Machlowitz Associates, a management development firm, New York.

Planning your leisure time

If you're like most people, there are lots of activities you'd like to do in your leisure time, but you never seem to get around to them. The solution is to plan—not so much that you feel like you're "on the job," but not so little that you fail to accomplish whatever is important to you, whether that means learning French or going dancing. Recommended:

☐ Create a "to do" list for your spare time just as you might for your workday. You probably don't want every hour accounted for, but you should at least list what you most want to do with each leisure evening or weekend.

☐ Allot some specific times on a regular basis when you will pursue the leisure activities that are most important to you. A scheduled time will help ensure the successful fulfillment of your plan.

☐ If it's culture you're after, consider getting at least one subscription series to eliminate some of the paperwork and phone calling that often accompany even leisure-time plans. (You will also avoid wasting time in line!)

☐ Set up regular social contacts, like monthly Saturday dinner with specific friends, so you spend less time coordinating your meetings and more time enjoying them.

☐ If you use too much of your recreation time for household chores, try delegating those tasks to professional help or family members. Or do it more efficiently and less frequently.

☐ If you often work in your leisure hours, consider that you may be more efficient if you plan, and carry out, pleasurable activities that energize you (and prevent work burnout).

☐ To keep your leisure-time plans active (not reactive to other people's demands on you), make appointments with yourself. You will be less inclined to give up your plans if someone else asks you to do something, since you have a previous commitment to yourself.

☐ Just as a "quiet hour" of uninterrupted time at the office increases your work efficiency, a "quiet" leisure hour enhances your nonwork time. On a fixed schedule, if possible, take some time each evening and weekend to meditate, listen to music, reflect, or just plain old "unwind."

☐ How can you find more hours for recreation? By setting your alarm clock only half an hour earlier on weekends you'll gain four hours a month. Become more efficient at work, so you can leave earlier (and not have to take work home as often). To find the time to read that mystery novel, try switching from showers to baths, and read in the tub.

Source: J. L. Barkas, Ph.D., author of *Creative Time Management*, Prentice-Hall, Englewood Cliffs, NJ.

47 inexpensive ways to have a good time

Having fun can't be calculated in dollars and cents. Sometimes the less money you spend, the more you enjoy yourself. Here are some inexpensive ways to have fun:

☐ Explore the beach and collect seashells.

☐ Visit the zoo and feed the monkeys.

☐ Go to a free concert in the park.

☐ Pack a picnic and drive to an attractive spot for lunch.

☐ Go skiing at your local park or a nearby mountain.

☐ Window-shop at your favorite stores.

☐ Eat early-bird-special dinners at local restaurants. Then go home and see a movie on TV.

☐ Hug each other more.

☐ Dress up with your favorite person and enjoy a formal dinner at home with fine food and wine.

☐ Go camping or backpacking.

☐ Go gallery-hopping. See the latest art exhibits.

☐ Enjoy your public library. Go to the reading room and catch up on the new magazines.

☐ Go for a drive on the back roads to just enjoy the scenery.

☐ Visit friends in a nearby city. (Arrive around lunchtime.)

☐ Eat dinner at home. Then go out for dessert and coffee.

☐ Instead of eating dinner out, eat lunch out over the weekends. It's less expensive.

☐ Seek out discount tickets and twofers for local entertainment.

☐ Take in the local museum's cultural events, including low-priced lectures and concerts.

☐ Invite friends in for drinks when a good movie is on TV.

☐ Take an afternoon walk in the park.

☐ Row a boat on the lake.

☐ Have a beer-and-pizza party for friends.

☐ Go back to the old family board games.

☐ Raise exotic plants or unusual herbs in a window box.

☐ Learn to paint or sculpt.

☐ Learn calligraphy.

☐ Take a long-distance bus ride.

☐ Go out to the airport and watch the planes.

☐ Visit the local amusement park and try the rides.

☐ Have friends over for a bring-your-own-specialty dinner.

☐ Become a do-it-yourselfer.

☐ Take an aerobic exercise course.

☐ Join a local political club.

☐ Go shopping for something really extravagant. Keep the sales slip and return the item the next day.

☐ Play cards for pennies, not dollars.

☐ Go to the races and place $2 bets.

☐ Explore your own city as a tourist would.

☐ Learn to be a gourmet cook.

☐ Treat yourself to breakfast in bed.

☐ Hold a family reunion.

☐ Attend religious services.

☐ Learn a foreign language.

☐ Join a local chorale or dramatic club.

☐ Watch local sports teams practice.

☐ Play golf or tennis at local parks or courses.

☐ Read everything in your area of interest at the library.

☐ Buy books. Get many hours of pleasure (and useful information) for still relatively few dollars.

To celebrate a really special occasion

☐ Take over a whole performance of a play or concert for your special guests. During the course of the event, have a prominent individual step out of character and tell the audience about you and your special day.

☐ Have a song written especially for the occasion.

☐ Run a tennis or golf party, with a name professional hired to give lessons to all.

☐ Hire a boat and bring along a large group for a cruise and buffet supper.

☐ Arrange a block party.

☐ Rent a hay wagon and a big barn for a square dance.

☐ Hire the museum or the lobby of a key office building in the downtown area for a huge buffet supper and dance.

☐ Hire a well-known singer to entertain at a party.

☐ Have a cookout on the beach, with the guests digging for related buried treasures.

☐ Take over a country inn for a day, and run a big house party.

☐ Fly a group of friends to a special place for a holiday.

The six best champagnes

☐ *Taittinger Comtes de Champagne*—vintage only. A rosé champagne that should go far to overcome Americans' prejudice toward this celestial brew. Taittinger also makes a fine blanc de blancs and a nonvintage brut.

☐ *Dom Perignon*—vintage only. Probably the most widely acclaimed champagne and deservedly so. Elegant and light, with delicate bubbles. The producer also makes, under its Moet et Chandon name, a vintage rosé champagne, a vintage champagne, a nonvintage champagne, and a nonvintage brut.

☐ *Perrier-Jouet Fleur de Champagne*—vintage only. This house produces champagne of the highest quality in a particularly popular style. The wine is austere, yet tasteful. It is also extremely dry without being harsh or acidic. Perrier-Jouet is introducing a rosé champagne.

☐ *Louis Roederer Cristal*—vintage only. Cristal's magic lies in its plays with opposites: Elegant yet robust, rich taste without weightiness. Roederer also produces a sparkling rosé, a vintage champagne, and a nonvintage brut.

☐ *Bollinger Vieilles Vignes*—vintage only. This is the rarest of all fancy champagnes. Its vines have existed since before phylloxera (a plant louse) killed most French grapevines in the middle 1800s. The wine is robust and rich flavored. Bollinger also makes a vintage champagne and a nonvintage brut.

☐ *Dom Ruinart Blanc de Blancs*—vintage only. Produced by Dom Perignon in Reims rather than in Epernay, it is a sleeper. It is held in low profile so as not to compete strongly with its illustrious co-product but is every bit as good. The wine is light (not thin), complex, very alive, yet velvety.

Source: Jack Lange, veteran of the wine business and vice president of 67 Wines and Spirits, New York.

Networking: Constructive, fun get-togethers

Do you often wonder how to get to know someone you've met in passing without seeming too pushy? Would you be interested in finding out about current issues from people who are actually involved in them? It is possible to do all of the above, and in addition expand your business and social contacts and have a great time, without spending a lot of money. Here are some suggestions from three veteran networkers:

Networking Dinners

☐ Have dinners for 13 to 15 people on Tuesday, Wednesday or Thursday at 6:30 so people can come straight from work and leave at a reasonable hour.

☐ Don't worry about the mix. There's a surprising commonality that develops among people of all ages and professions. Avoid inviting co-workers, couples or business partners. Candor diminishes when a guest comes with someone he sees all the time. Guests who spark conversation especially well: journalists, headhunters, celebrities.

☐ Use a modest typewritten or telephoned invitation. Ask guests to call your secretary. Send the invitations at least two weeks in advance.

☐ It's up to you, as the host or hostess, to get conversation started. Give informative introductions for each guest, mentioning at least three things people can ask questions about.

☐ A cozy, circular table keeps one conversation rolling rather than several private ones.

☐ The food needn't be fancy—only good, and plentiful, with lots of wine so tongues loosen. Chinese food works well because everyone seems to like it.

☐ Don't worry about inviting equal numbers of men and women. People are being matched for dinner, not for life.

Networking Salons

☐ Encourage guests to drop off their business cards as they enter. This serves as a conversation-opener and theme. Since business networking is the purpose, it is socially acceptable to go up to someone and ask, "What do you do?"

☐ People should be encouraged to exchange business cards. The cards you collect may become one basis for invitation lists.

☐ Hold salons on a regular basis, from 6 P.M. to 9 P.M. on Wednesday or Thursday. For example, every week it becomes a different, exciting mini-event with new people.

☐ People, not food, are the focus. You might have a simple but beautiful vegetable spread. The wine might be donated as a promotion.

Issue Discussion Groups

☐ Finding people to invite is not hard. And it gets easier as time goes on.

☐ Send out a list of topics six months in advance to those who've come to previous groups, and they often recommend others. At this point, many people know about the groups and call to ask about upcoming evenings.

☐ The key to success is active participation. Encourage guests to do homework, read relevant articles and bring copies with them.

☐ To begin, each person introduces himself or herself briefly, explaining why he's interested in the topic, and then presents an interesting fact unrelated to the main topic for a 15-second presentation.

☐ The groups should be held after dinner hour. Each guest might bring something for dessert. Eat after the discussion to give people an opportunity to socialize.

☐ Get ideas for topics from articles that you file based on what you predict will be newsworthy in six months. Try to plan evenings around upcoming events. Topics tend to grow out of each other.

Source: Machlowitz, Rubin & Yaffe

Bill Blass's favorite restaurants

Fashion designer Bill Blass has simple and very American gastronomic preferences. His top-rated restaurant choices:

New York

☐ *The Four Seasons*, 99 E. 52 St. (212) 754-9494. It is a beautiful place to have a quiet business lunch.

☐ *La Grenouille*, 3 E. 52 St. (212) 752-1495. The food is superb, and the flowers make it really special.

☐ *Mortimer's*, 1057 Lexington Ave. (212) 317-6400. A good place to see friends and enjoy good American cooking.

Boston

☐ *The Ritz Carlton Dining Room*, 15 Arlington St. (617) 536-5700. Its view of the Public Garden is splendid.

Chicago

☐ *The Cape Cod Room*, Drake Hotel, N. Michigan Ave. at Lake Shore Dr. (312) 787-2200. Excellent seafood.

Beverly Hills (Los Angeles)

☐ *The Bistro*, 246 N. Canon Dr. (310) 273-5633. A lovely setting for fine food.

San Francisco

☐ *Trader Vic's*, 20 Cosmo Place (415) 776-2232. Excellent Polynesian, Continental and American food.

Paris

☐ *The Ritz Hotel Dining Room,* 15 Place Vendôme, 260-38-30. Extraordinaire.

London

☐ *Connaught Hotel Restaurant*, Carlos Place, 499-7070. The ambience and attentiveness are tops.

Tipping guide

Restaurant tipping guidelines from leading New York restaurateurs:

☐ Waiter: 15% of bill (excluding tax).

☐ Captain: 5%. Note: If you write the tip on the check, the waiter gets it all, unless you specify how it is to be split. (Example: waiter $5, captain $2.)

☐ Headwaiter who seats diners: $5 or $10 or more at intervals for regular patrons. He should be tipped in cash.

☐ Sommelier: 10% of the price of the wine or 5% if the wine is expensive. $2 or $3 is a good tip.

☐ Bartender: $1 minimum or 15% of the check.

☐ Hatcheck: 50 cents to $1 per couple.

☐ Restroom attendant: 50 cents.

☐ Doorman (to get taxi): 50 cents normally. $1 in bad weather or rush hour.

☐ Other staff at a restaurant that is regularly used should be tipped once or twice a year: Hosts, switchboard operators (where the restaurant provides telephone service).

☐ Nightclubs: Headwaiter should get $2 to $10 per person, depending on the impression the party host wishes to make on his guests. (Higher tip usually ensures better service.)

Other Tipping:

☐ Limousine service: 15% to the driver. If service charge is included in the bill, tip an additional $5.

☐ Hotels: Valet, room service, bartender should get about 50 cents, depending on amount and quality of service. Bellboy: 50 cents per bag. Chambermaid: $1 per day.

☐ Sports arenas and racetracks: A $5 tip to an usher as you ask, Are there better seats available? will often give you and your guests access to reserved seats that are not being used.

How to taste a wine

Careful tasting allows you to evaluate and appreciate a wine's quality and value. It also helps you identify the components that make a wine pleasurable to you.

Proper wine tasting is performed in systematic steps that involve three senses...sight, smell, and taste.

Sight:

☐ Study the wine's color by tilting a glass of it away from yourself and toward a white surface. The color is your first indication of its quality. Be aware that a white wine gets darker and richer in color as it ages, while a red wine becomes lighter. So a lighter-colored red is older and presumably better than a very dark one.

Smell:

☐ Swirl the wine in your glass by moving the stem while leaving the base of the glass on the table. This lets the wine's esters accumulate in your glass.

☐ As soon as you stop swirling the wine, bring the glass to your nose (actually put your nose into the glass) and inhale. What does the wine smell like? Fruity? Woody? Your sense of smell affects your taste buds, giving them a hint of what is to come.

Taste:

☐ Sip the wine, being conscious of three stages in the tasting process:

The attack is the dominant taste in the wine, the one your taste buds respond to first. (If a wine is very sweet, for example, that will be the first taste impression.)

The evolution involves the other taste components that you become aware of after the attack. Notice the more subtle flavors such as bitterness and acidity.

For the finish, evaluate how long the flavor remains in your mouth after you swallow. What is the aftertaste? Is the wine memorable? And do you like it?

Source: Mary Ewing Mulligan, director of education, International Wine Center, New York.

Naming your poison: The hangover potential of various alcohols

Part of the reason you may feel bad after drinking stems from the congener content of the booze you consume. Congeners are toxic chemicals formed during fermentation. The higher their content in the beverages you drink, the worse you will feel.

Here's how various types of alcohol stack up:

☐ Vodka: Lowest congener content.

☐ Gin: Next lowest.

☐ Blended scotch: Four times the congener content of gin.

☐ Brandy, rum and pure malt scotch: Six times as much as blended scotch.

☐ Bourbon: Eight times as much as blended scotch.

How to reduce hangover discomfort

☐ Retard the absorption of alcohol by eating before and during drinking, especially foods containing fatty proteins, such as cheeses and milk.

☐ Use water as a mixer. Carbonation speeds the absorption of alcohol.

☐ If you get a hangover anyway, remember that the only known cure is rest, aspirin, and time. The endless list of other remedies—ranging from cucumber juice and salt to a Bloody Mary—have more to do with drinking mythology than with medical fact.

☐ Despite the preceding caveat, believe in a cure if you want to. Psychologists have found that believing something helps may actually do so.

Alternatives to alcohol

Fruit juices for adults come in wine-type bottles, are alcohol- and caffeine-free, and cost relatively little. Essentially sophisticated ciders and grape juices, these grown-up drinks come in sparkling and plain versions that range in taste from crisp to sweet.

Sparkling Juices

☐ *Grand Cru Cider*

☐ *Martinelli's Gold Medal Sparkling Cider.*

☐ *Challand French Sparkling Apple Juice.*

☐ *Ecusson Sparkling White Cider.*

☐ *Ecusson Sparkling Red Grape Juice.*

☐ *Meiers Sparkling Catawba.*

☐ *Meiers Pink Sparkling Catawba.*

☐ *Meiers Cold Duck.*

Still Juices

☐ *Grapillon French Grape Juice* (white or red).

☐ *Meiers Pink Catawba Grape Juice.*

☐ *Meiers Catawba Grape Juice.*

☐ *Lehr's Black Currant Beverage.*

☐ *Lehr's Pure White Grape Juice.*

☐ *Lehr's Pure Red Grape Juice.*

Lean cuisines

You can stay on your diet even while dining at your favorite restaurants. Here's how to order to avoid excess fat, sugar, cholesterol or salt:

☐ Italian: Pasta dishes with marinara (meatless) sauce. Baked or broiled chicken or veal. Pizza with mushrooms, bell peppers, and tomatoes (but ask them to go light on the cheese). Minestrone.

☐ French: Grilled swordfish. Chicken breast with wild mushrooms. Steamed vegetable plate. Salade nicoise (with dressing on the side). Poached salmon. Raspberries.

☐ Mexican: Chicken taco in a steamed corn tortilla. Tostadas (light on the avocado, sour cream on the side). Red snapper Vera Cruz. Avoid fried rice or beans.

☐ Chinese: Broccoli, scallops, and mushrooms sauteed with ginger and garlic. Stir-fried bean curd or chicken. Steamed fish and rice. Ask for preparation without MSG or soy sauce.

Source: Dr. Cleaves Bennett, author of *Control Your High Blood Pressure Without Drugs*, and Chris Newport, a Paris-trained nutritionist and chef, cited in *Los Angeles.*

Surviving weekend guests

Weekend guests can be a drag. They leave the lights on, show up late for breakfast and expect to be waited on. This is a checklist for the clever host or hostess who graciously but firmly takes charge and doesn't let guests become a nuisance.

☐ Be a benevolent dictator. The host or hostess has the right not to be put upon. If someone is cadging an invitation when you'd rather be alone, suggest another time. Set the dinner hour at a time that's most convenient for you.

☐ If you live without servants, tell guests what you want them to do— pack the picnic lunch, bring in firewood. You'll resent them if they're having fun and you're not.

☐ Don't let food preparation become a chore. Plan ahead to have options if you decide to spend the afternoon on the boat instead of in the kitchen. Have a dish you can pull out of the freezer, or a fish or chicken that will cook by itself in the oven or crockpot and maybe yield leftovers for other meals.

☐ Involve guests in preparation and cleanup. If guests volunteer to bring a house gift, ask for food. If guests have special diets that vary radically from your own, give them the responsibility for supplying and preparing their own food.

☐ Give guests a kitchen tour and coffee-making instructions so they can fend for themselves when they wake up.

☐ Present your own fixed responsibilities and activities. Don't be embarrassed to do something without your guests.

☐ Present optional activities for everyone. Mention anything you expect them to participate in. Discuss availability of transportation facilities and other amenities.

☐ Set up a way to communicate changes in schedules and important information (a corkboard for messages, an answering machine, etc.).

☐ Encourage independence. Supply maps, guidebooks, extra keys. And provide alarm clocks, local newspapers, extra bicycles.

Putting off unwanted guests

Favorite ploys of city dwellers who don't want to put up all the out-of-town relatives and friends who invite themselves: "We'd love to have you, but…"

☐ The apartment is being painted.

☐ We will be out of town ourselves.

☐ The house is full of flu.

☐ My mother-in-law is visiting.

☐ The elevator is out of order.

☐ The furnace is broken and we have no heat or hot water (winter version).

☐ The air conditioning is out, and you know how hot and humid it gets here (summer version).

How to make a party a work of art

☐ Serve only one kind of hors d'oeuvre on each serving tray. Guests shouldn't have to stop their conversations to make decisions about food.

☐ Don't overload hors d'oeuvres on your trays. Space them elegantly, and garnish the trays with attractive combinations of flowers, vegetables, greenery, or laces and ribbons.

☐ Small bouquets of flowers and greenery tied with a satin ribbon make a convenient decoration that can easily be removed and replaced in the kitchen as trays are returned to be refilled.

☐ A layer of curly green parsley makes a good bed for hors d'oeuvres such as stuffed grape leaves, which have a hard time standing up by themselves. Parsley also makes a good bed for somewhat greasy hors d'oeuvres.

☐ Don't limit yourself to conventional equipment. Woven baskets, wood trays, colored glassware, lacquered trays, an unusual set of pudding molds—anything beautiful can be put to use for serving hors d'oeuvres.

☐ Heavy glassware is a good idea at an outdoor party. Unusual glasses (such as colored Depression glass) make drinks interesting, as do offbeat combinations of glassware and drinks (using long-stemmed wine glasses for mixed drinks, for instance).

☐ Lights should be soft but not dim. Abundant candlelight or tiny electric spots can be very effective.

Surviving the cocktail party game

You can't avoid cocktail parties? How can you survive them? Five tips:

☐ If possible, attend with someone sociable and loquacious who will stand at your side and banter with passers-by as you think about tomorrow's headlines.

☐ Pick one interesting person, someone who seems to be eyeing the clock as longingly as you, and spend the next half hour getting to know that person as though you two were alone in the world. If you choose well, time will fly.

☐ Act as you would if the party were in your honor. Introduce yourself to everyone, and ask them about themselves head-on. People will be profoundly grateful for your initiative. They don't call you overbearing—they call you charming.

☐ Tell the host you have an injured leg. Then commandeer a comfortable chair and let people come to you. (They'll be glad for an excuse to sit down.) If no one does, find an oversized art book to browse through, or indulge in a few fantasies.

☐ Help the host. You'd be amazed at how overwhelmed a party giver can be

and how many small tasks need doing—even with hired help. You can pass the hors d'oeuvres, hang up coats, refresh the ice buckets and generally free the host for socializing. What's in it for you? A chance to move around (some call it "working the room"), the gratitude of your host and a nice feeling of usefulness.

Source: Letty Cottin Pogrebin, writer and editor for *Ms.* magazine, New York.

Hot tub etiquette

☐ Take a towel.

☐ If it's daytime and the tub is outdoors you might want sunglasses.

☐ If you're ambivalent about dress (or undress), take your cue from the host or hostess. It's like avoiding the awkwardness of using the wrong fork at a dinner party. Nudity works best with everyone doing the same thing, too.

☐ Nonchalance is absolutely *de rigueur*—a combination of Japanese politeness and California cool is recommended.

☐ Sustain the mood by maintaining eye contact with members of the opposite sex, especially when they are getting in and out of the tub.

☐ If you think it's getting too hot, speak up. Better still, get out.

Great party themes

☐ A Raj ball with decor, food, music, and costumes out of India.

☐ A Venetian masked ball, where the guests dress formally and vie for the best and most elaborate masks.

☐ A night in Montmartre, with red, white, and French blue decorations, wine, can-can dancers, and costumes from the Paris Left Bank.

☐ A Sunset Boulevard party: Decor and costumes are Hollywood, 1930s and 1940s vintage.

☐ A Kentucky Derby party around a TV set, with mint juleps and a betting pool.

☐ A speakeasy party: A password gets you in, the men wear wing collars, the liquor is drunk from cups, and hoods carry violin cases.

☐ A Wild West party: Dress is cowboys and cowgirls, and the room looks like an old saloon.

☐ An Old Customs House party: The invitations are in the form of passports, and guests wear costumes from their country of origin.

❏ A patriotic party: Guests wear red, white, and blue, and there must be fireworks.

❏ A Mexican party with strolling musicians, mariachis, waterfalls, and Mexican food and drink.

❏ A Moroccan dinner where guests sit on low pillows, eat roast lamb and couscous with their fingers and watch belly dancers.

❏ A bal blanc with balalaikas for music, an ice-palace decor, Russian food and vodka.

❏ A New Orleans jazz party with hot music and Creole food.

❏ A Viennese waltz party: The music reflects the theme and guests dress appropriately.

❏ A physical-fitness party: Hold it in a health club, and let guests work out, then eat a healthful meal.

❏ Celebrity look-alike party: Guests dress as famous people from the past or present and try to guess each other's identities.

Source: Sheelagh Dunn, associate, Gustavus Ober Associates, New York 10021, a public relations firm that specializes in business parties.

Parties on cruise ships

If you want to impress your friends, invite them to the ship for a bon voyage party. It can be quite elegant but remain inexpensive.

❏ Make all the arrangements through the shipping company.

❏ The ship will usually supply setups, soda and hors d'oeuvres at a very modest price.

❏ Expect to bring your own liquor when the ship is in port, but you can easily buy a few bottles from a local liquor store and take them aboard.

❏ The steward can serve drinks and other items to your guests in your cabin.

❏ If your crowd is large enough, ask for a section of one of the public rooms.

❏ Play expansive host by holding nightly parties while cruising, and it won't be too costly. The ship's staff will help you with parties in your room or in a public room at a fraction of the cost of a party in a hotel ashore. You also usually get the service of waiters and bartenders at no cost (but you provide the tips).

Overcoming dinner party jitters

❏ Define the goals of this dinner party. The main purpose may be to establish a professional connection or to bring together two people likely to be attracted to each other.

❏ Eliminate anxieties by verbalizing them. Ask your spouse or a close friend to listen while you describe your worst fears. Once verbalized, the actual possibilities will appear less of a problem than when they were vague apprehensions.

❏ Specify that the invitation is for dinner. It's not enough to say that you are having a get-together at 7:30.

❏ Let people know about dress— casual, nice but not formal, formal but not black tie.

❏ While phoning, mention one or two of the other guests, what they do and, if possible, what they are interested in. If a guest is bringing a friend, don't hesitate to ask something about the friend.

❏ Do not serve a dish you have never prepared before. Guests will enjoy what you prepare best.

❏ Have everything ready at least an hour before the party. Take a relaxing warm bath or shower. Allow extra time to dress and make up, and give yourself an additional 20 minutes to sit quietly.

❏ Arrange to be free from the kitchen when the first two or three guests arrive. They need the host's help to start up conversation.

❏ For the single host: Reduce last-minute anxieties by inviting a close friend to come over early, test the food and look over the arrangements.

Source: *Situational Anxiety* by Herbert J. Freudenberger and Gail North, coauthors, Anchor Press, Doubleday & Co., Garden City, NY.

Party size

The kind of entertaining you do depends on the length of your guest list and the dimensions of your house.

☐ For 10 or fewer people, a sit-down dinner is appropriate.

☐ For 25, a buffet is usually better.

☐ An open house—usually 1-4 P.M. or 3-6 P.M.—can accommodate more people. If your rooms for entertaining hold 90 to 100 people for a party, you can invite as many as 250 to an open house. Trick: Stagger the hours you put on the invitations.

☐ To entertain several disparate groups—family, business associates and/or social friends—consider giving separate parties on succeeding nights. It takes stamina, but it does save effort and expense. You buy one order of flowers and greens for decorating the house. You assemble serving dishes and extra glasses (borrowed or rented) just once. You arrange furniture one time only. And you can consolidate food, ice, and liquor orders, which, in bulk, can save money. Extra food from the first party can be served at the second.

☐ Remove some furniture—occasional chairs and large tables—to give you space and keep guests moving. Clear out a den or downstairs bedroom, and set up a food table or bar to attract guests to that room, too. If you have a pair of sofas facing each other in front of a fireplace, open them out so guests can easily walk around them. Use a bedroom or other out-of-the-way place for coats. (You can rent collapsible coat racks, hangers included.)

☐ Set up different foods at different parts of the party area. If you have open bars, put different drink makings at each set-up. A group drinking a variety of cocktails will not be able to congregate for refills in the same place.

☐ To avoid bottlenecks: Don't put a bar or buffet table in a narrow hall, for example, or at the back of a tiny room.

☐ To make the most of a small space, have waiters to take drink orders and a bartender to fill the orders in the kitchen or pantry. Waiters can also pass the hors d'oeuvres in tight quarters, saving the clustering at a food table.

☐ Count on seven hors d'oeuvres or canapes per person. Stick to finger foods. You'll want a variety of 8 to 10 canapes, but pass each separately, starting with the cold foods and bringing out the hot dishes later.

☐ For long parties where a turnover of guests is likely, arrange two cycles of passing food, so the later guests get the same fresh selections as the earlier guests.

☐ Figure that a 40-pound bag of ice will provide enough cubes for 50 people. Get more if you are also chilling wine.

☐ Use a bathtub to keep the ice in. (No matter what kind of holder you devise for ice, the container will sweat and you'll have a puddle.) A bathtub full of ice and chilling champagne can be a festive sight by itself. Or, you can decant from the tub to smaller ice chests for each bar. If the nearest bathtub is too far from the party area, buy a plastic garbage can to hold the major supply.

Source: John Clancy, chef, teacher, restaurateur and author of several cookbooks.

Hiring help for a party

☐ The ideal ratio is one tray carrier for every 10 guests.

☐ Two or three extra kitchen workers are sufficient.

☐ One extra person can tend bar for up to 30 to 40 guests.

☐ In the kitchen, set out a prototype of each hors d'oeuvre, and expect your helpers to make exact replicas.

☐ Servers should be neat and pleasant and should avoid conversing with guests.

☐ Serving people are responsible for maintenance—keeping the party attractive. Provide lots of ashtrays (if you permit smoking), and make sure servers are told to empty them frequently.

☐ Avoid hors d'oeuvres that lead to messy leftovers (for example, shrimp tails or skewered foods) if you don't have enough people to clean up after your guests.

☐ If you expect a caterer, empty the refrigerator and clear all kitchen surfaces. In an office, make sure all desks are cleared. Food should be prepared well in advance and, when possible, frozen.

❏ Stock wine and liquor a day or two ahead of time.

❏ Flowers and decorations should be in place two hours before the party.

Source: Martha Stewart, the coauthor of *Entertaining* and author of *Quick Cook* and *Martha Stewart's Hors d'Oeuvres*, all published by Clarkson-Potter, a division of Crown Books, New York.

How to enjoy holiday entertaining

Although everyone is supposed to look forward to the holidays, they can be a season of great strain, especially for those who are entertaining. To minimize the strain:

❏ Include nonfamily in your invitations. Reason: Everyone is then on "party manners." Snide comments, teasing or rivalries are held back. This is not the time for letting it all hang out.

❏ Accept help. Encourage your family and friends not only to make their favorite or best dish but to be totally responsible for it—heating or freezing or unmolding and serving. Meals then become a participatory event, rather than one or two people doing all the work and the rest feeling guilty or, worse still, awkwardly attempting to help. (The one who hates to cook can supply the wine or champagne.)

❏ Let the table itself set a mood of fun, not formality. Use place cards wisely and make them amusing with motifs appropriate for each guest, rather than names. Or, let one of the younger children make them with a sketch of each guest or hand lettering. Set them out with forethought. Make sure a particularly squirmy youngster is nowhere near an aunt known for her fussy table manners. If there are to be helpers, seat them so they can get up and down with ease. Put the famous spiller where the disaster can be readily cleaned up. If the light is uneven, seat the older people in the brightest section.

❏ Put everyone around a table. It creates a warmer, more shared meal than does a buffet, and it's amazing how tables can expand. Hint: Use desk or rental chairs, which are much slimmer than dining chairs. (Avoid benches for older folks.)

❏ Borrowing and lending furniture, such as tables, can help you to find room for everyone. It doesn't matter if the setup is not symmetrical or everything doesn't match. A ping-pong table covered with pretty new sheets can provide plenty of room, or you can have tables jutting into hallways or living rooms.

❏ Have some after-dinner games ready. Ping-pong, backgammon, chess and cards are among the favorites. You may want to buy the latest "in" game or a new word game.

❏ Bringing out old family albums can be fun.

❏ Gift exchanging is really a potential hazard. Children, especially, can grump all day if something they expected hasn't been forthcoming. Grandparents often ask what is wanted, but they may be unable to do the actual buying. Do it for them. A check is not a fun package to open. If you want to be sure no one overspends, set a limit. Or set a theme. Or rule out gifts altogether, except for the children.

Source: Florence Janovic, writer and marketing consultant.

Planning a big family reunion

Because a reunion brings together people of all ages, it presents special challenges. To make your party more enjoyable for everyone:

❏ Infants and toddlers. Parents will appreciate a place to change diapers and a quiet room for naps and nursing. Let them know if you can provide high chairs, cribs, safety gates or playpens. Toys: A box of safe kitchen equipment. Food suggestions: Mild cheese, bananas, crackers, fresh bread or rolls.

❏ Preschool children. Set aside a playroom. Best toys: Balloons, bubbles and crayons. Pay an older cousin or neighborhood teen to baby-sit.

❏ School-age children. A den or basement room and board games, felt pens and coloring books will keep them happy. Put them in charge of setting and decorating a children's dining table.

❏ Teenagers. Most teenagers find family reunions boring. For those who have to come, provide a room with a stereo, video games, and radio. Teenagers may be shy around relatives they don't know. When they come out of hiding, give them tasks that encourage their involvement with others, such as helping out grandparents.

☐ Older folks. They need comfortable chairs where they can hear and see what's going on without being in the way. Some may also need easy access to a bathroom and a place to rest or go to bed early. Food considerations: Ask if anyone needs a low-salt, low-cholesterol or special diabetic diet. Spicy foods are probably out.

☐ Make travel arrangements for those who can't drive so they don't worry about inconveniencing others.

☐ Now that you've seen to individual needs, how do you bring everyone together? Common denominator: Family ties. Make an updated family tree and display it in a prominent place. If you have an instant camera, take pictures as people arrive and mount them on the appropriate branch of the tree. Special: Ask everyone to bring contributions to a family museum. Suitable objects: Old photographs, family letters, heirlooms, written family histories, old family recipes. After dinner, gather around the fire and exchange family anecdotes. You may wish to record them.

Source: *Unplug the Christmas Machine: How to Give Your Family the Simple Joys of Christmas* by Jo Robinson and Jean Staeheli, co-authors, Morrow, New York.

Self-indulgent ideas for New Year's Eve

☐ Get away to a country inn and enjoy a peaceful respite away from home with your spouse.

☐ Have a white-tie party in your home, complete with champagne, caviar, an elegant menu, your stored wedding-present silver serving dishes and crystal and your fanciest table linens.

☐ Rent a batch of old movies for good friends to share throughout the night. Serve beer, popcorn and pretzels.

☐ Plan a dinner for people you haven't seen in at least five years and catch up on old times.

☐ Charter a yacht for a lavish but intimate supper-dance.

☐ Hire an artist to document your New Year's party with sketches.

☐ Run an ethnic party—French, Italian, etc.—with appropriate food, wine, music, and dress.

☐ Fly to Paris for the night on the Concorde, dine and sleep at the swank Hôtel Plaza Athénée, and return home the next day.

☐ Go to a ski resort for the weekend to enjoy the bracing air, good athletic activities, and grog.

☐ Run a masked ball, complete with fancy dress costumes and prizes for the best. Have plenty of room for dancing and include at least one waltz.

☐ Have a wine-tasting party for a group of appreciative friends. Or, design a meal around special vintages from your own cellar that you want to share with some fellow wine lovers.

☐ Have a country party with a caller and musicians for square-dancing.

☐ Take a group to Atlantic City or Las Vegas and gamble the evening away.

☐ Organize a literary evening; let each person recite or read from his or her favorite works. Or pick a favorite play and do a reading, with each guest taking a role.

☐ Invite close business associates for dinner to discuss the coming trends for the next 12 months—in business and in national and international politics.

Holiday shopping

Those wonderful but tiring gift-buying chores can be relatively painless with organization.

☐ Know what you're looking for. Browse through mail-order catalogs and department store catalogs before you go out.

☐ Shop during the early morning or at dinnertime, when stores are least crowded.

☐ Shop by yourself. One person travels more efficiently than two.

☐ Wear comfortable shoes.

☐ If it will be a long tour with lengthy stops at several stores, leave your heavy winter coat in the car.

☐ Write the names of recipients on the sales slips and save them. They may come in handy for exchanges.

☐ Keep a list of what you give to whom so you won't buy duplicate presents next year.

Guidelines for Christmas tipping

☐ Household help: The equivalent of a week's pay is standard. But much more elaborate gifts are appropriate for employees who have been in your service for a long time or to whom you are very close.

❑ Newspaper deliverer: $5 to $10.

❑ Garbagemen: $5 to $10 each if it is legal in your community; a bottle of liquor or fancy foodstuffs are an alternative.

❑ Mailmen: While it is technically illegal to tip the postman, many people give $5 to $10 to their regular carrier.

❑ Deliverymen: $10 per person for those who come regularly to your house, like the dry cleaner, the milkman or even your United Parcel Service man, if you get a lot of packages.

❑ Baby-sitter: A record or a book for a regular teenage sitter; a bottle of perfume or $10 to $15 for an adult.

For apartment dwellers:*

❑ Superintendent: $25 to $50.

❑ Doorman: $15 to $25.

❑ Elevator operator: $15 to $25.

❑ Concierge: $20 to $25.

❑ Handyman: $20.

❑ Porter: $15.

❑ Garage attendant: $15 to $20.

Outside the home:

❑ Restaurants where you are a regular customer: Maitre d', $20 to $40. Bartender, $10 to $15. Captain, waiter, busboy: Divide the average cost of a meal among the three of them.

❑ Beauty salon or barber shop: Give the owner-operator a bottle of wine or a basket of fruit. For employees who regularly attend you, $15 to $25.

❑ Butcher: $10 to $15 for regular good service.

❑ Tailor or seamstress: $10 or wine or perfume.

*If your building establishes a pool for tips that is divided among employees, you need only give an additional amount to those service people who have gone way beyond the call of duty for you this year.

How to fight the blahs

❑ Count your blessings.

❑ See a funny movie or TV show.

❑ Read a joke book.

❑ Go for a long, brisk walk.

❑ Spend a weekend in a deluxe hotel with breakfast in bed.

❑ Listen to beautiful music.

❑ Read a very good and engrossing novel.

❑ Exercise a lot.

❑ Rent a convertible and ride with the wind around you.

❑ Go to the airport and watch the planes land and take off.

❑ Buy a new and exciting game for your video machine.

❑ Look at old family albums.

❑ Sing songs around the piano with friends.

❑ Get a haircut.

❑ Go for a swim.

❑ Buy a dog or cat to keep you company.

❑ Get some new tapes or records.

❑ Buy something you have always wanted.

❑ Fix up your house.

❑ Go to an art museum.

❑ Meditate.

❑ Clean out your closets or bureau drawers.

❑ List your assets and accomplishments.

❑ Call a special friend who always makes you feel happy.

❑ Take a deep, warm, bubbly bath.

❑ Eat a large piece of chocolate cake.

❑ Blast the stereo and sing along at the top of your lungs.

❑ Spend some time at a religious retreat.

Fighting holiday blues

Visits to psychiatrists and physicians jump 25% or more during the holiday season that lasts from Thanksgiving to New Year's. The most common underlying causes of distress: Holiday depression, boredom, and burnout. Specifically:

❑ A longing for happier holidays (real or imagined) in days past.

❑ Loneliness. This is especially true for those in a new location or those who have recently lost a loved one or gone through a divorce.

❑ The feeling that holidays should be a happy time, that family life should be perfect, and that presents will bring your heart's desires.

❑ For those whose health is frail, a primitive fear of not getting through the cold, dark winter.

The best ways to combat the blues:

☐ Don't expect too much. Unrealistic anticipation only breeds disappointment. As expectations are reduced, every pleasant surprise becomes a bonus.

☐ Be selective about the festivities you attend. Enjoy the fellowship more than the alcohol.

☐ Try not to be alone. But spend your time with people who are comfortable and easy to be around.

☐ When the holidays seem too grim, take a trip or try some totally new experience. Perhaps volunteer work in a hospital, where the emphasis will be on bringing cheer to others.

☐ Skip those Christmas-shopping crowds by ordering your gifts by mail and visiting small, local shops or those in out-of-the-way places.

☐ Keep holiday entertaining simple. If traditions become too much of a burden, try something offbeat (for example, decorating with cut flowers instead of ornate evergreens). Or, go out. Above all, don't try to give huge, exhausting affairs.

☐ Unless you love to receive cards from others, save the bother and expense of sending them yourself.

How to get attention for your favorite charity event

☐ Hire skywriters to spread the message.

☐ Take a full-page advertisement in the local newspaper or advertise over a local cable TV station.

☐ Commission an artist to design a lithograph for the event.

☐ Have the mayor declare a special day and read a message from City Hall.

☐ Get a letter of congratulations from the President of the United States...or from the Governor of your state...or Senator...or Congressman.

☐ Run a special supplement of the event in your local Sunday newspaper.

☐ Videotape the event as news and offer it to your local TV station.

☐ Have special funny money printed with your face and message on it to give out as a token of the special event.

☐ Hire a marching band and have a parade.

☐ Arrange for displays of the event in the windows of local stores.

☐ Have cases of wine imprinted with a private label to mark the event.

☐ Have a special sandwich or dish named in honor of the event on the menu at a major restaurant.

☐ Have an automobile or train named in honor of the event.

☐ Hire the huge local stadium or concert hall.

☐ Have a street renamed for the day.

☐ Float specially designed and painted balloons all over town with the message you want to relay.

☐ Underwrite a special event—tennis, golf, marathon, polo, etc.

☐ Have the post office issue a stamp in your name. If this is not possible, print stamps designed by a major artist and have them affixed to all correspondence.

☐ Have a race horse named in honor of the event.

How to really appreciate movies

If you really want to appreciate movies, stray a little from the heavily beaten track. There are a number of good critics in small or specialized magazines who can alert you to fine—and unusual—new films, as well as notable revivals.

Movie buffs typically go through three stages in their appreciation of films:

☐ First, they find movies awe-inspiring magic.

☐ Second, they begin to realize those are actors up there and that all kinds of technology are involved. In this stage, which some people never leave, they become "fans." Many fans don't care about movies—they're just interested in following their favorite actors.

☐ Third, they realize movies aren't magic, that it may be a miracle they ever get made, but that they're a human achievement that also happens to be marvelous. At this stage they can start to look at movies critically.

To get the maximum enjoyment from movies:

☐ Watch a lot of them. Make a special effort to see foreign films. You'll begin to see what's original and fresh and what's stereotyped.

☐ Learn about movie forms and genres and the unique visual language of cinema.

☐ Read, follow other art forms. Read

about psychology, politics, history and other branches of knowledge.

❑ Avoid the rush. Don't dash off to see the latest blockbuster. It'll be around a while. See a film more likely to close soon, even though it was well-reviewed.

❑ Watch movies on cable TV and on cassettes. Both these forms have done a lot to make film scholarship possible and good movies accessible.

❑ Go to foreign films. More than a few are worth seeing, but most people aren't interested in them anymore. In the past, the "ooh-la-la" factor drew viewers. But now that American films are no longer censored, foreign films have lost their cachet.

Source: Andrew Sarris, film critic for New York's *Village Voice*, a professor of cinema at Columbia University, and author of *The American Cinema: Directors and Directions*, Octagon Press, New York, and *Politics and Cinema,* Columbia University Press, Irvington, NY.

How to enjoy a day at the races without going broke

The aim of a day at the track should be to enjoy every race while controlling your losses. Fifty dollars lost out of a hundred dollars played could be considered a highly satisfactory day.

❑ When betting, begin with the choices of the handicappers. Handicapping—the prediction of likely winners—is done by a track official who assigns odds to the horses in the morning races. Handicapping is also done by bettors in the course of the day (which causes the odds to change). One third of the favorites chosen by handicappers win their races.

❑ Decide on the amount of money you are willing to lose. Set aside one fifth of it for entertainment betting. The rest should be spent on serious betting. For about $20 you can bet on every race plus the daily double.

❑ Avoid the temptation to increase bets when losing in order to catch up. Also avoid the trap of betting more when winning to try to make a killing.

❑ To control spending, bet just 20% of your remaining capital each time you bet, whether your capital goes up or down.

❑ For fun betting, choose horse by name, jockey, appearance or any means you wish. You may get lucky and win one out of ten bets this way.

❑ For serious betting, pick the

appropriate races to bet on. Always eliminate maiden races (the horse's first year of racing), two-year-old races and races where it's indicated that the horses chosen won no race but their maiden race.

❑ To pick the two or three likeliest winners in the race, check handicappers' choices in local newspapers, racing forms and tip sheets sold at the track. Look especially for handicappers who predict in great detail how the race will be run, and those who tell you the front runners and the come-from-behind horse as well as the outcome.

❑ Late scratches (the elimination of contenders) can very much change the projected script of a race. If one of the two predicted front-runners is scratched, the remaining front-runner's chance is increased.

❑ Rain. In the racing charts, "mudders" (horses that have a history of doing well in the rain) are indicated with an asterisk. As the track is progressively softened by rain, the chances of mudders improve. The horse in the most adverse position on a rain-sodden track is a speed horse—a front-runner in the post position.

❑ Shifts in odds. Lengthening (higher) odds on a horse increase your chance of a good return. Observe the physical condition of your horse during the viewing ritual, when the horses are paraded at the rear of the track before each race.

You can place several types of bets:

❑ To win: Pays only if the horse comes in first.

❑ To place: Pays only if the horse comes in first or second.

❑ To show: Pays if the horse comes in first, second, or third.

Source: Peter Shaw, cultural critic, historian, college professor and occasional bettor.

Casino gambling: A matter of strategy as well as luck

Too many casino gamblers lack a good strategy for cutting the house's advantage to something reasonable—say under 2%. They don't bring enough money to ride out a losing streak. Worst of all, they don't know how to manage the money they do bring, win or lose.

To have any real chance of success in Nevada or Atlantic City, you must learn money management. Find out what your minimum bet can be, and bring at least 100 to 125 times that amount to last your total stay. With any less you won't be able to play comfortably.

☐ Divide your total stake into four parts. This leaves you $100 per gambling session—the bare minimum for survival at a five-dollar table. (Important: Never draw from one session's stake to replenish another.)

☐ If you lose the $100 quickly, leave the table, and the casino, to clear your head for the next session.

☐ If after 30 minutes of slow-but-steady losing, you find you're down to $50, cash in your chips and take at least a 30-minute break. Never play more than a half-hour at a losing session.

☐ If you're winning, preserve your profits. As soon as you've doubled your money (to $200), put your original $100 in your pocket, not to be touched until you see the cashier. Now you're in the ideal situation: Playing with the casino's money. If your luck sours, quit when you've lost 25% of your profits—in this case $25. If you manage to run your profits to $200, quit after losing $50, and so on. Although it's hard to leave when you're still ahead, this kind of discipline separates potential winners from inevitable losers.

Source: Lee Pantano, a professional gambler, teacher, consultant and editor of *Gamblegram*, Atlantic Highlands, NJ.

Traps in casino gambling

Casino gambling can be high-risk entertainment, if you're not careful. Avoid these common casino mistakes:

☐ Making "flat bets"—wagering the same amount each time. Since the odds are against you, your progress will soon resemble a sales chart in a recession...peaks and valleys, but down in the long run.

☐ Trying to get even by chasing losses with meal money...or the next month's rent. It's a big mistake to dig into your pocket after your stake is gone. You can't outspend the casinos.

☐ Flitting from craps to baccarat to the slots. It's better to stick with one game until you're comfortable.

☐ Taking too many long-shot bets (such as "proposition" bets in craps). They generally offer the worst odds.

☐ Staying at a "cold" table too long. If a new dealer is giving you terrible cards, or there's a loudmouth across the table or you don't like the smell of your neighbor's cigar, move on. The problem may be purely psychological, but it can throw off your game nonetheless.

☐ Accepting complimentary alcohol. When you drink too much you start making irrational "hunch" bets, and you get frivolous with your money.

☐ Playing when tired. The casino may stay open till 4 A.M., but you don't have to close the casino. Stick to your normal weekend hours.

☐ Getting caught up in the casino mentality. When everyone refers to $5 as a "nickel" and $25 as a "quarter," it's easy to treat money like plastic. Never forget that it's real money. Stick to your basic units and progressions.

☐ Viewing the dealer as a shark who's out to get you. At worst, the dealer is a mechanical device. At best, he can be your ally. Example: In a hot craps game, he may remind you when to take a bet down. To keep him on your side, don't forget to tip. (Dealers make two thirds of their income from tips.) Tactic: It's more effective to bet $1 for the dealer (giving him a stake in your game) than to give him $10 when you leave.

☐ Celebrating prematurely. Be happy when you win, but don't brag about it. You don't want to advertise that you're carrying a lot of money. And...don't play with a huge pile of chips in front of you. If you hit it big, convert to larger denominations, and put them in your pocket. (For safety, use the casino's valet parking. With a validated ticket it will cost you only a tip, and it's far better than walking three blocks to your car.)

☐ Forgetting what you came for. Take in a floor show and enjoy a good meal. If you lose at the tables, write it off as entertainment. If you're not a professional, that's the whole point of visiting a casino...to have a good time.

Source: Lee Pantano, a professional gambler, teacher, consultant, and editor of *Gamblegram*, Atlantic Highlands, NJ.

Winning at poker

Not so many years ago, every poker book told you the same thing: Play tight (fold bad hands). This is still good advice, as far as it goes. But there are other tactics to keep in mind:

☐ Be selective but aggressive. Ideally, you should end a hand by either folding or raising. Avoid calling bets with vulnerable hands, such as two pair.

☐ To own the table psychologically, so that other players are glancing at you every time they make a bet, be friendly, but at the same time confusing and unpredictable.

☐ Never gloat. You want your opponents to enjoy trying to beat you.

☐ In a low-to-moderate-limit game, you can win without mathematical genius or brilliant originality. Most of your profit will come from your opponents' mistakes. Their chief error: Calling for too many pots with mediocre hands.

☐ Bluffing is a poor strategy in a low-stakes game. Unsophisticated opponents won't even understand your intended deception. Second, they're likely to call you anyway, a habit you want to encourage. Try a strategic bluff just once, early in the session, as an "advertisement."

☐ Discipline is especially crucial in a low-limit game, when you need more hands to make up losses.

☐ Decide in advance how you will react in each of various situations. Never play a hand out of impatience or on a "hunch." Play it for a good reason.

☐ Monitor yourself carefully. If you make a mistake, admit it to yourself and get back on track. Don't let one bad play erode your entire system.

☐ Don't look for immediate revenge after an opponent burns you on a big pot. If you force the action, you're apt to get burned again.

☐ Stay later when you're ahead and leave early when behind. When you're losing, you lose psychological control of the game, too. Opponents try to bluff you out of pots and are less likely to call your good hands.

☐ Watch for and learn to read opponents' "tells"—the mannerisms they fall into that tend to give away whether their hands are good or bad. In general, follow the rule of opposites: Players usually act weak when their hands are strong, and they commonly act strong when their hands are weak.

☐ Look for reasons to fold just as eagerly as you look for reasons to call.

Source: Mike Caro, a gambling teacher and columnist for *Gambling Times* and, according to world poker champion Doyle Brunson, the best draw poker player alive. He is also the author of *Caro on Gambling*, published by Gambling Times, Hollywood, CA.

Successful poker: Reading your opponents

Bluffers generally:

☐ Breathe shallowly or hold their breath.

☐ Stare at their hands—or at you as you prepare to bet.

☐ Reach for chips out of turn.

☐ Bet with an authoritative pronouncement.

☐ Fling chips into the pot with an outstretched forearm.

☐ Show unusual friendliness toward opponents.

Players with powerful hands:

☐ Share a hand with a bystander (especially a spouse).

☐ Shake noticeably while making a bet. (This reflects a release of tension. Most players show obvious outward nervousness only when they feel they're in little danger.)

☐ Talk easily and naturally.

☐ Behave in an unusually gruff manner toward opponents.

☐ Lean forward in their seat.

☐ Bet with a sigh, shrug, or negative tone of voice.

☐ Ask, "How much is it to me?" or request another clarification.

☐ Glance quickly at the player's chips after receiving a (good) card.

Source: Mike Caro, author of *Mike Caro's Book of Tells—The Body Language of Poker*, published by Gambling Times, Hollywood, CA.

Darts: Tips from a champ

☐ Start off with a set of three brass darts with a one-piece plastic shaft and flight. Brass darts are big and easy to handle. They're also the most durable.

As you throw more, the dart will feel lighter.

☐ As your game improves, you'll want to buy tungsten darts. The darts are heavier, narrower, and a little harder to control.

☐ Buy a pressed bristle board. When you remove a dart from this material, it doesn't leave an indentation. Cork or wood boards are cheaper, but they'll disintegrate with heavy play.

☐ To play well, you need eye-hand coordination, good concentration, and good balance. Keep your head still so that your eyes stay on the target.

☐ When throwing darts, use your forearm, not your entire body. (It's like hammering a nail.)

☐ Stay loose and fluid on the follow-through movement after the dart leaves your hand. If you jerk your arm back, the dart won't reach the board.

☐ Most newcomers to the game overthrow to the left of the target. You can start by aiming a little to the right, but that's not a long-term cure. You must see the pattern of your throw and move accordingly on the toe line.

☐ Strategy: The two most important targets are the triple 20 and the outer double ring.

☐ Basic courtesy: Shake hands before and after play.

☐ Take your darts out of the board promptly.

☐ Be quiet when someone else is shooting.

Source: Nick Marzigliano, reigning singles champion of the Brooklyn (NY) Dart League.

Contest winners: Secrets of success

Cash, vacations, houses, cars, electronic equipment, cameras, and much, much more are the dream prizes that keep millions of Americans doggedly filling out entry blanks for contests. More than $100 million worth of prize money and goods are dispensed annually through an estimated 500 promotional competitions and drawings.

Dedicated hobbyists know that there is an advantage of a planned approach to overcome the heavy odds against each entrant.

Here are some winning strategies:

☐ Use your talents. If you can write, cook or take photographs, put your energy into entering contests rather than sweepstakes. Contests take skill, so fewer people are likely to compete…improving your chances. Photography contests have the fewest average entries.

☐ Follow the rules precisely. If the instructions say to print your name, don't write it in longhand. If a three-inch by five-inch piece of paper is called for, measure your entry exactly. The slightest variation can disqualify you.

☐ Enter often. Always be on the lookout for new sweepstakes and contests to enter. Sources: Magazines, newspapers, radio, television, store shelves and bulletin boards, product packaging.

☐ Make multiple entries. The more entries you send in, the more you tip the odds in your favor.

☐ For large sweepstakes: Spread out your entries over the length of the contest—one a week for five weeks, for example. When the volume of entries is big enough, they will be delivered to the judges in a number of different sacks. The theory is that judges will pick from each sack, and your chances go up if you have an entry in each of several different mailbags.

☐ Keep informed. Join a local contest club or subscribe to a contest newsletter. Either source will help you to learn contest traps and problems—and solutions. They'll alert you, too, to new competitions.

☐ Be selective. You must pay taxes on items that you win, so be sure the prizes are appropriate for you. If you don't live near the water, winning an expensive boat could be a headache. (Some contests offer cash equivalents, but not all do.)

☐ If you do win, check with your CPA or tax lawyer immediately. You must report the fair market value of items that you win, whether you keep them, sell them or give them away. This can be tricky. Also, if you win, you can deduct the expenses of postage, stationery, etc. that you have used to enter this and other sweepstakes and contests in the same year. These costs are not deductible if you don't win.

☐ Most contests and sweepstakes ask you to enclose some proof of purchase or a plain piece of paper with a product name or number written on it. Many people assume that a real proof of purchase will improve their chances of winning. Fact: In a recent survey, more than half the winners of major prizes reported that they had not bought the sponsor's product.

Source: Roger Tyndall, coeditor with his wife, Carolyn, of the country's largest circulation newsletter, *Contest Newsletter*, Fern Beach, FL..

Reluctant vacationers

Not everyone loves to get away from it all on a vacation. Some people really prefer to work. But families need vacations, and so do workaholics occasionally.

How to take yourself away from the office successfully:

☐ Make vacations somewhat similar to your year-round life, so that they offer continuity as well as contrast. If you enjoy a daily swim at the gym, be sure to pick a vacation stop with a pool. If you never step into art museums at home, don't feel you have to drag yourself to them when you're away.

☐ Leave your calculator, beeper, dictating device and briefcase at home.

☐ Avoid finishing lots of work at the last minute. It can leave you feeling frantic.

☐ Don't drive your staff crazy by leaving lots of lists and memos or calling continually. Limit yourself to two calls the first day and one a day thereafter.

☐ Take enough time off to recharge your energy. Two weeks may feel too long, but three days is too short.

Source: Dr. Marilyn Machlowitz, a New York organizational psychologist and consultant.

Don't let your vacation home cut into your leisure time

The most desirable thing to look for in a weekend house is ease of maintenance.

☐ Get rid of rugs in the summer.

☐ Ask the landlord to remove his accumulations of dustcatching peacock feathers and other decorator touches. Keep your own importations to a minimum.

☐ Cut down on weekend cleaning chores and outdoor work with hired help.

☐ Consider expanding leisure time by commuting with the laundry. That's cumbersome, but better than hours in a laundromat on a sunny afternoon.

☐ Cultivate the fine art of list-making. Shopping and menu planning can be almost painless if the list is done right.

☐ If you're planning a Saturday dinner party, don't rely on the local supermarket for the perfect roast unless you've ordered (and confirmed) in advance. The accompanying wines might be better purchased at home, too, unless you're sure of your local supplier.

☐ Don't forget to take the same precautions as you would for a trip— extra reading glasses and copies of prescriptions might save you an unwanted journey home.

Fishing a new lake

If you know where to start looking, you can fish any lake successfully.

Where bass congregate:

☐ Near trees that have recently fallen into the water.

☐ In hot weather: Under lily pads, especially in the only shallow spots around.

☐ In consistently mild weather: In backwater ponds and coves off the main lake. Best: Good weed or brush cover, with a creek running in.

☐ Any time at all: In sunken moss beds near the shore.

Source: *Outdoor Life.*

Portrait photography secrets

People are the most popular subject for photography. There are ways to turn snapshots of family and friends into memorable portraits. Techniques:

☐ Get close. Too much landscape overwhelms the subject.

☐ Keep the head high in the frame as you compose the shot. Particularly from a distance, centering the head leaves too much blank background and cuts off the body arbitrarily.

☐ Avoid straight rows of heads in group shots. It's better to have some subjects stand and others sit in a two-level setting.

☐ Pose subjects in natural situations, doing what they like to do—petting the cat, playing the piano, etc.

☐ Simplify backgrounds. Try using a large aperture (small f-stop number) to throw the background out of focus and highlight the subject.

☐ Beware of harsh shadows. The human eye accommodates greater contrast of light to dark than does a photographic system. Either shadows or highlights will be lost in the picture, usually the shadowed area.

For Outdoor Portraits:

☐ Avoid the midday sun. This light produces harsh shadows and makes people squint. Hazy sun, often found in the morning, is good. Cloudy days give a lovely, soft effect.

☐ Use fill light to cut shadows. A flash can be used outdoors, but it is hard to compute correctly. Best fill-light method: Ask someone to hold a large white card or white cloth near the subject to bounce the natural light into the shadowed area.

☐ Use backlight. When the sun is behind the subject (but out of the picture), the face receives a soft light. With a simple camera, the cloudy setting is correct. If your camera has a light meter, take a reading close to the subject or, from a distance, increase the exposure one or two stops from what the meter indicates.

☐ Beware of dappled shade. The effect created in the photograph will be disturbing.

For Indoor Portraits:

☐ Use window light. A bright window out of direct sun is a good choice. However, if there is high contrast between the window light and the rest of the room, use filter-light techniques to diminish the shadow.

☐ Use flashbulbs. A unit with a tilting head lets you light the subject by bouncing the flash off the ceiling, creating a wonderful diffuse top lighting. (This won't work with high, dark or colored ceilings.)

☐ Mix direct light and bounce flash. An easy way to put twinkle in the eyes and lighten shadows when using bounce light is to add a little direct light. With the flash head pointed up, a small white card attached to the back of the flash will

send light straight on to the subject.

☐ Keep a group an even distance from the flash. Otherwise, the people in the back row will be dim, while those in front may even be over exposed.

Making New Year's Eve a family or neighborhood affair

☐ Invite close relatives to spend the evening reminiscing and becoming a family again. Organize a slide show of old family photographs or show home movies to break the ice.

☐ If you are a runner, do an evening five miles with running friends and then see the new year in with a pasta feast. (New Yorkers can run in or watch a mini-marathon in Central Park, with fireworks at the finish line at midnight. Check for similar events in other cities.)

☐ Rent the local high-school auditorium and sponsor a band concert for the community. Or organize your own band with fellow musicians.

☐ Have a bake-in in your kitchen, with prizes for the best chocolate desserts.

☐ Have a multigenerational party for your whole family and friends of all ages.

☐ Spend New Year's Eve taking down holiday decorations, finishing your thank-you notes for holiday gifts, and otherwise cleaning the slate for the coming year.

☐ With your mate, make a list of do's and don'ts and resolutions for the new year.

☐ Organize a neighborhood "progressive dinner" with a different course in each house. Watch the time so you get to the last stop and the champagne by midnight.

☐ Rent a skating rink—ice or roller—for a big, many-family party with an instructor or two to get the fainthearted going smoothly.

How to solve caterer problems before they arise

☐ The ideal way to select a caterer is to attend one of his or her parties.

☐ If that's not possible, ask for recommendations from your most trusted and sophisticated friends and acquaintances.

☐ Another source of information is gourmet magazines. Local publications often write articles about caterers, too.

☐ Many caterers provide pamphlets or sample menus, but these are a poor substitute for a solid personal recommendation.

☐ Try, if at all possible, to sample the food each caterer offers. Keep in mind, however, the kind of party you are planning. Someone who prepares exquisite nouvelle cuisine may not be the best person to cater a large outdoor barbecue.

☐ When you have the names of a few reputable caterers, meet with each, preferably where the party will take place. Many hosts are distressed by caterers' tendency to "take over"—to dictate all arrangements and ignore the host's concerns. Know your own feelings about this and try to gauge the caterer's willingness to accommodate you.

☐ Never hire anyone who has a specific number of parties in her repertory and simply "does" party number six at your home. Even if the caterer is to take total control, you want her to approach your party as a unique situation.

☐ Ask at the beginning of the discussion whether the caterer herself will be present at the actual function. If she plans to send an assistant, meet that person and make sure you have confidence in her abilities.

☐ Be sure also to discuss clean-up arrangements with the caterer.

☐ Although most caterers actually only prepare the food and hire the service themselves, they can certainly make arrangements (and take responsibility for them) with liquor stores, florists, musicians, etc. They can also recommend people whom you can contact directly (possibly helping you to cut corners economically). Or, you can come up with your own choices.

☐ Never hire independent help to serve your caterer's food. After the quality of the food itself, service is probably the most important ingredient in a successful party. Your caterer should work with people she knows and trusts.

☐ The caterer should draw up a contract that spells out every cost and makes the caterer's list of duties clear.

☐ You will probably be asked to make a down payment for up to half the total cost.

☐ The caterer's price is all-inclusive; you are free to tip the staff if you should wish to, but you need not feel obliged to do so.

☐ The caterer will expect to find the scene of the party clean and ready for her to get started. Your equipment (serving trays, etc.) should be at its sparkling best.

☐ Now you should stand back and let her do her job. Don't make any last minute additions to the menu or suddenly rearrange the floor plan.

Source: Germaine and Marcel Chandelier owners and managers of Germaine's, Long Island City, NY.

How to make slot machines pay off

☐ Key to successful play: A basic understanding of slot mechanics. In Las Vegas, dollar slot machines return on average 88¢–98¢ per dollar invested. (At the high end, they compare favorably with the odds offered by craps, roulette, or any other game.)

These are long-term returns over six hours or six months…depending on the machine. The short-term return for a given player will vary tremendously— but not randomly. Every machine has a pay cycle and a down cycle. During its pay cycle, the machine will give back far more than you put in. It might stay "hot" for a hundred pulls or more, spilling out jackpot after jackpot. (At one machine, I hit a triple-bar jackpot— a $150 to $1 payoff—three times in a row.) But during a machine's cold cycle, you can easily drop $100 in less than an hour.

Finding Pay-Cycle Machines

☐ Observe before you play. If you see a player empty $100 or more into a machine (whether or not he hits a few small jackpots along the way) and walk away with nothing, step up and try your luck. There's a good chance the machine is near the end of a down cycle and entering a pay cycle.

☐ If you play a machine "blind," without prior observation, feel the coins in the tray after your first win. If the money is warm, it's probably been sitting in the machine for a time without a jackpot. Point: A down cycle may be ending. If the money is cool, move on.

☐ Ask a change clerk to steer you to a hot machine…with the unwritten understanding that you'll tip him/her 10% of your winnings on that machine. (Casinos tolerate this because it doesn't affect their overall take.)

☐ Play machines near casino entrances and exits. The house programs these slots to pay off the best, because their jackpots will attract the most attention. Also hot: Any machines near blackjack or other gaming tables. The casino hopes to lure to these machines wives who are watching their husbands play the other games. Colder: Machines isolated against the rear wall (and especially in the corners), where jackpots have less advertising value.

☐ Watch for empty coin racks—coin holders next to each machine used by players to stack coins for play or to hold winnings—and play the machine immediately to the left of one. An empty rack means the previous player busted. (When a player hits a jackpot, the rack is used to cart away the coins.) The more empty racks near a machine, the closer it is to a pay cycle.

☐ After I gave an extravagant tip, a casino mechanic once told me to look for three-reel machines with a cherry sitting in the middle reel. While worthless in itself, he said, the cherry was a sign that better times were coming. Since then, I've found that 75% of middle cherry machines return at least a small jackpot within five to six pulls. They're also good bets for a pay cycle.

☐ Your odds are best on single-line, dollar slots. Multiple-line machines offer a greater chance of hitting any jackpot, but the payoffs are much smaller. Also: For top value, play the maximum number of coins for each pull.

☐ "Progressive" slots, where the jackpot can build to $1 million or more, can be wildly profitable, but only if they're within their programmed payoff range.

Example: At the Sands in Las Vegas, a clerk told me (after a big tip) that one progressive machine always paid off when the jackpot reached between $48,000 and $64,000. I found it one night at $59,000 and pumped in $300 before I had to leave town. The next morning, the clerk called to tell me that the machine had been hit at 10 am, when its jackpot reached $62,000.

☐ If you ever see a new machine being uncrated, jump on it. Play it until it bursts. Casinos program new slots to pay particularly well for the first two days so they'll draw more business later.

Source: Dick Phillips, author of *Winning Systems on Slots,* Box 12336, Beaumont, TX 77706.

Secrets of doing crossword puzzles much faster

In order to successfully complete a crossword puzzle, follow these helpful hints…

☐ Start with the fill-in-the-blank clues. These are usually the easiest and the least ambiguous.

☐ Next, try to fill in an across answer in the top row or a down answer on the left side. You can then proceed to answers that start with a known letter …and they're always easier to solve than answers where the known letter is in the middle.

☐ In a thematic puzzle, the longest blanks on the grid always relate to the theme.

☐ When the clue is expressed in the plural, the answer is probably plural. Most clues that are expressed in the past have answers ending in *-ed.* Most clues that are expressed in the superlative have answers ending in *-est.*

☐ Remember that *e* and *s* are the most popular word-ending letters. Also, puzzles use a disproportionate number of common letters and very few rare letters, such as *q, z, x, j,* etc.

☐ When you are missing one or two letters in a word, scan the alphabet. Plug in all possible letters or combinations…one is bound to work.

Source: David Feldman, author of *How to Win at Just About Everything,* Morrow Quill, William Morrow & Co., 105 Madison Ave., New York 10016.

Bingo never was a game of chance

Most people play bingo as if it were a game of sheer chance—as if any set of cards had just as good a chance of winning as any other. They are mistaken. If you correctly choose the cards you play, you can significantly improve your odds of winning any bingo game.

The following system works with *straight* bingo (where you must cover five squares in a row—vertically, horizontally or diagonally), *coverall* (a jackpot game, in which you must cover every square on your card) or any other variation.

Key strategy: To get as many of the 75 numbers as possible on a given set of cards. There are 24 numbers printed on every bingo card. (There are 25 squares, but the center square is a nonnumbered free space.) If you chose three cards at random, their 72 numbered spaces would represent only 49 different numbers—the other 23 spaces would have duplicate numbers.

It is possible, however, to find sets of three cards with no duplicates—with 72 different numbers. (Time permitting, players can choose their cards freely at the beginning of any session.) If you were to play such a set, you would be 25% more likely to win a given game than a player with a random set. Depending on the size of the prizes, that edge can translate into hundreds—or even thousands—of dollars of winnings within a few weeks.

The truth about "lucky" cards:

Ironically, most players choose sets that are worse than random. They look for cards with one or two "lucky" numbers—7 or 11, for example. And they are especially drawn to cards where those lucky numbers are at the corners.

The results are devastating. In an average straight game with 1,000 cards in play, a bingo will occur after 15 numbers are called. That means that any given number—regardless of whether it is "lucky" or not—will be called in only one of five games. In those other four games, any set of cards with an uncalled "lucky" number is 25% less likely to win. (When a number is at a corner, it affects three lines—one vertical, one horizontal, one diagonal.)

Another advantage of choosing non-duplicating cards is that it makes it easier to keep track of the numbers you're covering—and harder to miss one by accident.

There are countless statistical systems favored by bingo players, but this is the only one I've found that generates consistent profits.

Where to play:

The only live variable in bingo is the proportion of money collected that is returned to the players. Most operators hold back at least 50% for overhead and revenue. (The percentage is usually posted on the bingo sheets or somewhere in the hall.)

Other games, however, return as much as 75% to the players. The more money that comes back, of course, the better your chances of coming out ahead.

Source: John "Dee" Wyrick, author of *Complete Authoritative Guide to Bingo,* Gambler's Book Club, Box 4115, Las Vegas, NV 89127.

The pleasures of organic gardening

There really is no need to use chemicals and gasoline-powered machines when gardening or tending to your lawn. Organic methods are just as successful and use only fertilizers and pest controls found in nature. Advantages:

☐ Creates a healthier environment by rebuilding the top soil, protecting ground water, and using less energy.

☐ Produces homegrown, organic (chemical-free) vegetables—fresher and cheaper than the ones you can buy in natural-foods stores or supermarkets.

Organic Fertilizers

While synthetic fertilizers feed the crop, they deplete the soil, then make future crops dependent on continued applications. Organic fertilizers feed the plants and nourish the soil. All plants need…

☐ Nitrogen for lush foliage.

Best organic sources: Homemade or bagged compost—decomposed plants or animal wastes rich in nitrogen and other trace minerals. Add up to two inches to each garden bed yearly. For fast results: Use blood meal and dried blood (by-products of slaughterhouses), or cottonseed meal (ground from seeds of the cotton plant).

☐ Phosphorus for flower and seed production.

Best organic source: Colloidal phosphate, a rock powder, also rich in lime and trace minerals. For fast results: Try bone meal—it's effective, but more expensive.

☐ Potash (Potassium) for strong roots and solid branches.

Best organic sources: Granite dust (a rock powder) and greensand (a mineral-rich deep sea deposit). For fast results: Try wood ashes left from a wood stove or fireplace.

Important: Soil conditions in your garden—and the specific needs of plants you want to grow—should determine your choice of fertilizer. Your local garden center or the US Department of Agriculture's cooperative extension service can test your soil and recommend the best organic fertilizer for your needs.

Organic Pest and Weed Control

☐ Insecticidal soaps: Spray every three to five days for about three weeks to eliminate most pests on specific plants or plant groupings.

☐ Fabric coverings: Sheets of very thin-woven polyester or thin-spun polypropylene, sold as "floating" row covers or super-light insect barriers.

Use only for vegetable gardens—not for ornamental plants…make sure plants have enough water—high temperatures under the fabric can make them dry…and remove covers over squashes, melons and cucumbers when the flowers start to bloom—in time for pollination.

☐ Beneficial insects: Bugs that kill harmful insects that eat your vegetables or plants. They can be purchased at local garden centers or by mail order.*

☐ Mulching: Cover the earth around each plant or row to deter weeds and conserve water with shredded bark mulch, wood chips, cocoa or buckwheat hulls. (Also use straw and shredded leaves for vegetable plants—but not for ornamentals.) Old mulch decomposes and can be worked into the soil. New mulch is spread after planting.

*Mail-order companies that sell these insects include: Gardens Alive!, 5100 Schenley Pl., Lawrenceburg, Indiana 47025 (812) 537-8650…Gardener's Supply Co., 128 Intervale Rd., Burlington, Vermont 05401 (802) 863-1700.

Source: Bonnie Wodin, of Golden Yarrow Landscaping, Heath, Massachusetts 01346, designs custom gardens and landscapes. She also lectures frequently on horticulture and landscaping.

How to get more out of your travel

☐ Take along a small tape recorder when you travel. This is easier than jotting notes or trying to find the time to keep a diary.

☐ Interview people you meet along the way. Ask them all about their lives, occupations, and backgrounds. This will preserve the facts and actual voices of interesting people you meet.

☐ Tape guided tours. Guides give out lots of information that is forgotten during the excitement of a tour but can be enjoyed later.

For very special occasions

Here are some very classy, exclusive hotels frequented by those who know the right places to stay when they travel. Make reservations a few months in advance.

☐ *Malliouhana Hotel in Anguilla, the Caribbean.* On a small little-known island with few tourists. This new hotel is the ultimate in luxury. Suites and private villas are available, some the size of private homes. Tennis courts, boating and all water sports, including scuba instruction, attracts a jet-set crowd of all ages.

☐ *Baden-Baden in Schwarzwald, Germany.* In the elegant style of a 19th-century spa. Extensive grounds, impeccable service, an excellent restaurant and hot springs where you can "take the waters." Attracts an old world, conservative crowd.

☐ *Hotel Los Monteros in Marbella, Spain.* On one of the Mediterranean coast's most fashionable stretches. Wide range of sports, spacious rooms and tropical gardens. Has a 1920s charm reminiscent of the Gatsby era. Ask for a room with an ocean view. Attracts all types, from young families to older couples.

☐ *Hotel San Pietro in Positano, Italy.* Picturesquely perched on top of a cliff, with all 55 double rooms overlooking rocky coast and sea. Scenic beaches. Secluded and elegant, it attracts a young to middle-aged highly sophisticated crowd. Open March 14 through November 3.

☐ *Mount Kenya Safari Club in Nairobi, Kenya.* A distinguished private retreat located halfway up Mt. Kenya. 100 acres of rolling lawns, waterfalls, gardens, a heated pool, sauna, three dining rooms, and safari excursions for both photography and hunting. Special events such as African barbecues and tribal dances. Dress is formal, with jacket and tie required for dinner. Guests tend to be families, couples and ultra-exclusive tours and groups.

☐ *Lake Palace in Udaipur, India.* Originally an 18th-century royal residence. Located on an island in the Middle of Lake Pichola, it has air-conditioned rooms, exotic suites, water sports, a marble-inlaid pool, and a restaurant serving Continental and Indian cuisine. Guests are all ages but tend to be very sophisticated.

☐ *Hotel de Paris in Monaco.* A superior hotel. Has an underground passage to the Casino and Le Club. Palatial rooms and facilities. Spa, sauna, two restaurants and a cabaret. Old money stays here. Frank Sinatra is a regular, and the Prince of Monaco often comes for tea.

☐ *Voile d'Or Hotel in St-Jean-Cap-Ferrat, France.* Overlooks the harbor. Its spacious, French provincial-style rooms all have balconies and marble baths. A favorite honeymoon spot, the atmosphere breathes intimate elegance. Gourmet cuisine. Open February to October.

☐ *Splendido Hotel in Portofino, Italy.* A super-deluxe classic hotel on high ground overlooking the sea. Charming rooms, suites, gardens, a seawater pool, sauna and health spa. Attracts all types and ages, including many businesspeople. Open March 29 to October 29.

Source: Francesca Baldeschi, manager, Ports of Call Travel Consultants, Inc., New York.

Plan for very special trips

If you're the type who finds the sameness of Holiday Inns comforting or prefers to have dinner at McDonald's—in Paris—this checklist isn't for you. But if you love country inns, a pot of coffee brewing in your room, four-poster beds, claw-legged bathtubs, lunch beside a swan pond, discovering the best wine cellar in Vermont or the trail that isn't on a map, then you might want to plan your vacations differently.

☐ Consult the guidebooks and travel agent last.

☐ Year round, collect information on all kinds of interesting vacation possibilities.

☐ Keep geographical files labeled Caribbean, West Coast, The South, New England, Europe, Israel, Japan, and Exotic Places, for example. You can make your own headings and add new folders when the catch-all category gets too full to be manageable.

☐ Subdivide your files into subject files labeled Ski Vacations, Tennis Vacations, Club Med Locations, Charming Inns/Elegant Small Hotels, Houses for Rent or Exchange and Great Restaurants in Other Places (to distinguish it from your home town restaurant file).

☐ File articles from airline magazines, newsletters, and the travel section of your newspaper.

☐ Interview friends: When you agree with your friends' taste in food, furnishings, theater or painting, chances are you can trust their vacation advice.

☐ Talk with neighbors, clients, friends at work.

☐ Think of exchanging visits with friends you meet on vacation.

☐ Save picture postcards from active travellers.

☐ Eavesdrop in an airport or restaurant, on the bus or train to work. If you hear a total stranger describe a perfect meal she had in Kansas City, or a rustic lodge in the Adirondacks with a gorgeous view of the sunset, jot it down. Check out the details later. (That's where guidebooks and travel agents come in handy.)

☐ Books, movies, magazines. In vacation terms, life can imitate art. You'll want to visit Big Sur if you've read Henry Miller.

Eight grand old hotels that are still magnificent

Some great old hotels have never lost their luster, and an increasing number of formerly faded dowagers have recently had facelifts, restoring them to their original beauty. Here are a few special places:

☐ *Adolphus Hotel, Dallas.* Texans used to describe this turreted pile of stone as "early beer baron," but their laughter turned to admiration when this Gothic revival hotel reopened in 1980 after four years of careful restoration to its original 1912 magnificence.

☐ *Bürgenstock Hotel Estate, Switzerland.* A splendid aerie 1,500 feet above Lake Lucerne. It artfully mixes modern meeting facilities featuring the latest electronic gadgetry with truly baronial accommodations. The guest rooms are luxurious, and the public spaces resemble museums. Open May-October.

☐ *The Connaught, London.* This landmark in the perennially stylish Mayfair district is elegance itself, and the service is as impeccable as only the finest English establishment could make it.

☐ *Four Seasons Olympic, Seattle.* This eclectic hotel in the center of Seattle had its ups and downs between its construction in 1924 and its renovation in 1982. The World War II blackout paint is now off the ballroom windows, the lobby is grandly furnished, and the rooms are modern yet luxurious.

☐ *Hotel Imperial, Vienna.* Built in 1867 on a fashionable boulevard as the home of the Duke of Wurttemburg, it has been a sumptuous hotel since 1873. Personalized service in the tradition of the Hapsburg empire still reigns supreme.

☐ *Hotel InterContinental, Paris.* Built for the 1878 World's Fair, it was taken over by InterContinental in 1968. Its public spaces gleam, and its guest rooms are sybaritic retreats with extras like hair dryers, minibars, bathroom scales and color TV with in-room movies. The Salon Imperial is a stately banquet hall, and the recently restored Garden Court is a tranquil oasis in the busy heart of Paris.

☐ *The Mandarin Oriental, Hong Kong.* Classic hotel in the center of Hong Kong's business district. All other hotels in the Orient are ultimately judged by this one. Lovely and luxurious, it sets the standard for impeccable service, superb cuisine and Oriental ambience combined with Occidental efficiency.

☐ *Hotel Seelbach, Louisville.* It was built in 1905 and hit a long, slow decline before closing in the early 1970s. The restorers (rather than the wreckers) took over, embarking on a three-year refurbishment to its original glory. This Louisville landmark reopened to rave reviews in March 1982.

Best hotels in the world

The world's premier travel accommodations, according to a poll of leading bankers, are (in order of preference):

- ☐ Bangkok, *The Oriental.*
- ☐ Hong Kong, *The Mandarin.*
- ☐ Tokyo, *Hotel Okura.*
- ☐ Zurich, *Dolder Grand Hotel.*
- ☐ Singapore, *Shangri-La Hotel.*
- ☐ Paris, *Hotel Ritz.*
- ☐ Hamburg, *Hotel Vier Jahreszeiten.*
- ☐ Hong Kong, *The Peninsula.*
- ☐ Madrid, *Ritz Hotel.*
- ☐ London, *Claridge's.*
- ☐ New York, *The Hotel Carlyle.*
- ☐ Paris, *Hotel Plaza Athénée.*
- ☐ Zurich, *Baur au Lac.*
- ☐ London, *The Connaught Hotel.*
- ☐ Rome, *Hotel Hassler Villa Medici.*
- ☐ Munich, *Hotel Vier Jahreszeiten.*
- ☐ London, *The Berkeley.*
- ☐ Washington, DC, *Four Seasons.*
- ☐ Vienna, *Hotel Imperial.*
- ☐ Washington, DC, *The Madison.*
- ☐ Manila, *The Manila Hotel.*
- ☐ Chicago, *The Ritz-Carlton.*
- ☐ Toronto, *Four Seasons Hotel.*
- ☐ Tokyo, *Imperial Hotel.*
- ☐ Paris, *Hotel Meurice.*
- ☐ Geneva, *Le Richmond.*
- ☐ New York, *The Pierre.*
- ☐ Paris, *Hotel George V.*
- ☐ London, *Four Seasons Inn on the Park.*
- ☐ Vienna, *Hotel Sacher.*
- ☐ Los Angeles, *Regent Beverly Wilshire.*
- ☐ Sydney, *Sheraton Wentworth.*
- ☐ Stockholm, *Grand Hotel.*
- ☐ New York, *The Park Lane Hotel.*

- ☐ Mexico City, *Camino Real.*
- ☐ Geneva, *Les Bergues.*
- ☐ Montreal, *Ritz-Carlton.*
- ☐ San Francisco, *The Mark Hopkins Hotel.*
- ☐ London, *The Savoy.*
- ☐ New York, *The Regency Hotel.*

Source: *Institutional Investor.*

Super executive travel

The best hotels to visit if you are on an expense account—or if money is no object:

- ☐ Amsterdam: The *Amsterdam Hilton* and the *Amstel.*
- ☐ Athens: *Athenaeum InterContinental* and the *Athens Hilton.*
- ☐ Berlin: The *Bristol Kempinski* and *Steignenberger.*
- ☐ Florence: *Excelsior, Savoy, Villa Medici* and *Rest Lorenzo de'Medici.*
- ☐ Geneva: The *Richmond* and the *Rhone.*
- ☐ London: The *Connaught* is tops, followed by the *Hyde Park, Ritz, Claridge, Churchill, Savoy, Dorchester Grosvenor House, Berkeley, Carlton Tower* and *Inn on the Park.*
- ☐ Madrid: Heading the list are the *Ritz* and the *Villa Magna.* The *Palace, Eurobuilding, Miguel Angel, Mindanao, Milia Castilla, Wellington, Princess Plaza* and *Luz Palacio* run close seconds.
- ☐ Milan: The *Excelsior Gallia* and *Principe e Savoia.*
- ☐ Paris: The *Ritz* or the *Plaza Athénée.* Next: The *Inter-Continental, Meurice, Lotti, George V, Bristol, Crillon* and *Prince de Galles.*
- ☐ Rome: The *Hassler-Villa Medici* is the best. Also highly recommended: *Le Grand Hotel, Excelsior, Jolly* and *Cavalieri Hilton.*

Source: The *1982 Michelin 20 Cities of Europe* guide.

Luxurious one-week trips

If you want to experience a magic vacation week—seven days to match your wildest fantasies—try any of these ideas:

- ☐ Travel first class by present standards and those of another age. Whip to London on the Concorde in three hours. Then settle into the new Orient Express for a leisurely trip to Venice. The legendary train (with its 1920s cars completely restored to their former polished-brass-and-crystal glory) makes the London-Paris-Milan-Venice run twice a week. Base your Venetian sight-seeing at the Hotel Cipriani before returning to London and flying home.

☐ Lose weight in luxury with the Lancaster Farm program at Brenner's Park Hotel in Baden-Baden, Germany. (The main building was a residence of Napoleon III.) Do water exercises in a Pompeiian pool. Have a daily massage, facial, body wrap, and beautiful meals that add up to only 1,000 calories a day. Makeup, manicures and pedicures are part of the program. Baden-Baden has colonnaded shops and a famous casino.

☐ See Burgundy by balloon. View the chateaus and vineyards of southeastern France from the gondola of a hot-air balloon (between terrestrial tours of the region by car). Stay in the Hotels de la Poste in Beaune and Vezelay, sampling the local wines. The great French Balloon Adventure leaves every Sunday from Paris starting in May and is organized by the Bombard Society in San Francisco. Airfare to Paris is extra.

☐ Charter a yacht—with crew—and cruise the Caribbean. Captain, cook, hands and provisions are included. Air-fare from New York to the Virgin Islands is extra.

☐ A villa or a castle for a week. Try Dromoland Castle in Ireland or an Acapulco villa.

☐ Entertain like a king (or a Comstock Lode heiress) in San Francisco by renting the penthouse suite of the Fairmont Hotel. Designed in the 1920s for Maude Flood, a gold and silver baroness, the suite has a walnut-paneled living room, a dining room that seats 50, a domed library, a mosaic-walled gameroom complete with pool table, three bedrooms and baths with gold fixtures. The kitchen is fully equipped. The bar is stocked. Dinnerware, silver and linens are included, as well as a vault, a baby-grand piano, books, artwork, a butler and a maid. Food is extra.

☐ Great hotels. Pick a city you want to explore and put yourself in the hands of a master innkeeper for a week. Some suggestions:

☐ California wine country, *Sonoma Mission Inn.*

☐ Colorado Springs, *The Broadmoor Hotel.*

☐ Paris, *The Plaza Athenee.*

☐ Beverly Hills, *The Beverly Hills Hotel.*

☐ New York, *The Helmsley Palace.*

☐ London, *The Savoy.*

☐ Dallas, *The Mansion at Turtle Creek.*

☐ Rio de Janeiro, *The Meridien Hotel.*

Getting VIP treatment on a cruise ship

☐ Get the word to the shipping line that you rate A-1 treatment. Your travel agent can do this by writing the shipping line. Also, the more expensive your cabin, the better service you will generally get.

☐ What you can expect when you're tagged for VIP treatment: Dinner at the captain's table, an invitation to the captain's special cocktail party, or perhaps flowers and assorted gifts in your cabin.

☐ Make sure to get a good seat in the dining room. Usually, that means in the center, close to the captain's table. Ask your travel agent to see if he can reserve a well-placed table for you in advance. If that can't be done, make sure that as soon as you go aboard ship, you tell the maitre d' what you want—with a tip.

☐ Have an early talk with your dining room captain and waiter. Ask them what the chef's specialties are. Order those far in advance for your dinners later on in the cruise. The trick is to know what the kitchen is good at and to give the chef time to prepare them.

☐ Tip the dining room captain and let him know there's more for him if the service is excellent.

☐ Also give the dining room waiter, in advance, half the amount you would normally tip him at the end of the cruise and indicate he'll get at least as much more for top-notch service. He's the man who can get you all sorts of snacks, like fruit, cheeses, sandwiches, iced tea, and ice cream—almost any time of day or night. Ask him what is available, and if there is a best time to order these items for your cabin. If you want ice cream at 11 P.M. every night, tell him in advance, so he can plan accordingly. Similarly, give your room steward half the tip in advance and let him know that good service will bring a reward.

☐ Book the second sitting for meals when on a cruise. That leaves you more time to get ready for dinner after a day of touring, a longer cocktail hour and less time to kill until the evening activities begin.

Best cruises

☐ Cunard Line, 555 Fifth Ave., New York 10017. (800) 221-4770, (800) 458-9000 for Sea Goddess. The Queen Elizabeth 2, one of the most palatial ships afloat, makes regular trans-atlantic crossings and offers free return flight on the Concorde to its Top of the Queen class passengers. The QE2 and the Sagafjord also offer round-the-world cruises, and Cunard's other ships offer itineraries in Caribbean and European waters.

☐ Renaissance Cruises, 1800 Eller Drive, Suite 300, Box 350307, Fort Lauderdale, FL 33335, (305) 463-0982, (800) 525-2450 for info, (800) 525-5350 for reservations. The eight Renaissance ships, each carrying about 100 passen-gers, sail everywhere from the Baltic to the Seychelles Islands. The ships are, on occasion, chartered by groups.

☐ Royal Viking Line, 95 Merrick Way, Coral Gables, FL 33134, (305) 447-9660, (800) 422-8000 for reservations. Royal Viking's changing itineraries may include a trip up the Amazon or a circumnavigation of South America. A formal atmosphere is maintained on these longer cruises.

☐ Home Lines Cruises, 1 World Trade Center, New York 10048, (212) 432-1414. Caribbean cruises originating in Fort Lauderdale. Incentive: Free round-trip airfare from principal US cities to Fort Lauderdale.

☐ Windstar Cruises, 300 Elliott Ave. West, Seattle, WA 98119, (206) 281-3535. The three elegant Windstar ships are powered mainly by the wind harnessed in giant computer-controlled sails. Itineraries include Polynesia, the Caribbean, and the Mediterranean.

☐ Seabourne Cruise Line, 55 Francisco St., Suite 710, San Francisco, (415) 391-7444, (800) 929-9696. Seabourne's two ships offer luxurious 100% outside cabins, and sail in Asia, the Mexican Riviera, and the Mediterranean.

How to get a cruise ship's best price

☐ Don't rely solely on travel agents. Not all of them are knowledgeable about cruises, and some promote only one or two lines.

☐ Instead, read the latest issues of *Travel Weekly*, especially the issues with a cruise guide. Then ask agents about specific cruises that interest you.

☐ Get prices from several agents. Surprisingly, prices often vary because of the many promotional gimmicks of the cruise lines.

☐ Ask about cash rebates, free airfare to the port of departure, flat rates for inside and outside cabins, free passage for third and fourth persons.

☐ Try checking with the steamship company itself, which may give you an even better deal.

Source: Daniel A. Nesbett, travel marketing consultant, Darien, CT.

Freighter and cargo cruises

These increasingly popular cruises can be taken only by people who can be away from business for long periods of time and have flexible schedules. They're very good for retirees.

There is no assurance that a ship scheduled to depart on a particular day will indeed leave that day. The first consideration of such ships is their cargo, and they will stay in port until they are completely loaded, even if that means waiting for weeks. The same holds true all along the route. You are protected on price, however. The longer the voyage, the lower the per diem costs.

Some advantages of cargo cruises:

☐ Costs are considerably lower than for other types of cruises. Everything is included in the price.

☐ Most ships carry only 8-12 passengers, so you have an excellent opportunity to get to know your fellow cruisers. (However, you risk traveling with people you don't care for.)

☐ You get more port time than with regular ships.

☐ The quarters are usually first-rate. The food is simple and good. Larger ships sometimes have their own swimming pools.

Points to keep in mind:

☐ There are certain restrictions on age and health on the smaller ships. On those with 12 or more passengers, a doctor is required, so they are more lenient about health restrictions.

☐ When you make your reservation, you pay a deposit. The balance of the cost must be paid by a month before scheduled sailing time. Cancellations are refundable if the ship company is able to resell your space.

☐ Book your trip through a travel agency familiar with this type of ship. A travel agency can help you with the many documents to be filed—and with refunds, if necessary.

Most popular freight and cargo lines:

☐ *Ivaran Line*, 111 Pavonia Ave., Jersey City, NJ 07310.

☐ *Blue Star North America*, 180 Howard St., Suite 560, San Francisco 94105.

☐ *Lykes Line*, 300 Poycras St., New Orleans, LA 70130.

☐ *Cast Freighter Cruises*, Box 188, Flushing, NY 11358.

☐ *Compagne Polynesienne de Transport Maritime*, 595 Market St., Suite 2880, San Francisco 94104.

Best months at top overseas tourist spots

Europe

☐ *Greece*. March-May, October and November.

☐ *London*. April-June, October and November.

☐ *Paris*. April-June, October and November.

☐ *Riviera* (Monaco, France, Italy). Christmas, New Year's and Easter holidays. Also: June-August.

☐ *Rome*. March-May, October-December.

☐ *Scandinavia*. May-September. Winter sports: February and March.

☐ *Switzerland*. Winter sports: December-April. Summer activities:

May-August.

☐ *Confederation of Independent States (former USSR)*. April-June, September and October. Summers are torrid, with no air conditioning. Winters are harsh.

☐ *Venice*. March-June.

Africa

☐ *Egypt*. Always hot and humid. Best: March-May, October-December.

☐ *Kenya*. Seasons are reversed. June, July and August are coolest. December, January, February and March are hot and dry.

☐ *Morocco*. The sun shines 300 days a year. In the south around Agadir and in Marrakech: December-March. Avoid visiting in August or September.

☐ *South Africa*. There are no extremes of climate. Capetown: January-March. Kruger National Park: June-September. Johannesburg: May-August.

Middle East

☐ *Israel*. Tel-Aviv: April-June, October-December. Jerusalem: January-June, October and November.

☐ *Jordan*. Hot and dry all year. Best: March-May, November and December

☐ *Saudi Arabia*. December-March.

Orient

☐ *China*. The country is vast, with a wide-ranging climate. The most visited cities are Peking, Tientsin, Nankin, Hangchow, Shanghai and Canton, where summers are hot and humid and winters are relatively mild. Best: April-June and October.

☐ *Japan*. April-June, October and November.

Asia and the Pacific

☐ *Australia*. Seasons are reversed. Melbourne, Sydney, Canberra: October-February. Darwin: June-August.

☐ *India*. The climate varies greatly. Best: November, December, February and March. Monsoons: June-September.

☐ *Malaysia*. March-July and September.

☐ *Nepal* (Himalayas). September-November.

☐ *New Zealand*. The weather is always cool and temperate.

☐ *Philippines*. November-March.

☐ *Singapore*. Always hot, with little variation in rainfall.

❏ *South Korea*. March-May, October and November.

❏ *Sri Lanka*. December-March.

❏ *Tahiti*. May-October.

❏ *Thailand*. November-April.

South America

❏ *Argentina*. October-March.

❏ *Brazil*. October-March.

❏ *Chile*. October-February.

❏ *Peru*. Lima: January-March. Mountains: June-September.

❏ *Venezuela*. December-March.

Closer to Home

❏ *Bermuda*. May-October. Also: Easter week.

❏ *Canada*. Winter sports: November-April. Summer sports and city vacations: May-September.

❏ *Caribbean*. November-April.

❏ *Florida*. December-April.

❏ *Hawaii*. Ideal all year.

❏ *Mexico*. October-April.

❏ *Puerto Rico*. November-April.

Best places to ski

California

❏ *Squaw Valley*. Developed for the Olympics, it includes an 8,200-foot ram. (916) 583-0121. Stay at: Squaw Valley Lodge.

Colorado

❏ *Aspen*. Ski Aspen Mountain, Ruthie's Run, Snowmass or Aspen Highlands. (303) 925-9000. Stay at: Aspen Inn, Aspen Lodge, The Gant or Hotel Jerome.

❏ *Vail*. A wide variety of runs is available in this movie-star ski capital. Alternate: Beaver Creek, just 12 miles farther on Interstate 70. (303) 476-5677. Stay at: Inn at West Vail, Sunbird Lodge, Vail Village Inn.

Idaho

❏ *Sun Valley*. An old-timer, but still going strong. Experienced skiers enjoy Mount Baldy and Dollar Mountain. (208) 622-4111. Stay at: Sun Valley Lodge.

Utah

❏ *Alta*. Experienced skiers attempt the High Rustler Run, with 40-degree slope, no trees and frequent avalanches. (801) 742-2040. Stay at: Alta Lodge.

❏ *Snowbird*. Known for powder skiing. Hidden Peak is 11,000 feet high. There are also runs for beginners. (801) 742-2000. Stay at: The Lodge.

Vermont

❏ *Killington*. Highest lift-served summit in New England. (802) 422-3333. Stay at: Mountain Inn, Summit Lodge.

❏ *Stowe*. Ski the demanding sectors of Mount Mansfield, Spruce Peak, Sterling Mountain. (802) 253-7321. Stay at: Green Mountain Inn, Stowehof, Topnotch.

❏ *Warren*. Excellent skiing is available at Mount Allen, Mount Lincoln Peak or Sugarbush Valley. (802) 583-2381. Stay at: Sugarbush Inn.

Western Canada

❏ *Vancouver area*. Ski the Black Comb and Whistler Mountains, with the highest vertical drop in North America. Heli-skiing is also available. (604) 932-3434. Stay at: Bayshore or Four Seasons.

Eastern Canada

❏ *Mount Tremblant*. 90 miles north of Montreal, in the Laurentians. (819) 425-2711. Stay at: Gray Rocks Inn, Mount Tremblant Lodge.

Austria

❏ *Innsbruck*. Twice an Olympic site, this 800-year-old city is surrounded by excellent ski areas. Austrian National Tourist Office, 500 Fifth Ave., New York 10017, (212) 994-6880. Stay at: The Europe, Goldener Adler, Sporthotel.

❏ *Kitzbuhel*. A favored, more chic ski spot in the lofty Austrian Alps. Stay at: Grand, Goldener Graf, Hirzingerhof.

France

❏ *Chamonix, Courcheval, Val d'Isere*. Ski the Haute Savoie chain of mountains, including Mont Blanc. French Government Tourist Office, 610 Fifth Ave., New York 10020, (212) 757-1125. Stay at: Carlton, Croix Blanche or Mont Blanc in Chamonix. Carlina, LeLana or Pralong 2000 in Courcheval. Christiania or Grandes Parades in Val d'Isere.

Italy

☐ *Cortina d'Ampezzo.* Downhill skiers are enthusiastic about the spectacular Dolomites, just north of Venice. Italian Government Travel Office, 630 Fifth Ave., New York 10020, (212) 245-4822. Stay at: Hotel Cristallo, Hotel de la Poste, Miramonti Majestic.

Switzerland

☐ *Swiss Alps.* The finest downhill skiing. Swissair, 608 Fifth Ave., New York 10020, (718) 995-8400. Stay at: Belvedere, Derby or Schweizerhof in Davos. Palace, Park or Residence Palace in Gstaad. Badrutt's Palace, Kulm or Suvretta House in St. Moritz. Monte Rosa or Mount Cervin in Zermatt.

Phone numbers in the US and Canadian sections are for area-information services that can take your reservation.

Best uncrowded resorts in Mexico

For the cheapest prices and probably the most exciting vacations, stay away from well-known, overcrowded resorts like Acapulco and Taxco.

Travelers who know Mexico well say they especially like:

☐ *Ixtapa*, 150 miles north of Acapulco on the Pacific. Warm, dry and uncrowded, the resort has one of the most luxurious hotels in Mexico, the Ixtapa Camino Real.

☐ *Merida*, the capital of Yucatan, is old, exotic and cheap. The elegant Montejo Palace costs much more than other hotels. Merida is the takeoff point for excursions to nearby Mayan ruins, where hotels are similarly priced.

☐ *Oaxaca* is near the site of some of the most beautiful pre-Columbian ruins. A 16th-century convent has been converted into El Presidente hotel.

☐ *Vera Cruz*, not touted by Mexico's tourist officials, is a picturesque old city on the Gulf of Mexico with some of the best food in the country. The six-hour drive from 7,200-foot-high Mexico City to sea-level Vera Cruz is spectacular. The beachside Mocambo Hotel is reasonably priced.

Best African safaris

Seeing the great animals of East Africa in their natural habitat is one of the most exciting and exhilarating vacation possibilities.

Modern safaris are well organized and comfortable, even for novice campers. Accommodations can be luxurious or basic and simple, but the food is usually good and dress is always casual.

Two prerequisites: You must be willing to get up early—that is when the animals are most active and fun to watch. And you must bring a camera—because the opportunities for photography will be irresistible.

Kenya and Tanzania are the major safari countries.

Make reservations for any of these safaris at least two months ahead:

☐ *National Audubon Society International Explorations*: 1 Empirous Park, Helena, AL 35080. (205) 428-1700.

Guided explorations of Kenya by safari vehicle. Stays in lodges and tented camps.

☐ *Overseas Adventure Travel*: 349 Bradshaw, Cambridge, MA 02139. (617) 876-0533. Camping safaris in Tanzania for the fit and active. Serengeti plains region: 19 days. Departures: All months except April and November. Selous: 17 days of bush camping and river boating in the game reserve, plus two days visiting Zanzibar. Departures: August, September, October.

☐ *Questers*: 257 Park Ave. South, New York 10010. (212) 736-3120. Unhurried travel by minibus. Comfortable stays in lodges or safari camps. Time: 17 or 23 days. Departures: July, October, February.

☐ *Mountain Travel Sobek*: 6420 Fairmount Ave., El Cerrito, CA 94530. (510) 527-8100.

All trips are for the adventurous and the athletic:

☐ A hiking safari in Kenya explores Mount Kenya and Tsavo National Park. Time: 18 days. Departures: June, July, August, September and December.

☐ A 20-day on foot safari in Kenya includes several days of walking with both Masai and Sambura guides.

☐ A safari in Kenya especially planned to include children. Time: 15 days.

Best gambling casinos in the world

We offer here the very best places to gamble, along with their best hotels.

Rates vary according to the season. It's best to book through a travel agent, since gambling packages are usually available at lower costs than the average room rates.

United States

☐ *Atlantic City, NJ*: Bally, Caesar's Palace, Claridge, Bally's Grand, Harrah's, Resorts, Sands, TropWorld.

☐ *Las Vegas, NV*: Caesar's Palace, Desert Inn, Las Vegas Hilton, Bally's Las Vegas, Mirage.

☐ *North Lake Tahoe, NV*: Hyatt Lake Tahoe.

☐ *Reno, NV*: Bally's, Reno, Harrah's.

☐ *South Lake Tahoe, NV*: Caesar's Tahoe, Harrah's Lake Tahoe.

Caribbean

☐ *Antigua*: Curtain Bluff, Halcyon Beach Cove Resort.

☐ *Aruba*: American Aruba, Aruba Concorde.

☐ *Curaçao*: Curaçao Caribbean.

☐ *Dominican Republic*: Casa de Campo at La Romana, Hotel Santo Domingo, Plaza Dominicana, Sheraton Santo Domingo.

☐ *Guadeloupe*: Meridien St.-François.

☐ *Martinique*: Hotel Meridien Trais-Ilets, Hotel La Bataliere.

☐ *Nassau/Cable Beach*: Carnival's Crystal Palace, Nassau Beach Resort Club.

☐ *Paradise Island*: Paradise Island Hotel.

☐ *Puerto Rico*: Caribe Hilton, Hyatt Dorado Beach/Hyatt Regency Cerromar Beach, Condado Beach Hotel El Convento.

☐ *St. Kitts*: Golden Lemon.

Europe

☐ *Baden Baden, Germany*: Brenner's Park Hotel.

☐ *Cannes, France*: Carlton, Martinez.

☐ *Deauville, France*: Normandy Le Royal.

☐ *Estoril, Portugal*: Palacio, Ritz Lisbon (in Lisbon, half an hour away).

☐ *Marbella, Spain*: Marbella Club, Los Monteros.

☐ *Monte Carlo, Monaco*: Hotel de Paris, Hotel Hermitage, Loews.

☐ *Venice, Italy*: Excelsior (Lido Beach), Gritti Palace, Royal, Royal Danieli.

Elsewhere

☐ *Macao*: Hyatt Regency Macao, Lisboa, Royal. (Macao is a Portuguese territory on the tip of mainland China, 40 miles from Hong Kong by jetfoil.)

☐ *Marrakech, Morocco*: Hotel Mamounia.

The best alpine ski resorts

Christmas (when most hotels insist on a minimum two-week reservation) and February in the Alps are booked up quickly by jet-setting regulars, but other weeks are open. Here are some top spots:

☐ *Badrutt's Palace* in St. Moritz is arguably the classiest ski resort hotel in the world.

☐ *The Goldener Graf* in Kitzbuhel is charming and luxurious—and located in the center of this stellar Austrian resort.

☐ *Hotel Christiania* in Val d'Isere. Good skiers in search of powder can do no better than skiing off-piste (off the patrolled courses) in the expansive terrain of Val d'Isere and Tignes.

☐ *Hotel Cristallo* and *The Hermitage* in Cervinia. The Cristallo has a spectacular view of the Matterhorn from the Italian side, and the Hermitage is a small and lovely chalet-style hotel in the center of Cervinia.

☐ *Swissair packages*. Billing itself as the airline of the Alps, Swissair packages accommodations and land transfers in conjunction with its plane tickets. Among the luxury leaders are the *Mont Cervin* in Zermatt, the *Palace* in Gstaad, the *Schwarzer Adler* in St. Anton and the *Annapurna* in Courchevel. Probably the best bargain among deluxe ski hotels is the *Sporthotel Igls* in a village outside Innsbruck.

Great golf vacations

A superior golf resort provides comfortable accommodations and special courses that offer unusual scenery, challenges and/or some history. Some exceptional ones:*

☐ *Casa de Campo*, La Romana, Dominican Republic. One of the best of the tropical golf resorts. Contact your travel agent for information and reservations.

☐ *Doral Hotel and Country Club*, 4400 Northwest 87 Ave., Miami, FL 33178, (800) 327-6334. Features four 18-hole golf courses and one nine-hole par-three course. The Blue Course is the home of the Doral Eastern PGA tour event.

☐ *Gleneagles Hotel*, Perthshire, Scotland. One of the great manor houses of the United Kingdom. There are three 18-hole championship courses, and a fourth course is presently under construction. Open April through October only.

☐ *The Greenbriar*, White Sulphur Springs, WV 24986, (800) 624-6070. Has three golf courses, one of them designed by Jack Nicklaus.

☐ *The Lodge at Pebble Beach*, 17 Mile Drive, Pebble Beach, CA 93953, (408) 624-3811. Home of the Bing Crosby Pro-Am. Pebble Beach also features two famous golf holes (the 7th and the 18th) that are known for their difficulty.

☐ *Pinehurst Hotel and Country Club*, Box 4000, Pinehurst, NC 28374, (800) 927-4653. Features six golf courses. The number-two course is among the best in the world.

☐ *Sawgrass*, 100 TPC Blvd., Ponte Vedra, FL 32082, (800) 457-4653. This resort is home to the PGA's Tournament Championship, the richest purse on the tour.

☐ *Seapines Plantation*, Box 7000, Hilton Head Island, SC 29938, (800) 845-6131. Three courses are available. One, the Harbor Town Links, is world class and is the site of the Heritage Golf Classic.

*Write or call for rates (they change seasonally).

Source: Stephen Birnbaum, editorial director, *Diversion*, New York, and author of the *Steve Birnbaum Travel Guide* series, updated yearly and published by Houghton-Mifflin, Boston.

Offshore fishing: Where to go when

April and May: Long-range party-boat season in Southern California. San Diego is the biggest port. Party boats in New York and New Jersey venture out for flounder, cod and other bottom fishing. Party boats and skiff guides are active in the Florida Keys.

☐ June: Head for the Gulf Stream from the Outer Banks of North Carolina for tuna and white marlin. It's big-game billfish season offshore in the Gulf of Mexico from Louisiana to Texas.

☐ July, August, early September: In New York through New England, fish for giant tuna (up to 1,000 pounds!). It's peak season for white and blue marlin in North Carolina. There's excellent fishing in the Florida Keys (not crowded) for sailfish and bonefish. Party and charter boats fish for salmon in the Pacific Northwest through Alaska.

☐ September and October: Catch bluefin tuna off Prince Edward Island, before they migrate south.

☐ October and November: Big game fishing is winding down in the North and in the Gulf. But it's great for bluefish from Massachusetts through Chesapeake Bay.

☐ September through November: For a glamorous trip, the black marlin fishing is tremendous off the Great Barrier Reef in Australia or New Zealand.

☐ December and January: Winter is winter, even in the Florida Keys, but sailfish like the cold, rough seas. (Dress warmly.)

☐ February and March: The weather is very changeable in Southern waters, so allow at least three to five days for a fishing trip. You may thus get one or two good days of fishing. There is still plenty of good fishing in the Caribbean even though it is not peak season. Try for marlin and billfish in the Bahamas.

☐ November through March: Cabo San Lucas, Mexico, is prime for marlin, sails, dolphin (the fish, not the mammal) and roosterfish.

Successful offshore fishing

Offshore fishing for big game fish requires the least amount of previous experience of any type of sportfishing. You don't have to rig your tackle, bait a hook, cast a line, or navigate. All you need is a good boat, a good captain, a competent crew and a strong back!

Once known as "deep-sea fishing" (a term now seen only in the brochures of tropical resorts), offshore fishing refers to sport-fishing for larger species: The billfish (marlin, sailfish, and swordfish), tuna, tarpon, cobia, and shark. The US offers excellent fishing off all three coasts.

☐ If time permits, visit the boat docks at sunset, when charters return. See what kinds of fish are being brought in. Talk with the passengers: Were their previous fishing experience and their expectations similar to yours? Did they have fun? Are they satisfied with their day's trip? Would they do it again?

☐ Talk to the mates. Are they pleasant? Enthusiastic about the captain?

☐ Inspect the boat. Is it clean and well maintained? Does it appear to have proper radio and safety equipment? Naturally, a boat will not look its best on its return from a day's fishing—but are the running gear and fishing tackle well kept? Or is tackle randomly stowed, paint chipped, hardware corroded?

☐ Check to see if the captain has been licensed by the Coast Guard.

☐ Boats that carry six passengers or fewer are not required to pass an annual Coast Guard inspection, but they must carry mandatory safety equipment. Boats that have undergone a voluntary inspection will display a Coast Guard sticker.

☐ If you're planning to bring a child along, ask if junior-size life preservers are available.

☐ For children, choose a charter geared toward variety fishing. Try a half-day charter first, and stay away from hard-core game fishing—it is boring to just watch Daddy fish all day!

☐ If you expect to be able to keep your catch, check with the captain beforehand to avoid a dispute at the end of the day.

☐ Variations in costs depend largely on how far the boat must travel to reach prime fishing waters.

☐ Regardless of whether fish are caught, tip the mate and captain.

Sources: Barry Gibson, editor, *Salt Water Sportsman*, Boston; John F. Klein, a charter captain out of Sarasota, FL.

Offbeat three-day weekends

For an extra-long weekend you will never forget:

☐ Ballooning. A great way to see the countryside. In most of the US, ballooning trips are available within 100 miles of major cities. You can also take a trip that includes gourmet picnics in France and Austria or wild-game-watching in Kenya.

☐ Spas. Most spa resorts include massage, aerobics, swimming, and succulent diet cuisine, and many feature beauty facilities for facials, pedicures, etc. Spas can be found in Florida, California, Arizona, Texas, New York, New Jersey and Illinois. A favorite: World of Palmaire, Pompano Beach, Florida.

☐ Iceland. Not too far a flight from most northeastern cities, Iceland offers swimming in naturally heated bubbling springs and quick flights to the smaller islands (which the US astronauts used to simulate the lunar surface). Reykjavik, the capital, features great Scandinavian restaurants and shops.

☐ Tennis ranches. Besides excellent tennis facilities, these ranches usually provide horseback riding and swimming.

☐ Snowmobiling. Many national parks have snowmobile trails and rental arrangements and lodging is available in cabins or lodges at low, off-season rates.

☐ Cruise to nowhere. Going (or actually not going) from various East and West Coast cities on a cruise ship can be great fun. All normal shipboard cruise facilities are available for a luxurious weekend.

☐ Paris weekend. For those who will spend a dollar to save a dollar, bargain hunting or Christmas shopping in Paris is the answer. Typical package deal: Airfare from an East Coast city, lodging at a *pension* on the Left Bank, breakfasts, and a list of recommended shops in the area. Major American credit cards are accepted in Europe, so you can charge away.

☐ Dude ranches. Most prevalent in the West and Southwest. Smaller private ranches and farms that take in guests are homier than the bigger ones. Families are especially welcome. An inexpensive get-away-from-it-all including riding lessons and home cooking.

☐ Biking tours. You can travel in the Berkshires, the Smokies, or any beautiful countryside.

Source: Carole M. Phillips, CTC, of Certified Travel Consultants, New York.

Unusual and adventuresome vacations

☐ Backpack in the West.
☐ Visit Australia's haunting Great Barrier Reef Islands.
☐ Take an air safari to East Africa.
☐ Heli-ski in the Canadian Rockies.
☐ Visit native villages in New Guinea.
☐ Canoe down the Amazon River.
☐ Balloon in California.
☐ Cruise the Mississippi.
☐ Ride the Colorado River on a raft.
☐ Barge through the rivers of Europe.
☐ See the unspoiled wildlife on the Galapagos Islands.
☐ Study-tour in Mexico.
☐ Go on a religious retreat.
☐ Work on a kibbutz in Israel.
☐ Explore Australia's outback regions.
☐ Visit the ancient city of Machu Picchu in Peru.
☐ Join an archaeological dig in China or Tunisia.
☐ Climb the Himalayas and visit Nepal.
☐ Go deep-sea fishing off the coast of Baja California.
☐ Visit Bali and learn about its ancient music.
☐ Learn a foreign language by living with natives.
☐ Explore the coral reefs of the West Indies.
☐ Visit Alaska's national parks.

America's best museums

California

☐ *J. Paul Getty Museum*, 17985 Pacific Coast Highway, Malibu. Extraordinary private art collection from Greek and Roman to 20th century.

☐ *Huntington Library, Art Gallery and Botanical Gardens,* 1151 Oxford Rd., San Marino. Gainsborough's Blue Boy, 18th-century British and European art.

☐ *Los Angeles County Museum of Art*, 5905 Wilshire Blvd., Los Angeles. Outstanding collection from antiquities to 20th-century art.

☐ *San Francisco Museum of Modern Art*, McAllister and Van Ness Ave., San Francisco. Fine collection of 20th-century European and American art.

☐ *Asian Art Museum of San Francisco*, Golden Gate Park, San Francisco. Finest collection of Oriental art in the Western world.

Colorado

☐ *Denver Art Museum*, 100 West 14 Ave. and Bannock, Denver. North and South American Indian collections.

Connecticut

☐ *Wadsworth Atheneum*, 600 Main St., Hartford. The oldest art museum in the United States and one of the best.

☐ *Yale University Art Gallery*, 1111 Chapel St., New Haven. John Trumbull's paintings of the American Revolution and much more.

District of Columbia

☐ *Corcoran Gallery of Art*, 17 St. and New York Ave. NW, Washington. Historic American paintings, European art.

☐ *Freer Gallery of Art*, 12 St. and Jefferson Drive SW, Washington. Far and Near Eastern art; Whistler's works.

☐ *Hirshhorn Museum and Sculpture Garden*, Independence Ave. at 8 St. SW, Washington. The entire collection—sculpture and modern art—of millionaire Joseph Hirshhorn.

☐ *National Gallery of Art*, 4 St. and Constitution Ave. NW, Washington. A jewel of a museum with a brilliant new wing by I.M. Pei. General European and American art collection.

☐ *National Portrait Gallery*, 8 St. at F St., Washington. Portraits of all the American presidents displayed in an 1840 Greek Revival building, the former US Patent Office.

Georgia

☐ *The High Museum of Art*, 1280 Peachtree NE, Atlanta. Renaissance of 20th-century American and European paintings, sculpture and decorative arts.

Illinois

☐ *The Art Institute*, Michigan Ave. at Adams St., Chicago. Outstanding Impressionists and post-Impressionists in a first-rate collection.

Maryland

☐ *Baltimore Museum of Fine Arts*, Art Museum Drive (near N. Charles and 31 St.), Baltimore. Fine French post-Impressionist works; mosaics from Antioch.

Massachusetts

☐ *Boston Museum of Fine Arts*, 465 Huntington Ave., Boston. The new I.M. Pei wing is impressive.

☐ *Fogg Museum*, 32 Quincy St., Cambridge. Harvard's extensive art collection.

Michigan

☐ *Detroit Art Institute*, Woodward at Kirby Ave., Detroit. Great masters and moderns.

Minnesota

☐ *Walker Art Center*, 725 Vineland Place, Minneapolis. Post-Impressionist and contemporary art.

New York

☐ *Albright-Knox Art Gallery*, 1285 Elmwood Ave., Buffalo. Splendid modern collection, as well as general collection.

☐ *Brooklyn Museum*, 200 Eastern Parkway, Brooklyn. Fine general collection with strong Egyptian art and American paintings.

☐ *The Frick Collection*, Fifth Ave. at 70 St., New York. One of the best private collections.

☐ *The Solomon R. Guggenheim Museum*, 1701 Fifth Ave. at 88 St., New York. Modern art and sculpture in a circular building designed by Frank Lloyd Wright.

☐ *Metropolitan Museum of Art*, Fifth Ave. at 82 St., New York. Probably the finest general collection in the US.

☐ *Museum of Modern Art*, 11 W. 53 St., New York. First US museum devoted to 20th century art—from paintings and sculpture to design and film.

☐ *The Pierpont Morgan Library*, 29 E. 36 St., New York. Illuminated Bibles, Rembrandts and other superb art.

☐ *Whitney Museum of American Art*, Madison Ave. at 75 St., New York. 20th-century US art.

Ohio

☐ *Cleveland Museum of Art* , 11150 East Blvd. at University Circle, Cleveland. All cultures. Strong in medieval and Oriental art.

Oregon

☐ *Portland Art Museum,* 1219 SW Park Ave., Portland. Appealing outdoor sculpture, mall, general collection.

Pennsylvania

☐ *The Frick Art Museum*, 7227 Reynolds St., Pittsburgh. Eclectic collection of Russian, Chinese, Flemish and French art and artifacts.

☐ *Philadelphia Museum of Art*, 26 St. and Benjamin Franklin Parkway, Philadelphia. Magnificent general collection.

☐ *Rodin Museum*, 22 St. and Benjamin Franklin Parkway, Philadelphia. Sculpture, sketches and drawings by this famous French artist.

Texas

☐ *Amon Carter Museum of Western Art*, 3501 Camp Bowie Blvd., Fort Worth. Extensive collection of Frederic Remington's and Charles Russell's work.

☐ *Houston Museum of Fine Arts*, 1001 Bissonnet, Houston. Fine general collection.

Offbeat museums around the US

☐ Ketchikan, Alaska: Totem Pole Heritage Center.

☐ Vermont: Two maple sugar museums.

☐ Baraboo, Wisconsin: The Circus World Museum recreates the glitter and razzmatazz of The Greatest Show on Earth with antique carousels, costumes and other memorabilia. Visitors can view a sideshow, participate in a Big Top performance and ride an elephant.

☐ New York City: The Songwriters' Hall of Fame.

☐ Sacramento, California: The California State Railroad Museum traces railroad history from early steam engines to modern diesel locomotives.

☐ Las Vegas, Nevada: The Liberace Museum houses some of the prized possessions of "Mr. Showmanship" himself—a fleet of customized cars, his flashy wardrobe and several rare pianos.

☐ Eureka Springs, Arkansas: The Hammond Museum of Bells.

☐ Nashville, Tennessee: The Country Music Hall of Fame.

New York City's most interesting churches and synagogues

Although Americans traveling to foreign cities usually make it a point to view the important cathedrals and churches, they often overlook them at home. New York City, for example, has more than 2,250 churches and 600 synagogues. Some of the most interesting:

☐ *Cathedral Church of St. John the Divine* (Episcopal), Amsterdam Ave. at 112 St., 316-7540. Open daily from 7:15 A.M. to 5 P.M. Services: Sunday at 8 A.M., 9:30 A.M. and 11 A.M. (the main service with choir is at 11 A.M.). Immense cathedral begun in 1892 and still not completely finished. Architecture: Diverse…but inspiring.

☐ *Central Synagogue* (Reform Jewish), 123 E. 55 St., 838-5122. Services: Friday at 5:30 P.M. and Saturday at 10 A.M. The oldest synagogue in the city, built in 1872. It is impressive with its onion domes and brightly stenciled interior walls.

☐ *Congregation Shearith Israel* (Orthodox Jewish), 8 W. 70 St., 873-0300. Open for viewing only during services, but call for tour information. Services: Daily at 7:30 A.M. and 6:30 P.M. (times may change with the seasons). A Portuguese and Spanish synagogue, home of the city's oldest Sephardic Jewish congregation.

☐ *Fifth Avenue Presbyterian Church*, Fifth Ave. at 55 St., 247-0490. Open daily from 8 A.M. to 9 P.M. Services: Sunday at 11 A.M. and 4:30 P.M. Call for schedule of concerts. An elegant, centrally located church built in 1875 in Scandinavian style. Dave Brubeck performs here in December.

☐ *Friends' Meeting House,* 137-16

Northern Blvd., Flushing, Queens, (718) 358-9636. Open the first and third Sunday of every month between 2 P.M. and 4 P.M. Oldest house of worship in the city. Used continuously since 1694. (Between 1776 and 1783 the British used it as a prison, storehouse and hospital.)

☐ *Grace Church* (Episcopal), 802 Broadway at E. 10 St., 254-2000. Open daily from 9 A.M. to 5 P.M. Services: Sunday at 8 A.M., 9 A.M. and 11 A.M. Designed by James Renwick Jr. in 1846 (he later designed St. Patrick's Cathedral). Considered one of the city's finest examples of Gothic Revival architecture.

☐ *Plymouth Church of the Pilgrims* (Congregational), Orange St. (between Henry St. and Hicks St.), Brooklyn Heights, (718) 624-4743. Service: Sunday at 11 A.M. Tours can sometimes be arranged to see the original Tiffany windows. Henry Ward Beecher's church from 1847 to 1887. A piece of Plymouth Rock is preserved in the arcade.

☐ *Riverside Church* (interdenominational), W. 122 St. at Riverside Drive, 222-5900. Open daily 9 A.M. to 5 P.M. (main building). Service: Sunday at 10:45 A.M. Ask about the regular organ recitals. Built in 1929. The architecture of the cathedral is modeled on Chartres, with gargoyles and marvelous stained-glass windows. There are two Sir Jacob Epstein statues—a 40-foot Christ in the nave and a large Madonna and Child outside. Four Henrich Hoffman paintings are in the church.

☐ *St. Bartholomew's* (Episcopal), Park Ave. at 50 St., 751-1616. Not open for viewing during the week. Services: Sunday at 9 A.M. and 11 A.M. A Byzantine splendor, with lovely terraced gardens designed by Bertram Goodhue.

☐ *St. Mark's-in-the-Bowery* (Episcopal), 10 St. and Second Ave., 674-6377. Open daily from 9 A.M. to 4 P.M. Services: Sunday at 10:30 A.M. Erected in 1799. Its graveyard contains the remains of Dutch governor Peter Stuyvesant.

☐ *St. Patrick's Cathedral,* Fifth Ave. between 50 St. and 51 St., 753-2261. Open daily from 7 A.M. to 9 P.M. Services: Daily at 7 A.M., 7:30 A.M., 8 A.M., 8:30 A.M., noon, 12:30 P.M., 1 P.M. and 5:30 P.M. Seat of the Roman Catholic archdiocese of New York. An adaptation of French Gothic architecture, designed by James Renwick

Jr. and William Rodrigue. Many of the stained-glass windows were made in Chartres and Nantes.

☐ *St. Paul's Chapel* (Episcopal), Broadway and Fulton St., 285-0874. Open daily from 8 A.M. to 3:30 P.M. Services: Sunday at 8 A.M., no Saturday service. A beautiful Georgian building, Manhattan's only pre-Revolutionary church (started in 1764). George Washington and Lafayette worshiped here.

☐ *St. Peter's Lutheran Church,* Lexington Ave. at E. 54 St., 935-2200. Open daily from 9 A.M. until midnight. Services: Monday through Friday at 12:15 P.M., Sunday at 8:45 A.M. and 11 A.M. Modern church with Louise Nevelson chapel in white. Famous for jazz vespers.

☐ *St. Thomas Church* (Episcopal), Fifth Ave. at 53 St., 757-7013. Open daily from 7 A.M. to 6 P.M. Services: Daily at 8 A.M., 12:10 P.M. and 5:30 P.M., Sunday at 8 A.M., 9 A.M.,11 A.M. and 4 P.M. French Gothic structure with opulent details. Built in 1914. Site of some of the most fashionable weddings (look for the "bride's door" with lovers' knot and dollar sign).

☐ *St. Vincent Ferrer* (Roman Catholic), Lexington Ave. at 66 St., 744-2080. Open daily from 7 A.M. to 7 P.M. Services: Daily at 8 A.M., 9 A.M., 12:10 P.M., and 5:30 P.M., Sunday at 8 A.M., 10 A.M., 1 P.M. and 5:30 P.M. Built in 1918 for the Dominican order. It has a priory and convent and is set back from the street with lovely gardens.

☐ *Trinity Episcopal Church,* Broadway and Wall St., 285-0872. Open Monday through Friday from 7 A.M. to 6 P.M., Saturday and Sunday 8 A.M. to 4 P.M. Services: Monday through Friday at 8 A.M. and noon, Saturday and Sunday at 8 A.M., 9 A.M., and 11:15 A.M. Founded by royal charter of England's King William II. It has been rebuilt twice. Fascinating old cemetery next door contains graves of Alexander Hamilton, William Bradford and other famous people.

Hours quoted are those in effect from September through the end of June. Summer hours may be more restrictive.

How to enjoy business trips more

Before you go:

☐ Learn about local hotels, restaurants and theaters, so you won't be at the mercy of bad recommendations. Go to an out-of-town newsstand for Sunday papers and "city" magazines.

☐ Talk with people who live in, work in or often visit your destination. Ask for recommendations of things to see and do on your off-hours.

☐ Schedule your first week back. Set up lunches and meetings in advance, to avoid losing time when you return.

☐ Tell your secretary exactly when you plan to call in. That way, she will surely be at her desk, with the necessary messages and materials at hand. She can also deal more effectively with callers or employees who need to know when they'll have answers from you.

What to tell children before a business trip

Children resent business trips and private vacations taken by parents. They feel you would rather travel than be with them.

To minimize hurt feelings:

☐ Explain the nature of your trip. Speculate on the problems they would encounter if they accompanied you.

☐ Leave behind a list of activities for them to do while you are gone. Perhaps lend them the family camera for taking pictures of what they do.

☐ Stash little gifts they can open on different days during your absence.

☐ Give each child a bonus of spending money.

☐ For young children, tape yourself reading a few favorite stories. The children can play them when they feel lonely.

Source: Kay Kuzma, author of *Prime-Time Parenting,* Rawson Wade Publishers, New York.

Making a business trip less stressful

☐ Take only work you can realistically do. Report writing that requires copious files and conferences with colleagues is out.

☐ If you like to bring back presents or postcards for your children, purchase these at the airport as soon as you arrive.

☐ Make things easy on yourself. Most

people will accommodate out-of-towners by driving to their hotels or holding meetings at airports. Trying to find your associate's suburban home by flashlight or dealing with downtown rush-hour traffic is frustrating.

☐ If you don't want to rent a car and can't justify hiring a car and driver, compromise. Cabbies will often agree to drop you off and pick you up throughout the day for just the fare plus a fat tip.

How to make the most of your time in unfamiliar towns

☐ Be a part-time tourist. An hour or two between appointments gives you enough time to check out the local aquarium, museum, library, antique district, park or waterfront. Major tourist attractions are often located near enough to a city's business district for you to mix meetings with pleasure conveniently.

☐ Have a great meal. Do some advance research, and equip yourself with a list of the best restaurants in each city on your itinerary. Then, when your free time coincides with a mealtime, invest instead in a delightful hour of gourmet adventure.

☐ Look up old friends. Perhaps you can share that gourmet meal with a college friend you haven't seen in years, or surprise an uncle or cousin with a call or visit.

☐ Take pictures. If you're into photography, you know that a new environment frequently yields new visions and special scenes and subjects. Keep your eyes open and your camera ready.

☐ Go gift shopping. On autumn trips, carry a list of holiday gift ideas for friends and family. Use even a spare 15 minutes to pop in on the local boutiques and specialty shops. Charge and send your purchases, and when you get home they'll be there, all ready for your December giving.

☐ Bring busywork. When you're too tired to kill time on the move—or it's raining or the neighborhood is threatening or everything is closed—you should have something to do in your hotel room other than watch TV and order room service. Try catching up on a pile of periodicals or going through seed catalogues.

Source: Letty Cottin Pogrebin, an editor at *Ms.* magazine and author of five books, most recently *Family Politics,* McGraw-Hill, New York.

Making the most of travel time

Some people claim that they can work on airplanes, trains or boats, but you may not be one of them. If you, too, are unable to concentrate while traveling:

☐ Go to sleep. Traveling is a natural soporific. Catching up on your sleep will give you an edge when you arrive.

☐ Find someone to talk with. Walk around and see if anyone who looks interesting has a copy of the *Official Airlines Guide* (which frequent travelers carry) or other travel guides. Start talking about travel, and you'll learn a few things.

☐ Clean out your wallet or briefcase. This is something you always mean to do but never get around to.

☐ Write letters. They don't take much concentration.

Killing time creatively at airports

☐ Make phone calls. Check into your office, pick up a dozen phone messages and return eight calls before being driven from the public phone by the furious stares of others waiting to use it.

☐ Write letters or pay bills. Bring notepaper, envelopes, bills and your checkbook. Use your briefcase as a desk.

☐ Shop for the unexpected. Airport gift shops are notoriously glitzy. And at first glance, the merchandise in every gift shop looks alike except for the city etched into the beer mugs. But you may well find a Pierre Cardin belt at a bargain price in Cleveland, live lobsters in Boston and sourdough bread in San Francisco.

☐ Read indulgently. Buy a spy novel if you usually lean toward business books. Pick up a foreign magazine and test your French. Indulge in a crossword puzzle magazine or cartoon book. Read the local papers.

☐ Get a haircut or shoeshine. Men have the edge here. Although airport barber shops sometimes advertise "unisex," I've never seen a woman in any of them. Bootblacks will gladly shine a woman's shoes.

☐ Jog. With throngs of people running to catch their planes, no one will know you are just jogging along the concourses to kill time. Leave your coat and carry-on bag under someone's watchful eye while you run.

☐ People-watch. This is a surprisingly diverting pastime, especially for hyperactive types who don't often stop to observe the world around them.

☐ Eavesdrop. Airports are great places to tune in on some fascinating conversations—one as melodramatic as a soap opera dialogue, another as funny as a Mel Brooks sketch.

☐ Think. If you're uninspired by the above alternatives, you can simply stare out at the landing field, letting your mind go blank. Or you can give yourself a specific problem to mull over. Sometimes the brain does a better job of thinking at rest than it does under pressure.

Source: Letty Cottin Pogrebin, an editor at *Ms.* magazine and author of five books, most recently *Family Politics*, McGraw-Hill, New York.

Saving time and money at hotels

☐ When you arrive at a hotel, check your bags. Then go to the pay telephone in the lobby and call the hotel. Ask to have your reservation confirmed, give them your charge card number and go on your way. You'll sidestep convention check-in lines.

☐ To avoid the long check-out line after the convention, go down to the desk very early in the morning, before official checkout time, and check out. You won't have to turn in your room key, and you can still use your room until official checkout time (usually around 1 P.M.).

☐ Don't stay glued to your hotel room if you're waiting for a call. If you ask, the hotel operator will transfer your calls to another room, interrupt the call you're on for a more important one or hold any calls while you run out for a soda.

☐ Save money by not paying for things you didn't order. Don't charge anything to your hotel room. It's too confusing when you're checking out to verify the list of room charges. And it's only too easy for the hotel to make a mistake. If you don't charge anything at all, you'll know that extra items on your bill can't be yours. How to do it: Use your

telephone credit card for calls, and pay cash for room service, laundry, etc. Use your credit card for food.

☐ Don't depend only on the hotel for services such as typing, film developing, etc. Call the local convention bureau. It's specifically set up to help out-of-town businesspeople, and every city has one.

Source: Dr. Barbara A. Pletcher, executive director of the National Association for Professional Saleswomen, is author of *Travel Sense*, ACE Books, New York.

How to speed hotel transactions when conventioneering

☐ When you reach your hotel, give your bags to the bellman.

☐ Go to the welcoming cocktail party or dinner. Then check in at 9:30 P.M. or so when the lines are gone.

☐ Check out early in the morning and avoid the lines at noon when most people check out.

☐ You may want to use the room during the morning, so check out at 9:00 A.M., but hand in your room key when you leave. Hotels usually don't rent their rooms until about 2:00 P.M.

☐ If you're assigned an undesirable room, ask for a better one. If necessary, be insistent.

Convention business is so important to hotels that they don't want unhappy convention-goers complaining about the accommodations.

Don't be a victim of hotel overbooking

It's not always the hotel's fault. Sometimes guests overstay. (Hawaii is the only state that allows hotels to compel guests to leave on time.) But hotels generally accept more reservations than they have rooms, betting that some reservation-holders won't show. Sometimes they bet wrong.

To keep from being a loser:

☐ Plan trips sufficiently in advance to get written confirmation of reservations. That gives you something extra to argue with should you need it. If there's no time for a written confirmation, try to get a confirmation number when the reservation is made.

☐ Get "guaranteed" reservations with a credit card. This does obligate you to pay for the room even if you can't make it. However, it reduces the incentive a hotel clerk has to sell your room to somebody else. American Express has an "assured reservations" program. Under it, the hotel that "walks" you has to pay for the first night's lodging in a comparable hotel room nearby, for a long-distance call to inform the office or family where you will be, and for transportation to the substitute hotel. Several chains have a similar policy.

☐ Arrive early in the afternoon, when last night's guests have checked out, but before the bulk of new arrivals.

☐ Take your case to a higher-up— probably the assistant manager on duty—since it's unlikely that the desk clerk will find a room after telling you he has none. The assistant manager might be persuaded to "find" one of the rooms that inevitably are set aside by luxury hotels for emergencies such as the arrival of a VIP. Make a loud fuss, some people suggest. This often works, since hotels try to avoid drawing public attention to their overbooking practices.

☐ If neither raving and ranting nor quiet persuasion moves the assistant manager, insist that he call other comparable hotels to get you a room, and at the same or lower price. The better hotels will usually do their best.

How to save on air travel

☐ Fly between 9 P.M.. and 7 A.M. Most airlines have cheaper night flights, especially on long distances.

☐ Plan business trips so that the schedule qualifies the business traveler for vacation excursion fares (discounts up to 50%).

☐ Fly out-of-the-way carriers looking for new business.

☐ Make sales or service trips, or tours of branch offices, using the unlimited mileage tickets offered by some airlines.

☐ Before making flight and car-rental arrangements, find out if a small commuter airline will make the hop to the traveler's final destination. It may actually cost less.

Source: Harold Seligman, president, Management Alternatives, Stamford, CT.

Getting a good airplane seat

Getting the seat you prefer on an airplane has become an increasing problem.

☐ If you're assigned to a seat you don't like, go back to the desk when all the prereserved seats are released (usually about 15 minutes before flight time). Prime seats for passengers who didn't show up are available then.

☐ If you discover on the plane that you don't like your seat, don't wait until the plane takes off to find a better one. Look around the plane, and the second before they close the door, head for the empty seat of your choice. Don't wait until the seat-belt sign goes on.

☐ Prereserve a single seat on a nonjumbo where the seats are three across and you'll increase the odds of getting an empty seat next to you.

☐ Ask for a window or aisle seat in a row where the window or aisle is already reserved by a single. The middle seat between two singles is least likely to fill up.

What the airlines don't tell you

☐ Never accept the first fare quoted. Half the time, some other airline's flight within hours of the one you booked has a special, less expensive deal.

☐ Take advantage of "illegal" connections. These are connecting flights usually less than 45 minutes apart—that usually do not even show up on the computer when your trip is being routed. Solution: Have your agent write up your flight in two separate tickets. The second is for the illegal connection that originates at your transfer point. To make fast transfers, travel with carry-on luggage.

☐ Use do-it-yourself searches with a CRT. Plug into the *Official Airlines Guide* data base and search out the flights available at the desired time. Using another code, find out what fares are available on each airline for the time period. If no asterisk is shown, it's possible to book the flight right up to the last minute. If there is an asterisk next to the airline flight number, ask the system what the restrictions are.

Source: Harold Seligman, president, Management Alternatives, Stamford, CT.

Bags for airline travel

American carriers now measure bags in total inches—that is, length plus height plus width.

☐ For international economy flights, the two checked pieces may add up to 106 inches, with neither bag exceeding 62 total inches. First-class passengers are allowed a total of 124 inches.

☐ In any class, a carry-on that adds up to 45 inches is acceptable.

☐ Some foreign lines limit luggage by weight—44 pounds for economy class and 66 pounds for first class.

☐ For domestic flights, the allowance is two checked bags, one no larger than 62 total inches and the other not exceeding 55 total inches, plus a 45-inch carry-on.

☐ To help spot your bags quickly, place a sticker, ribbon or special tag on the outside.

☐ Always put identification inside the luggage in case the outside tags are lost.

☐ Air travel with only a duffel bag eliminates the need to check baggage through. The flexible duffel contours to fit into the space under the seat. Pick a smooth-surface bag for easy sliding. Size of bag that can be taken aboard: One with total dimensions of 40-45 inches.

☐ To pack a duffel: Do not roll clothes. Fold them. Wear the bulkiest clothes, including boots. Segregate commonly used items such as toiletries, vitamins and prescriptions into small vinyl bags so they will be more readily available without emptying the contents of the large bag.

Source: American Society of Travel Agents, Washington, DC.

Know when not to fly

Avoid flying if you have had:

☐ A heart attack within four weeks of takeoff.

☐ Surgery within two weeks.

☐ A deep-diving session within 24 hours.

Don't fly at all if you have:

☐ Severe lung problems.

☐ Uncontrolled hypertension.

☐ Epilepsy not well controlled.

☐ Severe anemia.

☐ A pregnancy beyond 240 days or threatened by miscarriage.

Source: *Pocket Flight Guide/Frequent Flyer Package.*

How to cancel non-cancelable tickets

Problem: "Super Saver" tickets cost as little as 30% of regular airfares, but airlines say you can't get a refund if you change travel plans.

Solution: A cooperative travel agent. When you buy a ticket from an agent, the agent makes your reservation immediately. But it doesn't forward your money to the airline for a few days—in some cases not until a week later. That's because agents pay airlines only once a week. During the time gap a friendly travel agent will let you cancel the reservation and get your money back.

☐ Caution: Travel agents don't have to accommodate you. But if you're a good customer and the agent wants to keep your business, chances are good that you can get a refund.

☐ Helpful: Check with your agent to see if two round trip, noncancelable discount fares cost less than one full round trip ticket. Even if you use only half of each of the discount tickets, the cost for both may be less than a full fare ticket.

Source: Harold Seligman, president of Management Alternatives, travel management consultants, Stamford, CT.

Your ears and air travel

☐ Avoid flying with a cold or other respiratory infection. A cold greatly increases the chances of your suffering discomfort, additional fluid buildup, severe pain or even rupture.

☐ Take decongestants. If you must fly with a cold, or if you regularly suffer discomfort or pain on descent, decongestants can give real relief. For maximum effect, time them to coincide with the descent (which begins half an hour to an hour before landing). Use both oral decongestants and a spray for best results. Suggested timing: Take quick-acting oral decongestants two to three hours before landing or slow-release tablets six to eight hours in advance. Use nasal spray one hour before landing. Caution: If you have hypertension or a heart condition, check with your cardiologist about taking decongestants.

☐ Don't smoke or drink. Smoking irritates the nasal area, and alcohol dilates the blood vessels, causing the tissues to swell.

☐ Try the Valsalva maneuver. While holding your nose closed, try to blow through it as though you were blowing your nose. This will blow air through the ears. Do this gently and repeatedly as the plane descends. Warning: Don't use this method if you have a cold, as you'll be blowing infection back into the middle ear. Use the tried-and-true routines of yawning and swallowing instead. They can be quite effective if the problem is not too severe. Chew gum and suck candy. Aim: To activate the swallowing mechanism in order to open the eustachian tubes.

☐ If your ears are stuffed after landing, follow the same routine. Keep on with decongestants and gentle Valsalvas. Temporary hearing loss and stuffiness may persist for three to four weeks. If the symptoms are really annoying, a doctor can lance the drum to drain the fluid. If pain persists for more than a day, see a doctor.

☐ See a doctor before flying if you have a bad cold, especially if you have a history of ear pain when flying. If you absolutely must fly, the doctor can open the eardrum and insert a small ventilation tube that will allow the pressure to equalize. The tube should eject by itself in a few weeks…or you can go back to your doctor.

Source: Neville W. Carmical, M.D., attending otolaryngologist, St.Luke's-Roosevelt Hospital Center, New York.

Coping with high altitudes

One out of three travelers at altitudes of 7,000 feet above sea level (Vail, Colorado, for example) experiences some symptoms of altitude sickness. By 10,000 feet (Breckenridge, Colorado), everyone is affected.

Common complaints: Headaches, nausea, weakness, lack of coordination and insomnia.

To minimize the effects:

☐ Take it easy the first two or three days. Get plenty of rest and don't schedule vigorous activities.

☐ Eat a little less than usual. Avoid hard-to-digest foods such as red meat and fats. Carbohydrates are good.

☐ Drink more liquids than usual. (Breathing harder in dry air causes you to lose water vapor.)

☐ Avoid alcohol, smoking and tranquilizers. Their effects are compounded at high altitudes.

Flyer's health secrets

☐ Taking your mind off the motion can help your body restore equilibrium without drugs. How to do it: Close your eyes, or concentrate on a spot in front of you, and hold your head as steady as possible. Then focus your attention on your breathing or on alternately tensing and relaxing your muscles. Continue to concentrate until the nausea has vanished.

☐ The low air pressure in an airplane's interior can aggravate some medical problems unless precautions are taken. Gas trapped in the colon can expand, causing severe discomfort or cramps. People with heart or lung diseases should check with their doctor in advance to discuss requesting supplemental oxygen.

☐ Don't fly with a serious sinus problem. If a sinus is blocked, the trapped air inside expands and can lead to serious infection. Improve drainage prior to ascent and descent with decongestants or nose drops.

☐ The arid atmosphere of pressurized cabins encourages evaporation from the skin's surface, drying the skin. Remedies: Avoid beverages that contain alcohol or caffeine (they both have a diuretic action). Drink plenty of water during the trip and afterward.

Getting to and from the airport:

☐ Arrive early to avoid stress.

☐ Schedule an appointment at the airport. If you're in a strange city, try to get your last appointment of the day to meet you there a few hours before your plane leaves. Why should you be the one to do all the running?

❏ Join an airport club. Most airlines have them. Choose the one that belongs to the principal carrier flying from your city. Then you can relax in comfort while you wait for your flight. Benefits: Special services to members, such as a separate check-in desk.

Source: *Healthwise* and Commission on Emergency Medical Services, American Medical Association, Chicago.

Car rental tips

Car-rental competition is hotter than ever, especially among the small intracity and intrastate firms. What to keep tabs on:

❏ Does the price include fuel? Very few still do. Dry rate means the customer buys the gas. Find out where gas is cheapest. Fill up there, too, before dropping the car off.

❏ Special restrictions or charges for one-way rentals.

❏ Special weekend or weekly rates.

❏ When luggage space is important, make sure you're getting a large enough vehicle. (A compact or inter-mediate model may still be suitable.)

❏ Extra charge if a larger car is substituted. There shouldn't be one if the rental firm does the switching.

❏ Special corporate discount. Compar-ison shopping on this could hold surprises.

❏ Special fly/drive packages offered by airlines.

❏ The rental firm's policy in case of car trouble.

❏ In case of an accident, does the contract include primary liability coverage? (In California and Florida, only secondary coverage is required.)

Source: *Medical Economics*, Oradell, NJ.

When renting a car

❏ Give a rented car the once-over before driving away in it. Check the headlights, turn signals and brakes. Squirt the windshield washer to be sure that there is fluid. Check the oil level. Drive it around the block before taking it on the expressway.

❏ Don't pay for more insurance than you need on a rented car. Rental agencies routinely encourage customers to pay around $5 a day for optional collision coverage. Chances are, however, that your own personal-car policy may extend coverage to a

rented car. Check the insurance policy before signing up for unnecessary coverage.

Automatic drop-off can be a rip-off on late-night rented-car returns. Unlike normal rental-car check-in, where the clerk totals up the costs and gives you a copy of the bill, automatic drop-offs require you to return all copies. You often don't get a copy until your credit-card company has billed you. Protective alternatives:

❏ Return your rental car during business hours.

❏ Make a copy of the rental form before returning it, noting your entry of the final mileage.

❏ Don't pay your credit-card bill until you get the car-rental bill and make sure their figures agree with yours.

❏ If they have overcharged you, dispute the bill and let the credit-card company know about the problem.

Source: *Travel Smart for Business.*

How to avoid vacation time-sharing traps

Some owners of time-shares in beach- and ski-area condominiums are becom-ing disenchanted. Reasons: They find that committing themselves to the same dates at the same resort every year is too restricting. Or they find they overpaid.

To avoid problems:

❏ Locate one of the companies that act as brokers for swapping time-shares for owners of resort properties in different areas.

❏ Don't pay more than 10 times the going rate for a good hotel or apart-ment rental in the same area at the same time of year.

❏ Get in early on a new complex. Builders usually sell the first few apartments for less.

❏ Choose a one- or two-bedroom unit. Smaller or larger ones are harder to swap or sell.

❏ Deal with experienced developers who have already worked out mainte-nance and management problems.

❏ Pick a time in the peak season. It will be more negotiable.

❏ Look for properties that are protected

by zoning or geography. Vail, Colorado, for example, has a moratorium on further time-share development.

☐ Beware of resorts that are hard to reach or are too far off the beaten track. Your time-shares will be harder to rent, swap or sell.

If your tour is a disappointment

To get your money back:

☐ Go back to the travel agency or sponsor who promoted it with your evidence of a breach of contract.

☐ Keep all brochures or detailed itinerary that constitutes your contract.

☐ Keep evidence that the promises were not kept. Example: Out-of-pocket receipts, pictures you took of your hotel or room, etc.

☐ If you come to an impasse on the terms of the tour agreement, check with the American Society of Travel Agents in New York, for an explanation of standardized industry terms (first class, deluxe, etc.).

☐ Last resort: File a complaint with either small claims court or civil court. Advantage with either: You don't have to retain a lawyer. Judgments are made quickly.

☐ Final action: Class-action suits have been successful in cases where it's unclear who is at fault. Sometimes it's your only hope for recovering anything from wholesalers and suppliers that are hard to reach.

☐ Warning: If your complaint is with a travel agency that went out of business while you were on tour (such things do happen), your recovery chances are virtually nil against that business, no matter how far you take your case.

Source: Patricia Simko, Assistant Attorney General, New York State Bureau of Consumer Frauds, New York.

Essentials *before* you leave for overseas

☐ Check your health and accident insurance to see if you're covered for illness or injury abroad.

☐ Does your policy pay for transportation home if you're on a litter and need more than one airplane seat?

Although a number of companies will pay for treatment, transportation is rarely covered. Recommended: Check with your travel agent for a company that provides this kind of coverage.

☐ Leave a detailed itinerary with someone close to you—the more detailed, the better. If you fail to get in touch, this might be the only clue to your whereabouts.

☐ Be sure to fill in the section provided in your passport for a contact in case of emergency. Keep it accurate and up to date for each trip. Don't list your spouse if he/she is going with you. It can delay notification of your next of kin by the Department of State.

☐ Carry a copy of the prescriptions for any medications you're carrying. Don't carry large amounts of any prescription drug, as you might come under suspicion by foreign customs.

How to get a passport faster

If you seek a passport at the height of the tourist season, you'll inevitably face a long wait. But whenever you go for your passport, you can ease the delay by doing the following:

☐ Go to the passport office in person.

☐ Bring: Your airline ticket, two passport pictures, proof of citizenship (an old passport, voter registration or birth certificate), a piece of identification with your photo on it and the fee.

☐ Give the passport office a good reason why you are rushed.

If your passport is lost or stolen when you're traveling abroad, here's what to do:

☐ Immediately notify the local police and the US embassy or consulate. An overnight replacement is sometimes possible in an emergency.

☐ To hasten this process, know your passport number.

☐ Next best: Have a valid identification document with you. A photostat of your passport is best.

Source: *Travel Smart.*

THE SKILLED TRAVELER

How to "be prepared" when traveling overseas

☐ Before going overseas, write to the International Association for Medical Assistance to Travelers and ask for its free directory listing well-trained English-speaking doctors around the world. Important: Write six to eight weeks before your trip.

On an overseas trip take:

☐ String or mailing tape, wrapping paper and manila envelopes (for sending parcels home).

☐ A Swiss jackknife (to open wine, pare apples, or cut cheese).

☐ Scotch tape and epoxy glue (to mend tears or attach a shoe heel).

☐ A sewing kit.

☐ Basic first-aid items, such as Band-Aids, aspirin, Alka-Seltzer.

Source: *Living Abroad.*

If you lose your passport or credit cards overseas

☐ If your passport is lost or stolen, contact the nearest US embassy or consulate immediately. A consul will interview you.

☐ If he is satisfied of your US citizenship and identity, a new passport can be quickly issued. Most Americans are able to satisfy the consular officer on the basis of a personal interview and presentation of identification that was not stolen or lost with the passport.

☐ In some cases, the consul may find it necessary to wire the Department of State to verify that you had been issued a previous passport.

☐ The consul will be able to refer you to local offices of the major credit cards and travelers checks to report losses.

☐ If you lose all your money, the embassy will assist you in having funds transferred from a friend or relative in the US through State Department channels.

☐ The embassy will *not* lend you money.

Currency-exchange strategies

Even though the dollar has been strong, a sudden drop could leave you vulnerable while overseas. To protect yourself:

☐ Take about 40% of your travelers checks in commission-free foreign currency and the rest in dollars.

☐ Prepay your foreign hotel in its own currency to lock in the current rate.

☐ If you fly first class, business class, or on the Concorde, find out if you can pay for the return trip in foreign currency.

☐ Shop carefully before buying foreign currency. Even major US banks' conversion rates vary.

☐ Avoid changing dollars into foreign currency at overseas hotels and restaurants. Stick to banks.

☐ When shopping overseas, ask for prices in the local currency. Then request a discount if you intend to pay that way.

Customs rates on what you buy abroad

Your first $400 worth of foreign goods is duty-free. The next $1,000 worth costs a flat 10% in duty (except for designated countries whose articles are duty-free). Beyond that, rates vary by category as follows:

☐ Alcohol: 27¢–$3.40/gallon.

☐ Antiques over 100 years old: Free.

☐ Automobiles: 2.5%.

☐ Still cameras: 4.1%.

☐ Crystal: 7.1%.

☐ Furs: 3.4%–10%.

☐ Silver jewelry: 27.5%.

☐ Other jewelry: 7.9%.

☐ Leather: 1%–6%.

☐ Paintings: Free.

☐ Perfume: 5.6%.

☐ Tape recorders: 4.3%.

☐ Watches: 2.5%–5.4%.

Source: *Travel Smart for Business,* Dobbs Ferry, NY.

How to save customs duty

Declare more expensive items first if you expect to go over the duty limit in customs. The lower the value of an item, the less extra duty you will have to pay. For a list of duty imposed on popular items, write for a free copy of *Know Before You Go,* US Customs Service, Box 7118, Washington, DC 20044.

Clearing customs

Personal exemption: $400 ($800 from Guam, American Samoa or the Virgin Islands). The next $1000: A flat rate of 10% duty (5% from the US islands). Above this: Individual assessments are made on goods.

☐ Sending gifts: Duty-free, if marked unsolicited gift, value under $25. Gifts cannot be sent to yourself or to a traveling companion.

☐ Sending goods home: Duty must be paid on major items. They do not count as part of a personal exemption.

☐ Liquor and tobacco: You are allowed one liter of alcohol, 100 cigars and 200 cigarettes. (State laws take precedence over federal regulations.)

☐ Drugs: Medications obtained abroad could be seized.

What to do if you're arrested overseas

In a sample year, 3,000 Americans were arrested in 97 foreign countries for offenses ranging from narcotics and disorderly conduct to murder. If arrested, here's what you should do:

☐ Don't panic. Keep your wits about you.

☐ Ask to contact the US embassy. Be polite but persistent in making this request. (Normally, the local authorities will notify the US embassy anyway.)

When a consular officer comes to see you in jail, here's what he or she can do for you:

☐ Provide you with a list of local attorneys, including their specialties.

☐ Call an attorney for you if you are unable to make a call.

☐ Notify relatives or friends at home.

☐ Help you wire for funds.

☐ Make sure your basic health and safety needs are being met.

☐ Make sure you're not being discriminated against because you're an American.

☐ Do not expect the embassy to get you out of jail. You are subject to the laws of the country you're visiting.

Source: John P. Caulfield, Bureau of Consular Affairs, US Department of State, Washington, DC.

Offenses most likely to get you arrested abroad

When traveling, these are the major dangers that can land you in a foreign jail:

☐ Auto accidents. In many foreign countries, you can be arrested or imprisoned for driving while intoxicated or held criminally liable for an accident in which someone is injured.

☐ Narcotics. Those convicted of possession or trafficking in drugs usually spend from 2 to 10 years in jail, often with long waits in jail for a trial. Bail is generally not possible for narcotics offenses or other serious offenses in most foreign countries.

☐ Black marketeering. Selling unauthorized goods is a very serious offense in many countries and is often punished by a prison term. Also: Beware of black-market currency transactions. You could be robbed or wind up with counterfeit currency.

Source: John P. Caulfield, Bureau of Consular Affairs, US Department of State, Washington, DC

Tipping while traveling

Deluxe Restaurants

☐ Maitre d', $1–$15 every few visits (if you get special treatment).

☐ Waiter, 15%.

☐ Captain, 5%.

☐ Sommelier, 7% of the liquor bill or $2 for each bottle.

☐ Cloakroom, 50¢–$1 per coat.

☐ Doorman, $1 if he hails a cab.

Other Restaurants

☐ Waiter, 10%–15%.

☐ Coat check, 25¢–50¢.

Hotels

☐ Chambermaid, $1–$1.25 per room per night, or $7 a week.

☐ Dining room (American Plan), waiter gets 15% of the food bill for the total stay and the maitre d' a flat $10 for a stay of five to seven days.

☐ Room service, if service charge is not added, 10%–15%, depending on the amount of service given.

☐ Pool attendant, $1 per day.

☐ Waiter (snack bar, golf club, beach or tennis club), 15% of the bill.

☐ Locker attendant, 50¢–$1 a day.

☐ Bartender, 15% of bill.

☐ Doorman, 25¢–$1 unless baggage is handled, then 50¢–$1.

☐ Baggage handler, 50¢ per bag.

☐ Bellman, 50¢–$1 per errand.

☐ Taxi driver, 15% of bill, 25¢ minimum for small bill.

☐ In Europe and the Orient, tips are usually included in the form of a service charge of 10% to 15% of the bill. Be sure to check your bill before leaving additional money.

Cruises (Two in a Cabin)

☐ Cabin steward or stewardess, $3–$4 per day.

☐ Dining room steward, $3–$3.50 per day.

☐ Shoe cleaner, $5 at end of trip.

☐ Cabin boys, $1 per errand.

☐ Wine steward, 15% of total bill.

☐ Night steward, $2 per night if services are used.

☐ Deck steward, $10–$15 for the whole cruise.

☐ Bar steward, 15% of the total tab.

Personal Services

☐ Hairdresser, 15%–20% of his or her services (but do not tip the owner of a salon).

☐ Shampooer, $2.

☐ Manicurist, $2.

☐ Pedicurist, $4.

☐ Coat check, $1.

Caterers

☐ Party supervisor, $20.

☐ Headwaiter, $10.

☐ Head cook, $10–$15.

☐ Others, $5 each.

Miscellaneous

☐ Garage attendant, 50¢–$1.

☐ Valet parking, $1.

☐ Redcap, 50¢ per bag.

☐ Washroom attendant, 25¢–$1.

☐ Strolling musicians, $1–$2/single, $5/group.

Taking really good vacation photographs

The new fully automated cameras have taken technical burdens off the backs of amateur photographers.

Here are some practical suggestions:

☐ Get up close. A sure way to take boring pictures is to make all your shots "overalls." The details in a scene are what make it interesting and expressive. Don't hide behind your telephoto lens for close-ups. Move in close with a wide-angle lens, which gives a greater sense of intimacy, involvement and graphic drama.

☐ Make value judgments. Many amateurs take too many photos of boring things, especially boring landscapes. They walk into a market and miss the one gnarled vendor in fantastic ethnic clothing.

☐ Ask yourself…What does this subject symbolize? Is it the best evocation of this environment? Helpful: Pick out a symbol or idea that represents the country and come home with 15 or 20 photos as a treatment of that theme. Working on a theme keeps you intellectually alert, too.

☐ Study good photographs. Go to gallery shows and museum exhibitions. Buy books, and subscribe to publications that feature the works of leading photo artists. Try to understand the intent of other photographers even if you don't like their photographic effects. Take a photo workshop. Find a teacher whose style is different from your own—someone who will shake you up.

☐ Be flexible. Seek out opportunities to become photographically involved with people who may seem strange to you. Cities always have a place where people congregate on Sunday afternoons. Learn to relate to these people and to become quickly at ease with strangers. Then neither you nor they will feel threatened when you photograph them.

☐ Be physically flexible. Many travel photos are boring because they're taken from a standing position. Try climbing, stooping or lying flat on the ground to get a fresh angle.

☐ Practice at home. Don't expect to take great photos on vacations if that's the only time you use your camera. Take photos in your spare time and on weekends. Pretend you're a foreigner visiting from abroad, and be a travel photographer in your own backyard.

☐ Criticize your own work. Be as objective as possible about your failures and successes. Don't be afraid to be hard on yourself. A discouraging moment of dissatisfaction with your own work can be the first step toward style.

Source: Lisl Dennis, author, *Travel Photography: Developing a Personal Style,* Curtin & London, Somerville, MA.

Collecting seashells overseas

The most colorful shells are found near coral reefs in tropical waters. Many areas offer special arrangements for shell collectors, from boat trips to uncombed beaches to guided snorkeling or scuba diving.

Sanibel Island, Florida, is the best-known shelling spot in the US.

The best spots overseas:

☐ Costa Rica offers both Atlantic and Pacific varieties.

☐ The Philippines are known for their many local dealers and good values.

☐ Cabo San Lucas, Mexico, on the southern tip of the Baja Penninsula.

☐ The Portuguese Cape Verde Islands off Senegal.

☐ Keep in mind that much of Southern California and Australia's Great Barrier Reef are closed or limited for environmental reasons.

What you should put in your traveling gear box

A practical travel kit should include:

☐ Swiss army knife (complete with scissors, small screwdriver, nail file and clippers).

☐ Safety pins.

☐ Large Band-Aids.

☐ Styptic pencil.

☐ Small tin of aspirin.

☐ Two packets of antacid tablets.

☐ Dental floss.

☐ Two pairs of shoelaces.

☐ Small sewing kit.

☐ Sample bar of soap.

☐ Two packets of cold-water laundry detergent.

☐ Envelope of talc.

☐ Four feet of cord to tie your suitcase together if it has been damaged in transit.

Source: *Medical Economics.*

What men should pack for a long trip

The goal is to travel with only one carry on garment bag plus one carry on underseat case, with enough room to add new purchases. This list should carry you for a month.

☐ Lightweight black gabardine suit. Works as business suit and for formal wear.

☐ Blue blazer for business meetings and evening parties (with gray flannel slacks) or for casual occasions (with blue jeans).

☐ Pair gray worsted flannel trousers.

☐ Pair blue jeans.

☐ Two white broadcloth shirts, plain collar.

☐ White oxford-cloth shirt, button-down collar.

☐ White cotton-knit polo shirt.

☐ Black-and-gray-striped polo shirt.

☐ Gray cashmere V-neck sweater, long-sleeved.

☐ Black-white-and-gray-patterned silk tie.

☐ Solid maroon silk tie.

☐ Black silk evening bow tie.

☐ Five pairs black socks (silk, wool and cotton).

☐ Five sets of underwear.

☐ Pair pajamas or one bathrobe.

☐ Lightweight racing trunks.

☐ Black plain oxford shoes.

☐ Black slip-on loafers.

☐ Tan poplin raincoat with detachable lining (should be worn or carried over arm when boarding plane).

Source: Egon von Furstenberg, author of *The Power Look*, Holt, Rinehart & Winston, New York.

Preventing hotel burglaries

☐ Don't talk to strangers about gambling winnings, family finances or other money matters.

☐ Avoid disclosing your personal itinerary for the day.

☐ Make sure that sliding doors to balconies or patios are locked.

☐ When out of the room, leave a light on and the drapes slightly open.

☐ Never leave valuables in the room.

Source: *Travel Expenses Management.*

Traveling with a computer

Avoid mistakes that many people make. Be sure you:

☐ Carry a long extension cord…many hotel rooms have only one outlet.

☐ Use a padded carrying bag to protect the computer and its peripherals. Avoid models with name-brand advertising…they're targets for thieves.

☐ Carry your computer on the plane…checking it is begging for trouble.

Phoning from Europe

Four ways to cut down on often excessively high Europe-to-US hotel phone charges:

☐ Where high surcharges apply, make a brief call home just to leave your phone and room numbers—and have your party call you back.

☐ Use your phone credit card in countries where it is honored. Although there could be a surcharge, it is usually much less than a call charged to your hotel bill.

☐ Always check your hotel's surcharge policy. Countries notorious for rip-offs: Germany, Switzerland, Austria and Italy.

☐ Use telephone centers (usually in the post office or railway station) to skip middlemen and surcharges.

Source: AT&T, as reported in the *Journal of Commerce,* New York.

Taxi tips for you

☐ *London.* The famous black cabs can be hailed from the street. Tip: 15%.

☐ *Paris.* Taxis are hard to flag, except at hotels. Best bet: A taxi stand.

☐ *Rome.* Look for taxi stands at train stations, hotels and shopping areas. Tip: 10%-15%.

☐ *Tokyo.* Get help from your hotel in writing your destination in Japanese. Tip: Not expected.

☐ *Hong Kong.* Cabs are easily hailed on the street, but the driver's command of English will vary. Tip: Small.

Source: *Travel & Leisure,* New York.

The best zoos

☐ *Philadelphia Zoological Gardens.* The nation's oldest zoo (in Fairmount Park) now features the Tree House, where children can see the world from animals' perspectives.

☐ *International Wildlife Conservation Park,* formerly Bronx Zoo (*New York*). Outstanding natural habitat exhibits in Jungle World and Wild Asia.

☐ *Miami Metrozoo.* Monorail tours of more than 200 acres of plains, jungles and forests. Wings of Asia features more than 300 species of birds.

☐ *San Diego Zoo.* Wild Animal Park (30 miles north of the city) offers day or night safaris through a land of 2,200 uncaged animals.

☐ *Woodland Park Zoo (Seattle).* New bioclimatic zone replaces cages with a contoured, tall-grass terrain.

☐ *Cincinnati Zoo.* Attractions include the Cat House and a children's zoo for preschoolers.

☐ *Brookfield Zoo (Chicago).* Three daily tropical rainstorms, dolphin acts and a black rhinoceros.

☐ *St. Louis Zoo.* A grand legacy of the World's Fair of 1904, now moved to Forest Park.

Source: *TWA Ambassador.*

The most walkable cities

☐ *San Francisco.* Climbing the hills can be arduous, but the summit views are unsurpassed.

☐ *New York.* Manhattan is a never-ending street show, ranging from the elegant to the tawdry or hilarious. You'll find every possible ethnic snack along the way.

☐ *Venice.* The car-free streets are perfect for walking, the light and water enchanting. Pedestrian high spots: Piazza San Marco, Ponte di Rialto, Santa Maria della Salute.

☐ *Copenhagen.* You'll enjoy its seaside streets, flower-filled parks and storybook palaces. Shop along the famous Stroget (pedestrians only).

☐ *New Orleans.* The French Quarter is compact, historic and lively. Go to Bourbon Street for jazz and to the Mississippi River for port-town bustle.

Source: *The Washington Post.*

Clothing language

To psychiatrists, grooming, clothes, makeup, and all-around physical appearance are important clues to personality and mental health. Those clues can be useful, too, to people making hiring decisions or who otherwise want to be able to size people up.

Key: Appropriateness. Clothes and appearance have to be viewed in the context of a person's position and the milieu in which he operates.

Appearance clues:

☐ Overly meticulous. Constricted neat, not elegant neat. (Example: Very narrow, tight ties. Jackets always buttoned. People who arrange trouser creases each time they sit down.) Usually good indicators of an obsessive personality. Obsessiveness may be fine for employers seeking industrious, dependable types concerned with detail. It is not for those who want someone with creative capacity.

☐ Careless, torn, stained clothing and lack of attention to detail. These are signs of depression. Another trouble sign: Somber colors such as black or maroon, worn much or most of the time.

☐ Incongruous clothes that seem markedly inappropriate to the age of the person wearing them. This usually indicates a lack of friends and associates through whom he would have learned what to wear.

☐ Clothes that are too young: Short skirts or a "little girl" look on an older woman or the "preppie" look on a man obviously too old for the style generally indicates an image problem. Such a choice of clothes suggests an inability to tune into reality.

☐ Identification. People who go in for prestige symbols generally are using them as a means to inflate their self-esteem and for virtually no other reason.

☐ Focus. Attention-getting attire, particularly on men. Example: Going to the office (where such dress isn't expected) in jeans and workshirt. This is usually a sign of a narcissistic personality, a type that sees the world as revolving around him and what he wants.

☐ Very manly styles on women. Increasingly evident in women who have left their roles as homemakers and gone back to the business world, it may well indicate discomfort about leaving home and reversing women's traditional roles. Overdoing anything in a dramatic way, whether it's "looking businesslike" or some other posture is always a sign of conflict.

☐ Button wearers. Whatever the message of their buttons, they have a shaky sense of self-esteem (which they try to bolster by identifying publicly with a group).

☐ Wearing sunglasses unnecessarily. People trust others more when they can see their eyes.

Source: Dr. Michael Levy, psychiatrist, New York.

Dressing for success

Businessmen's concern isn't with fashion but with function—the impact their clothes have on people. Let's face it, clothes are a power tool. Wear the right clothes and you can "sell" yourself successfully.

☐ Successful dress is really no more than achieving good taste and the look of the upper-middle class. The traditional styling of Savile Row dominates the world of businessmen's clothing—the understated elegance of English tailoring.

☐ Designers have been responsible for many positive changes in men's clothing in recent years, and some liberalization of styles, patterns and colors has taken place, but this trend is basically confined to leisure wear. Designers have had little influence on the mainstream of American business dress.

☐ Business styles change with glacier-like slowness, and there's no point in risking career, income and social position by gambling on fads.

☐ The most important element in establishing a man's authority is his physical size. Large men tend to be extremely authoritative. But they can frighten people. The large man should avoid all dark suits. He should wear very soft colors: Medium-range gray suits, beige suits and very light suits in the summer. The small man has the reverse problem. The smaller man should wear high-authority clothing: Pinstriped suits, pinstriped shirts and vests.

☐ Expensive ties give authority to the young. Buy the kind of tie which would obviously not be bought by a boy.

Source: John T. Molloy, corporate image researcher and consultant and author of *Dress for Success* and *The Woman's Dress for Success Book*, Warner Books, New York.

Male body type: A factor in executive dressing

☐ For short men. The pinstripe contributes to an illusion of height. The vertical line formed by the classic three-button jacket will enhance the illusion, as will pockets that point inward and upward. No cuffs on trousers.

☐ For heavy men. Dark suits impart a lighter look. Best for men of ordinary height is a single-breasted jacket with a center vent. A double-breasted jacket is suitable for taller men—of any weight. Avoid pleats in trousers, as they add bulk. Darts are better for comfort and a well-tailored look.

☐ For thin men. Use pale, heavier-gauge fabrics to create a sense of bulk. Straight-legged trousers will give the legs a fuller appearance. Avoid tapered trousers, which conform to the shape of the leg.

For men: What to wear at the office

Successful men dress very carefully for the office:

☐ Dress conservatively, in a style as similiar to the style of those around you—and above you—as you can.

☐ Always wear a suit.

☐ To convey a stronger impression of authority, wear a darker suit—with a vest.

☐ To emphasize a financial aura, wear dark gray or blue pinstripes.

☐ Wear solid-color cotton shirts or conservative stripes. Avoid elaborate patterns and anything flashy, sharp or gaudy.

☐ The best ties are striped ("rep"), solid, dotted, "club," and "Ivy League" patterns. No flowers, foulards, or paisleys for office wear.

Source: John T. Molloy, author of *Dress for Success* and *The Woman's Dress for Success*, Warner Books, New York.

How to dress for success at your company

The key is to emulate your boss, but don't be obvious about it. General rules:

☐ Conservative-looking suit, white shirt (pale pastels if your boss and other senior managers wear them), matching tie.

☐ Muted colors connote trust, upper-middle-class status.

☐ Black, navy, pinstripe, and chalk-striped suits exude power, competence, and authority.

☐ Beware of loud pastels (gaudy); shades of pink (effeminate); gold or green-gray (unflattering); light blues, gray-beige (you're more likely to be liked than respected).

☐ Also out: European cuts; turtlenecks, clashing colors that hint of sloppiness or academia, sports clothes (save them for sports).

☐ Avoid styles or colors that threaten to become overpopular.

How to buy clothes that make you look good

☐ Choosing color to "go with" your hair and eyes is a mistake. It's your skin tone that determines how a particular color looks on you.

☐ The more intense and dark your clothing, the larger you'll appear and the less likely to blend into the environment.

☐ White tends to wash out the face and yellow the teeth. Soft ivory tones are somewhat better.

☐ Don't rule out whole color groups—all blues or all greens. Most people can wear certain shades of most color groups. Exceptions: A few colors, such as orange and purple, are really not good for many people in any shade.

☐ Pay attention to pattern or weave. People who are short or small-boned should not wear big prints or checks. They can wear small true tweeds. Slender, smallish men and women are overwhelmed by heavy fabrics. Light wools are better for them than heavy worsteds.

☐ Consider aging skin in choosing colors. Wrinkled skin is minimized by softer shades. Hard, dark, intense colors maximize the evidence of aging.

☐ The colors surrounding you in your home or office determine the way in which the eye perceives your skin and even your features. Some colors will produce deep shadows, enlarge certain features or produce deep facial lines because of the way they interact with your skin tone.

☐ Don't change makeup to "go with" clothes. Makeup should be chosen according to skin tone only. Using the wrong color makeup is worse than wearing the wrong color clothing.

☐ Most men can't wear madras or bold plaids. When men choose sports clothes, they go wild in the other direction from the conservative clothes they wear to work. Most have had little practice in choosing dramatic colors that are suitable.

☐ A tan does make you look healthier, but it doesn't change the basic effect of certain colors on your skin. With a tan, wearing colors you normally look good in is important, because that's when those colors look better than ever.

Source: Adrienne Gold and Anne Herman, partners in Colorconscious, Inc., Larchmont, NY.

Dressing for special occasions

Unusual circumstances may call for a thoughtful adaptation of basic dress rules. Learn as much as possible about the geographical, educational and socioeconomic background of the people you'll be dealing with and tailor your wardrobe to their expectations. Examples:

☐ Appearing in court. The main problem here is establishing credibility, and the best way to appear credible is to surprise no one. For maximum effectiveness, look just as others expect you to look.

If you are appearing as a high-ranking financial officer, you'll dress differently than if you're appearing as a technical expert—even though you may be both. The higher up the management pyramid you wish to represent yourself, the more quietly opulent your dress should be.

☐ Keep regional/local considerations in mind. A New Yorker, for example, testifying in Texas would be well advised to tone down his dress, keeping it low-key.

☐ Appearing at an IRS audit. The right image for this situation combines authority with humility—respectable and respectful, but not too prosperous. Keep it simple and conservative: Wear one of your older suits (a well-worn Brooks Brothers would be excellent), preferably two-piece, with a plain white shirt and a conservative striped tie. Avoid jewelry and other signs of affluence.

☐ Television appearances. The dress standards of a TV show host are a reasonable guide. Dress less conservatively. Wear lighter colors. Leave the three-piece suit and other power symbols at home. Keep accessories simple and understated. Wear solid colors. Avoid small patterns.

☐ Public speaking. If you know in advance what color the background will be (or if you can choose it), wear a suit (preferably dark) that will stand out. Wear a contrasting shirt (preferably light-colored) and a solid tie.

☐ Job interviews. Dress for the interview, not for the job. Even if you will be a field engineer, come to the interview in a three-piece suit.

Tailor the quality of your dress to the level of the position you seek. A recent college graduate will be forgiven a $200 suit. A candidate for an $80,000 management position will not.

Source: John T. Molloy, author of *Dress for Success* and *The Woman's Dress for Success*, Warner Books, New York.

What women hate about what men wear

No matter how differently women dress from one another, they are surprisingly unanimous about what looks bad on men. Results of an informal survey is a ten-point program:

☐ Socks are by far the most frequently mentioned item of annoyance. They must be long enough to cover the calf or "it's death to a woman's libido." Also "out" are socks with clogs, black socks with tennis sneakers, white cotton socks with business shoes and socks with holes in the heels.

☐ Comb-overs. Letting hair grow long at the side and combing it over a bald head was high on women's list of loathing. "Who does he think he's kidding?" they asked. Women don't dislike baldness per se. They do dislike comb-overs and other compensatory acts of denial and bravado. They like men who like themselves.

☐ Miami Beach macho. Even women who think men are nifty in manicures and pinky rings hate the men who expose five buttons' worth of chest and a gold medallion.

☐ Misfits. Women say clothes that don't fit advertise a guy who doesn't really see himself, which means he is probably oblivious to all his other flaws, too, or one who doesn't like himself enough to care how he looks, which means a woman will spend her life shoring up his self-image.

☐ Textures. Men shouldn't shine. Anything synthetic that glistens is too glitzy and anything naturally shiny is "pseudo-regal." As one woman put it, "Men need a matte finish."

☐ Affectations. Women opt for simplicity. They like their men unadorned, not gimmicky. "Playboy rabbit insignia drive me wiggo," said a normally subdued woman. "Full-dress fully-grown cowboys look ludicrous on Lake Shore Drive," said another. Also contemptible: Men wearing one earring (not to mention two); initials on shirts, tie clips or lapel pins promoting a lodge, Lions Club, PT-109, the American flag or God; sweaters with reindeer; leprechaun hats; and anything Tyrolean.

☐ Shoes. This is an easy one. Whether women were partial to men in Guccis or Adidas, cordovans or bucks, glove-leather wing tips or crepe-sole Hush Puppies, nobody loves tassel loafers.

☐ Color. Anything goes—except the too-bright tones. If it stops traffic...don't wear it.

☐ Gestures. Certain items of clothing inspire annoying gestures in men. The worst: "Shooting cuffs" (pushing arms out so that his sleeves show more of his shirt cuffs and ostentatious cuff links). "The mirror sneak"—checking and rearranging his tie in every looking glass. "The hoist"— the vaguely obscene lifting of the waistband of loose trousers.

☐ Underwear. The issue is settled by body type. The man with a "good bottom" and tight belly should wear jockeys. The well-muscled-shoulder man should wear sleeveless undershirts.

Source: Letty Cottin Pogrebin, writer and *Ms.* magazine editor.

How to prolong the life of your clothes

☐ Hang jackets on wooden or plastic hangers that are curved to the approximate shape of the human back.

☐ Remove all objects from pockets.

☐ Leave jackets unbuttoned.

☐ Keep some space between garments to avoid wrinkling.

☐ Allow at least 24 hours between wearings.

☐ Use pants hangers that clamp onto trouser bottoms.

☐ Remove belt before hanging up pants.

Hair care hints

☐ Baby shampoos are not as mild as special-formula shampoos for dry or damaged hair. Detergents and pH levels put baby shampoos into the middle range of hair cleansers, which makes them right for normal hair.

☐ People with oily hair need a stronger shampoo especially made for that condition.

☐ Wet hair should be combed, not brushed. Hair is weakest when wet and can be easily damaged then. Use a wide-tooth comb to reduce the chance of breaking your hair.

☐ Twenty-five brush strokes a day is optimal for best distribution of natural oils in the hair. More brushing can cause damage.

Men's hairstyles: The trend isn't trendy

Men's hairstyles today are short and genuine. Men want to look natural, not as though they just left the barbershop.

☐ The best stylist is nature. If we cut and comb our hair the way it wants to be cut and combed, it always looks good. If we try to imitate someone else's hairstyle, we always end up getting into trouble.

☐ A good barber makes the hair fit the customer's facial structure. He cuts the hair so the customer can take care of it himself. When the customer goes back to the office, his colleagues shouldn't realize that he just had a haircut. They should notice only that he looks better.

☐ A banker or Wall Street executive wants a conservative look. His hair doesn't come down over the tops of his ears. You shouldn't see a circle around the ear, either—just a perfect, neat haircut that tapers cleanly above the ear.

☐ Men in advertising can be a little more daring, with fuller, longer hair.

☐ The cosmetics company executive, who is in the business of making people look good, wants a little flair.

☐ Years ago, men who could afford it would get a toupee to cover bald spots. No more. If they do anything, they go for a transplant. But more and more, men want to look natural. They feel that if they have hair, good—if not, that's okay. As long as whatever they have is cut properly, they'll look fine. Hollywood reflects the change. Attractive middle-aged and younger stars are frankly balding: Jack Nicholson, Robert Duvall, or new star John Malkovich.

☐ Eighty percent of men in their early forties cover the gray. By that time a man may have a good executive position, but he's aware that if he loses his job or wants to change jobs there's still a stigma attached to looking old.

☐ The man who is 50 or 60 doesn't care anymore about gray. He's been around, and he's confident about who he is. It's important to color the hair discreetly, so it looks natural. Regular touch-ups are important. Even the most professional hair-coloring jobs start to fade quickly and must be touched up.

☐ Beware of the former barbershop that suddenly changed its name from Joe's Barbershop to Joe's Hairstylist. The change may be in name only. The best method is to ask someone whose haircut you consistently like where he got it done.

Source: Peppe Baldo, a New York City hairstylist for bankers, brokers, lawyers, advertising executives, and other corporate and media executives.

The secrets of a great shave

Treat your face to the most up-to-date equipment. It is false economy to buy anything less than the best, since the entire annual cost of shaving seldom exceeds $100. Also, blades and shaving creams are constantly being improved.

☐ Shaving cream: All types of cream (lather, brushless and aerosol in either lather or gel form) are equally efficient. Brushless shaving cream is recommended for dry skin. Buy three or four different kinds of shaving cream. Use different ones for different moods.

☐ Blades: Modern technology makes the current stainless-steel blades a real pleasure to use. The best type: The double-track blade.

☐ Proper preparation. Wash your face with soap at least twice before shaving. This helps soften the skin, saturate the beard and remove facial oils. Best: Shave after a warm shower.

☐ Shaving cream is more effective if left on the face for a few minutes prior to actual shaving. This saturation causes the facial hairs to expand by about one-third, which enhances the cutting ability of the blade.

☐ Except on the warmest days, preheat lather in the can or tube by immersion in hot water.

☐ The manufacturing process leaves a slight oil residue on the edge of the new blade. This can catch and pull the tender facial skin during the first couple of strokes. So start by trimming the sideburns, a painless way of breaking in the new blade. Always shave the upper lip and chin last. Why: The coarsest hairs grow here. Your skin will benefit from the extra minutes of saturation and wetness.

☐ When you have finished shaving, rinse the blade and shake the razor dry. Never wipe-dry a blade; this dulls the edge. When rinsing the blade, hold it low in the water stream for quicker results.

☐ After shaving: Save money by skipping the highly advertised aftershave lotions. Use witch hazel instead. It is odorless, less astringent, leaves no residue and is better for your skin than most of the aftershave lotions.

Men's fragrances

Today there is not only a greater variety of scents to choose from...but new styles of men's fragrances. Fragrance manufacturers, like wine merchants of a decade ago, are now leading their new clientele into more sophisticated territory.

Male executives are the population group most resistant to incorporating fragrances into their normal grooming and wardrobe habits.

☐ Aftershave lotion, which has a modest amount of fragrance, is designed to soothe freshly shaved skin. Use it right after shaving for its cooling and astringent effect.

☐ Cologne is more heavily scented and can be applied to the neck, chest, arms or anywhere else you like. Shake a little into the cup of one hand, rub your hands together, and then rub your hands wherever you want the fragrance.

☐ For the strongest effect, use both aftershave and cologne in the same scent.

☐ Try using aftershave and cologne of different but complementary fragrances. If one is woodsy and the other is spicy, for example, the combined effect can be very pleasant.

☐ For most men in a working situation, aftershave is enough in the morning. A little cologne applied in the afternoon will serve for an evening out.

Source: Robert Reardon, account executive with International Flavors and Fragrances.

Clean up

Best face-washing technique:

☐ Fill a sink with the hottest water your face can stand.

☐ Take a hard-milled soap, such as Grey Flannel (for men) or Old English Lavender (for women), and work up a rich lather.

☐ Work the lather into your face and throat with the tips of your fingers.

☐ Rinse by splashing with the sink's water, not running water. Never rinse with clear or cold water, which can dry skin or break capillaries. Hot water helps to both moisten dry skin by stimulating oil glands and dissolve excess surface oil if your face is oily.

☐ Blot gently (don't rub) with a towel, and let remaining moisture evaporate from your skin.

Source: James Wagenvoord, *Personal Style*, Holt, Rinehart and Winston, New York.

Test the state of your union

Below is a test to help you define the current state of your union. It may help uncover trouble areas, or it may reaffirm your strengths.

Test procedure: Each partner should write out responses to each item separately. Compare notes upon completion.

Expectations of a Marriage

Determine which ones apply to you and answer whether they are being met.

I expected a mate who would:

☐ Provide constant support against the rest of the world. Positive answer: My spouse always takes my side when I'm in trouble. Negative: When critical remarks are made against me, my partner never defends me.

☐ Be loyal, devoted, loving, and exclusive, a person I would develop with and grow old with.

☐ Provide sanctioned and readily available sex.

☐ Insure against loneliness.

☐ Attain a respectable position and status in society.

Psychological and Biological Needs

☐ Who controls whom in the relationship? Do you abdicate power to your spouse? Do you leave decisions to your partner and then complain about them? Are you competitive with your mate? Would you prefer not to be?

☐ How much closeness and intimacy do you want with your mate? An oft-heard complaint is that a spouse claims to desire closeness but pushes the partner away when true intimacy develops.

☐ Do you feel good about yourself? This truism is still valid: If you don't love yourself, you can't love others.

☐ Does your mate turn you on? Are the physical and personality characteristics you desire evident?

☐ Do you love your partner? Is that love returned?

Common Complaints

☐ Are you open and clear in speaking to and listening to each other?

☐ Are your lifestyles, interests, work and recreational activities similar? Do you need to agree to do things together?

☐ Are you in accord about child-rearing practices? (This is a persistent battleground between some spouses.)

☐ Are your children used in alliance against either parent? Is any child identified particularly as yours or your mate's?

☐ Are there differences over the control, spending, saving or making of money?

☐ Who initiates sex? How frequently? Are there alternative sex partners or practices? Is sex pleasurable and gratifying?

☐ Do you share friends, or does each partner have his or her own? Do you and your mate each have friends of the opposite sex? Does this cause problems?

☐ Do you share the same values? Include those related to sex and equality and to cultural, economic, and social class.

☐ Does gender determine the roles and responsibilities of each partner at home and socially?

☐ How do you react when you feel let down or deceived?

Source: Clifford J. Sager, M.D., clinical professor of psychiatry, New York Hospital–Cornell Medical Center, New York.

How to improve the quality of time you spend with your mate

Married couples today spend so much time apart that the little time spent together loses the richness it once had. They forget that the quality of time spent together is just as important as the quality in everything else.

Traps that can lower the quality of time together and what to do about them:

☐ Limiting conversation to terse exchanges of information. Instead: Speak in a way that conveys interest, involvement, a sense of love.

☐ Displaying affection only during full-fledged sexual interludes. Instead: Learn to appreciate a little physical contact, especially during very hectic or stressful periods. Don't be hesitant to touch…while shopping together, for instance, or while you're working around the house. It's important to let one another know you like each other.

☐ Choosing recreational activities that might prove stressful or draining, especially when work demands are heavy. Instead: Choose less taxing forms of entertainment at these times. For example, watch a football game on television instead of going to a crowded, cold, noisy stadium. Talk about the game and how you feel while watching it. Take advantage of the relaxed and familiar home environment. Fix a small drink...put your arm around your spouse.

☐ Looking on nonwork time as a void that must be filled with more work. Instead: Plan and share activities from which both can benefit...redecorate a room, take tennis lessons, cook a meal together, work in the garden.

☐ Being afraid to talk about your deepest desires and feelings. Instead: Verbalize aspects of your personality that aren't apparent in daily living. Sharing sexual fantasies, for example, can be both a means of communication and a way of revitalizing a relationship.

Source: Anthony Pietropinto, M.D., supervising psychiatrist, Manhattan Psychiatric Center, New York.

For a long-lived marriage

Various studies of successful marriages show that effective communication is the key ingredient. To weather the usual stresses of any close, long-lived relationship, experts recommend:

☐ Be specific in praising or criticizing a spouse's actions. Vague complaints always trigger arguments.

☐ Don't bring up long-past grudges and examples of misbehavior during a fight.

☐ Focus on one topic at a time and make preoccupations clear if they are interfering with current communication.

☐ Identify statements (often nagging) or actions (often angry responses) that almost always lead to escalating hostility. Stop the action when you catch yourself in such a scene. Cool down. Once these processes build up momentum, they are almost impossible to stop.

☐ Edit statements that needlessly hurt a spouse—even if they are true.

Family and career: The right mix

Professionally successful men and women are often failures in their personal lives. Just as common are the underachievers in the office who have rewarding family and love lives. Successful businesspeople who can balance their two lives are rare. Many traits useful in the office are counterproductive at home.

Here are some key differences:

☐ Business is goal-oriented in the sense that expectations are put on a schedule with emphasis on such end-products as promotion and money. By contrast, love, despite efforts to direct it, basically exists in the present for the sake of pleasure and well-being.

☐ Business requires efficient use of time. It is often difficult to quantify the value of time spent watching children play or caressing a lover.

☐ Business puts a premium on organization. Life outside the office, however, usually works best when it is disorderly. For example, in order to grow, teenagers need an environment of change and expansion where they can assemble the pieces of their own personalities.

☐ Business thrives on aggression and concentration. Love, on the other hand, is protective and spontaneous. In most cases, it just happens.

Many people caught in the conflict between their professional and personal lives try to minimize it by emphasizing one over the other. There are no magic formulas for recognizing the problem, and solving it is even more difficult. The best approaches are to:

☐ Monitor your motivation. Ask yourself if you need to put in 15 hours a day at the office. Are you doing it to get away from your spouse or because you fear failing as a parent?

☐ Confront problems head-on. If you are angry at a co-worker or child, do not work off the anger by jogging. Instead, put your energies where they count—into finding a solution.

☐ Consider professional counseling. Even though you may have just recognized the full impact of the office-versus-home conflict, it is a familiar problem to most counselors.

☐ See yourself in perspective. There is probably no ideal balance between rofessional and private lives. But onstantly striving for it can be one of ne most rewarding aspects of both.

ource: Jay B. Rohrlick, M.D., author of *Work nd Love: The Crucial Balance,* Summit Books, ew York.

Stay in touch with your children when you travel

you're a responsive parent and feel omfortable giving your children hoices, you have laid the groundwork or being able to meet your obligations ven while you travel. Not being there o respond can be detrimental to your hild, but parents can respond where-er they are.

☐ Minimize time away. Although you nay travel a great deal, make it a rule o try not to be away from home more nan one night at a time.

☐ Call children twice a day. When you re away, bracket the day with one elephone call in the morning and nother at night. Your presence is there ven if you're not.

☐ Plan children's time during your bsence. Before going on a business ip, try to set up the options your hildren will have while you're gone—a uest for dinner, an overnight visit at a iend's house. You participate in their ves even though you're not there. Vhile you're away, you're not upervising or controlling, but simply boking in to see what's going on.

☐ Gifts should be special. Parents houldn't be expected to bring back ifts. If you find something special, then s a surprise that says, "I was thinking f you." But bringing gifts every time ou make a trip becomes a ritual. Kids vho grow to expect a gift because they ave always received a gift can ecome ambivalent about their arents' traveling. The unfortunate esson: Materialistic values are more nportant than human values.

☐ When possible, take your children vith you. Missing a day or two of chool is well worth it for the benefits of amily closeness and the educational xperience of travel. For longer trips, rrangements can be made with the chool to take lessons along and to do pecial projects. (In fact, the trip itself nay provide the basis for a ersonalized school report.)

☐ Communicate your feelings about separation. Let your children know how much you miss them and that staying in hotels is a lonely business. When you telephone, say to your children, "I wish I were home with you."

☐ When you return, let the children know how happy you are to be home. It's nice if they can look forward to something special, like dinner out, to celebrate.

Source: The late Lee Salk, professor of psychology in psychiatry and professor of pediatrics, New York Hospital—Cornell Medical Center.

Dividing chores in the two-income family

Family ties are strongest when both husband and wife share household responsibilities as well as contribute to economic needs, according to an ad agency survey of married men:

☐ 32% of the men shop for food.

☐ 47% cook for the family.

☐ 80% take care of children under 12.

☐ The majority said they directly influence the decisions about which brands of disposable diapers, pet food, bar soap, and toothpaste to buy.

When both spouses work, a fair division of household tasks is crucial. One good approach:

☐ Select the mutually most-hated tasks and hire someone to do as many of them as possible.

☐ Negotiate the remaining disliked jobs.

☐ Don't alternate jobs. That only leads to arguments about whose turn it is.

☐ Schedule quarterly or semiannual review for adjustments and tradeoffs.

Source: Nancy Lee, author of *Targeting the Top,* Doubleday & Co., New York.

Why people have extramarital affairs

Common hidden motives for having an affair:

☐ Unwillingness to confront the possibility of a breakup. Outside excitement takes the partner's mind off the real problem, which may be a lack of intimacy, respect, or sexual satisfaction in the marriage.

☐ Need for emotional support and courage to break up a weak marriage. Rather than risk being left alone emotionally, the partner looks for a new attachment in the form of an extramarital affair before walking out on the old one.

☐ Fear of intimacy. Some people find that commitment and intimacy provoke anxiety. The only way they believe they can tolerate marriage bonds is by savoring the feeling of freedom that affairs give them.

☐ Need to show resentment or anger toward the spouse indirectly.

Source: Dr. Helen Singer Kaplan, psychiatrist, head of the Human Sexuality Teaching Program, New York Hospital–The Cornell University Medical College, New York.

Sex therapy

It isn't easy for couples who have sexual problems to seek professional help. The most common problems: Lack of interest. Trouble with erections and orgasms. Pain, real or imaginary.

When to consider therapy:

☐ When the problem becomes so great it jeopardizes the relationship.

☐ When preoccupation with the problem becomes so overwhelming that work suffers and enjoyment of life wanes.

☐ Especially dangerous: Trying to avoid the problem by drinking, abstaining from sex or turning to extramarital partners.

To find a reputable therapist:

☐ Ask your physician or county medical society for a recommendation.

☐ Review the directory of The American Association of Sex Educators, Counselors and Therapists. It sets education and training standards.

☐ Look for a therapist with degrees in a behavioral science (psychology, psychiatry) as well as training in sex therapy. Although sex therapy focuses primarily on sexual problems, a knowledge of psychology is essential because sexuality is so connected with total personality and life events.

☐ If a sex therapist doesn't ask at the first visit if you've had a medical exam, or refer you for one, find another therapist.

When you have to refuse a family member

This is the hardest kind of refusal to deal with. You not only need the interpersonal skills to say no gracefully, but you also have to rethink your real obligations to your family, so you can say no without guilt. Suggestions:

☐ Resist the hidden-bargain syndrome. Parents often operate under the assumption that since they've done all these wonderful things for their children to bring them up, the offspring owe them everything. Both young and grown children can be manipulated by this assumption. Remedy: Recognize that parents do nice things at least as much for their own benefit as for their children's sake.

☐ Recognize that a family member who acts hurt at a turndown—when it's for a legitimate reason—is torturing himself. You're not responsible for other people's reactions.

☐ Don't sit on guilt. As soon as you feel it, share it. Guilt pushers know better than anyone how awful it is to feel guilty. Frequently, just pointing out a guilt manipulation makes the other person back off. Once that's done, you're free to sit down and honestly discuss how making another person feel guilty hurts a relationship.

☐ Learn to say no to your children. Parents, more than anything, want their children to like them. But children need structure and limits in order to learn self-discipline and independence. Remind yourself that you are teaching him how to grow up rather than remain a perennial emotional infant.

Source: Barry Lubetkin, Ph.D., Institute for Behavior Therapy, New York.

Rules for family fights

Essential: Fighting fair. Every couple must develop its own rules of combat, but the following are generally sound:

☐ Never go for the jugular. Everyone has at least one soft, defenseless spot. A fair spouse attacks elsewhere.

☐ Focus on a specific topic. Don't destroy your spouse with a scorched-earth campaign. Fair: "I'm angry because you don't make breakfast before I go to the office." Unfair: "I'm angry because you're useless, and my mother was right—you're not tall enough, either."

☐ Don't criticize things that probably can't be changed. A physical blemish or a spouse's limited earning power is not a fair target. On the other hand, it's dangerous to stew in silence if your partner drops dirty socks on the floor or chews with mouth agape. Minor irritations fester.

☐ Don't leave the house during a fight. You'll be talking to yourself—your own best supporter. Result: A self-serving reconstruction of what happened, rather than an objective view of the situation.

☐ Argue only when sober. Alcohol is fuel for the irrational. Disagreements are beneficial only if you use reason.

☐ Keep your fights strictly verbal. A fight that turns physical intimidates rather than resolves.

☐ Don't discuss volatile subjects late at night. It's tempting to sum up your day at 11 o'clock. But everything seems worse when you are tired. And if you start arguing at 11, you'll be still more exhausted the next morning. Better: Make a date to go at it when both sides are fresh.

☐ Always sleep in the same room, no matter how bitter the fight. The bed is a symbol of the marital bond, and it's more difficult to stay angry with a spouse there.

☐ If you're getting nowhere after a long stretch of quarreling, simply stop. Don't say a word. Your spouse will have great difficulty arguing solo. You can always resume the next day.

☐ Don't sulk after the real fighting is over. Pride has no place here. The winner of the fight should be the one to initiate the reconciliation.

☐ Consider outside help. If you never seem to resolve an issue despite both parties' best efforts, use other resources…not necessarily a 10-week course or a formal session with a counselor. You might simply cultivate a couple whose marriage you admire and try to profit by their example.

☐ Don't give up too easily on either the fight or the relationship. A strong marriage demands risk-taking, including the risk of feeling and showing extreme anger. The intimacy of marriage is won through pain and friction as well as through pleasure.

Source: Kevin and Marilyn Ryan, coauthors of *Making a Marriage,* St. Martin's Press, New York.

Cooling down family fights

Dealing with emotionally violent situations within your family is one of the hardest things you will ever have to do since the peacemaker must try to stay emotionally uninvolved.

In a confrontation between a teenager and parents:

☐ One parent must step out of the fight and act as a negotiator. This involves sitting the other two down and listening to both sides.

☐ Say nothing while each is talking.

☐ Stop your spouse from cutting off the child.

☐ Restate what each one tells you, and always give each a chance to add comments.

☐ Recognize that it will be difficult to convince the teen you are unbiased.

☐ To end the fight, suggest a compromise solution. Phrase it carefully. (Example: Could we do this?)

☐ Make sure both the child and the other parent agree to accept the compromise, a date to start it, and the length of time the compromise solution will be tried.

When intervening in a fight between children:

☐ Avoid making one right and the other wrong.

☐ Involve both. Say, "I think it's better if John does not do this, and I think it would help if Jim does not do that."

Source: Peter Martin Commanday, consultant and security expert, New York City school system.

Day-care center criteria

A decent day-care facility offers clean quarters, good food, reasonable safety precautions and regular naps. Beyond that, parents should look for:

☐ A stable staff, with relatively little turnover…specialized training in child development or psychology…staff members assigned to specific children.

☐ A staff-to-child ratio of no less than one to three for infants, one to four for two-year-olds, and one to eight for children age three to six.

☐ Ambitious activities (trips to a zoo, a tour of the firehouse), but no heavy academic instruction.

☐ A welcoming attitude toward parental involvement, including unannounced visits.

Source: *Newsweek*.

Traps in accelerated early learning

The first three years of a child's life are the most important for future development. No wonder, then, that the parents of young children are presented with a dizzying array of elaborate early-learning programs.

Wanting your child to do better is very praiseworthy and understandable. But when you define better simply as bright, and you desperately reach out for almost any program that comes along, you're taking a great risk. Young children are heart as much as mind. Balance is the key. There's more to development than a surprising vocabulary. It's much easier to produce a bright, facile, obnoxious child than an unspoiled, likable, decent one.

☐ None of the accelerated-learning programs are useful in the development of a well-rounded child. (An exception is a low-pressure exercise instruction program for parents and their babies.) At best, they're superfluous to the child's natural learning process. At worst, they intrude on time and the child's need to develop social skills and motor skills.

☐ Too many parents come to value their children's achievement over the children themselves. Common results: Precocious, unhappy children who are socially incompetent.

☐ There's growing evidence that hurrying babies and young children intellectually often backfires in the future. David Elkind of Tufts University, a leader in the field of children's learning, has found that those who learn to read by the age of three are more likely to have reading problems later on. Key: Although these children learned the mechanics of reading, they understood little of its content. (In addition, Elkind found serious stress symptoms in three- to five-year-old early learners, including headaches and stomach aches.)

Some alternatives:

☐ As soon as your baby is ready to crawl (usually around seven months), encourage him to roam freely about the house. Don't confine your baby for long periods in playpens or jump seats. Instead, give the baby full access to the living areas (which have been childproofed for safety). In this way infants exercise their boundless curiosity, improve control over their bodies, and explore their new world.

☐ Young children don't need expensive educational toys. They receive wonderful stimulation from Ping-Pong balls, plastic measuring spoons, plastic containers—any small manipulable objects.

☐ Best books for the crawling set: Large ones with stiff cardboard pages. The literature is irrelevant; the point is to engage a baby's fascination with hinged objects.

☐ The best parents set up an interesting world for their child and then back off. Identify what your child is interested in rather than trying to focus his attention. It does no good to force learning on a child who is not interested at the moment. This only leads to boredom.

☐ Wait for the child to come to you. During the crawling stage, that will happen an average of 10 times an hour—whenever the child feels excitement, frustration or pain. Then you'll have a motivated student. In half a minute, you can offer a new idea with a phrase or a toy—and accomplish more than an hour's drill with flash cards.

☐ The best way to teach language skills is the same as it's always been…by simply talking, parent to child. Keep your talk concrete and in the present. Relate it to objects the baby can perceive…the sock you're putting on, the toy you're holding out. Never use baby talk. But keep in mind the child's limits. Most effective: Talking to children at or slightly beyond their apparent level of understanding.

☐ Reading aloud can also be useful, but only if the child is receptive. Best opportunity: Just before bedtime.

☐ Most important: Let children develop at their own pace. They need their parent's assistance, but certainly not some rigidly choreographed approach to learning. You may not end up with a five-year-old violin prodigy, but perhaps you'll get something better: A well-rounded, delightful person—short un and long-run.

Source: Burton L. White, author of *The First Three Years of Life,* Prentice-Hall, Englewood Cliffs, NJ.

Charting emotional development

The Swiss theorist Jean Piaget (1896-1980) paved the way for psychologists interested in charting the stages of human intellectual growth. Developmental psychologists have found that our cognitive capacities (language abilities, spatial skills, reasoning capacities, etc.) mature in a uniform, orderly sequence from infancy to adulthood.

A growing amount of evidence suggests that our emotional capacities also merge in an orderly progression. But the interaction between biological factors—the growth of the brain and central nervous system—and developing emotional and cognitive skills is highly complex.

The Stages of Emotional Growth

□ The first three to four months: The emotional reactions a very young infant displays are associated with the events he or she encounters. The introduction of a stuffed toy might provoke a reaction of interest. The sudden slamming of a door might cause an infant to startle. Distress is a response to physical discomfort; relaxation, to gratification. All are familiar emotions to new parents. However, mothers can easily misinterpret their babies' facial expressions and actions. An infant's pushing the mother away, for example, may be seen as anger rather than as distress or fright.

□ Four to twelve months: As the infant's mental ability develops, new emotions appear. Fear of unfamiliar adults and sadness or anxiety at separation from a primary caregiver are examples of emotions that require the ability to compare the events of the present with the events of the recent past. The removal of a favored toy may provoke anger, as the baby is able to relate the loss to another person as its cause.

□ One to four years: With the recognition of standards, including self-generated goals, comes an increased repertory of emotional reactions. A two-year-old may show frustration when he is capable of imagining a tower of six building blocks but can balance only four of them before they tumble to the floor. Likewise, he will show satisfaction at a successfully completed task.

Late in the third year comes the understanding that one could have acted otherwise: Guilt. By the fourth year, children can identify with people who lead them to feel pride in a parent's intelligence or shame at a sibling's dishonesty.

□ Five years and up: During the fifth and sixth years, a child begins to compare himself or herself with others on desired qualities. We then see the emergence of such emotions as insecurity and confidence. Problem: A child in a large peer group can compare himself with a pool of children and will find many children who have qualities superior to his own. He is therefore more likely to feel inferior if he is in a large peer group rather than in a small one. Better: Smaller classrooms with students of equal ability. Important: To be motivated, children need a reasonable expectation of success. Key: Reasonable goals.

□ Adolescence: The hormonal changes that occur in puberty permit a degree of sexual emotion not known in childhood. The adolescent also begins to examine his own beliefs for logical consistency and discovers many incompatible ideas and insoluble problems. Examples: Parents are all-knowing and always right, but my parents are not perfect. A person I love does not love me. Some illnesses are fatal. Result: A feeling of helplessness or depression, which may explain the moodiness associated with adolescence.

Source: Jerome Kagan, Ph.D., professor of developmental psychology at Harvard University and author of *The Nature of the Child,* Basic Books, New York.

How to pick the right school for your young child

□ Visit each school you're considering. Be wary of schools that try to sell themselves to you over the phone. The good ones will insist you judge their curriculum firsthand.

□ Talk with the director and the staff members who will be involved with your child.

☐ Ask to see the school's license, insurance contract, and health and fire department inspection forms.

☐ Be sure the school allows only approved persons to pick up your child at the end of the school day. The school should have a strict rule that if someone who is not on the list comes for the child, the parent should be called immediately.

☐ Check cleanliness and hygiene.

☐ Review the school's educational goals. The program should be designed to develop social, emotional, intellectual, and physical skills. See the teacher's lesson plans.

☐ Ask how students are disciplined.

☐ Observe the other children. Will they be compatible with yours?

☐ Ask yourself: "Could I spend a few years of my life here?"

☐ If possible, make surprise visits to the school at different times of the day after your child has been enrolled. If you're denied admission to areas you wish to see, be suspicious.

Putting your child on the right track

To nudge children onto a career track, parents must become aware of what helps and what hinders. Many traditional ways of dealing with children's vocational aspirations are counterproductive.

☐ The most common—and worst—mistake parents make is pressing their own vocational frustrations onto their children. They say things like: "I never went to college, so you're going to college," or "I've spent my life at this lousy 9 to 5 job—that's not going to happen to you." The most profound lessons children absorb from their parents are by example, not by proclamation. The lucky child gets to model himself after a parent who is happy and fulfilled in his work. This youngster will likely seek out rewarding work for himself.

☐ Self-esteem is the most important influence on the vocational aspirations of children. Parents should do anything and everything they can to raise a child's self-esteem. How: Learn to see whatever your child does well, and compliment him or her for it. Don't dwell on what he or she is not doing right. During the teenage years, it's especially important to affirm a child's skills and talents and help him to explore them further.

☐ Avoid making ironclad rules for your child. It's a mistake to pass on your own life lessons as mandates to young people. Example: The parent who has knuckled under to the system and insists that you have to cut corners and lie to get ahead will lose his child's respect. Share what you've learned, making it clear that your child is free to accept or reject your advice. State rules as possibilities. Advice about starting at the bottom, making sacrifices to get ahead and working for the future is much more palatable when prefaced by, "It may be necessary for you to do such-and-such."

☐ Give your child hope. This is the most valuable attitude a parent can hand down to a child. The message: You can do more with your vocation than people will tell you. If you make a misstep, such as choosing the wrong major in college or winding up in a career or job you don't like, you are not doomed. There's no such thing as a career mistake that forces you to live out the consequences the rest of your working life.

☐ Encourage children to ask whomever they meet about their work: What do you like most about your work? What do you like least about your work? How did you get into this field? Does anyone you know do this kind of work and enjoy it even more than you do?

☐ Instead of asking your child, "What do you want to be when you grow up?" ask, "Looking at all the people you know, whose job would you most like to have?" This makes the world of work more a reality than a fantasy.

Source: Richard N. Bolles, author of *What Color Is Your Parachute? Where Do I Go From Here With My Life?* and *The Three Boxes of Life and How to Get Out of Them,* Ten-Speed Press.

The artistic, intuitive child

A harmful mistake parents may make is depreciating a child's achievements in areas they don't understand. The parents may be very left-brained (analytical, good at figuring out what makes things tick). The child may be very right-brained (spontaneous, instinctively knowing the answer). So the parents disregard the child's rich intuitive skills, thinking they are not "marketable."

Interesting finding: When families are tested for brain bias, it often turns out that the parents and one or two children are very left-brained. These family members feel compatible. Then there will be one child whom no one understands. That's always the right-brained child—the artistic one who loves unstructured situations.

How to overcome this syndrome:

☐ Be alert to things your child does well for which you don't have talent, and compliment him.

☐ Recognize that you and the school system are biased toward left-brain skills—the rational, analytical, verbal, logical and mathematical talents. So when a child shows right-brain skills, such as artistic or musical ability, it's even more important to be encouraging.

☐ Don't overemphasize self-discipline. All skills fall into one of three basic groups: Functional skills—things we do with people or data or things (they usually end in "ing," like writing or organizing). Special knowledges—such as knowing how to fix a car. Self-management skills—which include self-discipline. Parents tend to come down hard on kids in the area of self-management, not recognizing that certain self-management skills go with certain functional skills. Artistic people work best in unstructured situations. They don't respond to supervision, and they seem undisciplined because they need to follow the impulse as it comes.

Your child could be in a TV commercial

This year, TV commercials will feature some 40,000 to 50,000 lucrative parts for youngsters. A child who appears in commercials may gross $25,000 to $30,000 a year. Stars make $100,000 or more. No previous experience is required. Prospective young commercial actors should meet the following criteria:

☐ Age: Child commercial actors range from three months to 17 years, but most parts go to kids from ages 7 to 12. Babies are always in demand unless they're teething.

☐ Personality: Poise, self-confidence and intelligence are essential.

☐ Location: It helps to be in New York City, where 60% of commercial work is generated, or Los Angeles. Most other work is in Chicago, Philadelphia and New Orleans.

☐ Appearance: Send clear, close-up photos of the child to 10 or 12 agents. Also include a personal cover letter and sheet supplying vital statistics (height, weight, clothes size, hair and eye color). The photo should depict the child naturally. Do not pose or costume the child.

Parents must devote:

☐ Time: Agents quickly stop calling parents who have to "play bridge" or "don't feel like" showing up with the child for auditions.

☐ Energy: As a rule, it takes 25 one-hour auditions to get one assignment. Assignments require at least a day of shooting.

☐ Love: Parental support helps children withstand the pressure, jealousy and rejection commercial work entails. Because 20 to 50 children audition for each part, self-esteem should never be linked to making it.

Source: James Peacock and Graham Chambers, coauthors of *How to Get Your Children into Television Commercials,* Beaufort Books, New York.

Understanding sibling rivalry

There are patterns in families that may help parents better understand how sibling rivalry is triggered.

☐ Where there is an intense, close relationship between the mother and a first-born daughter, the girl is usually hostile to a new baby. A year later, the children are likely to be hostile to each other.

☐ Firstborn boys are more likely than girls to become withdrawn after a new baby's birth. Children who withdraw (both boys and girls) are less likely to show positive interest in, and affection for, the baby.

☐ In families where there is a high level of confrontation between the mother and the first child before the birth of a sibling, the first child is more likely to behave in an irritating or interfering way toward the new baby.

☐ Where the first child has a close relationship with the father, there seems to be less hostility toward the new baby.

☐ A child whose parents prepare him for the birth of a new baby with explanations and reassurances does not necessarily react any better than a child who wasn't prepared. More important: How the parents act after the new baby is born.

☐ Inside the family, girls are just as physically aggressive as boys.

☐ Physical punishment of children by parents leads to an increase in violence between children.

☐ Breastfeeding the new baby can have a beneficial effect on firstborns. Reason: Mothers who breastfeed tend to find distractions for the older child during feeding. This turns a potentially provocative time into a loving situation where the first child is also cuddled up with the mother, getting special attention while the baby is being fed.

Source: Judy Dunn, author, *Siblings: Love, Envy & Understanding,* Harvard University Press, Cambridge, MA.

Dealing with sibling rivalry

☐ Don't blame yourself. Much sibling rivalry is unavoidable. There's no way you can blame a mother for an intense relationship with her firstborn child.

☐ Try to minimize a drop in attention to the first child. This change in attention is dramatic—not just because the mother is occupied with the new baby, but because she is often too tired to give the older child the kind of sensitive, playful focus he or she received in the past. (A month after a new baby was born, half the mothers in a recent study were still getting less than five hours' sleep a night.) Recommended: Get as much help as possible from the father, grandparents and other relatives and friends.

☐ Quarreling between siblings increases when the parents are under stress. Anything that alleviates marital stress will also quiet sibling rivalries.

☐ Keep things stable. A child's life is turned upside down when a new baby arrives. Toddlers of around two and three appreciate a stable, predictable world in which the daily schedule of events—meals, naps, outings—can be counted on. In families where the mother tries to keep the older child's life as unchanged as possible, there is less disturbance.

☐ Involve the older child in caring for the baby. In families where the mother draws the older child in as a helper for the new baby, there is less hostility a year later.

☐ Offer distractions to the older child. An older child gets demanding the moment the mother starts caring exclusively for the baby. Mothers who are prepared with projects and helping tasks head off confrontations.

☐ Recognize and avoid favoritism. Studies show that mothers intervene three times as much on behalf of a second child, although the second is equally likely to have been the cause of the quarrel. The first child's feeling that parents favor the second is often well-founded. Older siblings tend to hold back because they know their aggression is disapproved of, while younger ones often physically attack brothers and sisters because they feel they can get away with it.

☐ Be firm in consistently prohibiting physical violence. In the context of a warm, affectionate relationship, this is the most effective way to minimize sibling rivalry and to keep jealousies in check.

☐ Try to keep your sense of humor and your perspective when a new baby is born. Things will get better sooner than you think.

Source: Judy Dunn, author, *Siblings: Love, Envy & Understanding,* Harvard University Press, Cambridge, MA.

When you are invading your child's privacy

How much should parents know about their children's lives? The answer really depends more on maturity than on age. Children's lives become more and more their own business as they move away from parental supervision. It's part of growing up to have an increasingly greater private life and to feel you don't have to tell your parents everything.

☐ During the years when children are living under your roof, the key to keeping track is dialogue: If the relationship s sound and there are matters they don't want to share, they may have a good reason. Respect their privacy.

☐ It's an invitation to open up if parents talk about their own lives—especially if they admit that they, too, sometimes feel worried or embarrassed—or about feelings on something that is happening with the child. This helps create an atmosphere in which the child can talk about subjects he finds embarrassing.

☐ When you have something difficult to discuss with your children, do it in the car. No one can get up and walk out. You don't have to look at each other, if that is a problem. Pick a trip that will last at least half an hour. Try not to ask questions.

☐ Sometimes it is enough to give your opinion on a subject, even if you elicit no information. Example: A divorced father with custody of a 16-year-old daughter had this conversation about her relationship with a boyfriend: "You and David are getting very close, and I think that's fine. I don't know how active a sex life you're having, but I hope you will delay a full sex life. I think you're too young for that. But whether in six weeks or six years you do go all the way, the one experience I don't want you to have is getting pregnant. I want you to feel free to come to me to ask for the name of a doctor."

Her response: "We're not doing anything like that now." A month or two later, she said she was having problems with menstrual bleeding and asked for the name of a gynecologist. The father had expressed what he wanted to say and had opened the door. The child had not invited him in, but she had certainly received the message.

☐ Whether invasion of privacy is justified depends on the stakes. For parents to read a child's diary because they're curious about his or her sex life is indefensible. If the problem is something damaging to a child living under your roof, even if the child is 18, 19 or 20, you should intervene. Example: A parent who suspects a child is getting into drugs should search the child's room thoroughly.

☐ Movies: Some parents might be concerned about sexuality or violence in films. They wouldn't want a 12- or 14-year-old seeing a frightening or perverted horror film. They might, though, be more lenient about sex that isn't X-rated. For this age group: Strongly advise against an unsuitable film.

Refuse to pay for it. If necessary, prohibit seeing it.

☐ Friends: If you're going to press a negative opinion, have a good reason. Check yourself: Do I object because this is not my preference for a friend? Do I think no one's good enough for my child? Am I afraid of competition? If the association is dangerous, you can refuse to allow the friend in your house, but it is impossible to police whom your child sees outside the house.

☐ You can exercise more control about what goes on in the house than what takes place outside. If you don't know that your child is getting drunk at parties, there's not much you can do. If your 15-year-old comes home drunk, you can say, "You're grounded. This has got to stop." If you pass a prohibition ("You're not to get high any place at any time"), obviously you have no way of enforcing it.

☐ In general, keep the lines of communication open by expressing your own feelings and values. It may not always yield information, but at least it creates a receptive climate for exploring important issues.

Source: Howard M. Halpern, author of *Cutting Loose: An Adult Guide to Coming to Terms with Your Parents,* Bantam Books, New York.

Temper tantrums

Realize that tantrums are part of the process by which toddlers declare their individuality. They usually occur when the child is tired.

☐ A child's temper tantrum is best handled by simply walking away. This usually stops the display, as the child grows bored without the attention.

☐ Don't rush to the child and try to smother it with affection. This may make you feel better in front of onlookers, but it doesn't help.

☐ Don't automatically accept the blame for the problem.

☐ Don't berate the youngster.

☐ Best: Let the storm pass. Allow the child to have a nap, and don't mention the incident later.

Source: Dr. Dennis Allendorf, pediatrician, Columbia Presbyterian Medical Center, New York.

When a child needs a therapist

Children don't come to parents and say they need a therapist. They don't perceive the locus of the problem as themselves. They'll blame it on parents or school. Treatment revolves around helping children to see what it does have to do with them.

Most children get into therapy because a teacher or school psychologist suggests it to a parent. Parents often do not recognize deviant behavior until the child goes to school. But many problems can be corrected if they are caught early.

Major tip-off: A child is stuck in development and is not doing what one would expect of a child in his or her age group.

Signs of poor emotional development:

☐ A four-year-old in nursery school cries and misses his or her mother.

☐ An eight-year-old with no friends comes home after school and watches television.

☐ Rigid rituals: The child's bedroom has to be a certain way. Particular foods must be served on certain nights.

☐ Major sleep disturbances: Frequent nightmares, waking in the middle of the night.

☐ Lack of learning progress: The child is not performing at grade level in school.

☐ Psychosomatic illnesses: Whatever the root cause, ailments are exacerbated by stress (ulcerative colitis, asthma, etc.)

☐ When in doubt, ask the school psychologist or pediatrician to recommend a therapist. Don't bring the child in for the first visit. Request a consultation. In some cases, there may not be anything wrong with the child. The parents may be the ones who need help.

Source: Pearl-Ellen Cordon, Ph.D., child psychologist, New York.

How to talk with your child about sex

Parents who want to give their children mastery of the facts about sexuality have to start early in the child's life. That's when to begin, too, to build the attitudes they will need to enjoy themselves as sexual beings and to respect the sexuality of others.

A child is born sexual, just as he or she is born with the capacities for walking and for talking. Once you understand and accept your children's sexuality as normal and beautiful—the same as their other human endowments—you will be free to help them in their sexual socialization.

A child needs guidance and support in developing sexual behavior that fits in with his parents' value system. A proven approach:

☐ Establish a sense of intimacy and trust with a newborn by touching and holding. Do not stop the cuddling, kissing and hugging when the child reaches three, by which time some parents feel awkward with physical demonstrations of affection, especially with boys.

☐ When you start the game of naming parts of the body, include the sex organs. Avoidance of the area between the waist and the knees causes confusion and lays the groundwork for problems in adult life.

☐ Don't interfere with a child's natural discovery and enjoyment of self-pleasuring. At six or eight months, a child learns to put its hand where it feels good. Don't slap on a diaper, pull the hand away or look upset or disapproving. Leave the child alone.

☐ As the child gets older, teach what you consider appropriate sexual behavior. You don't want your child masturbating in the supermarket or living room even at 15 to 18 months, so you pick up the child and, smiling, carry him/her to its bedroom. Explain that the place to pleasure yourself is in your own room with the door closed—that sex is good but should be private.

☐ Parents need privacy, too. Tell children: "When our door is closed, you don't come in without knocking and being invited. When we see your door closed, we'll do the same for you. Everyone likes privacy during sex games." This is when you can introduce the idea that sex games are something people who love and respect each other can play together.

☐ Sex play between children is usual. If parents banish the play, it will only drive the child underground. It's better to keep the lines of communication open and to reinforce socially appropriate sexual play.

☐ Make sure your child knows that sex play with someone older is inappropriate. Child molestation is more commonly practiced by someone in the family or known to a child than by a stranger. The message: "You don't have to let anyone touch your body against your will. You are in charge and you can say 'No.'"

☐ Be aware that much sex education is transmitted before nursery school by attitudes and body language—how you react to scenes on TV, your tone of voice or facial expression in sexual conversations or situations, and significant silences.

☐ Children delight in affection openly expressed between their parents. Withholding such demonstrations can indicate sexual hang-ups.

☐ Don't avoid opportunities to discuss sex or to answer questions. Always speak only the truth. You may wish to withhold some of the details until later. Explain appropriate behavior outside the home. "In our family we are open with each other about sex. But most other families don't talk about it the way we do. So we keep what we do private. It's a good thing to respect what other people believe."

☐ A child who doesn't ask questions by the age of four or five has gotten the idea that the parent is uncomfortable about sex or that sex is not an open topic, or was not given straight answers. Initiate a discussion. One idea: Tell your child about your own questions when you were the same age. If there is no response, try again another day to prove you're available. Choose a time when you (or both parents) are alone with the child and have plenty of time. Be encouraging about behavior that is appropriate or shows maturation.

☐ Don't associate sexual parts of the body with dirt, ugliness or sin. Guilt and shame so transmitted will never be erased.

☐ Don't lie. You may have to tailor the truth to the level of the child. Example: To a three-year-old who asks, "Do you have to be married to have a baby?" the correct answer is, "No, you don't, but...." Then you go into your own value system about why marriage is important—on a level that a three-year-old can understand.

☐ You and your spouse should be clear on attitudes toward standards and rules and on what you agree and disagree. If there are differences of opinion, call them that, but try not to confuse the child.

☐ If you have laid the groundwork between birth and six or seven, you can take advantage of the major learning years until 12. Before puberty is when to pour in reliable information about sexually transmittable diseases, reproduction, etc.

☐ Keep the lines of communication open. Give opinions when they're asked for. Avoid judgments—they tend to close off discussions. Express your own values frankly and give sound reasons.

Source: Mary Steichen Calderone, M.D., former medical director of the Planned Parenthood Federation of America and co-founder and president of SIECUS (Sex Information and Education Council of the US).

Child sexual abuse: How to recognize the signs

Sexual abuse occurs when a child is forced or tricked into sexual contact with an older person. What constitutes sexual contact: Touching of the child's genitals. Requests that the child touch or look at the genitals of an older person...participate in oral-genital contact with an adult...undress and/or be photographed in sexual positions with other children or adults—witness the sexual activities of adults. Sexual abuse may or may not include actual penetration.

Parents have an important responsibility to educate their children about sexual abuse as part of their general sex education.* This responsibility cannot be left to the schools or the child's peers.

What Parents Should Communicate

☐ There is "good" touch and "bad" touch. If the child feels uncomfortable about any kind of touching by anyone, including family members, he or she has the right to say, "No. I don't want to." The child should be told that not all adults care about children's feelings.

*For educational materials, write or call the National Committee for the Prevention of Child Abuse, 332 Michigan Ave., Suite 1250, Chicago 60604, (312) 663-3520.

☐ If the child feels that something that just doesn't seem right is going on with an older person, whether it's a friend, family member or stranger, he or she should feel free to discuss it with you. No matter what kind of threats or promises have been made, you won't get angry or blame the child.

☐ Make it very clear that if by any chance the child doesn't feel free to tell you about a disturbing situation, he or she should talk to some other trusted adult. You might suggest a teacher, clergyman, friend or parent of a friend.

Reading Your Child's Signals

☐ Danger signs: Change in appetite, nightmares, acting out, or hyperactivity.

☐ The child avoids or reacts fearfully or abnormally to a person he or she has usually felt comfortable with.

☐ If you suspect sexual abuse, you will have to approach the child very carefully to get an honest answer. Questions such as "Is something wrong?" or "What's bothering you?" are likely to elicit simple denials. Better: "I know you're involved in something that's hurting, something you want to discuss, but maybe you're afraid I won't understand."

Be positive in your questioning. Show empathy, compassion and under-standing. If you come on like gang-busters, aggressively asking who, when, what and where, you'll frighten the child and get no answers.

If Your Child Has Been Sexually Abused

☐ React calmly. If you get hysterical or visibly angry, you'll frighten your child.

☐ Talk about specific details, but don't push the child to reveal more than he or she feels comfortable with at any one time.

☐ Reassure the child that he or she is not to blame, that you don't doubt his/her word and that you will protect him/her against any repercussions from the accused person.

☐ Report any case of child sexual abuse to your local social services or law enforcement agency. If the abuser is a family member, contact the local chapter of Parents Anonymous or Parents United.

Source: Dr. Vincent S. Fontana.

Helping a preadolescent

The transition to adolescence is a difficult time both for children and for parents. But parents can create an environment that will make it easier for everyone involved to weather this stressful preadolescent passage.

Entry into adolescence begins between the ages of 10 and 13. The process is earlier than it used to be and is much more condensed.

The parent is heading toward middle age at the same time the child is heading toward adulthood. That's often painful.

☐ Look for the physical changes, such as body growth, hormonal functioning and appearance. But right before that, changes usually show up in feelings and moods, an increase in sexual drive and aggressiveness. Children eat a lot more and are more self-centered. They regress. Example: Boys tell toilet jokes.

☐ Schools are often sensitive to dips in students' performances in the seventh and eighth grades. Parents need to be supportive but also must set limits so that the child doesn't go under completely. Be aware that there will be some slippage. That doesn't mean the youngster has suddenly become stupid or will never work again.

☐ In the uneasy transition to adolescence, youngsters are no longer involved in the simpler tasks of childhood. In fact, sometimes it looks as though it's all been lost. It hasn't been. The tasks of early adolescence are different.

☐ The major task for the child is disengagement from parents. He experiences a conflict between the upsurge of drive and the pullback to the early parental relationship. He acts older and then younger. He progresses and then regresses.

☐ The parent must disengage from the dependent child of the earlier period. Parents too often pull the child back into the nurturing, dependent status. The child may go along because it's hard to give that up.

☐ Resist "re-entering" adolescence with the child...by dressing like him, getting involved with his friends, becoming a participant. This does not help the child, although he may enjoy it at the moment. It keeps the child with the parent at a time when he needs support in disengaging.

□ Expect stress and conflict. No one disengages easily.

□ Let children know what you expect, but be reasonably tolerant. They are still not up to assessing the reality of the dangers of drugs, alcohol, or herpes. Rules and regulations for social life are important.

□ Try to work on a rational level first. But remember: You are the parent. You have a certain awareness of the child's needs. Ask yourself: Why do I need to keep the child as a baby (which is not going to help him)? What do I need to be a parent who knows what's safe and what's reasonable? It's the ability to recognize one's own motivation that distinguishes parents who can handle their child's adolescence from those who can't.

□ During this transition, parents must shift. They have to find new sources of gratification away from their children and accept limitations. They can't control as closely as they did earlier. The child will no longer tell you everything, which is actually positive. He won't be as responsive or as responsible.

Source: Pearl-Ellen Gordon, Ph.D., child psychologist, New York.

Managing teenagers

The trap for many parents of teenagers is not realizing that they can no longer communicate with their children as they did when the kids were younger. While teenagers might not show it, they're at the age when self-esteem is usually at a low point...as they prepare to move into the adult world. As youngsters they didn't mind having parents help run their lives. But now they resent obvious efforts to help them.

□ Just listen. That's the big thing a teenager wants—to be listened to. And this gives parents an overlooked opportunity to find out more about their children and boost their egos at the same time, simply by asking questions.

□ Don't be afraid to ask their opinion: Why do you think kids take drugs? But

never say: I bet the kids you hang out with take drugs.

□ You can help make your teenager feel more like a winner by helping him set goals. First ask him to list the things he's good at. You'll probably get a list of two or three activities. Remind him of other things he's good at. As the list grows, your child's self-esteem will be boosted—and so will the communication between you.

□ If you can't catch your teenager doing anything right, catch him doing something approximately right.

□ If you can't display affection, you're going to have real hassles. This is when a kid needs a hug the most. Kids who aren't touched feel they're not touchable—that they're not lovable. It's that simple. Parents are the only ones who can give total acceptance to their teenage children. The kids themselves tend to beat up on their peers, and their peers on them, because they're all so insecure.

□ Don't be afraid to put your foot down about misbehavior. You can be intolerant of intolerable behavior. Make it very unpleasant for him...for the first 30 seconds. But the last half of the reprimand is the most powerful. Tell him: "You don't need this in your life. You're a great kid, and you deserve a great life." The message that he's a good kid is one that he's not getting from his peers.

□ Too many parents tend to pay most attention when their kid is fouling up. That's the trap. He figures it out, and then it's worth fouling up to get that attention. That's why it's so important to look for opportunities to praise. Because if a kid likes himself, you'll have few, if any, problems.

Source: Dr. Spencer Johnson, author of *The One Minute Father* and *The One Minute Mother* and coauthor of *The One Minute Manager,* William Morrow & Co., New York.

How to deal with a defiant teenager

Adolescence is a period when children must separate from the family. At the same time, they still need guidance. Parents need to know how to exercise the right proportions of flexibility and supervision. How parents set limits will influence their success in maintaining them. Some suggestions:

□ Parents should have their own standards, but it's a good idea to check with other parents, and perhaps the school, about the prevailing views on curfews, use of alcohol and allowances. You can't always trust children to report accurately about regulations in other families.

☐ Parents should agree on a course of action and support each other. Kids will use every opportunity to take advantage of differences between parents.

☐ Discuss the rules with children. Explain your position calmly, and be prepared to back up your ideas. Remember: Things have changed a great deal since you were the age of your child. Listen carefully to your children, particularly to the oldest one, who usually has the toughest time because he is a trailblazer for those who follow.

☐ Rules must be geared to the ability of the child to handle responsibility. Development in adolescence is uneven not only physically but emotionally. One child of 16 may be able to manage a flexible curfew, but another may not be mature enough.

☐ If rules are being flouted, parents must first examine their own roles, expectations and motivations. Are they contributing to the problem? Are their demands arbitrary and unreasonable? Do they set the kind of example they wish their children to follow?

☐ What is the dinner-table ambience? Is it one a child would want to get away from?

☐ School grades: Are parental expectations realistic?

☐ Avoid hostile confrontation and open warfare. Create an atmosphere where attitudes are expressed, where there is a positive feeling about learning, the intellectual spirit and the arts. The child should feel home is a comfortable place to be and that his friends are welcome.

☐ Praise the child for what he is doing right before you tell him what he is doing wrong. If a child is told he is bad, he begins to live up to that reputation and is more likely to get into trouble.

☐ Defiant behavior is most often used to get attention or to test limits.

☐ It's all right to be angry if your anger is motivated by your concern for your child's safety. It is your job to protect him.

☐ Don't impose restrictions you can't enforce.

☐ Always give a warning before you punish.

☐ Don't make any threats for punishment you're not able or willing to carry out. Effective punishment requires the cooperation of both parents. What kind of punishment? Withholding part of the allowance or a planned trip or other treat is better than corporal punishment.

Let the punishment fit the crime. Lesser matters (untidy rooms) may not call for the same approach as more urgent ones (drugs, alcohol).

☐ Important: Do not discipline your child in front of other people, including siblings—and especially not in front of his friends.

Source: Clifford J. Sager, M.D., director of family psychiatry, Jewish Board of Family and Children's Services, New York.

Father/daughter talks: Men, dating and sex

When a daughter comes of age, it is often only the mother who has heart-to-heart talks with her concerning "life." But there is a role here for the father, too, since he can supply the male point of view on these vital topics.

These father/daughter discussions not only help the young woman in her understanding of life but initiate a healthy exchange of ideas and opinions that benefits both parties for the rest of their lives.

Important Prerequisites

☐ The tenor of a talk between a father and a 12- to 14-year-old daughter depends on their existing relationship. It is usually difficult for the father to take a young woman into his study and blithely talk about sex any better than he might with a son unless there is a feeling of trust and mutual understanding.

☐ The father must know what the mother has been telling the daughter about the facts of life.

☐ Begin the conversation along these lines: "You're getting to an age now where your mother and I notice your growing interest in boys and the facts of life and sexuality. Your mother has spoken to you about these things from the woman's point of view. I wonder if there are any questions you have about men, life, sex or anything else that you would like me to answer from the male view."

From here the discussion could include a range of subjects. Example: If the father worries about the type of people his daughter is socializing with, this is the time to air those misgivings.

❑ Reiterate the family attitudes toward sexuality. Background: Talk with other parents to explore their rules and regulations concerning dating and sex. This will help provide backup facts in case the daughter says, "Mary's parents let her go out any night she wants." Although the attitudes of other parents help in setting guidelines, the father still makes clear his views as to what is proper and healthy.

❑ Always level with your daughter and don't hide behind excuses. If she has been going out with older boys who drive cars, explain why this is a worry to you—the fear that she will be drawn into premature sexual relationships, drinking, and dangerous driving.

❑ Make clear that she need not feel pressured to go along with the crowd.

❑ Always welcome your daughter's male friends into your house. At times you may have to swallow hard before being polite. But if you turn them away, most likely she will see them outside your house—and you'll lose contact with your daughter.

❑ Guard against putting down her boyfriends. The jealousy of a father is often revealed in the disparaging remarks he makes about his daughter's male friends. Another sign of this jealousy: Overprotectiveness.

❑ Realize that it is not uncommon today for girls around the age of 16 to engage in sexual activity. Make sure that your daughter knows the truth about sex. Certain myths still persist. Example: In one survey made not too long ago, 30% of the youngsters age 14 to 16 believed that if you have sex standing up, the girl won't get pregnant.

❑ Explain that men, when sexually excited, have an imperative desire for an orgasm. Contrast: Young girls are usually satisfied with holding, kissing and some petting. Make sure she understands that a girl has a right to say that she is not ready for sex. The male will always want to go further because of his crushing need for orgasm.

❑ Be sure your daughter knows it is all right to enjoy sexual feelings. The pleasures of her limited sexual experiences are nothing to feel guilty about. If sex takes on a blind negativity, the daughter will not be able to enjoy the riches of conjugal love after she is married.

❑ A father can be surprisingly helpful to a daughter when she is breaking up with a steady boyfriend, especially if she feels she is hurting a decent person with whom she has shared a lot. The father can point out that since his daughter is a warm and giving person, her friend should be honored that he had the privilege of her exclusive company. Through this relationship, the daughter has learned more about love, men, and sex. Message: The love that lasts for a few months or a year or two is the love with which the daughter tests herself. It's part of learning about life.

❑ A formidable obstacle in a father/daughter relationship is the daughter's sexuality. The daughter he once kissed in greeting he now shies away from. Be aware of this sexuality, and don't be alarmed by it. If you kissed your daughter when you greeted her as a little girl, continue to do so when she becomes a young woman.

❑ The father is the first intimate male model the daughter has for the adult world. This is important in developing her sense of the opposite sex. Note: Although the father is a model, he must not fear showing his human frailty. At all costs, avoid hypocrisy. Be honest, even if it hurts—or makes you look like less than a god.

Source: Clifford J. Sager, M.D., director of family psychiatry, New York Hospital–Cornell Medical Center.

Building a good credit history for your child

The sooner your child starts to establish a good credit history, the easier it will be for him or her to have access to bank loans in the future.

State regulations on giving credit to minors vary, but even if your state is one of the more restrictive ones, you may still be able to get your child a credit card. Many bank credit-card firms and department stores skirt the issue by authorizing the use of cards to children of any age when parents are willing to assume responsibility for their debts.

Set guidelines at the time you authorize the credit card for a minor:

☐ Let the card be used only for purchases agreed upon in advance. Give permission purchase by purchase.

☐ Set monthly limits to the amount your teenager can charge.

☐ Insist that teenagers save receipts of purchases.

☐ Act as a co-signer on any charge card your teenager assumes, even if your signature isn't required for a purchase, so that you can monitor the child's spending.

☐ Require teens to pay for credit purchases with earned income and to use their allowances for daily expenses. This builds in an incentive for a teenager to supplement income for major purchases.

Source: Meredith Fernstrom, senior vice president, Office of Public Responsibility, American Express Co., New York.

Children and money

An allowance is an excellent means by which to teach children to manage money. But for it to work, parents, as well as children, must take responsibility.

☐ Be clear about what you expect an allowance to cover. If the child blows his allowance two days after getting it, he should have to do without until the next allowance day rolls around. Be flexible, however. If a special event comes up that your child wasn't planning for but really wants to attend, feel free to be generous.

☐ Don't use money to manipulate your youngster. Some parents are overly free with gifts and dollars to pacify a child they don't spend enough time with.

☐ Keep in mind that youngsters will learn their major lessons about money management by example. Suggested: Share your family's budgeting procedures with your child, showing in practical terms how the family's money is allotted. When he reaches adolescence, teach him how to balance a checkbook.

☐ When a youngster gets a job, it's time to discontinue his allowance and ask him to take on some responsibility for his own expenses. Suggest he start paying for his own school supplies, save for a trip, buy some clothing or put money away for college.

☐ If you are divorced, make sure the children don't start using money to play one parent against the other. To avoid it: The custodial parent gives the allowance, which should be part of the child support agreement. The noncustodial parent shouldn't undermine the arrangement by showering the child with money during visits. If there's joint custody, one parent should give the allowance.

☐ If you want a child to learn to save, give incentives. Example: Offer to add to his savings account if he saves an agreed-upon amount by Christmas.

Allowances: Resolving potential conflicts

An allowance often becomes the center of a power struggle between parents and children. Parental ambivalence about letting go often expresses itself in the allowance arena. Here's how to handle allowances without turning them into a battlefield.

☐ Allowances are for extras—junk food, records, entertainment with friends, small gifts for the family. Parents should provide the necessities—transportation to and from school, lunch at school, clothing, etc. When there's a conflict, use common sense.

Example: Your child says he hates school lunches and wants to eat with his friends at the local pizza place. If you agree that the school lunches are inedible, you might want to pay for the pizza. But if the school serves healthful, reasonably appetizing food, you might insist he spend his own money on lunch at the pizza place.

☐ Since part of giving an allowance is to impart a sense of values, parents have a responsibility to take a stand when a child spends allowance money on things you disapprove of, such as cigarettes and liquor. You can and should take money off the allowance if it's being spent on such items.

] Deduct money only if your youngster s doing something extremely self-destructive with it. Don't deduct for every minor xpenditure that you disapprove of, or r non-money-related misbehavior.

] Recognize that there are certain ultural pressures on your youngster. or example, the family that eats only ealth foods shouldn't punish a child r buying candy.

] Before you do any deducting, negoate. Talk over the issue with your child nd find out why he's doing something ou disapprove of. If you can convince im of your concern for his well-being nd acknowledge his need for independence, you may reach an agreement.

] You can use money to encourage a hild to display behavior you want to ee. But such "tokens" should not be onnected to the allowance. A certain mount should be considered as "base ay." Over and above this you can use e barter system, paying a child extra r doing extra chores, getting higher rades, etc.

] It's better to use money as a positive einforcement than as a negative one.

xample: You want your teenager to top smoking. Instead of deducting igarette money from his allowance, it's ore effective to pay him extra to stop moking.

] Start a youngster's allowance early— even is a good age—with a small mount, like $3 a week. Increase it nnually by a dollar or so. Take into ccount teenagers' need for extra noney for dating. Since dutch treat is a tandard operating procedure these ays, a teenage girl should get as uch as a boy.

] Always give the same amount on the ame day every week. An allowance hould be like a paycheck—something our child expects, not something he as to beg for.

] If your child complains that all the ther kids are getting more money, talk ith a few parents to check it out. If you an afford to, do give your child the mount customary among his choolmates. Any less will be seen as unishment and deprivation. If you eally can't afford the local average, on't give more than you can afford. xplain your financial situation to your hild so he doesn't take it personally.

ource: Robert F. Scherma, Ph.D., a school sychologist who has counseled teenagers and eir families in the New York City area for the st 18 years.

Teaching children the value of money

An appropriate timetable for allowances and money management:

□ Age 5. Start with a weekly or twice-weekly allowance of 50¢. (Regular expenses, such as school lunches or bus fare, would be in addition.)

□ Age 10. Increase to $2.50 to $3.00 weekly, allowing a small surplus that can be saved for future purchases.

□ Age 13. Change to a monthly allowance and encourage the child to prepare a simple budget.

□ Age 15. Children are ready to participate in family budget discussions. (But don't burden them with severe financial problems.) Handle their big expenditures (motorbikes, stereos, etc.) with loans. Don't set a schedule of steep payments that leaves the child with virtually no pocket money.

Basic guidelines:

□ Keep the allowance in line with what other children receive. Too much money can make the child wasteful and guilty. Too little creates resentment.

□ Hold fast to the agreed sum. Exceptions should be rare and clearly identified.

□ Encourage earnings. They are better than allowances and gifts. Don't pay for routine home chores. But do hire the kids for special work, instead of outside workers, as often as possible.

□ Withhold or cut the allowance as a punishment only when the offense is directly related to misusing the money.

□ Use money as a reward on a matching basis. For example, an improved report card earns a bonus equal to after-school earnings.

□ Give praise when the child does well and keep criticism low-key and constructive. Expect mistakes, anger and tears. This is a learning-by-doing process.

Source: *Your Money & Your Life*, AMACOM, New York.

Computerized children: Warning signs… and solutions

Computers are now being pushed on kids for many of the same reasons parents used TV—as a convenient, cheap baby-sitter. Dual-career couples and single parents find they can have a bit of peace at home (or time to do the work they brought from the office) if Johnnie is off working on the terminal. But TV is now considered "bad"…and computer work "good." Reality: Children are being encouraged to relate to a machine rather than to other human beings, just as they were with the TV screen. They're learning a narrow set of skills—and retreating from the more complex set of social skills that they need for healthy growth.

Symptoms of overuse of the computer:

☐ Edginess and crankiness—the result of mental fatigue.

☐ On and off communication patterns with parents and siblings…yes…no…yes.

☐ Impatience because parents take too long to get to the point…the book has too many descriptive words…the situation is too ambiguous.

☐ Few friends, little time spent out-doors, limited physical activity.

But as youngsters develop their computer skills and focus their attention on the computer during more and more of their "leisure" time, they're also increasing the negative impact of such work:

☐ Youngsters don't learn to deal with the inevitable negative feedback they'll get in real-life human relationships. As adults they may wind up being immobilized by criticism. The computer does not give negative feedback, but it does keep encouraging the computer worker to become more perfect, to stop making errors in the program, to work in a logical, deductive way.

☐ Young children (4-6 years) begin matching their thinking style to that of the computer—which is logical and deductive. Computer thinking is really quite simplistic and "dumber" than the natural thinking of children of this age, which is metaphorical. Metaphorical thinking is at the base of true genius and creativity.

Managing Kids and Computers

☐ Put limits on computer use—just as limits should be put on TV watching. It natural to lose a sense of time when working on the computer, so put a clock beside the terminal—and set an alarm to ring when the child must leav computer work.

☐ Train the child to recognize the sign of mental fatigue such as taking deeper breaths or making more mistakes. Explain that when he feels those symptoms—or when the alarm rings—he must stop working on the problem. Teach children to state the problem they're working on—either by logging it on the computer or writing it in a notebook that they keep near the computer. Goal: Write the problem down so that the child doesn't have to keep it in his short-term memory and continue to worry about it.

☐ Allow for a 20-minute (at least) transition time between computer wor and dinner or time for other family relationships. If this isn't done, the chil will spend half the time at the dinner table thinking about what he just left c the computer instead of conversing with those around him. By the time he ready to talk, dinner is over and everyone scatters again. Left alone, th child, looking for companionship, turn back to the computer—and still hasn' communicated with other members of the family.

☐ Don't let the computer substitute for time spent with your children. Though seems silly to have to say it: Spend nontechnological time with your children every day—not time spent watching TV, working on the compute terminal, working on the car, talking about new gadgets. Don't underestimate the value of simple playfulness and horsing around. And with older children, sit and talk for a fe minutes each day.

☐ Don't insist that your child work on a computer if he seems uninterested. Despite all the media publicity (much it stirred by manufacturers of computers), not all children take to computers automatically. At least one child in three resists learning to use them—even for playing games. There no reason to worry that such a child is scarred for life.

Source: Dr. Craig Brod, author of *Technostress* Addison-Wesley, Reading, MA.

Common problems in stepfamilies

Both partners in a remarriage usually have unrealistic expectations about their new roles. As parents, they are not prepared for the problems they will face when all their children are thrown together through various custody and visitation arrangements. The children, of course, are not prepared either.

Problems that frequently develop:

☐ Children, especially young ones, fantasize that the new parent will replace a deceased parent or provide something their custodial parent doesn't.

☐ A stepparent who has never had children anticipates becoming an ideal mother or father with an instant family. Being rejected by the children can be a real shock.

☐ Parents who have failed with their own children think they have a second chance. But they may not really understand why they failed, and they often end up making a similar mistake.

☐ Children vie for seniority. A child who has been the oldest in one family may now be number two or three. The usual results are rivalry, jealousy, and hurt feelings.

☐ The new stepparent is sought after by all the children, which causes conflict between that parent's loyalty to his or her own children and the need to relate to the stepchild.

☐ Blood ties tend to be pitted against nonblood ties. It is always more difficult to love, or even to get along with, someone else's children. A parent tolerates more inconvenience and conflict from a natural child than from a stepchild, and consequently suffers from feelings of guilt and hostility.

☐ Differences in parenting style. Watching one's spouse cope with a child in a way that you do not approve of can lead to marital problems. Example: A man who had longstanding problems with his adolescent son married a woman he thought would take care of these problems. She didn't consider it her role to be the disciplinarian. As she watched her husband tolerate abuse from his son, she began to lose respect for him.

How to be a better stepparent

Marriage and parenting are skills you learn from your own parents. You blunder along, imitating or rejecting their behavior. But most people never had any role models for stepparenting. Useful guidelines:

☐ Establish new rules. Some have to be negotiated between the parents. It is helpful to set times when the family gets together to work on those decisions the children can be included in.

☐ Realize that love is not instant. Someday you may learn to love stepchildren, and they may learn to love you—but not necessarily.

☐ Respect old ties. A new stepfamily has many complicated connections with relatives. A natural parent and child have a unique relationship. Allow children time to be alone with natural parents, grandparents or other relatives. Do not feel that a new family has to do everything as a group.

☐ The basis for any successful remarriage is for ex-spouses to be as considerate of the children as possible. Conflicts between parents should be dealt with by them. Children should not feel they are included in these problems.

☐ Realize that even the best stepparent can experience hostility from a stepchild for reasons that have nothing to do with the stepparent. For example, the child may feel that the natural parent won't approve if he likes the new stepparent.

☐ Children can love more than two adults as parents. It's an enriching experience for a child to have more than two parents, two sets of grandparents, etc. The natural family should understand that it may be better for the child to develop a close relationship with someone in the stepfamily.

☐ The couple relationship is primary. This is the core of the new family unit, in spite of the fact that each partner has strong loyalties to his or her family of origin. Children have to know that the new couple is an unshakable combination and cannot be broken up (which they often try to do in order to get their own parents back together again).

☐ Discipline. You cannot discipline even your blood children without a good relationship. It may take a year or

141

two before this happens with stepchildren. In the meantime, the natural parent should be the disciplinarian for his or her children. The authority of an absent natural parent should be vested in the stepparent. This must be made clear to the children.

☐ Ironing out discipline policy. Parents should discuss priorities and compromises. If they can't work out their differences, they should look into getting professional help.

Source: Barbara C. Freedman, C.S.W., director of the Divorce and Remarriage Counseling Center, New York.

Adopting a foreign child

Couples who want to adopt a US child often have to wait five years or so. Those who want a newborn of specific ethnic background have even greater problems. Many turn to foreign agencies. The waiting period is only 3 to 18 months, and children of all ages are easily available in some countries.

Trap: Some foreign agencies are unscrupulous. They deliver ill or crippled babies to couples who are not expecting to deal with those problems. Reputable agencies have the same standard of adoption that exists in the US.

☐ To find a reputable agency, ask the Adoptive Parents Committee (210 Fifth Ave., New York 10010). The organization helps parents during the adoption process and afterward.

☐ Steer clear of agencies that require a large part of their fee up front.

☐ Alternative: Deal directly with foreign orphanages and homes for unwed mothers. Information about them is available from foreign consulates in the US, and American embassies in foreign countries generally know about the reliability of these institutions.

☐ In South Korea, a major source, it's almost always necessary to use a US agency. One with a good reputation: Spence-Chapin (6 E. 94 St., New York 10028).

☐ Countries that work most closely with US adoption agencies are Chile, Colombia, El Salvador, Mexico, and South Korea.

☐ A big part of the total cost of adoption depends on whether the adoptive parents go to the expense of picking up the child in his or her home country. There's usually no advantage in doing so if the agency is reputable. But couples who have doubts should go to pick up the child and have him/her examined by an independent doctor. (US embassies and consulates have lists of recommended doctors.) The governments of Mexico and Colombia require adoptive parents to pick up the child.

☐ If there are problems, the would-be-parents are under no obligation to proceed with the adoption.

☐ The legal work for a Mexican adoption can be handled in that country. Suggestion: In Mexico, retain a lawyer (who can be recommended by the US embassy). Adoptions in other Latin American countries and in South Korea must be handled by US courts. Use a lawyer in the US who is familiar with foreign adoption procedures.

Re-establishing your marriage when the kids leave home

Initially, most parents are pleased when children leave home for college or an out-of-town job. But after the pleasure subsides, the new reality needs to be dealt with.

Some common sense steps to take:

☐ Realize that the parting is a signal that one chapter of your life is closed. The next chapter depends on how well you handle the transition.

☐ Say good-bye to the past without fear of grieving or of airing feelings of remorse, guilt and anger.

☐ Discuss with your spouse where you want to go in life.

☐ Congratulate each other on how well you have done with the children.

☐ Discuss resentments that have built up and start negotiating for changes.

☐ Set aside time to share activities and intimate conversation. Recognize that some interests are best pursued individually. Give each other leeway to do so.

☐ Ask yourselves, "How are we really different from the way we were at the beginning of our marriage? What are he implications of those differences?" To answer, take inventory of the bonds that connect you and your spouse— activities and interests, degree of intellectual closeness, physical attraction to one another, and the like.

☐ Assess the degree to which you have been nurturing or neglecting intimacy. One test of adequate intimacy is to find out how willing you are to share both good and bad feelings.

☐ If you and your spouse cannot re-establish a satisfying relationship, recognize the possibility that the presence of children may have masked a hollow marriage that is not worth salvaging. When this situation becomes apparent after children leave home, couples should discuss terminating the relationship. If this happens to you, seek services of a therapist or counselor. They can provide the necessary objectivity and support needed to confront the prospect of separation. Remember that the more valuable a relationship is, the more it is worth saving and the more useful counseling is likely to be.

Source: Gisele Richardson, president, Richardson Management Associates, Montreal.

Helping older children gain independence

Having the family all together for the holiday season may be cheerful. But togetherness can pall if it is overdone. And low starting salaries, high rents and a scarcity of apartments are keeping many young people at home and economically dependent on their parents well beyond graduation from college.

To encourage independence, parents should:

☐ Supplement their children's income at the outset so that they can live in their own quarters. There is no substitute for the experience of having to manage a household.

☐ Charge for room and board if children must live home. Some parents put this money aside as a stake for the child's marriage or business.

☐ Put a time limit on living at home: six months, a year or until the first salary raise. Whatever the arrangement, make it clear that independence is the goal.

☐ If you are not comfortable when your children bring sex partners home, say

so. Making feelings clear before a guest arrives avoids unpleasantness later.

☐ Ask grown children under your roof to help with chores and with family obligations, such as visiting relatives.

☐ After children mature, some parents want to simplify their lives by moving into a smaller house or apartment or nearer to work. Do not be deterred by sentimental arguments of the children. Independent parents foster independent children.

Source: Dr. Clifford J. Sager, director of family psychiatry for the Jewish Board of Family & Children's Services, New York.

Parents' guide to corporate training programs

What can you do to help your child land the right job offer? A corporate training program may be the answer, especially for liberal arts students.

☐ Recent graduates can earn while they learn. Most corporate training programs pay well. Starting annual salaries for trainees range from $15,000 to more than $30,000.

☐ Such programs give in-depth training in a specific industry while also offering a practical view of the corporate world. This hands-on training is useful in whatever field the student finally picks.

☐ Let your graduate know that you understand that competition for corporate training programs is fierce. Most applicants face a number of rejections before landing the perfect job.

How to Prepare

There is no such thing as too much preparation for a job interview. Encourage your graduate to first learn about the industry that interests him. Once he understands the industry and the key players, he can zero in on particular companies. He should study annual reports, recruitment materials and magazine articles. (Articles can be obtained by telephoning a company's public relations department to request a press kit.)

☐ Information interviews in advance of a job interview can also be helpful. Alumni from your son's or daughter's alma mater who are already working for that company or industry are often willing to take a few minutes—either over the phone or in person—to offer insights into what it's like to work there. Your own business contacts and friends may also be able to serve as informal career advisers.

☐ Questions the job hunter should ask contacts: What are the most satisfying aspects of your job? What are your priorities in an average work week? What do you wish you had known about this career field before you entered it? What about this employer?

Source: Marion Salzman, coauthor of *Inside Management Training: The Career Guide to Training Programs for College Graduates,* New American Library, New York.

Living better with adult children

We have entered the era of the nesters: Adult offspring (past age 18) who are living in the parental home. Largely because of economics, at least 25% more young adults today live with their parents than 15 years ago. Living with adult children can be stressful. But if you play your cards right, it can be rewarding for parents as well as children.

☐ Release your parental authority. When children reach adulthood, it's time to reshape old roles. This adjustment can be toughest for fathers, who often deal with their children as authoritarians.

☐ Don't be too generous with advice or financial aid. For many parents, excessive giving may be an unconscious attempt to gain control. Don't offer, but don't refuse. Try to find a solution that preserves the nester's responsibility. Co-sign a bank note.

☐ Communicate. The issue may be trivial—breakfast dishes that don't get cleared, ice-cube trays that are never refilled. But if resentment is allowed to build, the entire family suffers. Speak up about what's bothering you.

☐ Don't perform an adult child's personal business. As adults, they are responsible for walking their dog, getting up in time for work and paying their taxes. There will come a day when you won't be around to bail them out.

☐ Share household chores equitably. Make a written list. A 23-year-old bachelor's standard of cleanliness may not mesh with your own.

☐ Ask that they contribute something toward room and board. One survey found that nesters with full-time jobs pay an average of $75 a month. (One third pay nothing at all.) Fair formula: Propose that your nester pay 15% of take-home pay. Don't feel guilty about this. You're teaching a key survival skill: How to handle money and live within one's means. (If you really don't need the money, you can put it aside for a nest egg for when your nester leaves. But keep this a secret, or you'll defeat your purpose.)

☐ Remember that it's your roof and mortgage. If your adult children want to live in your home, they must abide by your rules and value system. If you feel uncomfortable with certain behaviors in your home, it's your right to forbid them. (Flexibility helps. Much as you might despise cigarettes, for example, you might let a nester smoke in his or her bedroom.)

☐ House rules stop at the front door. What nesters do outside is their own choice, unless they bring their problems home (no drunk driving or drug dealing condoned). Curfews are unrealistic. Like it or not, much of a young adult's social life happens after midnight.

☐ Reject the notion (quite popular in this culture) that nesters are failures.

☐ Set a target departure date before your adult child moves back home. This could be three months after college graduation or six months after a divorce. The date can be modified later on. Affirming that your nester's stay is temporary relieves much anxiety on both sides.

Source: Monica Lauen O'Kane, author of *Living with Adult Children,* Diction Books, St. Paul, MN.

Troubled parent and adult-child relationships

Parent and adult-child relationships that depend too much on rewards and punishments make both sides unhappy. If two or more of the following statements are true about how you think of your parents, problems are brewing.

☐ I let my parents have their way even though I know this is wrong.

☐ When I do something of which my parents disapprove, I feel very guilty.

☐ No matter what I do, I cannot get my parents to see what my problems are.

☐ I try to anticipate their every need.

☐ I am always fighting with my parents, but I know we love each other.

☐ I wish they would think about me sometimes instead of only themselves.

☐ I know they order me around, but that is really very good for me.

Source: Carol Flax and Earl Ubell, coauthors of *Mother, Father, You: The Adult's Guide for Getting Along Great with Parents and In-laws,* Wyden Books, Ridgefield, CT.

Helping parents with money problems

Your parents are faced with inflation and rising home maintenance bills. They refuse to sell their house and are too proud to take outright gifts. What can you do?

One solution might be to consider a nonamortized bank loan for your parents, using the house as collateral.

How it works:

☐ You negotiate a loan from a bank where you keep a minimum balance equal to the principal of the loan.

☐ Your parents pay interest on the loan and you arrange for the principal to be paid back after they die and the house is sold.

☐ With the loan, you buy annuities to supplement your parents' income.

For example, a mother is 65 and has a $120,000 house with no mortgage. She gets a loan from her son's bank for 80% of the house's net value ($96,000), at 15% interest. With the money, the son buys her a 20-year annuity that pays 15% interest. The annuity covers her interest payments and provides her with $1,000 a month. And by borrowing on the house, rather than selling it, the woman and her family hold onto its appreciation value.

Coping with elderly parents

Getting along better with elderly parents isn't easy. But it can be done. Here's how:

☐ Avoid criticizing, making demands or challenging their ideas. Instead, try to demonstrate support and concern.

☐ Do not bombard them with direct questions. Instead, search gently for their true feelings. Parents listen to you only if they are heard in return.

☐ Tell parents directly when they hurt your feelings.

☐ Give your parents a choice if you want their help as a baby-sitter, housesitter or whatever. Don't expect them to be at your beck and call.

Source: Carol Flax and Earl Ubell, coauthors, *Mother, Father, You: The Adult's Guide for Getting Along Great with Parents and In-Laws,* Wyden Books, Ridgefield, CT.

Coping with visits to elderly parents

Many adult children are reluctant to visit their elderly parents, particularly when the family relationship has been ridden with conflicts. Reasons:

☐ Problem parents are likely to become more so as they age. One who has always been a guilt provoker, excessively demanding or inclined to play the martyr's role will likely be more demanding and guilt-provoking in old age.

☐ Seeing parents aged and infirm threatens adult children by reminding them of the approach of their own old age and of their own mortality.

☐ Parents' aging usually reverses the parent-child role. The dependency and frailty of old parents, whether physical or psychological, may make them assume childlike roles. Adult children, in turn, experience a sharp loss because they recognize that they can no longer turn to their parents.

To deal with the reluctance you may feel about visiting your parents:

☐ Remember that a mature, parental response on your part is now in order. However enraged or frustrated you are by a parent's behavior, accept that a role reversal has taken place. Your parent now is actually dependent and helpless in some way and is not the same antagonist you remember from early-childhood conflicts.

☐ Visit regularly, so your parents can plan and look forward to your arrival. Remember, though, some parents lead busy, extremely independent lives and may not want too many visits from children.

☐ When going away for an extended

period, inform your parents of your return date, when they can expect to hear from you and how often you'll be in touch.

☐ Don't visit parents at the expense of your own adult priorities. Excessive guilt often pushes children into running themselves ragged visiting parents too often.

☐ Be aware that too much indulgence of a parent's wishes, or treating a parent as an infant, can impair the parent's will to continue assuming responsibility for his or her own life. Avoid placating behavior, which is a hangover from the childhood relationship. A realistic and caring attitude is better.

☐ During the visit, listen to your parents' problems, but also try sharing concerns of your own (if they are not overwhelming). Many parents would like to feel themselves still capable of giving advice and of having authority.

Source: Dr. Howard Halpern, author of *Cutting Loose: An Adult Guide to Coming to Terms with Your Parents,* Simon & Schuster, New York.

Helping aging parents care for themselves

Elderly people suffer emotionally and physically when facing dramatic changes. Ideally, preserve their daily routines and environment as long as possible, even in the face of growing infirmities.

Steps to take before considering a nursing home:

☐ Hire a cleaning person to come in once a week.

☐ Arrange with another elderly but healthier neighbor to share meals or visit daily.

☐ Sign up for Meals-on-Wheels delivery of hot meals daily.

☐ Register at neighborhood senior citizens' center.

☐ Schedule frequent visits from individual grandchildren.

☐ Find a smaller apartment with fewer stairs in the same building.

☐ List local stores that deliver phone orders.

☐ Familiarize parents with local public transportation routes.

☐ Purchase a pet as a present that provides company and diversion. The pet should require minimal care.

☐ Set definite limits on your own direct involvement in your parents' lives. Assume the role of creative coordinator. Involve a variety of others (neighbors, relatives, social agencies, friends, hired help) who can perform the jobs as well, and perhaps more cheerfully.

Source: Stephen Z. Cohen, M.D., and Bruce Michael Gans, M.D., authors of *The Other Generation Gap: The Middle Aged and Their Aging Parents,* Follett Publishing Co., Chicago.

Some alternatives to nursing homes

To keep parents functioning in their own homes as long as possible, consider:

☐ Adult day-care centers. They offer one meal a day, transportation to and from medical appointments and various programs to keep people healthy and alert. Get more information from your state's department of social services.

☐ Congregate homes. Apartment buildings or clusters of detached homes provide low-cost rental housing and essential services for elderly people who need minimal day-to-day help. Eligibility is based on income. For more information contact your local area office of the US Department of Housing and Urban Development.

☐ Home care. Services include convalescent care, nursing, household maintenance and Meals-on-Wheels. Most programs are run by the state or the community.

Source: Joseph Michaels, author of *Prime of Your Life,* Quarto Marketing, New York.

How to select a nursing home

Placing a troubled, dependent relative in a nursing home is a heart-wrenching ordeal. To ease the way, know when a nursing home is the only answer. Deciding factors: When there is a loss of control of body functions, a loss of memory or an inability to perform the basic activities of daily life such as shopping, cleaning and dressing.

People do not age physically and emotionally at the same rate.

Never coerce a person into a nursing home. Rather, open the decision for discussion. When possible, have the person accompany you when you shop for the proper home.

The nursing homes with the best reputations, highest staff-to-patient ratios and longest waiting lists are nonprofit. That is, they are run by churches, fraternal orders, and charities. Hitch: Only about 25% of all homes are nonprofit.

The majority of nursing homes are for profit, or proprietary. Other differences among homes:

☐ Health-related facilities emphasize personal, not medical, care. These are generally nonprofit homes.

☐ Skilled nursing facilities are for patients with serious mental and physical disabilities. Most of these places are proprietary.

☐ Nonprofit homes usually charge a flat, high monthly fee with no extras for added services. Proprietary homes ask a lower monthly fee with extra payments for services. Always be certain that you understand the rates and service charges.

☐ Many proprietary homes don't take Medicaid patients. The amounts paid by the state and federal health plans aren't always enough to cover the costs. Patients without any money should be placed in a nonprofit home.

To select a home, start by asking the patient's physician, relatives and friends who have gone through a similar experience for information. Also, get information from the state departments of health and social services.

Begin the search long before it becomes necessary to find a home. Caution: Many emotional problems among the elderly occur during the waiting period because of the stress of being in limbo.

Since this is an emotional experience, take a close friend with you when you inspect nursing homes. The person will look for things that you forget.

What to seek in a home:

☐ Good location. The right home is close enough for convenient visits. Avoid places in run-down or dangerous neighborhoods. Best: A residential area with gardens and benches.

☐ Well-lit, cheery environment. Doors to the room shouldn't have windows. This is a home, not a hospital.

☐ The home's affiliations with hospitals and associations. Find out how many patients are on Medicaid. If the number exceeds 50%, the home is not likely to provide adequate care.

☐ A professional staff. There should be a fulltime or regularly visiting doctor with specialized knowledge in geriatrics. The total number of registered nurses, licensed practical nurses and nurses' aides should be at least 40% of the number of beds.

☐ The residents. Nothing speaks better for a nursing home than active, vital patients. Observe the staff to see if they treat residents with respect. Talk to the residents and ask for their complaints. Bad signs: If more than 3% of the residents are in the hospital at one time. If patients are still in bed or in bedclothes at 11 A.M. If many residents are catheterized to avoid linen changing. Ask what happens when a patient is hospitalized. Is the nursing home bed still available afterward?

☐ Handrails in hallways and bathrooms.

☐ Smoke alarms in public areas and each room. Ask to see the latest fire inspection report and note the date.

☐ The dining room should be clean, bright and inviting, with no dirty trays around. Are special diets adhered to?

☐ The residents' rooms should be comfortable and attractively furnished. Be sure the room can be personalized with pictures, plants, knickknacks. Drawers should be lockable.

☐ Happy patients are those plugged into the outside world. Newspapers and large-print books should be readily available. The home should show movies, bring in entertainers and provide outside trips. Other necessary activities: gardening, workshops, education courses, lecture series and discussion groups. Find out about religious services and provisions for voting.

☐ Special services should include visits by a licensed physical therapist and workable therapy equipment that the patients can use. Visits by other specialists: Speech therapists for stroke victims, audiologists, dentists, psychiatrists, optometrists and podiatrists.

What to watch out for:

☐ Patients who are sedated to keep them quiet.

☐ The home asks for a large sum of money up front.

☐ Doctors who hold gang visits (they see 40–50 patients during each call).

☐ You are denied visiting rights to the kitchen, laundry, and library.

☐ The Patient's Bill of Rights isn't displayed.

Before you leave: Stand in the home and feel the ambience. Ask yourself if you would like to live there. Return to the place several times. Arrive at least once unannounced. The best time to visit is 11 A.M. or 7 P.M.

To monitor nursing homes for abuses: Put small pen marks on the patient's body and bandages to check frequency of bathing and bandage changes. Visit at mealtime. Get weekly weight checks of the patients to be sure nutrition is adequate. Learn the names of nurses and aides on all shifts to determine who's responsible for the patient's care.

Source: Texans for Improvement of Nursing Homes, Houston.

Making a deal with a nursing home

Putting a relative or loved one in a nursing home is becoming even more difficult as the federal government cuts back programs and medical costs soar. Making a good deal with a nursing home requires a grasp of current federal and state laws and knowledge of how nursing homes operate.

Medicare is an insurance program subsidized by the federal government and administered by private insurance companies for people over 65. It is fairly adequate for covering doctor and hospital bills, but it does not take care of long-term custodial care.

In theory, Medicare covers the first 100 days of nursing-home care, but in practice, most of these claims are disallowed. Why: Medicare administrators say they will pay only for skilled care, something they deny that nursing homes supply.

Medicaid is the federal health-care program of the indigent, a person with assets of only $1,500 to $3,000, depending on the state of residence. Medicaid is a federal program, with each state having the option to buy into it and administer it. At present, only one state, Arizona, does not have Medicaid.

Most nursing-home patients eventually wind up on Medicaid when their assets run out. Major problem: Discrimination against the Medicaid patient. The home's income from a Medicaid patient is 15% to 40% less than the private-patient fee.

Most nursing homes charge $20,000 to $40,000 per year, depending on the degree of medical care provided. Even at these steep rates, private-patient waiting lists are long. Additional pressure is caused by Medicare, which often refuses to pay for hospitalization of patients awaiting nursing-home admission, on the ground that they are hospitalized inappropriately. Patients who cannot get into nursing homes are being billed by the hospital (sometimes at $300 a day or more), putting tremendous pressure on the patient's family to do whatever possible to get the patient into a nursing home quickly. Many nursing homes are quick to take advantage of this pressure.

When you are facing a $300 per day hospital bill, a $5,000 voluntary contribution to a nursing home's building fund to facilitate admission can seem like a bargain. These contributions, whether made by a corporation or an individual, are tax deductible but are not applied to the patient's bill.

Contracts with nursing homes are often too broad in scope. They basically state: You give us all your money and we'll take care of you for the rest of your life. Some states have outlawed such agreements because of rampant abuses. A patient who paid a home $100,000 and later wanted to move when he discovered the food was dreadful could not get his money back.

Many homes demand payment of one or two years' fees in advance. This practice, too, has been outlawed in some states.

Yet another practice is for sponsoring contracts to be signed with the patient's children, who guarantee that the nursing home will be paid for periods up to about two years. Often, these contracts are a way of circumventing laws that forbid a home to accept more than two to three months' payment in advance.

The noninstitutionalized spouse has to pay only the first six months of nursing-home care for the institutionalized partner. Then, if the person paying refuses to pay more, the institutionalized spouse is eligible for Medicaid. Problem: The noninstitutionalized spouse can be sued by the local agency for support. This is not always as bad as it seems, because disputes are settled in family courts where support payments are ordered on the basis of what can be afforded, just as in child support. One strategy: If you do not use a trust fund, transfer all assets immediately to the healthy spouse as soon as the other becomes ill.

Joint savings or checking accounts are not recommended because they are usually construed as belonging fifty-fifty to each depositor.

Source: Charles Robert, lawyer with Robert & Schneider, Hempstead, NY.

When the money runs out

When the nursing-home patient's assets run out, Medicaid should take over. It is illegal for a home to evict a patient who can no longer pay privately, although many homes use devious tactics to do just this: A patient gets a high fever in the middle of the night, is dropped off at the local hospital and is then refused readmittance to the home when the fever subsides.

❑ Except for the very rich, it is unlikely that any family can support for many years an annual nursing-home bill of $30,000. Since almost all nursing-home patients eventually wind up on Medicaid, it is imperative to protect your assets (and your children's inheritance) by making sure Medicaid takes over as soon as possible.

❑ Problem: Almost all states have laws that forbid the transfer of assets during a time (usually two years) prior to nursing-home admission. Since it is impossible to predict when nursing-home care will be needed, advance planning is crucial.

❑ A trust fund is one good way to move assets of $50,000 or more out of an elderly person's direct ownership. It can also help with taxes and the problem of children who cannot be trusted with a lot of money.

Essential: Set up the trust in a way that minimizes the potential of its being attached as an evasion of Medicaid rules, a federal crime. This difficult and complicated matter is best handled by a lawyer experienced in the field.

Lost relatives

The Salvation Army, known for saving souls, has an impressive record of finding them as well. Its little-known missing-persons service is devoted to reuniting scattered families. Four regional offices coordinate cases for the United States. The New York bureau has processed 10,000 inquiries in the past 10 years and concluded 4,000 of them successfully.

Working through local chapters throughout the US and in 85 other countries, the Army carries on a heavy correspondence with government agencies such as the Social Security Administration and the IRS, checks local phone books and places ads in its own publications.

"We don't help wives track down missing husbands to collect alimony, nor do we do much work with runaway children," says Major Mary Jane Shaw, director of the New York bureau. "And if someone doesn't want to be found, we respect that."

Many requests come from overseas families trying to locate relatives who emigrated and lost touch. "People who move to a foreign country get busy and neglect to keep up with their families until their lives are more established," says Major Shaw. Her proudest moment was the reconciliation of a patriarch with his surviving heirs after 50 years of separation.

Easing the impact of relocation on employees

Be cognizant of the fact that transfers may create serious problems, especially in these situations:

❑ Midlife crisis. A relocation that coincides with a period of personal transition adds to emotional confusion if you are already trying to cope with changes in life goals and lifestyle.

❑ Career-oriented spouse. There is a good chance your working spouse will greatly resent the career interruption and show it. One solution is to ask your

149

employer to help your spouse find rewarding work at the new location or help pay for more education.

☐ Adolescent offspring. Children of other ages cope better with a move than do teenagers.

☐ Repeated relocations. Even an adaptable family resents moves that occur every few years.

Your company can alleviate the problems by:

☐ Encouraging your family to discuss their reactions to the transfer openly.

☐ Helping them make a clean break.

☐ Bidding fond farewells to you and your family, perhaps throwing an informal send-off party.

☐ Providing extensive information to your family on their new area.

☐ Checking back after the move for a progress report.

Source: *The Effective Manager,* Warren, Gorham & Lamont, Boston.

How your company can help you buy/sell a house when you're transferred

Companies are increasingly underwriting housing costs to encourage their executives to relocate when they have to give up a low-interest fixed-rate mortgage.

Three ways your employer can help:

☐ Cover the loss you suffer from trading the old mortgage for a new one.

For example, you sell a house with a $50,000 balance on a 7% mortgage. You then buy a new house with a 15% mortgage. The company reimburses you for the extra interest, usually for the next three years. Calculation: $50,000 (old mortgage balance) times 8% (difference in interest rates) equals $4,000 a year. Total payout: $12,000.

☐ Company financing. It can offer interest rates below market levels but high enough to minimize losses.

☐ Purchase the new home jointly with you and share the profits from its future appreciation. This is similar to a bank's share appreciation mortgage.

Source: Patricia E. Matteson, marketing director, Merrill Lynch Relocation Management, Inc., White Plains, NY.

Choosing the right breed of dog for your family

When contemplating buying a puppy, your first consideration should be the type of dog, rather than size. Many large dogs actually need less room than smaller ones. The original function for which the breed was developed often dictates the animal's need for space and influences his temperament.

☐ Scent hounds (beagle, basset, dachshund, bloodhound). Well-suited to city living and children.

☐ Sight or gaze hounds (saluki, Afghan, Irish wolfhound, Scottish deerhound, greyhound). Originally bred for running down prey and killing it, they still need lots of room to be happy.

☐ Sporting dogs (spaniels, setters, pointers, retrievers). Originally bred to locate game and retrieve it. Need a little less room than sight hounds. But with the exception of Labrador and Newfoundland retrievers, sporting dogs are not especially protective or good with children.

☐ Working dogs (German shepherds, malamutes, huskies, collies, sheepdogs). Probably the most intelligent and protective of all groups. Large (60–150 pounds) and used to outdoor work, but they adapt nicely to city life if exercised twice a day. Actually require less space than smaller, more active dogs like terriers.

☐ Terriers (Airedale, Scottish, Welsh, West Highland white, fox, schnauzers). The most alert and active dogs. Also tenacious, extremely protective and often aggressive. Need space. Good with children and older people, as long as they can cope with the terrier's high level of activity.

☐ Toy dogs (Pekinese, toy poodle, Yorkshire terrier, Maltese, Italian greyhound, Pomeranian). Charming companions for adults. But strongly not recommended for small children. No matter how adorable these dogs may look, they're much too fragile.

☐ Nonsporting dogs is a catch-all group with no special characteristics. Includes unrelated breeds, such as the poodle, French and English bulldogs, Boston terrier, chow chow and dalmatian.

Most dog owners strongly prefer one sex over the other. General pros and cons:

❑ Males (called dogs by breeders) tend to fight, wander, chase cars and display aggressive dominant behavior toward people.

❑ Females (bitches) are more protective and gentle. They neither wander nor fight but if they're not spayed, they can become pregnant. Even if they're kept locked up, living through their semiannual heat periods is difficult because of all the unwanted attention from neighboring dogs.

How to select a puppy

The main thing is to buy from a breeder rather than a pet shop. Don't buy a puppy on impulse. Consider the following points:

❑ It's best to see both the pup's parents or their photographs at the breeder (chief reason to buy there rather than at pet store). Not only will you see what the puppy will look like as an adult, you will also be able to judge its genetic inheritance by the health of its parents.

❑ Buy a puppy at 6 to 12 weeks of age. That's when they make the best adjustment to a new home.

Try these quick and easy visual tests:

❑ Shine a pocket flashlight at the pup.

❑ Show it a mirror.

❑ Roll a ball toward it.

❑ Wave a sheet of white paper.

❑ Drag an object along on a string.

Similarly, here are some hearing tests to be done out of the puppy's sight):

❑ Blow a police whistle.

❑ Honk a car horn.

❑ Clap hands.

❑ Blow a kazoo or noisemaker.

❑ Body sensitivity is important in training. Gently pinch the puppy's ear between the ball of the thumb and the forefinger. Then push down its hindquarters, forcing it to sit. A puppy that doesn't react has little body sensitivity and won't feel corrections. A puppy that whines, cowers, or runs away is so sensitive that it will fear corrections and be difficult to train.

❑ Temperament can be tested by seeing the puppy's attitude toward strangers. Jump right in front of the puppy. It should show neither fear nor anger. Surprise followed by friendliness is a good reaction.

Training your puppy

Some suggestions:

❑ Don't encourage a puppy to chew on facsimiles of valued objects. You can't expect it to tell an old shoe from a new one.

❑ Never place your hand or finger in a puppy's mouth when playing. That biting might seem cute today, but you won't enjoy it a year from now.

❑ Allow the puppy to climb and jump on you only when you're seated on the floor. If you let it jump on you when you're in a chair, you're teaching it to sit on furniture.

❑ Never encourage a puppy to bark on command. This can lead to excessive barking and a dog that "talks back."

❑ Puppies become bored and anxious easily. If you leave your puppy alone too long and too often, you must expect destructive behavior.

❑ Praise the puppy when it's good. Treat bad behavior with a stern *No* and a shaking or a harsh noisemaker. Physical abuse will teach a dog only fear.

What to feed your dog

Commercial dog foods usually contain parts of an animal that a dog would never eat in the wild. Sometimes these foods include diseased animal parts rejected for human consumption. To provide your pet a good diet:

❑ Feed it table scraps, including meat, vegetables, grains, fruit, and even salad.

❑ Avoid sugars and other sweets, except as treats.

❑ For variety, mix scraps with a little commercial food. (Buy only products that contain no additives.)

❑ Give your dog trimmings, tripe, spleen, kidney or liver served raw or partially cooked. (The entrails of a freshly killed animal are the first thing a wild dog eats.)

❑ Always supplement the diet with

minerals and multivitamins, especially vitamins C and E.

Source: Wendell O. Belfield, D.V.M., author of *How to Have a Healthier Dog,* Doubleday, New York.

Getting your pet into TV commercials

☐ Get your animal an agent. Like any other model, he needs an agent to get jobs. In bigger cities, there are animal talent agencies. In smaller cities, animal trainers are usually the contact for commercial producers.

☐ What agents look for:Trained animals that photograph well. At a minimum, dogs should respond to basic obedience commands—*sit, down,* and, most important, *stay.*

☐ Prepare your pet with a test many agents use: Make him stay in a busy corridor where there are many distractions. (The set for a commercial shoot is a noisy, bustling place.)

☐ Other important tricks: Fetching and carrying a product gently by mouth, "speaking" on command.

☐ For pet-food commercials, a healthy, indiscriminate appetite is essential. Few ads are completed on the first take, so the animal may have to eat several times.

☐ If you have a cat that does tricks, you may have an advantage because trained cats are rare.

☐ To audition your pet, make an appointment for an interview. Take along pictures. Color snapshots are fine if they are clear and show the animal close up, at eye level. Bring a resume that includes the pet's vital statistics, its training and special tricks, and your phone number.

☐ Payment: There is no union for animals, so fees vary widely. In general, TV pays more than print work.

Pet breeding

Pets can usually give birth without assistance. In fact, cats and dogs generally do better when not disturbed. A veterinarian should be called, however, in the event of a problem delivery.

Signs of problems:

☐ The pet's temperature reaches 103° and stays there.

☐ She seems very excitable or has seizures. It may be eclampsia ("milking fits"), a metabolic disorder.

☐ The pet strains for an hour or more without breaking the placenta.

☐ The placenta breaks (a clear fluid drains out of the vulva), but no kitten or pup has been born, and the mother hasn't strained for an hour. A dead or wrongly positioned pup or kitten may be blocking the rest of the litter.

☐ The mother is resting more than 10 minutes or so between births.

☐ The mother's milk is brown, green, o bloody instead of clear and creamy.

Source: Michael W. Fox, D.V.M.

What your pet can do for you

Here are some reasons why your pet can be your best friend—in ways you've never dreamed!

☐ Patients who watch an aquarium in their dentist's office before having oral surgery have substantially lower blood pressure (and less need for analgesics) than those who don't.

☐ The single factor that improved survival rates of heart attack patients most was pet ownership—even more than having a spouse.

☐ The simple act of stroking any anim lowers our blood pressure.

☐ Pets act as social lubricants. Pet owners are perceived as friendlier tha the norm. More people will approach and talk to a person who is walking a dog than one who is wheeling a baby carriage.

☐ For the shy, a pet may be an ice-breaker—a pleasant, neutral topic to start a conversation.

☐ Some of us can learn how to love (and accept love) through our pet.

☐ Many couples have taken a preliminary step toward parenthood b learning to care for an animal.

Source: Susan Cohen, director of counseling and chairperson of the Animal Medical Center Institute for the Human/Companion Animal Bon New York.

Norman Vincent Peale's 10 rules for getting along with people

☐ Remember their names.

☐ Be comfortable to be with. Don't cause strain in others.

☐ Try not to let things bother you. Be easygoing.

☐ Don't be egotistical or know-it-all.

☐ Learn to be interesting so that people will get something stimulating from being with you.

☐ Eliminate the "scratchy" elements in your personality, traits that can irritate others.

☐ Never miss a chance to offer support or say "Congratulations."

☐ Work at liking people. Eventually you'll like them naturally.

☐ Honestly try to heal any misunderstandings and drain off grievances.

☐ Develop spiritual depth in yourself and share this strength with others.

Source: *Time Talk*, Time Management Center, Grandville, MI.

How to build a personal support system

Individuals need not only a few intimate friends but also a network of friendly relationships that make anyone more effective. To build a support system:

☐ Join groups: Participate in self-help groups—not so much for the help as for the support, to get a sense of community and belonging.

☐ Pursue with other people some of the activities you like. A runner can join a running club; a photographer can take a photography course. This way, you weave your interests into a friendship network.

☐ Reciprocate acts of friendship. If someone waters your plants, you'd better be prepared to do the same for him. Reciprocity—both giving and accepting—is part of keeping any kind of friendship. People who have problems with accepting favors should remember that other people feel good doing things for them.

☐ Mentor friends. The younger person ordinarily seeks out the older one.

However, the older person might do well to encourage such a relationship because there's something in it for him or her, too—a revitalization that comes from dealing with a younger person with ambition, enthusiasm, and a fresh education.

What nourishes and what poisons friendship

Key nourishing qualities:

☐ Authenticity. Inauthentic behavior is contrived and false. Authentic behavior is spontaneous and unpremeditated. Being freely and deeply oneself is important to friendship.

☐ Acceptance. A sound friendship permits the expression of anger, childishness and silliness. It allows us to express the various facets of our personality without fear of harsh judgment. A feeling of being valued promotes our fullest functioning with other people.

☐ Direct expression. Coaxing, cajoling, dropping "cute" hints, manipulating and beating around the bush are all barriers to clear communications. When people know what they want from each other, they establish clear communication and contact. They're in a position to attempt an agreement regarding their desires. They may also realize they're too different to get along and that they may be less frustrated if their relationship is more casual.

☐ Empathy. This involves an effort to understand another's beliefs, practices and feelings (not necessarily agreeing with them). Empathy means listening, trying to understand, and communicating this understanding to the speaker.

What poisons friendships:

☐ Blame. Blame shifts responsibility and also can be a way of avoiding self-examination. The antithesis of blame and defensiveness is to assume responsibility for one's own feelings. If a person is honest enough to admit his mistakes and finds he's forgiven, he can then be tolerant of his friends' foibles.

☐ Excess dependency. Some people have lost touch with their values and their strength and need other people to lean on. This kind of person feels unable to be alone. In the dependent friendship, growth and development are stifled rather than enhanced.

Source: Dr. Joel D. Block, clinical psychologist and author of *Friendship: How to Give it, How to Get It,* Macmillan, New York.

All about nerds

Nerds get attention by being obnoxious. They don't pay attention to the signals other people send them.

How not to be a nerd:

☐ Let people finish what they are saying.

☐ Don't always insist that you know more than other people about the subject under discussion.

☐ Slow down on advice-giving.

☐ Open up to new ideas.

☐ Let yourself change your mind once in a while.

When a nerd starts to realize that much of his behavior stems from anxiety about being accepted and loved, he is well on his way to being a nerd no longer.

Source: Doe Lang, author of *The Secret of Charisma,* Wideview Books, New York.

Making friendships stronger

Even the best of friendships can have their ups and downs. How to minimize this type of stress:

☐ To move closer to a friend, take him or her into your confidence. Share your thoughts and feelings. There's no guarantee that this approach will produce positive results, but the probabilities increase dramatically when you give what you want to get.

☐ Use compromise to resolve differences. The only other alternatives are domination by one and the consequent resentment on the part of the other or withdrawal. Compromise restores the reciprocity needed in friendship.

☐ Avoid a mismatch. It's foolish to pursue a friendship with someone who isn't interested in you. Friendship involves mutual feelings.

☐ Observe the Golden Rule. Most of us want the same things in our friendships—honesty, a sharing of good feelings and thoughts, empathy, support, fun. If you're not getting these, ask: Do I offer the same things to others that I want for myself?

Source: Dr. Joel D. Block, a clinical psychologist, and author of *Friendship: How to Give It, How to Get It,* Macmillan, New York.

Changing an enemy into an ally

If there's someone in your business with whom you're always at odds:

☐ Think of this person as someone you like, someone who can work with you.

☐ Create in your mind an image of the relationship restored.

☐ Treat this person as a valued friend and associate.

☐ You won't see immediate results, but over time, you'll find that this person is responding to you in a more positive way.

☐ The lesson: Be aware of your expectations of others. People are likely to deliver what you expect them to deliver.

Source: Dr. Norman Vincent Peale, author and lecturer, New York.

How to say no to anyone

Many of us say *yes* more often than we'd like. Whatever the reason, if you find yourself saying *yes* because you feel too guilty about saying *no,* here are some practical measures to help you protect yourself.

☐ Stall. This gives you precious time to work up an honest rationale for a total refusal. Simply say: I don't know. I need time to think about it—give me an hour (or a day, or whatever seems reasonable).

☐ Use humor.

☐ Try flattery.

☐ Tell white lies, if necessary.

Source: Barry Lubetkin, Ph.D., Institute for Behavior Therapy, New York.

How to forgive and forget

To forgive another is the greatest favor you can do—for yourself. It's the only way to release yourself from the clutches of an unfair past. Beyond that, opens the possibility of reconciliation, often a gift in itself.

What to do:

☐ Take the initiative. Don't wait for the other person to apologize. (That cedes control to the one who hurt you in the first place.)

☐ If the forgiven person wants to re-enter your life, it is fair to demand truthfulness. He or she should be made to understand, to feel the hurt you've felt. Then you should expect a sincere promise that you won't be hurt that way again.

☐ Be patient. If the hurt is deep, you can't forgive in a single instant.

☐ Forgive "retail," not "wholesale." It is almost impossible to forgive someone for being a bad person. Instead, focus on the particular act that hurt you. (It might help to write it down.)

☐ Don't expect too much. To forgive doesn't mean you must renew a once close relationship.

☐ Discard your self-righteousness. A victim is not a saint. You, too, will need forgiveness some day.

☐ Separate anger from hate. To dissolve your hate: Face your emotion and accept it as natural. Then discuss it either with the object of your hatred (if you can do so without escalating the hatred) or with a trusted third party.

☐ Forgive yourself. This may be the hardest act of all. Candor is critical. Admit your fault. Relax your struggle to be perfect. Then be concrete and specific about what is bothering you. Your deed was evil. You are not.

☐ To make self-forgiveness easier: prime the pump of self-love. Do something unexpected (possibly unappreciated) for a person you care about. By acting freely, you'll find it easier to think freely.

Source: Lewis B. Smedes, author of *Forgive & Forget*, Harper & Row, New York.

How to read people

Much of people-reading involves making elementary, commonsense observations and then acting on them.

Observation tips:

☐ Don't generalize. Conventional wisdom says that if someone slumps in his chair, he's not very commanding, or he leans forward, he's ready to make a deal. However, I've seen a lot of erect, attentive types who hung on my every word but never made a move. Any useful observation must be considered in the context of the particular situation.

☐ Learn the difference between posture and posturing. Look out for people who lean in toward you, who push things back on the desk at you, who sit back and strike poses, who dress pretentiously, who do strange things with lighting, or who have your chair placed lower than theirs. All those things are keys that you're dealing with a phony, someone who's more concerned with appearance than with accomplishment.

☐ Look at the eyes. People communicate with their eyes in situations where silence is called for. The next time you're in a meeting with people you don't know, notice the eye contact of the participants. It will tell you who's allied with whom, who is most influential, and, if you're the speaker, whether you're boring everyone to death.

☐ Use ego to your advantage. Most successful people are one giant ego with a couple of arms and legs attached. But a giant ego isn't necessarily a strong ego. It may be compensating for low self-esteem. Or someone who seems to have a weak ego may simply be low-key. When you know these things, you can work with them or around them.

☐ Make inferences from co-workers and subordinates. For example, if someone seems unwilling to commit himself to even minor details, it may be that his boss is a person whose ego demands that he make all the decisions.

☐ Take the fish out of water. People tend to reveal themselves in unexpected ways when outside their usual settings. For this reason I favor breakfast, lunch and dinner meetings. Even the way someone treats a waiter can be very revealing.

Source: Mark H. McCormack, author of *What They Don't Teach You at Harvard Business School: Notes From a Street-Smart Executive*.

How to spot a liar

Less than 5% of the population are natural liars...performers who lie flawlessly and make no mistakes. But research shows that the majority of people are fooled by liars. Clues to look for:

☐ The single biggest giveaway is a series of inconsistencies in the lie.

☐ Watch for changes in patterns of speech, especially when a person has to pause and think more often than usual to answer a simple question.

☐ Look for signs that the person is deviating from a usual pattern of behavior. Liars may use a monotonous tone of voice or change inflection less frequently when they lie. They may also use fewer hand and body motions than usual.

☐ A smile is the most common mask of a person's true feelings.

☐ Liars sometimes lie just for the thrill of telling a successful lie. Giveaways: Widening of the eyes and a trace of a smile.

☐ Ask questions when inconsistencies start to pop up in a story. Most people become willing prey to liars because they don't want to act suspicious or don't think they have the right to ask questions.

Source: Dr. Paul Ekman, professor of psychology, University of California, San Francisco, and author of *Telling Lies*, W. W. Norton & Co., New York.

More on lying

When we lie, we feel varying degrees of discomfort. Some people feel actual fear—others, the mildest tension. But at least to some degree, our feelings are expressed in our behavior. We may control our words, our voice, our face or our posture. But we cannot control everything. Here's how we give ourselves away to an astute observer:

☐ Sometimes the giveaway is only a "micromovement"—a brief, minimal change in facial expression.

☐ The voice is a rich source of information. People who are lying tend to talk slowly. (By definition, they're not spontaneous.) They speak in shorter sentences than usual. They realize that the more they talk, the more likely they are to slip up.

☐ Liars cut back on gestures and eye contact. The less exposure, the better. They sit sideways, rather than face to face. They rarely lean forward toward their listeners.

☐ Liars are more self-conscious. They shift in their seats, adjust their clothing and scratch themselves. Often, they bring a hand to the face—another way to reduce exposure.

☐ A very reliable sign is body stiffness. Look for a rigid posture (whether the person is standing or seated), with strict symmetry of limbs.

It should be noted that these signals can appear in someone who is not lying. The person may simply be uncomfortable—either about saying something or about saying it to a particular individual.

Source: Albert Mehrabian, Ph.D., professor of psychology, UCLA, and author of *Silent Messages*, Wadsworth Publishing Co., Belmont, CA

Disarming difficult people

To deal with infuriating people, what counts is your response, not what they do. If you don't confront them, you end up making a negative judgment on yourself. Familiar types:

☐ The person who keeps repeating negative remarks about you made by others.

☐ The person who keeps referring to everything he has done for you.

☐ Those who insist you act in a certain way: "Isn't my daughter Frannie wonderful?" (demanding applause). Or those who tell a joke or story and wait for you to laugh on cue.

How to handle such people:

☐ Avoid recriminations.

☐ Don't attribute bad motives or bad character.

☐ But make the point that you have as much right to your response—or lack response—as the speaker does to his. You'll put a stop to the annoyance, and in most cases you'll also improve the friendship.

☐ Understand that if this doesn't work and you lose a friend, that's better than to be in a state of constant, impotent fury.

Source: Dr. George Weinberg, author of *Self Creation*, Avon Books, New York.

Better one-to-one conversations

It's been said before, but the surest way to improve your one-to-one conversations is…to become a better listener. Listening skills may seem simple enough, but many people (particularly men) need to work on them.

☐ Live in the present moment. Resist distractions. Don't let your mind wander to your bank balance or to after-dinner plans.

☐ Stay alert and concentrate on what your "partner" is saying—not only the words, but the emotions behind them. Rephrase what you've heard in your own words (mentally or verbally).

☐ Maintain consistent eye contact.

☐ Lean toward the person if seated.

☐ Nod or smile in response.

☐ To handle a long-winded anecdote or complaint: Steer the conversation to a mutually interesting subject. Or…approach the old subject from a new angle.

☐ When it's your turn to talk, think about the point you want to make before you start speaking.

☐ Get to the point in as few steps as possible.

☐ Consider your audience. Make what you're saying relevant to the particular person you're addressing.

☐ Don't be afraid to ask a "dumb" question about a subject that's new to you.

☐ If your conversations seem bland, maybe you're suppressing honest disagreements. A dispute shouldn't hurt an exchange (or a friendship), as long as a certain etiquette is respected.

☐ Give the other person credit for something before you disagree. Never say, "How can you think something like that?" Better: "That's a good point, but I see it differently…." Or, first point out areas of similarity: "We agree that world peace is vital—therefore…."

Sources: Mark Sherman, associate professor of psychology, and Adelaide Haas, associate professor of communications, State University of New York, New Paltz.

To rescue yourself from embarrassing situations

What to do:

☐ Simply and quickly apologize. That gives you time to think, if nothing else. But don't overdo it. Apologizing profusely just makes the other person uncomfortable.

☐ Don't put yourself down by saying "I'm so clumsy" or "I can't seem to do anything right." If you go overboard, you might wind up convincing the other person that there really *is* something wrong with you.

☐ If you're habitually tactless, ask yourself if you felt enmity or anger toward the person you insulted…if something about him made you uncomfortable or envious.

☐ How to apologize: Don't play innocent by insisting your remark was unintentional. The other person knows you meant to hurt because that was the result. If you apologize honestly, telling the other person about your angry feelings, you're much more likely to be forgiven.

☐ Make a joke about your mistake. It relieves the tension of the moment and shows you're a good sport. The other person also feels less embarrassed. Sharing a good laugh about something that could have created a rift can even improve rapport.

When you get in a tough, embarrassing spot:

☐ If you have personality traits that make you feel awkward in certain situations, ask a friend for feedback about how you're really coming across. You might be very self-conscious about some traits, such as your shyness or a tendency to talk too much. But others most likely won't even notice.

☐ Change the subject when it seems that you've put your foot in your mouth.

☐ Agree to disagree. One of the most awkward moments for people is disagreement, especially about personal matters. Acknowledge that you have differences, but make it clear that you still like and respect that person.

☐ Don't relive the embarrassing moment, wishing you'd done it differently. Forget it. Don't spend the rest of the day telling everyone what a fool you made of yourself, and don't keep bringing up the incident whenever you see the person it happened with.

Source: Dr. Judith Meyerowitz, Ph.D., a psychotherapist in private practice in New York.

Dating for mature and successful singles

When you meet someone you might like to know better:

- ☐ Avoid talking too much about a former spouse.
- ☐ Re-examine your priorities, and try to be more flexible.
- ☐ Don't judge another person in the first 10 minutes of a date. Stay open.
- ☐ Keep a sense of humor.
- ☐ Listen to what the other person is saying. Be interested, not only interesting.
- ☐ Be realistic and learn from your past experience.

How to start a conversation with a stranger

- ☐ Pay attention to the person's name when introduced. Repeat it. If it's unusual, ask about its origins.
- ☐ Look directly at the person. Lean forward a bit.
- ☐ Ask the person something about her/himself in a flattering way.
- ☐ Ask encouraging questions as the person talks about himself.
- ☐ Don't interrupt. If you have an interest in keeping the conversation going, let the other person talk about himself and his interests. Don't immediately begin talking about yourself. Be patient.

Source: James Van Fleet, author of *A Lifetime Guide to Conversation*, Prentice-Hall, Inc., Englewood Cliffs, NJ.

Tactful flirting

Matchmaking is a thing of the past, so if you hope to find that special someone, you have to know how to go about it. Luckily the art of flirting can be learned.

To initiate contact with a stranger you think you would like to know better:

- ☐ Don't come on with obvious lines or a standard act. You'll be seen as crude or a phony.
- ☐ Don't get too personal. Make your conversational opener about something neutral, or you may be seen as pushy.
- ☐ Do pick up on an innocuous topic and comment on it. Good: That's a lovely ring you're wearing. Is it Art Deco? Poor: You have the most beautiful hair.
- ☐ Do make eye contact—but not for too long. According to a psychological

study, three seconds is optimal to indicate interest without seeming to stare.

- ☐ Don't touch the person right away. Women especially are very put off by men they consider "grabby." You might even move away to create allure.
- ☐ Do show vulnerability. People love it when you're not Mr. or Ms. Self-Confidence. If you're nervous, say so. Your candor will be appealing. Also: Your admission will allow the other person to admit that he or she is nervous, too. This breaks the ice, and then you both can relax.
- ☐ Do ask for help as a good conversation opener. Example: I don't know this area well. Could you recommend a good restaurant around here?
- ☐ Don't feel you have to be extraordinarily good-looking. If you have confidence in yourself as a person, the rest will follow. Whatever your type may be, it is certain to appeal to someone.
- ☐ Do be flexible. The same approach won't work with everyone. If you're sensitive and alert, you can pick up verbal and nonverbal cues and respond appropriately.
- ☐ Don't oversell yourself or feel compelled to give all your credits. Make the other person feel like the most important person in the world to you at that moment. Being interested is just as important as being interesting (if not more so). Really listen. Don't just wait until the other person finishes a sentence so you can jump in with your own opinion.
- ☐ Don't let your confidence be shattered by a rejection. It may not have anything to do with you. You may have approached someone who is married, neurotic, recovering from a devastating love affair, in a bad mood, or averse to your eye color. The best remedy: Try again as soon as possible.

Source: Wendy Leigh, author of *What Makes a Woman Good in Bed*, *What Makes a Man Good in Bed*, and *Infidelity: An American Epidemic*, William Morrow, New York.

What men like in women

- ☐ Brunettes come in first with 36% of the men surveyed.
- ☐ Blondes come in second at 29%.
- ☐ Hair color is unimportant to 32% of the men surveyed.
- ☐ Favorite eye color: 44% select blue,

21% like brown and 20% prefer green.

☐ By two to one, men choose curly hair over straight.

☐ The trait men first associate with a beautiful woman: 42% say personality, 23% think of the smile, 13% say eyes and only 6% zero in on the body.

☐ Favorite look: Striking and sophisticated is first, with 32%.

☐ Biggest turnoffs: Heavy makeup, 26%; excess weight, 15%; arrogance, 14%.

Source: *Glamour.*

Talking to women

A survey of 1,000 women revealed that they liked most to talk about (in this order):

☐ Family and home, including children and grandchildren.

☐ Good health.

☐ Work or job (if a working woman).

☐ Promotion and advancement (if employed).

☐ Personal growth.

☐ Clothes and shopping.

☐ Recreation.

☐ Travel.

☐ Men (especially single women).

Subjects that were least liked:

☐ Sports such as baseball, football, and boxing.

☐ Politics.

☐ Religion.

Source: James Van Fleet, author of *A Lifetime Guide to Conversation*, Prentice-Hall, Inc., Englewood Cliffs, NJ.

How to talk with men if you're a woman

The topics men most like to talk about are strikingly similar to those women like:

☐ Family and home, including children and grandchildren.

☐ Good health.

☐ Work or job.

☐ Promotion and advancement.

☐ Personal growth.

☐ Recreation.

☐ Travel.

☐ The opposite sex (especially young single men).

☐ Sports.

☐ Politics.

Men generally dislike to talk about:

☐ Religion.

☐ Clothes, fashion, or shopping.

Source: James Van Fleet, author of *A Lifetime Guide to Conversation*, Prentice-Hall, Inc., Englewood Cliffs, NJ.

Personal ads: A woman's view

The personal classified ads in *The New York Review of Books, New York* magazine and *The Village Voice* are becoming an increasingly useful social medium.

Here are some tips on answering and placing ads:

☐ Don't lie. Even white lies do damage. Don't say you're a college professor if you really teach occasional courses in night school at several local colleges. Stretching the truth sets up unrealistic expectations, and your "date" is certain to be disappointed. Important omissions also count. If you weigh 300 pounds, it's better to say so.

☐ Look in the mirror. Don't say you're handsome, beautiful or very attractive if you're not. You have a better chance being honest because different people want different things.

☐ Don't ask for photos. When it comes to wallet-size portraits, they lie at worst. At best, they say nothing. When you like someone, that person becomes better-looking to you. And when you don't like someone, it doesn't matter how good-looking he is. Besides, some very attractive people photograph badly…and vice versa. You'll get the best sense of a person from the letter, not from the picture.

☐ Try humor. It always gets a better response.

☐ Avoid attractiveness requirements. Just on general principles don't answer any ad by a man who asks for a "very beautiful" woman or a woman with a "fabulous figure." If he's preoccupied with looks, he's superficial.

☐ Don't limit yourself with age requirements. Why do men in their fifties consistently ask for women in their twenties and thirties? Unless you want children, don't limit your possibilities.

☐ Don't brag. This unpleasant trait

159

breeds skepticism and distaste in the reader.

☐ Be sincere. Nothing catches a woman's attention more surely than a sincere, straightforward, informative letter. When you answer an ad that looks inviting, let the person know why. Respond to the particulars in the ad in a warm and personal way. Talk honestly about yourself, your likes and dislikes, favorite vacations, funny anecdotes, etc. And never, never, never send a photocopy response.

☐ If you really liked a woman's ad but she hasn't answered your response, write again. Persistence is a virtue.

☐ Don't be discouraged. Chances are you won't be attracted to 99.9% of the people you meet this way. But that will also be true of singles you meet other ways. This is more efficient, however, since people are already preselected. They're singles who want to meet someone—just like you.

How to enjoy relationships

☐ Accept people as they are. Nothing kills a relationship faster than the expectation that you can change someone. It's impossible. The best you can do is to become more tolerant and flexible yourself, encourage an atmosphere for change, and then hope for the best.

☐ When you give, give freely. If you expect people to give the same back, measured by the cup, you'll always be disappointed. If they respond, that's great. And if they don't, that's all right, too.

☐ Be honest with the people you care about. Get rid of petty irritants. Don't suffer in silence until you finally explode.

☐ Honesty needn't be cruel. Good rule: Be as tactful with your spouse and children as you are with friends and distant relatives. Most people are wonderful in courtship but later get careless. Love is not a license for rudeness.

☐ Don't use your family as an alibi when you fall short of goals. Stop underestimating these people. They're much more flexible than most people assume. You can make your dreams real if you want them enough—and

share them with the people you love. But if you never say, "Let's go to Nepal!" you'll never get there.

☐ It's a gamble to be vulnerable. But you never really lose because the risk itself reminds you how richly you are living.

Source: Leo Buscaglia, author of *Loving Each Other*, Holt, Rinehart and Winston, New York.

Terminating a relationship

In terminating either a business or personal relationship, those who initiate the termination have the upper hand. They also have the bulk of the responsibility.

To walk away from the termination with a sense of moral clarity, it is essential to have made a genuine attempt to come to some degree of accommodation with the other party, whether employee or spouse. Terminators should meet with those terminated to share their dissatisfaction when they are still open to finding a solution.

Terminators should answer these questions:

☐ What do they need from the other party to continue the relationship?

☐ What support are they prepared to give the other party?

☐ What is an acceptable time frame for the changes to be made? A reasonable period should be allowed for making changes and adjustments. Announcing requirements for change on Friday, and then deciding on Monday that the relationship won't work, is unfair.

☐ What don't the terminators want?

☐ What aren't they prepared to give?

☐ How would they describe the consequences if satisfactory changes aren't made? People often resist making major changes not because they fear what's ahead but because they are unwilling to give up what they have. The same fear hinders organizational change as well as change in personal life.

Source: Gisele Richardson, president, Richardson Management Associates, management consultants, Montreal.

Are you ready for love?

Love Resume

Here is a way to consider—and maybe rethink—what you really want in a loving relationship and what you respond to. Think of this as a love resume. Sometimes just the act of writing can change your thinking. Like a work resume, it may show a tendency toward instability. Or it may show a logical progression from one "job" to the next. You can discover your own patterns in relationships.

Write a detailed report* about your three (or more) most serious relationships, including:

❏ A description of the person and what you did and didn't like.

❏ What worked and what didn't work.

❏ How it ended and how you got over it.

❏ What you think you should have done differently.

❏ What your partner would say worked or didn't work, and why it ended.

❏ Would you be attracted to such a person today?

Write a description* of the person you would like to meet now, including:

❏ Is this person like the ones in past relationships? If not, why not?

❏ What sort of relationship you want (marriage, a companion for weekends, an escort, etc.)

❏ Characteristics you would avoid.

❏ Your three highest priorities.

*Do this before going on to read the scoring section that follows.

Scoring

Scale 1: Use a red pencil to underline the times you have written *I* or *me.* Count them, and put the score in a box.

Use a blue pencil to underline the times you have written *he, she, we, us* or *both.* Count them. Put this score in another box.

Add the numbers in both boxes. Divide the total into the number of red underlines. If the percentage is anywhere up to 35%, you're available for a relationship. From 36% to 50% means you are borderline (okay on short-term dating but unable to sustain long-term relationships). Over 50%

indicates a counterfeit lover. Your concern for yourself and lack of empathy for others almost guarantee that nothing will work, no matter who the partner is.

Source: Abby Hirsch, founder and director of The Godmothers, a dating service.

Being single...again

Being involuntarily single after years of marriage can deal a serious blow to the ego. Essential to cushioning it is to start leading the single life immediately.

❏ Force yourself to make a date at least once a week, even if it is only having dinner with someone from work.

❏ Do not expect too much from yourself too soon. Scars of a broken marriage take at least a year, usually two, to heal. You are probably deluding yourself if you believe you are ready for a permanent relationship before that time.

❏ Brief sexual encounters are normal during this period, and they can be useful in rebuilding the ego. Do not be alarmed if periods of celibacy follow periods of sexual activity. These are also normal and useful in the healing process.

❏ Older people are often surprised to discover that achievement makes them attractive to the opposite sex. Not only is prestige an aphrodisiac; age itself is frequently attractive. But although younger people often have affairs with those older than themselves, usually they want permanent partners closer to their own age.

❏ Transitional partners, with whom you form a nurturing though transitory relationship, often occur during the first year of being single. This type of partner is also part of the healing process. You may feel guilty about breaking off the relationship, but do not. You may well be someone else's transitional partner.

❏ Your best chance for meeting new partners is in the normal course of business and social events. However difficult it may be at first, ask your friends to introduce you to eligible acquaintances.

❏ Once you have been introduced to a new person, avoid harping on your ex-spouse and introducing your new friend too quickly to your children. Many dates will discourage you from talking about your former spouse, but may enjoy hearing about children.

☐ Although they may remind you of pain you would like to forget, it is essential to continue being a good parent to your children, maybe even a better one. Remember, the divorce or separation may have been harder on the children than on you.

☐ Expect your children to take a keen interest in your new life and be curious to know about your new day-to-day routine. After meeting some of your new friends, children may even suggest that one of them seems marriageable. Sometimes they are right.

Source: Richard Schickel, author of *Singled Out*, Viking Press, New York.

Successful marrying and remarrying

Today, with the statistical probability that two out of every three marriages will end in divorce, couples who marry or remarry need all the help they can get.

Here is some advice for a good start:

☐ Choose the right person for the right reasons. Too often, people make the wrong choice because they have needs they don't admit even to themselves. They know what they want, but even though the person they plan to marry doesn't fill the bill, they think he/she will change.

☐ Have realistic expectations about the marriage. Another person can do only so much for you. No one person can fill every need. It is important for both partners to develop their own lives and interests and not depend solely on each other.

☐ Learn to communicate. Get issues out on the table and talk about them. Try to reach conclusions regarding conflicts rather than let them stay unresolved.

☐ Respect the other person's style of communication. People express affection in different ways. Instead of expecting a spouse to react as you do, try to be sensitive to what he or she is telling you in his/her own way.

☐ Respect the other person's feelings about space and distance. Many

people have difficulty understanding someone else's needs for privacy and time alone. Conflicts about space needs can be resolved by trial and error—and patience.

☐ Create a new lifestyle. Each partner comes with different concepts about customs, handling money, vacations, etc. One may be used to making a big thing about celebrating holidays and birthdays, the other, not. Combine the best elements to get a richer blend that is distinctly your own.

Source: Barbara C. Freedman, CSW, director of the Divorce and Remarriage Counseling Center, New York.

Most common sexual concerns

Among men:

☐ Premature ejaculation. It is easier than you think to control the timing of ejaculation. You have to find the point at which you can no longer stop yourself from ejaculating. During masturbation, practice ways in which you can decrease or increase feelings of arousal. Discover which fantasies or behavior triggers your excitement and what diminishes it, and learn how to focus on the latter, in order to postpone ejaculation. But don't use the old-fashioned trick of thinking about baseball scores or work, which can be destructive to sexuality. Instead, focus on any minimally sensual thought, which at least keeps you in the realm of being sensual (but not at the peak of excitement).

☐ Sexual deviations and fetishes. Men are very much concerned with what they consider unnatural desires, such as the wish to be spanked by women or to wear women's clothes. These desires arise from deep psychological needs, such as the need to be punished for feeling sexual or a wish to be "close to Mommy" by dressing like her. If these kinds of problems are causing disruptions in your life, seek professional counseling.

☐ A desire for more sexual aggressiveness from female partners. A great many men wish that their wives or lovers would take the sexual initiative and behave less passively.

Unusual infertility cure

Weight gain may cure infertility in some women. Women below their medically ideal weight may experience reproductive-cycle shutdowns which make pregnancy less likely or impossible. Eighty-five percent of women studied who had been unable to conceive for four years became pregnant after gaining an average of eight pounds through a well-balanced diet—and without the use of hormones, drugs or surgery….

Source: G. William Bates, MD, professor of obstetrics and gynecology, Medical University of South Carolina, Charleston.

The physical and psychological roots of impotence

Many factors can cause impotence. Contrary to the opinion that has prevailed since Masters and Johnson did their research, not all impotence is caused by psychological problems. New research shows that a variety of physical problems can cause impotence and that these are treatable. Included are hormonal problems and vascular and neurological conditions.

Impotence may be caused by medical or organic factors if:

☐ Medications are being taken to lower blood pressure, or antidepressants, tranquilizers, antihistamines, or decongestants.

☐ A man drinks heavily. Alcohol has very strong negative effects on sexual function, including possible long-term problems such as reduced production of the male hormone, decreased sperm production, and reduced sex drive.

☐ There is a major illness, especially diabetes, thyroid disease, or arteriosclerosis. Illness doesn't dictate erection problems but should be considered as a possible cause.

☐ The man has lost sexual desire (as well as capacity).

Impotence is likely caused by psychological factors if:

☐ A man has firm erections under some circumstances (waking at night or in the morning, during masturbation, etc.). This indicates that the physical mechanism is in good working order and that the difficulty probably stems from emotional factors.

☐ Firm erections are lost just before or after entry. The odds here greatly favor an emotional cause.

☐ The problem started suddenly, over a period of a month or less. Most likely this is an emotionally caused impotence, since physical problems affect sexual function more gradually. There are exceptions, however. Emotional causes are not always sudden in their effect. And medical causes can surface quickly, especially if a drug is prescribed.

☐ The problem started after a very stressful emotional experience (the death of a spouse, the loss of a job, a divorce, rejection by a partner).

☐ Penis size. A very common concern, disguised with euphemisms such as "I have a handicap." (Translation: I think my penis is too small.) The solution is to understand that psychologically the small penis is not a deterrent to sexual pleasure. It is important to find out what penis size means to you or your partner and the ways it affects your desire and pleasure.

Among Women

☐ Not having orgasms. The first part of the solution is to learn not to focus on the missing orgasm—if it is missing. Studies show that at least half the women who think they don't have orgasms in fact do have them, but they're looking for some ideal of an orgasm that they've heard about. Genuinely nonorgasmic women can often overcome this problem by learning to achieve orgasm via masturbation. After acquiring the capacity to accept the sexual pleasure she has learned to give herself, a woman can usually go on to the next step, the pleasure of orgasm with a male partner.

☐ Conflict over the way they're treated in relationships with men. Men are much more concerned with sexual performance and physical fears than are women. Women care far more about the psychological and emotional aspects of relationships than do men. Many women still settle for "half a loaf" in a relationship. The first step out of this trap is to reject the false security of relationships that offer very little satisfaction.

☐ Problems integrating the role of parent and lover. It isn't only men who suffer from the madonna-prostitute complex (separating women into categories such as the "pure madonna" and the "sexy enticer"). Women also suffer from this syndrome. The most common example is the woman who has a child and thus comes to feel she isn't sexy and shouldn't feel sexy because she is now a mother. She may avoid sex on the grounds of fatigue, a problem with the baby or concern over money.

Among Both Sexes

☐ Whether it's healthy to get involved in a sexual relationship with someone much older or much younger. There usually isn't a great deal wrong with this sort of thing, even though such pairings are often a holdover from incestuous childhood desires. When such desires are acted out by two adults, it can be taken as psychological information, but nothing else.

Source: Dr. Judith Kuriansky, clinical psychologist and sex therapist, New York; Saul H. Rosenthal, M.D., editor of *Sex Over Forty.*

Misconceptions about sex after fifty

Middle age can be an opportunity to make sex better and more satisfying than ever before. People of mature years have had more experience in lovemaking. The pressures of career building are less frantic, leaving couples with more time to share. The children have grown up and left home, giving adults more privacy and fewer demands on their time. And as men age, they lose the pressure to get right to intercourse and a quick climax. They can concentrate on a fuller sensual and sexual experience in lovemaking.

Most common myths about age and sex:

☐ That your sex life is essentially over by the time you're in your fifties. Society tends to reinforce this notion with its emphasis on youth. People behave according to the expectations that the culture sets for them and begin to give up on their sexual lives at middle age. This is, in many ways, the equivalent of giving up on life itself.

☐ That the physiological changes affecting sexual function spell the end of your sex life. This is particularly damaging, because most changes can be readily accommodated. For example, many men age 55–60 or

over, worry when they don't get a spontaneous erection seeing their partner undress as they did when they were 20 or 30. But this does not mean sexual function is over for them. It means only that they now require more direct stimulation. Many men put off having intercourse until they get a spontaneous erection for fear their wives will think they have some sexual problem. Sex in these circumstances becomes less and less frequent, and this is what causes wives to fear that their husbands are no longer interested in them.

☐ That sex requires a climax every time. As men get older, they need longer and longer periods between ejaculations. A man in his sixties may require a full day or even several days between ejaculations. This does not mean that he cannot enjoy intercourse and lovemaking in between. Sex partners get into serious trouble when they think climaxes are essential and that the male, particularly, must have one. (The man feels he must because his partner expects it. The woman feels that if he doesn't, he no longer cares for her.) You can enjoy all the sensations of sexual arousal without climax.

Source: Saul H. Rosenthal, M.D., editor of *Sex Over Forty.*

What to expect from sex therapy

☐ If you're married, it's more effective to undergo therapy as a couple. Reasons: Since successful therapy may mean a change in sexual practices, your spouse will inevitably be involved. Moreover, many sex difficulties, such as lack of interest and failure to be aroused, are often the result of a breakdown in communication between partners.

☐ In some states, therapists use a surrogate partner (a paid partner) during treatment. A person with sexual difficulty is taught how to overcome it during supervised foreplay and other sexual activities with the surrogate. But many therapists consider the use of a surrogate inappropriate.

A typical session lasts one hour, nd therapists usually recommend ne session per week. Most difficulties an be successfully treated in three to x months. Some people are helped gnificantly in a single session be- ause they only think they have a roblem. Example: A woman who ils to have an orgasm during sexual tercourse. Or a man who feels guilty hen his partner fails to have an or- asm during intercourse. The fact: ost women *do not* have orgasms uring intercourse.

Lack of sexual interest, the most ommon problem, takes longer to treat. herapists now recognize that although ome declining interest is normal uring a relationship, it's often ggravated by depression, stress, or motions that build up at home.

The most common mistake couples nake is assuming that sex must always e spontaneous. Few things in life eally are. Most couples wince at the lea of scheduling sex. It works, say ne therapists. And it's one of the implest and most effective ways out of ne problem.

The therapist may recommend that a ouple experiment at home with ctivities designed to heighten sexual nterest. Examples: Different kinds of oreplay, verbal excitement, different ositions during intercourse. Lack of nterest often develops because a ouple haven't been communicating neir preferences in sexual activity to ach other.

ource: Dr. Shirley Zussman, president, merican Association of Sex Educators, ounselors and Therapists, Washington, DC.

ntimate relations

Couples rate talking to each other bout their own relationship as the #1 opic to avoid…especially couples in ne "romantic potential" stage (in etween a platonic friendship and an ntimate relationship).

Most couples are afraid of revealing neir differing levels of involvement. The artner who is more committed fears caring the other away, while the less committed may fear hurting the other erson.

ource: Study by Leslie Baxter, Lewis and Clark college, and William Wilmot, University of Montana.

Affection expressed physically but not necessarily sexually is important to a love relationship. Nonsexual physical affection nurtures feelings of caring and tenderness and opens new avenues of communication. The new-found closeness can give your sex life, as well as your relationship, new vigor.

Source: Dr. Bernard Zilbergeld, clinical psychologist and co-author of *Male Sexuality,* Bantam Books, New York.

☐ Men today welcome a woman's sexual initiative, contrary to the macho myths of the past that have put men in charge of initiating sex. Most men prefer to take turns taking the lead because they enjoy feeling desirable and giving sexual decision-making power over to their partners at least some of the time.

Source: Donald L. Mosher, PhD, professor of psychology, University of Connecticut, Hartford.

☐ Foreplay works best if a woman takes more responsibility for her own arousal. Problem: Many women believe it's the man's duty to arouse them. What works: Being honest about needs and desires…not worrying about the kids, jobs, etc…being specific about technique.

Source: Judith E. Steinhart, sex therapist, in *Medical Aspects of Human Sexuality,* Secaucus, NJ.

The fine art of touching

Touching and being touched can solve many of our problems. You can increase your sense of general well- being and rejuvenate your relationship by learning the language of touch. Here's how a couple should get started:

☐ Have sessions in which they alternate touching each other without sexual intercourse.

☐ Each partner gets to initiate sessions …and to be both passive and active.

☐ Learn to be selfish and communicate what you like—eventually developing a nonverbal language of touch.

Helpful suggestions

☐ Don't insist on separating sex and affection. Women complain that when they just want to be affectionate the man will turn it into foreplay. Problem: We fail to see affection and sex as a continuum. We're too used to turning ourselves off during affectionate mo- ments because we had to as children when we kissed and hugged our par- ents. And now we have to as parents with our own children. But you should remember that the affectionate hug or kiss with your spouse is exactly the same physical act that turns you on during sex.

☐ Communicate with your body. If you can't say *I love you* with your body, there's a whole dimension lacking in your relationship. How you express yourself is an individual matter.

☐ Sleep in the nude to create a sense of intimacy.

☐ Be flexible…in terms of touch, body contacts, positions…and where you touch each other in the house.

☐ Don't make it a power struggle. People who have trouble touching each other often toss accusations back and forth, such as *I always touch you—how come you never touch me?* The one who's having trouble gets more resistant because he or she feels forced. Solution: Take it in small steps. Keep touching your partner for your own gratification, no matter what the response. Eventually your partner will stop feeling threatened and reciprocate of his or her own accord.

☐ Don't forget about usually untouched areas. If I don't tell my clients to touch heads and feet, they'll forget about them. Licking toes and massaging feet can be very sensual.

Source: Dagmar O'Connor, author of *How to Make Love to the Same Person for the Rest of Your Life—and Still Love It,* Doubleday & Co., Garden City, NY. Ms. O'Connor is director of the sexual therapy program at St. Luke's-Roosevelt Hospital Center in New York City.

Therapeutic separation

Living apart temporarily can help couples on the verge of divorce resolve their differences. Most couples who try living apart temporarily remain married—and eventually resume cohabitation.

How to do it:

☐ Both spouses must be committed to using the time apart to work through their differences.

☐ During separation, keep a diary of experiences and insights.

Source: Dr. Norman Paul, psychiatrist, Lexington, MA.

Will this marriage survive?

Five premarital indicators that marriage will last:

☐ Economic stability. Neither spouse should feel they are making a great financial sacrifice or will have to overwork to maintain an unrealistically high standard of living.

☐ Maturity. Spouses should be able to minimize selfishness and practice selflessness comfortably.

☐ Commitment. A committed pair will be more able to compromise.

☐ Compatibility. A couple must like to do things together, enjoying each other's company.

☐ Parent success. Spouses who come from happy families with stable marriages have a better shot.

Source: Dr. John Curtis, Valdosta State College.

Effective discipline guidelines

If you must discipline someone, follow these guidelines:

☐ Discipline should be exercised immediately after the infraction is committed.

☐ The application of discipline should be consistent for each infraction.

☐ Warning should be provided of what constitutes an infraction and what punishment can be expected.

☐ Disciplinary punishment should be given impersonally to all offenders. It's the infraction, not the person, that's the problem.

Source: *The Art of Disciplining Your Employees* by DePaul University professor James A. Belohlav, Prentice-Hall, Englewood Cliffs, NJ.

How to stay fit while you sit

Exercises to do at your desk to keep mentally alert, tone sagging muscles and relieve muscle strain:

] Tummy slimmer. Sit erect, hands on knees. Exhale, pulling abdominal muscles in as far as possible. Relax. Inhale. Exhale as you draw in stomach again. Repeat 10 to 20 times.

] Head circles. Drop head forward, chin on chest, shoulders relaxed. Slowly move head in large circle. Reverse direction. Do 5 to 6 times each side.

] Torso twist. Raise elbows to shoulder level. Slowly twist around as far right as possible, then reverse. Do 10 to 12 turns each way.

] Heel and toe lift. Lean forward, hands on knees. Lift both heels off floor, strongly contracting calf muscles. Lower heels, lift toes high toward shins. Do 10 to 15 complete movements.

Source: Doug MacLennon, The Fitness Institute, Willowdale, Ontario.

Exercising when you don't have time

] While you talk on the phone, do leg raises, arm exercises or isometrics.

] Park your car far from the building and walk.

] Do things the hard way (walk the long way to the office, take six trips carrying things upstairs instead of saving items for one trip, shovel snow instead of using the snow blower).

] Exercise while watching TV (run in place, skip rope, use an exercise machine or do yoga, isometrics or toe-touching).

Source: Stephanie Bernardo, author of The Ultimate Checklist, Doubleday, New York.

Fitness vs. health— they are two different things

Exercise will make you physically fit— fitness being defined as the capacity to do physical activity comfortably. But, contrary to popular misconception, fitness and health are two separate things. Don't fool yourself into thinking that exercise is an all-benefit, no-risk proposition.

Three main myths about exercise and coronary health:

☐ Myth: Exercise makes your heart healthier. Exercise *does* make your heart mechanically more efficient—it makes it possible to do more physical activity more comfortably. But your heart isn't healthier just because it's beating more slowly. This would be true only if each of us were allotted a certain number of heartbeats per lifetime. There is no such allotment. There are people in their nineties who have had fast heartbeats all their lives.

☐ Myth: Exercise improves your coronary circulation. Exercise does not stimulate your body to grow collateral blood vessels around the heart. The only thing that does this is the clogging of your original arteries. The original idea that exercise improved coronary circulation was based on an early-1950s study done with dogs under highly artificial conditions. The tests had nothing to do with anything resembling human life.

☐ Myth: Exercise reduces your coronary-risk factors. Most hyper-tension specialists would agree that the likelihood of reducing blood pressure to a significant degree via an exercise program is very small. A California study of trained distance runners found that they had the same range of blood pressure as nonrunners.

Common misconception: That lower heart rate means lower blood pressure. One has nothing to do with the other. So far, a low-fat low-cholesterol diet is the only reliable way to lower choles-terol levels. It's been claimed that there are several types of cholesterol: HDL (high density lipoprotein), the "good" cholesterol…and the "bad" ones, LDL (low density lipoprotein) and triglycer-ides. The latest evidence suggests that even when your HDL goes up after exercise, it may be the wrong kind of HDL. Some studies show that HDL doesn't go up with exercise and that triglycerides and LDL don't go down. There's even an important study that shows the opposite actually occurs.

☐ Myth: Exercise makes you live longer. No one really knows why some people live longer than others. Innumerable factors contribute to it, including genes, marital status, number of social contacts, resistance to stress and educational level. There's never been an unflawed study showing that exercise prolongs life. An interesting book called *Living to Be 100* analyzed 1,200 centenarians. Avoidance of stress was a common denominator.

☐ Myth: Exercise makes you feel better. Although many claims have been made that exercise alleviates depression and anxiety, the data are contradictory. Some studies claim benefits, others don't. Some studies comparing the benefits of exercise with those of meditation and relaxation have found no difference.

Source: Henry A. Solomon, M.D., author of *The Exercise Myth*, Harcourt Brace Jovanovich, San Diego.

Moving gradually into a fitness program

☐ Before launching any fitness program, have a complete physical examination, including an electro-cardiogram. Your doctor should schedule a stress test to check on the heart's capacity.

☐ Don't let your new enthusiasm for getting fit make you too competitive. If you try to get back to the level of achievement you reached as a college athlete, you risk severe injury to ankles, knees, and hips.

☐ Don't jump into a racquet sport or a basketball league. Instead, prepare your body with a six-month program of walking, stretching and perhaps light jogging and weight training.

☐ Choose a sport you like as a primary activity and a complementary activity to go along with it. A swimmer might walk or jog two days a week. A runner could work with weights.

Source: Everett L. Smith, director of the Biogerontology Laboratory, Department of Preventive Medicine, University of Wisconsin, Madison.

Working up to rigorous exercise

It takes middle-aged men and women six months of regular exercise (fast walking, light jogging, weight training, etc.) to work up to rigorous exercise.

Even then, they should move gradually into each workout. The steps to follow:

☐ Walk or jog in place for two or three minutes.

☐ Do 10 minutes of stretching.

☐ When you move into your sport, take the first five minutes at a slow pace (a relaxed volley in tennis, for example) until you break into a light sweat.

☐ For the first few months, aim for 40% to 60% of your maximum heart rate. After six months, go for 70%. After nine months, shoot for 85%.*

☐ Take 10 minutes to cool down with slow jogging and more stretching.

☐ Recognize when you've done too much (if it aches to take a step the next day).

*To calculate these goals, subtract your resting heart rate from your maximum rate—220 minus your age—and multiply by the desired percentage. Then add your resting rate to get your goal. Example: A 45-year-old man has a maximum heart rate of 175 and a resting rate of 60. To perform at 70% of maximum, he should reach a rate of 140.

Source: Everett L. Smith, director of the Biogerontology Laboratory, Department of Preventive Medicine, University of Wisconsin, Madison.

Swimming: The best exercise of all

Swimming helps the entire musculature of the body, particularly the upper torso. It tones muscles (but does not build them). Greatest benefit: To the cardiovascular system.

☐ Best strokes for a workout: Crawl, butterfly, and back strokes are the most strenuous.

☐ Less taxing: The side, breast, and elementary breast strokes.

☐ The elementary back stroke is best for survival. The face is clear of the water for easy breathing, and the limited muscle use saves energy.

☐ The side stroke is traditional for lifesaving. It can be performed with one arm, which leaves the other free to tow someone. It is very relaxing—and effective.

☐ To build up the legs: Hold a kickboard while swimming. This forces propulsion by the legs alone. Or swim with the flippers favored by divers. Their surface increases the resistance to the water, making the legs work harder.

Source: James Steen, swimming coach at Kenyon College, Gambier, OH.

Aerobic ratings of sports

☐ Best for cardiovascular fitness: Stationary bicycling, uphill hiking, ice hockey, rope jumping, rowing, running, and cross-country skiing.

☐ Moderately effective: Basketball, outdoor bicycling, calisthenics, handball, field hockey, racquetball, downhill skiing, soccer, squash, swimming, singles tennis, and walking.

☐ Nonaerobic: Baseball, bowling, football, golf, softball, volleyball.

Source: Dr. Franklin Payne, Jr., Medical College of Georgia, Augusta, GA.

Walk for good health

Exercise doesn't have to be strenuous or punishing to be effective. Despite its economy of muscle use, walking is considered by most experts to be one of the best exercises. Benefits:

☐ Preventative and remedy for respiratory, heart, and circulation disorders.

☐ Weight control. Walking won't take off pounds, but it keeps weight at a desirable level. (Particularly effective in keeping excess pounds from coming back, once they have been dieted off.)

☐ Aids digestion, elimination, and sleep.

☐ Antidote to physical and psychological tensions.

Best daily routine:

☐ Time. Whenever it can be fitted into daily routine. (A mile takes only 20 minutes.) People doing sedentary office work usually average a mile and a half in a normal day. Stretch that by choosing to walk down the hall to a colleague instead of picking up the interoffice phone.

☐ Place. Wherever it's pleasant and convenient to daily tasks. Walk at least part way to work. If a commuter, walk to the train. Walk, not to the nearest, but to the second or third bus or subway stop from the house. Get off a stop or two from the usual one. Park the car 10 blocks farther away. Walk 10 blocks to and from lunch. Walk after dinner, before sitting down to a book, TV or work.

☐ Clothes. Comfortable and seasonal, light rather than heavy. Avoid thin-soled shoes when walking city pavements. It may be desirable to use metatarsal pads or cushioned soles. (The impact on concrete weakens metatarsal arches and causes callouses.)

☐ Length. Walk modest distances at first. In the city, the number of streets tells you how far you've gone. But in the country, you can walk farther than you realize. Consequences: Fatigue on the return trip. Instead: Use a good pedometer.

☐ Walking for exercise should feel different from other kinds of walking. Set out at a good pace. Use the longest stride that's comfortable. Let arms swing and muscles stretch. Strike a rhythm and keep to it.

☐ Don't saunter. It's tiring. Walking at a good pace allows the momentum of each stride to carry over into the next.

☐ Lengthen the customary stride by swinging the foot a little farther ahead than usual. Lengthening the stride speeds the walking pace and also loosens tense muscles, puts other neglected muscles to work and provides continuous momentum that puts less weight on feet.

☐ Most comfortable pace: Three miles per hour. It generally suits the average male and is the US Army pace for long hikes. With the right shoes and unconfining clothes, most women will be comfortable at that pace, too.

Source: Aaron Sussman and Ruth Goode, authors of *The Magic of Walking,* Simon and Schuster, New York.

Everyday ways to walk more

How to get more exercise from day-to-day activities:

☐ Park the car farther away from the office or train station and walk.

☐ Quit taking elevators. Daily climbs of

18 floors or more will increase fitness, studies show.

□ Eat lunch in a restaurant at least 10 blocks from the office and stride briskly both to and from.

□ Instead of driving to the shopping center, walk there. If it's too far, ride a bicycle. If there's too much to haul home, make a second trip.

□ Carry your own golf clubs. And skip the golf cart, even if you're the lone walker in your foursome.

Source: *The Cardiologists' Guide to Fitness and Health Through Exercise,* Simon & Schuster, New York.

Jogging and Achilles tendinitis

The repetitive impact of running often causes inflammation, degeneration and small tears in tendons. Orthopedists from Boston University Medical School suggest these preventive steps:

□ Decrease weekly mileage.

□ Cut down on uphill workouts.

□ Prepare for running by stretching the tendons. With heels flat and knees straight, lean forward against a wall and hold for 30 seconds.

□ Warm heels and tendons with a heating pad before running. After running, apply ice for 10-12 minutes.

□ Elevate heels by placing small felt pads inside running shoes. They relieve tension on the Achilles tendon and contiguous structures.

□ Monitor wear on outer sides of shoes. Tendons are stressed when shoe sides give no support.

□ If these measures fail, consult a physician about immobilization and anti-inflammatory drugs.

Source: *American Journal of Sports Medicine.*

Easy exercises to strengthen your back

Strengthening the back and stomach muscles is the best protection against a back injury. If you have back trouble, consult your doctor before starting this, or any, exercise program.

□ Flexed-knee sit-ups. Lie on your back, with knees bent and arms at your side. Sit up slowly by rolling forward, starting with the head.

□ Bent-knee leg lifts. In the same position as the sit-ups, bring one knee as close as you can to your chest, while extending the other leg. Alternate the legs.

□ Knee-chest leg lifts. Work from the bent-knee sit-up position, but put a small pillow under your head. Use your hands to bring both knees up to the chest, tighten the stomach muscles and hold that position for a count of 10.

□ Back flattening. Lie on your back, flex the knees, and put your arms above your head. Tighten your stomach and buttock muscles and press the lower back hard against the floor. Hold this position for a count of 10, relax and repeat.

□ Don't overdo the exercises. Soreness is a sign to cut back.

□ Never do these exercises with the legs straight.

Source: *American Journal of Nursing,* New York.

Indoor exercise machines

Indoor exercise machines can provide excellent exercise. Certain types of machines are best suited to particular muscle groups and fitness regimens. Here's a rundown of the main types:

□ Multipurpose gyms: To develop major muscle groups, not cardiorespiratory fitness. Check for: Smoothly tracking weights. A sturdy, level bench. Padded levers. Steel pulleys. Coated cables.

□ Stationary cycles: For cardiovascular fitness, injury rehabilitation and lower-body strength. Check for: A rigid frame. A heavy flywheel. A seat post that can be locked into position.

□ Treadmills: For cardiovascular fitness through running or walking. Check for: Comfortable, secure footing.

□ Rowing machines: For cardiovascular fitness, all major muscle groups and injury rehabilitation. Check for: A smoothly sliding seat. A track that allows full leg extension. Oars with equal resistance. A covered flywheel.

□ Skiing machines: For cardiovascular fitness, major muscle development.

Source: *Changing Times,* Washington, DC.

Realities of exercise equipment

The sophisticated machinery that has turned old-fashioned gyms into today's health clubs is designed to offer continuous resistance during each of the movement exercises you use it for.

☐ Using machines is a much faster, more efficient way to build muscle strength than using weights.

☐ Doing all the exercises for all the muscle groups on a regular basis does not make you perfectly fit.

Strength and fitness are not equivalent. Although muscle strength is a component of fitness, you also need flexibility and heart-lung capacity. Stretching exercises make you flexible, and aerobic exercises such as running and bike riding build up your heart muscle and your lung capacity.

☐ Strengthening exercises do not turn fat into muscle. It doesn't work that way. People who are overweight need to follow a calorie-restricted diet and do aerobic exercises, which trigger the body to use up fat. Working out on machines only builds up muscle under the fat layer. However, combining a weight-loss program with strengthening exercises can improve body tone as the weight comes off.

☐ The machines are safe if you learn the proper technique for using each machine, including proper breathing, before you are allowed on the equipment alone. On the Nautilus, for example, all the straps must be secured before you start. If one is broken or missing, don't use the machine. Poor form on the machines can lead to serious injuries. So can using the wrong weight settings.

☐ Good rule of thumb: Use a weight setting that lets you do 8–12 repetitions comfortably. If you must struggle to get beyond five, the setting is too heavy. If you complete 10 without feeling any fatigue at all, it is too light. You will have to experiment with each machine to get the right setting. Then, from time to time, you can adjust the weights upward. But be cautious. Pushing yourself too hard not only invites injury, but also discourages you from sticking to the program on a regular basis.

How to pick a stationary bicycle

A good in-home stationary bicycle should be made from sturdy steel (not lightweight aluminum).

Check that it has:

☐ A comfortable, adjustable-height seat.

☐ Smoothly rotating pedals.

☐ A selector for several degrees of pedal speed and resistance (simulated "uphill" pedaling that makes your heart work harder).

☐ A heavyweight flywheel, which creates a smoother and more durable drive system.

Sophisticated electronic gadgets, such as "calories-burned" or "workload" meters are frills.

To choose the right cycle: Visit a large sporting goods store and try a variety of models. The one that works you hard and still feels comfortable is right for you.

Source: Eastside Sportsmedicine Center, New York.

How to use a stationary bicycle

To ride without pain or injury:

☐ Check with your doctor, especially if you have any heart, knee, or leg problems.

☐ Raise the seat on your cycle high enough so that in the downward position your foot just reaches the pedal with your knee slightly bent. This is the proper mechanical position for cycling.

☐ Always warm up and cool down with your bicycle set on a low resistance level. After a three- to five-minute warmup, set a constant pedal speed and increase the resistance to the level of difficulty at which you want to work. Cool down with a lower resistance setting, again for three to five minutes.

☐ When you begin a stationary bicycle program, work at 60% of your predicted maximum heart rate. If your heart is beating faster, then you are overdoing it. As you become more fit, you can work at up to 80% of your predicted maximum heart rate. But remember to keep the increase slow and gradual.

☐ Start cycling in 10-minute sessions. Then increase to 15, then 20, and then 25 or more minutes per session. Gradual increases over a period of weeks help prevent injury to muscles and joints. Once you build up your physical strength, pedal for as long as you feel comfortable.

Source: Eastside Sports Medicine Center, New York.

To get into shape for skiing

Being physically fit makes skiing more fun and helps prevent soreness and injuries. What to focus on:

☐ Muscle tone and flexibility. Stretching exercises keep your muscles long and pliable. They also warm muscles up for strenuous sports and help relax them afterward. Always stretch slowly. Hold the extended position for 20 to 30 seconds. Don't bounce.

☐ Do sit-ups with your knees bent to strengthen abdominal muscles (they can take stress off the back).

☐ Practice any active sport, from swimming to tennis, for three one-hour sessions a week.

☐ Jogging builds up the muscles of the lower torso and legs. Running downhill strengthens the front thigh muscles, essential to skiing. Running on uneven terrain promotes strong and flexible ankles. Biking builds strong legs and improves balance.

How to improve your tennis

Here are some secrets that help tennis pros on the court:

☐ Psych yourself up for a big point by triggering the adrenaline response. Here's how: Open your eyes wide and fix them on a nearby object. Breathe deeply and forcefully. Think of yourself as a powerful, aggressive individual. Exhort yourself with phrases like "Fight!" Try to raise goose bumps on your skin—they signal a high point.

☐ To switch from one type of playing surface to another, practice easing the transition. If you're moving to fast cement from slow clay, for example, practice charging the net before the switch. If it's the other way around, spend extra time on your groundstrokes.

To play well against a superior player:

☐ Suspend all expectations. Avoid thinking about the situation. Watch the ball, not the opponent.

☐ Play your game. Don't try to impress your opponent with difficult shots you normally never try.

☐ Hit the ball deep and down the middle. The more chances for your opponent to return your shot, the more chances for him to err.

☐ Concentrate on your serve. No matter how outgunned you may be, you can stay in the match if you hold your serve.

Source: *Tennis* and *World Tennis.*

How to play good singles tennis after 40

Older tennis players can win and avoid injuries by using the right strategies and techniques. Pancho Gonzales, the former champion who is now a leading Seniors player, advises playing a "thinking man's" game:

☐ When hitting, watch the ball right up to the point where it hits the strings of the racket.

☐ Aim for consistency rather than winners. Older players often hit too hard.

☐ For power and pace, shift your body weight forward on every stroke. At impact, the weight should be completely on the front foot.

☐ Anticipate your opponent. Example: If you hit a shot to your right, it will probably be returned to your left. Be ready to move left, but don't commit yourself until the ball has been hit.

☐ Get the racket back quickly and all the way before each shot.

☐ Try to swing the same way on every shot, both for consistency and for deception. Your opponent shouldn't be able to tell from the swing if the shot is hard or soft.

☐ Try to hit flat shots deep to the corners, rather than underspin slices, which provide more time for your opponent to reach the ball.

☐ Always change a losing game. Lob frequently against opponents who are dominating plays, especially if they have a winning net game. Against winning base line players, hit drop shots to force them to come in and play the net.

Save energy. Take plenty of time between points and before serving.

Work on a consistent second serve. The resulting gain of confidence will lead to improvement of the first serve.

When practicing the serve, spend time on the toss. Practice with a bucket placed where a perfect toss should fall.

Beware of the topspin serve. Though effective, it is hard on the back muscles.

Return serves as early as possible, and keep them low.

Adopt sound health and conditioning practices.

Do some weekly running and exercises. Squeeze an old tennis ball a few minutes a day to build up arm muscles, and jump rope to improve footwork.

Rest before and after playing.

Use a warmup jacket to speed the loosening of the muscles before play.

During play, run with bent knees to reduce shock to knees.

After play, apply lotion to the palm of your racket hand to keep it from scaling and blistering.

Use the right equipment for your changed style of play. Choose a flexible wood racket, which jars the arm less than a metal racket.

Try a lighter-weight racket more loosely strung.

Source: Pancho Gonzales, author of *Tennis Begins at Forty,* Dial Press, New York.

How to play better tennis doubles after 40

Here are some more hints from Pancho Gonzales:

Agree on strategy and signals with your partner before playing. Most important signal: Net players must let their partners know when they plan to cross over to intercept the return of a serve. (A clenched fist behind the back is often used.) During this move and all other moves, remember you both should be in motion...one to make the shot and the other to cover the exposed part of the court.

Agree that the weaker player should take the forehand court. This player should be assigned to serve when the wind and sun are behind the server.

Make sure the weaker player plays closer to the net. Reason: It is easier to volley in this position.

Keep in mind that one player normally concentrates on setting up shots. This person hits the ball low to force the opponents at the net to hit up on the ball.

The second player has the job of making the put-aways.

Source: Pancho Gonzales, author of *Tennis Begins at Forty,* Dial Press, New York.

Martial arts schools teach more than martial arts

The martial arts offer more than a simple exercise program. They build both physical and mental strengths. Students learn the skills to extricate themselves from dangerous situations and, if necessary, to defend themselves.

Styles and Systems

Tai Chi Chuan uses slow, graceful movements.

Karate employs powerful, focused techniques.

Judo and Aikido make use of joint locks and throws.

Finding the Right School

To get a list of schools, talk with friends and check out the ads in your local *Yellow Pages.*

Visit the schools to observe a few classes before you sign up.

Clarify your goals before you make a choice—do you want mainly a physical fitness and self-defense program, or are you interested in the mental/spiritual aspects?

What to Consider

A balanced approach to both the mental aspects (such as concentration and focus) and the physical aspects of the particular martial art.

The temper of the fighting classes, if the school has them. Make certain that care is taken to minimize injuries. Fighting is a part of most martial arts, and you should be comfortable with the school's fighting program.

☐ Thoughtful answers to your questions. If the school is evasive in its explanations, it is probably not a good bet.

☐ Instructors create the training environment of the school. Make certain they suit you. Some people like a "marine sergeant," while others might prefer a more temperate teacher.

☐ Students should be brought into the regimen slowly in a progressive process. Only as a student gets used to one style should new techniques be added to his repertory.

☐ Make sure the school accommodates different levels of athletic ability and different ages. Inflexible standards may only frustrate you.

☐ Attitudes of students. Do they encourage and help each other? Or are they bullying? The attitude of the instructor is passed on to his students.

☐ Facilities. Is there room to practice in between classes? Does the school have exercise equipment such as weights and jump ropes? Are the locker rooms big enough for the number of students? Are there showers?

☐ Schedule. If you will have a hard time getting to the workouts, you probably won't go often enough.

Source: Ken Glickman, third degree black belt and chief instructor, American Self-Defense Institute at the World Seido Karate School, New York.

How to get back in shape after 40

Americans over 40 are not very physically fit. Recent Gallup polls indicate that people are more interested in exercise than ever before…and that about 40% of adults exercise aerobically three times a week. I'd say the real number is probably closer to 15%–20%—and that's too few people exercising regularly.

The physiological benefits of regular exercise—weight loss, improved HDL (good) cholesterol, lower blood pressure, decreased coronary risk, etc.—are well known. Many people, however, are not aware of the psychological benefits of exercise. Since 1977, we've done psychological testing of all patients coming to the Cooper Aerobics Center. We've found that those who are physically fit are less depressed, have a better self-image

and a more positive attitude toward life. These people are just plain happier than their non-exercising counterparts.

Yet despite all the good reasons to do aerobic exercise, many people over 40 believe it's too tough, too risky or too late to start.

Nothing could be further from the truth. Surprisingly, even a modest increase in your present activity level can make a world of difference in your health and the overall quality of your life.

Whether you're beginning a fitness program for the first time or want to get back into shape, there are some important steps to follow—and pitfalls to avoid…

☐ Get your doctor's okay. Make sure your doctor endorses your plan. Ideally, you should first be given both a resting and a stress cardiogram. These tests should be repeated every three years or as often as your doctor recommends.

☐ Go slow. Don't rush into exercise. It may have taken you 20 years to get out of shape, and if you try to get back into shape in 20 days, it can be dangerous …and potentially fatal.

☐ Aim for just 30 minutes of sustained activity, three times a week. Even an exercise program that modest will greatly enhance your level of health and fitness.

THE PROGRAM

I've created a six-week starter program, which is ideal for men and women over 40. I have found that even people with advanced heart disease or who have had bypass surgery can follow this routine with medical supervision.

☐ Weeks 1 to 3: Walk for 15 minutes. Don't worry about how far you get, even if it's just a couple of blocks. It's best to do this the first thing in the morning—exercise tends to be most consistent when it's done before breakfast. If that's not feasible, take a brisk walk an hour or two after dinner with your spouse, a friend, or your dog. Do this three times a week, more if possible.

☐ Week 4: Walk for five more minutes, totaling 20 minutes each time.

☐ Week 5: Walk for 25 minutes each time.

☐ Week 6: Walk for 30 minutes each time. Alternatively, instead of walking for longer and longer periods, you may find it more challenging—and fun—to work on decreasing the time it takes you to cover two miles. Take it slow—at first it might require 45 minutes to complete the two miles. Gradually decrease your time to 30 minutes, three times a week, over a six-week period. Caution: Walk, don't run or jog during this phase.

If, after the end of the six weeks, you don't develop any symptoms or problems—chest pains, musculoskeletal problems—you may then want to move on to a more vigorous program of slow jogging. Aim to reduce the time it takes you to cover two miles from 30 minutes to 20 minutes. Again, do it gradually, over a six-week period. Caution: Make sure you get your doctor's okay before increasing the intensity of your exercise program.

Walking and slow jogging are the easiest and least expensive exercises. They can be done anywhere.

But you may prefer to try something else, and there are three activities—cross-country skiing, swimming, and cycling—that will produce equal, or even better, aerobic benefits.

The more varied your exercise program, the more likely you'll stick with it. It takes much more discipline to maintain the same routine month after month, year after year.

Exercise is important, but it's no panacea. I endorse a program of total wellness, including a low-fat/low-calorie diet, the elimination of smoking and stress management.

If you do just 30 minutes of sustained activity three times a week, you'll substantially reduce most major causes of death—heart attack, stroke, diabetes, and even cancer. What's more, you'll look better, feel better and dramatically improve the quality of your life.

Source: Leading fitness and health expert Kenneth H. Cooper, MD, director, Cooper Aerobics Center in Dallas.

Exercises that can harm you

The most important benefit of exercise is that, properly done, it increases longevity. But exercises that promote a single aspect of the body, such as form, stamina, coordination, speed, or strength, generally have a negative impact. Especially dangerous are:

☐ Muscle-building exercises. They can harm joints and connective tissues. Weight lifters are not known for longevity.

☐ Skill-producing activities. Ballet, handball, and squash require arduous training and stopstart patterns. Both are negatives for long life.

☐ Marathon sports. Jogging, swimming, cycling, and strenuous walking can work the body to the point of exhaustion. This is dangerous because stress and injury occur more easily during body fatigue.

☐ Speed-oriented activities. Those that require lots of oxygen, such as sprinting or speed swimming, can be fatal, especially for those who have not trained extensively for them.

Source: Dan Georgakas, author of The Methuselah Factors: The Secrets of the World's Longest-Lived Peoples, Simon & Schuster, New York.

Alternative exercises

☐ Housework (scrubbing, waxing) demands as much energy as walking three miles per hour or cycling five miles per hour.

☐ Climbing stairs equals playing doubles tennis or jogging five miles per hour.

☐ Jumping rope is equivalent to swimming 45 yards a minute or running at six miles per hour.

Source: James S. Skinner, exercise physiologist, Arizona State University, Tempe.

Fitness facts

☐ Easy fitness plan: Walk at least one mile a day at three miles per hour. Your body will thrive—and without the injury risk of running, the knee strain of bicycling, or the inconvenience of swimming. Optimal plan: Walk a mile twice a day at four miles per hour.

Source: Dr. Henry A. Solomon, a New York cardiologist, in Signature.

☐ For every week you've laid off because of illness or vacation, allow one week to return to your full exercise program.

Source: Michael L. Pollock, director of cardiac rehabilitation and sports medicine, Universal Services Rehabilitation and Development, Inc., Houston, TX, in Mademoiselle.

Exercise tips

☐ Aerobic exercise can lower mildly high blood pressure to normal within two months.

Source: Research by John E. Martin, a behavioral psychologist with the Veterans Administration Medical Center, Jackson, MS.

☐ For post-workout showers, keep the water at about body temperature. A hot shower is relaxing, but it slows circulation and leaves you sluggish. A cold shower, although bracing, can strain the heart.

Source: John Cantwell, MD, a team physician for the Atlanta Braves in *Esquire*.

☐ After a heavy workout, drink two to four glasses of water to replace lost fluids. Follow the water with a chaser of orange, apricot, pineapple, or grapefruit juice for electrolytes, potassium and added energy. If you really want a beer, drink it after a few glasses of water. Otherwise the alcohol can interrupt the release of hormones that hold water in the body. This leads to excessive urination, which can leave your body more dehydrated.

Source: *Women's Sports and Fitness*.

☐ Stationary bicycling burns off almost as many calories per hour as running. Example: 700 calories per hour for a 150-pound runner at an eight-minute-mile rate vs. 655 calories per hour for a stationary cyclist pedaling 15 miles per hour.

Source: *Maximum Personal Energy* by Charles Kuntzleman, quoted in *The Runner*.

Body building after 40

Weight training offers just as much body building, fitness and sense of well-being to the middle-aged as it does to the young. It will change the shape of your body faster than any other sport, with visible results in just six to eight weeks.

Common Myths

☐ I can't build muscle at my age. You can still "bulk up," although not as quickly.

☐ I'll hurt myself. Exercising incorrectly can lead to physical injury at any age. At midlife you do need to think more about your back, knees, and shoulders. But if you start out slowly and learn the proper techniques, weight lifting will actually help cure orthopedic problems.

(It is often used for rehabilitation.)

☐ The muscle that I build will turn to fat if I stop training. Muscle doesn't turn to fat. When you stop training you experience less energy and have to adjust your diet to take in fewer calories.

Equipment

☐ Free weights (barbells and dumb-bells): These give the quickest results but they take some time to learn properly

☐ Universal gyms: Weights and pulleys are arranged around a single large machine in "stations." Each station works a different set of muscles.

☐ Nautilus machines: These operate with a unique mechanical action geared to the natural strength curve of each working muscle group. Each machine works a single muscle group

The best weight-training programs include all three types of apparatus.

Source: Bill Reynolds, editor-in-chief of *Muscle and Fitness* magazine.

Unexpected health club hazard

Number and motility of sperm cells are decreased for up to six weeks after a dip in a hot tub.

☐ Shocking: Only one hour of soaking in water 102.4 degrees or hotter (most health clubs keep tubs at 104 degrees causes immediate harm to sperm.

☐ Fertility low point: Four weeks after bath, when sperm that were immature upon bathing mature.

☐ Remedy: Patience…sperm life span is 75 days, so all damaged sperm are replaced within that time frame.

Source: Dr. Richard Paulson of the University of Southern California School of Medicine.

Winter sports pointers

☐ Ice skating is an underrated exercise that works all your muscles. It's also easy to learn…most people can glide around the rink after three or four sessions.

☐ Skier's hazard: Sunburned corneas, caused by the sun's ultraviolet rays. (Snow reflects 85% of those rays, compared with 10% from water and 5% from grass.) Recommended: Goggles or wraparound glasses made of impact-resistant polycarbonate.

Source: Dr. Paul Vinger, a Boston ophthalmologist and eye/medical consultant to the US Olympic Committee, in *Executive Fitness Newsletter*.

The healthy gourmet

☐ Cut fat in your favorite recipes by 25% to 50%. Example: If the recipe suggests one cup of oil, try ¾ cup. If that works, try ⅔ cup the next time. In many casseroles and soups try eliminating butter or margarine completely.

☐ Instead of sautéing vegetables in oil or butter, add several tablespoonfuls of water or broth and steam them in a covered pot.

☐ Compensate for lost fat flavor by adding spices and herbs.

☐ Use skim or low-fat milk instead of whole milk…evaporated skim milk instead of cream.

☐ In sauces that call for cheese, stick to grated Parmesan or Romano (about 25 calories per tablespoonful).

☐ Rather than starting sauces with a fatty "roux," add cold milk or fruit juice to the flour or cornstarch.

☐ Substitute veal, skinless poultry, or flank or round steak for fat-marbled cuts of beef.

☐ Slice meats thinly and add more vegetables to the meal.

Source: *Tufts University Diet & Nutrition Letter*, New York.

How to reduce the fat in your food

☐ Sauté vegetables in a few tablespoonfuls of soup stock rather than in fat.

☐ Sauté and fry foods less often. Steam, broil, bake, and poach instead.

☐ For salads and cooking, use corn, safflower or olive oil—sparingly.

☐ Substitute egg whites or tofu for egg yolks.

☐ Use low-fat yogurt instead of sour cream or mayonnaise.

☐ Try low-fat cheeses such as part-skim mozzarella in recipes.

☐ Use ground turkey or crumbled tofu in place of ground beef.

☐ Thicken cream-style corn with a mashed potato or uncooked oatmeal.

☐ Replace nut butters with bean spread for sandwiches and snack dips.

Source: *Medical Self-Care*, Inverness, CA.

To protect your immune system

Your immune system is made up of white blood cells. To give optimal protection, these cells should be working 24 hours a day. They're directly affected by the quality of food you eat,* the way you behave, and the nature of your thoughts.

Dangers to the immune system:

☐ Excessive sugar.

☐ Inadequate protein.

☐ Inadequate zinc, iron, or manganese.

☐ Inadequate Vitamin C or Vitamin E.

☐ Diet and psychology are intimately related. Be especially cautious during times of stress, bereavement, sorrow, and trauma. They often translate into suppression of the immune function.

☐ Monitor magnesium intake. Most people don't get enough magnesium in their diets. And a magnesium deficiency can create anxiety symptoms. The minimum amount necessary is usually 300 to 500 milligrams a day. Under conditions of high stress, you would need more magnesium (since it's utilized very rapidly at such times). Best sources: Green leafy vegetables, lean meat, whole grains.

☐ Exercise enhances the function of your immune system by reducing stress.

☐ Examine your expectations about health. Do you expect, and accept, a couple of bouts with colds or flu each year? Instead, focus on strengthening your immune system. Sickness a couple of times a year is inevitable only if your immune system has been compromised.

*The amount of nutrients you need is best determined on an individual basis. To find out how much you need, consult a physician who specializes in disease prevention. Also useful: *Nutrition Against Disease* by Dr. Roger Williams, Bantam Books, New York.

Source: Jeffrey Bland, Linus Pauling Institute of Science and Medicine, Palo Alto, CA and author of *Nutraerobics*, Harper & Row, New York.

All calories aren't equal

Dieters myth: A calorie is a calorie is a calorie. Reality: Fat calories are more fattening than carbohydrate calories. A single fat calorie has a greater chance of being converted into body fat than a single carbohydrate calorie.

☐ Reason: The body burns up 25 of every 100 carbohydrate calories converting them into fat—net gain, 75 calories. But it burns up only 3 calories of every 100 fat calories—net gain, 97 calories.

Source: Dr. Jean-Pierre Flatt, of the University of Massachusetts Medical School.

Dr. Dean Ornish clears up the confusion over cholesterol

Despite all that's been said and written about cholesterol in recent years, many Americans remain understandably confused on the topic. While most of us know that too much cholesterol in the bloodstream can cause heart disease, many people remain unclear on certain subtle but very important issues…

What's a healthy cholesterol level? For years, the American Heart Association and the National Institutes of Health have recommended an optimal total serum cholesterol level of less than 200 milligrams per deciliter.

But we now know that roughly one-third of all heart attacks occur in individuals with cholesterol readings between 150 and 200. In fact, only when cholesterol falls to 150 or lower does heart disease cease to be a meaningful risk.

Unfortunate: The average American has a cholesterol level around 220… and the average American develops heart disease.

What about "good" and "bad" cholesterol? Total serum cholesterol is made up of two different compounds—low-density lipoprotein (LDL) cholesterol …and high-density lipoprotein (HDL) cholesterol.

☐ LDL (bad) cholesterol forms fatty plaques inside your coronary arteries, which can lead to heart attack.

☐ HDL (good) cholesterol is what the body uses to remove excess LDL from the bloodstream.

Doctors sometimes use the ratio of total cholesterol to HDL as another means of gauging heart-disease risk.

Example: Someone with a total cholesterol count of 200 and an HDL level of 50 has a ratio of 200/50 or 4:1. In general, a ratio of 3.5 (200/57 is 3.5:1) or lower puts you at minimal risk for heart disease. The lower the ratio, the lower the risk—at least for people eating a traditional fatty, cholesterol-rich diet.

Exception: Vegetarians and others on a very low-fat, low-cholesterol diet with less than 10% fat and virtually no cholesterol. Because they consume less fat and cholesterol and thus have less LDL in their blood, their bodies don't need to make as much HDL. Consequently, they may have high ratios yet they have a reduced risk of heart disease.

What causes high cholesterol? The single biggest factor is simply eating too much saturated fat and cholesterol. In fact, in the traditional American diet, roughly 40% of calories come from fat…and foods rich in fat are often rich in cholesterol. In countries where people eat much less cholesterol and less fat and where cholesterol averages around 130, heart disease is very rare.

Eating too much fat causes not only heart disease, but also has been linked with cancers of the breast, prostate, and colon, as well as stroke, diabetes, osteoporosis and, of course, obesity.

There is a genetic variability in how efficiently or inefficiently your body can metabolize, or get rid of, dietary saturated fat and cholesterol. On one end of the spectrum, some people are so efficient that they can eat almost anything and not get heart disease. On the other end of the spectrum are people who may get heart disease no matter what they eat. Ninety-five percent of people are somewhere in the middle. If your cholesterol level is less than 150, then either you're not eating very much fat and cholesterol or your body is very efficient at getting rid of it. Either way, your risk is low.

If it's above 150, begin by moderately reducing the amount of fat and cholesterol in your diet. If that's enough to bring it down below 150, that may be all you need to do, at least as far as your heart is concerned. If not, then continue to reduce the fat and cholesterol in your diet until your cholesterol stays below 150…or you are following a low-fat vegetarian reversal diet.

Which foods contain cholesterol? All foods derived from animals, including meats, poultry, fish, and dairy products. Meat is also high in iron, which oxidizes cholesterol into a form that more quickly clogs arteries. Skim milk has almost no fat and virtually no cholesterol. "Low-fat" milk is not really very low in fat. Foods derived solely from plants contain no cholesterol.

Caution: Some plant foods, including avocados, nuts, seeds and oils, are rich in saturated fat.

Just because a food is "cholesterol-free" doesn't mean it's good for your heart. All oils are 100% fat, and all oils contain at least some saturated fat, which your liver converts into cholesterol.

How often should I have my cholesterol checked? About once every two years, starting as early as age two. To insure a reliable reading: Find a testing lab certified by the Lipid Research Clinics. Use the same laboratory each time. Be sure to fast* for at least 12 hours prior to your test.

How can I get my cholesterol under control? Exercise—it raises HDL cholesterol.

Stress raises LDL cholesterol, as does eating a high-fat, cholesterol-rich diet.

So the best way to raise HDL and lower LDL is to get regular exercise, avoid smoking, practice meditation or other stress-management techniques and eat a healthful diet.

If you have heart disease: Eliminate all animal products except egg whites and nonfat dairy products…and all high-fat vegetable products, including oils, nuts, seeds, avocados, chocolate and other cocoa products, olives and coconut. In most cases this "reversal" diet not only keeps heart disease from progressing, but also reverses its course.

Eat more vegetables, fish, and skinless chicken. Use skim milk instead of whole milk. Use as little cooking oil as possible. Avoid oil-based salad dressing. If after eight weeks your cholesterol remains high, go on the "reversal" diet.

What about cholesterol-lowering drugs? I prescribe cholesterol-lowering drugs for people with heart disease who make only moderate changes in diet and lifestyle. Why? Several studies have shown that people with heart disease who only follow the American Heart Association guidelines tend to show worsening of their disease. People who follow the reversal diet—or who take cholesterol-lowering drugs—often can stop or reverse heart disease. Diet is preferable, because you avoid the high costs and side effects (both known and unknown) of drugs.

Source: Dean Ornish, MD, assistant clinical professor of medicine and an attending physician at the School of Medicine, University of California, San Francisco and at California Pacific Medical Center. He is the author of *Dr. Dean Ornish's Program for Reversing Heart Disease.* Ballantine Books, 201 E. 50 St., New York 10022.

How to read nutrition labels

Cutting down on cholesterol, sugar and salt requires a close reading of nutritional labels.

A simplified guide to understanding the fine print:

☐ Ingredients: They are listed in descending order, according to their weight.

☐ Sugar: Whether it's called sugar, dextrose, sucrose, corn sweetener, corn syrup, invert sugar, honey, or molasses, the food has little nutritive value if it's among the first three ingredients. When listed as a minor ingredient, a combination of two or more sugars may mean a hefty sugar count.

☐ Cholesterol: Avoid coconut and palm oil. They are more saturated than animal fats. Nonspecified vegetable oils frequently mean palm or coconut. When purchasing margarine, choose the brand with liquid vegetable oil as the primary ingredient. It contains less saturated fat.

☐ Salt: While sodium levels are not shown on many ingredient lists, look for brands that list sodium by milligrams. Rule of thumb: No one should consume much over 4,000 milligrams of sodium daily. Those on restricted diets should have considerably less than that amount.

Cholesterol basics

Results of an exhaustive, 10-year National Heart, Lung and Blood Institute study have put to rest any doubts about the links between high blood cholesterol levels and heart disease.

*Drinking water is OK.

For most Americans, careful diet can keep cholesterol in control, particularly the dangerous low-density-lipoprotein (LDL) cholesterol. Keys: Cut cholesterol consumption to 300 milligrams or less per day. Keep the percentage of calories from fats to 30% or less of the daily intake. Substitute polyunsaturated fats for saturated fats in the diet.*

☐ No foods that come from plant sources contain cholesterol.

☐ The most concentrated sources of edible cholesterol are egg yolks (one yolk from a large egg has 252 mg), and organ meats (three ounces of calf's liver has 372 mg).

Bacon (2 slices)	15
Beef (3 oz. lean)	77
Beef kidney (3 oz.)	315
Butter (1 tbsp.)	35
Cheese (1 oz. cheddar)	30
Chicken (3 oz. light meat, no skin)	65
Cottage cheese (½ cup 4% fat)	24
Cottage cheese (½ cup 1% fat)	12
Cream (1 tbsp. heavy)	21
Flounder (3 oz.)	69
Haddock (3 oz.)	42
Ice cream (½ cup)	27
Milk (1 cup skim)	5
Milk (1 cup whole)	34
Pork (3 oz. lean)	75
Salmon (4 oz. canned)	40
Sardines (3 oz.)	119
Turkey (3 oz. light meat, no skin)	65
Yogurt (1 cup lowfat)	17

While many fats per se have no cholesterol content, certain types of fats actually raise the cholesterol levels in the blood even if the rest of the diet contains very little cholesterol.

☐ Saturated fats. You can recognize these by their tendency to harden at room temperature. They contribute most to a buildup of LDL cholesterol. They include meat fats, butter, chicken fat, coconut and palm oils, vegetable shortening and even some margarines (read the label).

☐ Monounsaturated fats. These play a more neutral role in cholesterol chemistry, although, like all fats, they should be eaten in moderation. These are the fats found in avocados, cashews, olives and olive oil, peanuts and peanut oil.

☐ Polyunsaturated fats. When kept to a limited part of the total diet, these actually lower the amount of LDL cholesterol in the blood. Good fats: Corn oil, cottonseed oil, safflower oil, soybean oil, sunflower oil, and fats from

*Recommendations of the American Heart Association.

nuts such as almonds, pecans and walnuts.

☐ If you are overweight, reducing will lower your cholesterol level.

☐ Certain fiber foods such as carrots, apples, oats and soybeans also help reduce cholesterol.

☐ Aerobic exercise can cut down the percentage of LDL cholesterol in the blood.

The right middle-age diet

It's not too late to change the eating habits of a lifetime when you reach middle age. As a matter of fact, it's probably a necessity because of the changes the body is going through at that time. Most obvious change: Slowing of the metabolic rate. Individuals who don't reduce their caloric intake after age 45 commonly gain 10 pounds a year, regardless of the amount of exercise they do. It takes 12 hours of tennis to burn off 3,500 calories, roughly equivalent to one pound.

☐ Steak is highly caloric, and its fat content has been linked to coronary disease and colon cancer, two potentially fatal disorders that plague older people. Chicken and fish are more healthful alternative sources of proteins.

☐ Because bones begin to grow progressively brittle after age 30, the body needs more calcium. But this important mineral can be absorbed effectively only by reducing the intake of protein (from meats) and phosphorous (from carbonated soft drinks). To prevent the brittle-bone problem, a calcium supplement of one gram a day is recommended by most nutritionists.

☐ Because many older people secrete less hydrochloric acid, they have difficulty absorbing iron and, therefore, are more vulnerable to pernicious anemia. The best source of iron is meat, especially liver. But to avoid eating too much meat, you should turn to iron-fortified foods, especially cereals. Absorption of iron is helped by intakes of vitamin C, which is abundant in citrus fruits, broccoli, kale, red peppers and brussels sprouts. For some older people, taking an iron supplement may be necessary.

☐ The bodies of older people often

have trouble absorbing vitamin B-12, which can actually be destroyed in the body by large doses of vitamin C. B-12 deficiency can lead to anemia, particularly among vegetarians, because the vitamin is found exclusively in animal products (especially liver) and shellfish. Multivitamin supplements may be needed to insure that you are getting the right amount of each vitamin.

☐ Digestive problems associated with aging make fiber especially important to persons over 45. Sources: Whole grains, fruits, vegetables.

☐ Although all the evidence is not yet in, most nutritionists advise against taking vitamin megadoses. In the case of vitamins A and D, megadoses are highly dangerous. Exception: Vitamin E, large doses of which may help with colon cancer and the painful blood vessel spasms in the legs that older people often experience. Even with this vitamin, consult a physician before considering taking megadoses.

Source: Dr. Brian Morgan, Institute of Human Nutrition, Columbia University College of Physicians & Surgeons.

8 ounces of milk

Types of milk vary in taste, fat content and nutritional value. Here's the breakdown:

☐ Buttermilk: 90 calories, two grams of fat. Easily digested, since active bacteria break down the milk sugars.

☐ Dry nonfat milk: 80 calories, less than one gram of fat. As nutritious as whole milk, but with a flat taste.

☐ Low-fat (2%) milk: 120 to 140 calories, five grams of fat. A good choice when fat restriction is important but calories are secondary.

☐ Skim (nonfat) milk: 80 calories, less than one gram of fat. Best for dieters and those on a strict low-fat diet.

☐ Whole milk: 150 to 180 calories, eight grams of fat. Best only for children under two years old.

Source: Berkeley Wellness Letter, published by the University of California, Des Moines, IA.

How to get along without cream and mayonnaise

Fat is the enemy of both the heart and the waistline. Learn to substitute yogurt and other low-fat milk products. They are tasty as well as healthy.

Yogurt

☐ Thicken commercial yogurt. Line a sieve with a paper coffee filter and place it over a bowl. Pour in the yogurt and let it drain until it is the consistency you want…that of light, heavy or sour cream.

☐ Use the drained yogurt as a base for any dip that originally called for sour cream. (If the yogurt seems too thick, beat a little of the drained whey back into it.)

☐ In cooking or baking, replace each cup of cream or sour cream with ¾ cup of drained yogurt mixed with 1 tablespoonful of cornstarch. The yogurt should be at room temperature.

☐ In dishes such as beef Stroganoff, where the yogurt-cornstarch mixture replaces sour cream, fold it gently into the beef at the last minute…and let it just heat through.

Basic Recipes

☐ Light mayonnaise: Mix ⅓ cup thickened yogurt into ⅔ cup mayonnaise.

☐ Light salad dressing: Mix ⅔ cup slightly thickened yogurt into ⅓ cup mayonnaise.

☐ Mock sour cream dressing*: Mix 1 cup drained low-fat yogurt with 2 tablespoonfuls of wine vinegar. Add a dash of sugar (or substitute), a bit of garlic powder, and ¼ cup vegetable oil. Mix and chill.

Other Good Substitutions

☐ Replace the cream in cream soups with buttermilk, which is satisfyingly rich, yet low in calories. To eliminate any hint of buttermilk's slightly acidic taste, add a liberal amount of mild curry powder.

☐ Mix 1 cup skim milk with ½ cup dry skim milk. Add to soup to thicken it. This works with all cream soups, including vichyssoise.

*The Low-Cholesterol Food Processor Cookbook by Suzanne S. Jones, Doubleday, Garden City, NY.

Just when you thought it was safe to eat salt…

The vast majority of foods sold in stores are laden with salt. Since we've eaten these foods for most of our lives, we're conditioned to expect the taste of heavily salted foods.

To cut down on salt intake:

☐ Reduce salt gradually. When people are abruptly placed on a very low-sodium diet, they develop cravings for salt that cause them to revert to their former eating habits. But a gradual reduction of salt will change your taste for salt…so much so that food salted to its previous level will taste unpleasant. Time: Allow up to three months to adjust to a salt-free diet.

☐ Keep daily records of the amount of sodium you eat. This is now relatively easy because federal law requires most grocery store foods to be labeled for sodium content. A pocket calculator is sometimes useful as you shop, but don't think you'll have to keep count for the rest of your life. After a couple of months, separating high from low-sodium foods will be almost automatic.

☐ Substitute other flavor enhancers, especially herbs and spices.

☐ If you have children, start now to condition their taste by not feeding them salty foods. For the first time, low-sodium baby food is now on the market.

Source: Dr. Cleaves M. Bennett, clinical professor, University of California at Los Angeles, and author of *Control Your High Blood Pressure Without Drugs*, Doubleday, New York.

Tasty, low-salt, low-fat cooking

If your doctor puts you on a no-salt, modified fat, cholesterol and sugar diet, with limited alcohol consumption, you might feel as though you're in a gastronomic straitjacket. However, the benefits are enormous—no more edema, a reduction in blood pressure, considerable weight loss and a feeling of well-being—and you can increase your food intake without increasing your weight.

Basics of the Diet

Do use:

☐ Low-sodium cheeses.

☐ Seltzer.

☐ Trimmed meat.

☐ Stews and pan drippings skimmed of all fat.

☐ Fish, poultry without skin, veal and lamb.

Don't use:

☐ Eggs, except those used in food preparation.

☐ Sugar. Drinks made with sweet liqueurs. Soft drinks.

☐ Canned or packaged foods.

☐ Sodas with high salt content.

☐ Rich and/or salty products—bacon, gravies, shellfish, organ meats, most desserts except fruit and fruit ices.

Tricks to Fool the Taste

☐ The sweet-and-sour principle. A touch (sometimes as little as half a teaspoonful) of sugar and a dash of vinegar can add the sweet-and-sour flavor needed to fool the palate.

☐ Garlic. Essential in salad dressings and tomato sauces. Use it with rosemary to transform broiled chicken, broiled fish or roast lamb.

☐ Fine or coarse black pepper. When broiling and roasting meats and chicken, use as much as a table-spoonful for a welcome flavor. Use a moderate amount in soups, stews and casseroles (the pungent nature of pepper will not diminish in these as it will with broiling and roasting).

☐ Crushed hot red pepper flakes. A good flavor distraction or flavor addition. Not for every palate.

☐ Curry powder. Use judiciously and without a large number of other spices. Combine it only with a bay leaf, green pepper, garlic or black pepper. Add smaller amounts for rice, more for poultry or meat.

☐ Chili powder. Similar to curry, but you might want to add more cumin, oregano or garlic. Also try paprika, ground cori-ander, ground hot chilis. They're good with almost any dish made with tomatoes.

☐ Homemade hot-mustard paste. Dry mustard and water does wonders for salad dressing and grilled foods.

☐ Freshly grated horseradish. Goes well with fish or plain yogurt.

☐ Bottled green peppercorns. A wel-come touch for bland foods.

☐ Plain boiled or steamed rice, cold yogurt relish, chutneys and other sweet relishes are a good foil for spicy dishes.

Cooking Techniques

☐ Charcoal broiling helps compensate for lack of salt.

☐ Steaming is preferable for fish and better than boiling for vegetables.

☐ No-salt soups are difficult to make palatable. Solution: A stockpot going on the back of the stove, to which you add bones, cooking liquid, vegetables. The more concentrated the broth, the greater the depth of flavor. Use only the freshest, ripest vegetables.

Source: Craig Claiborne, food critic.

"Good" foods that can be bad for you

☐ Blood-sugar-sensitive types who experience a temporary lift from sugar followed by fatigue should be cautious about fruit juice intake. Six ounces of apple juice contain the equivalent of more than five teaspoonfuls of sugar— 40% more sugar than a chocolate bar. Recommended: Eat a whole apple or orange instead of drinking juice. The fiber dilutes the sugar impact. Alternative: Eat cheese, nuts or other protein with juice.

☐ Nondairy cream substitutes, often used by those on low-fat diets, usually contain coconut oil, which has a higher fat content than most dairy products.

☐ Decaffeinated coffee can lead to significant stomach acid secretion, causing heartburn and indigestion in many persons. Caffeine was assumed to be the culprit. A new study shows that decaffeinated coffee is even worse. The effect is seen in doses as small as a half cup of decaffeinated coffee. People experiencing ulcer symptoms, heartburn and dyspepsia should avoid decaffeinated as well as regular coffee.

☐ Most commercial products billed as alternatives to salt are based on potassium chloride. Problem: Although potassium chloride does enhance flavor, it leaves a slightly bitter or metallic taste. And excessive potassium may be as bad for your health as too much salt. Alternatives to the alternatives: Mrs. Dash, a commercial blend of 14 herbs and spices; Lite Salt, a half-sodium, half-potassium blend. Or try adding parsley.

☐ One of the few proven substances that can bring on flare-ups of acne is iodine. Excessive, long-term intake of iodine (a natural ingredient of many foods) can bring on acne in anyone, but for people who are already prone to the condition, iodine is especially damaging. Excess is excreted through the oil glands of the skin, a process that irritates the pores and causes eruptions and inflammation. Major sources of iodine in the diet: Iodized table salt, kelp, beef liver, asparagus, turkey, and vitamin and mineral supplements.

☐ Chronic diarrhea, gas and other stomach complaints are often linked to lactose intolerance, the inability to digest milk. One of every four adults suffers from this problem. Their bodies don't make enough lactase, the enzyme that breaks down milk sugar in the intestinal tract. Among the offending foods: Milk, ice cream, chocolate, soft cheese, some yogurts, and sherbet. Lactose is also used as a filler in gum, candies and many canned goods.

☐ People on low-sodium diets should check out tap water as a source of salt intake. Some local water systems have eight times the amount of sodium (20 milligrams per quart) that people with heart problems or hypertension should use.

☐ Health-food candy is really no better for you than traditional sweets. Comparison: Health-food candy often contains about the same number of calories. The fat content is often as high or higher. Bars made of carob are caffeine free, but the amount of caffeine in chocolate is negligible. And the natural sugars in health bars have no nutritional advantage over refined sugars.

Source: *Journal of the American Medical Association*, Chicago; *Dr. Fulton's Step-By-Step Program for Clearing Acne*, by J. E. Fulton, Jr., M.D., and E. Black, Harper & Row, New York; *The Sodium Content of Your Food*, Consumer Information Center, Co.

Best whole-grain breakfast cereals

Whole-grained breakfast cereals are a rich source of protein, vitamins, minerals and fiber. Bonus: They have relatively low percentages of cholesterol, fat and calories. Added bonus: Often the cheapest cereals are the best nutritionally.

What to look for:

☐ Cereals in which the first listed ingredient is a whole grain—whole-grain wheat, oats (rolled or flour), whole corn kernels or bran.

☐ Cereals with three or more grams of protein per serving.

☐ Avoid cereals with sugar or other sweeteners (honey, corn syrup, fructose) as a main ingredient. Guide:

Four grams of sugar equals one teaspoonful.

☐ Also avoid: Cereals with dried fruits. They are concentrated sources of sugar. Best: Add your own fruits.

Caffeine facts

☐ Low doses of caffeine can increase alertness and motor ability, reduce drowsiness and lessen fatigue. Small to moderate amounts of caffeine pose no health danger, according to the Clinical Nutrition Section of Boston's University Hospital. Heavy doses produce ill effects—nervousness, anxiety, irritability, headache, muscle twitch, and insomnia.

☐ Tolerance to caffeine varies widely from person to person. Two cups of caffeine-rich coffee make some people nervous. Others cannot survive the day without several cups. Most sensitive to caffeine's effects: Children and the elderly.

☐ The caffeine quantity in coffee depends on how it is brewed. The drip method produces a higher caffeine content than the percolator. Instant coffee contains much less caffeine than brewed coffee. Tea contains half as much caffeine as coffee, and cola drinks have even less.

How much is too much: Four cups of coffee a day (500 milligrams of caffeine) is a heavy dose for most people.

☐ There is no evidence that caffeine is a causal factor in either arteriosclerosis or heart attacks.

☐ Caffeine does not increase the blood pressure of regular users.

☐ Caffeine does not seem to be a cancer hazard, but other compounds (found in negligible amounts) in beverage coffee are known carcinogens in animals.

☐ Caffeine is a much less important factor than cigarette smoking in heart disease, hypertension, bladder cancer, peptic ulcers, and cystic breast disease.

☐ Caffeine stimulates the central nervous system and can help reduce boredom from repetitive tasks. It increases the body's muscle strength.

☐ Caffeine can relieve certain types of headaches by dilating blood vessels and reducing muscle tension.

Source: American Council of Science and Health, Summit, NJ.

Caffeine count

☐ A five-ounce cup of drip-brewed coffee contains 146 milligrams of caffeine.

☐ Regular instant coffee has 53.

☐ Decaffeinated coffee has 2.

☐ Most soft drinks range between 33 and 44. (Diet citrus drinks, root beer, ginger ale and tonic water contain little or no caffeine.)

☐ A one-minute brew of tea has half the caffeine of a five-minute brew. (Steeping for five minutes can take a cup to 50 mg., depending on the leaf used.)

☐ Exceptionally high in caffeine: Non-prescriptive stimulants. The average dose is 200 mg. Even higher, diuretics and weight-control drugs.

Long-term weight loss

The diet mentality just doesn't work when it comes to long-term weight loss. The straitjacket approach will probably backfire as soon as you go off the strict regimen. To be successful, you have to analyze your eating habits and change them gradually.

First, look at what's going on when you're eating. Awareness is all-important. Start keeping a daily food diary, and review it after a week:

☐ Where did you eat? Do you have food stashed in your car's glove compartment, in your nightstand and in your desk at work? Maybe you eat in too many places. Best: Keep food only in the kitchen.

☐ What position were you in while eating? Do you eat while standing up in the kitchen, lying in bed, sitting in front of the TV, or at your office desk? Learn to eat only when sitting at the table.

☐ With whom did you eat? Food can be a crutch for social interactions, such as business lunches or family dinners. If you pinpoint such times, you can learn to deal with them.

☐ What was your emotional state while eating? Were you feeling anger, stress, etc.? Did you feel the need for security, protection or comfort? Find out what food means to you.

☐ Were there any visual cues associated with eating? Some of us eat when the clock says noon, rather than waiting until we're hungry. If you eat at noon every day, put lunch off for half an hour and see what happens.

❏ What was your eating style? Paradoxically, many overeaters don't really savor their food. They gulp it down quickly, as if they wanted to get the process over with. Practice eating slowly. Taste each bite and savor each flavor. If you pace your eating, you'll consume less but enjoy it more.

❏ Did any practical factors influence your eating? Were you late for work, missing breakfast in the process? Did you eat an enormous lunch instead? Did you overeat when you came home from work because you were too busy for lunch? Rearrange your schedule to permit planned, unhurried meals.

Making Realistic Changes

❏ After you became aware of how, when and why you eat, start making some behavioral changes in ways that you find most comfortable:

❏ Don't avoid food—manage it. There are no "good" foods or "bad" foods. You can eat small amounts of those favorite foods of yours that are forbidden by traditional diets—but be in control.

❏ Pay attention to portion size. We tend to use restaurant-portion sizes as a gauge. But restaurants serve much larger portions, especially of entrees, than most people really need. Suggested portions: Three ounces of meat, fish, or chicken, rather than the customary six to eight ounces.

❏ Pay attention to quality. You might just be satisfied with one small piece of Swiss chocolate as with two cheap candy bars. Half a glass of really fine wine goes a long way. A tablespoonful of real Vermont maple syrup on French toast is a pleasant substitute for drowning it in an inexpensive syrup. Develop a discriminating palate. Bonus: Quality foods will make you feel you're treating rather than depriving yourself.

❏ Keep in mind that spices don't have calories. Use garlic, pepper, vinegar, curry and other herbs and spices liberally and creatively to add sparkle to your meals.

❏ Be creative. Today's markets offer a multitude of products that are low in calories even though they're not in the diet-food section. Suggestions: Exotic fruits and vegetables. Whole-grain bread products (they're tasty, and have more fiber and fewer calories than white bread).

❏ Make imaginative substitutions. For example, vanilla yogurt flavored with cinnamon and nutmeg is as good as fruit yogurt and has 50 fewer calories. Half an English muffin with mozzarella cheese and tomato sauce toasted under the broiler is a delicious pizza substitute.

Source: Janet K. Grommet, a doctor of nutrition and administrator of the weight control unit (a pioneer in treating obesity) at St. Luke's–Roosevelt Hospital Center, New York.

How to get thin and stay thin forever

Just about everyone knows how to lose weight—most people have successfully slimmed down at some time in their lives. Unfortunately, the vast majority regain the weight they've worked so hard to lose because they never learned how to keep the excess pounds from creeping back on.

Overweight isn't just unattractive—it can kill. More than 20 years ago, after seeing my parents and sister die of weight-related illnesses, I decided it wasn't going to happen to me, and I lost 40 pounds. And…I never regained the weight because I developed and followed five principles of weight control. They will work for anybody, regardless of your present weight or age, or the number of times you've dieted in the past…

1. Take responsibility. You made yourself fat—nobody else did it—and you can make yourself thin. You don't have gland problems…you have eating problems.

2. Make a plan before you take the plunge…to maximize your chances for success. You want this to be the last time you have to lose weight. Carefully consider how you're going to accomplish that—what you will and will not eat, what your exercise program will be and how often you will work out. Opt for a sensible, varied menu. Avoid what I call the one-sided diets—for example, eating only cottage cheese or only carbohydrates. You'll get bored quickly and lose motivation.

Helpful: Don't think of this as a diet. The trouble with diets is that they begin and end…and once they end, you usually return to the eating patterns that got you overweight to begin with. Choose a program you can follow comfortably forever.

3. Play the trade-off game. If you know

you'll be going out to a special restaurant tonight, then eat a little less than usual at breakfast and lunch. "Bank" your food by eating carefully during the week so that you can have cake and champagne at your friend's wedding Saturday night.

Your biggest—and best—trade-off: Swapping the instant gratification of eating something now for the long-term pleasure of a slimmer body.

Caution: Never skip meals. You'll be hungry—and that may lead to a binge.

4. Go slow. Plan so that you deliberately lose your weight at a moderate pace—one to two pounds per week is best. If you see that you're dropping more than that each week, add extra food to your diet, no matter how hard that may be for you. It will help you learn to moderate your intake so you don't fall back to the quick loss/quick regain patterns of the past.

5. Have your favorites…in moderation. Never let yourself feel deprived—this is your life, not just a quickie diet. Once a day, eat something that really gives you food satisfaction. Knowing you'll permit yourself four french fries at lunch or one chocolate-chip cookie after dinner can actually keep you in control all day long.

You'll notice that I never specifically say what you should and shouldn't eat. That's because you know what foods— and in what quantities—made you overweight, and which ones will make you thin.

Far more important than a particular menu plan, you need mental preparedness to lose the weight and keep it off. I'm convinced that once you're psychologically ready to slim down, any sensible food plan will work for you.

And…

☐ Dine…don't just eat. You can feast on a piece of grilled meat or poultry and sautéed vegetables, served on good china…or you can eat your tuna fish right out of the can. Make mealtime a pleasure, especially if your servings are smaller than usual.

☐ Eat as well as your budget allows…and you won't be tempted to overeat. Whenever I've had a particularly bad meal, my first thought is usually: Thank goodness, there's ice cream in the freezer! That won't happen if you make the best food choices that you can afford. You can enjoy lobster and shrimp, exotic fresh fruit, luscious sorbets…and

much more. Nobody says that you have to live solely on cottage cheese and lettuce. You can eat very well, feel totally satisfied…and still lose weight.

☐ Don't let your business meals be an excuse to binge. Focus on the business, not on the food. Get to know the maitre d' at one or two of your favorite restaurants and ask to be served the same low-calorie/low-fat meal each time. Or just make sensible choices— there's a pasta-and-veggies or grilled-fish dish on most menus.

☐ Avoid "diet" foods—sugar-free candies, low-cal frozen meals, etc. They taste mediocre at best and take away from the joy of living.

☐ Make exercise a part of your life. It's possible to lose weight without exercising, but it will take longer and be a lot harder. If you hate the idea of exercise, change your perception of what exercise is. Try thinking of it as something prescribed by your doctor, or as a new challenge for yourself. The most pleasant and easy-to-do exercise for nearly everyone: Walking.

Helpful: Instead of making a drink or dinner date, plan a "walking date" with a friend. You'll both appreciate the shift from food to fitness.

Bottom Line

The most important thing about losing weight is not how fast you can get thin, but how long you can *stay* thin. Take your time losing weight and do it sensibly—and you may never have to diet again.

Source: Carole Livingston, author of *I'll Never Be Fat Again!*, Barricade Books/Publishers Group West, 4065 Hollis, Emeryville, California 94608.

Artificial sweeteners and weight gain

Women who use artificial sweeteners gain more weight—and put it on more quickly—than women who don't.

Theory: Artificial sweeteners cause the body to crave sugar by stimulating those receptors on the tongue.

Source: Survey of 80,000 women conducted for the American Cancer Society, reported in *The Walking Magazine*, 711 Boylston St., Boston 02116.

Expert views of artificial sweeteners

Scientific opinion varies both about the advisability of using artificial sweeteners and about which ones are safe and which aren't.

◻ Using artificial sweeteners simply perpetuates your sweet tooth and doesn't teach you to like less sweet foods. There are too many tempting foods that will never be made with an artificial sweetener, such as pecan pie, imported chocolate or even most ice creams. If you don't reduce your sugar cravings across the board, you'll always be vulnerable to the temptation of calorie-laden sweets.

◻ No artificial sweetener has ever been proved to help people really lose weight or to help diabetics control their disease.

◻ Laboratory tests of aspartame show that it changes the level of neurotransmitters in the brain (crucial chemicals that carry nerve messages from one cell to another). Its effect on behavior and intelligence isn't really known. Phenylalanine, one of its breakdown chemicals, is known to cause mental retardation when used in large quantities, and perhaps it is dangerous to those who are sensitive to it. There have been hundreds of reports to the FDA from people who claim that aspartame has caused all kinds of neurological symptoms, including dizziness, depression and headaches. Although the FDA has dismissed these reports as inconsequential, the Centers for Disease Control have analyzed them and suggested that they require more careful clinical analysis.

◻ Aspartame poses the additional hazard of breaking down into dangerous substances when heated. Although instructions say to use it only in cold foods, people are bound to try it in hot foods such as coffee.

Choosing the right sweeteners

◻ It is a myth that brown sugar and raw sugar (unrefined sugar) are more healthful than white (refined) sugar. Nor is turbinado, a partially refined sugar, any more nutritious than the others.

◻ The corn sweeteners—dextrose, corn syrup and high-fructose corn sweetener (HFCS)—are all refined from corn starch and are as nutritiously bankrupt as cane and beet sugars.

◻ Maple sap straight from the tree is only 3% sucrose (and quite delicious), but the syrup made from boiling down the sap is 65% sucrose. Imitation maple syrup is 97% sucrose. Although pure maple syrup contains some calcium and potassium, it is not a prime source of either.

◻ Blackstrap molasses (made from sugar cane) and sorghum (made from the sorghum plant) have varying amounts of iron, calcium, potassium and B vitamins. The darker the color, the better the nutrition.

◻ Honey has small amounts of minerals and vitamins.

Better Choices

◻ Vegetables such as parsnips, carrots, winter squash and beets have 4%–9% sucrose plus fiber, vitamins and minerals.

◻ Fresh fruits have 10% to 25% fructose and glucose, plus fiber, vitamins and minerals. Dried fruits are much sweeter, but they do contain iron.

◻ Date sugar (dried and crushed date particles) can be substituted for other sugars in baking. Use half as much date sugar as the recipe calls for in regular sugar. Grind it in a coffee mill or food processor to get a smooth consistency. You can buy date sugar at natural-food stores.

◻ Complex carbohydrates—whole grains, whole-grain flours and seeds such as sunflower and sesame—are a good source of glucose plus other important nutrients. Grain-based syrups such as barley malt, rice syrup, wheat syrup, and amasake (made from fermented brown rice) are somewhat more nutritious than other sweeteners and can be used in baking.

Source: Leslie Cerier, a personal-fitness specialist, Charlemont, MA.

To avoid food poisoning

◻ Never let food cool to room temperature before putting it in the refrigerator. Slow cooling encourages the growth of bacteria.

◻ Do not thaw frozen foods for hours at room temperature. Allow them to thaw slowly in the refrigerator, or, wrap them in plastic and soak in cold water.

◻ Bacteria in raw poultry, fish or meat could contaminate your cutting board. Scrub the board after each use.

◻ Do not use cans that bulge or that contain off-color or unusual-smelling food. Dangerous: Tasting the contents to see whether they are bad.

□ Lead poisoning can result from storing food in open cans. The solder that seals the tinned-steel can leaches into the contents. Most hazardous: Acidic foods, especially juices. They interact quickly with metal.

□ Although cooking spoiled food destroys bacteria, it does not remove the poisons the bacteria produced.

Source: *Modern Maturity.*

Secrets of better meat freezing

Improper freezing and thawing of meat can ruin it, or at least alter its flavor and affect its texture. Correct procedures:

□ Rewrap the meat in heavy-duty aluminum foil or laminated freezer paper. Reason: Unprotected meat loses moisture when exposed to the dry cold of a freezer for a long period of time. Result: "Freezer burn," which causes a loss of flavor and nutritional value.

□ During freezing, restrict spacing to three pounds of meat per cubic foot of freezer space. Leave room for air to circulate around each package as it freezes. Proper temperature: Zero degrees or lower. After the meat is frozen, push the packages tightly together to save cooling costs.

□ Don't cut pieces larger than your family will use at one meal.

□ Label each package with its type of meat and the date you froze it.

□ Thaw the meat in the fresh food compartment of the refrigerator—not at room temperature. Reason: Bacteria can grow rapidly during thawing if the temperature is too warm. Warning: Fast cooking (for people who like rare meat) may not kill these organisms.

Source: Tom Flaherty, merchandising specialist, the National Live Stock and Meat Board, Chicago.

Drugs vs. nutrition

Don't overlook the interaction of medication and nutrition.

□ Chronic aspirin users can suffer microscopic bleeding of the gastrointestinal tract, a condition that also causes loss of iron. Aspirin can also

increase requirements for vitamin C and folic acid.

□ Laxatives may deplete vitamin D.

□ Antacids can lead to a phosphate deficiency.

□ Diuretics prescribed for hypertension can promote the loss of potassium.

□ In all these cases, vitamin and mineral supplements may be the solution.

What vitamin manufacturers don't tell you

While vitamins can have beneficial effects on your health, they can be dangerous if used improperly. You should know that:

□ Vitamin B-6 can poison you. Those one-gram B-6 tablets sold in health stores far exceed the body's need of one or two milligrams a day. Overdose may lead to loss of sensory and motor control.

□ Vitamin E should be used with restraint. High doses can cause blood clots, phlebitis, hypertension, severe fatigue, breast tumors and reproductive disturbances. A daily intake of more than 100 to 300 units of "active tocopherol" is excessive.

□ Vitamins A and D are not passed out of the body through the kidneys when taken in excess. They are stored in fat and in the liver, where they can cause cirrhosis, dry, itchy skin, fatigue, painful muscles, and loss of body hair. Limit supplementary intake of these vitamins to the recommended daily dietary allowances.

□ Consumers are frequently short-changed when they purchase vitamins. Many compounds both off the shelf or through mail order houses are far less potent than their labels claim. Buy vitamins with expiration dates on the labels and avoid vitamins that contain a long list of stabilizers and preservatives. Return vitamins that have a strong, rancid odor or that crumble easily.

□ Niacin is not a tranquilizer, despite the stories about its calming effects. Taking niacin tablets in search of tranquility can cause niacin toxicity.

Symptoms: Flushed face and blotchy skin on arms.

Source: *New England Journal of Medicine, Journal of the American Medical Association, The Health Letter*, and Dr. Jeffrey Blanc, professor of nutritional biochemistry, University of Puget Sound, Tacoma, WA.

Avoiding the lure of megavitamins

When it comes to vitamins, the old advice is still the best: There is no reason to take more than the recommended dietary allowance (RDA) of any vitamin, except for relatively rare individuals who cannot absorb or utilize vitamins adequately. If you want nutrition "insurance," take a regular multivitamin capsule containing only the RDA of vitamins.

A megadose is 10 or more times the RDA. This is the level at which toxic effects begin to show up in adults.

Some of the medical problems adults may experience as a result of prolonged, excessive intake are:

☐ Vitamin A. Dry, cracked skin. Severe headaches. Severe loss of appetite. Irritability. Bone and joint pains. Menstrual difficulties. Enlarged liver and spleen.

☐ Vitamin D. Loss of appetite. Excessive urination. Nausea and weakness. Weight loss. Hypertension. Anemia. Irreversible kidney failure that can lead to death.

☐ Vitamin E. Research on E's toxic effects is sketchy, but the findings suggest some problems: Headaches, nausea, fatigue and giddiness, blurred vision, chapped lips and mouth inflammation, low blood sugar, increased tendency to bleed, and reduced sexual function. Ironically, one of the claims of vitamin E proponents is that it heightens sexual potency.

☐ The B vitamins. Each B has its own characteristics and problems. Too much B-6 can lead to liver damage. Too much B-1 can destroy B-12.

☐ Vitamin C. Kidney problems and diarrhea. Adverse effects on growing bones. Rebound scurvy (a condition that can occur when a person taking large doses suddenly stops). Symptoms are swollen, bleeding gums, loosening of teeth, roughening of skin, muscle pain.

Vitamin C is the vitamin most often used to excess. Some of the symptoms of toxic effect from Vitamin C megadoses:

☐ Menstrual bleeding in pregnant women and various problems for their newborn infants.

☐ Destruction of Vitamin B-12, to the point that B-12 deficiency may become a problem.

☐ False negative test for blood in stool, which can prevent diagnosis of colon cancer.

☐ False urine test for sugar, which can spell trouble for diabetics.

☐ An increase in the uric acid level and the precipitation of gout in individuals predisposed to the ailment.

Source: Dr. Victor Herbert, author of *Nutrition Cultism: Facts and Fictions*, George F. Stickley Co., Philadelphia.

Cleaning up your drinking water

Pure drinking water piped into the home can no longer be taken for granted. If your water has an odd taste, color or smell, it may be contaminated by heavy construction or a sewer installation in the area, a change in pesticide use or antiquated water-treatment facilities.

What to do:

☐ Have the water department or board of health test the water. If they won't, consult the *Yellow Pages* under "Laboratories—Testing" for a lab that handles water samples. Cost: Up to $175.

There are a number of ways to get cleaner drinking water. These might include using:

☐ Bottled water. Keep in mind that some do contain traces of harmful substances. In one New York City test several years ago, two brands that scored cleanest were Great Bear and Deer Park.

☐ Water filters. The only effective ones contain granules of activated carbon. Filters are good against trihalomethanes only, not lead or arsenic. Never use filters that fit over the faucet. The water runs through too quickly to be properly filtered. Note: Filtered water is not necessary for such functions as dish washing.

☐ Distillers. They boil the water and recondense it without the contaminants. Fractional distillers prevent contaminants from recondensing with the water vapor.

☐ Quick fixes. Run the water for two or three minutes full force first thing in the morning to get rid of water that sat in pipes all night. Agitate drinking water in blender to eliminate dissolved chlorine gas.

Source: Carol Keough, author of *Water Fit to Drink*, Rodale Press, Emmaus, PA.

Rating the waters

Connoisseurship apparently knows no limits. Many people who used to ask for whiskey by the brand do the same with sparkling water.

Four boxes, excellent; three, very good; two, good; one, fair; zero, must suit tastes other than mine.

☐☐☐☐ *San Pellegrino*, Italy: A real charmer with a lively, gentle fizz. Clear, spring-like flavor is balanced and sprightly.

☐☐☐ *Saratoga*, US.: There's a bracing lilt to the soft fizz. The clear, neutral flavor has a slightly dry, citric pungency.

☐☐☐ *Perrier*, France: Dependably neutral when cold, but a mineral taste develops. Overly strong fizz softens quickly.

☐☐☐ *White Rock*, US: Moderately strong fizz. Sunny lemon flavor is pleasantly astringent, if a bit distracting.

☐☐ *Poland Spring*, US: Fizz is a bit overpowering. Generally acceptable flavor with some citric-sodium aftertaste.

☐☐ *Canada Dry*, US: Despite an overly strong fizz, this has a fairly neutral flavor with mild saline-citric accents.

☐ *Appolinaris*, West Germany: Strong, needling fizz and a warm, heavy mineral flavor that suggests bicarbonate of soda.

☐ *Calistoga*, US: After the gently soft fizz, it's all downhill. Musty, earthy flavor has salt-sodium overtones.

Seagram's, US: Sugar-water sweetness is a real shocker. Citric bitterness develops later. Moderate fizz.

Schweppes, US: A prevailing citric-saline bitterness makes this dry in the mouth. Fizz is extremely strong.

Source: Mimi Sheraton, writing in *Time*.

How bad is snacking before meals?

For most people, a low-carbohydrate, high-protein snack is good, since it promotes weight loss. For example, a cup of chicken soup (only 50 calories) about 20 minutes before a meal, stimulates the release of the hormone cholecystokinin (CCK) in the small intestine, creating a sense of fullness.

Source: Steven Peikin, MD, associate professor of medicine, Thomas Jefferson University, and author of *The Feel Full Diet*.

Candy bar myth

Many people think that candy bars are a good "quick energy" source. Not true; in reality, the high amount of fat in chocolate slows absorption of the candy bar. The tired person looking for a pick-me-up should opt for fruit or a bagel.

Source: Bonnie Liebman, director of nutrition, Center for Science in the Public Interest, Washington, DC.

Foods that can give you a headache

MSG is not the only culprit. Look out for tyramine-containing foods like:

☐ Aged cheese.

☐ Chicken livers.

☐ Chocolate.

☐ Pickled herring.

☐ Beer.

☐ Champagne.

☐ Red wine

☐ Sherry.

☐ Ice cream. A brief, but intense pain in the throat, head or face sometimes results from biting into ice cream. The pain is a physiological response of the warm tissues of the mouth to the sudden cold. The pain is sometimes felt throughout the head because cranial nerve branches in the area spread the pain impulse along a broad path. Prevention: Allow small amounts of ice cream to melt in the mouth before eating successive large bites.

Source: Joel R. Saper, M.D., and Kenneth R. Magee M.D. coauthors *Freedom from Headaches*.

Eight rules for staying healthy

Some people work too hard at making themselves healthy. Actually, the human body is an intricate organism with feedback mechanisms to maintain itself in a healthy state. Eight ways to help your body do its best:

☐ Eat a well-balanced diet. For most people, diet should be high in fiber content.

☐ Maintain a comfortable weight. Being too thin is not healthier than maintaining your normal weight.

☐ Do not take vitamin supplements if your diet is proper.

☐ Learn to cope with stress. The best ways to achieve this are through relaxation exercises, biofeedback courses or, if necessary, psychotherapy.

☐ Exercise all muscle groups daily without excessive strain.

☐ Avoid sleep medications. If anxiety or depression causes poor sleep patterns, come to grips with the underlying problems.

☐ Establish good rapport with a physician you can trust.

☐ Listen closely to your body. Good health is a combination of using common sense and allowing the body to heal itself. By avoiding all the good things in life, you will not live longer. It will only seem longer.

Source: Dr. Bruce Yaffe, fellow in gastroenterology and liver diseases, Lenox Hill Hospital, New York.

Health hints

☐ Before buying vitamins: Check Vitamin A and D dosages. Safe limits are 10,000 International Units for A, 400 for D. Signs of overdosage: Irritability, fever, bone pain (Vitamin A); lethargy, loss of appetite, kidney stones, or kidney failure (Vitamin D).

☐ Don't take Vitamin C and aspirin together. Studies at Southern Illinois University indicate that combined heavy doses produce excessive stomach irritation which could lead to ulcers (especially for those with a history of stomach problems).

☐ Eye care: Use eyedrops sparingly, especially commercial brands. They relieve redness by constricting blood vessels so eyes will look whiter. If used frequently, varicose veins can develop and eyes will become permanently reddened.

☐ The best cold medicine may be no medicine at all. No capsule or pill can cure a cold or the flu and may actually prolong the discomfort and hinder the body's own inherent ability to fight off the virus. Best advice: Rest and drink fluids.

Source: *Harvard Medical Health Letter*, Cambridge, MA.

Making a plan for wellness

Passing an annual physical exam was once enough to satisfy most people about their health. But today an increasing number strive beyond that—for optimal health or the condition of "wellness." How to set up a wellness plan for yourself:

☐ Try to clarify your most important reasons for living and write them down in a clear and concise fashion.

☐ With these in mind, identify the health goals that bolster your chances of living longer and healthier. Be specific: Do not plan to lose weight but to lose 20 pounds in six months. Other possible goals: Lowering blood pressure by a specific amount, accomplishing a dramatic feat, such as riding the Snake River rapids or completing a marathon.

☐ List supportive actions for each goal. Example: Joining a fitness club, training for long-distance running.

☐ Also identify the barriers to each goal and how they can be overcome.

☐ List the payoffs for each goal, whether they are new energy at the office or more fun at the beach.

☐ Before starting the program, list friends you can rely on for bicycle rides, tennis or other activities in the plan. Virtually no one can hope to stay on a wellness plan without support from friends.

☐ Once the plan is under way, set realistic quarterly benchmarks to track your achievements. A log or diary is usually helpful.

Source: *14 Days to a Wellness Lifestyle*, Donald B. Ardell, Whatever Publishing, Inc., Mill Valley, CA.

The major threats to your life

The biggest, most deadly risks today are smoking and drinking.

☐ Smoking's association with lung cancer is well-known, but perhaps more startling is the fact that the habit *doubles* your risk of death from coronary heart disease (which accounts for 40% of all deaths these days).

☐ The deleterious effects of alcohol are less well-known. Even though wine consumption lowers your risk of heart disease, the overall impact of drinking is that three drinks before dinner regularly *doubles* your risk of premature death. The major causes of alcohol-related deaths are auto accidents, cirrhosis, suicide, gastrointestinal diseases.

Source: John Irquhart, M.D., a former professor of physiology and bioengineering and coauthor (with Klaus Heilman, M.D.) of *Risk Watch: The Odds of Life,* Facts on File Publications, New York.

Health secrets only the insurance industry knows

Actuarial tables prepared by the life insurance industry to predict mortality rates show that:

☐ A larger abdomen than chest (when expanded) is the most dangerous type of obesity.

☐ Death rates at all ages are more than twice as high among smokers.

☐ The death of both parents before they reach age 60 increases the mortality risk in children up to one third.

☐ Overweight people have a markedly lower suicide rate. But being underweight generally leads to a longer life.

☐ It is much more dangerous to your health to live alone than in a stable relationship.

☐ The wealthy live longer, in large part because they get the best medical care, hygiene and nutrition.

☐ A stroke before age 60 becomes less and less of a mortality factor the longer the person lives uneventfully after it. Getting insurance is virtually impossible for those who have a stroke after 60.

☐ The nearsighted are unusually prone to anxiety.

☐ Obsessive personality types (compulsively neat and thorough) are especially likely to become depressed and kill themselves in later life.

☐ Severe drunkenness once a month doubles the risk of mortality. So does getting boisterously drunk every weekend.

☐ Those involved in kinky sex are much more likely to die violently or to kill themselves.

☐ Susceptibility to fear seems to correlate with blood coagulation associated with phlebitis.

☐ About one insurance applicant in 10,000 is denied coverage because of a hazardous occupation. About one in 250 has to pay a surcharge because of occupation.

☐ Farmers, college teachers and Anglican ministers are extremely good risks.

Source: Andrew Tobias, author of *The Invisible Bankers: Everything the Insurance Industry Never Wanted to Know,* Simon & Schuster, New York.

Life's real risks

Although we live in an era of low risk, with people living longer and healthier lives than ever before, we nevertheless seem to feel *more* at risk than we used to. Not all of our fears are well founded.

Here are some common myths many of us believe—and the realities:

☐ Myth: People were healthier and life was safer in "the good old days." Reality: Your chance of premature death 50-75 years ago was much higher than it is today.

☐ Myth: Pollution is a serious risk that never existed in the past. Reality: Pollution has shown no statistical sign of being a serious risk. If pollution were a big risk, you might expect a rise in certain cancers in the general population, like cancer of the bladder, since many substances that go into the body come out in concentrated form in urine. This hasn't happened.

☐ Myth: Death or injury by criminal violence has increased greatly. Reality: Life in London in the 18th century, *Tom Jones* vintage, included cutthroats and cutpurses just like today. Although murder is on the rise in our cities today, much of it is confined either to people who know each other or to young males in the lower socio-economic brackets.

☐ Myth: We're having a cancer epidemic. Reality: The opposite is true. We're having an epidemic of one kind of cancer—lung cancer caused by cigarette smoking. If lung cancer is removed from the statistics, fewer people than ever are dying from cancer. The perception of an increase in cancer is due to the increased longevity of the population. Cancer is an age-related disease: The longer you live, the more likely you are to get it.

☐ Myth: The risk of dying in an auto accident is greater today than 50-75 years ago. Reality: In England, although there are 10 times as many cars on the road as 50 years ago, and 30% more people, the same number of people are killed in cars today as in the 1930s. US statistics are similar. This is because people drive better, roads are better, cars are safer and medical care is better.

☐ Myth: We shouldn't use nuclear energy to produce power because the risk of an accident is too great. Reality: More people die in mining accidents every year than in nuclear power plants. The actual problems of nuclear power are minimal compared with the environmental damage from fossil-fuel generation (including destruction of the land by strip mining, of the seashore by oil drilling and of the forests by acid rain).

Source: John Urquhart, M.D., a former professor of physiology and bioengineering and coauthor (with Klaus Heilman, M.D.) of *Risk Watch: The Odds of Life,* Facts on File Publications, New York.

How to sit correctly

Even if you have the perfect office chair, you can develop physical problems from prolonged sitting unless you align your body properly.

Suggestions:

☐ Keep your neck and back in a straight line with your spine. Bend forward from the hips. Do not arch your lower back.

☐ Use a footrest to relieve swayback. Your knees should be higher than your hips.

☐ Move your neck and shrug your shoulders to relieve the tension that results from prolonged sitting.

Source: Joel Makower, author of *Office Hazards: How Your Job Can Make You Sick,* Tilden Press.

Heart disease risks and prevention

Heart disease is a major concern for millions of Americans. New and often conflicting information is published almost daily on the causes and cures.

Here are some points of clarification:

☐ High cholesterol, along with smoking and hypertension, is considered to be one of the three major risk factors. People with high cholesterol and a low HDL* fraction are apparently more susceptible to heart attacks. Problem: A large proportion of heart attack victims and people with arteriosclerotic heart disease have relatively normal levels of cholesterol and HDL. High cholesterol and low HDL can be altered 13%–20% with diet, exercise and medication. But altering a cholesterol level that's within normal range is difficult, if not impossible, and the drugs used to lower cholesterol are highly unpleasant. It's unclear whether lowering your cholesterol will lower your risk anyway.

☐ Hypertension is alterable. People who have it are more likely to get arteriosclerotic heart disease and coronary artery disease. As with high cholesterol, however, a large number of heart attack victims don't have hypertension.

☐ Smoking is a very strong risk factor. And the evidence is unequivocal. Smoking definitely increases the risk of developing heart disease and reduces the longevity of heart attack victims.

☐ Genes are not commonly listed as a major risk factor, but their influence is highly significant. Many heart attack victims have relatively normal cholesterol and no hypertension, and they don't smoke. Most of this group have bad family histories. If your father and uncles died of heart attacks at age 40, you may be in big trouble. And there may not be much you can do to alter this risk factor.

☐ Obesity, strangely enough, is not one of the major risk factors. However, insurance company statistics show that

*HDL is high-density lipoprotein, one of the breakdowns of cholesterol that can be measured in the bloodstream.

very overweight people don't live as long as normal-weight people. Although heart disease may be one reason, respiratory illness, diabetes and other diseases are contributing factors.

☐ Salt intake may not be a factor. The link between salt intake and heart disease is tenuous. It can't hurt to reduce your salt intake. But it may not help either.

☐ Stress and the type-A personality are probably minor risk factors. Whether type As (continually wound up) can be changed, or want to be, is questionable. If possible, reduce the stress. It's easier than changing your personality.

☐ Hormones protect women, who apparently peak with heart disease 10-15 years after men. This difference is presumably hormone-related.

☐ Reduce your weight to low normal if possible, especially if you've already had a heart attack. Weight loss will lower cholesterol and decrease hypertension. If you need to diet, do go on a moderate reduced-calorie diet that includes all the major food groups.

Source: Edward J. Berman, MD, chief of cardiology, Gardena Memorial Hospital, Gardena, CA.

Preventing a heart attack

Get an annual heart checkup:

☐ Complete blood workup, including tests of cholesterol, triglycerides, sugar, and uric acid. All provide clues to heart troubles.

☐ Chest X-rays—with emphasis on the heart.

☐ Two kinds of EKGs—one at rest and one under stress.

☐ Don't smoke. That's the best advice. Non-smokers clearly have the best chances.

☐ Get your weight down. It's not as important as smoking, but it's advisable. If you're having a hard time, consider joining Weight Watchers, which has a good success record.

☐ Get regular exercise—the kind that challenges the cardiovascular system—with the key word being "regular." Avoid strenuous competitive sports if you aren't in good shape. Any new exercise program should be reviewed by your physician.

☐ If you suffer from hypertension (high blood pressure), have it treated by your physician.

Building your stress-resistance

☐ Change your expectations. The difference between expectations and perception of reality is the measure of how much stress you will experience. Example: If you begin the day with an attitude of "the world is changing, finances are fluctuating, nothing stays the same," and you perceive that to be so, you'll experience very little stress. If, instead, you assume that tomorrow will be the same as today and that things will go as you planned, you'll experience a lot of stress if your expectations aren't met. Either the environment or your own performance will displease you. Remedy: Be more realistic about your expectations and pay attention to your perceptions of reality.

☐ You won't be able to deal with stress if you feel that your past performances have been inadequate. You'll just assume that you'll fail again. Remedy: Find out the average or expected performance for any given job and gear yourself to that. People under stress tend to feel extremely anxious and afraid. These feelings often come across to others as *anger* rather than fear. If people see you as hostile (even though it is not really so), it may adversely affect any evaluation of your performance.

☐ Seek a socially cohesive work situation. In England during World War II, there was less illness and higher performance among Londoners who weathered the bombings than before, or after, the war. Great social cohesiveness was provided by an external enemy. That same kind of cohesiveness occurs in any organization geared toward a strong goal.

☐ Do relaxation exercises.* The purpose is to get the focus on a *nonlogical* part of the body. It's the constant logical planning and rumination that keep

*Recommended: Herbert Bensons's *Relaxation Response;* Stroebel and Hartford's *Quieting Response;* Patricia Carrington's *Freedom in Meditation.*

stress going. Best: Approaches that focus on breathing. Proper breathing triggers other parts of the body to relax. The body is born with the *innate ability* to counter stress. These exercises allow you to activate that mechanism, and eventually you'll be able to call upon it at will.

☐ Make time to do something relaxing. Take some time away from your desk to window-shop or do something "silly." Eat lunch out of the office. Plan something pleasurable each week, and then follow through. Caution: If you eat while under stress, you'll have a 50% higher cholesterol level after the meal than if you were relaxed.

☐ Physical exercise helps only if you do it right. For instance, if jogging is just another chore that you don't enjoy, but you squeeze it into a heavy schedule because you feel you should, it only puts an extra load on your heart. Exercise while under stress can be dangerous. But if you see the trees and smell the air and feel high and good after running, you're doing it right. Exercise that makes you feel good is as helpful as any relaxation technique.

Source: Dr. Kenneth Greenspan, psychiatrist and Director of the Center for Stress and Pain-related Disorders, Columbia Presbyterian Hospital, New York City.

Attitudes that combat stress disease

In today's fast-moving, success-oriented world, it seems as though one must be able to withstand a very high stress level in order to get ahead and stay ahead. Many ambitious people put themselves under a crushing stress burden for years, eventually paying the price in heart disease, ulcers and so on.

But there *are* busy, high-achieving people who are seemingly immune to stress.

You can be one of them:

☐ Seek out and enjoy change. See it as a challenge. This is extremely important. How we view a stressful event determines how our bodies and minds react. If an event is seen as a threat and we feel victimized, the actual physiology of the body changes to meet the threat. If we see change as a challenge, with potential for growth and excitement, the body's response is entirely different.

☐ Don't be overly self-critical. Perfectionists—a very stress-vulnerable group—are always condemning themselves for not having coped well enough in the past. When a new challenge comes along, they view it as just another threat to their self-esteem.

☐ Identify with your work. When your work seems an extension of your personality it ceases to be an alien threat. Work-related stress then becomes less dangerous because it's for something you've *chosen.*

☐ Have a sense of control over your life. If you participate in the planning of a project and handle your part in its execution you will have a sense of control and get a sense of completion when the job is complete. This is why top managers are under less stress than middle managers.

Source: Dr. Kenneth Greenspan, psychiatrist and Director of the Center for Stress and Pain-related Disorders, Columbia Presbyterian Hospital, New York City.

How to reduce stress at your desk

You'll get more work done and feel better if you make your working environment comfortable. Try these techniques:

☐ Make certain that your chair is comfortable.

☐ Quiet your telephone's ring.

☐ Alter the lighting to reduce glare…or increase brightness.

☐ Personalize your work space with photos, prints, etc.

☐ Adopt at least a partial closed-door policy for your office. (If you have no way to be alone in your office, find a place elsewhere in the building where you can take breathers.)

☐ Avoid tight collars…they can cut blood flow to the brain and result in light-headedness and even panic attacks. Tight belts are troublesome, too.

☐ Establish a regular time for meals, especially lunch.

Source: Stephen Cohen, author of *The Termination Trap,* Williamson Publishing, Charlotte, VT.

Identifying disguised stress

Busy managers are often unaware of the amount of stress they are really under. They deceive themselves into ignoring stress by believing that whatever is bothering them isn't all that bad.

Some stress can be good, for example when it's the basis for motivation, excitement, creativity, and satisfaction. Too much is always harmful.

Signs of stress:

☐ Irritability, being bothered by little nuisances.

☐ Increased use of alcohol, caffeine or tobacco.

☐ Decline in clarity of thought.

☐ Reduction of work quality and efficiency.

☐ Physical discomforts such as headaches, neckaches, backaches, tense muscles, and skin irritations.

☐ Overeating.

☐ Sleep disturbances.

☐ Anxiety or timidity.

☐ Anger, dissatisfaction, bitterness.

☐ Confusion, a sense of being swamped with work.

☐ Depression.

Source: Herbert W. Greenberg, author of *Coping with Stress,* Prentice-Hall, Englewood Cliffs, NJ.

How to warm cold hands caused by stress

Cold hands are often a sign of stress if you are indoors and there is no reason for them to be chilled. Biofeedback research indicates that techniques to warm hands can also reduce the stress load. What works:

☐ Close your eyes and imagine yourself holding and playing with something soft and warm.

☐ Touch your cheeks, which are usually warm, and imagine the warmth flowing into your fingers.

☐ Interlock fingers, squeeze gently for one second, release for one second.

☐ Repeat sequence several times.

Source: Robert Hall, president, Futurehealth, Inc., Bensalem, PA.

Executives' ranking sources of stress

What bothers executives most:

☐ Failure of subordinates to accept or carry out responsibilities: 92% of those responding to a survey listed this as their most serious problem.

☐ Inability to get critical information: 78%.

☐ Firing someone: 48%.

☐ Incompetent co-workers: 47%.

☐ Owner or board of directors challenging recommendations: 33%.

☐ Subordinates who question decisions: 5%.

☐ Conducting performance reviews: 3%.

Source: The Atlanta Consulting Group, Atlanta, GA.

The best ways to control stress

☐ Work at something you enjoy (not always easy to do, but a goal to strive for).

☐ Express your feelings freely.

☐ Relax (another tough order for some people).

☐ Identify and prepare for events or situations likely to be stressful.

☐ Talk to relatives, close friends or others about personal matters. Don't be afraid to call on them for help.

☐ Participate in group activities (such as church and community organizations) or hobbies that you enjoy.

Source: National Health Information Clearinghouse, Washington, DC.

To eliminate fatigue

☐ Analyze your lifestyle. Write down what you do every day. Be sure to include the amount of physical exercise you get and the kinds of demands (emotional and otherwise) that are made on you. Include your time with people and your time working alone. Document the times when you feel fatigued. Is it at work or at home? Is it better or worse around other people? Correlate your fatigue diary with your activity record, and look for patterns.

☐ Try some small changes in your work style. If your job puts you under constant pressure, take minibreaks to do some gentle stretches. If you spend a lot of time with other people, make some private time for yourself. If you do paperwork alone, schedule some social breaks.

☐ Pay attention to diet, and eat regularly. A breakfast of complex carbohydrates such as whole-grained toast and protein will keep you going until lunch. People who skip meals or have an erratic eating pattern are more fatigue-prone.

☐ Stick to a regular, moderate exercise regimen—not weekend overexertion. The best exercise is walking. Besides being healthful and safe, it also gives you time alone to notice the outside world and reflect on your inner life. Aerobic exercise stimulates the brain to produce endorphins, the body's natural painkillers and antidepressants.

☐ Look within yourself. Do you like your job, friends, home life? Could you admit it to yourself if you didn't? If for the next two weeks you could do anything you wanted, what would it be? Is there a way of incorporating that fantasy into real life? What's the biggest price you have to pay for your current lifestyle?

☐ Once you identify problems, see what you can do about them. For example, if you like your job but hate the long commute, maybe you can stagger your hours to work fewer days a week—or move closer to the office.

☐ Get a physical checkup. Although there is no physical basis for fatigue in 99% of the people who visit doctors complaining of it, occasionally a health problem is a factor. The most common medical cause of fatigue is mild low thyroid, which occurs more commonly in women.

Source: Mary E. Wheat, M.D., an internist at Mt. Zion Hospital and Medical Center, San Francisco.

Improve the quality of your sleep

☐ Researchers cannot easily determine how much sleep is optimum for a specific person. They have determined that, on average, people need seven or eight hours of sleep a day.

☐ Keep a diary of sleeping patterns for at least 10-14 days. If you feel productive and alert, the average sleep time during that period is probably the amount you need.

☐ Establish a regular bedtime and wakeup schedule. Stick to it, even on weekends and holidays.

☐ Avoid trying to make up for loss of sleep one night by sleeping more the next. Sleep deprivation of two to four hours does not severely affect performance. Having the normal amount of sleep the next night compensates for the loss without changing the regular sleep pattern. And that has long-term benefits.

☐ Relax before bedtime. Good ways to unwind. Take a bath, read, have a weak nightcap or snack (milk is ideal for many people), engage in sex. Avoid late-night exercise, work, arguments and activities that cause tension.

☐ Knowing the reason for insomnia is the only way to start overcoming it. If the cause is not quickly obvious, see a doctor. Many emotional and physical disorders express themselves as sleep disturbances.

☐ Avoid sleeping pills. On a long-term basis, they are useless and sometimes dangerous. And when taken infrequently, they may produce a drug hangover the next day.

☐ Avoid naps in the middle of the day to compensate for lack of sleep the previous night. Take them only if you do it regularly and feel refreshed, instead of groggy, after a nap. Test: If you dream during a catnap, it is likely to delay sleep that evening or to cause insomnia.

☐ Don't attempt to reduce the total amount of sleep you need. Carefully researched evidence from monitoring subjects in sleep laboratories indicates these schemes are not only ineffective but unhealthful. The daily biological cycle cannot be changed by gradually cutting back sleep over a period of months. Older persons apparently need slightly less sleep, but even here the exact difference is not yet known.

Source: Dr. Charles P. Pollak, codirector, of Sleep-Wake Disorders Center, Montefiore Hospital, New York.

Good sleep demystified

People spend almost one third of their lives asleep. The primary sleep disorder is insomnia. That's difficulty falling asleep, trouble remaining asleep or early-morning awakening. Causes:

☐ Depression is often the cause of early awakening.

☐ Sexual stresses lead to nighttime insomnia.

☐ Boredom.

☐ Some medications, such as drugs for asthma and heart and blood-pressure pills, cause poor sleep.

☐ More than moderate alcohol intake usually disturbs the sleep cycle.

Ways to promote better sleep:

☐ Follow a good physical fitness program.

☐ Sleep in a quiet, dark, well-humidified room and in a comfortable bed.

☐ Avoid late-night physical or mental stress, snacks, coffee, cola, or drug stimulants.

☐ Do relaxing exercises or biofeedback exercises.

☐ Don't take sleeping pills.

Source: Dr. Bruce Yaffe, fellow in gastroenterology and liver disease, Lenox Hill Hospital, New York.

The straight story on sleep

☐ There's nothing particularly natural or inevitable about daytime sleepiness. Americans have developed an unhealthy tolerance of daytime sleepiness and fatigue.

☐ Both drowsiness and fatigue during the daytime hours are usually the result of sleep disorders of which sufferers often aren't aware. There are also chronic sleep disturbances of which the sleeper may not be aware. Example: Loud noises from aircraft or a nearby highway that disturb sleep regularly even though people don't always waken.

☐ Contrary to common notions, the inability to get a refreshing night's sleep is rarely caused by stress or anxiety. For people younger than 15 or older than 50, the main cause is usually a physical one. In older people, the most common problem is apnea, a disorder that causes them to stop breathing periodically during sleep. Other frequent problems: Asthma and chronic disease.

☐ A cool bedroom is not necessarily better for sleeping than a warm one. No temperature (within a normal range) has been proved better than another for sleep.

☐ Some people who have insomnia do sleep, and much more than they think they do. The real test of sleeping well: Whether you feel fully alert the next day, not the number of hours you've slept. If you sleep just five hours and you don't feel tired the next day, you don't have a sleep disorder.

☐ Heavy snoring followed by daytime sleepiness is virtually a sure sign of apnea. In this condition, episodes of impaired breathing or failure to breathe at all causes the apnea sufferer to wake up many times a night. Most vulnerable to sleep apnea: Middle-aged males (particularly those who are overweight) and people with large adenoids, a deviated septum or polyps. Some apnea sufferers are so used to their condition that they're not aware of their wakening, only of their daytime fatigue.

☐ A cigarette before bedtime is likely to keep you awake (in addition to creating a fire hazard). Nicotine is a stimulant to the central nervous system.

☐ The position in which you lie when going to sleep is not important. Fact: Everybody moves around many times during sleep.

☐ A couple of stiff drinks every night will not help your sleep. Stiff drinks before bedtime will more likely cause you to wake up in the middle of the night, when they wear off. Small quantities of alcohol (one drink) may help on a particularly difficult night, however.

☐ Drink a glass of milk and eat a light snack before going to bed. Reason: Hunger can disturb sleep. Avoid rich or spicy foods or stimulants such as coffee, tea, cola, drinks, or sweets. (Sugar is a stimulant.) Eating the wrong foods before bedtime may not actually keep you from falling asleep, but it will often wake you within a few hours.

☐ Check to see if there are noises that may be disturbing your sleep without your being aware of them. Mute the sounds by putting up heavy curtains or by using earplugs.

☐ Avoid too much mental stimulation in the period before you go to sleep. Don't discuss family problems or finances, and don't take up unfinished work problems before bedtime. Instead: Do some light reading or watch a television show that relaxes you.

☐ If you wake up in the middle of the night and can't get back to sleep right away, don't lie there. Get up, put the light on and use the time, perhaps to read. Lying in bed and trying to sleep without success only makes you more tense.

☐ Avoid strenuous physical exercise within a few hours of bedtime. It can cause excessive stimulation and stress, which can disturb sleep. Exercise can benefit sleep if taken in the afternoon or early evening. Morning exercise is of no great help in inducing a good night's sleep.

Source: Dr. William C. Dement, director, Sleep Disorders Center, Stanford University School of Medicine.

Sleep can be disturbed by...

Only about one third of people wake up refreshed. While many sleep problems for the other two thirds are caused by anxiety, these factors can also reduce the quality of sleep:

☐ Alcohol. Can affect both dream and deepest-sleep stage. Best: Make your drink with dinner the last of the evening.

☐ Room temperature. A cold room does not make you sleep better. Ideal: 60–65°.

☐ Exercise. Aches and pains from strenuous exercise can keep you awake.

☐ Sex. Unless it is both physically and mentally rewarding, it can inhibit sleep.

☐ Caffeine. Effects linger 6 to 7 hours.

☐ Smoking. Nicotine is a strong central-nervous-system stimulant. Heavy smokers who quit usually sleep dramatically better within days.

☐ Irregular schedule. The body functions on a regular rhythm.

Source: *Executive Fitness Newsletter.*

How to stop snoring

☐ Put a brick or two under the legs at the head of your bed. Elevating your head will keep the airway open.

☐ Don't use extra pillows. They'll only kink the airway.

☐ Avoid all depressants a few hours before bed. Take no alcohol, tranquilizers, sleeping pills or antihistamines late in the day.

☐ Lose weight. Three of four snorers are at least 20% over their ideal weight.

☐ Wear a cervical collar. It keeps the chin up and the windpipe open.

☐ Wear a "snore ball." Cut a small, solid-rubber ball in half. Using two patches of Velcro, attach the flat side of the half-sphere to the back of your pajama top. If done right, it should keep you off your back—the position for virtually all snoring.

Source: *Prevention,* Emmaus, PA.

How to fall back asleep

Agony: Awakening in the middle of the night and not being able to fall back to sleep. Prime cause: Advancing age. People over 50 tend to middle-of-the-night insomnia. Those under 50 often have difficulty falling asleep.

How to cope:

☐ Don't become angry when you find yourself awake at 3 A.M. Anger only excites you, preventing sleep. Fix your mind on a single relaxing image. Example: Visualize a flickering candle.

☐ If you are still awake after 30 minutes, go to another room. Watch an old movie on TV, or read a book or magazine.

☐ When you feel sleepy, return to bed. If sleep still eludes you, go back to the other room and read some more.

Preventive steps:

☐ Eliminate daytime naps if they have been a habit.

☐ Do not go to bed too early. This only increases the chances of middle-of-the-night insomnia.

☐ Set your alarm an hour earlier than usual. This makes you more tired for the following night. Advance the alarm by 15-minute increments until you are sleeping through the night. Then slowly extend your sleep period until you are back on a normal schedule.

Source: *A Good Night's Sleep* by Jerrold S. Maxmen, Contemporary Books, Chicago.

How to become an ex-insomniac

☐ Condition your sleep environment. Learn to associate your bed and your bedroom with sleep.

☐ Pay attention to bedroom conditions, such as light, heat, noise. Shut off telephones if necessary. Keep temperature cool (around 68°). Make sure your mattress and your sleep clothing are comfortable.

☐ If you don't fall asleep right away, get up, leave the bedroom, and go do something else. Don't lie awake thinking about it or you'll begin to associate your bed and your bedroom with trying to get to sleep.

☐ Stick to a regular bedtime schedule. Go to bed at the same time every night—weekdays and weekends. Don't expect to catch up on missed sleep on the weekends. You can't do it. Trying simply disrupts your biological rhythms.

☐ Exercise early in the day. Late in the evening it's too stimulating.

☐ Sexual activity, within a comfortable relationship where no tension or anxiety exists, is helpful in inducing sleep.

☐ If you think widely advertised insomnia cures like vibrating beds, prerecorded cassette tapes, and sleep masks will relax you, try them.

☐ Don't take nonprescription, over-the-counter sleeping pills. Studies have shown "sugar pills" to be just as effective.

☐ If you have a particular emotional or physical upset, see your doctor.

☐ If sedatives are prescribed, use for no more than a week or two. Expect that the first night or two after stopping the pills will be very disturbed sleep. That's perfectly normal.

Source: Dr. Frank Zorick, clinical director of the sleep disorder center at Cincinnati Veterans Administration Hospital and the University of Cincinnati.

How to buy a mattress

The quality of sleep makes the quantity less important. To enable you to relax, your mattress must provide proper support for your body, yet be resilient enough for comfort.

Basic considerations:

☐ Mattress prices. Depend on the materials, quality of construction, size, number of layers of upholstery and the store's markup. (May be lower in small neighborhood stores.) Queen-size innerspring sets cost $325–$800, sometimes discounted to $225–$500. A high-density queen-size foam mattress costs about $300.

☐ Construction. Innerspring or foam rubber are the basic types. Top-quality innerspring mattresses have covered metal coils, cushioning material and an insulator between the coils to prevent them from protruding. Foam mattresses are made of a solid block of urethane, high-resiliency foam or laminated layers of varying density sandwiched together (preferably 5–6 inches thick).

How to shop for a mattress:

☐ Sit on the edge of the bed. The mattress should support you without feeling flimsy, and it should spring bac into shape when you get up. A reinforced border increases durability.

☐ Lie down. (If the bed is to be used b a couple, both partners should test it lying down.) Check several different firmnesses to choose the one you're most comfortable with.

☐ Roll from side to side and then to the center. The mattress should not sway, jiggle or sag in the middle. If you hear creaking springs, don't buy it.

☐ Examine the covering. The best is sturdy ticking with a pattern woven in, *not printed on*.

☐ Check for handles on the sides for easy turning, small metal vents to disperse heat and allow air to circulate inside, and plastic corner guards.

☐ Don't forget about the boxspring which bears up to 80% of the sleeper's weight. When you need a new mattress, both the mattress and spring should be replaced to ensure that the support system is specifically designe for the mattress.

☐ Buy a sleep set made by a manu-facturer with a good reputation and sold by a reputable dealer. Be very wary of advertised bargains.

How to buy shoes that really fit

Shoes should provide a lot of cushioning. The running shoe is the most physiologic shoe made. Soft and malleable, it provides cushioning and a little bit of support.

☐ If you're a woman and you wear a high-heeled, thin-soled shoe, have a thin rubber sole cemented onto the bottom to cushion the ball of the foot.

☐ Fit shoes with your hands, not with your feet. There should be an index finger's breadth between the tip of the toes and the front of the shoe.

☐ Tell the salesperson to start with a half-size larger than you usually wear and work down. The shoe shouldn't be pushed out of shape when you stand. The leather should not be drawn taut.

☐ An ideal heel height for a woman is 1½–2 inches. This is not a magic number, simply the most comfortable. a man wore a 1½–inch heel, he'd be more comfortable than in the traditional ¾-inch heel.

❑ If you have flat feet, look for low-heeled shoes that feel balanced. They should not throw your weight forward on the balls of your feet or gap at the arches.

❑ Buy shoes in the late afternoon when your feet have had a full day's workout and are slightly spread. Shoes that you try on first thing in the morning may be too tight by evening and uncomfortable for all-day wear.

Source: John F. Waller, Jr., M.D., chief of the foot and ankle section, Lenox Hill Hospital, New York.

Lead poisoning warning

The danger of lead poisoning is greater than most of us think. Biggest source: Lead plumbing or copper plumbing soldered with lead. If your water pipes are a dull gray color instead of copper, or if they have dull gray soldering at the joints, you have a potential lead problem. Protection:

❑ Let the water run for at least three minutes before using it for drinking or cooking. That allows water that's been sitting in the pipes collecting lead to drain off.

❑ Drink and boil only cold water. Hot water dissolves lead much more quickly.

Source: *Tufts University Diet & Nutrition Letter.*

What to do if you're mugged

Getting mugged these days is a real and personal threat, not something that happens just to other people. Fortunately, most muggings are simple robberies in which neither the criminal nor the victim is hurt. However, the possibility of violence is always there.

Recommendations:

❑ Cooperate. Assume the mugger is armed. No matter how strong or fit you are, you are no match for a gun or knife. Remember that your personal safety is far more important than your valuables or your pride.

❑ Follow the mugger's instructions to the letter. Try not to move too quickly or too slowly—either could upset him.

❑ Stay as calm as possible, and encourage companions to do the same.

❑ Give the mugger whatever he asks for. Don't argue. But if something is of great sentimental value to you, give it to him, and only then say, "This watch was given to me by my grandfather. It means a lot to me. I'd be very grateful if you'd let me keep it."

❑ When he has all he wants of your valuables, ask him what he wants you to do while he gets away—stay where you are, lie face down, whatever. If he dismisses you, leave the scene immediately, and don't look back. Don't call the police until you are in a safe place.

Some important don'ts:

❑ Don't reach for your wallet in a back pocket without explaining first what you plan to do. The mugger might think you are reaching for a gun.

❑ Don't give him dirty looks or make judgmental remarks.

❑ Don't threaten him with hostile comments.

❑ Don't be a wiseguy or a joker. Even smiling is a dangerous idea. He may think you are laughing at him.

❑ Don't try any tricks like carrying a second empty wallet to give to a mugger. This could make him angry. Some experts even recommend that you carry at least $50 with you at all times to keep from upsetting a mugger.

Source: Ken Glickman, chief instructor, American Self-Defense Institute, New York.

VDTs and eye strain

You can minimize eye strain when working with a video display terminal by:

❑ Placing the terminal no higher than eye level.

❑ Tilting it back 10–20 degrees.

❑ Keeping it about 18 inches away.

❑ Adjusting the brightness control for minimum glare.

Source: *Popular Science.*

Vaccines for adults

More than half of American adults fail to take advantage of available vaccines. Important: Don't count on your doctor to keep track for you. Recommended:

❑ Tetanus and diphtheria immunity: Important for all adults. Requires an initial series of three shots (usually given in childhood) and boosters every 10 years.

❑ Measles vaccine: Should be given to any adult born after 1956 who has not had either a documented case of the disease or an injection with live virus vaccine. Caution: The killed-virus vaccines available between 1963 and 1967 are ineffective. If you're unsure, it is advisable to have a live-virus vaccine administered.

☐ Rubella vaccine: Should be given to all adults who were not immunized as children. Most in need: Women likely to become pregnant. (Rubella severely damages developing fetuses.)

☐ Hepatitis vaccine: A good idea for those who are routinely exposed to blood and blood products.

☐ Influenza vaccine: Should be given annually to everyone over 65. Others at high risk because of poor health or frequent exposure to people sick with the disease should also consider vaccination.

☐ Pneumococcal pneumonia vaccine: For everyone over 65 and others at high risk. This vaccination is relatively new, effective and vitally important. (Pneumonia is a major cause of death among older people.)

Additional protection (against malaria, polio, meningitis, etc.) may be necessary if you plan to travel outside the US. Contact your state's health department for instructions appropriate to your destination.

Source: Steven Wassilak, MD, medical epidemiologist, division of immunization, Center for Disease Control, Atlanta.

Toilet-seat danger

You can catch diarrhea, intestinal bugs and hepatitis from toilet seats. Trap: When toilets are flushed, a fine mist of water that could contain contagious fecal bacteria rises and lands on toilet seats and flush handles. Best defense. Clean your toilet three times a week with disinfectant…avoid using public rest rooms—especially the most popular middle stall…stand before flushing.

Source: Dr. Charles Gerba, University of Arizona

Wash away poison ivy

Poison ivy can be nipped in the bud if you wash the resin off your skin within 10 minutes of exposure.

Source: *The Pharmacist's Prescription: Your Complete Guide to the Over-the-Counter Remedies That Work Best* by F. James Grogan, Pharm. D., Rawson Associates, 115 Fifth Ave., New York 10003.

f you think you're having a heart ttack

Don't wait for pain to send you to the octor.

If you have any symptoms, such as a uttering in the chest or skipped eartbeats, seek medical help.

If your doctor is not immediately vailable, go to a hospital emergency om at once.

If the pain is bad, rest and have omeone else call.

Above all, don't ignore the signs of ouble. Most victims do ignore the first gnals out of fear or denial.

Don't be embarrassed about calling e doctor at an inconvenient time, ven if you think the pain may be only digestion or a muscle cramp.

Although chest pain is the most ommon symptom, it's not the only ne. So don't dismiss pain in the eck, shoulder, or arms. Also, the ain may not be great, and it may ome and go.

ealing with a nedical emergency

a medical emergency, emotions can n high. Knowing how to get someone the hospital quickly and efficiently an not only calm the patient, it may ven save his life.

Call your local municipal emergency umber for a public ambulance. The esponse time is usually quicker than r a private ambulance.

Answer all the dispatcher's questions s completely as possible. The nswers determine the priority of your all. A broken leg, for example, may ot get assistance as quickly as a heart ttack.

Tell the dispatcher exactly what ondition the patient is in, as clearly nd calmly as possible. Simply saying think he is having a heart attack" is ot enough. Try to be specific about all e symptoms you have observed.

Don't hang up until the dispatcher oes. Let him decide when he has nough information.

Give the dispatcher your phone number even if he doesn't ask for it. If something happens to delay the ambulance, he may need to reach you.

Give careful directions that include your street address, prominent landmarks and any other information that will help the ambulance crew find your location quickly.

Tell the dispatcher that you will have someone wait outside, put the porch light on, or hang a bed sheet out the window so the driver can see where you are right away.

Stay with the victim or at least keep him in sight.

Gather all relevant information, such as insurance numbers, medical history, medications currently being taken (the actual bottle of pills is even better) and anything else that concerns the patient's condition.

You can usually ride in the ambulance with the patient, unless the patient needs emergency procedures en route.

In that case, get the name and address of the hospital and the care unit where the patient will be admitted, to go there on your own. (Don't speed or run lights.)

At the hospital, find out who is caring for the patient. Let the floor nurse know that you are there. Offer to expedite the admitting office paperwork.

Source: Brian Maguire, director of training, BRAVO (Bay Ridge Ambulance Volunteer Organization), NY.

Thorough check-up for men

A man's thorough physical includes these procedures:

Blood pressure test (most important).

Eye and eye pressure exam.

Check of lymph nodes and thyroid for swelling.

Stethoscopic exam of heart and lungs.

Stress tests (particularly for vigorous exercisers).

Examination of the aorta.

Testicle examination.

Reading of pulse in legs.

Proctoscopic exam of rectum and lower large intestine.

Prostate examination.

Stool sample for blood.

☐ Superficial neurological exam (reflexes and muscle strength).

☐ Laboratory test: Blood sugar, cholesterol, uric acid, complete blood screening (every three years), triglyceride, kidney function and calcium.

Source: *M* magazine.

Headache relief without drugs

Relief from incapacitating tension, vascular and migraine headaches is possible without drugs, using a self-administered form of acupuncture know as acupressure.

The technique:

☐ Exert very heavy thumbnail pressure (painful pressure) successively on nerves lying just below the surface of the skin at key points in the hands and wrists. As with acupuncture, no one's sure why it works.

Pressure points to try:

☐ The triangle of flesh between the thumb and index finger on the back of your hands (thumb side of bone, near middle of the second metacarpal in the index finger).

☐ Just above the protruding bone on the thumb side of your wrist.

Operations that are often unnecessary

Major surgery is too often thought of as an easy way to deal with certain ailments. But as medicine becomes more sophisticated, some operations that were once routine have been replaced by less radical treatments or should be performed only when there is clear cause.

Examples:

☐ Tonsillectomy. Now prescribed only for recurring ear infections that cause loss of hearing, after a series of strep throat infections, or when enlarged tonsils substantially impair breathing.

☐ Hysterectomy. To relieve profuse bleeding or back pain ostensibly caused by a large or displaced uterus. Be certain that the uterus is indeed to blame and that the problem cannot be stopped by other means.

☐ Ruptured disc surgery. Symptoms can often be relieved completely with bed rest, painkillers, muscle relaxants, and traction. Before an operation,

make certain that X-rays prove that the disc is indeed ruptured.

☐ Exploratory surgery prompted by chronic abdominal pain. Modern X-ray and other diagnostic testing have made this operation virtually obsolete.

Source: George D. LeMaitre, M.D., author of *How to Choose a Good Doctor,* Andover Publishing, Andover, MA.

Questions to ask a surgeon

To protect yourself against unnecessary surgery, get a second opinion. Then, ask the physician these important questions before you have an operation:

☐ What are the risks?

☐ What is the mortality rate for this operation?

☐ What is the likelihood of complications?

☐ How long will it take to recover?

☐ Are there ways to treat this condition medically (that is, nonsurgically)?

☐ How many people have you seen with similar symptoms who have chosen not to have surgery? What happened to them?

☐ How many of these operations have you done in the past year?

Understanding hospital talk

When you're hospitalized, it's easy to be confused by the jargon used by hospital personnel. Here are some commonly used terms:

☐ NPO: Sign placed by the bed of a patient who is not supposed to get anything to eat or drink.

☐ Emesis basin: Basin brought to patients who are sick to their stomach.

☐ Ambulate: Take the patient for a wal.

☐ Force fluids: Encourage intake of lo of liquid.

☐ Void: Urinate.

☐ IV: Intravenous.

☐ OOB: Out of bed.

☐ IPPB: Intermittent Positive Pressure Breathing machine to aid breathing.

☐ HS: Medication before sleep.

☐ BP: Blood pressure.

☐ HR: Heart rate.

Preparing yourself for anesthesia

The use of anesthetics during surgery to produce a pain-free, unconscious state is over a century old, but no one yet understands how these drugs work. Nevertheless, anesthesia is now a very safe procedure when performed by well-trained anesthetists.

Anesthetic drugs can cause upsetting postoperative side effects in some patients. Nausea, vomiting, chills, prolonged hallucinations, euphoria, sleepiness and impaired judgment are the most common ones. (These effects do eventually disappear.) Best news: Methods to alleviate or prevent these side effects exist.

☐ Insist on a preoperative discussion with the anesthetist before surgery (except in emergency situations, of course). Open discussion of worries before the operation is the most effective way to alleviate postoperative side effects.

☐ Tell the anesthetist about any previous problems with anesthesia. Be specific about dosages of all current medications, including tranquilizers. Such information helps an anesthetist determine the right kind and amount of drugs to use.

☐ Caution: Ketamine, a safe new drug good for short operations, occasionally causes unpleasant dreams and hallucinations for hours afterwards.

☐ Encourage the use of local anesthesia when possible. For many operations, patients can choose a local anesthetic or spinal-nerve block over general anesthesia of the whole body. Benefit: Postoperative side effects usually do not occur. The old fear that a spinal could cause paralysis is unfounded with today's techniques.

☐ The power of positive thinking works wonders (especially for nausea and vomiting). A patient who assumes that his recovery will be smooth will most likely have one.

☐ Physical fitness helps. A body in poor condition does not function as well immediately after anesthesia.

☐ Blankets. Patients often feel cold for several hours after an operation because temperatures normally drop below 98.6° during surgery. Solution: Plenty of blankets. Hint: Hospital blankets may be scarce. A family member or friend should procure them from busy nurses or aides.

Source: Jack Neary, chief nurse anesthetist, Sharon Hospital, Sharon, CT.

Considering plastic surgery

Plastic surgery for cosmetic reasons is surrounded by a lot of hype. The fantasy that your life will be magically transformed by surgery can play into the hands of the unscrupulous. If you know what questions to ask yourself before you make a commitment to surgery, you'll save heartache—to say nothing of money.

☐ Do I really need plastic surgery? Be objective when you look in the mirror. Some people want surgery for a couple of wrinkles that are barely noticeable to anyone but themselves. Their vulnerability to the power of perfection may make them easy marks. Criteria to follow: Would repair of an imperfection that bothers you enhance your well-being? Does that imperfection actually exist?

☐ What will it accomplish for me? The psychological factor in cosmetic surgery must be approached realistically. Many people delude themselves into believing that their difficulties will instantly be overcome if their physical defect is corrected.

☐ What's realistic? Improvement in self-image. People who have lost a lot of weight, for example, are almost always thrilled with the removal of excess skin, even though such surgery can cause extensive scarring that may actually look worse than the loose skin. Since loose skin is visible testimony to former obesity, however, removing it can go a long way toward improving self-image.

☐ How do you find your plastic surgeon? Stay away from high-pressure advertising. Best: Referral from other satisfied patients. If you don't know anyone who has had the type of surgery you want, ask your family doctor or internist for a recommendation. If you have a good relationship with your primary physician, there will be quality control. Your doctor can't afford to have his name smeared by an incompetent doctor.

☐ Do I ask for a second opinion? There's no other area where second opinions are more valuable. Only another doctor can confirm that you actually need the surgery and that the particular procedure your surgeon wants to do is reasonable for the result you seek.

Source: Neal B. Schultz, M.D., clinical assistant dermatologist, Mount Sinai Hospital, New York.

What to ask your plastic surgeon

No matter how many questions you have or how trivial you feel they are…ask!

☐ Realistically, what will be done? Not what can be done, or what you can hope for, but what you can expect.

☐ What will happen if you don't get the result the doctor promises? How will he remedy that situation? Will you have to pay for the unsatisfactory job? Will he do a corrective procedure at no cost? Crucial: Preoperative and postoperative pictures taken by the same photographer. Only with photos can you prove that you didn't get the promised result.

☐ What is the chance of real damage, and if it happens, what might the extent of it be? Plastic surgeons aren't gods. They are physicians who have had extensive training in delicate repair of skin; but nobody can break the integrity of normal skin without leaving a mark. If you have a big growth in the middle of your cheek, you can't expect the doctor to cut it out without leaving a mark. Other areas of concern: The chances of infection and other complications.

☐ Where will the surgery be done? Although many reputable plastic surgeons operate out of their own offices, surgery done in a hospital inevitably offers more quality control. There's much less room for nonprofessionalism in a hospital, where nurses and operating room teams are provided by the institution and there is peer review of a surgeon's work. Generally safest bet: A doctor who is university affiliated and teaches in a hospital or medical school.

☐ May I see your book of "before and after" pictures? You may want to speak to a surgeon's other patients, but since this might violate confidentiality, he may only be willing to show you before and after pictures. If he offers you a whole book of good results, you can feel confident.

☐ Can the surgery be done in stages? Why that can be important: A male model had facial moles treated with liquid nitrogen. His skin darkened, and there were brown spots and scars. The surgeon hadn't done a trial on one mole, but had treated them all at one session. Suggestion: If you have many of the same defects, have one corrected first to see if you like the result.

☐ Is there a less serious procedure that will produce a similar result? Collagen injections available today can sometimes eliminate both wrinkles and acne scars. Suction lipectomy can remove fat pockets. Look into such lesser procedures before undergoing full-scale surgery.

☐ How much will it cost?

☐ How much time will it take?

☐ How long will I be out of work or away from home?

What to look for in eye checkups

You should have a professional eye examination by an ophthalmologist or optometrist every two years, even if there has been no noticeable change in your vision since your last visit.

The examination should include:

☐ Full medical history, including details on previous or existing eye disease or injury in yourself and your family (first visit).

☐ Measurement of visual acuity, with and without corrective lenses.

☐ Tests for color blindness and stereopsis (binocular vision).

☐ Examination of the eyes' ability to track a moving object (usually with a tiny flashlight).

☐ Examination of the pupils' ability to constrict and dilate in response to changes in illumination and viewing distance.

☐ Screening for defects in the visual field (peripheral vision). This important test could indicate the presence of tumors, brain damage or a detached retina.

☐ Microscopic examination of the external portions of the eye, as well as the lens, optic nerve, retina and other interior structures. (Your eyes will be dilated for this step.)

☐ Screening for glaucoma.

Source: Richard L. Abbott, M.D., associate clinical professor, department of ophthalmology Pacific Presbyterian Medical Center, San Francisco.

A skilled eye examination checks more than vision

By looking carefully into the eyes, a skilled physician can detect clues to literally hundreds of different systemic illnesses. The eyes can act as an early warning system for diseases that may not otherwise be apparent:

☐ High blood pressure: Changes in the eyes can include blood vessel spasm or narrowing and microscopic hemorrhages within the retina. Swelling of the optic nerve in the back of the eye indicates severe high blood pressure that requires emergency treatment.

☐ Diabetes: A patient might experience blurriness of vision and sudden sightedness. This change occurs because high blood sugar affects the water content of the lenses, causing them to swell. Distance vision improves and near vision deteriorates. Once the sugar problem is corrected, vision often returns to normal. Examination of the retina can reveal vascular changes, some of which respond to laser therapy. This could prevent visual disability in the future.

☐ Heart valve infection: This is most characteristic in patients who have run a low grade fever over a period of time and may have a history of childhood heart disease or rheumatic fever. How it happens: From a wound or infection somewhere else in the body, the bloodstream is temporarily seeded with certain bacteria that can settle on a heart valve, especially if it was previously damaged. The bacteria slowly grow like vegetation on the valve. The symptoms can be very subtle, including headaches, sweating and low-grade fever. Occasionally little infected blood clots with bacteria on them travel to the eyes. Called Roth spots, these might be the only clue to a heart-valve problem that could be cured with intensive antibiotic therapy.

☐ Strokes: Episodes of amaurosis fugax (temporary blindness) can be evidence of an impending stroke or an indication of atherosclerosis of the carotid artery (the large artery in the neck).

☐ Brain tumors and other neurological problems. Some can come to light as a result of vision problems, such as loss of peripheral vision.

☐ Thyroid disease. This can cause swelling and increased prominence of the eyes. Sometimes only one eye seems to bulge, or there may be a too-wide stare or an eyelid lag.

☐ Inflammatory diseases. Rheumatoid arthritis and certain back diseases occasionally cause the eyes to be red and very dry, sandy, and scratchy.

☐ Hereditary defects. On occasion, metabolic disorders can be seen in the eyes. It may be possible to examine an entire family to see who is at risk for a particular genetic disease.

☐ Infectious diseases. Long-term syphilis and other abnormalities in the bloodstream may affect the eyes.

☐ Don't be frightened if the ophthalmologist recommends a medical checkup. Very often there are minor or unimportant findings that require confirmation of your general health.

Source: B. David Gorman, M.D., adjunct ophthalmologist and coordinator of resident education at Lenox Hill Hospital.

Recognizing and treating detached retinas

About one out of 10 people develop small holes in their retinas, the lining in back of the eye that receives images and transmits them to the brain. In very few of these cases, the condition causes the retina to detach when the fluid in the eyeball oozes through the hole and separates the retina from the back of the eye. If untreated, blindness can result.

☐ Most vulnerable: Very nearsighted people, those with high blood pressure and those who have had cataract surgery. Besides annual eye check-ups, there are no preventive measures.

☐ Earliest symptom: A flash of light in the peripheral field of vision, something like a flashbulb going off a few tables away at a restaurant.

☐ Next: Dark dots or other shapes that move from the side toward the center of the vision field. (These are not the same as the translucent "floaters" many people see.)

☐ If symptoms occur, consult an ophthalmologist immediately.

☐ To keep from aggravating the problem, avoid jolts to your body or head.

☐ Treatment: A laser can be used to fuse the retina to the back of the eye.

Alternatively, the hole can be "frozen" shut with a probe that goes around the side of the eyeball. Both operations can be performed in the doctor's office. The only after-effect is a temporary, minor irritation that can be relieved by eyedrops.

☐ For a severely detached retina, a major operation called scleral buckling is required. Surgeons put a piece of plastic or sponge behind the torn area, pushing the wall up toward the retina, and then freeze them together.

☐ Subsequent risk: People who suffer one retinal detachment are vulnerable to recurrence in that eye and are more susceptible to a detachment in the other.

Source: Dr. Jacob Rosenbaum, M.D., specialist in retinal diseases, New York.

How to buy contact lenses wisely

As contact lenses become more sophisticated, the options for wearers seem endless and the differences confusing. Before buying lenses, take into account your budget, your lifestyle and the degree of vision correction you need.

Regardless of the type of lenses you end up with (hard, gas-permeable, soft, or extended-wear), follow these guidelines:

☐ Select a professional eye-care specialist you trust and who comes well recommended.

☐ Be wary of discount commercial eye-care establishments. They deal in quantity, not quality, and emphasize product, not service.

☐ Be aware that physical changes can take place in the eyes as a result of wearing contacts. Your eye-care professional should carefully monitor such changes and adjust for them, if necessary.

☐ Ask about a service (or insurance) contract that offers replacement lenses at reduced fees. This is usually worth the modest price, as you may well lose a lens every year or so.

☐ Follow the cleaning/disinfecting procedures recommended by your eye-care professional. If you take shortcuts, you could shorten the life of your lenses and/or damage your eyes.

☐ Although you may wear your lenses every day, keep an updated pair of glasses to wear in emergencies.

Source: Robert Snyder, O.D., an optometrist in private practice, Beach Haven, NJ.

Current options in contact lenses

Hard Lenses
☐ Oldest type of contact lens.

☐ Made of rigid plastic, which some people find uncomfortable.

☐ Good for people with astigmatism.

☐ Must be removed each night and soaked in a sterile solution.

☐ Can be tinted to enhance eye color and make lost lenses easier to find.

☐ Can be worn 10 to 14 hours per day after initial familiarization period.

☐ Should be professionally cleaned and polished each year.

☐ Last several years.

Gas-Permeable Firm Lenses
☐ Variation on hard lenses—made of plastic and silicon.

☐ Lenses "breathe," thereby letting more air flow to the eyes.

☐ Can be worn 14 to 18 hours per day.

☐ Also good for people with astigmatism.

☐ Care and replacement schedule similar to that of hard lenses.

Soft Lenses
☐ Made of spongelike plastic.

☐ More comfortable than hard or gas-permeable lenses for most people.

☐ Can be tinted.

☐ Good for those who engage in active sports, since they are less apt to pop out from a rough blow.

☐ Less prone to dust particles and other eye irritants.

☐ Must be removed and sterilized every night, either with a heat machine or chemical disinfectant.

☐ Can be worn virtually round the clock, so long as they are cleaned and disinfected every day.

☐ Last up to two years.

Bifocal Soft Lenses
☐ New type of lens.

☐ Similar to regular soft lenses, especially for bifocal wearers.

☐ Not suitable, though, for everyone who needs bifocals, so must be carefully prescribed and fitted.

Extended-Wear Soft Lenses
☐ Have higher water content than regular soft lenses, so transmit even more oxygen to eyes.

] Very comfortable for most people.

] Can be worn all day and night (that ;, can be left in during sleep).

] Easily wearable for a week at a tretch, and sometimes longer, lthough wearing for a month without leaning is not advisable.

] Can be tinted.

] Especially good for very nearsighted people or those with cataracts.

] Special lenses can be made for stigmatic eyes.

] Must be replaced every 1½ to 2 ears.

] Similar cleaning procedures as for egular soft lenses must be followed, lthough much less frequently.

Source: Robert Snyder, O.D., an optometrist in private practice, Beach Haven, NJ.

Contact lens cautions

] Avoid wearing lenses in the barber shop if hair sprays or other irritating vapors are in the air (including fumes from nail polish remover).

] Don't use any sprays (deodorant, hair, foot) after inserting lenses.

] Make sure there's no soap or shampoo on fingertips.

] Insert your lenses before shaving to avoid contaminating them with after-shave products applied with the hands.

Helping the hard of hearing

] Always speak in full view of a nonhearing person. Don't talk while rocking in a chair, chewing gum or eating.

] If the person has a hearing aid, move closer and speak normally. If not, raise your voice without shouting.

] To get attention, gently tap the person's shoulder or come into full view before speaking.

] When in a group, avoid whispering or covering your mouth while talking.

] Never speak about hearing-impaired people in their presence. (They might pick up more than you assume.)

] Be sensitive to facial expressions. They'll tell you if you're getting through.

Source: *For Your Good Health,* Overlook Hospital Foundation, Summit, NJ.

How to take your temperature

□ Take your temperature first thing in the morning for the most accurate reading.

□ Wait 30 minutes after eating, drinking, smoking, or exercising so your mouth will be neither cooled down nor heated up.

□ Shake down the thermometer to below normal—mercury rises from the last reading.

□ Relax.

□ Hold the thermometer under the back of your tongue for four minutes.

□ Don't move your tongue, breathe through your mouth or talk.

□ When using a rectal thermometer on an infant, lubricate it with water-soluble jelly and hold the baby's legs so a quick movement won't dislodge it or break the glass.

□ Leave the thermometer in at least two minutes. Don't use the new disposable thermometers. They're not very accurate. Better: The old-fashioned kind.

How to treat fever

□ Take aspirin or acetaminophen only when your temperature is over 102° and you're uncomfortable.

□ Dress lightly enough so that body heat can escape.

□ Sponge with tepid water, not alcohol (the vapors can be dangerous).

□ Take a bath and wash your hair if you feel like it—the evaporating water may lower your temperature.

□ Drink eight to twelve glasses of liquid a day to avoid dehydration.

Fever: When to call the doctor

Call the doctor for a fever when:

□ A child's temperature goes above 102° or an adult's over 101°.

□ The fever persists for more than 24 hours with no obvious cause.

□ The fever lasts for more than 72 hours, even if there's an obvious cause.

□ An infant under three months old has any temperature elevation.

□ There is a serious disease involved.

□ In short, call the doctor when you feel really sick (even if you haven't got a fever).

What to do about colds

Doctors cannot cure a cold. But sufferers can help themselves by keeping in mind what is known about the ailment. Essentials:

☐ Chills don't cause colds, but they encourage existing viruses to multiply.

☐ Colds spread most effectively by direct contact and are most contagious in their early stages before the symptoms are even noticeable.

☐ The body's process of curing a cold requires about the same energy as hard physical labor. Keep vigorous exercise to a minimum so your energy goes toward fighting the cold.

☐ Taking vitamin C may help. Advocates suggest one to three grams a day at the outset of a cold and 500 milligrams daily throughout its duration.

☐ Avoid stress during a cold. It reduces antibody production in the nose and mouth.

☐ Don't numb pain by drinking alcohol.

Source: *Executive Fitness Newsletter,* Emmaus, PA.

The office cold is a myth

People pick up relatively few cold viruses from their associates at work. An office may have many people nursing colds, but chances are few of them have the same virus strain. The majority of colds are caught at home. And the main carriers are children, who are exposed to the most viruses through close association and direct physical contact with their playmates. Parents then catch the cold from the sick child.

☐ Shaking hands with someone who has a cold and then rubbing your eyes can be riskier than standing directly in front of a sneezing person. Current research indicates that most colds are probably spread by direct physical contact. The viruses grow in the nose and eyes (but not the mouth). When infected people wipe or blow their noses sloppily, some of the cold virus can get onto their hands. Outside the body, the virus can survive as long as a day. Result: Unless washed off, it spreads to toys, furniture, drinking cup and other people's hands.

☐ Colds are contagious, beginning wit the onset of symptoms until the symptoms vanish. Worst period: The first two to three days.

☐ Use a tissue or handkerchief when covering coughs and sneezes. Bare hands pick up the virus and spread the cold.

☐ Wash your hands frequently when around people who have colds, especially after touching things they have handled.

☐ Keep hands away from noses and eyes immediately after contact with a person with cold symptoms.

☐ Do not rely on household sprays to disinfect objects. Their value is unproven.

Source: Jack Gwaltney, Jr., M.D., professor of internal medicine, University of Virginia Medical School.

Sinusitis: What you can do to prevent it

A common cold can lead to sinusitis, inflammation of the sinus cavities. In its acute stage, sinusitis causes swelling of the membranes inside the sinuses, pressure, headache, low-grade fever and a general feeling of misery.

The cold or upper respiratory infection brought on by bacteria or a virus sets up an inflammatory condition of the nose and the sinus cavities that obstructs the flow of secretions. Infection follows, producing more swelling of the mucous membrane, which in turn produces more blockage—and a vicious cycle ensues

☐ Once you've got full-blown sinusitis, see a doctor. He'll probably prescribe an antibiotic, which will usually knock out the infection quickly. Penicillin compounds are the most commonly used, but different antibiotics are required for different types of bacteria.

☐ If antibiotics alone don't clear up the problem, you may need to have your sinuses opened surgically. Most of the time, this is an office procedure.

☐ You may be one of the 10% to 15% who need an in-hospital operation. A deviated septum may have to be corrected. Or it might be necessary to make an opening between the nose and an obstructed sinus for maximum drainage.

☐ To avoid sinusitis, take decongestants and use nasal sprays when you have a cold. They reduce the amount of swelling and inflammation, preventing the sinuses from becoming blocked and infected.

☐ But don't overdo them. They also dry up the secretions that fight infection. Nasal sprays shouldn't be used for more than 48 hours. Both sprays and decongestants should be administered under the care of a doctor.

☐ Use a humidifier or vaporizer when you have a cold.

☐ Don't sleep in a hot, dry room. Dry heat is the worst thing for the sinuses. Leave your bedroom window open, even if you live in a cold climate.

☐ Avoid cigarettes and alcohol. Both are irritating to the nasal passages and sinuses.

☐ If you have hay fever or other allergies, be sure to have them treated.

☐ Eat a balanced diet and get plenty of exercise. Exercise is particularly important for promoting proper nasal and sinus function.

Source: Stanley M. Blaugrund, M.D., an ear, nose and throat specialist and director of the Department of Otolaryngology, Lenox Hill Hospital, New York.

A cough: Getting rid of it the old-fashioned way

Skeptics of cough medications say home remedies may be more effective and less risky. Try these:

☐ Chicken soup.

☐ Fruit juices.

☐ Vaporizers and humidifiers.

☐ A drop of honey on the back of the tongue.

Source: Dr. Sidney Wolfe, M.D., and others, quoted in *Executive Fitness Newsletter,* Emmaus, PA.

Cough medicines that don't do what they advertise

The Federal Drug Administration is beginning to agree with an increasing number of doctors who say commercial cough remedies interfere with the body's natural way of clearing the respiratory tract, which is coughing. Doctors are especially concerned with:

☐ Antihistamines, which they say work by thickening, not thinning, lung secretions. Good only for allergies.

☐ Decongestants, which might be good for extreme stuffiness but are otherwise of doubtful effectiveness.

☐ Expectorants, which drug companies say loosen mucus and phlegm, although the evidence is scanty.

☐ Suppressants, which suppress the brain's cough reflex. They are especially hazardous for people with asthma or bronchitis who rely on coughing to breathe when their lungs are not clear.

Source: *Executive Fitness Newsletter,* Emmaus, PA.

Battling migraines

The best way to deal with recurrent, intense migraine headaches is to try more than one solution. Chronic sufferers (estimated at between 8 million and 12 million Americans) can try one or more of the following:

☐ Keep a headache diary. Note the times a headache starts and stops and what you were doing, eating and thinking. The records help a doctor evaluate the condition and help patients discover causative factors.

☐ Avoid aggravating foods and drinks. These include edibles containing tyramine (nuts, chocolate, aged cheese), sodium nitrate (frankfurters), and alcoholic beverages.

☐ If you take birth-control pills, consider switching to another contraceptive method.

☐ If aspirin doesn't provide relief, ask your doctor about propranolol (marketed by Ayerst Laboratories under the name Inderal). This is now considered the safest, most effective antimigraine medicine on the market.

☐ Get more opinions. Ideally a neurologist should verify that the condition is indeed a migraine.

Simple causes of backache

Backache may be caused by discomfort and tension arising from poor everyday living habits.

☐ Clothing should never be tight. This

applies to pajamas and nightgowns, as well as to everyday dress.

☐ Avoid narrow-toed shoes. They tense the leg muscles, which in turn affect the back. Heels should not be too loose or too tight. Either extreme produces ankle sway, which works its way up to the back and neck. Women's high-heeled shoes shorten the hamstring and calf muscles, causing the tension that frequently leads to backache.

☐ Toes of socks and stockings should not be tight. You should be able to wiggle your toes freely.

☐ Too high or too tight a collar can cause a stiff neck. Wear collars half a size larger and, if your neck is short, stick to soft, narrow collars.

☐ Narrow shoulder straps of brassieres can cause shoulder and upper back pain, especially if they are pulled too tight.

☐ People with wide shoulders who sleep on their sides require bigger pillows.

☐ Foam rubber pillows often force the neck into a rigid position. Use a feather pillow.

☐ Never sit in one position for more than an hour or two. Get up and move around.

☐ On car trips, stop frequently to stretch and move.

☐ Instead of tensing when the phone rings, make it a practice to shrug the shoulders before reaching out to pick up the receiver.

Source: Hans Krause, M.D., author of *Backache, Stress and Tension,* Pocket Books, New York.

Back strain and driving

The probability of spinal disk problems is three times greater for those who spend a big part of their work lives driving. To reduce the strain on your back:

☐ Keep your head and shoulders erect while driving. Place a 1½-inch-thick pillow, or a wicker back support, at the small of the back. Keep the back pressed against it.

☐ Change driving position often.

Take frequent breaks to stretch your legs and do one or two of these exercises:

☐ Grab your wrists, and raise your arms to shoulder height. Try to pull your arms apart for a count of six. Repeat three times.

☐ Hold your forehead, then push your head against your hand. Repeat for each side of the head. Do slowly three times.

☐ Lace your fingers behind your head and press back against them. Do slowly three times.

☐ Using the car to steady you, do at least four deep-knee bends when you stop for a rest.

Source: Shirley Linde, author of *How to Beat a Bad Back,* Rawson, Wade Publishers, New York.

Kicking the cigarette habit

Tactics for giving up cigarettes vary according to the underlying motivation for smoking. Keys to the right strategy:

☐ Habitual smokers reach for a cigarette in response to such cues as talking on the phone or drinking. First step: Make the cigarettes difficult to reach, or put them in a hard-to-open package.

☐ Positive-effect smokers actually enjoy smoking. First step: Find an equally enjoyable activity that can't be done while smoking.

☐ Negative-effect smokers smoke because of nervousness or depression. First step: Professional advice on the basic problem.

☐ Physically addicted smokers should quit cold turkey. The reactions to quitting are always unpleasant. But the worst of them will be over in a week.

Source: *Executive Fitness Newsletter,* Emmaus, PA.

Smoking restrictions at work

Companies can legally discriminate against smokers. More companies are doing so because it may actually head off trouble in the form of lawsuits brought by nonsmokers who demand a healthful, smoke-free work environment.

Here are some measures companies have taken:

☐ Total ban. Employees may smoke only in the company parking lot, and then only during work breaks and on lunch hours. And it applies to everyone, including top management, visitors and customers.

☐ Work station ban. Smoking is prohibited in working areas but allowed during work breaks in specified areas. Softer policies such as dividing the work area between smokers and non-smokers. However, these rarely work well.

Source: Dr. William L. Weis, Albers School of Business, Seattle University, writing in *Personnel Journal.*

Prescription-drug addiction

For every person addicted to heroin in the US, there are 10 hooked on prescription drugs. And withdrawal can be as painful as from any in the illicit-drug world.

Why addiction happens: The doctor prescribes a psychoactive drug (one that affects the mind or behavior) to relieve a physical ailment. By altering your moods, psychoactive drugs can affect your ability to make judgments and decisions. Some drugs mask the symptoms of serious ailments or can impair your physical activity. These drugs have their place among useful medications (generally for short-term relief), but they do not cure physical ailments.

Most commonly abused psychoactive drugs: Codeine, Valium, Librium, Demerol, Dalmane, and Nembutol. Worse: Mixing drugs or combining a drug with alcohol.

☐ If your physician is reluctant to make a specific diagnosis or refuses to explain the effects of drugs, find another doctor.

☐ Question every prescription you're given: Will it cure the ailment or will it just relieve the symptoms?

☐ Before accepting a drug for an emotional problem, seek another solution: a vacation, exercise, counseling.

☐ If the problem is physical, ask why this drug is being prescribed rather than another treatment.

If you've become dependent on prescription drugs

☐ Cut drug dependency gradually, under a doctor's supervision. Stopping the pills immediately is sometimes possible. But it is often accompanied by insomnia, muscle twitches, a burning sensation of the skin or even seizures.

☐ Expect withdrawal symptoms to occur days after you stop taking the drug. When they occur, don't fall into the trap of believing you're overstressed and resume taking the drug that caused the problem in the first place.

☐ Sign up for a detoxification program. There are many throughout the country, from low-cost therapy offered through most state and local health departments to luxury "spas." To find out about detox programs, contact: Center for Substance Abuse Treatment Hotline, 11428 Rockville Pike, Rockville, MD 20852. (800) 662-4357.

☐ At various points in your withdrawal from drugs, you may decide it is not worth the effort. Except for those people with chronic, incurable physiological (not psychological) pain, it is worth it. If you have any doubts, ask a former addict.

Source: Josette Mondanaro, M.D., Santa Cruz, CA.

Sexual side effects of high-blood pressure medicines

Many illnesses can themselves cause lack of libido and impotence, but in other cases, it is the medication used to treat the illness that brings on changes in sexual desire and capability. Research in this area is scanty, and the sexual side effects of many drugs are not universal. Discuss your own situation with your doctor. The following drugs are known to have affected the sex lives of many who take them regularly:

☐ Esimil and Ismelin (guanethidine) may cause impaired ejaculation and lack of potency in men.

☐ Aldomet, Aldoclor, and Aldoril (methyldopa) can decrease sexual desire and make holding an erection difficult for men. In rare cases, they cause a man's breasts to develop.

☐ Diupres, Exna-R, Rau-Sed, Regroton, Salutensin, Ser-Ap-Es, and Serpasil (reserpine) can cause reduced libido and potency, delayed ejaculation and enlarged breasts.

☐ Catapres (clonidine) may produce impotence in men and failure to achieve orgasm in women.

☐ Eutonyl and Eutron (pargyline) may bring on impotence, delayed ejaculation or delayed orgasm.

☐ Inderal and Inderide (propranolol) rarely cause side effects, although difficulty with erections has been reported.

Source: Joe Graedon, pharmacologist and author of *The People's Pharmacy* and *The People's Pharmacy–2,* Avon Books, New York.

Sexual side effects of mood altering drugs

☐ Librium and Valium have quite opposite effects on different individuals. For some, these drugs reduce inhibitions and increase sexual desire. In other cases, they decrease libido.

☐ Depression itself often causes a lack of interest in sex. Antidepressant drugs sometimes increase libido and sometimes decrease it. Other sexual side effects vary widely and are not well recorded. Possible problems include impotence, testicular swelling, breast enlargement and milk secretion, impaired ejaculation in men and delayed orgasm in women.

☐ Many medications used to treat psychosis have adverse sexual side effects that have not been fully documented. Among the symptoms are impotence, difficulty in ejaculation, irregular menstruation, abnormal lactation, increased and decreased sexual desire and even false positive pregnancy tests.

☐ Sleeping pills reduce the desire for sex. As administered in therapy, barbiturates often diminish sexual inhibitions, which raises sexual enjoyment. But chronic use of sleeping pills causes difficulty in reaching orgasm. More dangers: Men can become impotent, and women may suffer menstrual problems.

Source: Joe Graedon, pharmacologist and author of *The People's Pharmacy* and *The People's Pharmacy–2,* Avon Books, New York, and Dorothy DeMoya, RN, and Dr. Armando DeMoya, M.D., both of Georgetown University, writing in *RN,* Oradell, NJ.

Precautions when you need blood

There are certain steps individuals can take to insure against getting contaminated blood in hospitals:

☐ Prior to surgery, make a specific request of your physician to use only volunteer-donor blood. Volunteer blood does not cost any more than commercial blood. And commercial (paid-donor) blood has a much higher incidence of contamination.

☐ Better still, arrange beforehand to donate your own blood to be used during your surgery.

☐ If your blood type is rare, join the National Rare Blood Club*, which has 16,000 volunteer donors throughout the U.S. who will supply blood without charge in an emergency.

☐ Despite your precautions, you may still get commercial blood. Hospitals cannot be held liable if they have no volunteer-donor blood and must, in an emergency, give paid-donor blood to a patient who requested volunteer-donor blood only. Several states, including California, Illinois and Oklahoma, have outlawed the use of commercial blood.

*The rare blood types are B+, O, A, AB+, B, AB.

Cancer survival rates

For most cancers, patients who survive five years have an 85% chance of surviving 20 years. Of all cancers diagnosed this year, 50% will prove curable. (Curable means the patient will survive as long as an age-matched person without cancer.)

☐ With the aggressive lymphomas, such as advanced Hodgkin's disease, cure rates a patient pronounced "cured" will survive as long as an age-matched person without cancer are up from 5% in 1973, to 70% today.

☐ With testicular cancer, the most common cancer in young men, the rate is up from 10% in 1973 to 70% today.

☐ Thyroid: 92% survive after five years.

☐ Endometrium (uterine): 87% survive after five years.

☐ Melanoma: 79% survive after five years.

☐ Bladder: 72% survive after five years.

☐ Prostate: 67% survive after five years.

☐ Uterine cervix: 67% survive after five years.

☐ Larynx: 66% survive after five years.

☐ Lung cancer: Lung cancer is the most common form of cancer in men, and now exceeds breast cancer as the leading cause of cancer death in women. Overall only 9% of lung cancer patients live five years or more after diagnosis.

☐ Colon and rectal cancer: Although these cancers are second in incidence to lung cancer, and there have been no real changes in treatment, five-year survival rates are up from 43% to 51%. Surgery is the most effective treatment. Many victims fear a permanent colostomy, but only 15% of cases detected early will need one.

☐ Breast cancer. A woman with breast cancer today has about a 73% chance of being alive in five years. It was 63% in 1975. Also, in many cases less mutilating procedures (particularly removing just the lump itself or part of the breast) in combination with radiation therapy provide the same five-year survival rate as radical mastectomy.

☐ Cancer in children. Although there were only 6,000 new cases in 1984, making it a rare childhood disease, cancer is still the chief cause of death by disease in children between the ages of 3 and 14. However, leukemia is no longer the death sentence it once was. With improved chemotherapy, survival rates have risen from 5% in the 1960s to 50% today. The latest statistics show that with leukemia, once five-year survival is reached, relapse is unheard of. Survival rates for other childhood cancers vary considerably, depending on the site, but the overall death rate of children with cancer is about half the 1950 rate.

Source: Gregory A. Curt, M.D., medical oncologist, division of cancer treatment, National Cancer Institute, Bethesda, MD.

Testicular cancer

Without prompt treatment, 29% of men who have testicular cancer will die from it. But virtually all could be cured if treated within a month of the onset of symptoms. To lower your chances of being a victim:

☐ Give yourself a testicular self-exam once a month. The exam takes only three minutes. The best time to do this is after a warm bath or shower, when the scrotum is most relaxed.

☐ Technique: Examine the testicles separately, using fingers of both hands. Put your thumbs on top of the testicle and your index and middle fingers underneath. Roll the testicle gently. (If it hurts, you're applying too much pressure.)

☐ Be aware that a normal testicle is firm, oval and free of lumps; behind it you'll feel the epididymis (sperm storage duct), which is spongier.

☐ If you feel a small, hard, usually painless lump or swelling on the front or side of the testicle, you could have a problem. When in the slightest doubt, see a doctor.

Source: *Prevention*, Emmaus, PA.

Skin cancer alert

Malignant melanoma, a form of skin cancer, has doubled in incidence in the past 10 years. If the cancer is caught and excised in the earlier stages of development, the patient can be cured. But if the malignancy goes too deep, the cancer invades the body, and neither radiation treatment nor chemotherapy is effective.

☐ Malignant melanoma can develop independently as a dark tumor in the skin or it can come from a potentially malignant lesion, the "dysplastic atypical mole."

☐ People with dysplastic moles should be checked by a dermatologist at least every six months.

Characteristics of malignant melanoma and dysplastic moles:

☐ Bigger in size than a pencil-eraser head.

☐ A mixture of colors in the same mole.

☐ Asymmetrical shape.

☐ Bumpy texture.

☐ Irregular or notched borders.

☐ Development of malignant melanoma is directly related to the sun. It is more common in fair-skinned, blue-eyed people, who are more sensitive to the sun. Many victims of malignant melanoma had a severe, blistering sunburn in childhood or adolescence, and areas such as the back that get weekend sunburns are often affected. Malignant melanoma and dysplastic moles also tend to run in families.

☐ Myth: A mole that suffers trauma (such as a cut during shaving) or sprouts hair will become cancerous.

Source: Harold T. Eisenman, M.D., a dermatologist and dermatopathologist in private practice in West Orange, NJ.

Using your mind to fight cancer

Your beliefs can be powerful allies against cancer. The body produces billions of cells and routinely identifies and kills cancerous ones. Once the major cancer-removal job is done by surgery and chemotherapy, your body can take over. But you must free up energy to mobilize your body to fight cancer.

☐ Express your feelings. Patients who express anger and sadness survive the longest. Expressing your feelings reduces stress and releases energy. Suppressing feelings uses up valuable energy that should be mobilized to fight the cancer. Example: In a study at Johns Hopkins, patients with metastatic breast cancer who survived more than a year were those who expressed their depression, anxiety, and sense of alienation. They were also judged by their doctors as being poorly adjusted to the disease and as having negative attitudes toward their doctors.

☐ Avoid blame, guilt, and self-criticism. You are not being punished for wrong-doing. The question *Why me?* should be replaced with *What can I do about it now?*

☐ Seek support. Discuss your situation with a therapist, family member, or support group. Important: Talk with a former cancer patient who has been pronounced cured or has survived for years with the disease. This can be a powerful combatant of negative feelings.

☐ Take positive steps to help yourself. Recognize that your life has changed, probably forever, and that your old ways of coping are no longer viable and may even be implicated in your illness. What must change: Gratification from compulsive goal-seeking. The cancer patient must start to develop a sense of self-worth that comes from within rather than from outside goals such as success, money, or sexual conquests.

☐ Learn to say no. Every moment is precious. Why waste it on trivia or worrying about whether an extra phone call will bother your doctor.

☐ Speak the unspeakable. The relatives and friends of cancer patients often feel certain subjects are taboo. This leads patients to suppress their feelings in order to protect their loved ones. But when patients and the people they're close to talk openly about their feelings, it can be an enormous relief and source of strength.

☐ Participate in choosing your treatment to reduce the stress of feeling like a passive victim. You may feel emotionally and physically debilitated by the side effects of chemo-therapy and slip into thinking that you *have* to take these drugs for your doctor. Remind yourself that you are taking the drugs because they are powerful allies of your body.

☐ You must choose a doctor you feel has some concern for you as a human being and who takes your values and life goals into consideration when medical decisions are made. Your doctor should give you information about treatment plans and alternatives and be open to negotiating alternative with you rather than assuming a "take or leave it" attitude.

Source: Neil A. Fiore, Ph.D., a psychologist who works for the University of California and has a private practice in Berkeley. He has worked with many cancer patients, and is the author of *The Road Back to Health: Coping With the Emotional Side of Cancer,* Bantam Books, New York.

Even moderate drinking can be harmful

Even moderate drinking may be bad news for some people (susceptibility varies widely). Some typical problems

☐ Sleep disorders. Sleeplessness and awakening early. Reason: Alcohol depresses body functions for four to six hours. So an evening drinker may awaken at 4 A.M. or 5 A.M., as the body begins to rebound. Lunchtime drinker may get nervous by late day and decide to have another drink.

☐ Anxiety. Agitated depression, guilt and sense of inadequacy can occasionally result. Reason: Alcohol's depressive effect on mental condition parallels that which it has on the body

☐ Muddled mind—loss of memory, lowered aptitude and trouble organizing thoughts. Unlike other body tissues, brain cells do not regenerate.

☐ Special danger for women: A highly regarded medical journal, *The Lancet* suggested that the incidence of breast cancer among mild drinkers may be 1.5 to 2 times that of nondrinkers. The reason has not been established.

Source: Dr. Robert Millman, psychiatrist, New York Hospital.

Hangover help

No magic formula prevents the headache and general malaise that follows an evening of drinking too much alcohol too quickly. Some measures, however, can keep a night on the town from being a total disaster.

❏ Eat fatty or oily food before you have the first drink. That lines your stomach and slows the body's absorption of alcohol. (Cheese and nuts are good choices.)

❏ Eat starches while you drink to soak up the alcohol. (Bread or crackers work.)

❏ Avoid spirits with high levels of cogeners (additives that can cause toxic effects). Brandy, red wine, dark rum and sherry have the most. Vodka and white wine have the least.

❏ Take charcoal tablets to speed up the removal of the cogeners (four tablets if you are small and up to six for large people). Cabbage and vitamin C are reputed to help in this area, as well.

❏ Drink plenty of water to replace lost fluid.

❏ Alcohol depletes the system of many nutrients, particularly vitamins A, B, and C and minerals such as niacin, calcium, magnesium and potassium. Take a multivitamin that includes minerals.

❏ Work the alcohol out of your system with a little exercise. It increases your intake of oxygen, and oxygen speeds up this process. So does the fructose found in honey and fruit juices.

❏ For pain or nausea, over-the-counter analgesics or antacids are the antidote.

❏ "A little hair of the dog that bit you" is an old cure that has some basis in reality. The brain cells affected by alcohol can return to normal quite suddenly. This explains the supersensitivity to noise and smells associated with hangover. A small amount of alcohol (one to one-and-a-half ounces) can ease your brain back into awareness. Recommended: If you try this panacea, mix the spirits with something nutritious like cream. Other possibilities: A can of beer. A Fernet Branca, a packaged alcoholic mixture that includes herbs and folk-medicine standbys like camomile and aloe.

Source: David Outerbridge, author of *The Hangover Handbook,* Harmony Books, New York.

How to treat varicose veins

Varicose vein sufferers should consider surgery only as a last resort. Surgery is not a permanent solution. The condition will reappear unless the underlying causes are corrected.

Before surgery:

❏ Change your diet to include a high proportion of whole grains, seeds, nuts, vegetables and fruit.

❏ Avoid constipation, too much sitting with crossed legs, too much standing, tight clothing.

❏ Use a slant-board and elevate the foot of your bed.

❏ Walk and swim.

❏ Use elastic support stockings if the condition is severe.

Source: Paavo Airola, author of *Every Woman's Book,* Health Plus, Phoenix, AZ.

Reducing the risk of Alzheimer's disease

Alzheimer's disease is a progressive degenerative disease referred to as senile dementia. There is much that is unknown about the disease at this point. Any suggestions for preventing Alzheimer's are speculative. An elevated level of aluminum has been found in the nuclei of the nerve cells affected by Alzheimer's disease. The aluminum seems to produce damage that prevents normal utilization of calcium ions, which are essential for neuronal function. It's not necessarily true that aluminum is toxic in itself. Rather, aluminum apparently prevents normal metabolism of calcium and possibly of other essential nutrients.

❏ It's foolish to think that if you throw away your aluminum pots and stop using baking soda, aluminum foil, aluminum-containing antacids, or aluminum-containing deodorants that you'll be safe from Alzheimer's disease.

❏ Someone who is developing Alzheimer's disease, however, would probably be wise to cut back on the use of aluminum-containing products, since it's possible that a lot of aluminum might accelerate the progress of the disease. But the general population should follow common sense. If it's just as easy to wrap food in plastic and take nonaluminum antacids, you might as well.

❏ There may be some value in zinc, which has been used experimentally to prevent some of the damage done by aluminum. This doesn't mean one should take in too much zinc, but rather eat a well-balanced diet that includes normal amounts of zinc.*

☐ Over indulgence in alcohol helps aluminum from the normal diet to enter the brain. So, cutting down on alcohol may be helpful. The old rule about moderation is a good one—avoid extremes.

*The US recommended daily allowance is 15 milligrams.

Source: Dr. Leopold Liss, an M.D., in neuropathology and professor of pathology and psychiatry at Ohio State University, Columbus.

Smoking and Alzheimer's

In a health study conducted by Harvard University, it was observed that individuals who smoked more than one pack of cigarettes a day were four times as likely to develop Alzheimer's disease as those who smoked less. Reason: Unknown.

Source: Stuart L. Shalat, ScD, assistant professor of epidemiology and medicine, Yale University School of Medicine.

Hemorrhoids (much too much about them)

Just about everyone gets a hemorrhoid occasionally. Although they are uncomfortable and worrisome, with good medical and dietary management, you can almost always avoid surgery.

What we think of as hemorrhoids are actually enlarged blood vessels in the anal canal. These blue swellings are entirely normal and are suspected to have something to do with maintaining control of bladder and bowels. Hemorrhoids occur when these vascular cushions protrude in some way and become enlarged, ulcerated, inflamed and bleeding. If you should experience rectal bleeding:

☐ First, get a medical checkup to rule out malignancy.

☐ Increase your intake of dietary fiber, mainly by eating high-fiber cereals (those with at least eight grams of fiber per serving). In a 24-hour period you should have close to 20 grams of fiber.

☐ In addition to the cereal, which you must eat religiously, also eat whole-grain bread, a daily salad, and fresh fruits and vegetables.

☐ Avoid refined foods.

☐ Avoid irritants such as alcohol and spicy or constipating foods during an attack.

☐ Be aware that with a change in diet there may be some initial discomfort, including cramping, an increase in gas, and more bulky, more frequent stools. This will improve as your intestine gets used to the increased fiber.

☐ Don't use medical stool softeners unless the high-fiber diet turns out to be really intolerable and your doctor prescribes them.

☐ If you have pain and irritation, take warm baths, which are soothing to the area and keep it clean.

☐ Take mineral oil to lubricate the bowel movement. Mineral oil is harmless in the short run—but don't use it for more than two weeks.

☐ Use any over-the-counter preparation that gives you relief, except steroid preparations. Simply using petroleum jelly as a lubricant when wiping is often adequate.

☐ Moderate exercise has a generally beneficial effect on colonic function. However, very strenuous exercise, such as weightlifting, can aggravate hemorrhoids.

☐ If you experience complications such as thrombosis, which is caused by a blood clot in the hemorrhoid, or prolapse (protrusion of the hemorrhoid), seek medical treatment. Several outpatient procedures have been developed in recent years that minimize the need for in-hospital surgery.

☐ If you need a doctor, find one with extensive experience in hemorrhoid treatment. General surgeons and proctologists are your best bets.

Source: Thomas A. Stellato, M.D., general surgeon and assistant professor of surgery, Case Western Reserve University, Cleveland, OH.

Problems that respond to acupuncture

Acupuncture has gained in respectability in this country in recent years. You may wish to consider this treatment for a variety of conditions.

The sensation of the needles varies

among patients. Some feel only the slightest prick and others find them painful. The more pain a patient feels, the more resistance and stress there are in the related part of the body. As in deep massage, where the patient must "work through" the pain to get real relief, patients are asked to get through the painful part of acupuncture until they get some positive effect.

☐ Back pain. First acupuncturists ease the discomfort by working on the circulation in the spinal area. Then, they try to analyze the cause of the problem—posture, weight, or a poor mattress. Or, the patient may need a better diet and more exercise. The object is to keep the pain from recurring. Success rate: 95%.

☐ Insomnia. Acupuncturists try to relax the natural functions of the body through the nerve system to get the patient into a natural rhythm of feeling energetic when he wakes up and sleepy at night. Success rate: 90%.

☐ Addictions. Whether the substance is cocaine or nicotine, the user must want to shake the habit. Acupuncture can help people get into a healthier, more energetic cycle. Success rate with patients who want to quit: 80%.

☐ Excess weight. Business people do a lot of nervous eating. Acupuncture relaxes them and strengthens their sense of well-being. They can then better burn off fat and control eating. Success rate: 80%.

☐ Depression. Many people tire and get nervous too easily. Acupuncturists attempt to give them more energy with acupuncture and a combination of herbs and vitamins. Success rate: 80%.

☐ Hearing loss: Acupuncture can help the problem is the result of some (but not all) kinds of nerve damage. Success rate for hearing improvement: 80%.

☐ Impotence. Sometimes people lose sensitivity and desire because they are tired. Acupuncture can contribute to general well-being and appetite and can specifically stimulate the nerves of the sex areas. Success rate: 70%.

☐ Hair loss. Acupuncture can increase circulation to the scalp and may be helpful to men under 50.

☐ Look for an acupuncturist who is certified by your state's licensing board. If you find a practitioner by word of mouth, be sure he has the proper credentials.

Source: Zion Yu, a 20th-generation acupuncturist who came to the US from Taipei in 1970 and now directs a private clinic in Beverly Hills, CA.

Before you have any teeth extracted

Eye teeth (canines), the large, pointed teeth on either side of the upper jaw, are strong teeth, the cornerstone of the mouth's arch, and are essential to maintaining the ridge of the mouth. Other important teeth: Front teeth. When they are removed, they cause a collapsed-looking mouth, particularly in areas of the lips and nose.

☐ When any teeth are removed, the bony structure around them shrinks up and inward.

☐ Before allowing teeth to be removed, get two other dentists' opinions. It is important to try to keep teeth even if it is obvious they can last only a few years more.

☐ The only reason to consider teeth hopeless: When the bone around them has been lost to the degree that it cannot hold the teeth.

☐ Nonvalid reasons for extracting teeth: Abscesses, decay, pain. These conditions can be corrected with treatment.

What you should know about dentures

One-third of all Americans end up losing all their teeth in an arch requiring a full denture. This is a horrible statistic since people need not lose all their teeth.

☐ Upper dentures can usually be worn satisfactorily and comfortably.

☐ Lower dentures always pose much more severe and continuous problems than do uppers. Why: Uppers hold much better because they rest on a palate and a wide ridge. Lowers have only a very thin ridge to adhere to, and the tongue tends to displace the dentures. (Lowers cost more because of the additional problems with fitting.)

☐ An immediate denture is a prosthesis inserted at the same time the teeth are extracted. This is done to avoid going without teeth for any period of time. Usual effects: Swelling and discomfort for a few days.

☐ Within the first six weeks to three months of the time teeth have been pulled, shrinkage of bone and gums in that area accelerates rapidly. Significance: The original denture no longer fits and must be relined with acrylic to fill in areas that have shrunk.

☐ At the end of the first year, an entirely new denture (or dentures) should be made. This second denture has a better fit and appearance than the original, which had to be molded while real teeth were still in the mouth.

☐ Denture wearers should be checked by a dentist at least once a year, and their dentures regularly relined, even if the denture does not feel loose. Why this is important: The better the denture fits, the less the bone around it will shrink away.

☐ Denture teeth should look as natural and individual as possible, not perfectly symmetrical. It is a mistake to insist on completely even picket-fence or piano-key teeth.

☐ Look for a dentist who stresses natural and individual-looking teeth and who gives detailed attention to planning an aesthetic appearance and proper balance of dentures.

☐ The materials used in dentures do not vary much or cost much. What does vary from dentist to dentist is expertise, time, and attention to aesthetic considerations.

Source: Arthur S. Brisman, D.D.S., dentist, New York.

Dentures may not be for you

People prone to problems with dentures:

☐ Diabetics or people with poor general health. They tend to have more bone disappearance after their teeth have been pulled.

☐ People with a very high palate (tapered arch), a result of thumb-sucking in childhood or of genetic inheritance. They tend to have trouble retaining even an upper denture.

☐ People whose psychological approach or sensitivity to the feel of dentures is negative. They will probably never adjust to them properly.

☐ People with bony projections sticking out from the palate. Most people who have them are not aware of them. They can be removed surgically, before the denture is fitted.

How to protect yourself from your doctor

The best doctors are sometimes the ones with the poorest personalities. Bedside manner is not necessarily a relevant criterion. The prime do's and don'ts:

☐ Do ask questions. Many patients are intimidated by the doctor's professional status. Don't be. Ask your prospective doctor about his medical philosophy. Pose specific questions—for example, does he believe in taking heroic measures in terminal cases? Look for a doctor who is attuned to the patient/doctor relationship. Be wary of a doctor who puts you off, who takes a question as a personal affront, or who says things like, "Don't worry, I'll take care of it."

☐ Don't be impressed by the diplomas on the wall. Many are probably from organizations that the doctor joined for a fee. What you should know: Is the doctor *board certified* in his specialty?

☐ Do find out about the doctor's hospital affiliation. Is he on the medical staff of a hospital? Is a local hospital of good reputation?

☐ Don't go straight to a specialist when you're having a problem. Specialists can be blind to any ailment that doesn't fall into their specialty. Have a generalist or internist assess your problem and send you to the appropriate specialist.

Source: Leonard C. Arnold, MD, JD, Chicago.

Tip-offs to quackery

The problem: A massive, widespread, well-organized and lucrative web of *consumer* fraud (taking money under false pretenses) known as "quackery"…the promotion and selling of questionable therapies, remedies, and diagnostic tests—advertising them to be safe and effective. At the heart of the problem: Staggering profits—and clever deceits.

The frequent use of the language of fear is one common tactic used to deceive the consumer. You may be told that "establishment" doctors are really unenlightened butchers, that hospitals are death traps, that surgery is actually "cutting" and radiation is "burning," that our food supply is "poisoned" with additives.

The New York State Department of Agriculture found the same pesticide residues in food sold in health-food stores as in similar foods sold in supermarkets, but the "health food" was twice the price.

Source: Dr. Victor Herbert, professor of medicine and chairman, Committee to Strengthen Nutrition, Mount Sinai Medical Center, New York, and chief, Hematology and Nutrition Laboratory, Veterans Administration Medical Center, Bronx, NY.

Very, very, very aesthetic dentistry

Until recently, there wasn't much a dentist could do to create teeth that were beautiful as well as healthy. Now dentists can close the spaces between teeth, cover stains, repair chips, and create caps and dentures that look real. Choices:

☐ Bonding. How it works: The tooth is roughened with a mild acid. Next, a liquid material (the best is porcelain laminate) is painted on in layers and set by an intense white light. Then a tooth-colored bonding material of a puttylike consistency is sculpted onto the tooth. This material will not set until an intense white light is applied to it.

☐ Porcelain over gold is considered the ideal crown or bridge replacement today. Leading edge: cast ceramic. The process, developed by Corning Glass, uses ceramic material cast the same way as gold. It's almost as strong as metal and looks much better.

☐ The newest thing in bridges is the Maryland bridge. Instead of grinding down and ruining the teeth on either side of a space in order to attach a bridge, dentists can now bond metal to the backs of the adjoining teeth so that it doesn't show and attach a porcelain tooth in between. This prevents the destruction of good teeth. Problem: For people who have strong bites or large spans of missing teeth the Maryland bridge is not advisable.

Source: Irwin Smigel, D.D.S., the founder and president of the American Society for Dental Aesthetics, author of *Dental Health, Dental Beauty*, M. Evans & Co., Inc., New York.

Drug interaction dangers

There is a real danger in this age of multiple drug therapy: Drug interactions. Some of them are potentially life-threatening. Always ask your doctor or pharmacist about interaction hazards whenever you begin a new medication…and before you take any over-the-counter medication.

The most-likely-to-be-encountered drug interactions and what to do to prevent them…

Add-On Interactions

"Add-on" interactions are the most common type and can be the most dangerous. These occur between drugs that have similar effects, either depressant + depressant or stimulant + stimulant. Some of these combinations have proven fatal.

Depressants include: Alcohol, antianxiety agents, tranquilizers, anticonvulsants, antihistamines, certain high blood pressure drugs, muscle relaxants, narcotics, and the popular pain-reliever propoxyphene (e.g., Darvon).

Stimulants include: Antidepressants (MAO* inhibitor type), appetite suppressants, some asthma drugs, caffeine, nasal decongestants, methylphenidate (Ritalin) and pemoline (Cylert).

Always ask your doctor or pharmacist about this type of interaction before you take a new medication.

Antihistamine Interactions

☐ Seldane + Antibiotics. Seldane, one of the new nonsedating antihistamines (prescription-only), has become very popular for relief of allergies. Recently, a dangerous drug interaction was identified between Seldane (terfenadine) and antibiotics—ketoconazole (an antifungal agent with the brand name of Nizoral), erythromycin, and troleandomycin.

These antibiotics can increase the amount of Seldane in the blood. Seldane is broken down for elimination in the liver. Antibiotics interfere with this process. That has led to life-threatening, abnormal heart rhythms. Also at risk are individuals with liver disease (whose bodies may not eliminate Seldane properly)—and those who take excessive doses of the drug.

On the heels of the Seldane revelation came reports of a similar risk with Hismanal (astemizole), another nonsedating antihistamine. In this case, no interactions with other drugs have been reported, but taking more than the recommended dose of 10 mg (one tablet) daily has caused heart-function abnormalities.

*Monoamine oxidase.

If you experience fainting, dizziness, palpitations or any other unusual symptoms while taking Seldane or Hismanal, the Food and Drug Administration (FDA) advises you to contact your physician immediately.

Interactions Involving Food

☐ Fruit juices + Antibiotics. Penicillin and erythromycin, the interacting antibiotics, are used for microbial infections such as strep throat. The effect of the antibiotic may be decreased by the acidity of the fruit juice—and the infection may not be eradicated.

Self-defense: Avoid taking antibiotics with fruit juices.

☐ Salt + Lithium. Lithium is prescribed for manic-depressive illness. A diet too low in salt may cause lithium toxicity. Be alert for symptoms such as dizziness, nausea, dry mouth, weakness, confusion, appetite loss, abdominal pain, loss of coordination.

A diet too high in salt may reduce the effect of lithium so that the condition treated may not be properly controlled.

Self-defense: Avoid extremes in salt intake. Table salt (sodium chloride) is found in numerous foods.

☐ Milk/dairy products + Tetracycline. Tetracycline is an antibiotic used for microbial infections such as urinary-tract infections. Milk may decrease the effect of the antibiotic—and the infection may not be eradicated.

Self-defense: Take tetracycline antibiotics one hour before or two hours after ingesting milk or other dairy products.

☐ Carbohydrate-rich foods + Acetaminophen. Foods such as bread, crackers, jelly, and pasta may blunt the pain-relieving and fever-reducing effects of the widely used over-the-counter drug acetaminophen (e.g., Tylenol, Tempra, Datril).

Self-defense: Limit servings of high-carbohydrate foods while taking acetaminophen.

☐ Monosodium glutamate + Phenytoin. Phenytoin (brand name Dilantin) is used for seizure disorders such as epilepsy.

The adverse effects of monosodium glutamate (MSG)—a flavor enhancer often found in Chinese food and other foods—may be increased. Watch for symptoms such as weakness, numbness at back of the neck, heart palpitations.

Self-defense: Avoid foods high in MSG.

☐ Amine-containing foods + MAO inhibitors. MAO inhibitors are used in some cases of clinical depression. This can be a life-threatening combination that may result in a dangerous rise in blood pressure with severe headache, fever, visual disturbances and confusion, possibly followed by brain hemorrhage/stroke.

Self-defense: Avoid amine-containing foods, even for several weeks after stopping a MAO inhibitor-type antidepressant.

Amine-containing foods: Avocados, baked potatoes, bananas, bean pods, beer, bologna, broad beans, caviar, cheese, chicken liver, canned figs, instant soup mixes, meat tenderizers, nuts, pepperoni, pickled herring, raspberries, salami, sauerkraut, summer sausage, sour cream, soy sauce, wines, yeast, and yogurt.

Over-the-Counter Drug Interactions

☐ Antacids + Quinidine. Quinidine is used for heartbeat irregularities. Brand names include Cardioquin and Quinidex Extentabs. Antacids (e.g., Maalox, Mylanta, etc.) are used for indigestion or stomach ulcers.

The adverse effects of quinidine may be increased. Result: Possible fall in blood pressure, vertigo, heart block, and a serious heart irregularity called ventricular fibrillation.

Self-defense: Your physician should monitor quinidine blood levels and symptoms, and lower the quinidine dose as needed. (An aluminum-only antacid may not interact—e.g., AlternaGEL, Amphojel.)

☐ Antacids + Iron. Iron is an essential mineral found in many over-the-counter vitamin/mineral products. Antacids can decrease the effect of iron so those in need of iron supplementation may not receive its full benefits.

Self-defense: Take the two at separate times, as far apart as feasible.

☐ Antacids + Aspirin. Aspirin is used for pain, fever and inflammation. Antacids may hamper the effect of aspirin. Result: The condition treated may not respond properly.

Self-defense: Use a higher dose of aspirin as needed.

Source: Richard Harkness, PharmD, a consultant pharmacist in Ocean Springs, Mississippi and the author of several books on drug topics, including Drug Interactions Guide Book, Prentice Hall, Business and Professional Books, Rt. 9W, Englewood Cliffs, NJ.

Expand your thinking power

Over the past few years, there have been important developments in our understanding of effective thinking and how to teach it.

You can improve your reasoning skills by:

❏ Using analogies and metaphors. Deliberately ask yourself, What am I assuming? If art is creative, for example, does that mean business is noncreative? This will lead you to think about the real meaning of creativity.

❏ Not getting bogged down in a particular line of reasoning. Deliberately step outside it. Suggestion: Take 10 minutes to think of the problem in a completely different way. If that doesn't work, you've lost only a little time.

❏ Paying more attention to the aesthetic aspects of the problem than to the pragmatic ones. If you're designing an inventory system, for example, it shouldn't only be functional but should also solve certain difficulties in keeping track of things in an easy, elegant way.

❏ Looking at how you're being conventional. Break that conventional set. Watch out for cliches. Avoid timeworn and obvious answers.

❏ Being self-conscious. It's a myth that self-consciousness is a barrier to effective thinking. Be aware of the way you do things. Do you brush aside problems, or do you take them seriously? Do you look for opportunities to think about something a little longer, or do you pass them by?

❏ Opening up to ideas. Don't dismiss suggestions with *That's just common sense* or *I already do that.* Common sense isn't always common practice, and if you think you already do it, you probably don't. Research on actual behavior tells us that people don't accurately perceive whether or not they follow their own advice. Typically, they don't.

❏ Taking a course in thinking. Look for one that requires a lot of small-group work over a 6-to-20-week period. Investigate the course carefully, including the teacher's credentials, before taking it.

Source: David N. Perkins, Ph.D., senior research associate in education, Graduate School of Education, Harvard University, author of *The Mind's Best Work,* Harvard University Press, Cambridge, MA.

Relaxation: The key to concentration

Ironically, when people know they must concentrate on a task, they often fail because they make the mistake of concentrating on concentration. They focus on the mechanism of getting the job done rather than the objective itself. The result is anxiety over the task, which only leads to further distractions.

Ways to help concentration:

❏ Recognize what type of thinker you are—one who focuses broadly and can juggle many ideas or one who does best by focusing narrowly on one aspect of a problem. Try to take on only those tasks that match your abilities. If this isn't possible, ask for support in troublesome areas.

❏ Don't be afraid to take a little longer than usual to finish a job. Good concentration doesn't necessarily mean you will work faster.

❏ If concentration slips during a project, boost your adrenaline level by taking a short rest, exercising, meditating or bringing in others who wouldn't ordinarily be involved in the job.

❏ Avoid thinking about the consequences of not getting a job done or how the result will be viewed by others. Just focus on the work at hand.

Source: Dr. Ari Kiev, a psychiatrist and founder of the Life Strategy Workshops, New York.

Scheduling time to concentrate

❏ Time budget should include "quiet hours" when you have a chance to think without interruptions. Best time in the office is early morning before official hours begin.

❏ If possible, work during noon hour when interruptions are rare because most others have gone to lunch. Go out to eat at 1 PM or later.

☐ When scheduling your day, schedule the interruptions, as well. Try to restrict all calls on routine matters to a certain time of the day. If calls come in at other hours, have your secretary say you'll call them back. (Even VIPs will accept this if you establish a reputation for returning calls when promised.)

☐ Spend a few "office hours" at home. Use an answering machine to cover telephone calls so you won't be interrupted.

Use your intuition to improve your thinking

Intuition, the spontaneous generation of fresh ideas for solving problems, can help you in your work and personal life. Here are some ways to use intuition and evaluate its effectiveness relative to other methods of making decisions:

Keeping a journal will enable you to discover successful intuitions. For each intuition, record at the moment it happens:

☐ The date and time.

☐ Content.

☐ Type (future prediction, creative insight, problem solution, etc.).

☐ Description (verbal, visual, a faint idea, etc.).

☐ Vividness.

☐ What you were doing and how you felt immediately before and after having it.

☐ Your initial reaction (skepticism, belief, etc.).

Later, add the following to your journal:

☐ Was the intuition a departure from custom, authority or logic?

☐ Was it something you wanted or didn't want to hear?

☐ Did it return at various times?

☐ Did you analyze it, try to verify it, seek other opinions?

☐ Were you under pressure to come up with a decision?

☐ Did it represent a high risk?

☐ How did it work out in the end?

☐ If you went with an intuition that was wrong, do you understand why?

☐ Leave room in your journal for random thoughts and observations.

☐ Note any patterns that you may come across.

Source: Philip Goldberg, author of *The Intuitive Edge,* Jeremy P. Tarcher, Inc., Los Angeles.

Real problem solving

Management's job isn't simply to predict the problems—many of them can't be predicted, no matter how well the project is planned. What is critical: The way managers respond to inevitable problems.

☐ Seeking a victim and assigning blame is the most common response to a problem—and the least effective way to solve it. Inevitable result: Everyone avoids blame and argues if others had done what they should have, the problem wouldn't have come up.

☐ Not putting the emphasis on blame creates the atmosphere for making rolling adjustments and changes in plans and specifications in any new venture. This will not take place if individuals feel that concessions will be held against them or are an admission of guilt for originating the problem.

☐ Don't gloss over problems and figure mistakes can be fixed up later. Solve problems when they first surface.

Source: Dr. Leonard R. Sayles, Center for Creative Leadership, Greensboro, NC.

Finding solutions to problems

We all have a tendency to underestimate our most serious problems and to overestimate less serious ones. Often there are serious problems that we simply refuse to face by denying that they exist.

One big mistake is waiting for a problem to solve itself. To wait is to waste time and opportunity.

☐ If the solution to a problem lies in getting help from some other source, don't hesitate to ask for that help.

☐ Insulate yourself from the negative forces and negative personalities that constantly surround you. How many imes has a positive idea been slaughtered, strangled, or sunk with the words *No way*?

❏ Attack your problem with courage...and the possibilities with enthusiasm.

❏ Ask your mind and heart what your real motives are and what price you're willing to pay.

❏ Add up your strengths. You're stronger than you think you are.

❏ Adjust your mind to change.

❏ Accept the irrevocable negative realities.

Source: Robert H. Schuller, founding pastor of Crystal Cathedral, Garden Grove, CA, and author of 15 books, the most recent of which is *Tough Times Never Last, But Tough People Do!*, Thomas Nelson Publishers, Nashville.

Problem solving: Some traits that get in the way

Would-be problem solvers often run into trouble because they:

❏ Cannot tolerate the ambiguity associated with a complex problem and believe all problems must be clear-cut.

❏ Stick to a preconceived belief and reinterpret inconsistent data to fit it.

❏ Hesitate to ask questions for fear of appearing ignorant.

❏ Give in to unrealistic anxiety about failing without systematically doing worst-case scenarios.

Roadblocks to creativity

❏ Assuming that creative means new. Borrowing and modifying the ideas of others is just as useful.

❏ Relying too heavily on experts or self-styled creative types, who often are blinded by traditional approaches.

❏ Believing that only a few gifted people can be creative.

❏ Confusing creativity with emotional instability. What is needed instead is the ability to let the mind wander without fear of losing control.

❏ Failing to promote ideas voluntarily. Not pointing out achievements to superiors (a common failing of fired executives).

❏ Waiting for inspiration. Concentration and fact-finding are the most solid bases for innovation.

❏ Getting bogged down in technology. Look for solutions that can be accomplished with existing hardware and systems.

Source: M. LeBoeuf, *Imagineering: How to Profit from Your Creative Powers*, McGraw-Hill, New York.

Fears that stifle creativity

❏ Making mistakes.

❏ Being seen as a fool.

❏ Being criticized.

❏ Being misused.

❏ Standing alone.

❏ Disturbing traditions.

❏ Breaking taboos.

❏ Not having the security of habit.

❏ Losing the love of the group.

❏ Truly being an individual.

Learning how to remember

Contrary to the conventional wisdom, memory doesn't work like a muscle. You can't exercise your way to a perfect memory. But you can learn tricks and techniques that can give you a far better memory than you'd believe. Here are the best ones:

❏ Chunking: That's the basic technique for short-term memory improvement. How it works: Grouping apparently isolated facts, numbers, letters, etc., into chunks. Thus, the series 255789356892365 turns into 255 789 356 892 365.

❏ Sleep and remembering: There is some evidence to indicate that things learned just before sleep are retained better.

❏ Spacing: Don't try to memorize by swallowing the whole thing down in one gulp. Instead of a three-hour study marathon, try two 1½ hour spans. Experiment to see what time period is best for you.

❏ Reciting: Vocalizing provides a kind of feedback as you literally hear (in addition to seeing) the words. It also forces you to organize the material in a way that is natural for memory improvement.

❏ Story system: A very effective way to remember some obviously unrelated objects. Just make up a silly story, using each of the objects in the story.

Thus, if you want to remember the words paper, tire, doctor, rose, ball, try this story:

The paper rolled a tire down the sidewalk, and it hit the doctor, knocking him into a rose bush, where he found a ball.

Source: Kenneth L. Higbee, author of *Your Memory: How It Works and How to Improve It*, Prentice-Hall, Englewood Cliffs, NJ.

Improving your short-term memory

Memory exercises are most useful for those who face special short-term tasks such as the memorization of facts for a presentation. These tasks can be accomplished through the application of a few simple techniques.

Basic steps:

☐ Before resorting to memorization, use such aids as shopping lists, memos, or charts.

☐ When you do need to memorize, do so in the kind of environment in which you function best. Learn whether you concentrate better in total silence, with background music, etc.

☐ Arrange for short, frequent periods of study. Memory flags during long sessions.

☐ Outline what you need to learn, and carry your notes with you in a small notebook.

☐ Refer to your notes at every empty interval during the day—waiting in line, riding the bus, etc.

How to remember people's names

To remember the names of people to whom you have just been introduced, the classic system is best:

☐ Take an interest in the person.

☐ Concentrate by looking directly at him or her. Notice appearance and dress.

☐ If you forget the name right after hearing it, ask immediately for it to be repeated.

☐ Repeat the name to yourself every few minutes. Over the next few days, keep calling the name to mind.

☐ Gradually decrease the frequency of repetition.

Source: Alan Baddeley, author of *Your Memory: A User's Guide*, Macmillan, New York.

Remembering faces and names better

There are no special gimmicks to remembering important names and faces. You need only apply a few simple techniques:

☐ Take every opportunity to study lists of names that are important to you. It takes time, but it's worth it.

☐ Look through the names carefully, taking time to study each one and recollect when, and if, you ever met the person.

☐ If a name looks familiar, try to recall something about the person.

☐ Jot a friendly note to the person thanking him for the donation or order. The act of writing the note reinforces your memory of the person.

Source: Joseph F. Anderson, vice president for communications and development, Hamilton College, Clinton, NY.

How to develop intuition

We all have intuition, though we may not be aware of it and tend to devalue it as irrational. But many of the greatest scientific and creative people in history including Einstein and Mozart, relied heavily on intuition.

To develop intuition, the first step is to accept that it isn't a gimmick. Intuition is spontaneous. It can't be contrived or programmed. However, you can create the conditions under which it's most likely to occur:

☐ Promote inner calm. An agitated, tense mind creates too much mental noise for intuition to operate. Stress-management techniques help people to be more intuitive, though this isn't their stated aim.

☐ Relax your mind by allowing it to wander. Take a walk on the beach, watch fish swim in a fishtank, take long baths, go away for the weekend. Some people have had their best intuitions while shaving or washing the dishes.

☐ Don't keep working harder and harder, struggling desperately for an answer to a problem. Like having a word on the tip of your tongue, the answer will come of its own accord hen you're thinking of something else. he old saw, Sleep on it, really works.

☐ Approach problems in a flexible way. Many people acquire such rigid thought patterns that they effectively inhibit intuition. Loosen up. Be prepared to go with your feelings. Improvise. Get started before you know where an idea is going.

☐ Avoid outlining a project before you begin. This method can extinguish the spontaneity crucial to intuition.

☐ Don't feel you have to defend every idea rationally. Suspend judgment long enough to keep the idea as a possibility, to let it take concrete form. No idea is too bizarre to consider.

☐ Try brainstorming. Do for yourself what is generally done in groups. Sit quietly and let ideas pass without evaluating them. You can analyze and evaluate them later.

Source: Philip Goldberg, author of *The Intuitive Edge,* Jeremy P. Tarcher, Inc., Los Angeles.

How to use fantasy as a creative tool

An active fantasy life is as crucial to the mental health of adults as it is to children. We tend to think that as we grow up we must leave our fantasies behind. But without fantasy, we would never dare to push or grow psychologically. We would become bland and constricted half-people. Fantasy has many useful functions in our lives. Here are some of them:

☐ Fantasy lets us "try out" new roles. For example, anyone who contemplates a job or career change first fantasizes what it would be like to do other kinds of work.

☐ Fantasy is a way of testing concepts and ideas, from new products to financial systems.

☐ Fantasy helps us master negative emotions and events. If we're very

depressed over a loss or other unhappy event, we can allow ourselves to feel better by imagining something that makes us feel good.

☐ Fantasy can relieve boredom or an unpleasant experience. We've all fantasized through a traffic jam.

☐ Fantasizing can mean the difference between life and death in truly traumatic situations—war, solitary confinement, etc. Diaries of concentration camp survivors and prisoners of war attest to this.

☐ In sex, fantasy has been touted as an enhancer of pleasure, and shared sexual fantasies can indeed do this. But unshared fantasy during sex can be one way of tuning out and avoiding intimacy with the other person.

☐ Love relationships are predicated on fantasy. We project onto the loved one our fantasy of the ideal lover. This is an obstruction in one way because it keeps us from seeing the real person, but if we didn't do it we wouldn't fall in love at all.

☐ Fantasy displaces fear. We displace frightening things through fantasy as adults, just as we did as children. Thus, we imagine that harmful things will happen elsewhere—that someone else will have a car accident or get cancer.

While fantasy has many benefits, it's important to temper fantasy with reality. When we retreat into a fantasy world untempered by reality, there is the real danger of becoming nonfunctional— not getting out of bed in the morning or not taking care of the routine matters that ensure our daily existence.

Source: Dr. Simone F. Sternberg, a psychotherapist and psychoanalyst in private practice in New York.

To develop genius

Geniuses are made by sheer hard work more often than by simple inborn talent. Steps toward developing genius:

☐ "Falling in love" with a particular subject.

☐ Sharpening skills with time and effort.

☐ Mastering a personal style, with the goal being excellence rather than praise.

Source: Study by education specialist Benjamin Bloom, University of Chicago, cited in *Success!*

The mind-body relationship

☐ Mental abilities don't deteriorate with age, contrary to popular belief. Wisdom —the ability to use past experience to judge a problem for which there is no correct answer—grows at least through a person's sixties. And the ability to grasp new relationships slows down, but can remain strong. Helpful mental exercise: Challenging reading, adult education courses, games.

Source: *University of California Wellness Letter.*

☐ An understimulated brain will often attempt to counter boredom by causing back pain, obesity, hypertension and even cancer. Most susceptible: Once-active people who feel they've seen it all. Recommended: Seek out the new and fresh in the ordinary— even a new way to brush your teeth.

Source: Dr. Augustin de la Pena, University of Texas Medical School, in *New Age Journal.*

☐ An energy slump (postprandial dip) affects many people between 2 p.m. and 4 p.m. Although it often follows lunch, it doesn't seem to be caused by eating or digesting. To combat the dip: Run a physical errand, rather than doing purely mental work.

Convert worry into productivity

Reduce worrying by disassociating it from common worry-inducing situations. Techniques from Penn State psychology researcher Thomas Borkovec:

☐ Set aside a half-hour worry period each day.

☐ When you start to worry, put it off until the worry period.

☐ Replace worrisome thoughts with task-oriented thoughts.

☐ Use the worry period to think intensively about current concerns.

All about happiness

Sometimes happiness seems like a terribly elusive goal. We tend to forget that it doesn't come as a result of getting something we don't have, but rather of recognizing and appreciating what we do have. Some steps on the pathway to happiness:

When you think about time, keep to the present. Those who are excessively future-oriented often score very high in despair, anxiety, helplessness, and unhappiness. As much as practical, focus on the here and now.

Don't dwell on past injustices. You'll be unpopular company. No one wants to hear about how you got a raw deal in your divorce or how your boss doesn't appreciate you.

Develop the habit of noticing things. An active mind is never bored. Make a resolution to notice new things each day—about nature, people, or anything else that interests you. Ask questions. Don't assume you know all the answers or that showing curiosity will be considered prying. Most people love to talk about themselves or their interests.

Don't wear too many hats. Focus on one thing at a time. Set time aside for your family, yourself, your golf game, etc.—for having fun.

Drop your bucket where you are. Take advantage of what you already have. There are already interesting, stimulating adventures waiting in your own backyard. Get to know your own children, for example.

Source: Dr. Frederick Koenig, professor of social psychology, Tulane University, New Orleans.

Words of wisdom

Here are the mottoes and proverbs that helped the following celebrities get to—and stay at—the top:

Isaac Asimov, writer:

"Laugh, and the world laughs with you; Weep, and you weep alone; For the sad old earth must borrow its mirth, but has trouble enough of its own."

Helen Gurley Brown, editor, *Cosmopolitan:*

"I don't remember any motto or saying that was valuable to me when I was 'getting there,' but there is one I like now (not that it helps, but it just happens to be true.) 'There is no free lunch.'"

Midge Decter, former director, Committee for the Free World:

"The perfect is the enemy of the good."

Jean Louis Dumas-Hermes, chairman, Hermes:

"Patience and time do more than force and anger."

Rose Kennedy, matriarch of the Kennedy clan:

"To whom much is given, much will be required." (St. Jude)

Edward Koch, former mayor of New York City:

"Be not afraid."

Jack La Lanne, pioneer physical fitness expert:

"*Pride* and *discipline.* If you use those two words, you can't fail."

Leonard A. Lauder, president, Estee Lauder, Inc.:

"Anything can be done as long as everybody gets the credit."

Willard Scott, weatherman on NBC's *Today* show:

"If a job is once begun, do not leave 'til it is done. Be it great or be it small, do it well or not at all."

Carl Spielvogel, chairman, Backer Spielvogel Bates Worldwide:

"Do unto others as you would have others do unto you."

Gloria Steinem, founder of *Ms.* magazine and author of *Outrageous Acts and Everyday Rebellions:*

"If there's no dancing, it's not my revolution!"

Some tough questions

Before you can make the right decision about more job responsibility, a new venture, travel, or a big move or change, you must identify your own strengths, interests, goals, needs and priorities. Ask:

☐ To whom do I owe what? How do job-related responsibilities (to stock-holders, employees, customers) rank in priority with family responsibilities? Most big jobs preclude giving equal rank to both.

☐ Do I feel good about my work, the people in my life, myself?

☐ Do I waste valuable time and energy on things that don't really matter?

☐ When is the last time I ___ (fill in two or three activities you enjoy for pure fun)? If it's been too long, something's wrong.

☐ Is the desire for "bigger, better, more" causing me to work harder without joy?

☐ What should I be doing differently in my work to be happier, more productive, less frustrated or bored? The answers will be an adventure in self-discovery.

Benefits of a personal philosophy

Developing a personal philosophy of life is crucial for meeting crises to be faced day by day. (And those crises can get more complicated as one grows older.) The virtues are:

☐ It provides a guideline for living.

☐ It sounds an alarm when one's behavior is inconsistent with one's beliefs.

☐ It supports the ability to make a rational explanation of life's events, including the most disruptive or seemingly senseless ones.

What's required in a personal philosophy:

☐ It must be comprehensive. Ideally, it will provide an ability to meet all life's normal crises in a balanced way.

☐ It requires one's full commitment. Personal philosophy can't be taken on and off like a coat. It has to provide a sense of worth.

Meeting the challenge of personal growth

☐ Personal growth is a positive commitment that is aided by in-depth reading and conversations with those who have done it. Search out people who are skilled in a field in which you wish to advance. Learn about the dedication required and the attitudes that will help to make your effort fruitful.

☐ Never forget the level of application demanded. Depressing cycle: Beginners start out wildly enthusiastic, eager to master a chosen endeavor, such as playing the violin or unraveling the secrets of Zen. But they have been oversold on self-development without effort, and they quickly become discouraged at the first patch of difficulty. Do experimental trials before making the total commitment. Try a class, session, interview, or book. Be certain you are ready to give yourself to the project.

☐ Persevere when the spirit is weak. Many creative people develop mental blocks from the fear of defeat or failure. The term *writer's block*, for example, describes a creative person who has temporarily lost the courage to take the risks that writing entails. A negative attitude is a defense employed by people hoping to avoid the pain of failure by rejecting their chances of success.

☐ You are more likely to be courageous when you have a positive mind set. And, it will be easier to find purpose and the strength to accomplish the objective.

☐ Knowing your limits and accepting yourself. That is also part of realizing your potential.

Source: Martin G. Groder, M.D., a practicing psychiatrist, business consultant and author of *Business Games: How to Recognize the Players and Deal with Them,* Boardroom Books, Springfield, NJ.

Becoming a more complete person

Many executives neglect personal growth in favor of career.

Penalties for failing to develop other interests:

☐ Produces a feeling that life has gone stale.

☐ Lowers the ability to love or take interest in family and community.

☐ Leads to despair. You pretend that you don't mind being so job-oriented, but you do.

Rewards of extending your interest:

☐ You drop some psychological defenses and use that energy to enjoy life more fully.

☐ You lose the anxiety, confusion, and identity crises of youth. You ppreciate the joys that being older rings.

Source: Richard C. Hodgson, in *Business uarterly*, published by the School of Business dministration, University of Western Ontario, ondon, Ontario.

How to enjoy ourself by yourself

he problem most people have with oing things by themselves is a hold-ver from when they were teen-gers—being alone meant nobody ved you. Remember that being lone doesn't mean rejection. A lot of eople who are with someone would ather be alone.

o avoid loneliness or boredom when ou're alone, try these activities:

] Go out to eat. Make a reservation at nice restaurant, dress well and tell ourself: "I'm going to ask for a good able and enjoy myself!" Once you get here, you might ask another nteresting-looking person eating alone o join you.

] Go to the movies. Many people void going to the movies alone when hey're in their hometown. One dvantage is that no one is constantly whispering comments to you, asking uestions about the movie, or stealing our popcorn.

] Look in stores. Shopping just for the un of it is another thing busy people on't often do. Look around. There's lways something to learn about roducts and merchandising.

] Take a tour. Pretend you're a tourist, nd see your town through others' yes. Best: Walking tours. You see a lot nd get exercise.

] Meander by yourself. Discovering n unfamiliar place is fun. And doing it t your own pace is wonderfully elaxing.

Growing-up realities

] Negative events in infancy do not reversibly damage the mental health f the adult. Some repair is possible if he environment becomes more enevolent.

] The behavior of an infant does not rovide a good preview of the young dult. A one-year-old's tantrums don't reshadow teenage delinquency, for xample. Many infantile qualities dis-ppear as their usefulness is outgrown.

Adult behavior becomes more pre-dictable after the age of five than it was before.

☐ Human beings are not saddled with a fixed "intelligence" or "temperament" in every situation. These qualities are related to context and can vary in different circumstances.

☐ A biological mother's physical affec-tion is not basic to a child's healthy emotional growth. More important is consistent nurturing from primary caregivers, related or not, female or male. The key is a child's belief in his own value in the eyes of the care-givers.

Source: Dr. Jerome Kagan.

Four revelations of middle age

Psychologists say that many of the crises and traumas associated with middle age are really simply a dropping away of illusions. Well-adjusted and effective adults are those who understand that life can still be enjoyable and productive even if some of their assumptions and beliefs have been proven wrong.

What most people find are no longer reasonable expectations:

☐ Rewards for doing worthwhile things will come automatically.

☐ In most situations, rationality prevails.

☐ Most people are committed to what they are doing and will put forth their best effort.

☐ There is always one best way to accomplish one's goals or the organization's objectives.

Turning fifty

Life on the 50-year-old plateau is a time of great change for many people. Those who are going to advance to positions of influence in their professions have more or less already done so. Children have grown up; grandchildren may be on the way. Parents are likely to have passed away, creating a sense for the first time among 50-year-olds that they are now the older generation.

The big shifts:

☐ Reconciliation of dreams with reality. What many individuals fear about their fiftieth birthday is the sense of resigna-tion about limitations and giving up lifelong dreams. The good side is comfort in accepting oneself even without those dreams. Recognizing that now is a good time to reassess and set new, more appropriate, goals for the next 20 years.

☐ Greater appreciation of time. It takes most people until 50 to learn that most goals do not become reality as rapidly as expected. The result is a greater sense of leisure and enjoyment of things that exist in the present. The pressure to reach goals eases. An important realization is that it is not so important to achieve goals as it is to use them as standards to structure a life.

☐ Spiritual awakening. Although there is an initial disappointment in giving up the notions of egotistical immortality cherished since youth, many people begin to see themselves as links in the chain between past and future generations. There is a common energy shift from social and political activities to more spiritual and aesthetic concerns. Even relentless decision making seems less important.

☐ Renewal of friendships. Acceptance of oneself often generates a recognition of dependency on other human beings. People become more caring about others. This is a time of settling down with one's spouse, of intensifying friendships and appreciating basic human relationships. Some people find opportunities to teach in order to pass on their knowledge to the younger generation.

☐ Increase in flexibility. Most people bend away from the authoritarian views they held to during their younger years. Parents realize that they cannot force knowledge on their children through discipline, and that the best they can do is set an example and encourage them to learn from experience.

☐ Appreciation of the basics of life. Good health becomes something for which one is thankful. Status symbols (the big house, the fancy car, professional awards) lose their importance.

Source: Dr. Ari Kiev, psychiatrist and originator of the Life Strategy Workshops, New York.

How to make the most of midlife crisis

A midlife crisis involves self-examination sparked either by internal awareness of mortality or by an outside event, usually involving a loss of some kind. Common triggers are a divorce, loss of a job, death of a friend or family member, children leaving home. Midlife is the time to find a sense of balance within yourself. How to do it:

☐ Stop measuring success by money. Ask yourself what you missed in the making of the buck. Realize when you've made enough and can begin to spend it.

☐ Don't dive into anything. It took you lots of years to get to where you are. You don't have to make any instant decisions. Lifetime family and friendship networks are very important and should be preserved if at all possible.

☐ Learn to grow up. Recognize that changing your life doesn't have to be an either/or decision. Life is neither good nor bad. Today it's one thing, tomorrow another. Life involves balance plus movement.

☐ Head off a crisis. If your job is going poorly, for instance, get out on your own terms before the ax falls.

☐ Learn to undo whatever narrow force has been controlling your life so far. If you've spent your life giving to others and sacrificing yourself, start seeing what you can give to yourself. If you've spent your life focused on yourself, start paying attention to others.

☐ Don't be afraid to fantasize. When you really want something, your energies go in that direction. If you don't fantasize, you won't make a move.

☐ Don't break up your marriage over an infidelity. You may have to come to terms with your spouse's having had an affair. If he or she is a good husband or wife and loves the children, and something solid and good still exists between you, you don't have to break up.

☐ Learn to be open with your spouse. There are many ways to do this. Trust each other with your inner thoughts and feelings. Share sexual fantasies. Join a therapy group for couples.

☐ Learn to be who you are rather than who you "should" be. People who live what Thoreau called "lives of quiet des eration" are doing what they think (or someone else thinks) they should do rather than what they really want to do.

Source: Milton M. Berger, M.D., a psychiatrist and codirector of the American Short-Term Therapy Center in New York.

The power of positive imaging

One of the most important elements of positive thinking is positive imaging. That is, creating a picture in your mind in which you actually visualize yourself doing whatever it is you want to do. These pictures—and the suggestions they generate—can have a powerful effect.

☐ Set reasonable goals.

☐ Believe you're capable of reaching them.

☐ Work at changing your thought habits.

☐ You won't always accomplish everything you visualize, but you'll do much better than you would believing you'll never reach your goals.

Source: Dr. Norman Vincent Peale, minister, author and lecturer, New York.

Stopping unwanted thoughts

The average person has more than 200 negative thoughts a day—worries, jealousies, insecurities, cravings for forbidden things, etc. (Depressed people have as many as 600.) You can't eliminate all the troublesome things that go through your mind, but you can certainly reduce the number of negative thoughts. Here's how:

☐ When a negative thought begins to surface in your mind, pause. Just stop what you are doing for a few seconds. Don't say anything—talk reinforces the bad feeling.

☐ Take five deep, slow breaths. By taking in more oxygen, you flush out your system and lower your level of anxiety. If you do this correctly, you will approach a meditative state.

☐ Concentrate on a pleasant, relaxing scene—a walk on a breezy beach, for example. Take two to three minutes for a minor trouble, up to 10 minutes for a serious upset.

☐ Use this technique continuously until the upsetting thoughts begin to decrease. Then practice it intermittently.

Source: Elior Kinarthy, Ph.D., professor of psychology, Rio Hondo College, Whittier, CA.

The tough job of setting your personal priorities

How you already allocate your own time is the best indicator of what's important to you. It tells you what your priorities really are. Anxiety about personal time management comes from confronting what you are doing with what you think you should be doing.

☐ Confront your real needs and time values and be honest about what you see.

☐ Resist the temptation to be sucked into other people's needs. Face the risks inherent in not answering some phone calls, not answering certain letters, not jumping when someone asks you to do something.

☐ Beware of the open door policy at the office. People who report to you need something more important than ready access.

☐ Be honest about how you feel about meetings. Many executives complain about them as time-wasters but actually call many meetings themselves because they enjoy chairing them, being the center of attention and putting other people's ideas down.

☐ Consider cutting down on dictated formal letters. Dictation is inefficient but ego-satisfying. Most memos and letters can be answered by a handwritten note or comment across the original. And people appreciate the quick turnaround much more than the perfectly typed memo or letter.

Source: Charles E. Dwyer, Wharton School, University of Pennsylvania, Philadelphia.

Evaluate your goals

Many people get so wrapped up in the means that they forget about the ends.

☐ Ask yourself from time to time: "Why am I doing this? Am I working hard because I love my work or because I think money will buy happiness?" Maybe you'd really like peace of mind or recognition or job satisfaction. These can be more immediate, attainable goals.

☐ If you're working yourself to the bone because you think money will eventually buy contentment, maybe you can discover that you don't really need a million dollars. Making enough money to buy a small country retreat might do the trick.

☐ Accept what you cannot change. As we get older, we have to accept our limitations. At some point in life we all must recognize that we'll never be president of General Motors, a Nobel Prize winner, a *Time* cover subject, a perfect "10," or whatever else we thought was crucial to happiness. At this point, you have to be able to say sincerely, "So what!"

☐ Establish a regimen for yourself. This will give you a feeling of control. If you can stop smoking, lose weight, exercise, stick to a schedule, etc., you'll gain a sense of mastery. Anything that proves you can affect your own life will give you a positive sense of self.

☐ Make time for yourself. Everyone needs at least 20 minutes a day for quiet reflection—just thinking time. If you think while walking or running, leave the radio home. Let your thoughts drift to who you are, how you feel, what you're doing, how your life is going.

☐ Learn to like yourself. The best way to think positively about yourself is to think positively about others. They will then reflect back to you how wonderful you are, which will make it a lot easier. Our sense of self is a reflection of other people's responses to us.

Source: Dr. Frederick Koenig, professor of social psychology, Tulane University, New Orleans, LA.

Fitting priorities into categories

Even some of the most efficient managers sometimes lose ground because they don't accurately weigh the relative importance of their activities. To prevent this problem in your life, categorize activities carefully according to priority, and revise the categories daily.

☐ Category A. Important and urgent.

☐ Category B. Important but not urgent.

☐ Category C. Urgent but not important work. This category is usually the big trap because the crisis nature of the activity makes it seem more important than it is.

☐ Category D. Neither urgent nor important. For example, cleaning drawers, straightening files.

☐ Activities will vary in urgency as time passes, so it is important to revise the priority list each day.

☐ Tackle the A and B priorities, and then the C tasks, if you have the time. If you never get to the D jobs, what has been lost?

Source: Milton R. Stohl, president, Milton R. Stohl Associates, Farmington Woods, CT.

Selfishness is not necessarily a sin

The whole notion of sacrificial relationships is wrong, whether you are sacrificing yourself to other people or vice versa. What's essential to relationships is *exchange.*

Selfishness, or honoring the self, means:

☐ Be aware of yourself and the world.

☐ Think independently and have the courage of your own perceptions.

☐ Know what you feel and accept your right to experience such feelings...fear, anger or other emotions we often consider negative.

☐ Accept who you are, without self-castigation or pretense.

☐ Speak and act from your innermost convictions and feelings.

☐ Refuse to accept unearned guilt. Attempt to correct the guilt that you have earned.

☐ Commit yourself to your right to exist. Acknowledge that your life does not belong to others and that you were not put on earth to live up to someone else's expectations.

☐ Be in love with your own life and with your own possibilities for growth, joy and the process of discovering your human potential.

Source: Dr. Nathaniel Branden, a Los Angeles psychologist and author of *Honoring the Self,* Jeremy P. Tarcher, Inc., Los Angeles.

Avoiding needless personal sacrifices

A fair number of men and women remain workhorses for their entire lives

234

o avoid the stigma of selfishness. Example: A middle-aged man who is bored with his career may want to switch to another career that will give him personal fulfillment. If the change involves a drop in family income, he is often accused of being "selfish."

The steps to change involve having the courage to face up to the following:

☐ Human relationships should be based on an exchange of values, not of sacrifices. Here a market analogy is apt (without implying that human relationships are meant to be materialistic): If you want something someone else has, you must offer value in exchange that will be perceived as roughly equal, appealing to the self-interest of whomever you wish to trade with. Formula for respect: Never ask anyone to act against his or her self-interest.

☐ Other human beings are not put on earth to satisfy your needs, wishes or expectations. You are not put on earth to live up to someone else's needs, wishes or expectations.

☐ What we call our fear of being selfish is really our fear of disapproval or our fear of being condemned for perfectly honest and legitimate forms of self-assertion.

☐ When we do sacrifice ourselves to others, we hate them for it and make them pay for it in all sorts of indirect and underhanded ways.

Source: Dr. Nathaniel Branden, a Los Angeles psychologist and author of *Honoring the Self,* Jeremy P. Tarcher, Inc., Los Angeles.

How to say "no"

Say *yes* quickly. Say *no* slowly. When a letter or conversation begins with a rejection, the other person usually ignores the rest of the discussion, including the reasons for the negative decision.

The pattern to follow when saying no:
☐ Review the facts and reasons for the decision without revealing it.
☐ Build an argument in a step-by-step, fact-by-fact manner.
☐ Provide information to support the decision. (The goal is to have the other person acknowledge the validity of the rejection.)
☐ Say no politely.
☐ Always say something good about the rejected idea, organization or

person. Acknowledge the problem and the difficulty of its solution.

Source: William C. Paxson, *The Business Writing Handbook,* Bantam Books, New York.

How to get out of a rut

No matter how old you are or what kind of rut you're in, there is a way out.

☐ Accept that no one is going to do anything for you. It is your responsibility, and yours alone, to change your own life.

☐ Start thinking constructively about what you want rather than moaning about what you don't have.

☐ If you're upset about your career, stop complaining and ask yourself: What do I really want to do? Where do I want to do it? With whom? Under what circumstances? What are my skills? (Include not only business experience but also hobbies, interpersonal skills and non-job-related skills.)

☐ Ask yourself: What are my short-term goals? Long-term goals? Think long and hard and in great detail about what would make you happy. Don't be afraid to fantasize or hatch grandiose schemes. You may be able to make at least parts of your fantasy come true.

☐ Give yourself an imaginary $10 million and think about what you would do with it. Be specific. Then use your brain to see how much of your fantasy you can turn into reality. Sample fantasy: To live on a South Sea island and spend all my time sunbathing, fishing and picking coconuts. It may not be possible to move to the South Seas and loll about all day, but if you're living in a cold climate and really love the tropics, you might be able to get a job in Florida and spend all the spare time that you choose sunbathing and fishing.

☐ Change your job without leaving the company. Negotiate a move to another state. Redesign your job so you can focus on your strengths and hand over other tasks.

Source: John C. Crystal, head of John C. Crystal Center, New York, which offers intensive courses in creative life/career planning.

Breaking an undesirable habit

☐ Before trying to break a habit, take at least a few days to observe it in action.

☐ Then try to stop completely instead of tapering off. Performing the act reinforces it, while abstaining strengthens the habit of *not* doing it.

☐ Don't fret over lapses. It takes time to establish new patterns.

☐ Be aware that you cannot change just any habit. Work hardest to change those that both annoy others and violate your own standards. You can improve yourself only if the changes sought are in accord with your own moral and ethical standards.

Source: Dr. George Weinberg, author of *Self Creation*, Avon Books, New York.

Rid yourself of nervous gestures

Audio-video cameras are an excellent way to check yourself for nervous physical gestures that can interfere with your ability to communicate effectively. Record a conversation with another person or the draft of a talk you are about to deliver. Look for:

☐ Repetitive phrases such as "you know."

☐ Cracking your knuckles.

☐ Rubbing your nose.

☐ Pulling your ear.

☐ Adjusting your glasses.

☐ Stroking a mustache.

☐ Jingling change in a pocket.

☐ Leaning too heavily on the lectern.

☐ Pacing back and forth all the time.

☐ Shifting weight from one foot to the other.

☐ Using a chart pointer excessively.

Source: James K. Van Fleet, author of *Lifetime Conversation Guide*, published by Prentice-Hall, Inc. Englewood Cliffs, NJ.

If you want a drastic change in your life

☐ Start your own business. This does not have to be a total gamble.

Overlooked clue to success: Research not only your venture but yourself. Too many people go into businesses they are personally unsuited for. Example: The couple who dreams of running a little hotel in the mountains won't make a go of it if they're shy, retiring types.

☐ Start communicating openly with your family. This hardly sounds like a prescription for drastic change. However, lack of communication is the primary reason for a marital rut. It can be an exciting, startling and totally new experience to find out what your spouse and children really think.

☐ Consider going to a weekend marriage workshop, sometimes called a "marriage encounter." This is a group of couples with an experienced leader. Spouses are taught how to be open with each other. It can be more effective than marriage counseling, which is often the last stop before the divorce.

Source: John C. Crystal, of the John C. Crystal Center, NY. The Center offers intensive courses in creative life/career planning.

How to plan a major change in your life

The change that's needed to execute any major personal plan: Willingness to accept less than 100% perfection. Set the parameters of performance: The ideal level and the acceptable level. Then aim for performance with that range. That's easier said than done.

Between the recognition of what has to be done and the courage to change, you must do some hard work.

☐ Sit down with an accounting spread sheet and, on the vertical axis, write down all the things you want to do in your personal life. On a separate list, write down all the things you want to do in the business.

☐ Spend two to three days working out this list.

☐ Think audaciously, creatively, freely. For instance: I want 2,000 people working for me. Or: I want to run a $1 billion company. Or: I want to be married to Michelle Pfeiffer.

☐ After the list is made, mark the items A, B or C, using this ranking:

A: Top priority—the things that need to be done tomorrow (or at least sometime in the future).

B: The things impacting today.

C: Lowest priority—the things that I should have done yesterday, but didn't.

☐ Rationale: You have to change the tempo of what you do. And you must do it on paper. You can't change what happened yesterday—so it gets lowest priority. The only thing you can really affect is what happens tomorrow. That's where to put all the energy and skill.

☐ Ask yourself, of everything listed, what tasks can be done by someone else.

☐ On the horizontal axis, assign the tasks.

☐ Work out some sensible (not grandiose) time schedule for meeting all the goals you really plan to meet.

How to push for change

To improve the likelihood that a recommendation for a change will be accepted:

☐ Demonstrate a thorough knowledge of the status quo, including essential figures.

☐ Make claims for improvement absolutely accurate. Quantify them whenever possible.

☐ Do not play down the real costs of change.

☐ Investigate the less obvious effects a change could have in some areas, in order to head off a quick rejection because of the side effects.

☐ Find someone to play devil's advocate and test the validity of the proposal before presenting it.

☐ Bring copies of supporting data to the proposal meeting.

Source: *Purchasing,* Boston, MA.

Making realistic changes

Before you initiate a major life change:

☐ List your greatest strengths, the past achievements of which you're proudest, and your future goals.

☐ Examine the pattern of contradictions that may become apparent. That pattern provides clues to what changes, if any, should be made.

☐ Caution: Beware of unrealistic expectations that add stress. Examples: Trying to please everyone (some call it the formula for failure) and trying to change other people. Neither one can be done. You can only change yourself.

☐ Set priorities. Despite media hype, it's rare to have all the good things in life—a luxury home, sports car, world travel, country club, Ivy League schools for the children, job satisfaction, peer approval, *and* perfect health.

Source: Professional Practice Consultants, Great Neck, NY.

Focusing on your strengths

Some evening at home, go into your bedroom and close the door. Tell the family you need some time alone.

☐ Take off your clothes and stand in front of the mirror. You'll feel absurd. Everyone does.

☐ Talk to yourself. You'll feel even more absurd. Everyone does.

☐ Ask yourself what you *like* about what you see. Most people are very hard on themselves. I'm too fat. Too gray. Too many wrinkles. You have to get over that—and you only can do that if you stick to it. Keep talking: My arms are strong. My legs aren't too bad. My back is straight.

☐ The lesson, both personal and professional: Don't focus on improving the flaws. Accept the flaws and identify the strengths that you have to work with.

☐ In business, too, achieving the goals you want to achieve is a process. The process is using the company's strength—and your own.

How to beat self-defeating behavior

☐ Write down the things you feel are inhibiting your growth.

☐ Ask yourself if you've tried to deal with the problem or simply fantasized it away.

☐ Realize that *you* may have to change for your life to change. A close friend might be able to suggest something you haven't considered.

☐ Don't get stuck in self-pity. Recognize that your approach to life simply isn't working.

☐ Concentrate on what's right about your life. See if what has worked for you in one area can be applied successfully to another.

Pushing toward peak performance

You have undoubtedly had the experience at one time or another of finding yourself in a high-pressure situation and performing way above your usual level.

A few people—call them peak performers—seem able to turn on the superchargers almost at will. Studies reveal that to be a peak performer you must be:

☐ Deeply and unambiguously committed to your goals.

☐ Confident of your ability to perform well.

☐ In control of your actions.

The Commitment Connection Is Fundamental

☐ If you're not doing what you really want to do, it's not likely that you will give your best attention and energy to what you do.

☐ True commitment requires that you be in touch with your true desires.

☐ Pay attention to your most unguarded daydreams. Take note of these with an open mind and, in a tranquil moment, reflect on what they're telling you about you innermost desires. Give them credence. Don't edit. As you begin to act in accordance with those desires, you should find your performance improving.

Build or Enhance Confidence by Controlling Fear

☐ When you feel fear taking hold, extricate yourself immediately from the bog of undefined apprehension and get a firm grasp on the concrete realities of the situation.

☐ Measure the difficulty of the problem. Make a mental or written profile of exactly what has to be accomplished. It is almost invariably much less than your undefined fears projected.

☐ Rate the problem on a scale of one to ten. This further serves to put the problem into realistic perspective, making it concrete rather than abstract.

☐ Compare your problem with others you have handled successfully in the past. Reflect on past instances in which you have performed well on similar or even more difficult problems.

☐ Imagine the worst. Define as objectively as you can the worst possible consequences that could result from completely "blowing it."

☐ A reality check won't alter the reality, but it will help to interrupt the self-perpetuating cycle of fear that keeps you from doing your very best. It will help you to act.

The importance of control in high-pressure performance is largely a matter of momentum and efficient use of energy.

☐ Distinguish between elements you can control and those you can't, and focus on what you can do.

☐ Choose an action (a can-do) that is concrete, that can be embarked on immediately, and that is in your power to carry out. As one can-do follows another, the task will be rapidly completed and the problem solved.

Source: Robert Kriegel, Ph.D., coauthor with Marilyn Harris Kriegel, Ph.D. of *The C Zone: Peak Performance under Stress,* Anchor Press/Doubleday, Garden City, NY.

How good a leader are you?

How good are you at inspiring excellence in others? The following questions should give you a clear idea of your capabilities in this important area:

☐ Have I spelled out what's expected in terms of results?

☐ Have I discussed these results with my subordinates?

☐ Have I told employees where they stand?

☐ Do employees understand how to do the work?

☐ Do I give employees adequate support?

☐ What have I done or not done to cultivate positive relationships?

Do employees know why their jobs re important, how they fit into the verall company structure and the ffects of poor performance?

Do I keep employees informed on what is going on in the department and he company? (Not just need-to-know ems but nice-to-know.)

Do employees have adequate reedom in which to work?

Do I too often put employees in a defensive position regarding performance?

What have I done to get employees mentally and emotionally involved in heir jobs?

Have I let employees participate in etting goals and deciding how to achieve them?

Have good aspects of performance eceived adequate and periodic ecognition?

Have I shown adequate concern for he employees as individuals? For their personal goals?

Am I willing to listen to employees and give them a chance to implement deas and suggestions?

Have I ever consciously assessed employees' strengths and weaknesses with the idea of structuring work to capitalize on those strengths?

Are employees adequately and reasonably challenged?

Source: Burt K. Scanlan, professor of management, University of Oklahoma, in *Personnel Journal*, Costa Mesa, CA.

What leaders do best

Leaders make the people who follow them feel secure and give them a sense of harmony.

A leader should be able to:

☐ Handle social occasions well.

☐ Use stress constructively.

☐ Be smooth and unruffled in tense situations.

☐ Rally a group to a common goal.

☐ Feel comfortable when faced with diverse points of view.

☐ Make decisions that support independent behavior by members of the group within organizational limits.

☐ Learn more about individuals in the group to better match their tasks to their goals and abilities.

☐ Review recent decisions objectively.

If too many were risk-free, it could be a danger sign that the leader is failing to lead.

How to sell ideas

Creative people often find it easier to do original thinking than to sell their ideas to others.

Before presenting an idea to a group:

☐ Look for reasons why others might oppose the idea.

☐ Seek out early supporters.

☐ Decide on goals. Ask yourself if the acceptance of the idea is more important than getting credit for it.

☐ Downplay originality. Instead, discuss similar concepts that have been successful. Never assume that others want innovation because they say they do. Most people prefer the status quo.

☐ Play politics. Get an unpopular staffer to oppose the idea. Or point out that competitors might use it first.

☐ Throw out decoys for opponents to shoot down. Once their negative impulses have been satisfied, bring up the real idea.

☐ Be detached and appear uninterested. Depriving opponents of a victory reduces their joy in taking the idea apart. Or be the first to point out the idea's flaws, then listen as others solve them.

☐ Make sure that others' perceptions of the idea are accurate. Otherwise they may reject what they think the innovation is, not what it really is.

Source: Thomas J. Attwood, managing director, Cargill Attwood International, *Management Review*, New York.

Coping with disappointment

We have become addicted to the notion that personal change is a simple, painless matter. TV and the movies always present a dramatic crisis and then a resolution. Advertising tries to convince us that this car or that perfume will make us powerful or sexy. Even psychology has contributed by spreading the fiction that a book or weekend seminar will profoundly and quickly transform our lives. But true change doesn't happen overnight. It takes time, commitment, energy, and courage.

Disappointment Styles

There are four basic disappointment styles. Once you identify your patterns, you can start to deal with the problems it causes you.

☐ Acquiescent. She (it's most often a she) responds not from her inner needs but from a desire to please. Disappointment results from the impossible attempt to meet all the demands, real or imagined, of others.

☐ Deprived. This type was deeply disappointed in early life and has developed a defensive posture based on always expecting the worst. Typical premises: "Life is pain" and "You never get what you want."

☐ Romantic. This is a variation of deprived. Romantics were emotionally deprived in childhood and so became attached to unrealistic fantasies of being rescued by love. But since they feel undeserving of intimacy, they sabotage relationships and then cling to the anguish long after a relationship has ended. They are constantly disappointed as each successive lover ultimately fails to fulfill their ultra-romantic expectations.

☐ Self-important. These individuals view themselves as special and there-fore different from others. They expect the world to recognize their superiority and to treat them accordingly. Having been raised by families that convinced them they were favored beings, they are disappointed when the rest of the world doesn't treat them the same way.

To Prevent Disappointment

☐ Maintain flexible expectations. Flex-ibility allows you to plan for the future in a realistic manner while maintaining your excitement and enthusiasm. The key: When you find your expectations aren't being met, change them.

☐ Put more into "assessment" and less into "wish." Every expectation is a combination of an assessment (what you've determined will probably happen) and a wish (what you want to happen). Often our wishes exceed our assessments, and our expectations are therefore unrealistic. But you can change your attitudes to avoid future disappointment. How to go about it: Know what you expect from your family, job, friendships, etc. Then make sure your expectations are realistic. Ask yourself: Has this expectation ever been met before? What were the conditions under which it was met? Do I have control over those conditions?

☐ Have fewer expectations. The ability to live in the present without precon-ceived notions of how life should be is a great gift. If you can accept life in the here and now, enjoying whatever comes your way, you'll experience much less disappointment and much more fulfillment.

Source: David Brandt, Ph.D., a clinical psycholo-gist and author of *Is That All There Is? Overcom-ing Disappointment in an Age of Diminished Expectations,* Pocket Books, NY.

Recovering from a disappointment

Some steps that will help you to recover from disappointment:

☐ Acknowledge the pain and allow yourself feelings of loss and dispossession.

☐ Take a step back to gain perspective. No single hoped-for event is necessary to your survival. Remember some of your past disappointments and realize that life went on—that you achieved satisfaction without fulfillment of those particular expectations.

☐ See the positive side. Disappointment is a lesson in reality. It tells us what's possible and what isn't. It may tell you to give up a certain set of expectations or to change your behavior in order to make what you expect actually happen.

Coping with a major loss

The death of a loved one, the loss of a job, separation, or divorce, all involve change and loss. A sense of loss accompanies all major changes in life, even when the change is positive, such as a job promotion, marriage or a job transfer.

Stages by which people respond to a major loss:

❏ Shock or denial.

❏ Fear and paralysis.

❏ Anger, at others or at oneself.

❏ Sadness and depression.

❏ Acceptance and reformulation of goals.

All the stages are important to the process of adaptation:

❏ The omission of any single stage can result in depression or incomplete adjustment because the energy needed to cope with the present remains bound up in the past.

❏ The longer people have to rehearse a new situation and work through feelings about it, the less stress there will be and the less time it will take to adapt. For example, research among widows shows that those whose husbands died after a long illness, such as cancer, had a much less difficult time making the transition to widowhood than those whose husbands died unexpectedly, in a car crash, for example.

Learning from failure

Sooner or later, everyone who is ambitious will experience a failure. Many don't recognize, however, that failure is necessary. You can't succeed without struggle. But if you're able to learn from what went wrong, you can do it right the next time.

❏ Evaluate honestly what stands between you and success, both in the outside world and within yourself.

❏ Find a mentor who will be open with you about his or her own struggles with such blind spots.

❏ Read biographies of people who overcame their own fears to become successful.

Taking criticism

❏ Don't read more into the criticism than the speaker intends.

❏ Don't be deaf to positive comments.

❏ Separate legitimate from inaccurate criticism.

❏ Don't argue about the critic's feelings rather than the facts of the situation.

❏ Delay a direct response until you have figured out whether the critic is trying to come off better by putting you down.

❏ Make sure the critic knows enough to make an intelligent observation about the subject. Then, pick your response to fit the circumstances.

Source: Dr. Jack E. Hulbert, North Carolina Agricultural and Technical State University, Greensboro, NC, and Dr. Barbara Pletcher, director, National Association for Professional Saleswomen.

How to save face while encouraging criticism

While most people agree that dissent and discussion are vital, many bristle when their own ideas are challenged or criticized. How to be open and avoid ego damage:

❏ Ask for *specific* ways to strengthen or improve an idea rather than for a general opinion.

❏ Meet in individual sessions rather than in a group. Opposition is easier in private.

❏ Solicit reactions to only one part of the proposal at a time.

❏ Ask for written criticism. It can be less traumatic and can be put aside for a calmer moment.

Source: *Personal Report for the Executive*, Research Institute of America, New York.

How to profit from criticism

You can improve yourself by encouraging friends to criticize you, and learning how to take criticism. Your critics may not always be right. But if you don't get the truth from others, you may never find out.

❏ Let your critic finish what he has to say before you answer.

❏ Don't go into the reasons for your actions or behavior. This is really just a way of excusing them.

❏ Don't jest. It is insulting to the critic.

❏ Show that you have understood (whether or not you agree) by briefly repeating the criticism in your own words.

❏ Let your critic know that you understand how your behavior has caused inconvenience or made him feel.

❏ Don't open yourself to criticism for what you are—only for what you do.

You are not responsible for anything but your actions. It is by changing these that you can change yourself.

Source: Dr. George Weinberg, author of *Self Creation*, Avon Books, New York.

Dangers in perfectionism

Emotional perfectionists believe they should always be happy and in control of their feelings.

They believe they should never:

☐ Feel insecure…so they worry about shyness, thus adding to their anxiety.

☐ Feel ambivalent about a commitment…so they're unable to make a decision in the first place and then feel miserable about their vacillation.

☐ More reasonable goal: To have general control of emotions and accept emotional flaws as part of our humanity.

Source: Dr. David D. Burns, cognitive therapist, Presbyterian—University of Pennsylvania Medical Center, Philadelphia.

How to change Type A behavior

Here are some ways to modify dangerous Type A behavior:

☐ Walk and talk more slowly.

☐ Reduce deadline pressure by pacing your days more evenly.

☐ Stop trying to do more than one thing at a time.

☐ Don't interrupt other people in mid-speech.

☐ Begin driving in the slow lane.

☐ Simply sit and listen to music you like while doing nothing else.

Big drains on personal energy

Unwillingness to face up to emotions leads to fatigue. Normal energies are expended in the effort to repress sadness or anger. Some common instances:

☐ Grieving that hasn't been attended to. Surprising, but typical, examples are getting a new job and moving to a new city. The event can be exhilarating.

But, the new situation still implies some loss. This holds true for promotions or getting married—which mean saying goodbye to certain freedoms, contacts options. People who don't deal with the negative aspects of even the most positive changes are vulnerable to psychological fatigue. Some of their energies remain bound up in the past.

☐ Situations of acknowledged loss, i.e. the death of a loved one or the fact that the children have grown up and left home, or having to face the fact of limited potential (executive's sudden realization that he'll never fulfill career objectives).

Recognizing fatigue for what it is

Fighting fatigue is a concept of success-oriented people that actually makes them fatigue-prone. Fatigue is a symptom the purpose of which is to get your attention—to tell you there's something wrong with the way you live. The main cause of fatigue is a monolithic lifestyle, in which the rational sense is used to the exclusion of the other senses, movement, and the emotions. To beat fatigue, you have to get your life back in balance.

What Is Fatigue?

The tiredness we feel after jogging for instance, is not fatigue. Fatigue is an absence of energy, *joie de vivre*, interest…It's a blunting of sensation, a shutting out of stimuli.

Behavioral clues:

☐ Difficulty in getting going or persevering.

☐ Not having the energy to do things you know you enjoy.

☐ Having trouble waking up or getting to sleep.

☐ Taking too many naps.

Most Vulnerable

People who:

☐ Do virtually the same thing all day, every day. The classic case is the executive who spends his work hours hunched over a desk, grabs a sandwich at lunch, takes a break only to talk to co-workers about business, and goes home to a set routine with his family each evening.

☐ Have lifestyles contrary to their natural inclinations. Each of us has a rhythm of activity with which we are most comfortable. If a natural doer is forced to lie on a beach in the Bahamas for two weeks, he'll come back exhausted.

Source: Mary E. Wheat, M.D., an internist and counselor on fatigue at Mt. Zion Hospital and Medical Center, San Francisco.

Are you a workaholic?

People who love their work passionately and spend long hours at it are not necessarily work-addicted. True workaholics cannot stop working even in non-work situations. They make all other activities and relationships secondary to work. While the reasons differ widely, almost all work addicts share these traits:

☐ Oriented to activities involving skills and skill development. Averse to activities where skill is not a factor.

☐ Strongly analytic. Focus on precise definitions, goals, policies, facts, lists, measurements and strategies.

☐ Aggressive and unable to leave things alone. An urge to manipulate and control their environment to gain a sense of satisfaction.

☐ Goal-oriented, product-oriented. Uninterested in the sensations of the present unless they yield products or contribute to their creation.

☐ Concerned with efficiency and effectiveness. Severely upset by waste and loss. Ironically, many work addicts are inefficient because they are perfectionists and refuse to delegate authority.

Source: Jay B. Rohrlick, M.D., *Work and Love: The Crucial Balance*, Summit Books, New York.

Recognizing psychological fatigue

As a rule, if a person has been overworking for some time and then takes three or four days off and sleeps adequately, he should be refreshed.

But often rest is not the answer. People whose tiredness is psychological need stimulation. The more rest such a

person gets, the more tired he becomes.

Who's prone to psychological fatigue:

☐ People who are unwilling to ask for what they want or who keep waiting for people to guess.

☐ People who refuse to say what they don't want. Nothing saps energy and produces fatigue as much as unacknowledged resentment.

☐ If chronic tiredness persists and the doctor says there's no physical cause, acknowledge the problem is a psychological one.

☐ Explore the feelings engendered by work or by important relationships.

☐ Figure out what unmet needs and wants you have in these areas.

☐ Determine which expectations are realistic and which aren't, and how to go about resolving that draining aspect of your life.

Source: Gisele Richardson, management consultant, Richardson Management Associates, Montreal.

Tension-reducing techniques

Basic rules for tense individuals:

☐ Wake up early to avoid hurrying and getting keyed up before leaving the house.

☐ Take a short walk after lunch. Do it any time that tension is high. (Just say, "I'll be back in five minutes," and go.)

☐ Have a daily quiet hour. No phone calls or visitors.

☐ Plan social engagements to allow for a short relaxation period between the end of the business day and the start of the evening's activities.

☐ Always be prepared for those tense moments during the day and, when they come, concentrate on breathing slowly and deeply.

Source: *Personal Health*.

Reducing pain-producing jaw tension

Five exercises to ease discomfort:

☐ Start by opening the mouth wide, then closing it. Do this repeatedly and as rapidly as possible.

☐ Continue the same motions, but now place the palm of your hand beneath the chin when opening the mouth, and above it when closing. This offers a slight resistance.

☐ Repeat the same two steps with a sideways motion of the lower jaw, first doing it freely and then doing it against the resistance of the palm of the hand.

☐ Go through the same steps with a motion that protrudes the jaw.

☐ Chew a piece of gum alternately on each side of the mouth, then in the center of the mouth. Do each exercise for three to five minutes.

Source: Patricia Brown, R.N., *American Journal of Nursing*, New York.

How 9 celebrities handle anxiety

Many successful people have developed their own special ways of dealing with anxiety with a significant emphasis on physical activity. Their approaches may be worth a try for you.

☐ *Yogi Berra,* baseball great:

"I spend lots of time on the golf course, often with my son, who is also a ball player. And I like to play racquetball."

☐ *Jane Brody, New York Times* science writer and author of the bestselling *Jane Brody's Nutrition Book* and *New York Times Guide to Personal Health:*

"I find the best way to avoid anxiety is to exercise. I drop everything and do something physical—jog, swim, whatever. I clear the slate and calm down. When I come back, things don't seem so bad. Another thing—I keep a continuing calendar and try not to let too many things pile up at once. And I have also learned the fine art of saying No."

☐ *Joyce Brothers,* psychologist and TV personality:

"Whenever I get anxious, I swim. (Studies indicate that 15 minutes of strenuous exercise have a more tranquilizing effect than strong drugs). Another good way to fight stress and anxiety is take a long, brisk walk."

☐ *Dr. Frank Field,* NBC science editor:

"The key word, for me, is 'awareness.' Once I am aware of my anxiety, I stand back and look at it. If someone tells me that I am shouting, I try to do something about it—not just deny it. I get swept up with so many things that often I am unaware that I am becoming anxious.

So then I take control of myself."

☐ *Eileen Ford,* Ford Model agency:

"I do yoga deep breathing. The tension just flows from my body."

☐ *Roger Horchow,* founder of The Horchow Collection:

"I don't have much anxiety in my life. When I do, I guess it is when I eat too much. But mostly, I try to work harder to eliminate what is bothering me…try to accomplish more and deal with the source."

☐ *Reggie Jackson,* baseball great:

"My best cure for anxiety is working on my collection of old cars. I also enjoy building cars, and I find that doing physical work can relieve stress for me. Reading the Bible also puts my mind at ease and gives me spiritual comfort."

Ann Landers, syndicated columnist:

"My work is not anxiety-producing, but occasionally, if there is a hitch, I get into a hot bath, take the phone off the hook and count my blessings. I have a great deal to be thankful for, and I know it."

Dr. Ruth Westheimer, prominent sexologist:

"When I get anxious, I say, 'Ruth Westheimer, get hold of yourself.' The important thing is to recognize your anxiety. Sometimes this makes it go away. If it were a really serious anxiety, would go for professional help."

Depression myths and realities

Common as it is, depression is shrouded in popular misconceptions. Whether short-term and mild or more serious and longer-lasting, those feelings of low self-esteem, aimlessness and purposelessness afflict many people periodically. You'll be able to cope with depression better if you understand the major fallacies about it.

☐ If you're feeling depressed, the cause must be psychological. Fact: Not necessarily. Many psychiatrists consider much emotional distress to be caused by genetically inherited body chemistry. Also, a variety of physical illnesses, such as viral infections, can cause low psychological moods.

☐ People who lack ego strength and character are more likely to get depressed than those with strong personalities. Fact: If anything, it's the trongest characters who are most ubject to feelings of depression and ow periods. Strong personalities have ery high standards of success and norality and suffer most from a loss of elf-esteem.

Men and women are equally usceptible to depression. Fact: Women are more likely, by a ratio of two o one, to develop feelings of epression. On the other hand, men end to have more serious depressions nd a higher rate of suicide.

Depression will affect you sychologically but not physically. Fact: rolonged and serious periods of epression can result in weight loss, leeplessness and other stress that can nake the sufferer vulnerable to serious hysical problems, such as heart ttack and multiple sclerosis.

Falling in love will lift you out of epression. Fact: People who are eeling low and emotionally distressed re too internally preoccupied to be ither very interested or successful in andling relationships. Feelings of epression also cause a decrease in ne sexual impulse.

Help for depression can come only om long-term psychotherapy. Fact: here are ways of combating epression effectively that don't require ong-term therapy. Anti-depressant drug therapy may help in several veeks. People who are having a mild, hort-term depression may profit from eeing a therapist or a counselor everal times. However, serious and disabling depression that lasts for nonths does call for continuing professional treatment.

Tranquilizers will help you combat eelings of depression. Fact: Valium and alcohol are both depressants hemselves, as are all tranquilizers. The only medications that work are antidepressant drugs, which must be carefully prescribed.

The cause of your depression is usually obvious. Fact: The cause that seems most obvious is most often not he real one. Reason: Depression has o do with unconscious conflict. For example, one of the frequent causes of depression is repressed hostility. When hat hostility is acknowledged, the depression usually lifts.

You always know when you are depressed. Fact: There are common orms of depression in which people do not know how they feel. Such people express their depression in other ways. Obese people and alcoholics often may not feel depressed, but their obesity or drinking are the equivalent. People who feel their depression have an advantage because they, at least, have a chance to do something about it.

☐ There are usually some after-effects from depression. Fact: It's possible, after a period of feeling depressed, to jump right back to where you were with no residuals. Depression does not change the psyche.

Source: Michael Levy, M.D., psychiatrist, New York.

How to cope with depression

☐ Avoid isolation. Talk with someone who can provide counsel.

☐ If a period of depression lasts for more than a few weeks, or if your ability to function is impaired, more professional help is needed.

☐ Recognize that your outlook during a low period is going to be pessimistic and distorted. In such a period, your judgments of yourself, of your situation and of other people are not based on reality.

☐ Difficult as it may be, try to be active, do things and see people. People who are most successful at coping with feelings of depression are those who fight them.

Source: Michael Levy, M.D., psychiatrist, New York.

Rules of thumb

Rules of thumb are useful because they cut down on the time needed to get information and figure things out ourselves. Some especially helpful and little-known ones:

☐ Extracurricular. Don't expect any more than one third of any professional-club members to attend a meeting. Build up a large membership so enough members are around to make up for those away.

☐ Horses: To get the best price on a riding horse, the best time of year to buy is fall.

☐ Walking. Without a pack, you should be able to walk 25 miles a day without serious strain. With a pack one-fourth your weight or less, 15 miles a day is reasonable on an average trail.

☐ Dieting. Most overeating happens at

night. If you can't diet all the time, diet after dark.

☐ Most for your money. You can mail five sheets of average paper for 29¢.

☐ Holiday time. To find out how many lights a Christmas tree needs, first multiply the tree height by the tree width measured in feet. Then multiply this figure by three.

☐ Determining your frame size. You can determine your body frame by wrapping your thumb and index finger around your wrist. Small frame: Thumb extends past the index finger. Average frame: Thumb and index finger just meet. Large frame: Thumb and index finger don't meet.

☐ Fixing up. It takes the average person one hour to paint 1,000 square feet plus one hour for each window or door.

☐ Bad weather. Second gear is best for driving on ice and snow.

Source: *Rules of Thumb* by Tom Parker, Houghton Mifflin Co., Boston.

How to make the most of the time in your life

Write a game plan for the rest of your life. It should include answers to the following questions:

☐ What things are really important in your life?

☐ What practical considerations have to be taken into account (earning a living, raising children, lifestyle)?

☐ What are your greatest personal strengths? Rank them.

☐ What are your most limiting shortcomings? Rank them, too.

☐ What are the activities you most enjoy and most dislike?

With these lists as a guide, make three sets of goals:

☐ Long-term—assume normal retirement age, plus 20 years.

☐ Mid-term—from today until retirement.

☐ Short-term—the next one to five years.

Long-term goals tend to be general (they should be), and short-term goals tend to be overly ambitious. A typical long-term goal is "Happiness." A

typical short-term goal is "To get out of this rat race and open my own business."

Source: *Overcoming Executive Mid-Life Crisis*, John Wiley, New York.

Easy ways to get organized

The most efficient people usually use systems that have two things in common—they're easy to set up, and they can be used consistently.

☐ Part-time employees are the key. Intelligent and motivated students will work for relatively low wages. Young mothers, too, are often looking for part-time work, and a note posted in pediatricians' waiting rooms will help them find you. Use them to prepare your tax returns, match paint swatches, address invitations to a party, collect the RSVPs, deliver collection envelopes for your favorite charity and wait in your home for the appliance repair service to arrive.

☐ As soon as you can each morning, make two lists of things you want to accomplish that day. The first list is activities that absolutely must get done. Reserve the second list for the wouldn't-it-be-nice-if jobs. You'll probably accomplish everything on the priority list. Consider yourself lucky if you make even a dent in the wish list.

☐ Find ways to get something done, no matter where you are. Carry notebooks to jot down ideas as they occur to you, or keep required reading material close at hand to review whenever a spare moment crops up.

☐ Don't force the issue if you're working on one thing but really want to be doing something else. Work on what you feel like doing.

☐ Create a master list—one place to write everything of importance that you need to remember. Include things to do, important names and phone numbers, good ideas. Use a spiral notebook instead of a pad so pages won't fall off.

Source: Dr. Marilyn Machlowitz, author of *Workaholics: Living with Them, Working with Them*, The New American Library, New York, and Gerard R. Roche, Executive Recruiter.

How to develop good time-use habits

All of us can make more of ourselves if we take the trouble to cultivate good time-use habits until they are second nature. Habits automatically steer our lives. When habits become time-thrifty, people get better use of their time for the rest of their lives, automatically.

To develop better time-use habits:

☐ Pick those habits that are good and drop bad ones. Make a list of times and places to substitute a new habit for an old one. It takes a month or more until a new habit is second nature.

☐ Concentrate on using the new technique as often as possible. Every time you use a new habit, give yourself a mental pat on the back. Otherwise, a mental kick is in order.

☐ Put weekly reminders to change habits on a calendar. When the reminders come up, evaluate your progress. Then list additional times and places to apply the new habit.

☐ Announce your intentions to develop new habits to other people. This strengthens your motivation to finish the job.

Source: Robert Moskowitz, time-management consultant, Canoga Park, CA.

Hard-nosed ways to manage time

☐ Concentrate on the best ways to spend time, instead of worrying about saving it.

☐ Keep an accurate log of activities to identify and define work patterns.

☐ Have only one chair (besides yours) in your office. Keeping people standing saves time.

☐ Each meeting should have an announced time limit.

☐ Have all calls screened. Make a list of who should be put through immediately.

☐ Arrange your office with your back to the door.

☐ If someone asks, "Do you have a minute?" say, "No."

☐ List tomorrow's priorities before leaving the office today.

☐ Don't rush needlessly. It takes longer to correct a mistake than to avoid making one.

Source: Merrill E. Douglass, director, Time Management Center, New York.

Avoiding the obligation overload

The prime cause of the overload syndrome is outside pressure to accept too many work or volunteer obligations. Another factor is the initial receptiveness of certain personality types to taking on tasks. Those people are particularly prone to guilt feelings.

Overload symptoms:

☐ Fear that the additional responsibilities (which suddenly seem overwhelming) won't be met.

☐ Inability to make decisions.

☐ Difficulty in communicating with family. The usual excuse is exhaustion.

☐ Isolation. Discarding the usual recreational outlets and exercise habits on grounds that there is no time.

What it takes to say no:

☐ A clear awareness of priorities. It's easier for a responsible person to say no if it's clear what's at stake: Obligations to family and personal health.

☐ The strength to accept temporary feelings of guilt.

Dealing with details

When your mind is cluttered with details, use one of these techniques to redirect energy and improve organization:

☐ Take a mini-break. A short walk or a minute of relaxation and a drink of water. Or, simply breathe deeply for 30 seconds with your eyes closed (this can help concentration when you shift from one subject to another).

☐ Keep your schedule on paper. Resist the temptation to keep it in your head.

☐ Avoid interruptions. Work away from the office and keep your distance from the telephone.

☐ Delegate details. Rely more heavily on your secretary. Let subordinates handle routine jobs. Let them attend most of the less important meetings.

☐ Set time limits. If a task isn't completed within an allotted time limit, come back to it later.

Source: *International Management*, New York.

While standing in line

☐ Do isometric exercises.
☐ Listen to instructional tapes.
☐ Read a paperback.
☐ Watch your miniature TV set.
☐ Meditate.
☐ Meet your neighbors in line.
☐ Plan the week's schedule.
☐ Plan an upcoming trip.
☐ Bring along a dictionary to expand your vocabulary.
☐ Make a list of people you want to meet to improve your business or social life.

The basics of speed-reading

Speed-reading is not a miracle. It is a skill that takes commitment, concentration and practice. Nor is it appropriate for all kinds of reading. Poetry, for example, was never meant to be whizzed through.

Good speed-reading courses employ a variety of techniques designed to make your reading more efficient and effective. The more you train yourself to use these techniques, the faster—and more productive—your reading will become. The basics:

☐ Skim material from which you want only the main ideas.

☐ Go slowly when you need to take in all the details.

☐ Concentrate. Reading is a mental process. If you are distracted while reading, you will proceed slowly and not remember what you have read.

☐ Use typographical clues to get the general content. Headlines, boldfaced lead-ins, bullets, etc. guide you through the material, indicating what you can

skip and what you need to concentrate on most.

Source: Robert de Vight, adjunct associate professor of communications at New York University.

Speed-reading: Fact vs. fiction

What To Be Wary Of

☐ Any system that *guarantees* increased reading speed. The most deceptive thing about a guarantee is the false sense of confidence it gives to the individual with low verbal skills. If you don't start out with basic skills, you will not learn them in speed-reading.

☐ Anyone who suggests that you can read 900 or 1,000 words a minute. Impossible, except when reading extremely easy material. Average reading speed is around 250 to 300 words per minute. Some reading specialists claim 600 to 800 is the maximum for good reading comprehension.

How Reading Can Be Speeded Up

☐ Preview material. Skim for key words and phrases. Then decide which memos, reports, surveys, business and professional journals you should keep to read.

☐ Read flexibly. Most experts believe learning to read flexibly is the real key to speed-reading. A fast look is valuable when you need to get through repetitive material that doesn't require you to take in every word. It is also helpful when you're trying to locate a specific fact or phrase. Adjust to a slower reading tempo when the information on the subject is unfamiliar.

☐ Read a lot. It's necessary to keep good reading habits sharp by practicing.

Source: Dr. Charles Shearin, president, Vicore, Inc., Arlington, VA.

Conversation basics

Here are some ways to keep good conversation flowing:

❏ When talking with someone from a field you either don't know or don't care anything about, steer the conversation toward feelings rather than facts or details. By focusing on emotions that everyone shares, you can feel secure discussing anything.

❏ Make sure both people have equal power to bring up topics, change the subject and demand attention. Avoid common conversational mistakes:

❏ Bombarding the other person with questions.

❏ Being too quick to give advice.

❏ Giving too many personal details.

Sources: *Better Communication* and Gerald Goodman, associate professor of Psychology, UCLA, quoted in *US News and World Report.*

Conversation killers

Intimate talks will be more pleasant and productive if you avoid the following:

❏ Sentences that start with the accusatory *You* or the inclusive *Let's* or *We.* (Instead, try to begin more sentences with *I,* to make your honest feelings known.)

❏ Absolute statements. Example: "That was a stupid movie."

❏ *I don't know.* (You probably have some inkling of an answer, even if it's only to add, "Let me think about it.")

❏ *I don't care.* (Even a weak preference should be voiced.)

❏ *Ought, should, must, have to.* Instead, try *I might, I would like to* or *I want to.*

❏ Questions beginning with *Why,* such as "Why are you feeling that way?" Better: Begin with a *What,* as in "What is bothering you?"

❏ *Always* and *never.* More flexible phrases are *up to now* and *in the past.*

Source: Dr. Theresa Larsen Crenshaw, *author of Bedside Manners,* Pinnacle Books, New York.

How to be a better conversationalist

❏ Don't start with your name. A name exchange gives a conversation nowhere to go. Instead, mention something in the environment that you can both talk about, such as "How's the cheesecake in this restaurant?"

Then pay attention to the cues to find out whether the other person wants to talk with you. Consider tone of voice, facial expression and body language.

❏ Develop your descriptive power. The well-told anecdote or story will express your personality and convey warmth and charm. Many people are afraid to express their feelings when it comes to description. They stick to a dry recitation of facts instead.

❏ Be sensitive to the other person. Pick up on messages about how that person is feeling. Watch body language as well as listening to what's being said. Don't be one of those insensitive, endless talkers who fear that if they stop, their partner will get bored and want to leave.

❏ Don't use boredom as a defense. People who always claim to be bored are usually just erecting a defense against rejection. If you're at a party and don't talk to anyone because you tell yourself they're all boring, you've just insulated yourself against failure. If you feel you're boring to others, that's just another excuse for not trying and therefore not failing.

❏ Don't keep asking questions. Constant queries to keep a conversation going can be a crutch. The other person will finally realize that you're not really listening but are thinking up the next question. People dislike feeling interrogated and resent answering questions under those circumstances. Ask a question only when something genuinely sparks your curiosity.

Source: Arthur Reel, who teaches the art of conversation at New York City's Learning Annex and at Corporate Communications Skills, Inc., an executive training center in New York.

Learning to listen

Here are some simple techniques to help you improve your listening ability:

❏ Relax and help the speaker relax, too. Give your full attention to what's being said. Stop everything else you're doing. Maintain eye contact.

❏ Don't let the speaker's tone of voice or manner turn you off. Nervousness or misplaced emotions often cloud the message the speaker is trying to get across.

❏ Prepare beforehand for the conversation. Take a few minutes to read or consult information pertinent to the discussion. That also helps you to quickly evaluate the speaker and the subject.

☐ Allow for unusual circumstances (extreme pressure or disturbing interruptions). Judge only what the speaker says, given the conditions he's faced with.

☐ Avoid getting sidetracked.

☐ Listen very closely to points you disagree with. (Poor listeners shut out or distort them.)

☐ Mentally collect the main points of the conversation. Occasionally, ask for clarification of one of the speaker's statements.

Bad listening habits

If you want to be a better listener, try to avoid:

☐ Thinking about something else while waiting for the speaker's next word or sentence. The mind races ahead four times faster than the normal rate of conversation.

☐ Listening primarily for facts rather than ideas.

☐ Tuning out when the talk seems to be getting too difficult.

☐ Prejudging, from appearance or speaking manner, that the person has nothing interesting to say.

☐ Paying attention to outside sights and sounds when talking with someone.

☐ Interrupting with a question whenever a speaker says something puzzling or unclear.

Source: John T. Samaras, University of Oklahoma.

How to listen to a complaint

Many people don't hear anything that doesn't fit their own assumptions. If someone comes to you with a complaint or claim, listen—just listen.

☐ Don't answer or explain.

☐ Take notes on exactly what's said.

☐ Try to imagine that the person is right, or at least justified.

☐ Put yourself in the other's place and imagine how you would feel in the same situation.

☐ Give yourself time to think the matter over before making any decision.

☐ Nobody can see all sides of an issue immediately. New facts or ideas take time to sink in.

Source: Levinson Letter, Cambridge, MA.

How to get information from others

☐ Speak softly. This encourages others to take center stage where they should be if you want to learn something from them.

☐ Look responsive. Most people don't use nearly enough facial expression. Raising one eyebrow a little and smiling slightly makes you seem receptive. Eye contact and a calculated pause will invite the person you're talking with to elaborate.

☐ Give reinforcement. Comments such as "Very impressive!" or "Excellent!" can be dropped into the discussion without interrupting the flow.

☐ Follow up and probe. If someone fails to explain the reasons for an action that you're curious about, try a casual follow-up question.

Source: Richard A. Fear, author of The Evaluation Interview, published by McGraw-Hill, New York.

Hidden meanings in what people say

Key words tell what people are really trying to communicate. These words and phrases may be spoken repeatedly or hidden in the middle of complex sentences. But they relay the true message being delivered through all the chatter of conversations, negotiations and interviews.

What to watch out for:

☐ Words that jump out at you. The speaker may be mumbling, but suddenly a word (or proper name) is emphasized or spoken loudly.

☐ Slips of the tongue, especially when denied by the person who made them. Example: "We won't leave this room until we have reached a derision" (instead of decision). The speaker is mocking either you or the subject under discussion.

☐ Embedding. The repetitive use of words or slogans manipulated to reshape your thinking. Embedding can be insidious. Example: At a meeting of parties with irreconcilable differences, one side keeps repeating the word consensus. "After we reach a consensus, we'll break for lunch." This one concept is repeated relentlessly by the speakers and members of their

...eam until it dominates the meeting. This is a mini-version of the Big Lie.

❑ Hostile words and phrases. Any statement that hurts or sounds hostile is an affront, even when pawned off as a joke.

❑ Unstated words. These key words are those not spoken. Prime example: The husband or wife who can never say "I love you" to the mate.

❑ Metaphors. The turns of expression people choose often signal their inner thoughts. Example: A metaphor such as "We'll cut the opposition up into little pieces" takes healthy competition into the realm of aggression.

Source: Martin G. Groder, M.D., psychiatrist and business consultant, Durham, NC.

How people say "yes" but mean "no"

Here are some apparently acquiescent verbal expressions that really mean "no":

❑ "Yes, but…"

❑ "I don't know why, but…"

❑ "I tried that, and it doesn't help."

❑ "Well, to be perfectly honest with you…"

❑ "But it's not easy…"

❑ "I know, but…"

❑ "I don't remember."

Spot the unspoken thought behind the poker face

Watching people's actions can bring you a lot closer to the truth than merely listening to what they say.

Here are some typical feelings and mental machinations—and their common outward expressions:

❑ Openness: Open hands, unbuttoned coat.

❑ Defensiveness: Arms crossed on chest, crossing legs, fistlike gestures, pointing index finger, "karate" chops.

❑ Evaluations: Hand to face, head tilted, stroking chin, peering over or playing with glasses, cleaning glasses, cleaning or filling a pipe, hand to nose.

❑ Suspicion: Arms crossed, sideways glance, touching-rubbing nose, rubbing eyes, buttoned coat, drawing away.

❑ Insecurity: Pinching flesh, chewing pen, thumb over thumb, biting fingernail, hands in pockets.

❑ Cooperation: Upper body in sprinter's position, open hands, sitting on edge of chair, hand-to-face gestures, unbuttoning coat.

❑ Confidence: Steepled hands, hands behind back, back stiffened, hands in coat pockets with thumbs out, hands on lapels of coat.

❑ Nervousness: Clearing throat, "whew" sound, whistling, smoking, pinching flesh, fidgeting, covering mouth, jiggling money or keys, tugging ears, wringing hands.

❑ Frustration: Short breaths, "tsk" sound, tightly clenched hands, wringing hands, fistlike gestures, pointing index finger, rubbing hand through hair, rubbing back of neck.

❑ SOS: Uneven intonation of voice, wringing of hands, poor body posture, or failure to make eye contact.

How not to be put on the defensive

Criticism from fellow workers or superiors on the job can escalate if you react defensively. How to avoid this instinctive reaction:

❑ Paraphrase an accusation as a way of slowing down reaction time and giving the accuser a chance to retreat. Accuser: How come that report isn't ready? Can't you ever get your work done on time? Response: Do you really think that I never get my work done on time?

❑ Describe in a tentative fashion what appears to be the other person's psychological state. In response to a scowling superior, say: I'm uncomfortable. I don't understand what your frown means.

❑ Ask for clarification. Accuser: This proposal isn't what I asked you to design at all. Response: Is nothing in the proposal acceptable?

❑ Use a personal response to assume responsibility. Accuser: This is entirely wrong. Response: I guess I didn't understand. Can I review the instructions again?

Source: Gary P. Cross, management consultant, Cross Names & Beck, Eugene, OR.

Arguments: Keeping your cool

☐ Don't fear to negotiate, even when the difference with the other person is so huge that agreement seems impossible.

☐ If the issue is important, you probably cannot accurately predict when and how a resolution will finally be made. The outcome may become apparent only after extensive discussions.

☐ Avoid the temptation to start off in a hostile manner out of anger at the other person's extreme stance.

Source: Dr. Chester L. Karrass, Karrass Seminars, Santa Monica, CA.

When to offer a solution to a dispute

Let the two sides clear the air by exchanging accusations and expressing pent-up resentments over extraneous issues, not just the one now on the table. Any trained mediator waits for this venting of feelings and buildup of frustrations before exercising influence.

☐ The best (often the only) time to recommend an innovative solution comes when desperation peaks. Both sides know they have a problem. And both know they can't settle it without third-party help.

☐ To be a hero, deliver a solution where mutual goals are not being met and where all parties already recognize that there is a gap between expectations and performance.

Build trust during a discussion

☐ Begin with a positive statement, for example, "I have been looking forward to talking with you. Joe Smith said if anyone could help us, it's you."

☐ Avoid pulling rank.

☐ Don't make veiled threats.

☐ Don't offer a reward.

☐ Show yourself to be an expert.

☐ Associate yourself with someone the other person respects.

☐ Restate the other person's opinions or feelings periodically. But do not preface the restatement with "you said" or "you think." The other person may

quibble over what is attributed directly

☐ Share something personal about yourself if the other person is wary.

☐ Point out ways the information you need will help you.

☐ Indicate ways you can help the other person.

☐ Make a commitment to action, and then ask for a commitment in return.

Source: Pamela Cumming, author of *The Power Handbook,* CBI Publishing, Boston.

Choose your words carefully

Avoid:

☐ Using popular but vague modifiers, such as exceptional or efficient, without defining precisely what is meant. For example, an exceptional record can be either exceptionally good or bad. Describing something as efficiently designed does not say enough. It's better to use facts, numbers, details.

☐ Exaggerating. Overstating a fact is acceptable (and common) in conversation, but it destroys credibility in writing because readers take it literally.

☐ Generalizing. Do not use absolutes, such as: All, right, wrong, true, false, always, never. Instead, say this is true under such-and-such conditions.

Source: William C. Paxson, author of *The Business Writing Handbook,* Bantam Books, New York.

Write as clearly as you think

Concentrate on simplifying your sentence structure. It's the easiest way to say what is meant and to make sure the message gets across. Three basic rules:

☐ Keep sentences short. They should be no more than 17 to 20 words. If an idea has multiple parts, use multiple sentences.

☐ Vary the length of sentences. The 17 to 20 word rule is the average. When sentences drone on at unvarying lengths, the reader's attention begins to wander.

☐ Vary the punctuation. Include plenty of commas, as well as a sprinkling of semicolons, to go with the necessary periods. Well-placed punctuation is a road map, leading the reader comfortably and accurately through the message.

Source: Paul Richards, author of *Sentence Control: Solving an Old Problem,* Supervisory Management, New York.

How to measure the clarity of your writing

Use the "Fog Index" to measure how clearly you write letters, memos, and reports.

☐ Count off a 100-word section.

☐ Count the number of sentences and divide 100 by that number, which gives average words per sentence.

☐ Count the words with more than two syllables. Add this figure to the average words per sentence.

☐ Multiply the total by 0.4 to get the Fog Index (indicating minimum school grade level a reader needs to comprehend it).

The lower the index, the better. A score of 11 to 12 is passable for most business writing. (The Fog Index for this item: 7.6)

Source: *Time Talk,* Grandville, MI.

How to write a persuasive letter

☐ Grab your reader's attention by fitting in with his interests, either personal or in business. Tell him how he is going to benefit by doing as you ask.

☐ Give proof of what you say. The best proof is to suggest that the reader get in touch with others who have benefited from your suggestion. (Of course, you must make sure that you have people who will back you up.)

☐ In the next-to-last paragraph, tell the reader exactly what he must do to take advantage of the benefits you're offering.

☐ Close with a hook. Encourage the reader to take action by telling him about a loss of money, prestige or opportunity if he does not act at once. (A time penalty is one of the best ways to get the action you want.)

Source: James Van Fleet, author of *A Lifetime Guide to Conversation,* Prentice Hall, Inc., Englewood Cliffs, NJ.

Help readers understand your report

Readers understand a report better when they are carefully led through it. Use the right words or phrases to signal a shift of subject or emphasis:

☐ To get your reader to stop and consider alternatives. Use: However, but, by contrast, nevertheless, on the other hand, still, despite, notwithstanding.

☐ To expand the idea. Use: Actually, realistically, at the same time, unexpectedly, perhaps.

☐ To concede to a limitation. Use: Sometimes, to be sure, possibly, to some extent, conceivably.

☐ To make an aside. Use: Incidentally, digressing for a moment.

☐ To move ahead in the same direction. Use: Additionally, also, besides, moreover, furthermore.

☐ To make a comparison. Use: Similarly, in the same way.

☐ To strengthen an assertion. Use: Indeed, in fact, certainly.

☐ To signal importance. Use: Significantly, notably, remarkably.

Source: A. Weiss, author of *Write What You Mean,* AMACOM, New York.

Speeches with impact

Only rarely is it possible to change your audience's deep-seated attitudes or beliefs. Aim no higher than getting the listeners to question their attitudes.

☐ Avoid alienating an audience by pressing points too hard.

☐ State conclusions.

☐ Call for action.

☐ When you have to speak extemporaneously, develop a theme early and stick to it.

☐ Use silence to underline a point.

☐ End a speech with a short, emotional, conviction-filled summary of the main points.

Source: Michael Klezaras Jr., director of research and planning, Roger Ailes & Associates, Inc., New York.

Delivering an important speech

☐ Find out what common bonds unite the audience so that the speech can be directed to meaningful subjects.

☐ Remember that your audience is interested first in people, then in things, finally in ideas.

☐ Start by tape-recording a spontaneous flow of ideas. Don't attempt to be logical or to follow an outline. This initial tape is the raw material to prepare the final speech.

☐ Avoid opening with a joke. Most jokes backfire. The best grabbers are a question, personal story, famous quote, vital statistic, comparison, or contrast.

☐ Use questions throughout.

☐ Avoid unnecessary phrases such as "Now let me explain…." Or: "The point I want to make is."

Audience attention drops off sharply after 20 to 30 minutes, so no presentation should run beyond that. If it's necessary to fill more time:

☐ Use slides when appropriate.

☐ Have a question and answer session after the speech.

Public speaking: Secrets of success

Contrary to a lot of advice about making a speech, there is no need to memorize, rehearse, rely on extensive notes or spend weeks getting ready. The key is to keep the presentation spontaneous.

The only requirements for spontaneous speaking:

☐ Thorough knowledge of the subject.

☐ Self-confidence.

☐ An assured manner of delivery.

To make sure the speech does not sound overrehearsed or canned:

☐ Don't use notes because you'll have no more than two seconds to look down, find the place in the notes and speak to the audience. You'll end up looking, reading, memorizing and reciting, but not communicating.

☐ Instead of notes, use one- to three-word "triggers" instead of notes. Triggers are facts or concepts designed to spark off the next train of thought. Using triggers allows you to deal easily with what is to be said. The result is that you'll gesture more, be more animated and vary your tone of voice.

☐ As a structure for the speech, adopt the same format that people use to communicate every day: State the purpose, support it with details, then recommend what should be done.

☐ Start with a 15- to 30-second grabber. The grabber explains the purpose and stimulates the audience. Work through the details by using the triggers. About five of these should suffice.

☐ End by telling the group something specific to do. If questions follow the talk, restate the recommended action at the conclusion.

☐ Stand in front of the lectern and as close to the audience as possible. This makes the talk seem more like a conversation. In a big auditorium, use a lapel microphone to avoid getting stuck at the lectern. Establish eye contact with people one at a time. Don't look at the wall.

Talking effectively to small groups

☐ Meet personally as many people as possible beforehand.

☐ Get right to the point. The first 15 seconds is what grabs the listener. Don't start with "Thank you" and "I'm very happy to be here."

☐ Make eye contact with everyone in the audience at some time very early in the presentation.

☐ Support main points with factual information and examples.

☐ Repeat the main points to be sure the listeners have gotten them.

☐ Look for a creative conclusion—a provocative thought or action-suggesting statement.

☐ Never let a talk end with an answer to a question from the audience. After answering questions, always return to the main point of the presentation. The last word is important. It shouldn't be yielded to a questioner.

☐ Never ask the audience, "Any questions?" If there aren't any, the silence will be embarrassing. Instead, suggest, "There may be some questions." It makes a difference.

☐ Limit use of notes because it inhibits spontaneity. Write out key words or short phrases to jog thoughts. Alternate lines with different color ink to facilitate quick focusing on material.

☐ Rehearsing is usually not recommended. Unrehearsed presentations have the advantage of freshness and spontaneity which only come from thoughts uttered for the first time.

Source: Dr. Roger Flax, communications training consultant, Motivational Systems, South Orange, NJ.

Using humor successfully

☐ Avoid humor when speaking out of doors. The laugh tends to get lost, leaving people with the feeling it wasn't funny at all.

☐ Avoid puns, even though they may go over well in a parlor. They almost always cause the audience to groan more than laugh.

☐ Leave enough time for the laugh before proceeding. Audiences sometimes react slowly, especially if the humor was unexpected. To a nervous speaker, a second's delay seems like an hour.

☐ Be prepared to carry on smoothly and self-confidently if the audience doesn't laugh. The audience will quickly forget that the speaker laid an egg if he remains calm.

Source: Paul Preston, *Communication for Managers*, Prentice-Hall, Englewood Cliffs, NJ.

How to tell jokes like a pro

Henny Youngman, the well-known master comedian and king of the one-liners, offers the following advice:

☐ Genuinely like the jokes you tell. If you don't, you'll nearly always have trouble telling them, not to mention remembering them.

☐ Practice. Memorize your jokes thoroughly. If you fumble for words in the middle of a joke, it will always fall flat.

☐ Always give your audience time to laugh. Then just as the laughter starts to die down, start another joke or resume the conversation. Timing is easier than you might think.

☐ Avoid off-color jokes. There are plenty of funny stories around that aren't dirty.

☐ Be wary of very long jokes. The longer they are, the greater the risk of failure.

☐ Stick to simple, short jokes on subjects we normally like to laugh about.

Source: Henny Youngman, renowned comedian.

How to testify before Congress

Congress holds thousands of hearings a year on subjects vital to your community and business. Can a company or civic or non-profit organization hope to influence legislation by testifying? Chances are against it.

But testimony can sometimes make a difference, particularly on a subject with which legislators are unfamiliar. And an organization or company can raise its profile if an appearance before a Congressional committee is covered by the news media.

If you wish to testify, follow these steps:

☐ Write a letter asking to appear to the committee chairman, whose name appears in the *Congressional Directory*.

(You can find this book at your local public library.)

☐ In your letter, focus on your organization's expertise. Point out that its views differ from those already presented. (To protect themselves, committees look for a cross section of views.)

☐ Submit a detailed summary of testimony for committee members to review before the hearing. (Some committees require it 24 hours in advance.)

☐ At the hearing, limit testimony to two or three major points, then open it up to questions. The impact of testifying lies in the face-to-face exchange with committee members. Brief testimony is more likely to be covered by the press.

☐ To improve your chances of being asked to testify, keep in touch with committee staff members, also listed in the *Congressional Directory,* and the representatives from states where your organization is active.

Also useful is the *Congressional Record,* which gives advance notice of hearings.

Source: *The Directory* and the *Daily Record,* available from the Superintendent of Documents, US Government Printing Office, Washington, DC 20402.

255

How to come across well on radio or TV

If you're asked to be a guest on a radio or TV program, perhaps to promote a charity or civic group with which you're associated or to talk about the local business scene, don't say no for fear of doing poorly. Follow these five simple rules, and you'll do fine:

☐ Set the tone right away. Explain at the outset why the subject is important.

☐ Don't stray from the subject.

☐ Keep answers tight. Allow time for more questions and answers, and thus more information.

☐ On television, don't look at the cameras. Look directly at the show host.

☐ On radio, sit close to the microphone. The audience will lose much of what you're saying if you're too far away.

Source: Richard Goldberg, president, *You're On!* Visual Communications Consulting, Brighton, MA.

How to make an effective presentation

Presentations don't have to be speeches. Other possibilities:

☐ An interview format, with one person questioning another.

☐ A discussion among several people, one acting as leader and outlining a project, one strongly in favor, another doubtful, another opposed—thus presenting every point of view.

☐ You might even try a skit, if your people can make the time to learn the lines.

☐ Don't conduct a meeting with nothing but speech after speech. Creative presentations are much better remembered.

Source: *Successful Meetings*.

Planning ahead for summer jobs, internships and study programs

It's not too soon for your college youngster to make plans for the summer. A variety of good resources to start with is listed below.

Publications

☐ *Federal Jobs*, Box 1438, Leesburg, VA 22075. A listing of federal job opportunities, state by state.

☐ *Summer Jobs in Federal Agencies*, Office of Personnel Management, 1900 E St., NW, Washington, DC 20415. Government internships, paying and nonpaying.

☐ *Vacation Study Abroad*, Institute of International Education, 809 UN Plaza, New York 10017. Nearly 1,000 summer programs sponsored by US and foreign organizations.

☐ *Wanted Abroad*, Council on International Educational Exchange, 205 E. 42 St., New York 10017. Job openings in France, Germany, Great Britain, Ireland, and New Zealand.

☐ *Work, Study, Travel Abroad: The Whole World Handbook*, Council on International Educational Exchange, 205 E. 42 St., New York 10017. Summer and whole-year jobs and academic programs.

Agencies

☐ College career placement offices have information and applications for competitive summer internships in government and industry.

☐ State information offices will provide lists of state government internship programs.

☐ The National Society for Internships and Experiential Education, 3509 Haworth Dr., Suite 207, Raleigh, NC 27609. Gives students information on programs in particular areas of business.

Source: Dr. Peter Shaw, author.

Tuition tactics—it pays to be a resident

Students who attend a state college or university outside their home state pay much higher tuition than do residents of that state. In addition, nonresidents do not have access to statewide scholarship and student aid programs.

However, the Supreme Court has ruled that although state colleges and universities can charge nonresidents higher tuition, those students must be allowed to earn residency status during the period of their enrollment.

Although requirements for residency vary from state to state, most follow similar patterns. All states require continuous residence for a period of time immediately preceding application—usually one year, but as little as six months in a few states.

Basic questions a residency applicant is asked:

☐ Have you filed an income tax return in the state?

☐ Are you dependent on your parents for support, or are you financially independent?

☐ Have you registered and voted in the state?

☐ Do you have a driver's license or car registration in the state?

☐ Do you have a record of employment in the state? (Students who are seeking financial aid are expected to earn some money through summer and part-time employment.)

State universities that welcome out-of-staters

State universities and colleges were founded primarily to provide low-cost higher education for residents of the state. However, a number of top-flight state universities and colleges welcome students from all over the country. Out-of-state students are charged higher tuition than residents of the state, but frequently, the total still represents a higher-education bargain.

Some first-class institutions that welcome out-of-state students:

☐ *College of William and Mary*, Williamsburg, VA. This is the second-oldest institution of higher learning in the country. Located in historic Williamsburg, the college admits about 30% of its student body from out of state.

☐ *Indiana University*, Bloomington, IN. Founded in 1820, the university draws

20% of its students from out of state.

☐ *New College of the University of South Florida*, Sarasota, FL. Founded in 1960 as a private liberal arts college, it is now an honors-type campus of the university. Nearly half of its students are from outside the South.

☐ *University of Michigan*, Ann Arbor, MI. One of the most prestigious state universities, it has long been popular with students from around the country.

☐ *University of North Carolina at Chapel Hill*, Chapel Hill, NC. This is the nation's first state university. Most of its students come from the South, but it is also popular with students from other parts of the country, particularly the Northeast.

☐ *University of Virginia*, Charlottesville, VA. Thomas Jefferson founded this school and designed its beautiful campus. UVA has considerable social prestige—admirers claim that Princeton is the UVA of the North.

☐ *University of Wisconsin*, Madison, WI. Long popular with students from the Eastern seaboard, it has always been generous, too, in accepting students from the Midwest.

☐ *Virginia Polytechnic Institute and State University*, Blacksburg, VA. This is a rarity—a land-grant university that seeks a national student body. Although the majority of its students come from the South, substantial numbers are from the Northeast, especially at its school of engineering.

☐ The University of California at Berkeley and the University of California at Santa Cruz do not actively recruit a national student body, but both schools admit substantial numbers of out-of-state students.

A selection of fine Canadian colleges

If your child is college or graduate school hunting, don't overlook Canada, which has 58 universities offering quality education at relatively low cost for Americans, especially at times when the Canadian dollar is weak. Here are some of the best Canadian schools (designated "E" or "F," according to whether curriculum is conducted in English or French):

☐ *University of British Columbia*, Vancouver, B.C. (E)

☐ *University of Alberta*, Edmonton, Al. (E)

☐ *University of Calgary*, Calgary, Al. (E)

☐ *University of Regina*, Regina, Sask. (E)

☐ *University of Manitoba*, Fort Garry Campus, Winnipeg, Man. (E)

☐ *Laurentian University of Sudbury*, Sudbury, Ont. (E)

☐ *University of Ottawa*, Ottawa, Ont. (E, F)

☐ *University of Toronto*, Toronto, Ont. (E)

☐ *University of Waterloo*, West, Waterloo, Ont. (E) (Canada's M.I.T.)

☐ *University of Western Ontario*, London, Ont. (E) (Excellent business school)

☐ *Universite Laval*, Quebec, Que. (F)

☐ *McGill University*, Montreal, Que. (E)

☐ *University of New Brunswick*, Fredericton, N.B. (E)

☐ *Nova Scotia Agricultural College*, Truro, N.S. (E)

☐ *Nova Scotia College of Art & Design*, Halifax, N.S. (E)

☐ *University of Prince Edward Island*, Charlottetown, Prince Edward Island (E)

☐ *Memorial University of Newfound-land*, St. Johns, Nfld. (E)

Bargains in private colleges

Skyrocketing tuition costs have caused many parents and students to turn away from private institutions and opt for publicly supported schools. But state colleges and universities do not provide the only bargains in higher education.

Most of the colleges listed below are small liberal arts institutions founded by religious denominations. The large majority have become independent of church control. All of these colleges rank in the top 10% of the nearly 1,500 four-year, regionally accredited institutions in the US. They are grouped by tuition costs.

The percentage of students receiving financial aid ranges from 50% to 80%. The average amount of aid ranges from 60% to 120% of tuition costs.

☐ *Creighton University*, Omaha, NB 68178. Founded by Jesuits, now independent. Requires six hours of theology.

☐ *University of Dallas*, Irving, TX 75060. Conducted by the diocese of Dallas/Ft. Worth. No religious requirements.

☐ *Furman University*, Greenville, SC 29613. Southern Baptist. Requires one course in religion.

☐ *Hofstra University*, Hempstead, NY 11550. Founded as a commuter school for Long Island students. Now has residence halls for half its students. Seeks students from other parts of the country.

☐ *LeMoyne College*, Syracuse, NY 13214. Jesuit. Requires two semesters of nondenominational religious studies.

☐ *Marquette University*, Milwaukee, WI 53233. Jesuit. Theology courses are required of all students: The number varies with the particular college attended.

☐ *Stetson University*, De Land, FL 32720. Southern Baptist. Requires one course in religion, plus another course in religion or philosophy.

The percentage of students receiving financial aid ranges from 60% to 90%. The average amount of aid covers 60% to 90% of tuition costs.

☐ *Coe College*, Cedar Rapids, IA 52402. Independent, though historically related to the United Presbyterian Church.

☐ *Fordham University*, Bronx, NY 10458. Founded by Jesuits, now independent. Two or three courses in religious studies are part of core requirements.

☐ *Hamline University*, St. Paul, MN 55104. United Methodist. No religious studies are required.

☐ *Illinois Wesleyan University*, Bloomington, IL 61701. Independent, though maintains ties with its founding United Methodist Church. Requires one course in religion.

☐ *Luther College*, Decorah, IA 52101. American Lutheran. Requires two courses in religion.

☐ *Rose-Hulman Institute of Technology*, Terre Haute, IN 47803. Independent school of science and technology.

☐ *University of Santa Clara*, Santa Clara, CA 95053. Founded by the Jesuits, now independent. Choice of any three courses in religion required.

☐ *Rhodes College*, Memphis, TN 38112. Presbyterian. Two courses in religion and humanities required.

☐ *Ursinus College*, Collegeville, PA 19426. Independent, though maintains ties with United Church of Christ. No religious requirements.

☐ *Wabash College*, Crawfordsville, IN 47933. Independent, no religious requirements.

The percentage of students receiving financial aid ranges from 54% to 75%. The average amount of aid ranges from 58% to 101% of costs of tuition.

☐ *Albright College*, Reading, PA 19604. United Methodist. Requires nine credits in philosophy and religion.

☐ *Allegheny College*, Meadville, PA 16335. Independent (historic ties with United Methodist Church). No religious requirements.

☐ *Cornell College*, Mount Vernon, IA 52314. Independent (historic ties to United Methodist Church). No religious requirements.

☐ *Earlham College*, Richmond, IN 47374. Church-related (Friends). Requires two courses in philosophy and/or religion.

☐ *Gustavus Adolphus College*, St. Peter, MN 56082. Lutheran. Requires one course in religion.

☐ *College of the Holy Cross*, Worcester, MA 01610. Jesuit. No formal religious requirements.

☐ *Illinois Institute of Technology*, Chicago, IL 60616. Independent school of engineering. No religious demands.

☐ *Kalamazoo College*, Kalamazoo, MI 49001. Founded by American Baptists, now independent (maintains ties with the church). Requires two quarter courses in philosophy and/or religion.

☐ *Macalester College*, St. Paul, MN 55105. United Presbyterian. Although church-related, Macalester makes no religious demands on students, and from a religious standpoint its student body is remarkably diverse. Substantial grants from the Reader's Digest Foundation in recent years have helped the college to raise and maintain academic standards.

☐ *University of Notre Dame*, Notre Dame, IN 46556. Founded by Congregation of the Holy Cross, now independent. Requires six hours of theology.

☐ *Ripon College*, Ripon, WI 54971. Independent. No religious demands.

☐ *St. Olaf College*, Northfield, MN 55057. American Lutheran. Requires three courses in religion.

☐ *Syracuse University*, Syracuse, NY 13210. Founded by Methodists, now independent. No religious demands.

☐ *Whitman College*, Walla Walla, WA 99362. Independent. No religious demands on students.

Source: James Cass and Max Birnbaum, coauthors, *The Comparative Guide to American Colleges*, Harper & Row, New York.

Lesser-known colleges that merit attention

The institutions listed below are far above the national average in quality of academic program. They are small (500-2,000 students). Most are liberal arts colleges. A substantial percentage of their graduates go on to graduate and professional schools.

☐ *Allegheny College*, Meadville, PA 16335. Emphasis on preparation for professional school. Maintains historic relationship with United Methodist Church, but is nonsectarian and makes no religious demands on students.

☐ *Beloit College*, Beloit, WI 53511. Retains ties with United Church of Christ, but has always been nonsectarian. Strongly committed to liberal arts, along with an emphasis on preprofessional and career-oriented studies.

☐ *Clarkson University,* Potsdam, NY 13676. Two thirds of students major in engineering, business and management. Three fourths of graduates go into business and industry.

☐ *Coe College*, Cedar Rapids, IA 52402. A liberal arts college where one quarter of graduates go into business and industry. College maintains a relationship with its founder, United Presbyterian Church.

☐ *Cornell College*, Mount Vernon, IA 52314. Students choose a traditional liberal arts course of study or a nontraditional combination of standard courses, independent study, work-service and travel. College retains some ties to the United Methodist Church.

☐ *Earlham College*, Richmond, IN 47374. A Quaker college that places primary emphasis on a "living fellowship" and individual development. Earlham has become increasingly popular with Eastern

students in recent years. Two courses in religion and/or philosophy are required of all students.

☐ *Goucher College*, Towson, MD 21204. A sturdy survivor of the vanishing breed of women's colleges. Goucher has a strong cooperative program with Johns Hopkins.

☐ *Hamilton College,* Clinton, NY 13323. A reputation for high-quality academics and professors who know how to teach. More than 40% of its graduates go on for higher degrees.

☐ *Hamline University*, St. Paul, MN 55104. Founded by the United Methodist Church, Hamline maintains ties to the church. Essentially a liberal arts college, the university also includes a school of law. Cooperative programs with neighboring colleges.

☐ *Haverford College*, Haverford, PA 19041. Founded by Quakers and one of the top academic colleges in the country. The Quaker influence is felt in a student-monitored honor code that governs campus life.

☐ *Knox College*, Galesburg, IL 61401. A venerable liberal arts college. One of the most productive institutions for its size in developing corporate executives.

☐ *Macalester College*, St. Paul, MN 55105.

☐ *Manhattanville College*, Purchase, NY 10577. Founded as a Roman Catholic college for women but now coeducational and independent. Its location (25 miles north of New York City) attracts students who prefer to live in a rural environment with easy access to a major cultural center.

☐ *Mills College*, Oakland, CA 94613. A women's college that says it will stay that way. Attracts a geographically diverse student body. Half of its graduates pursue careers in business and industry.

☐ *Millsaps College*, Jackson, MS 39210. Church-related (United Methodist). Millsaps requires three hours of religious studies for graduation. Notable for its strong liberal arts program, combined with considerable emphasis on preprofessional studies.

☐ *Ohio Wesleyan University*, Delaware, OH 43015. In recent years the college has deliberately reduced the size of the student body while making admissions more selective. Top entering students and leading upperclassmen get preference in financial assistance awards.

❑ *Pitzer College*, Claremont, CA 91711. Youngest of the Claremont College Group, now coed. Advantages of a small college environment with access to the facilities of a large university.

❑ *Rollins College*, Winter Park, FL 32789. Florida's first institution of higher learning. A liberal arts college where nearly half the graduates major in business and management.

❑ *St. Lawrence University*, Canton, NY 13617. One of the largest institutions listed here. The nearest major city is Ottawa, Canada. Attracts students from many parts of the country.

❑ *Scripps College*, Claremont, CA 91711. One of only two women's colleges on the West Coast. Scripps students enjoy the advantages of membership in the Claremont Group.

❑ *Simon's Rock Early College*, Great Barrington, MA 01230. Simon's Rock assumes that many high school juniors and seniors are capable of doing college work. It admits qualified students after the 10th and 11th grades (as well as after grade 12).

❑ *Skidmore College*, Saratoga Springs, NY 12866. Skidmore went coed in 1971 and offers a broad liberal arts program with special emphasis on fine and applied arts and preprofessional studies.

❑ *Wabash College*, Crawfordsville, IN 47933. One of the few remaining men's colleges in the Midwest. A strong liberal arts program and notable for ranking among the top schools of comparable size whose graduates become corporate executives.

❑ *Wells College*, Aurora, NY 13026, Still a women's college, Wells sends about one third of its graduates on to graduate and professional school.

❑ *College of Wooster,* Wooster, OH 44691. A liberal arts college founded by the United Presbyterian Church, Wooster is now independent. Sends its graduates on to a wide range of professional and business careers.

How to get better test scores

❑ Most people do better on tests if they do not cram. Keep current during the semester. Prepare for tests as if they occurred without prior notice. Instead of memorizing the subject matter, paraphrase it and integrate it into your total store of knowledge.

❑ Bring several pens and pencils to the test.

❑ Arrive a few minutes early. A little excitement may improve your performance, but do not let anxiety interfere with clear thinking.

❑ Quickly scan the entire test. Ask the instructor immediately about any unclear phrasing.

❑ Be sure to follow all instructions exactly. Example: If a list is requested, do not compose an essay.

❑ Ask if wrong answers will be penalized. If not, guessing may improve your score slightly.

❑ Mentally schedule your answers. Set priorities. For example, if the test lasts two hours, answer at the rate of 1% each minute. This pace gives you a little reserve time for the more difficult questions and for the all-important review.

❑ Study each question carefully and plan your answer. Conserve time by avoiding repetitions. Examples: Label (do not write out) each question. Give as much detail as is requested, but no more. Omit side issues, especially if they encroach on other questions. Do not write out the same answer to more than one question. Cross out wrong answers (instead of taking time to erase them). Exception: Computer-scored tests require complete erasures of mistakes.

❑ Avoid dogmatic presentations. In an essay on a controversial issue, give all sides before justifying your view.

❑ Shortcuts: In an objective test, choices are usually wrong if they contain such words as *always* or *never*. A statement is false if *any part* of it is wrong.

❑ Don't belabor the obvious. For example, don't write that a company should set goals. Instead: Specify what goals are appropriate. Try to cover all bases, but briefly. Most teachers disdain padding.

❑ Use clear expressions. Define technical terms so that a person who is not familiar with them would understand. Example: "A computer's byte equals eight bits" conveys nothing at all to someone who knows little about computers.

❑ Allow time for review.

261

□ Use the test as a springboard for further learning. Don't blame the teacher or text if your grade is lower than you hoped. Pinpoint and remedy the weakness.

Source: Dr. Harold W. Fox, professor at Ball State University, and George A. Ball, business consultant, Muncie, IN.

Getting into a top college with ordinary grades

Perfect grades and board scores are no guarantee of admission to top schools. A student with board scores in the 500s and a B average can get in anywhere, if he promotes himself correctly.

Specific things a student can do to improve his chances.

□ Give the admissions office a reason to vote for you. On a typical day, the admissions office reviews all the applications from the same high school or geographic area. Use the essay, interview and recommendations to distinguish yourself from the mob. Emphasize work or volunteer experience, interesting sports or hobbies, unusual interests, anything you're really good at.

□ Don't feel you have to be the well-rounded kid. Most good colleges are looking for the well-rounded class. It's much better to do really well at one thing than to be mediocre at a dozen things.

□ Go prepared to the interview. Use it as an opportunity to distinguish yourself.

□ Don't waste the essay. It's your one real opportunity to set yourself apart, to give the admissions committee a reason to remember you. If your essay is dull or it contains misspellings or grammatical errors, you've killed your chances.

□ Ask only teachers and employers for recommendations. Parents often think it's important to get a recommendation from an influential neighbor or politician. This can hurt your chances. Recommendations from anyone who hasn't taught or supervised you will be considered padding.

□ Take the right courses in high school. Grades are more important than board scores, but the quality and level of courses count more than grades. It's better to get a B in an advanced placement or honors course than an A in a regular course.

□ Don't take the college boards more than twice. More than that shows you're a little bit too neurotic and pushy. Do read the review books and take review courses. If you show improvement on your second score, that helps.

□ Take advantage of colleges' desire for diversity. A good student from a small Midwestern town has a better chance of getting into Harvard than one from a big city. All the schools look for geographic diversity.

□ Apply to unlikely schools. One Catholic school looked very favorably on Jewish students because so few applied. It's easier for a Catholic to get into Brandeis and a Jew into Fordham than vice versa.

□ Don't dismiss a school just because your parents went there. It helps admission chances considerably to have an alumnus parent. Harvard's freshman class averages 22% children of alumni.

Source: Steve Cohen, author of *Getting In! The First Comprehensive Step-by-Step Strategy Guide to Acceptance at the College of Your Choice*, Workman Publishing, New York.

College applications: Easing the anxiety

The pressures and anxieties of finding the right colleges and then filling out application forms make a child's senior year in high school a difficult time for the whole family. Parents can offer support and assistance without adding to the turmoil if they are discreet.

□ Learn from your friends. People who have gone through the application process recently have valuable information and first-hand experience. Find out what books they found most helpful (for example, *Comparative Guide to American Colleges* by James Cass and Max Birnbaum or *Selective Guide to Colleges* by Edward B. Fiske) and provide them for your child. Filter out your friends' personal biases about particular schools. Relay only factual information about the housing crunch for freshmen at an urban college or the attitudes toward women at a formerly all-male campus.

□ Encourage an early deadline for finishing applications. Thanksgiving is a good target date. Then, the child can concentrate on his schoolwork before the end of the semester and keep his rades up. First semester senior-year grades are important to colleges.

☐ Make copies of all the finished applications and correspondence. Most colleges acknowledge the receipt of completed papers with a postcard, so you will know if anything is missing. too much time passes without such an acknowledgement, call and check. Having a copy on hand saves time and trauma.

☐ Consider early-action applications or at least one or two schools with rolling admissions to get early decisions. Neither admissions policy commits your child to a particular campus, but knowing before April 15 that at least one school wants a student can take the pressure off.

☐ Talk to the high school guidance counselor. Be sure your child is applying to schools where he has a better than average chance of being accepted. One or two long shots are reasonable, but young egos are badly damaged by a series of rejections. Find out what the counselor can and will do if the worst happens and your child is not accepted anywhere. (It does occur—even to good students.)

☐ Subscribe to the newspaper published by the students at the colleges in which your child may be interested. Tune in to both the problems and the good points.

☐ Budget for campus visits to potential colleges. If time and money are a consideration, save the visits for after the acceptances come in and real choices have to be made. Be sure your youngster sees the college while it is in session. Admissions offices will arrange for dormitory stays and opportunities for going to class if your child doesn't know anyone at the school.

☐ Let your child know now that he can transfer from one college to another with no loss of face if the first choice doesn't work out. In fact, some colleges are easier to get into as a transfer student than as a freshman.

Source: Florence Janovic, writer and partner in Sensible Solutions, Inc., book marketing consultants.

College tours

Visiting prospective colleges is important to your teenager. It helps narrow the choices and gives the student exposure to "real life" on campus.

Some ground rules:

☐ Visit six or eight schools at most. Save for last any colleges where tuition costs may be a problem or your child's chances of getting in are slim. (They may fade naturally from consideration.)

☐ If possible, begin touring soon after your child's sophomore year in high school. You'll have more time and energy the following year for a second look at the top contenders.

☐ Try to visit during the fall, when the campus is more populated than in the summer.

☐ Visit only one school per day. Jot down notes to help recall details.

☐ Let your child take the initiative in questioning student guides or admissions officers. But don't refrain from asking about fees, expenses and student aid.

Source: *Business Week.*

How to turn the college interview to your advantage

☐ Do research. In particular, find out as much as you can about the college.

☐ Prepare questions to ask the interviewer.

☐ Be ready for two inevitable questions: Why do you want to come here? What can I tell you about our school?

☐ Give them a reason to want you. Link who you are with what the school is.

☐ Practice the interview beforehand with a friend or parent.

☐ Ask for an on-campus interview (as opposed to one in your hometown with an alumnus), especially if you live less than 200 miles from the campus.

Source: Steve Cohen, author of *Getting In! The First Comprehensive Step-by-Step Strategy Guide to Acceptance at the College of Your Choice*, Workman Publishing, New York.

College housing: New investment opportunity

On many college campuses where housing is in short supply, parents find they can save money by spending money—investing in a condominium for their student children. For middle-class families who can afford the down payment, the tax advantages and appreciation pay off even in the short term of a four-year education.

How it works:

☐ Tax break: Initially, all the mortgage interest and part of the maintenance fee are deductible.

☐ Bonus: The child finds a roommate to share the apartment which brings down the monthly cost.

☐ If several students share your child's condominium, the rental income may be high enough for the apartment to be treated as ordinary investment rental property, with big deductions for depreciation. The test is whether income from the other students represents fair market value for rent. *Caution:* The Tax Reform Act of 1986 classifies all property rentals as "passive" activities and limits the deductibility of losses. Check with your tax advisor.

☐ After four years of school, the apartment is sold at (or above) the original price, and the initial investment is recouped—usually with a profit. Moreover, if you had losses in previous years and were unable to deduct them because of the "passive" loss rules, these losses become fully deductible in the year of the sale.

Considerations:

☐ Dormitory costs: The average cost of college housing runs upward of $1,500 a year. Obviously, the higher the cost, the more incentive there is to find an alternative.

☐ Campus restrictions: Some colleges have sufficient housing for their students, so the need for off-campus housing is minimal, making the condominium investment riskier.

☐ Responsibility: Investment real estate must be maintained to keep its value. Your child's willingness and ability to take care of an apartment full of other students should be a factor in your decision. The responsibility might be more appropriate for graduate school than for the undergraduate years, when campus social life is more important.

Best graduate schools

The graduate school with the best overall academic reputation is the University of California at Berkeley. Here are the graduate schools that rank first in the subjects listed, as determined by a survey of US faculties.

☐ *California Institute of Technology:* Chemistry, geoscience, physics.

☐ *University of California, Davis:* Botany.

☐ *University of California, San Francisco:* Physiology.

☐ *University of Chicago:* Sociology.

☐ *Harvard University:* Classics, philosophy, Spanish language and literature, zoology.

☐ *MIT:* Biochemistry, cellular and molecular biology, economics, electrical engineering, linguistics, mechanical engineering, microbiology.

☐ *University of Minnesota:* Chemical engineering, geography.

☐ *New York University:* Art history.

☐ *Princeton University:* German language and literature, mathematics.

☐ *Stanford University:* Computer sciences, psychology.

☐ *Yale University:* English and French language and literature, political science.

Source: A study by The Conference Board of Associated Research Councils.

Send your children to college without sending yourself to the poorhouse

By the year 2004, the cost of a full college education will range from $100,000 at a state school to more than $240,000 at an elite private college.

Payment Plans

☐ To help families cope with college costs, many schools now have programs to enable parents to start paying while future students are still infants. Others have loan and aid plans to make education possible for those who otherwise couldn't attend.

☐ The tuition future: Parents make a one-time investment with a school in the expectation that when the child is 18, that's where he'll go to school. That one-time investment, compounded over time, pays for all four years of college. The younger the child when you make the investment, the less you have to pay.

☐ Traps: No one has examined the tax implications…How will the investment—and earnings on the investment—be taxed?…Who's liable for taxes, the donor or the college?…What happens if, 18 years after the investment is made, the child decides not to attend that school?…What if the child wants to attend, but doesn't meet the school's academic requirements?…And from the college's point of view, does accepting the investment mean that the student's been accepted "sight unseen?"

Other innovations:

□ Private colleges that make up the difference between the costs of attending the private college and the cost of a state school (Bard College, Annandale-on-Hudson, NY, makes the offer to applicants in the top 10% of their high school class).

□ Tuition prepayment, where freshmen lock in prices by paying for their second, third, and fourth years at the beginning of freshman year.

Prior Planning

Recommended:

□ Estimate college costs for each of your children. What type of school—public or private—will they probably attend? (College costs will probably increase about 6%–7% per year.)

□ Project your income and expenses to estimate eligibility for financial aid. To these calculations figure in an annual income increase of about 4%.

□ Calculate the gap between what you've saved, your current earning capacity, your probable financial aid and projected college costs. The gap will be the amount you'll need to borrow in order to pay for college.

Strategies

□ The ideal scenario for a family with a newborn baby and a good income:

Set aside as large a sum as possible—say, $10,000—and add to that about $500/month for the next 18 years. You'll wind up with about $250,000 assuming 7% annually compounded interest after taxes).

□ Alternative: Put $50,000 in a zero coupon bond now yielding about 8%. When it matures in 18 years, you'll have set aside about $210,000.

More modest advice:

□ If your child is academically qualified or one of the elite schools, don't let insufficient income discourage him/her from applying. The top schools have larger endowment funds—and, hence,

better financial aid offerings—than more modest schools.

□ Overall, qualified students now can attend the college of their choice by putting together a package of loans, grants, student aid, and campus jobs that will finance four years of education.

Source: R. Jerrold Gibson, president, and Gayle Speck, vice president, Pacesetter, an educational financial planning service, 73 Trapelo Rd., Box 78, Belmont, MA 02178.

Refinance your home to pay for your child's education

Interest on student loans is no longer a tax deduction for you and your child.

□ Convert this nondeductible interest into a deduction. How: Take out an equity loan on your home and use this money instead of a student loan to pay for college. It's permitted under a special exemption that allows an interest deduction for home equity loans up to $100,000.

Deductible school costs

□ Courses to maintain or improve your skills on the job are deductible. But the deduction for transportation is limited to travel between your place of employment and the school. Transportation between home and school is not deductible. Exception: If the school is located beyond the general area of your business location (for instance, 50 miles out of town), you can deduct the cost of all transportation between that general area and the school.

□ If you attend school away from home, you can deduct all travel expenses, including board and lodging. The rules are the same as for business trips.

□ Since travel for education is a form of business travel, you can deduct all actual car expenses or take the regular IRS mileage allowance for business travel.

Caution: You can never deduct the costs of education to prepare you for a new or different occupation. For example, you couldn't deduct the cost of attending law or medical school.

What colleges offer in financial aid

When you contact the admissions office of a school that you're considering, ask these questions:

☐ Is there a per-student limit on aid? Some schools set ceilings, such as $2,000 a year per student.

☐ Must financial need be shown to earn assistance? Some schools won't provide aid unless the student's family demonstrates a need for $500–$800 or more to meet education costs.

☐ Does the school have an application cutoff date for assistance?

What's usually available:

☐ Low-interest loans.

☐ Installment tuition-payment plans allow parents to avoid writing out a single large check each semester. Tuition costs are paid in installments.

☐ Academic scholarships, based on scholastic achievement, not on financial need, are awarded by almost 1,000 colleges in the US. Awards amount to as much as $10,000 per year. They're based on such criteria as admission-test scores, grade point averages and class standings.

☐ Part-time employment can be found for many students through college placement offices.

☐ Middle income assistance in the form of loans, tuition breaks and rebates are offered by many schools when the student's family can demonstrate financial need. Special consideration is often given when another family member has already attended the school.

☐ Federally backed student loans are sometimes still available, even to upper-income families, when the school attended has tuition costs that are more than the family can pay. But these loans don't cover nontuition expenses. Interest rates and eligibility are subject to change at any time.

For more information about student assistance, including material on the aid programs provided by various institutions:

☐ *The A's & B's of Academic Scholarships*, Octameron Press, Alexandria, VA. Also, *The Ambitious Student's Guide to Financial Aid*, same publisher.

☐ *Scholarships, Fellowships and Loans*, Bellman Publishing, Arlington, VA.

Source: Robert Leider, education-aid consultant and president of the Octameron Press, Alexandria, VA.

How to look for college scholarships

Grants for students with quirky talents or particular names are numerous. They make up a sizable portion of the $15 billion in grant money identified by scholarship search services.

Exciting as they may sound, these scholarships should not be a student's first priority in the search for college.

After the family has studied the college's financial aid package, it might want to try tracking down additional help through scholarships.

☐ Your local community can be helpful.

☐ A parent's employer or social organization often sponsors scholarships, and more and more grant dollars are being awarded through high schools to college-bound seniors.

☐ Look at the financial aid section of college catalogs in your local library.

☐ Check the library's scholarship listings (a collection of notices, pamphlets and other materials) and how-to-find-financial-aid manuals such as *Don't Miss Out.**

☐ High school guidance counselors should be able to provide materials on scholarships.

☐ Another useful tool is a scholarship search service. Most require a detailed application. Going on the information you provide, they send you a relevant listing of which scholarships you may qualify for. Scholarship listings are constantly updated, and the good services provide counseling and tips

*Octameron Press, Alexandria, VA.

or applying. The best services do your research for you, but they make no guarantees of success. The worst ones can be just a waste of your money. The two that are by far the biggest, most trusted and best-known are the National Scholarship Research Service and the Scholarship Search Service.

☐ Private and business sectors are becoming the best sources of untapped scholarship aid. With diligence and research, almost any college freshman can get some private-sector scholarship help.

Source: Mary Armbruster, director of financial aid, Sarah Lawrence College, Bronxville, NY; Joseph D. Gargiulo, National Scholarships Research Service, Box 2516, San Rafael, CA 94912; Mary Ann Maxin, Scholarship Search Service, 407 State St., Santa Barbara, CA 93101.

Financial help for military families

☐ Army Emergency Relief Assistance Program. Loans and scholarships for needy, unmarried independent children of current or former members of the Army. Department of the Army, 200 Stovall St., Alexandria, VA 22332.

☐ The Navy Relief Society. Loans for unmarried, dependent children of present or former Navy or Marine personnel. 801 N. Randolph St., Suite 1228, Arlington, VA 22203.

☐ Retired Officers Association, for children and wards of present or former officers in any of the uniformed services. Funds are awarded only after the applicant has shown that all other sources have been investigated. 201 N. Washington St., Alexandria, VA 22314.

Helpful financial services for everyone

☐ College Student Financial Aid Services, 600 S. Frederick Ave., 2nd floor, Gaithersburg, MD 20877, 301-258-0717.

☐ College Quest, c/o Peterson's Guides, Box 2123, Princeton, NJ 08543, 609-243-9111.

☐ National Scholarship Research Service, 2280 Airport Blvd., Santa Rosa, CA 94901, 707-546-6777.

Each of these services charges a price ($50-$75) for reports or printouts that attempt to match you with useful funding sources.

How to beat the SATs

SAT scores don't really measure aptitude, intelligence or academic potential. They show only how good you are at taking the test. Keys to doing well: Good preparation and a thorough knowledge of how the test works.

Where To Begin

Determine whether the colleges you're interested in require SAT scores. If so, take two months before your test date to:

☐ Study an SAT preparation book such as *Ten SAT's* (The College Board, 45 Columbus Ave., New York 10023, $11.95). This contains tests given over the past couple of years.

☐ Take a course on preparing for the SAT that offers good feedback. This will give you an idea of what areas you need to work on most.

☐ Don't depend solely on math and English teachers for help. They teach only academic math and English…not "SAT math" and "SAT English."

Taking The Test

☐ Eliminate the wrong answers first—leaving only the right answer.

☐ Guess if you have to. Once you've eliminated one or more of the wrong answers, guessing works in your favor.

☐ Take the test slowly. Rushing results in careless mistakes that can hurt your score.

☐ Questions are usually in order of difficulty. But skip topics in which you're weak to get to those in which you excel. Reason: All questions are weighted equally.

☐ Use the scrap paper provided—especially for math questions—to avoid careless errors. Also: Don't waste time erasing mistakes in calculations.

☐ If you don't know the answer to a question, leave it and move on to the next one. Don't waste time pondering.

☐ Give the answer you feel the test

authors are looking for, even if you think it's incorrect.

☐ Look out for deceptively easy questions that can cause you to make mistakes. Hint: Each section of the test is divided into thirds—easy, medium-hard, and hard, in that order. Questions that seem easy but have a twist appear on the boundary between the easy and medium-hard thirds.

☐ Save the reading section for last. Reason: It is a time-inefficient section because it involves reading long passages. Hint: The passages are based on fact, so you can eliminate answers based on your knowledge or common sense.

Source: John Katzman, director of the Princeton Review (an intensive eight-week course in preparation for the SAT) and author of *Cracking the System: The SAT*, Villard Books, 201 E. 50 St., New York 10022.

Developing your own image of success

☐ Recognize that you have talents and skills that are ingredients of success. Focus on these and forget your bad points entirely.

☐ Concentrate your energy. One way to focus energy: Split up your day into the smallest possible segments of time. Treat each segment as independent and get each task done one at a time. This will give you the feeling of accomplishment and will fuel your energy.

☐ Take responsibility. Be willing to accept personal responsibility for the success of your assignments, for the actions of people who work for you, and for the goals you have accepted. Seize responsibility if it is not handed over easily. There are always company problems that are difficult to solve and that nobody has been assigned to—take them for starters.

☐ Take action instead of waiting to be told. Listen to other people's problems and link their ambitions to your goals. Then deliver what you promise.

☐ Nurture self-control. Don't speak or move hastily. Don't let personal emotions color decisions that must be hard and analytical. Before taking a major action, ask yourself, "What's the worst that can happen?" Let that guide your next step.

☐ Display loyalty. No matter how disloyal you feel, never show it. Show loyalty to your boss, your company, your employees. Be positive about yourself and about others. Never run anybody down.

☐ Convey a successful image. Move decisively—walk fast and purposefully, with good posture. Look as if you are on the way to something rather than moping along.

☐ When you sit, don't slump. Sit upright and convey alertness. Choose a chair of modest dimensions. A large chair makes you look small and trapped. The chair should have a neutral color and be of a material that doesn't squeak or stick to your body.

☐ Avoid large lunches—they deprive you of energy. Successful people tend to eat rather sparingly.

Source: Michael Korda, author of *Success! How Every Man and Woman Can Achieve It*, Random House, New York.

Are you really as ambitious as you think you are?

To test your ambition quotient, rate the following statements on a scale of 1 to 5 to indicate how much the statement applies to you. A rating of 1 means it doesn't apply at all, and 5 means it applies very much.

☐ I truly enjoy working.

☐ Given free time, I would rather be out socializing with people than sitting home watching television.

☐ My first response to a problem is to attempt to figure out the most practical solution.

☐ One of the things I like best about work is the challenge of it.

☐ I believe very strongly in the work ethic.

☐ I have a strong desire to get things done.

☐ When there's a difficult situation, I enjoy assuming the responsibility for correcting it.

☐ I frequently come up with ideas—day and night.

☐ I'm not satisfied with the success I already enjoy.

☐ I rarely miss a day of work because of illness.

☐ I enjoy vacations, but after four to five days I look forward to getting back to work.

☐ I can usually get along with six hours of sleep.

☐ I'm interested in meeting people and developing contacts.

☐ I set high standards for myself in almost everything I do.

☐ All in all, I consider myself a lucky person.

☐ I'm not afraid to rely on my instincts when I have to make an important decision.

☐ I can think of very few situations in which I don't have a great deal of control.

☐ I recover from setbacks pretty quickly. I don't dwell on them.

☐ I'm not afraid to admit it when I make a big mistake.

☐ Achieving success is very important to me.

Scoring: 85-100 indicates very high ambition. With the right skills, you're almost certain to achieve your goals.

70-84 means higher-than-average ambition, and chances of achieving goals are very good. 55-69 is about an average score. If you achieve your goal, it won't be on ambition alone. A score below 55 indicates that success isn't an important goal for you.

Source: Robert Half, author of *Success Guide for Accountants,* McGraw-Hill, New York.

Setting goals for success

The lack of a clear goal is the most common obstacle to success, even for people with large amounts of drive and ambition. Typically, they focus on the rewards of success, not on the route they must take to achieve it. Remedy:

☐ Whenever possible, write down your goals, forcing yourself to be specific.

☐ Periodically make a self-assessment. Take into account your education, age, appearance, background, skills, talents, weaknesses, preferences, willingness to take risks and languages spoken.

☐ Ask for feedback from others.

☐ Don't try to succeed at something for which you have no talent.

☐ Try out your goal part-time. If you dream of owning a restaurant, work in one for a while.

Targeting success

☐ Visualize the results you intend to achieve and write them down. Example: I will increase output 10%.

☐ List the personal benefits that reaching the goal will confer.

☐ Jot down at least 10 obstacles and try to find three possible solutions for each.

☐ Set a target date.

☐ Start tackling the problems, beginning with the easiest.

Source: Audrey Cripps, Cripps Institute for the Development of Human Relations, Toronto.

Climbing to success without stumbling

The behavior our parents reinforce in us when we are children always encourages us to strive for bigger and better things. We gain approval for achievement and disapproval for failure. As adults, we keep striving because our developmental makeup says "You've got to have more."

To avoid rising to your level of incompetence:

☐ Take your life and your job seriously. But don't take yourself seriously.

☐ Don't spend your life climbing and acquiring. Instead, combine accomplishment and satisfaction.

☐ Climb to a level that you find fulfilling stay there for a long period, and then move forward.

☐ Approach promotion avoidance indirectly. One successful ploy is to display some charming eccentricities that in no way effect your work performance, but which might discourage a promotion.

Source: Dr. Laurence J. Peter, whose latest book is *Why Things Go Wrong, or The Peter Principle Revisited,* William Morrow & Co., New York.

Overcoming obstacles to success

Personality traits can be a straightaway or a dead-end—on the road to success.

Don't be caught in the following common traps:

☐ Inability to let go. People often stick with a dead-end job out of pride, stubbornness or unwillingness to admit that they made a mistake. Sometimes the comfort of the familiar is just too seductive. To start letting go: Take small, safe steps at first. Start talking to friends and associates about possible new jobs. See what's available during your vacation. Shake things up at the office by suggesting some changes in your current job. Take some courses and learn new skills.

☐ Lack of self-esteem. This is an enormous stumbling block. But, in fact you may be judging yourself by excessively high standards.

☐ Procrastination. Like alcoholism, procrastination is a subtle, insidious disease that numbs the consciousness and destroys self-esteem. Remedy: Catch it early, but not in a harsh, punitive, self-blaming way. Look at what you're afraid of, and examine your motives.

☐ Shyness. If you're shy, the obvious remedy is to choose an occupation that doesn't require a lot of public contact. But even shy salespeople have been known to succeed. As long as they're talking about product lines and business, a familiar spiel can see them through. Concentrate on getting ahead by doing a terrific job rather than by being Mr. or Ms. Charming. Or take a Dale Carnegie course. They are helpful.

☐ Unwillingness to look at yourself. If you're not willing to assess yourself honestly, success will probably forever elude you. People tend to avoid self-assessment because they feel they must be really hard on themselves. Realize you've probably taken the enemy into your own head—you've internalized that harsh, critical parent or teacher from your childhood. Instead, evaluate yourself as you would someone you love, like a good friend whom you'd be inclined to forgive almost anything.

Source: Tom Greening, PhD, clinical supervisor of psychology at the University of California at Los Angeles and a partner in Psychological Service Associates, Los Angeles.

Common sense business and social manners

A common error today is the failure to realize that there are at least two sets of manners—one for the business world and another for the social world. In the business world, it is not vulgar to talk about money or to brag. But the social world is just the opposite.

☐ In business, manners are based on rank and position, not on gender. The business lunch or dinner check, for instance, belongs to the person who initiated the invitation or the superior in the office. The gender of the person does not alter this tradition.

☐ Never worry about what service people (waiters, maitre d's, hotel clerks) think of you. If you use the wrong fork, it is up to the waiter or bus boy to supply you with another. Don't worry about what he thinks of you.

☐ If you are critical of someone while at a dinner party, only to discover that the person you are belittling is the father (or close relative or friend) of the person with whom you are speaking, make a quick and complete U-turn. Add to the defamatory statement, "Of course, that's the basis of my admiration for him." Remember dinner table conversation doesn't have to be logical.

☐ The notion that it is unhealthy to disguise your feelings has helped lead to a decline in manners and social health. One advantage of a little disguise: You will have more feelings to share with intimates.

Source: Judith Martin, otherwise known as Miss Manners.

Power lunching

Power lunching tactics can turn a restaurant meal into an occasion to impress your lunch partner.

Power lunching aims to impress without letting the luncheon become a tasteless display of ego and one-up-manship.

Here are some tips:

☐ Patronize restaurants that have a reputation for business lunches and where you're known. Select restaurants with excellent service and plenty of space between tables. Eat in restaurants that important people frequent.

☐ Avoid luncheon invitations to other people's private dining rooms. You lose power on their turf.

☐ Call the maitre d' personally to make reservations. Tell him where you want to sit and how long you expect to stay. The more details you give the maitre d', the more his staff will be in tune with your needs.

☐ Don't order drinks served with a paper umbrella or a lot of vegetables or fruit. Draft beer is appropriate, but bottles look tacky. The "fancy waters" are wimpy now…club soda is a power drink.

☐ Order food that's easy to handle. Example: Steak instead of lobster so that you can do a lot of talking without fumbling. Power foods: Black bean soup, fresh oysters and clams, brook trout, calves' liver, London broil, paella, venison and gumbo. Wimp foods: French onion soup, fried oysters and clams, corned beef, coquilles St. Jacques, chicken a la King, lasagna, shrimp de jonghe.

☐ Pay the bill with cash, if possible. Next best is a house charge. You don't have to wait for a credit card to be processed. You can quickly sign the check and leave before your guest becomes anxious to get back to the office.

☐ Tip 20%.

Source: Power Lunching by E. Melvin Pinsel and Ligita Dienhart, Turnbull & Willoughby, Chicago.

Good business communication

☐ *What happened?* is the question to ask when something's gone wrong. Don't try to blame someone for the mistake right at the start. Asking *What happened?* focuses on the mistake itself, not on the person who did it, and is much more likely to lead to useful information. Contrast: *Who did it?* is a phrase that can turn off information flow.

☐ Oral orders are usually all that's needed to correct a basic mistake. If the oral order changes an existing policy, though, confirm it in writing as soon as possible to prevent future confusion.

☐ Tuesday is the best day for having a serious heart-to-heart discussion with an employee concerning job performance. Friday risk: Person broods all weekend about the conversation and comes back embittered on Monday. After the Tuesday talk, find a way by Wednesday to indicate that there's no ill will.

☐ Discuss serious problems with a subordinate in *your* office where your authority is evident. Minor matters can be handled in the subordinate's office as long as there's privacy and quiet.

☐ Value of a dumb question or a simple and honest *I don't know* is that you'll probably learn something you don't know now…and that you couldn't find out any other way. "It's what you learn after you know it all that really counts," said President Harry S. Truman, an expert at turning seeming modesty into great strength.

Source: James Van Fleet, former US Army officer, manager with Sears, Roebuck & Co. and US Gypsum, and consultant on the psychology of management, writing in *Lifetime Conversation Guide*, Prentice-Hall, Inc., Englewood Cliffs, NJ.

Secrets of success

Top performers in all fields have these qualities in common:

☐ They transcend their previous performances.

☐ They never get too comfortable.

☐ They enjoy their work as an art.

☐ They rehearse things mentally beforehand.

☐ They don't bother too much about placing blame.

☐ They are able to withstand uncertainty.

Source: David A. Thomas, Dean of Cornell University, Graduate School of Business.

What successful men think makes them successful

☐ Bill Blass: "I guess it is my ability to concentrate and a dedication to the best in design—first fashion, and then the best in design for other things."

☐ David Klein, Dav-El Limousines, New York: "Even when I was a kid in New Rochelle, New York, I had more paper routes than the rest of the kids. Then I began to run parking lots at the local country club, graduated to being a chauffeur and continued to work, work and work more. I really do love to work."

☐ Tom Margittai, co-owner, Four Seasons restaurant, New York: "Determined professionalism combined with high standards of quality. Also, a lot of hard work. We try to understand the psychology of our market and to be first in everything."

☐ Mickey Rooney: "Through the years, it has been my great faith in God, and lots and lots of energy. At last I have it all together. I guess my good health is also a factor. I've been luckier than a lot, and I have always taken a positive outlook."

☐ Carl Spielvogel, Backer Spielvogel Bates Worldwide: "I think getting in early and staying late and not taking the 5:15 to Greenwich is one reason [for my success]. Also, being where the business is. As Lyndon Johnson once said, you have to press the flesh. People you do business with want to know you and to be with you socially."

☐ Ted Turner, head of Cable News Network and sportsman: "Every day I try to do my very best. When you wish upon a star, your dreams really do come true."

How to be known as an expert

Improve your chances for promotion and attract outside job offers by displaying expertise and calling attention to yourself.

Some ways to do it:

❑ Write an article for a key trade journal.

❑ Join an association of peer professionals. Get to know your counterparts and their superiors in other companies. Run for office in the association.

❑ Develop a speech about your work and offer to talk to local groups and service clubs.

❑ Teach a course at a community college.

❑ Write letters to the editors of trade journals, commenting on or criticizing articles that they publish in your field.

❑ Have lunch with your company's public relations people. Let them know what your department is doing, and see if they know of some good speaking platforms for you.

❑ Use vacation time to attend conferences and seminars.

❑ Write to experts, complimenting them (when appropriate) on their work and their articles. Whether or not they reply, they'll be flattered and they'll probably remember your name.

Source: Errol D. Alexander, president, Profiles, Inc., Vernon, CT.

Putting yourself on TV

Public access (PA), a noncommercial form of cable television established expressly for amateur programming, is now available in hundreds of communities nationwide. And if your community has cable, chances are it also has PA facilities just waiting to be used.

❑ Contact the local PA coordinator first. Although most PA programs are administered by the cable company that will cablecast them, in some cities the public library, school district or some municipal government office coordinates things.

❑ Ask around to find out exactly how PA works in your community. Don't get started with specific plans until you have let the appropriate people know exactly what you would like to do.

❑ Plan carefully in advance. Deciding upon a suitable topic is the first step toward creating a successful PA program. Other issues that need

settling: How long will the program be? Will it be an ongoing series, or merely a one-shot deal? Who's going to operate the camera and the editing equipment? Will you need to film on location, or can all the necessary footage be shot in the studio? Will you need furniture and props for a set?

❑ Keep in mind that it takes much longer to produce a program than you've probably anticipated. You'll probably need to devote a couple of weeks, at least, to learning the television ropes before even beginning to produce your program. Usually, however, it takes much longer.

❑ Set specific goals. Decide if you simply want to convey information, to educate or to entertain. Don't try to do too much in a single show.

❑ Polish your program. Decide before you go into the studio exactly what you hope to accomplish. Rehearse your program carefully and then time it.

❑ Learn production techniques. Most PA organizations require that you demonstrate proficiency in the use of equipment before they turn you loose in the studio. Don't try to get around this requirement. Technical knowledge is crucial, even if you plan on leaving the nuts-and-bolts end of things to someone else. You can't be an effective director or producer if you're not sure what the equipment can and cannot do. Besides, the instruction is usually free.

❑ Secure sponsorship. Most of your expenses will be assumed by the cable operator—but not all. Particularly for more ambitious projects, you may want to secure outside funding from a local business or philanthropic group to help with production costs and publicity. Although PA guidelines prohibit advertising per se, there's a good chance you'll be able to list sponsors on the air. Before approaching potential sponsors, find out exactly what you can promise them.

❑ Get the message out. Many PA users concentrate so singlemindedly on getting their programs finished that they neglect one of the most important things: Getting people to tune in. So tell your friends to watch and have them tell their friends. Ask the cable operator to include your program, along with its air date and time, in the monthly schedule it distributes to its viewers. Call your local newspaper and radio stations, and even take out ads if you want to reach as many people as possible. (Of course, you'll have to foot the bill for this yourself.)

Source: Sue Buske, Executive Director, National Federation of Local Cable Programmers, Washington, DC, and James McElveen, Director of Public Affairs, National Cable Television Association, Washington, DC.

Who gets promoted first

The four most important factors in determining how fast you are promoted:

☐ How top management feels about the person who recommended your promotion.

☐ Your exposure and visibility to those in higher management.

☐ Your background, education, work experience.

☐ How well you perform in your present job.

Capitalizing on early success

Early career success can be followed up by even further success if you:

☐ Stay ambitious.

☐ Are willing to make sacrifices on the way up.

☐ Acknowledge mistakes. Avoid covering up or passing the buck.

☐ React to a setback by honestly identifying what went wrong.

☐ Behave consistently during a crisis.

☐ Don't become abusive under stress—or refuse to negotiate.

☐ Regularly reassess personal career strategies.

☐ Broaden skills—and learn new ones when necessary.

☐ Resist the temptation to become arrogant with success.

Source: Morgan W. McCall Jr. and Michael M. Lombardo, authors of *Off the Track: Why and How Successful Executives Derail,* The Center for Creative Leadership, Greensboro, NC.

How to negotiate a big raise

The best way to get a sizable raise:

☐ Start campaigning for it on the day you're hired. Don't talk dollars then, of course, but set up standards of performance that will be the basis for future wage negotiations with your new boss.

☐ Find out if there are ways you can influence company standards so that your strongest qualities are rewarded.

Gauge the company's raise-granting profile by finding out:

☐ Pattern of raises for your type of job.

☐ Extent to which pay is part of a fixed budget process.

☐ How much autonomy your boss has in granting raises.

☐ Business conditions in the company and in the industry.

When the time comes to request a raise:

☐ Don't let your request be treated in an offhand manner. Make a date with your boss to talk just about money. If he puts it off, persist.

☐ To negotiate successfully: Narrow down obstacles until the supervisor is holding back because of one major factor ("Things are tough this year"). Let him cling to that, but in the process make sure he assures you that your performance has been excellent. Then attack the main obstacle ("Are things really that bad?"), pointing out that your capabilities should be rewarded in any case.

☐ Unless you're quite sure of your ground, don't threaten to quit. Even if you are a ball of fire, the boss may welcome your departure because he's scared of you.

Source: John J. Tarrant, author of *How to Negotiate a Raise,* Pocket Books, New York.

Secrets of successful job hunting...now

Even during tricky times, many companies are willing to open the hiring door for a person who can improve operations and increase profits.

The secret to job-hunting success during times like these is to convince a potential employer that you are that person.

Reality: Most job seekers don't work

hard enough—it's a full-time job—or intelligently enough.

Each week my investment banking firm receives many resumes from highly qualified applicants—rarely from one who has done the necessary research to learn exactly what this firm does and can suggest ways we might do it better.

Here's the three-step job-hunting plan that worked for me when I was job hunting—and has helped others to whom I have suggested it over the years:

☐ Decide what it is you do best and focus your job hunts in that direction. Be realistic and thorough in identifying your strengths.

Example: At one point in my career, I was dissatisfied with my job in the operations end of an electronics manufacturing firm. But I liked immensely one of the tasks of my job—reviewing potential corporate acquisitions—and was very good at it. That knowledge and experience gave me the confidence to leave manufacturing and become an investment banker. Bonus: I brought to my new career real-life experience in running a business—skills very few of my new competitors had.

☐ Research. Research. Research. Learn as much as possible about the companies you're targeting in your job search.

Information sources, available in most public libraries, include…Standard & Poor's, Value Line, Dun & Bradstreet, company annual reports, business magazines—*Business Week, Forbes* and *Fortune.*

Also speak to major customers of the companies you're researching. Managers in purchasing, engineering or other departments of customer companies can often be valuable sources of information and are often very helpful if you clearly explain what you're doing.

☐ Find a company problem—and solve it. Distinguish your letter and resume from those of other applicants by suggesting a specific idea to improve the company's business.

Example: Years ago, when applying for a job with a manufacturer, I proposed marketing plans for four new production applications—and was hired within days.

Try to identify a manager you might be working for if hired. That's the person most familiar with a job's requirements, most likely to know about openings and best able to evaluate your proposal. Avoid the company's personnel department. Don't write to the chief executive officer, either.

Even if this three-step job-hunting plan doesn't result in an offer because a company has a hiring freeze on, it will usually result in an interview. You'll build up a network of contacts that can be valuable as you build your career.

Source: Arthur P. Gould, president of the merchant and investment banking firm of Arthur P. Gould & Co., 1 Wilshire Dr., Lake Success, New York 11020.

When to change jobs

It's time for you to leave the company when you:

☐ Realize management is neglecting its basic business.

☐ Your company has had a sensational run for several years. (A downturn is inevitable. It's best to leave as a winner.)

☐ You're being excluded from sharing in the company's success.

☐ Your firm isn't keeping up with the competition.

☐ You've run out of interest.

☐ You've run out of ideas.

☐ You start aiming at a position a relative of management might want.

☐ You don't know why you're there. (Sketch out a career plan and find the job that will be your next step up.)

Source: Tom Hopkins, author of *The Official Guide to Success,* Warner Books, New York.

Triumphing in a job interview

Job seekers often don't like the interviewer. But usually, they won't be working for the person who does the first interview or even some of the subsequent ones. The goal: To be successful enough in each interview to finally reach the person you will be working for—the one you're going to have to relate to.

But first, even if there is no "chemistry," you have to win over the lower-echelon people.

☐ Practice by going to as many interviews as possible.

☐ Practice at home. Sit before a mirror and answer stock questions ("Tell me something about yourself") into a tape recorder. Gradually, you will improve and be more at ease during real interviews, even if the stock questions don't come up.

☐ Be pleasant, polite and friendly—but not too friendly. Remember, you have something to sell.

☐ Don't eliminate the job on the basis of lower-level interviews. You might not know enough to make a choice until you move up to the next level.

☐ Tailor your resume for the job you're going after and make it easier for the interviewer to pick out the highlights that apply to that particular opportunity.

☐ If the interviewer steers you into an area where you are weak, take charge, and steer the conversation in another direction—toward a strength.

☐ Make yourself as comfortable as possible at an interview. If the sun is in your eyes, the interviewer may have set it up on purpose (though probably not). Ask permission to move your chair or to sit somewhere else.

☐ Arrive on time. If it's a hard-to-reach place, do a dry run in advance. It's better to come early. You will be more relaxed that way.

☐ Try to avoid being the first person interviewed. Studies show that the first person has much less of a chance of getting the job. Although you can't always control this, avoid Mondays, in any case. Mondays and Fridays, the most disorganized days in an office, are also the worst for an interview.

☐ Don't smoke. It can't do you any good—and it can do you harm.

☐ Try to learn something about the interviewer, especially as you move to higher levels. You will be able to make more meaningful comments and you will be more relaxed.

☐ If the interviewer is getting a lot of phone calls, suggest coming back another day. He will either refuse further calls or accept your offer. Many on-the-spot decisions like these are a matter of being considerate, as you would be with a friend.

☐ If the interviewer stops talking, ask a specific question, such as, "Is there anything else you'd like to know about me?" Don't ramble your way into trouble.

☐ Somewhere near the end of the interview, tell the interviewer that you like the job, that you like the company and that you'd like to work for him/her. Also: Impress the interviewer with your confidence. Say, "I know I can do the job. I won't let you down. You can count on me."

☐ Follow up by sending a note to the interviewer. Send a note of thanks to that person's secretary, too. The secretary might mention it to the boss.

☐ After the interview, analyze what went wrong. Work on the assumption that something did. We're all amateurs at job interviews. If you can honestly figure out your mistakes, you won't make them again at the next interview.

Source: Robert Half, President, Robert Half International, Inc., executive recruiters, San Francisco.

How to handle the silent treatment at an interview

A popular technique in interviewing a candidate is to clam up somewhere in the middle of the interview. This takes candidates off guard, and they sometimes get into trouble with too much loose talk and lots of nonsense.

How to keep from being derailed by the silent treatment:

☐ Be prepared with interesting and pertinent ideas.

☐ Shift the conversation to your strengths. In the event of the silent treatment, talk about these strengths as they apply to the company and to the function for which you're being interviewed.

☐ Sell your abilities. Instead of feeling ill at ease, consider a pause a benefit. Pick your own subject.

☐ Don't talk too long. After a few minutes, ask the interviewer if he wants you to continue or would like to ask you a question. If you are told to go on, do that for another several minutes and then ask again if you should continue.

☐ Remember, the interviewing process is a game. It's to your advantage to play it skillfully.

Source: Robert Half, president, Robert Half International, Inc., executive recruiters, San Francisco.

Being prepared (but appearing casual) at a job interview

❏ You should do about 85% of the talking in the interview. If an unskilled interviewer is doing too much talking, gracefully try to make your points. Otherwise, the interviewer will discover after you left that he knows very little about you.

❏ Study up on the company but don't appear too prepared. A skilled interviewer will be cautious that you are keying your replies to what you know the company wants.

❏ Try to find out what happened to the last person who had the job without asking a direct question. Encourage the interviewer to tell you about the job, what the best people did right and what mistakes others made, etc. The information may come out anyway.

❏ Don't prepare long, rehearsed answers to questions such as "Why didn't you make better grades in college?" Answer briefly and with confidence.

Source: Richard Fear.

How to check out your job interviewer

❏ Find out in advance the name of your interviewer.

❏ Dig into his background for education, former jobs and outside interests.

❏ If you know his co-workers, quiz them about his personality and reputation in the company.

❏ Armed with this information, you may be able to maneuver the interview to your advantage. At least you'll have an idea about his priorities and interests.

Eleven most common reasons job applicants aren't hired

❏ Too many jobs. Employers are suspicious of changes without career advancement.

❏ Reluctance of applicant or spouse to relocate if necessary.

❏ Wrong personality for the employer.

❏ Unrealistic salary requirements.

❏ Inadequate background.

❏ Poor employment record.

❏ Unresponsive, uninterested or unprepared during the interview. (Being "too aggressive" is not a serious handicap.)

❏ Negotiations with employer handled improperly.

❏ Little apparent growth potential.

❏ Long period of unemployment.

❏ Judged to be an ineffective supervisor.

Source: National Personnel Associates.

Negotiating salary in a job interview

Negotiating salary is often the hardest part in a job interview.

Here are some suggestions:

❏ Avoid discussing salary in detail until you're close to getting an offer. If the first interviewer asks what salary you want, respond, "Salary is important, but it's not the most important thing. Why don't we develop an interest in each other and then we'll see."

❏ If the interviewer insists, mention your current salary and suggest using that as a guideline.

❏ When you are actually offered the job, you are in a much stronger bargaining position. That is the time to negotiate.

❏ Do not demand more than the market will bear. It's a mistake to lie about what you have been earning, especially if you're unemployed. The higher the salary, the fewer the jobs.

Source: Robert Half, president, Robert Half International, Inc., executive recruiters, San Francisco.

How to evaluate a job offer

Questions you must ask (yourself and the recruiter) to increase the chance that you land in a job that offers opportunity for promotion, mobility, power, personal growth:

☐ Who's in the job now?

☐ What is the average length of time people have stayed in the job?

☐ Where do they go?

☐ How old do people get to be in that job?

☐ Ask to talk to people holding the same or similar jobs. Find out what other people in the company think about the job. If they think the job is dead-end, don't consider taking it. You may think you can overcome and be the "pleasant surprise." But chances are excellent that you will fail.

☐ Will the job give me a chance to know other people in the organization doing lots of different jobs?

☐ Will I represent the department (or group or section, etc.) at meetings with people from other parts of the organization?

☐ If the job is in the field, do I get much chance to meet with managers from headquarters? Does the job have too much autonomy? (Working on your own too much can be the kiss of death for upward movement if no one else gets to know you and your abilities.)

☐ Is this job in an area that solves problems for the company? The best jobs for getting power (and promotions) fast always have a sense of danger. Jobs in safe areas where everything is going well offer a slower track to promotion.

Best days to job hunt

Most job-seekers think Monday is the best day to look for a job because there are more jobs advertised in the papers on Sunday. But jobs advertised on Sunday actually become available the previous Wednesday.

Recommendations:

☐ Look every day of the week.

☐ If you have to skip one day, Monday is the best choice. You will not be slowed down by the same hordes of competition on other days.

☐ The best job-hunting may be when the weather is bad. Again, there are fewer competitors. Management may well believe that the bad-weather candidate is more interested in employment and will work harder with less absenteeism. However, interviewers may be depressed and executives busy filling in for absent staff when the weather is poor.

Source: Robert Half, president, Robert Half International, Inc., executive recruiters, San Francisco.

The art of getting fired

☐ Restrain your anger. Don't scream at your boss (he'll be your first reference) or threaten to sue the company.

☐ Apply for unemployment compensation immediately. It's nothing to be ashamed of, and the money will buy time to plan your next move.

☐ Find out precisely why you were fired. It may help to reevaluate your personal style for your job hunt and beyond.

☐ Don't withdraw out of self-pity. Share your feelings with your family and friends. They can sustain you in this difficult time.

☐ Reassess your career goals. It may be time for a modification—if not an outright switch.

Source: Frank Louchheim, Chairman of Right Associates, a re-employment counseling firm, Philadelphia.

What to expect from an outplacement service

If you are dismissed from your job and your company provides you with outplacement counseling, you are several steps ahead of the game in finding your next job.

What you can expect:

☐ Counseling to help with personal problems, such as how to handle family and neighbors.

☐ Assessment of your skills and achievements, including psychological and aptitude tests.

☐ Help in staying focused on the future rather than dwelling on the past.

☐ Instruction in how to re-enter the job market.

☐ Guidance on how to handle job

interviews, write an effective resume and letters, negotiate salary and, most of all, respond to the question, "Why were you fired?"

Source: T.B. Hubbard, chairman, and E. Donald Davis, president, THinc Consulting Group International, Inc., New York.

Assess your chances of being a successful entrepreneur

Your chances of being a successful entrepreneur are best if:

☐ Both your parents were self-employed.

☐ You were fired more than once in your career.

☐ You began operating small businesses before you were 20 years old.

☐ You have spent most of your career to date in firms with less than 100 employees.

☐ You are the eldest child in your family.

☐ You are married.

☐ You have a B.A. degree but no advanced degrees.

☐ Your relationship with the parent who provided most of the family income was strained rather than comfortable.

☐ You are easily excited by new ideas, new employees, new financial plans.

☐ You enjoy being with people even when you have nothing planned.

Source: Joseph R. Mancuso, founder and president of The Center for Entrepreneurial Management, New York.

What it takes to have an entrepreneurial edge

The traits of successful entrepreneurs:

☐ Work for results, not praise. Don't fall into the trap of expending energy to please people who have nothing to do with your success.

☐ Continue to set higher performance goals for yourself than your boss does.

☐ Don't be afraid to take on more responsibility and the control that goes with it.

☐ Stand back occasionally from day-to-day work so you can plan strategically.

☐ Hone your ability at communications and selling.

☐ Rehearse in your mind a successful process and a successful outcome. The process helps supply the mental and physical reserves needed to get through tough situations.

☐ Learn to overcome occasional loss and rejection.

☐ Think of failure as a lesson rather than as a blow to your self-esteem. Then quickly get back on the right track.

☐ Be forthright in claiming ownership for your ideas.

☐ Assess risks by setting up a worst-case scenario. If you can cope with a negative outcome, consider taking the risk.

Source: Dr. Charles A. Garfield, professor of psychology, University of California Medical School in San Francisco.

Deciding if a blue-sky idea is worth pursuing

☐ What are the assumptions on which the idea is based?

☐ What tests can be applied to these assumptions?

☐ If the project goes ahead, what are the likely financial results? (For maximum success, for partial failure, for total failure.) What criteria will be used to make these forecasts?

☐ Is the trade-off between the maximum gain and the maximum loss acceptable?

☐ How will this project be managed?

☐ What are the likely weak points at which difficulty could be experienced?

☐ At what point should we abandon the project?

Source: Robert Heller, author of *The Supermanagers,* Truman Talley Books (E.P. Dutton, Inc.), New York.

Entrepreneurial burnout

The mistakes that can bring a budding entrepreneur's career to a halt are seldom unique. And the big ones can be avoided with a minimum of effort if you know what to look for.

Common traps to avoid:

☐ Spreading yourself too thin. Entrepreneurs often think they can be all things to all people. They convert a real asset—their flexibility—into a liability by pursuing too many directions at once. Narrowing your focus and becoming the best in a small area is the key to success.

☐ Substituting business contacts for a social life. People who work alone often forget to make the effort to develop a social/recreational world outside work. They then confuse fleeting business contacts with recreational friendships. This diffuses their business concentration and judgments. Remedy: Planned social encounters such as regular lunches or dinners with friends. Take the initiative to meet new people.

☐ Enjoying only the anticipation of the next accomplishment. Don't motivate yourself by putting down your past achievements and concentrating only on the next big project. After a while, you forget what you have accomplished and lose any sense of yourself. To prevent this form of burnout: Savor your accomplishments as they occur.

Source: Dr. Srully Blotnick, author of *The Corporate Steeplechase: Predictable Crises in a Business Career,* Facts on File Publications, New York.

Setting yourself up as a consultant

☐ Take on assignments after-hours while still with the company. Accumulate so many clients that the only way to handle them is to leave your employer.

☐ Volunteer for a sophisticated task with a prestigious nonprofit organization. Make it clear you are doing it for a reference and on a limited basis. Tell your employer, if possible.

☐ Cultivate contacts. Do favors. Pass along helpful information to people who may be in a position to help you later on.

☐ Discreetly mention finders' fees for leads that actually result in business.

How to get others to support your position

☐ Give them your cooperation and support first.

☐ Be ready to accept blame when you are wrong.

☐ Use witnesses and objective outsiders to prove your points.

☐ Ask for their ideas on how to get the job done.

☐ Be a buffer between those whose support you need and others who might threaten them.

☐ Say, "I need you."

Source: James K. Van Fleet, author of *Lifetime Conversation Guide,* published by Prentice-Hall Inc., Englewood Cliffs, NJ.

Career crisis points

A study of executives on the fast track revealed they tended to fail when they were:

☐ Moved up during a corporate reorganization but were not evaluated until the reorganization was complete.

☐ Lost a boss who compensated for missing skills or gaps in personality.

☐ Promoted into a job for which they were not prepared.

☐ Shifted to a new boss with an unfamiliar style of management.

☐ Moved into a new area where composure and control under pressure and stress were essential.

Source: Morgan W. McCall, Jr., and Michael M. Lombardo, co-authors, *Off the Track: Why and How Successful Executives Derail,* The Center for Creative Leadership, Greensboro, NC.

If a rival beats you to a promotion by a hair

Assuming that you and your rival are very much alike in experience, education and service with the firm, you need to find out why you lost. The reasons can affect your future with the company. Areas to explore:

☐ Your rival appeared more committed to the company. Management judged you ready to bolt for a better opportunity.

☐ Your rival had a sponsor higher up in the company of whom you were unaware.

☐ Your boss personally prefers your rival's company.

☐ Your boss saw your rival as less of a threat to his job.

☐ You are being saved for something bigger down the road, but no one thought to tell you.

☐ You failed at an assignment that you thought was insignificant, but your boss judged you likely to fail again.

☐ You have been too active politically within the company outside your department.

☐ You are perceived as untrustworthy by some, or they question your loyalty to your boss.

Source: Marilyn Moats Kennedy, author of *Career Knockouts: How to Battle Back,* Follett Publishing Co.

Mid-career work problems

The most important problems mid-career executives face on the job can produce stress-related illnesses:

☐ Overload. Putting in too many long hours because of taking on too much work.

☐ Confusion about work role. This ambiguity exists when managers are unclear about job objectives.

☐ Job conflict. Employees find themselves doing what they don't want to do. And performing work they feel is not part of the job specification. The greater the authority of the people sending the conflicting role messages, the more the job dissatisfaction among the managers.

☐ People pressure. Those who are responsible for people suffer more stress than those in charge of things, such as equipment or budgets.

☐ Boss's attitude. Those who work for a considerate boss feel less pressure than those under the command of managers who pull rank, play favorites, and take advantage of their employees.

☐ Executive neurosis. This occurs when managers are promoted beyond their abilities and overwork in a desperate attempt to hold on to the top job.

Source: Cary L. Cooper, University of Manchester, Manchester, England, in *Mid-Life,* Brunner/Mazel, Inc., New York.

Dealing with political infighting

☐ Don't decide that one of the infighters is "right" and the other is "wrong." That encourages the winner to pick more political fights in the future, while it leaves the loser spoiling for revenge. On the other hand, deciding that neither is right and that they must compromise leaves both parties unhappy and convinced that the boss wasn't fair.

☐ Look for a third choice that both parties can live with, without each one feeling that he's lost or that the other one has won. The ideal "third way" incorporates all the important points of both sides. Only the irritants are omitted.

☐ The person who leads the way to a solution comes out stronger.

Source: *The Effective Manager,* Warren, Gorham & Lamont, Boston.

High-level incompetence

High-level incompetence has many faces and lurks in some heretofore unsuspected areas:

☐ Physical incompetence. A person who is professionally or technically competent may develop such anxiety over his work that he gets ulcers or high blood pressure. And that results in a poor attendance record. His boss and co-workers assume he's really very competent but just has health problems. In reality, he is physically incompetent to handle the strain of the job.

☐ Mental incompetence. This occurs when a person is moved to a level where he can no longer deal with the intellectual requirements of the job.

☐ Social incompetence. A person who is technically competent may be unable to get along with others. Or, problems may arise if he is promoted in an organization where a different class of social behavior is required when moving up the ladder.

☐ Emotional incompetence. A technically competent person may be too unstable emotionally to deal with a particular job. Creative types, who tend to be insecure, are particularly prone to this type of incompetence when promoted to administrative positions.

☐ Ethical incompetence. Richard Nixon is a good example. Only when the White House tapes revealed his dishonesty beyond a doubt was it clear that, in office, he had reached his level of ethical incompetence. His brand of manipulative persuasiveness, an asset in local politics, became a liability in the highest office in the land.

Source: Dr. Lawrence J. Peter, author of *The Peter Principle*.

Sexual harassment on the job

Sexual harassment on the job is unlawful and a violation of fair employment practices. Supervisors who allow it to occur in their offices, even though they themselves don't commit any offensive acts, can be charged.

If you think someone is sexually harassing you at work:

☐ Keep a diary and write a brief description of each event right after it happens. Note the time and the place, the people involved, the names of any witnesses.

☐ Confront the offender. Tell the person that you think the remark or action is harassment.

☐ Write a letter to the offender, describing the event and noting that you consider it sexual harassment. Send the letter "personal receipt requested," which means the Post Office will only deliver it to the person to whom it is addressed and give you a receipt that the person signs. Or, hand the letter to the person in the presence of a witness you can trust.

☐ Report the event to management and explain the actions you have taken.

As a supervisor:

☐ Take every complaint about sexual harassment seriously. Document the actions taken in response to a complaint.

☐ Write a policy statement against sexual harassment which defines it, condemns it and provides a way in which employees can bring events to management's attention.

☐ Don't condone a regular practice of sexually-oriented conversations and jokes in the work place. And certainly don't make such remarks to the people you supervise.

☐ Don't permit employees to post sexually-oriented pictures or cartoons in the work place.

☐ Never tie sexual favors to job performance—not even in jest.

☐ Never touch an employee in a sexually-oriented manner.

Source: Howard Pardue, director of human resources, Summit Communications, Inc.

How to keep from burning out on the job

Burnout is a clear loss of interest in work. It's the feeling that work no longer has purpose. Those most vulnerable to burnout are:

☐ The workaholic, whose life is consumed by the job.

☐ The person who quickly tires of routine and can't maintain enthusiasm without constant challenge.

☐ The individual trying conscientiously to master a job that runs counter to temperament and talent.

To rekindle the joys of work:

☐ Get more rest, since stress plays a big role in burnout.

☐ Exercise regularly to get into better physical shape.

☐ Introduce as much variety as possible into your daily routine. One method is to trade some duties with colleagues.

☐ In extreme cases, consider changing your job or career. Make the decision to quit during an emotional high, rather than a low, when everything seems hopeless.

Source: *Working Woman*, New York.

The 10 best companies to work for

Based on employee evaluations of pay, benefits, job security, opportunity for advancement and ambience:

☐ Beth Israel Hospital (Boston).

☐ Delta Air Lines.

☐ Donnelly.

☐ Federal Express.

☐ Fel-Pro.

☐ Hallmark Cards.

☐ Publix Super Markets.

☐ Rosenbluth International.

☐ Southwest Airlines.

☐ USAA.

Source: *The 100 Best Companies to Work for in America*, Doubleday, New York.

Avoid unnecessary overtime

Many experts feel that regular late hours at work signal inefficient, disorganized work habits, not ambition. Ways to accomplish your work during office hours:

☐ Do not linger over an office breakfast or a long lunch.

☐ Keep visits and phone calls to a minimum.

☐ Establish times when your door is shut so that you can concentrate on your work without interruptions.

☐ Before a late afternoon meeting, make it clear that you have to leave at a specified time. Most meetings will proceed more quickly.

☐ Before taking on a new job, find out if any overtime is required, aside from normal emergencies. Weigh this against the rewards of the job.

Source: *Bottom Line,* Boardroom, Inc., New York.

Executive stress profile

Try to change the way you operate at work if you:

☐ Plan the day unrealistically.

☐ Are the first to arrive, and last to leave.

☐ Are always in a hurry.

☐ Make no plans for relaxation.

☐ Feel guilty about doing anything else but work.

☐ Treat any unforeseen problem or setback as a disaster.

☐ Are "polyphasic" in your thinking, involved in one activity when thinking of several others. You talk fast and interrupt often.

☐ Have an overwhelming need to be recognized. Winning is the end-all. But there's no prize in winning or enjoyment of it. As a result, you seldom enjoy recognition, money and possessions.

Source: Rosalind Forbes, author of *Corporate Stress,* Doubleday, Garden City, NY.

How to reduce work-related stress

☐ Recognize the aggravating aspects of your job. Stop fighting them.

☐ Identify your emotional needs and accept them. Most executives are competitive, need to be liked, need to vent anger. They should have outlets for each of these needs.

☐ Practice listening. Listening is more relaxing than talking, and it can help you know what's really going on in the organization.

☐ Be sensitive to change. Recognize when it's occurring on the job and figure out what adjustments are necessary. By consciously recognizing change, you make it manageable.

☐ Keep alcohol consumption under control. Excessive drinking creates the illusion of dealing with stress, while in fact adding to it.

Source: Rosalind Forbes, author of *Corporate Stress,* Doubleday, Garden City, NY.

Most common job-search mistakes

☐ Failure to look within before looking outside. Self-assessment is the key to a successful job search. Before you begin, take the time to look inside and ask, "What have I to offer?"

☐ Failure to approach the job search as a multifaceted process. A good campaign mixes at least three of the following methods: Personal networking, using employment search firms, answering classified ads, doing research, conducting a direct-mail campaign and targeting (the thorough analysis of one or two companies). Do some of each, but be sure that you spend at least half of your time on personal networking. Studies show that about 70% of all jobs are filled through personal contacts. Most people know

200-500 people, though they seldom realize it. Some can be valuable to you.

☐ Failure to plan and organize a campaign. Map out each week ahead of time.

☐ Failure to keep careful records of everything you do and everyone you speak to. A month from now, you may be talking to someone whom you've spoken to before, and you might not remember what was said in the initial meeting. Information is the job seeker's most powerful tool.

☐ Failure to maintain the ideal job seeker's attitude: Nonjudgmental. Treat everyone with warmth and courtesy. Realize that in a job search you get back what you put in. If you're putting out positive energy, you will connect with people much more easily.

☐ Failure to spend enough time on the telephone. Productivity in any campaign is directly related to the number of calls you make. It is easy to fall into a campaign of sending resumes and writing letters. Spend 50% of your time on the telephone. That's the way everything happens. It's more personal. It also forces you to call people whom you know—essentially doing the networking that you might otherwise neglect. If you have a goal of meeting 10 people a week, the only way that you can do it is by using the telephone.

☐ Failure to maintain your vitality during a campaign. Work to keep mentally and physically fit. A good campaign is a combination of work, rest, exercise and good diet. Some people think that if six hours a day of job searching is good, 10 hours will get the job that much faster. But such people usually burn themselves out.

☐ Failure to prepare ahead of time for interviews. Simply go to the library and get an annual report. Find out: The size of the company, its products or services, and any problems in the company or in its industry. You'll be ahead of 90% of the other applicants if you know something about the company before the interview.

☐ Failure to maintain good grooming and personal appearance. Take care of your appearance, even when dressed informally for networking. First impressions are hard to change.

☐ Failure to send thank-you notes to people in the network who have helped you—and to people who have interviewed you.

☐ Failure to follow up…and follow up…and follow up.

Getting a job is a social process. The interaction among people is what makes jobs happen.

Source: William Ellermeyer, president of Career Management Services, Irvine, CA.

Saving-time checklist

To protect your time:

☐ Ask your secretary to screen all calls and drop-ins. Or swap with a colleague so he takes your calls and you take his or perform some other service.

☐ Actually leave the premises. I know people who come in in the morning, make their presence known, and then take their papers to a coffeeshop or public library for an hour or so.

☐ Put a sign on your desk or office. Avoid the cold, unfriendly *Do not disturb* in favor of something more pleasant, such as *Person at work from 9 to 10:30. Please come back later.*

To minimize interruptions while remaining flexible:

☐ A fair number of interruptions come from people walking by your office on their way to and from the Xerox machine, restroom, etc. If your desk is situated in such a way that you make eye contact almost every time you raise your head, people tend to stop and chat. If you angle your desk a little to prevent automatic eye contact, it can make a substantial difference.

☐ Since you are to some extent closing off your time to your staffers, it's important to set up open-house hours so your subordinates and colleagues know that you're essentially available during other times when they should be able to drop in without an appointment.

☐ For an informal meeting, try to go into the other person's office. It's a lot easier to excuse yourself from someone else's office than to get someone out of yours.

☐ If someone does come into your office for a quick meeting, stand up. Be courteous, but don't give the person a chance to sit down. People will conduct their business more quickly if you're standing.

☐ Set a time contract. Respond to interruptions with something like, "I can't see you now, but how long might this take? Oh, good—I have 20 minutes at 3:30.'

Source: Stephanie Winston, president, The Organizing Principle, a management consulting firm, New York. Her most recent best-selling book is *The Organized Executive,* Warner Books, New York.

Characteristics of a good boss

❏ Directs and communicates clearly.

❏ Rewards good performance.

❏ Is encouraging.

❏ Keeps a finger on all important areas of work.

❏ Is responsive to requests for aid.

❏ Is predictable.

❏ Is fair.

Key skills for managers

❏ Interest in improving the way things are done.

❏ Continuing desire to initiate.

❏ Confidence in abilities and goals.

❏ Ability to develop, counsel and help others improve.

❏ Concern with the impact managerial actions have on the activities of others.

❏ Capacity to get others to follow the manager's lead.

❏ Knowledge of how to inspire teamwork.

❏ Faith in others.

❏ Skill in oral and written communication.

❏ Spontaneity of expression.

❏ Tendency to put organization needs before personal needs.

❏ Objectivity in a dispute.

❏ Knowledge of own strengths and weaknesses.

❏ Adaptability to change.

❏ Stamina to put in long hours.

❏ Logical thought.

Source: *International Management*, New York.

Behaving like a top professional

You can reap a great deal of self-esteem and a wide variety of other rewards by learning how to behave like a real professional.

Essentials:

❏ Sense of responsibility for clients (or customers). People who are cynical about their work, who despise the people they have to deal with, demoralize themselves and generally perform badly in the long run.

❏ Avoid rules of thumb, quick answers and rigid thinking. Be on the lookout for exceptions—incidents where theories don't seem to fit the facts. This is an opportunity to perform creatively.

❏ Stay current. Take additional training and/or coursework. Force yourself to work on tough problems, do heavy business-related reading.

❏ Be thoughtful about trade-offs in making difficult decisions that often involve several contradictory factors.

❏ Approach complex problems with a general strategy plus the readiness to change as the situation unfolds or new factors develop.

❏ Think more about task accomplishment than about hours spent accomplishing it. Professionals aren't clock watchers. They're driven by goals that they've set for themselves. And because these are, in large part, their own goals, they're motivated to attain them.

❏ Be responsible for developing subordinates. You'll end up with better people, increase loyalty and motivation, and experience the pride of seeing someone you've trained advance from neophyte to polished performer.

❏ Understand that excellence isn't an end state. It's a process of continuously striving to meet more challenging goals, learn new things and become more adept at solving difficult problems. Suppress the temptation to take destructive shortcuts or gain selfish advantage.

Source: Dr. Leonard Sayles, Center for Creative Leadership, Greensboro, NC.

Personal mistakes managers make

❏ The worst mistake made by talented managers in their early years is to underrate the boss. The danger: Bosses will almost always detect that attitude. And it's the kind of offense that's hard to forgive. The young manager makes an enemy. Or, even more likely, the boss writes the manager off as yet another of those fad-followers who's not really so bright after all.

❏ Young managers often fail to understand how the boss receives information best. Communication depends as much on the recipient as it does on the sender. Typical: The young manager sends along a brilliant 64-page analysis and plan of action, doesn't get a reaction and blames the boss. What the subordinate has failed to recognize is that the boss is a listener, not a reader.

☐ The first big promotion—especially one to headquarters or to a position close to senior management—often presents the opportunity for the third big mistake: Trying to do too many things. Enthusiastic, and with bountiful reserves of energy, managers at this level splinter themselves. They mistake busyness for progress and performance.

☐ The right thing to do: Concentrate on performance, not on credibility.

☐ Don't assume that everyone understands what it is they have to accomplish. Winning tactic: At least every nine months ask: On whom do I depend for information and support? And who depends on me? Make sure each of these people is kept up to date on what you're doing and what you need.

☐ A top manager must use two basic ways of gathering information—reading analytical reports and walking around. Managers can rise to the top because they're excellent at either one of these techniques. But once there, they must force themselves to do both. Report readers will lose touch with the urgent realities of running the business. And managers who rely on their perceptions often fail to check those perceptions against hard analysis. Either one comes to grief, sooner or later.

☐ The most fatal flaw of all in top managers: Compromising before understanding what the right decision really is. At the top, managers won't succeed if they substitute energy and a coach's half-time exhortations for making hard decisions.

Source: Dr. Peter F. Drucker, a leading consultant to top companies around the world and author of *Innovation and Entrepreneurship,* Harper & Row, New York.

How to prevent mistakes in decision making

☐ Never make unnecessary decisions. All decisions involve risk. It can occasionally be wiser to leave well enough alone.

☐ Identify recurring problems. Resolve them once and for all.

☐ Don't develop grandiose schemes to solve simple problems. Evaluate

solutions in terms of costs.

☐ Don't delay the decision. Moving quickly allows more time to correct the decision if it turns out wrong. And it frees you to tackle other problems.

Source: Don Caruth and Bill Middlebrook, Caru Management Consultants, Carrollton, TX, authors of *Supervisory Management,* Saranac Lake, NY.

Preparing for a crisis

You may not be able to plan for a crisi but you can prepare.

☐ Be alert. The best way to handle a crisis is to anticipate it.

☐ Stay flexible. Make a commitment to change swiftly, if necessary. Make provisions ahead of time for doing so.

☐ Know the options. Options must be developed before a crisis interrupts a personal routine.

☐ Establish clear communications with all those involved to reduce panic, ease tension, and make quick change possible.

☐ Recognize a crisis. It may create opportunities, as well as problems. Pla up any such advantages, rather than be content simply to survive.

Source: Walter Johnson, president of Quadrant Marketing Counselors, Ltd., New York.

New projects: Keep them exciting

New ideas have a way of exciting people, then fading away. To maintain interest:

☐ Pump in emotion and excitement by remaining personally involved.

☐ Organize schedules so that people working together have a sense of directed action.

☐ Remind everyone of the target. Mak it stand out clearly as the common goa

☐ Show respect for all participants by continuing to listen to their comments and ideas to improve ongoing projects

Source: Craig S. Rice, author of *Secrets of Managing People,* Prentice-Hall, Englewood Cliffs, NJ.

What makes committed employees

Committed people get a great deal of personal satisfaction from their accomplishments. They totally immerse themselves in a project and often need a brief break to recover emotionally before a new assignment.

In addition, they:

☐ Assess the feasibility of a task and speak up when they think the odds are bad. Uncommitted people take on anything without caring whether it is possible.

☐ Back up and cover for co-workers and supervisors without concern for who is responsible.

☐ Understand the underlying plans and objectives of a project. Know how to proceed without checking with supervisors at every point.

☐ Feel apprehension and anxiety at the possibility of failure. Unhesitatingly ask for help from supervisors when it seems necessary.

Source: W.C. Waddell, author of *Overcoming Murphy's Law,* AMACOM, New York.

Characteristics of a good helper

☐ Works well with colleagues.

☐ Is systematic. Sets priorities well.

☐ Gives a stable and predictable work performance.

☐ Accepts direction well.

☐ Shows up regularly and punctually.

☐ Detects problems in advance and refers to them when necessary.

MBA schools as talent sources

Chief executive officers of the country's largest companies ranked business schools as sources of talent for their own companies in the following order (the percentage indicates how many chose that school as number one):

☐ Harvard (33%)

☐ Stanford (18%)

☐ Pennsylvania/Wharton (7%)

☐ Michigan (5%)

☐ Dartmouth/Tuck (5%)

☐ Chicago (4%)

☐ Texas (4%)

☐ Northwestern (3%)

☐ MIT/Sloan (3%)

☐ Purdue (2%)

☐ Columbia (1%)

Source: Arthur Young Executive Resource Consultants, *The Chief Executive: Background and Attitude Profiles,* New York.

Hiring tips

For jobs that require judgment, initiative and good sense, seek the following personality traits in potential employees:

☐ Ability to anticipate what might go wrong and to plan for it.

☐ Readiness to listen to and accept good ideas from others.

☐ High energy and perseverance.

☐ Flexibility in communicating with a variety of people.

Hiring secrets

☐ Write a clear job description. Keep this information in hand along with the applicant's resume before he or she is interviewed.

☐ Let the candidate do about 85% of the talking in a 60- or 90-minute interview. Untrained interviewers fall into the trap of doing most of the talking themselves.

☐ Avoid talking too much yourself by working with a detailed interview guide to remind you where there are blanks in information.

☐ Don't interview anyone who hasn't filled out the company's own application form. Trained interviewees are taught to stall on the forms, hoping to present themselves in their own way first. Don't fall for that routine.

Learn how to spot the "pros" who have been professionally coached. Clues:

☐ Knowing "too much" about the company and positioning their pitch exactly to show how they could make a contribution there.

☐ Trying to take control of the interview, especially from an untrained interviewer.

☐ Asking what happened to the last person who had the job.

☐ Expecting a question-and-answer type of interview and having prepared answers to such questions as, What are the reasons we should hire you? or, Why didn't you make better grades in college?

☐ Don't assume that applicants who do any one of these things have necessarily been coached. But if they give themselves away in several areas, the chances are good that they've been professionally trained.

☐ Assume control with some broad lead-off statements, such as: Begin by telling me about your previous jobs, starting with the first one and working up to the present. Tell me about your education.

Source: Richard A. Fear, a consultant with the Selection Systems Division of Mainstream Access, Inc., a New York consulting firm specializing in outplacement, and author of *The Evaluation Interview*, McGraw-Hill, New York.

Why managers fail ...and succeed

People who fail in business usually have no trouble finding external reasons for their failure—economic conditions, discrimination, politics, uncooperative employees.

Although these play a part, internal factors are frequently as important.

In my psychiatric practice, I have observed that powerful unconscious issues affect work just as they do other areas of life.Our interactions are guided by a whole spectrum of beliefs and behavior styles developed over many years.

What we learned growing up influences the way we react to challenges in adulthood. Understanding and grappling with these issues can make a significant difference in job performance.

Personality style is one of the major internal factors in managerial performance. Three leadership styles are responsible for the most serious managerial problems…

The Narcissistic Leader

Characteristics: Narcissists are drawn to leadership positions by a deep need for power and prestige. They are often highly talented, hard-working and charismatic. But feelings of inferiority lead to self-aggrandizement and the need for constant, unconditional affirmation and positive feedback from others. Narcissists also tend to have a low tolerance for frustration.

Consequences: The narcissist inspires people to action, but can't always follow through. By surrounding himself/ herself with yes-men—people who idealize him and reflect back exactly

what he wants to hear—he is unlikely to anticipate and prepare for potential trouble spots as his ideas are executed. The narcissist's need to be in the spotlight makes it hard for him to build an effective team. He may resent and even sabotage employees whose creativity threatens to overshadow his own.

Most dangerous, the narcissist fails to encourage balance and diversity of opinion. The result can be disastrous, both to him and the company, as he inspires others to pour resources into implementing his brilliant—but unworkable—ideas.

Issues: The narcissist is likely to have grown up in an environment where nothing he did was ever quite good enough. He never developed a strong sense of self-esteem. To mask this sense of inferiority, he learned to rely on self-aggrandizement and seeks out only those people who will reassure him that he's wonderful.

The narcissist needs to develop a more complete sense of self—one that is not dependent on others' perceptions or on always being the best. He needs to recognize the value of clear, attainable goals that are reached step by gradual step. Skills to develop…

☐ Share credit. Use the words we and us rather than I and me.

☐ Be generous in giving praise instead of always expecting to receive it.

☐ Rather than relying on co-workers for affirmation, explore ways to meet that need outside work. Put time into developing family relationships and satisfying hobbies.

The Authoritarian Leader

Characteristics: The authoritarian personality has an obsession with order, with being right and in control. This type of manager is poorly attuned to the emotional needs of employees. He relies on a competitive, rather than affiliative, model of work relationships.

Consequences: Though corporations and departments do need an authority figure in order to function efficiently, the authoritarian's excessive need for control can lead to numbing bureaucracy and a rule-bound, by-the-book decision-making style.

Autonomy and creativity are stifled— which can spell disaster when a crisis arises that requires quick, effective decisions.

The authoritarian manager is unlikely to build loyalty or team spirit among staff. He may appear petty and defensive…employees respond with feelings of dislike and by doing the bare minimum required of them.

Issues: Authoritarians learn this style by growing up in families where control and rules are valued…and emotions are ignored or denied. The authoritarian leader must work to become more aware of how he feels, not just what he does…and recognize that intellect and emotion can work together. Skills to develop…

❏ Learn to listen carefully, without interrupting or becoming defensive.

❏ Practice seeing things from a subordinate's point of view. You may come across more harshly than you mean to.

❏ Welcome criticism instead of rejecting or punishing it. Invite feedback from others.

❏ Share credit for positive results.

The Emotionally Isolated Leader

Characteristics: The emotionally isolated manager is so uncomfortable with social interaction that he becomes almost invisible—business is carried out via subordinates, other managers or committees.

This type of leader is so afraid of making a mistake that he'll avoid taking action or making a commitment—which could turn out to be the greatest mistake of all.

Consequences: Subordinates may form small groups or pairings, seeking the direction and support that is lacking from above. Since each group is likely to have its own agenda, the organization may become fragmented. This is not an environment that fosters lively, productive collaboration and interchange.

In some cases, a more socially skilled peer or subordinate will act as a kind of buffer between the manager and the rest of the organization, helping to create a responsive climate for employees. Having a gifted co-worker interpret and carry out the leader's ideas may be enough. But the leader risks being left behind as the department or company grows beyond him.

Issues: Emotionally isolated leaders lack confidence in their ability to lead or even communicate with others. They are uncomfortable with the concept and enactment of power. Some dislike people and prefer the world of ideas…others are simply shy.

Many of them have been high intellectual achievers all their lives—but received little modeling or encouragement from their parents in getting along with peers. Skills to develop…

❏ Read about and take courses in assertiveness training to become more comfortable with collaboration, leadership and basic social skills.

❏ Learn to see mistakes as a way of finding out what is and isn't effective. Errors can be corrected.

❏ Fight inaction by recognizing that there's always more information to be gathered—but that's no reason to postpone action indefinitely. Helpful: Set deadlines. Resolve to stop research and to make decisions based on data gathered by that date.

Source: David W. Krueger, MD, clinical professor of psychiatry at Baylor College of Medicine and author of *Emotional Business: The Meaning and Mastery of Work, Money, and Success,* Avant Books, Slawson Communications, Inc., 165 Vallecitos de Oro, San Marcos, California 92069.

How to avoid errors in hiring

Many mistakes in hiring are obvious and can be avoided easily, specifically: Failing to describe jobs adequately to prospective candidates.

Other mistakes, however, are less obvious and therefore harder to avoid:

❏ Hiring overly qualified people.

❏ Too little information in help-wanted ads. Include required skills, duties, type of business and location, benefits, advancement opportunities and name of specific person to contact.

❏ Failure to prescreen applicants before scheduling interviews. This can result in time wasted interviewing unsuitable candidates, while good prospects are overlooked.

❏ Inadequate interviewing. This is a task for someone with plenty of skill and time. Interviewers should explain the interview's purpose and company policies and encourage applicants to ask questions.

❏ Unchecked references. This applies especially to those who claim success in previous jobs.

❏ Rejection because the applicant might not stay a long time. Good employees benefit the company even in short stays.

☐ Delays in making the hiring decision. If an applicant is going to be rejected anyway, the company should use its time to find other prospects. If the applicant is going to be hired, delay cuts productivity.

☐ Hiring friends or relatives who are not qualified. A uniform hiring policy boosts morale among those already employed.

Source: Alan Leighton, vice president, Cole Associates, management consultants, Short Hills, NJ.

How to be a better interviewer

When interviewing a job candidate:

☐ Spend a few minutes in small talk.

☐ Use ideas from the resume or the application form to frame your questions.

☐ Speak softly. This encourages applicants to take center stage, where they should be.

☐ Look responsive. Most people don't use nearly enough facial expression. Raising one eyebrow a little and smiling slightly gives an expectant look that makes an interviewer seem receptive. Eye contact and a calculated pause will invite the speaker to elaborate.

☐ Give reinforcement. Some people call it stroking or giving a pat on the back. Comments such as "Very impressive!" or "Excellent!" can be dropped into the discussion without interrupting the flow.

☐ Maintain control. If someone runs on too long, interrupt gently after a thought seems to be complete but before the applicant actually finishes the sentence and starts another one.

☐ Follow up and probe. If someone fails to explain the reasons for leaving a job, bring this up in the form of a casual follow-up question. If an applicant indicates that detail work is less satisfying, probe to find out how strongly that applicant dislikes detail work.

☐ To find out why people liked or disliked a previous job, use soft phrases such as "How did you happen to…? What prompted your decision to…?"

☐ Use double-edged questions to get at people's shortcomings. Example: "What about tact? Do you have as much of that as you would like, or is this something you could improve a little bit?" Most applicants find it much easier to discuss things that they could improve rather than qualities that they lack.

Source: Richard A. Fear, a consultant with the Selection Systems Division of Mainstream Access, Inc., a New York consulting firm specializing in outplacement and author of *The Evaluation Interview,* McGraw-Hill, New York.

Getting essential information from a job candidate

Even more important than finding out what people liked or disliked about a previous job is finding out why.

☐ Focus on asking people what they would like to improve. Most applicants find it much easier to discuss improving themselves than admitting they lack essential qualities or skills.

Questions to ask a job candidate— legally

Five questions to avoid:

☐ What is your religion?

☐ Do you have school-age children?

☐ How long have you been living at your current address?

☐ Are you married?

☐ Were you ever arrested?

What to ask instead:

☐ Will there be any problems if you have to work on a weekend?

☐ Are there any reasons why you might not be able to make an overnight business trip?

☐ What is your address?

☐ Defer questions on marital status until after the employee has been hired. Then they are completely proper if asked in connection with such purposes as insurance, etc.

☐ Were you ever convicted of a felony? (Ask only if the question is job-related.)

Source: Hunt Personnel, Ltd., New York.

What to ask a job applicant about his previous job

☐ What problems came up at your last job?

☐ How did you plan for them?

☐ What did you do?

☐ Raise a contrary point of view and observe whether the applicant thinks it through or simply responds with a knee-jerk acceptance or rejection.

☐ Identify a candidate as one with high energy if he talks comfortably and zestfully.

Source: Dr. Leonard R. Sayles, Center for Creative Leadership, Greensboro, NC.

The art of checking references

Checking references is becoming more difficult because many companies, as a matter of policy, no longer give out information other than dates of employment. This is because of the danger of being sued by a disappointed job-seeker. You'll have to be more subtle and tenacious than in the past, but you should aim to:

☐ Avoid vague questions that can be met with equally vague answers. Instead of asking, "What kind of guy is Ed?" ask for concrete instances of what Ed did. For a marketing director applicant, ask "What was Ed's contribution to any new products put out during his tenure?"

☐ Listen carefully to the former supervisor's tone of voice over the phone. Hesitations or false heartiness may be warning signs. But do not jump to this conclusion. Many managers are unused to giving recommendations and they respond awkwardly.

☐ Try not to settle for a reference from the personnel department. It knows almost nothing about the applicant's day-to-day performance.

☐ For key positions, take the reference source to lunch, if possible. Frankness is likelier in a face-to-face situation.

☐ Do not solicit references by letter or request written responses. Very few companies are willing to put much in writing these days.

☐ Double-check an overly negative response to a reference call, since the supervisor may personally dislike the applicant.

Making best use of subordinates

☐ Ask the secretary to keep a list of things to be done so she can check on your progress. (Especially good for chief executives; it gives them someone to "report to.")

☐ To make sure a typist picks up all corrections, always make them in color.

☐ Discourage excessive reporting by subordinates. Most memos contain information you don't need. One solution is to have subordinates report only when results deviate from a plan you have both approved.

☐ Have a secretary or assistant sit in at meetings; take minutes of action items; distribute to those concerned; follow up to make sure action items are actually completed; report to you if they aren't.

How to deal with excuse-makers

People who make excuses chronically aren't lazy. They're troubled—driven by a fragile sense of self-worth and fearful of any error or criticism.

To deal with habitual excuse-makers:

☐ Stress their importance to the organization (or family) and the repercussions of their irresponsibility.

☐ Refuse to hear out their recital of excuses.

☐ Keep a record of missed or late assignments.

☐ Get tough with excuse-makers if it finally becomes necessary.

Source: *Executive Productivity.*

How not to waste time on committees

It is usually flattering to be asked to serve on a committee. What it takes to turn down such invitations is a clear sense of personal direction and a strong sense of security. If you're asked:

☐ Accept appointments only to committees that are doing work you believe in.

☐ Restrict your contribution to the area of your expertise.

☐ Whenever possible, delegate time-consuming chores to paid committee assistants.

Source: Lillian Vernon, president, Lillian Vernon Corp., Mount Vernon, NY.

Forming a successful committee

Some helpful suggestions to point a committee in the right direction:

☐ Three or four members can function effectively. More participants mean members won't feel personally responsible for results. Fewer limits the input.

☐ Assign definite responsibility to each member.

☐ Rotate membership on standing committees periodically. That provides a steady flow of ideas and breaks up stagnant thinking patterns.

☐ Balance membership between experienced participants and relative newcomers.

☐ Set goals. To solve a problem (rather than merely move it elsewhere), aim for specific results. A committee that isn't expected to produce a substantial result won't.

☐ Review level of cooperation. A committee dominated by one member often produces insignificant results and frustrates other members.

☐ Set a time limit for work to be completed.

☐ Get periodic progress reports if the assignment is a multi-stage one.

☐ If committee proposals are rejected, the reasons for that rejection should be explained carefully.

☐ If the proposals are accepted, implement them promptly, so the committee can see the effects of its efforts.

How to create a committee that really works

☐ Give the committee the power to act on their own decisions.

☐ Make membership voluntary.

☐ Encourage members to speak freely.

☐ Match members' skills to problems. Don't make automatic appointments to subcommittees or task groups.

☐ Choose members of somewhat equal status. Otherwise, the powerful dominate, and the less powerful agree or don't participate.

Setting an agenda

☐ Begin and end with the least controversial matters.

☐ Schedule seven items per two-hour session.

☐ Never have a meeting run more than three hours.

☐ Agenda items one and two should be the minutes of the last meeting and any announcements. This fills time while latecomers arrive.

☐ Items three and four should be fairly simple, with low potential for controversy. (At the end of item four, one third of the meeting time should have been used.)

☐ Item five should be the most controversial and the one needing the most time. Allow one third of the meeting for this matter.

☐ Follow the controversial agenda item with a break, so members can unwind.

☐ Item six should be something that doesn't require immediate action.

☐ Item seven should be a topic on which everyone can agree. That way the members will leave with a feeling of having been part of a consensus.

Source: *Directors and Boards,* McLean, VA.

How to chair a committee

☐ Be aware of every member's interests, hopes, and suggestions for the committee. Meet privately beforehand with invitees to ascertain their points of view. This will insure against unpleasant surprises during the session.

☐ Handle housekeeping details efficiently. Be sure agendas and supplies are distributed on time. Welcome members at the door to relax them.

☐ Don't let talkative members dominate and quiet ones fade into the woodwork. Privately urge quiet people to speak up. Or, get permission to state their views.

☐ Remain neutral. Avoid granting individual favors or advancing narrow causes. Chairpersons are judged by how their committee performs as a whole, not by personal contributions they might make.

☐ Stress the blending of divergent opinions into a consensus. Be wary of advancing too many opinions from the chair.

❏ Check the final report with the full committee before submitting it to make sure it accurately represents the group's findings.

Source: Dr. John E. Tropman, professor of social work, University of Michigan, writing in *Directors and Boards*, McLean, VA.

Running a meeting

f you have to run meetings—of staff members, trustees, committees—the following techniques may be useful:

❏ Pick the proper-size room. If the group can't fit comfortably, see, hear, and breathe, the meeting will fail. It's worth the money to seek outside premises, but try to avoid hotels or other facilities that have many meetings at the same time. Your people may lose a lot of time finding their way through crowds or waiting for elevators.

❏ Check the sound system, lighting, projection equipment, and ventilation far enough in advance so there is time to get backups and replacements if necessary. Check on seating, tables, water, ashtrays.

❏ Be sure that those who aren't invited to a meeting know that it's because there's no need for them to be there. And make sure that everyone who ought to be present is invited.

❏ The purpose of a meeting should be an exchange of ideas and information. This requires structuring and planning: Who is to speak, on what, for how long.

❏ Those making presentations should be briefed well in advance to make sure their talk will generate discussion. Adequate time should be allowed for audio-visual aids. But don't get carried away by technology. Be sure that slides, tapes, charts, and other materials are really essential and that they're properly cued into presentations.

Source: Charles Bleich, vice president, Committee for Economic Development, New York.

Seizing the right moment at a meeting

❏ During the first half-hour of a large meeting, members need to establish their credentials or argue about agenda.

❏ Once this nonproductive muddling is over, the group is ready for constructive problem-solving.

❏ The time is right when the group is receptive to solutions, when there is a consensus on the definition of the problem and the relevant issues.

❏ The best moment is at hand when everybody is desperate for the one bright idea that will resolve the quarreling and solve the problem that has been defined.

❏ Grab the opportunity. Offer your idea now! Agreement on minor matters is self-perpetuating as larger, more important issues come up. Ideas that would have been rejected earlier are now accepted.

Group decision making

When a few individuals dominate group decision making, it is important, and often useful, to force participation by the rest. One way is a silent treatment that resembles secret balloting:

❏ State the problem clearly.

❏ Ask the participants to write down their own list of possible solutions, without revealing their identities.

❏ Do not permit talking during this exercise. This gives the more reticent group members an equal shot, which the open discussions (perhaps owing to protocol) had denied them.

❏ The chairperson then selects one idea from each list, records it on a flip-chart sheet, and opens up the meeting to verbal give-and-take on each idea's pros and cons.

❏ Every member ranks the solutions, again in a no-talking written exercise, on a one-to-ten scale.

❏ After the votes are tallied, the idea with the highest cumulative score wins.

Silence is the golden rule at two critical junctures. So the technique hinges on having a strong leader in the chair who can enforce it.

Source: William P. Anthony, Ph.D., author of *Participative Management*, Addison-Wesley, Reading, MA.

Running a problem-solving session

❏ Encourage several definitions of the problem before driving toward a solution.

☐ Do not treat new problems as recurrences of old ones. Direct the group away from comments like "I remember how we handled that before."

☐ Discourage evaluation of ideas early in the meeting. Criticism inhibits creativity.

☐ Do not jump at the first good answer. Groups often try to finish their business quickly because unresolved problems create anxiety.

☐ Seek out dissent and minority opinions to avoid the common group-think trap.

Organize a time- and travel-saving teleconference

Linking up managers in branch offices or in different plants via a teleconference keeps everyone in touch, alerts them to emerging problems, and allows them to exchange ideas about solutions. For most conferences, simple audio connections are enough; video is rarely needed.

☐ Identify the purpose of the meeting in one clear sentence to keep the focus sharp.

☐ Limit the agenda to a single item or, at most, to four items. (Hold the conference to half an hour so that participants don't lose concentration.)

☐ Arrange to tape the meeting, if you want a record of the discussion.

Source: Darome Connection, Chicago.

How to negotiate more effectively

☐ Don't allow the negotiations to be hurried by the other side. Clarify everything that seems fuzzy.

☐ Have the facts to back up every objective. If no facts are available, use opinions from experts as support.

☐ Maintain flexibility in every position. It avoids making the other side overly aggressive and always leaves a way out of dead ends.

☐ Look for the real meaning behind the other person's words. Body language tells a lot. Looking away when discussing a key point can indicate a lack of commitment.

☐ Don't focus only on money. Loyalty, ego, pride, and independence can be more important than dollars to many people.

☐ Be alert to the other side's priorities. Don't assume that the two sides are going to have the same priorities. Bending on a point that's important only to an adversary is one of the fastest ways to speed the process.

Key negotiation phrases

☐ *Please correct me if I'm wrong.* (Shows you're open to persuasion by objective facts...defuses confrontations.)

☐ *Could I ask you a few questions to see if my facts are right?* (Questions are less threatening than statements.)

☐ *Let me see if I understand what you're saying.* (Once a person feels understood, he or she can relax and discuss the problem constructively.)

☐ *One fair solution might be...*(Keep it open-ended and worthy of joint consideration.)

☐ *Let me get back to you.* (Resist psychological pressure to give in right away.)

Source: Roger Fisher, author of *Getting to Yes*, Houghton Mifflin, Boston.

How to answer questions while negotiating

Knowing what to say and *not* to say is the key. Correct answers aren't necessarily good answers and may be foolish. Rules for good answers:

☐ Take time to think. Never answer until you clearly understand the question.

☐ Stall on the basis of incomplete knowledge or failure to remember.

☐ Evade by answering a different question. Or answer only part of a question.

☐ Prepare by writing down in advance those questions most likely to come up during negotiations.

☐ Use an associate as devil's advocate.

Source: Dr. Chester L. Karrass, Karrass Seminars, Santa Monica, CA.

Patience as a negotiating tool

Patience is the most powerful tactic in negotiating. Don't rush to finish things quickly. Take the time to:

❑ Divide the other side's team.

❑ Lower their expectations.

❑ Tire them out.

❑ Bring new problems to the surface.

❑ Buy time to find their weaknesses.

Source: Dr. Chester L. Karrass, Karrass Seminars, Santa Monica, CA.

Signs that the other side is ready to make a deal

It's valuable to know as early as possible that the other side is preparing to settle. It allows strong points to be pressed home and helps avoid overkill. Clues to look for:

❑ The discussion shifts focus from the points of contention to the areas of agreement.

❑ The two sides are significantly closer together.

❑ The opposition starts to talk about final arrangements.

❑ A personal social invitation is made. At this point, agreement is almost always just a formality.

❑ Other side starts to make notes. Follow through at once, even if nothing but a napkin or envelope is at hand to write on.

❑ Don't handle the signing of the formal agreement through the mail. Both parties should sign it together. This adds importance to the event and helps cement the ties that were formed during the final stage of negotiation.

Source: D.D. Seltz and A.J. Modica, coauthors, *Negotiate Your Way to Success,* Farnsworth Publishing Co., Rockville Centre, NY.

Using an ultimatum

This is a risky tactic. For it to succeed, especially in the latter stages of a negotiation, an ultimatum must be:

❑ Presented as softly and palatably as possible.

❑ Backed by documentation or some form of legitimacy.

❑ Phrased so it leaves the other side with very few alternatives except to accept or walk away.

Reneging as a negotiating tool

Going back on a deal right after it's made and demanding a higher price is a common, very effective and somewhat unethical negotiating tactic. The trick, called *escalation*, works because the other side has come too far to walk away.

Best defense: Anticipate such a move and plan for it.

❑ Get a large security deposit or performance bond.

❑ Ask the other side for other assurances against escalation.

❑ Persuade as many high-level people as possible to sign the agreement, which will make it more difficult to escalate the terms.

Source: Dr. Chester L. Karrass, Karrass Seminars, Santa Monica, CA.

Planning tips for office routine

Make your office run smoother with these techniques:

❑ Arrange routing lists alphabetically. This avoids hierarchical irritations that arise when one person's name is placed below someone else's.

❑ If there is a way to avoid written memoranda, use it. Eyeball-to-eyeball response is important in gauging how information is received and how it will be acted upon.

❑ Brevity is the essence of good communications.

❑ Boil down ideas and reports to less than one minute, if possible.

❑ Try not to hire assistants, even when the work load gets heavy. Assistants add a layer of bureaucracy, which reduces contact between managers and subordinates. They rarely expedite matters since they cannot make decisions in the boss's absence.

❑ Consider secretarial pools rather than personal secretaries. That way, letters can be dictated either to a machine or a person.

Source: Robert Townsend, author of *Robert Townsend Speaks Out,* Advanced Management Reports, Inc., New York.

Cutting telephone chitchat

☐ Preset time limit: "Yes, Tom. I can talk for three minutes."

☐ Foreshadow ending: "Bill, before we hang up…"

☐ When calling a long-winded party, time the call for just before he goes out to lunch or leaves for the day. Gives him a reason to keep the call short.

☐ Never hold the phone waiting for someone.

☐ Eliminate "hello" from telephone answering habits. It just wastes time and adds confusion. Answer by identifying yourself instead—it starts conversation with no lost motion.

☐ Don't return all calls the minute you get back to the office. Spot the crucial ones. Half the rest will be from people who've already solved their problems; the rest will get back to you soon enough.

☐ When asking someone to call back later, suggest the best time. This avoids repeated interruptions at inconvenient moments.

When your secretary places a call

When a secretary places a call, tell her in advance:

☐ If there's anyone else to ask for if the person wanted isn't there.

☐ Whether to ask that the call be returned.

☐ To find out the best time of day to place the call again.

☐ To suggest the other party call back at a specified time.

Minimizing paper problems

Neither sloppiness nor quantity is the root cause of office paper gluts. The real problem is a shortfall in decision making. The solution is to decide which of these four categories a piece of paper belongs to:

☐ Toss. Figure out the worst thing that could happen if you threw the paper away. Toss liberally.

☐ Refer. Many documents fall into the bailiwick of secretary, boss, subordinate, colleague or specialist. Make individual "discuss" folders for key colleagues. (For general referrals, use the "out" box.)

☐ Act. These are your own tasks—writing letters, planning, etc. Put them in an "action" basket or a designated location on your desk. Process the "action" basket daily.

☐ File. For future reference. Jot a "toss" date on papers that will become obsolete.

This is the TRAF system of paper management, shorthand for the key concept of traffic—what moves in must move out.

Source: Stephanie Winston, president of The Organizing Principle and author of *The Organized Executive*, W.W. Norton & Co., New York.

Thoughts on problem-solving

The process involves the question of priorities and available time.

☐ Convoluted decisions consume time and energy.

☐ Do not shy away from sticky problems, but be realistic about investing effort in either the trivial or the intractable.

Political view:

☐ Association with certain decisions determines your track record, but not all decisions will stick in others' minds.

☐ Beware of involvement in messy problems that have no good solutions—but that others are likely to remember.

Source: *Whatever It Takes* by Morgan W. McCall Jr., Center for Creative Leadership, Greensboro NC, Prentice-Hall, Englewood Cliffs, NJ.

Antiques: Spotting the real thing

Guidelines to help you get the antique you think you're paying for:

☐ Wedgwood. The only way to determine if a piece of Wedgwood is old or recent (assuming it bears the impressed mark of Wedgwood) is by close examination of the raised relief molding. The earlier works have greater depth and more delicacy.

☐ Porcelain. The Chinese made porcelain a thousand years before anyone else. Pieces that were copied at a later date may have had the original identifying marks copied also. Only a real expert can distinguish between the old and the very old.

☐ Pewter. The alloy of tin and other metals is easily identified by its color and appearance, which are more mellow and subtle than silver or silver plate. If a piece called pewter is marked Dixon or Sheffield, with a number on its underside, it is not pewter at all but Britannia metal, a substitute.

☐ Ironstone. Mason's ironstone, found largely in jugs made for the home and in dinner service, is the original only if the words Mason's Patent Ironstone China appear in capital letters on the bottom.

☐ Enamels. The term "Battersea enamel" has come to be used for old enamels made mostly in Battersea and other English towns in the 18th century. However, the piece could also have been produced within recent years in a factory in Birmingham, or even in Czechoslovakia. The originals are of copper, surfaced with an opaque glass that was then hand decorated with inked paper transfers taken from copper plates.

☐ Silver. Old Sheffield plate will show the copper where the silver plating has worn off. This generally means that the piece was made before 1850. Once a piece has been resilvered by modern electroplating methods, it is just about impossible to differentiate it from other kinds of silver.

☐ China. The patterns are not always an indication of age since copyright is a relatively new idea. In years gone by, one porcelain maker cheerfully borrowed the pattern of a predecessor. The only way to cope with the resultant identification problem, say the experts, is to look carefully until you become savvy enough to recognize a Staffordshire printed earthenware plate by the flowers of its border.

Antique auction do's and don'ts

Even inexperienced auction goers can find quality items—and not pay too much for them—if they know what to look for and how to proceed. Some simple guidelines:

☐ Examine the items carefully at the pre-sale exhibition. Take along a tape measure and flashlight.

☐ Beware of wooden furniture with legs of a different wood. Chances are it has been put together from two or more pieces.

☐ When an item catches your interest, ask the attendant what price it is likely to bring—usually a pretty good estimate of what it will go for.

☐ If you can narrow your choice down to one item of each type, you don't have to attend the auction. Simply decide on the maximum you are willing to pay and place your bid in advance. If a piece isn't bid up to your price, auctioneer will execute it for you at the next level of bidding.

☐ Understand auction terminology. Antique means only that an object is 100 years old or older. Style means only that; it does not mean it's from that period.

☐ Buyers do best in June, July, August and December, slow months at auction houses.

☐ Auctioneers never take anything back. They are not responsible for bidders' errors. If in doubt, take an expert along.

☐ Don't be overeager. It encourages bids from "phantom" buyers, bidding you up. Best not to open the bidding.

☐ Don't worry about bidding against dealers. They have to buy low enough to cover their overhead and make a profit.

Collecting firearms

Firearms are among the oldest and most distinguished collectibles. (Henry VIII was a keen collector, as were George Washington and Thomas Jefferson.) And because firearms have been made since the 14th century, the field is vast. No individual can be expert in every aspect.

☐ Most US collectors concentrate on Americana. For the past 40 years, they have tended to specialize—even down to a single gun series. A collector might choose the Colt Single Action Army group, the guns you see in Western movies, for example. They were called "the peacemakers" and "the thumb busters." The US Army adopted this series as a standard sidearm in 1873.

The Criteria for Collecting

☐ Aesthetics play a great role. The finer guns are exquisite. The engraving can be compared with the work of Faberge.

☐ Historical relevance is important, and so is condition.

☐ But quality and maker count more. Even excellent condition cannot make an ugly gun desirable.

☐ The big four are Colt, founded in 1836; Remington, founded in 1816; Winchester, founded in 1866 but really dating back to 1852, the same year as Smith & Wesson. (The last two companies trace their origin to the same firm.)

☐ Pairs are more valuable than singles. Also triplets: A rifle, a revolver and a knife made as a set, for example.

☐ Some collectors specialize in miniatures. These tiny weapons were a test of the gunsmith's art, and they were made for fun. (You can fire the little guns, though it's not advisable.) A society of miniature-collectors exists.

☐ Modern engraved guns are also very collectible. In the last 10 years, they've become a $15-million-per-year business. Colt, Remington and Winchester (among others) make them. The craftsmanship is magnificent. Some are the equal of anything done in the past. These are not replicas, and owners do not discharge them. One reason for collecting modern firearms is assurance of authenticity. However, after 1840, most US firearms were given serial numbers. If you own a weapon made after that date, a factory may have it on record.

Caring for a Collection

☐ Rust is the great enemy. Try a light film of oil. Put on a pair of white cotton gloves, spray oil on the palm of one glove and rub the gun with it. If you use a rag, sweat from your hand will eventually mingle with the oil.

☐ Never fire a fine weapon. Well, hardly ever—only if the antique arm is not of much value. Black powder, outdated in the 1890s, is still available for shooting today. It is corrosive to metal and scars wood.

Do You Need a License?

☐ Generally not, if they were made before 1898, the federal cutoff. But check with local authorities.

Source: R. L. Wilson, historical consultant for Co
Firearms Division.

The best books on restoring antiques

The care and repair of fine treasures from the past is a craft in itself and a satisfying hobby to many collectors. The following books are excellent guides to repair techniques. Most are out of print but can be found in large public libraries and museum libraries.

☐ *China Mending and Restoration: A Handbook for Restorers* by Cual & Parsons, London, 1963.

☐ *The Painter's Methods and Material.* by A.P. Laurie, New York, 1960.

☐ *Pigments and Mediums of the Old Masters* by A.P. Laurie, London, 1914.

☐ *Antiques, Their Restoration and Pres ervation* by A. Lucas, London, 1932.

☐ *The Artist's Handbook of Materials and Techniques* by Ralph Mayer, New York, 1957.

☐ *The Care of Antiques* by John Fitzmaurice Mills, Hastings House, Ne York, 1964.

☐ *Care and Repair of Antiques* by Thomas H. Ormsbee, Medill McBride Co., New York, 1949.

☐ *The Preservation of Antiques* by H.J Plenderleith, New York, 1956.

☐ *The Art and Antique Restorer's Handbook* by George Savage, Praeger, New York, 1967.

☐ *Restoring and Preserving Antiques* by Frederick Taubes, Watson-Guptill, New York, 1963.

☐ *Handbook of American Silver and Pewter Marks* by C. Jordan Thorn, Tudor Publishing Co., 1949.

❏ *How to Restore China, Bric-a-Brac and Small Antiques* by Raymond F. Yates, Harper, New York, 1953.

Source: David Rubin, antique expert, Springfield, MA.

How to hang an investment quality oriental rug

Done the wrong way, hanging may distort the shape and diminish the value of a valuable rug. To do it right:

❏ Top-stitch two rows of the hook side of hook-and-loop Velcro fabric fastener to the back of one end of the rug.

❏ Hot-glue the loop side to a board cut to match the rug's width.

❏ Bolt (not nail) the board to the wall.

The Velcro will hold the rug evenly without letting it stretch out of shape.

Book collecting: A time-tested hedge against inflation

As with other investments, book values act according to the laws of supply and demand. But over the years, quality books almost always appreciate in value. In addition, like art, books offer a return in aesthetic pleasure above and beyond monetary investment.

Investors who know what they're doing often have collections that appreciate in value by 20% annually.

Four principal ways to invest:

❏ First edition classics. Collecting these books is much like collecting art masterpieces. You are competing against professionals and prices are very high. The likelihood of finding bargains is remote.

❏ First edition nonclassics. Try to anticipate which of today's first editions will be highly valued in the future. Because these books are not yet classics, the investor risks only the book's current market price. Look for authors or subjects you like. If the book doesn't appreciate, at least you have an enjoyable item.

❏ Specialize in books by or about one author or subject. By choosing a slightly unusual author or topic, one can build a valuable collection even though it isn't in first editions. And the cost isn't exorbitant.

❏ Book clubs. These make for a much less time-consuming way to collect. You don't have to have great hunches or compete against professionals. But you must be sure to join the right club. Recommended: The Limited Editions Club (551 Fifth Ave., New York 10017). Because it prints only 2,000 copies of the 12 books it puts out each year (a member is required to buy all 12), each book is automatically rare. It also gets top artists to illustrate them. They are all autographed by the authors or artists. Membership is limited to 2,000, so you may have to be put on a waiting list.

Basic investment guidelines:

❏ Only invest if you love books. Book collecting is not a sure thing for everyone, and an investor must get pleasure from his books in noneconomic ways.

❏ Don't follow the crowd. If you decide to collect books by or about an author or subject, be sure to avoid the obvious choices. Shakespeare and the Civil War are two examples of subjects so popular and widely printed that it's unlikely most collections will appreciate. Don't invest more than 10% of your investable assets.

Source: Louis Ehrenkrantz, Ehrenkrantz & King, New York.

Caring for fine books

Proper care is essential to preserve them, but it need not be a burden. Some basic information:

❏ Store them in a bookcase that is protected from direct sunlight. Sunlight fades the print and can cause the printing to transfer.

❏ Keep them in a room that is cool and not too dry. Overheating warps books and yellows the pages.

❏ Bookworms are not a serious problem. If they turn up, seal the book in a large plastic bag with some paradichlorobenzine mothballs for a month. (Put the mothballs in a small cardboard box with holes in it, so that the mothballs don't touch the book itself.)

❏ Dust the books regularly.

❏ Use bookmarks.

❏ Never lay a book face down—that cracks the binding.

Source: Louis Ehrenkrantz, Ehrenkrantz & King, New York.

Getting started investing in art

The art market isn't out of the small investor's price range. There are still investment-quality prints going at auction for a few hundred dollars. Some 16th- and 17th-century oils attributed to known artists can be had for around $5,000. Lesser-known American Impressionists' paintings run $1,000-$2,000.

Collect what's appealing. Become an expert on a period, an artist, or a school. How to do it:

☐ Visit museums, art shows, and galleries. To find an artist to your taste, flip through a museum's print collection.

☐ Ask curators about the artist, which galleries sell the paintings, and their recent selling prices.

☐ Buy two or three works right away. Plunging-in speeds learning. Bargains are the artist's early work, drawings, watercolors, smaller canvases, and, frequently, posters announcing an exhibition of the artist's work.

☐ Develop relationships with galleries. Use business trips to visit major dealers in other cities. Many galleries have work by living artists that's not on display but worthy of attention. Ask to see it.

☐ Visit auctions and begin to bid. Remember: Dealers mark up by 100% the art they buy at auctions. Overbidding a dealer by a few dollars results in a big saving.

☐ Avoid mail-order prints. They may be part of multiple editions with only minor variations, which have little, if any, real investment potential.

Finding bargains in art

Primary advice: Buy what you like, but buy quality—the best examples that you can find and afford.

☐ Because of the preference for oil paintings in today's art market, drawings and sculpture are better buys.

☐ Less popular subjects—some portraits, animals, religious paintings, violence—are often less expensive.

☐ Paintings that are under or over the most popular size (two feet by three feet to three feet by four feet) tend to cost less.

☐ Works that are not in an artist's most typical or mature style are usually less expensive.

☐ Avoid the currently stylish. Investigate the soon-to-be stylish.

☐ Works of western art that are not attributed or authenticated can be cheap, but they are bad investments. A work with an authentic signature and date is always worth more than one without them.

Source: Steven Naifeh, author of *The Bargain Hunter's Guide to Art Collecting*, New York.

Insuring paintings

☐ If you have art holdings valued at over $5,000, insure them separately. The standard homeowner's policy does not list artworks individually, and valuation isn't made until after the object has been lost, making it difficult to settle a claim. Also: Standard policies do not take into account the tendency of art to appreciate rather than depreciate in value.

☐ A fine-art floater can be purchased as an extension of your regular policy. This will list each object at its appraised value, providing all-risk coverage that includes all loss and damage.

☐ Have your art collection reappraised every two or three years. Change the policy accordingly.

☐ Buy all-risk insurance, including loss and damage.

☐ If you plan to lend a work, get "wall-to-wall" coverage, which insures the work from the moment it leaves your custody until its return.

☐ Standard exclusions in art policies: Damages from wear and tear or stemming from restoration, moths, normal deterioration, war and nuclear disaster.

Source: "Investor's Guide to the Art Market," *AM Newsletter*, New York.

Collecting bronze sculpture

In the world of our grandparents and great-grandparents, no home was without its bronzes. Even families with modest incomes could afford these commercially produced pieces.

A recent revival of interest in sculpture of all kinds has created a lively market in old bronzes as well. They are plentiful, decorative and easy to take care of (with a feather duster).

Collecting Categories

☐ Academic or salon sculpture. These realistic 19th-century bronzes from Europe and America were cast in a variety of subjects—portrait busts, prancing putti of India, laboring peasants and nudes. They provide a good starting point for beginners. Important sculptors: Jean Baptiste Carpeaux, Jules Dalou, Achille d'Orsi.

☐ Animal sculpture. A school of French artists led by Antoine-Louis Bayre produced sculptures of horses, dogs, lions and hunting scenes that are prized for their fine modeling and realistic movement. Important artists: Pierre-Jules Mene, Georges Gardet, Emanuel Fremiet, Alfred Dubucand. Attractive pieces are available starting at about $100, though name artists command more.

☐ Art Nouveau and Art Deco. Popular with collectors who specialize in all designs of these periods, these styles are subject to current fashion. Modest Art Nouveau and Art Deco pieces, particularly by American designers, can be found for $500-$5,000. Many Deco bronzes are of athletes. ("Pushing men" bookends are typical and popular.)

☐ American West sculpture. The peak of this craze has passed, but prices are still very high for this area of Americana. Frederic Remington's work is out of most collectors' reach. Western sculpture by other artists is a less secure investment, but, of course, it is also less expensive.

☐ Impressionist and Early Modern. Bronzes by established artists of this era are considered fine art rather than decorative objects and are available only through auctions and galleries. Works by Rodin, Daumier, Degas, Maillol, Picasso, Henry Moore, Brancusi, etc., have proved to be sound investments, but they are extremely expensive—from $100,000 to well over a million dollars.

☐ Museum specialties. Medieval, Renaissance, baroque, oriental and African bronzes require study and connoisseurship and attract only a few independent collectors. Expert advice is essential if you consider buying one of these.

Factors That Affect Value

☐ Fame of artist or founder. Signatures or foundry marks should be crisp and clear. (Fakes abound.)

☐ Edition. A rare and limited edition is more valuable than a common one. But records of most 19th-century bronzes are sketchy. Many pieces then were cast in thousands. And the records vary for established artists.

☐ Condition. Original condition is preferable. However, it is acceptable to have 19th-century bronzes repatinated or repaired in a reputable foundry if necessary.

☐ Size. This is a matter of fashion. In recent years, the demand (and prices) is greatest for very large pieces appropriate for outdoor settings.

Spotting Fakes

☐ A piece slightly smaller than an original (made from a cast of the original) is probably a forgery. Fakes also may vary in color, weight and clarity of detail.

☐ Bronzes that have been epoxied to a marble base so you can't check the hollow interior.

☐ An unnaturally even "Hershey-bar brown" color.

☐ Color that can be removed with nail-polish remover or scratched with a fingernail.

☐ A ghost impression around the signature or foundry mark.

☐ Air bubbles, bumps and craters around the base (good 19th-century craftsmen would have hand-finished such imperfections).

Source: Alice Levi-Duncan, Jody Greene, and Christopher Burge, Christie's, New York.

Collecting coins for investment

Collector-investors approach their coins with a higher level of commitment than hobbyists. Main difference: They spend significant amounts of money in the hope of reaping financial rewards.

Salient Facts About the Market

☐ The market for US Treasury-minted coins was once fairly steady, since only collectors bought and sold. But starting in the mid-1960s, noncollecting investors began to move cash in and out of the market, buying and selling coins as speculative investments much as they might stocks and bonds. This injection of volatile money transformed a relatively steady market into one of cycles, with booms and busts.

☐ Experienced collector-investors and dealers sometimes use their expertise to take advantage of the novice investor and stick him with junk.

How to Avoid Being Skinned

☐ Study before making major money investments. Background knowledge helps keep you from being cheated. There are a number of books about each major US coin series. These volumes discuss the historical background of the coins. Examples: How well the coins were struck and the condition of the dies when the coins were made. The rare years and common years for the coins and dozens of variations that make each coin distinct from others.

☐ Check prices. The coin books often give values for the coins, but these are usually out of date. For the latest figures, consult coin collectors' newsletters.

☐ Learn from dealers. Get acquainted with several to gain a sense of them as people. Be alert to their willingness to protect beginners from their own errors.

☐ But do not depend on the advice of dealers for long. To wean yourself away, spend lots of time at coin shows and auctions. Learn to identify and grade individual coins and note their sale prices. Subscribe to and study the literature read by professionals.

Other Guidelines

☐ Sell part of your collection every year. This shows you whether or not you knew what you were doing when you

bought. Sell duplicates for which you have better samples, coins from periods that no longer interest you, and samples that have lost their fascination.

☐ Take good care of your coins. The value of a coin does not depend entirely on the market cycle. It can drop rapidly from poor handling or cleaning or even from coughing on the coin. Avoid plastic holders made from polyvinylchloride (PVC). This material breaks down with time and releases an oil that oxidizes the copper in coins, turning them green and oily. (Although damaged coins can be cleaned, they never look the same to an experienced eye.)

Source: Dr. Martin G. Groder, consultant to a coin dealership in Durham, NC.

Collecting movie posters

Movie posters shouldn't be purchased primarily as investment items. They are fun items for movie fans rather than graphic art collectors.

☐ By 1911 there were 10,000 movie theaters, with posters promoting films of scenery, exotic places, romance, comedy and sexy dances. These historical posters are rare and expensive.

☐ Pick a movie type. Epics, adventure stories, comedies, Western melodramas, "problem" stories, romance-sex subjects, literary classics mysteries and crime are each a popular collecting category. Movie studios began to produce features, five-reel films that ran for over an hour in 1912. (The first epic, *The Birth of a Nation*, appeared in 1915.)

☐ The silent films produced in the era following WWI are a relatively untapped area for poster collectors.

☐ Favorite movie stars may be the major reason collectors go hunting for posters. When a star has caught the imagination of many, the supply of posters becomes scarce.

☐ The impact of television in the past two decades has caused the number of new movies and the theaters showing them to dwindle drastically, greatly reducing the number of posters produced. Particularly scarce are posters for blockbuster movies such as *Star Wars* and the gory horror pictures that appeal to teenagers, who quickly gobble up the supply. Contemporary osters may grow in value if the trend continues.

☐ Prices of movie posters do not necessarily increase with age as they do with other paper collectibles. Supply and demand determine cost, which can run from $10 to $1,000.

☐ Perfect condition raises prices.

☐ Reproductions costing $6-$10 are available for some of the most popular lms of the past, but these are not valuable.

☐ New York and Los Angeles have the argest supply of movie memorabilia. Ads in film magazines can provide eads to local stores and mail-order sources.

Source: Ernest Burns, owner of Cinemabilia, which sells movie memorabilia.

Collecting color posters

Posters caught the public's fancy in the 1880s and have retained a fascination for collectors ever since.

☐ Categories for collectors: Circus, theater, ballet, movies, music halls and both world wars.

☐ Posters in constant demand: Those connected to avant-garde art that combine strong typographic design with photomontage.

☐ Rare finds: Work from the 1920s associated with the Bauhaus, the Dada movement and Russian Constructivism. Constructivist film posters made in 1925-31 most often measure about 40 inches by 28 inches. Classic example: Any of the few advertising the film *The Battleship Potemkin*.

☐ Best buys: Automobile posters (except those for American cars, which are not of very good quality). Star: The Peugeot poster by French artist Charles Loupot.

☐ Beginners should look at Japanese posters made from the mid-1970s to the present. Also recommended: Post-World War II Swiss posters for concerts and art exhibits. Posters of note since World War II include those of Ben Shahn and the San Francisco rock posters of the 1960s.

☐ Best: Stick to recent foreign posters made in limited editions and not distributed beyond their place of origin.

☐ Poster condition: Creases and small tears in the margin are acceptable.

Faded posters are undesirable. (The quality standards are not quite as stringent for posters as they are for prints.)

Source: Robert Brown, co-owner of Reinhold Brown Gallery, New York

Collecting bottles

Collecting bottles is one of the most popular pastimes in the field of antiques. Besides the age-old allure of glass itself, bottles offer a collector a wide variety of types to choose from, generally moderate prices and a range of sizes and colors.

Prime sources of collectible bottles include attics and basements, barns, flea markets and antique dealers.

Although there are many subdivisions to specialize in, most bottles available to a collector fall into the following categories:

☐ Spirits bottles. Large, crude, dark-colored bottles in which whiskey was shipped to the American colonies from England; "seal" bottles to hold smaller quantities of liquor; ribbed and swirled pint-sized flasks made by the Pitkin Glassworks in Connecticut in the 1780s; 18th and 19th century decanters.

☐ Medicinal bottles. 19th century patent medicine bottles; bitters bottles; pharmaceutical bottles, including the deep blue ones that held poisons.

☐ Household bottles. Late 19th and early 20th century bottles that held everything from mineral water to soda pop to vinegar to ink. Milk bottles are especially popular.

☐ Personal bottles. Late 19th- and early 20th-century bottles for such substances as cologne, smelling salts and ammonia.

Tips for collecting:

☐ Because prices vary widely, consult a reputable dealer before buying.

☐ Keep in mind that condition is a major determinant of price.

☐ Guides to collecting, including price guides, are available at libraries and bookstores.

☐ The Corning Glass Museum in Corning, NY, is a superb place to see a wide variety of bottles.

☐ Subscribe to a newsletter, such as *Antique Bottle World*, Chicago.

Source: William Delafield, Bottles Unlimited, New York 10021.

Collecting seashells

Seashell collecting is a just-for-the-fun-of-it hobby, not something to do if you have investment appreciation in mind.

Begin by collecting as many types of shells as appeal to you. This way you can learn their names and become familiar with the distinctive qualities of each type. Most collectors are eventually drawn to one or two species and narrow their scopes.

Prices within every species range from 25¢ to several thousand dollars. But it is easy to put together a very broad collection of several thousand shells for $1-$10 apiece, with an occasional splurge into the $20-$25 range.

Most popular species:

☐ Cones (Conus): Cone-shaped shells that exhibit an astonishing variety in pattern and color.

☐ Cowries (Cypraea): Very rounded shells, with lips rolled inward to reveal regularly spaced teeth. Naturally so smooth, hard and glossy that they appear to have been lacquered, they are often considered the most pleasurable shells to handle.

☐ Murexes: Swirling shells favored for their pointy spines, though many are delicate and hard to store.

☐ Scallops (Pectens): Shaped like ribbed fans in surprisingly intense reds, oranges, yellows and purples.

☐ Volutes (Voluta) and Olives (Oliva): Equally popular species.

Other hints:

☐ Stay away from lacquered shells.

☐ Avoid ground lips (an edge that has been filed will feel blunt rather than sharp).

☐ Get a label to accompany each shell with its scientific name and location information.

Source: Jerome M. Eisenberg, The Galleries at La Jolla, and William Gera, The Collectors' Cabinet, New York.

Art appraisal: Some definitions

What's it worth? In an art appraisal, the word "value" can have several different meanings.

☐ Fair market value: The price at which an item would change hands between a willing and informed seller and a willing and informed buyer.

☐ Replacement value: The amount it would cost to replace the item with a similar one.

☐ Estimated value: Fair market value, but taking into account local conditions at the time of the sale (i.e., is the item "hot" right now?)

☐ Liquidation value: An item's value if it had to be sold today. Often the lowest determinable value.

Surviving the over-the-counter stock market

Over-the-counter stocks, being small and often not well followed by many brokers, are especially susceptible to rumors and false reports. Stockbrokers and underwriters flourish on heavy trading and are usually themselves the source of misleading reports. Basic wisdom: When a company sounds too good—its product will replace toothpaste—watch out!

☐ Rule of thumb: If you don't know why you own a stock—or why you're buying—or why you're selling—then you're in someone else's hands. This makes you more vulnerable to the caprices of the market.

☐ OTC stocks, particularly new issues, are usually short-term plays. One should never buy without having a sell target in mind.

☐ If the selling price is reached, even within a week of buying, stick to the sell decision unless there is some major mitigating factor you hadn't considered before.

☐ About 80% of all new issues will be selling below their issue price within 18 months. Reason: Most new issues are overpriced in relation to existing companies. But they are all destined to become just another existing company within a year.

☐ In evaluating a new issue, find out who the people involved are. If the underwriter is or has been the target of the Securities and Exchange Commission's investigations, this is often mentioned in the prospectus. The SEC prints a manual of all past violators. Avoid underwriters that have had lots of SEC problems. The strong companies rarely use them to go public.

☐ Check out the auditors of a new-issue company. (They will be named in the prospectus.) If the auditor is not well-known or is in trouble with the SEC, question the numbers in the financial reports.

☐ A danger in over-the-counter stocks is a key market maker who crosses buy and sell orders among its own brokerage customers so that the market price is artificial. If such a broker collapses, so will its main stocks. This illustrates the danger of buying a stock dependent on only a single market maker. To avoid such a problem, invest in stocks quoted on NASDAQ, where by definition there are at least two strong market makers, and hopefully a lot more.

☐ Spot companies just before they decide to go onto NASDAQ. When they do, their price inevitably rises because of the increased attention. Very often the managements will simply tell you if they have NASDAQ plans or not. Tip-off: If they've just hired a new financial man, it's often a sign of a move to NASDAQ.

Source: Robert J. Flaherty, editor of *The OTC Review*, Oreland, PA.

Techniques for evaluating over-the-counter stocks

☐ Growth potential is the single most important consideration. Earnings increases should average 10% over the past six years when acquisitions and divestitures are factored out.

☐ Cash, investments, accounts receivable, materials, and inventories should be twice the size of financial claims due within the next year.

☐ Working capital per share should be greater than the market value of the stock (an $8 stock should be backed by $10 per share in working capital).

☐ Long-term debt should be covered by working capital, cash, or one year's income.

☐ The balance sheet should show no deferred operating expenses and no unreceived income.

The criteria for final selections include:

☐ Ownership by at least 10 institutions reported in *Standard & Poor's Stock Guide*.

☐ Public ownership of between 500,000 and one million shares, with no more than 10% controlled by a single institution.

☐ Continued price increases after a dividend or split.

☐ Strong likelihood of moving up to a major exchange. (A good sign is strong broker and institutional support.)

Avoid companies that are expanding into unrelated fields, where they lack the required management experience and depth, and have stock selling at prices far below recent highs. This sign of loss of investor support can take months to overcome.

Source: C. Colburn Hardy, *Physician's Management*.

Takeover fever

If you own stock in a target company: Wait 24 to 48 hours to see how the stock price is affected by the takeover announcement. If the price is near or just below proposed offer: Bidding is at a fair price—sell all stock and take your profits. If stock exceeds offer price within 48 hours: Bidding will probably go higher—sell 20% to 50% of holdings to hedge against the deal falling through. Advice for non-holders of target stocks: Don't buy after the announcements. Individuals don't have access to the information needed to evaluate the high risks.

Source: A round-up of portfolio managers quoted in *The New York Times*.

Pointers from professional traders

Here's a collection of suggestions from some of Wall Street's savviest traders:

☐ If the market has already risen for five to six weeks, it is almost always too late to make new purchases with safety. Possible exception: The first months of a fresh bull market.

☐ Strongest short-term market periods: Last trading day of each month and first four trading days of the subsequent month. Days before holidays often show good market strength, too.

☐ If a stock has not made a new high within a five- to six-week period, there is a good chance that its intermediate trend is about to turn down.

☐ If a stock fails to make a new low five to six weeks after a decline, there's a good chance its intermediate trend is about to turn up.

☐ Count the weeks from one significant market bottom to another and from one significant market top to another. Strong market advances often start at intervals of from 20 to 26 weeks. Severe declines often start at the same intervals.

☐ Before buying preferred stocks of blue chip companies, investors should consider that the same company's bonds may yield ¼% to ½% more.

Reading index futures for stock market signals

Trading in stock index futures contracts is too volatile for many investors. But they can be used as a reliable forecaster of short-term market swings and, therefore, can be valuable.

How index futures relate to day-to-day trading:

☐ Index futures generally lead the stock market. If the market is down for the day but the price of contracts is up expect the market to swing upward. Conversely, if the market is up but index futures are down, expect the market to turn down within a day or two.

☐ When the *Value Line* and *Standard & Poor's* indexes gain more than the contracts, the market is bearish. If the indexes lose less than the contracts, the market is bullish.

☐ If futures contracts continue to rise after the stock market closes, expect a good opening for stocks the next day. If they fall after the stock market closes, expect the market to open mixed or down the next day.

☐ The market will often change direction when the premium paid for futures contracts exceeds or falls below the actual market indexes by about 2.5% to 3%. If the stock market rises but premiums for futures contracts decrease, expect a downside market reversal within a day or two.

☐ Caution: These trends apply to short-term market swings only.

Stock market advisory letters

You should buy market letters on the basis of their performance success, not investment philosophy.

Bear in mind:

☐ Stocks most recommended by investment advisers as a group consistently underperform the Dow Jones industrial and *Standard & Poor's 500* averages. This has proved true in all time periods checked.

☐ Stocks that are recommended by the best-performing market letters slightly outperform the averages.

☐ Equities owned by investment advisers—as distinct from those they merely recommended—consistently outperform market averages.

◻ Even when advisory letter recommendations drive up the price of a stock, as they often do, the odds of making a profit favor those who sell those stocks within three months of the original recommendation. After that, stocks decline from lack of interest or are overtaken either by events or by more recent recommendations. Caution: Investors should not necessarily dump a premier growth stock based on market letter recommendations. There are always other fundamentals to consider.

◻ Investors who buy a stock they know little about just because a market letter is pushing it should be aware that the push soon dissipates. Moreover, advisers often fail to tell subscribers when a previous pick goes sour.

◻ Low-priced issues (those under $10) outperform high-priced stocks.

◻ Stocks with a high price/earnings ratio outperform low p/e ratio stocks. This finding goes against traditional Wall Street wisdom. Possible explanation: Stocks for which investors have high enough hopes to pay a premium generally tend to fullfill those hopes.

◻ Market letters have a huge bias toward buy advice as opposed to sell recommendations. This is particularly true of market letters published by big brokerage houses. These letters are highly edited to make sure they don't offend clients in other areas of the firm's business.

◻ Limit stock purchases to issues recommended by the top-performing advisers in industries recommended by the best-performing forecasters.

Source: George H. Wein, publisher *Select Information Exchange*, New York.

Following insider stock trading

No one knows a company better than those who run it—the officers, directors and, usually, owners of large chunks of stock, too. Fortunately for investors, the law requires these insiders to report stock trades within their own companies. Investors who follow those insider trades generally outperform the market significantly over time. But watching insider trading is a sophisticated art, full of pitfalls for the unwary.

◻ Widespread insider buying in the open market (not through the exercise of stock options) is a clearer market signal than insider selling. That's because people have many reasons for selling. They might need cash for their children's college or a down payment on a home. But they buy largely for one specific reason—they have inside information that leads them to believe that the price of company stock will go up.

◻ About 35% of insider transactions on the open market are usually buys, and 65% are sells. When this ratio changes significantly, it's an important signal for investors to follow the same trend.

◻ Volume of insider trading is far less important than the direction in which the insiders are moving. Unanimity of direction is very significant.

◻ Look at who is buying and who is selling. In general, trades made by the company president or its chairman are most significant.

◻ Insider trading is easier to read in smaller companies than in big ones.

◻ Insider trading is valid as an indicator for all industries except the brokerage industry. Reason: It has so many insiders with so many kinds of private purchases that there are normally very few buyers and lots of sellers. This makes data too confusing to interpret.

◻ Insider trading is not an infallible indicator of future stock prices. Over the entire market, it's accurate about 75% of the time. Important: Insider buying will push stock prices relatively higher than insider selling will cause a price drop.

◻ Stock moves generally follow insider trading gradually over 12 to 24 months. Investors can often climb aboard even if they're acting on information that's several months old.

◻ Insider trading can also be used to anticipate broad trends across the entire market, not just for individual stocks.

◻ As an aggregate indicator, insider trading is usually early by several months.

Source: Norman Fosback, publisher of the bimonthly newsletter *The Insiders*, Fort Lauderdale, FL.

How to spot a market decline before it starts

Strong market moves frequently end in one- or two-day reversal spikes. Those spikes often provide advance warning of significant market turning points. Checkpoints that show when a market decline may be coming:

☐ The market will rise sharply in the morning on very high volume running at close to 15 million shares during the first hour of trading.

☐ From 10:30 A.M. (Eastern time) on, the market will make little or no progress despite heavy trading throughout the day.

☐ By the end of the first day, almost all the morning's gains will have been lost, with the market closing clearly toward the downside. Occasionally, this process will be spread over a two-day period.

☐ Steps to take: When you see the pattern, either sell immediately or await the retest of the highs that were reached during that first morning. Such a retest often takes place within a week or two, on much lower trading volume. This may prove to be the last opportunity to sell into strength.

How bear market rallies can fool you

Bear market rallies are often sharp. They're fueled, in part, by short sellers rushing to cover shares. However, advances in issues sold short often lack durability once short covering is completed.

Here is what you need to know about bear market rallies:

☐ They tend to last for no more than five or six weeks.

☐ Advances often end rapidly—with relatively little warning. If you are trading during a bear market, you must be ready to sell at the first sign of weakness.

☐ The first strong advance during a bear market frequently lulls many analysts into a false sense of security, leading them to conclude that a new bull market is underway. The majority of bear markets don't end until pessimism is widespread and until the vast majority is convinced that prices are going to continue to decline indefinitely.

☐ Although the stock market can remain "overbought" for considerable periods of time during bull markets, bear market rallies generally end fairly rapidly, as the market enters into "overbought" conditions.

☐ Price/earnings multiples for the group soar far above historical norms.

☐ Heavy short selling appears. Early short sellers of the stocks are driven to cover by sharp rallies. Their covering of shorts adds fuel to late rallies within the group. (Short sellers who enter the picture later, however, are likely to be amply rewarded.)

Trading tactics that work for professionals:

☐ Exercise extreme caution, first and foremost.

☐ Place close stop orders on any long and/or short positions taken.

☐ Enter into short sales only after these issues have shown signs of fatigue and of topping out, and then only after recent support levels have been broken.

☐ Wait for a clear sign that the uptrend has ended before selling out.

Spotting the bottom of a bear market

Here's how sophisticated investors recognize that a bear market is near its last phase:

☐ Downside breadth increases. That is, market declines become broader, including even stocks that have been strong before. More issues are making new lows.

☐ "Oversold" conditions (periods in which the market seems to decline precipitously) extend for longer periods of time. Technical recoveries are relatively minor.

☐ Pessimism spreads, but analysts and bullish advisories still discuss "bargains" and "undervalued issues."

☐ Stocks continue to be very sensitive to bad news. The market becomes very unforgiving of poor earnings reports and monetary difficulties.

☐ Trading volume remains relatively dull. Prices seem to fall under their own weight, the result of a lack of bids rather than urgent selling.

Important: The bear market isn't likely to end until pessimism broadens into outright panic, and until public and institutional selling become urgent. One of the most reliable nontechnical signals that the bear market is over is when the mass media begin to headline the fact that the stock market is hitting its bottom.

How to make money in market declines

Mistake: Most investors tend to place capital into the stock market following important market advances. This increases your risks.

Instead:

☐ Adopt a planned strategy of making investments in phases as the market declines. Market declines of greater than 10% are relatively unusual during bull markets and investors should look upon them as an opportunity.

☐ Don't take quick profits early in intermediate advances and reinvest quickly into new stocks. You miss the really good moves and simply incur additional commission costs.

☐ Prepare for market advances during periods of market decline. Determine which groups are best resisting market decline, and plan to purchase into such groups upon a 10% market decline. Hold for a minimum of several weeks, preferably months.

☐ Don't chase stocks that have already risen sharply in price, particularly when the price rise has been based upon speculative expectation.

☐ Try to ferret out true value—stocks in companies that feature solid balance sheets, regular earnings growth, increasing dividend payout.

☐ Avoid stocks with institutional followings. They tend to underperform the market.

☐ Study the market on days when trading is quiet. If such days show positive closing action, you can presume that the professionals are positioning themselves for market advance.

How to buy stock in an up market

Basic rule (expressed in exaggerated form here): There is never a second chance to buy a good stock. However,

if the stock is genuinely strong, any downward correction is usually minor, so the longer you wait the more you'll pay. Don't be too concerned about getting in at the lowest price. If it's a good stock (and a steady rise in price confirms that), it will probably be good even if you have to pay a bit more by not jumping in.

To handle that dilemma of either waiting for a correction or chasing it up:

☐ Consider that a stock has gotten "too far away" if it has already advanced three days in a row or gained 15% in price or both. You should have acted before the rise. But if you missed that point, wait.

☐ Stocks typically fall back by about 50% after a strong rally. (If the stock has grown from 25 to 30, a 50% retracement of that 5-point gain would mean back to about 27[2/3].)

☐ In order not to miss a stock you really want (one that didn't dip back to the buy-order level), jump on it the moment the stock shoots up past 30 (its prior high point) because that usually means the stock is on its way up again.

Knowing when to wait before buying

Investors often think they are buying stock at a bargain price, only to see it fall further because of an overall market falloff. Signs that such a falloff is ahead:

☐ Just before the decline, the market advance becomes very selective. Gains are recorded in just a few industry groups rather than across the board.

☐ Speculative interest runs high in the American Stock Exchange and over-the-counter markets.

☐ During the first phase of the decline, the stocks that failed to participate at the end of the previous advance show the most severe declines. The strongest industry groups tend to keep rising on short-term rallies. This pattern traps unwary traders who believe that stocks are at bargain levels.

☐ During the second phase of the decline, most groups participate, but the previously strong groups decline only slightly.

☐ During the final stages, even the once strong industry groups fall sharply. Odds are that the decline will soon come to an end. Wait for evidence that all segments of the market have declined before stepping in to buy.

☐ As a general rule, groups that were strongest during the previous rally will advance sharply when the market starts to recover, although they may not remain in the forefront throughout the next market cycle.

☐ Strong market rallies often take place at quarterly intervals.

☐ Leaders of one quarter often do not maintain leadership in the next upward cycle.

How to avoid selling too soon

If you're nervous about the direction of stock market movement, adopt the following method to avoid selling securities just as the market may be gathering upside momentum:

☐ Each week, record the number of issues making new highs for that week on the New York Stock Exchange. (These and other key data are recorded in *Barron's,* among other sources.)

☐ Maintain a moving four-week total of the number of issues making new highs on the NYSE.

☐ Presume that the intermediate uptrend is intact for as long as the four-week total of issues making new highs continues to expand. Investors can hold long positions in most issues without fear until the four-week total turns down.

Source: *Timing and Tactics,* Ventura, CA.

Selecting stocks: A disciplined approach

☐ Consistency: You want to see six consecutive years of 10% earnings growth in adjusted pretax earnings. To do this, eliminate interest income and gain or loss from the sale of property, plant or equipment. If accounting procedures change, adjust earnings so performance is comparable over the years. You are trying to strip away all illusion and get to the real numbers.

☐ Magnitude: Over the six-year period, adjusted pretax earnings (exclusive of acquisition and divestiture) must have shown a 20% annually compounded growth rate.

Working capital: Look for very strong ratios and require:

☐ Two-to-one or better current ratio.*

☐ One-to-one or better quick asset ratio.**

☐ Working capital in excess of market valuation (shares outstanding multiplied by current market price).

☐ Corporate liquidity: Long-term debt must be covered by working capital, by cash and equivalents or by the latest 12-month cash flow.

☐ Accounting procedures: Eliminate companies if they follow deceptive, unconservative accounting practices. Examples: They defer operating expenses or prematurely realize revenues.

☐ Owner diversification: Investment company ownership should be no more than 10% of outstanding shares.

☐ Price/earnings multiple: This must be under 10 times estimated earnings for the current fiscal year.

*The ratio of current assets to current liabilities. The ratio determines how able the company is to pay its near-term debts (those due in a year or less).

**The ratio between existing liabilities and quick assets (cash and receivables without inventory). This is another measure of how able a firm is to pay off its liabilities rapidly with available funds.

Source: Barry Ziskin, The Opportunity Prospector, Brooklyn, NY.

Questions to ask before buying a stock

You'll want a yes answer to just about every one of these questions before taking a long position in a stock.

☐ Is the price/earnings ratio of the stock (price divided by latest 12-month earnings) well below the price/earnings ratio of the average listed issue?

☐ Have earnings of the company been rising at a steady rate over a period of years, preferably at a rate exceeding the rate of inflation?

☐ Has the company had a recent history of steadily rising dividend payouts?

☐ Has the stock recently risen above a clearly defined trading range that lasted for at least five weeks?

☐ If not, has a recent sharp decline ended with the stock trading on extremely high volume for that issue, without the price falling further?

☐ Have insiders of the company purchased more shares of the company than they have sold?

☐ Has the company recently

purchased its own shares on the open market?

☐ Has the stock remained relatively undiscovered by the advisory services and brokerage houses? (One sign that an issue is near the end of a rise is that many advisory services suddenly begin to recommend its purchase.)

Source: Gerald Appel.

Blue chips

Buying cheap stocks, as measured by low stock prices in relation to the earnings per share, is a classic contrarian method of buying cheap, out-of-favor issues. The big hope: As the market recognizes the stock as a substantial performer, or earnings begin to rise, the market "votes" it a higher multiple. Therefore the stock price rises.

Applying the technique to blue chip stocks:

☐ Stick with low-priced blue-chip companies that offer high yields and are strong financially. These issues give you a better chance of being well-positioned for a market rally and also provide a strong defensive position in case the market falls.

☐ When the market declines, blue-chip low price/earnings ratio issues tend to go down less than the high flyers. While many fast-track investors may be down 20% or even 40% during a market pullback, most low p/e ratio portfolios decline considerably less than the *Standard & Poor's 500* as a whole.

☐ Preserving capital during a bear market is at least as important as enhancing it during bull markets. Investors who stay fully vested, with their capital basically intact, are ready for the next market move upward. That prepares the low p/e ratio investor to take advantage of the strong beginnings of a market rally.

Source: David Dreman, author of *The New Contrarian Investment Strategy* and managing director of Dreman, Gray & Emby, a New York-based investment firm.

Investing in penny stocks

Penny stocks come in four basic types, each of which requires a separate strategy:

☐ Stocks trading on the New York Stock Exchange and the American Stock Exchange for $5 or less. Look for long-term turnaround candidates, takeover and merger candidates, and stocks trading well below book value.

☐ Stocks traded over the counter, computer-listed by the National Association of Securities Dealers. Focus on traditional growth stocks.

☐ Stocks traded over the counter, not NASDAQ-listed, for which individual brokers make markets. Study growth stocks doing 250,000 to 300,000 shares in trading volume weekly. Get research reports from a variety of penny-stock brokers on such companies, and compare the views on each company.

☐ Stocks offered by underwriters in initial public offerings. Evaluate the assets and growth potential of the companies going public. Avoid those raising money to refinance existing debt. Read prospectuses carefully.

Other points to remember:

☐ Be careful to check the track records of the underwriters and brokers handling penny stocks of interest.

☐ To hedge your bets, diversify your penny-stock holdings.

Source: Jerome Wenger, publisher, *Penny Stock Newsletter*, Columbia, MD, and John Spears, general partner, Tweedy Browne, Inc., New York.

How professionals spot a low-priced stock that is ready to bounce back

A top-quality large company selling at a high price/earnings multiple is less attractive than a lesser-quality company selling at a depressed price in terms of its past and future earning power, working capital, book value, and historical prices.

What to look for:

☐ Stocks that have just made a new low for the last 12 months.

☐ Companies likely to be liquidated. In the liquidation process, shareholders may get paid considerably more than the stock is selling for now.

☐ Unsuccessful merger candidates. If one buyer thinks a company's stock is a good value, it's possible others may also come to the same conclusion.

☐ Companies that have just reduced or eliminated their dividends. The stock is usually hit with a selling wave, which often creates a good buying opportunity.

□ Financially troubled companies in which another major company has a sizable ownership position. If the financial stake is large enough, you can be sure that the major company will do everything it can to turn the earnings around and get the stock price up so that its investment will work out.

There are also opportunities in stocks that are totally washed out—that is, situations where all the bad news is out. The stock usually has nowhere to go but up.

How to be sure a stock is truly washed out:

□ Trading volume slows to practically nothing. If it's an over-the-counter stock, few if any dealers are making a market.

□ No Wall Street research analysts are following the company any more.

□ No financial journalists, stock market newsletters, or advisory services discuss the company.

□ Selling of the stock by company's management and directors has stopped.

Signs of a turnaround:

□ The company plans to get rid of a losing division or business. If so, learn whether the company will be able to report a big jump in earnings once the losing operation is sold.

□ The company is selling off assets to improve its financial situation and/or reduce debt.

□ A new management comes on board with an established track record of success with turnaround situations.

□ Management begins buying the company's stock in the open market.

□ Form 13d statements filed with the SEC. (A company or individual owning 5% or more of a public company must report such holdings to the Securities and Exchange Commission.) If any substantial company is acquiring a major position in a company, it's possible a tender offer at a much higher price is in the wind.

Source: Robert Ravitz, director of research, David J. Greene & Co., New York.

Making profits on a stock split

When a stock splits, the average profit to an investor is 20%. But the greatest profits are generally made in the three to six months before the split is announced. The general pattern is that the price stays high for two days after the split announcement and then declines.

To spot a candidate for a split, look for:

□ A stock price above $75. A split moves it into the more attractive $35 to $50 range.

□ A company that needs to attract more stockholders, diversify, or attract additional financing.

□ A takeover candidate (heavy in cash and liquid assets) whose management holds only a small percentage of the outstanding shares. (Companies with concentrated ownership rarely split stock unless there are problems with taxes, acquisitions, or diversification.)

□ A stock that was split previously and price has climbed steadily since then.

□ Earnings prospects so strong that the company will be able to increase dividends after the split.

□ Likely prospects are over-the-counter companies with current earnings of $2.5 million, at least $2 million annually in preceding years, and less than 1 million shares outstanding (or under 2,000 shareholders). A stock split is necessary if management wants to list on a major exchange.

Source: C. Colburn Hardy, *Dun & Bradstreet's Guide to Investments*, Thomas Y. Crowell Co., New York.

Picking small-company stocks

Most investors prefer recognized names and are willing to pay a big premium for them. Smaller, less-well-known companies can sell at a substantial discount from their private worth.

A company's private worth is what another company would pay to buy it outright.

Small companies have more room to grow. And because they are more likely to be controlled by the original owners management's interests coincide with shareholders'.

□ Main investment criterion: Cash flow in excess of what it needs in the business. Excess cash flow builds up pressure in the company—pressure to repurchase stock or go private, to make acquisitions, to increase dividends or to be taken over. Point: All of those are factors that can cause the private worth of the company to be realized.

☐ Buy many different stocks (at least 20), and be prepared to hold them for as long as three to five years. When you buy stock in an undervalued small company, you cannot be sure what will be the trigger that causes private worth to be realized…and how long it will take to happen.

☐ Look for above-average return on assets, combined with a below-average ratio of price to book value.

☐ Small does not necessarily mean high-tech. Investors traditionally overpay for high-growth, high-technology stocks. Mundane companies are much more likely to be undervalued.

☐ Don't pay much attention to earnings. They're only one component of cash flow. Down earnings can mask a fundamental positive change going on underneath.

☐ Don't bother trying to "get a feel for management." Management either produces decent results or it doesn't.

☐ Don't waste time trying to understand all the minutiae of a company before investing. Even little companies are extremely complex, and situations can change very rapidly.

☐ Don't try to time the market. No one out there has a long-term investing record built on market timing alone. The investors who have made money over the long term are the ones who have made broad economic bets based on value.

Source: Charles M. Royce, president, Pennsylvania Mutual Fund, Inc., and Royce Value Fund, Inc., New York.

How to spot a small growth company—I

An analyst with an exceptional performance record tells how he spots attractive small companies. They usually have these specifics:

☐ Unconventional managers willing to take risks. Strong chief financial officer, marketing manager, research director. Executives who can and do play devil's advocate to the boss's ideas.

☐ A focus on where the company is going rather than where it has been. Be sure that the company is spending heavily from current revenues on the development of new projects.

☐ A company in a period of healthy transition. Good sign: Rising earnings after several years of flat results due to heavy R&D and marketing expenses.

What to avoid:

☐ Companies run by lawyers. To grow, a young company needs a chief executive who is willing to take risks. Such an approach is anathema to most legal minds.

☐ A management that responds to tough questions in a vague way.

Source: Bob Detwiler, partner, Fechtor, Detwiler, Boston.

How to spot a small growth company—II

When you want a small growth company, look for:

☐ Current ratio (current assets to current liabilities) of 2:1 or better, a large amount of cash, and little debt. Keep a wary eye on long-term lease obligations, which are, in effect, a form of indebtedness. Learn how heavy such obligations are and whether they will put an undue burden on the financial resources of the company.

☐ No recent accounting changes that artificially boost earnings.

☐ Inventories accounted for on the most conservative basis (LIFO rather than FIFO).

☐ Fast inventory turnover.

☐ Small number of shares outstanding. This will prevent institutional investors from taking a position in the stock, which can be disastrous if they decide to sell all at once.

☐ A return on equity of at least 17% and profit margins that are high in relation to industry norms.

☐ The company's tax rate. Be sure that if the company is paying less than the usual 46% tax rate, an increase in the rate isn't likely for several years. A big tax bill could wipe out any earnings gains for the year.

☐ Company annual reports for four to ten years. See if actual results live up to management's predictions.

Source: Charles Allmon, publisher, *Growth Stock Outlook*, Bethesda, MD.

Picking the right industry at the right time

In addition to studying individual stocks, you should know which industries are likely to prosper and which are likely to suffer at various stages of the economic cycle.

When inflation fears predominate:

☐ Strong groups: Metals, gold, silver, natural-resource stocks, oil and gas, and timber.

☐ Weak groups: Utilities, banks, finance companies, and other interest-sensitive groups. Long-term debt instruments are dangerous.

When recession fears predominate:

☐ Strong groups: Drugs, insurance, and basic food stocks.

☐ Weak groups: Autos, chemicals, steel, auto parts, textiles, appliance manufacturers, and other cyclical industries.

When a recession is many months old:

☐ Strong groups: Autos, chemicals, and other cyclical industries that usually move upward in anticipation of an economic turnaround.

☐ Weak groups: Defensive stocks.

☐ At a time of strong economic recovery marked by sharply falling interest rates—the most favorable market climate of all—the most volatile industry groups usually do their best.

Stocks that benefit when oil prices fall

☐ Airlines. Fuel prices will be lower.

☐ Homebuilders. Interest rates fall because lower oil prices add liquidity to the system. Lower interest rates boost home-building activity.

☐ Restaurants. The nondiscretionary portion of the average paycheck is 86%. With more discretionary income, people will eat out more.

☐ Motel chains. There will be more au travel.

☐ Automobiles. Lower gasoline prices

☐ Retail industry. Another area buoye by more discretionary spending.

☐ Brokerage industry. People may invest some of that extra money.

☐ Interest-rate-sensitive stocks. As rates fall, these companies benefit.

☐ Japan. The yen will rise and the Japanese economy becomes healthi due to lower oil prices.

Source: Barry Sahgal, managing director of research, Ladenburg Thalmann & Co., New Yo

Investing in biotechnology companies

☐ Look at the company's valuation relative to its science and potential products. Does the company have a sound scientific staff working on products that address a solid market? Do the scientists have a good publishing track record in their field?

☐ Look at the competition. Is the company just another "me-too" firm trying to get a piece of an already heavily sliced pie?

☐ Look at the management. Who's running the company? Well-meaning scientists or skilled executives with a scientific background? Read what management says in the press, in annual reports and during meetings. managers are talking through their hats, they probably won't be able to pull rabbits out of them.

☐ Look for staying power. Does the company have the cash to stay in the game for the long haul—through R&D (as well as a few years of clinical trials in the case of human pharmaceuti-cals)? Does the company have at lea four times its R&D budget as cash in the bank?

☐ Look at the price of the stock. The higher the price, the more difficult it w be for investors to recoup their investment—and then make a profit.

☐ Look at trends in the industry. Biotech abhors a vacuum. If there is a need, the industry will fill it.

☐ Look at the company's joint venture Biotech R&D burns up cash quickly. Joint ventures with big companies are pipelines to money—and staying power. Remember: The big companie had a good, inside look at the company before forming a partnership. If they were impressed by what they saw, it might be worth your time to consider investing in that firm, too.

Source: *Breakthrough*, Boardroom Reports, New York.

Questions to ask before buying utility stocks

Utility stocks, more than most issues, are purchased for reliable income by conservative investors who may require current income from investment holdings.

Here are some guidelines to help avoid unpleasant surprises:

☐ Is the utility located in a state with a favorable regulatory climate? Some states make it very difficult for utilities to pass along rising costs to consumers; some states are more permissive. Typically, a state will grant the utility approximately two-thirds of the rate increase requested.

☐ Does the utility have ample earnings from which to pay interest on any bonds outstanding? Utility companies are generally heavy borrowers of capital for expansion. Should a cash flow bind develop, dividend payouts may have to be suspended, since bondholders hold first call on company assets. Earnings for the company should amount to at least 2.5 times the interest payments due on corporate notes, preferably more.

☐ Does the utility have earnings sufficient to cover projected dividend payouts?

☐ What is the relationship of the price of the shares to book value? If the company has plans to issue more shares, the price should be no lower than book value. Otherwise, shareholder equity will be diluted by such distribution.

☐ Is the company paying out too high a percentage of earnings in dividends? Approximately 65% to 70% is average. The lower a percentage of earnings in dividend payout, the more protected the dividend.

☐ Does the utility have excessive debt? Check the balance sheet for favorable asset-to-liability ratios.

Your broker should be able to provide the above information either via in-house research or access to *Standard & Poor's* ratings of corporations and corporate debt.

Source: *Electric Utilities 1977*, Prescott, Ball & Turben, Cleveland, OH.

Buying new stock issues

☐ Don't expect general stockbrokers and wire houses to service you on new issues as well as they do on conventional stock transactions. Find a source that specializes in such stocks by monitoring the formal announcements of new issues (called tombstone ads) that appear in *The Wall Street Journal*.

☐ Identify the lead underwriter (the first name listed among the brokers handling a new issue), and keep track of what happens to the issues brought out by that underwriter over time. If prices in the aftermarket hold a premium above the issue price on a fairly consistent basis, call that underwriter directly.

☐ Ask for the firm's biggest producer. When an issue is really hot, you can buy only so much. The superstar's allotment, however, is bigger. Tell him that you want to be on his primary mailing list for prospectuses. Aim: To get them as soon as they are issued.

☐ Read the prospectuses carefully. Note people or firms (lawyers, accountants, etc.) where you have contacts. Ask them about the company. While they probably will not say much directly helpful, with experience you can do some very valuable reading between the lines.

☐ Don't buy at the new-issue broker, hold the stock for a short time as the price runs up and then sell it through a wire house. If everyone runs out after the first day or week, the reputations of both the stock and the original underwriter are hurt. Suggestion: Tell the broker that you need some liquidity as soon as possible, and ask what you can sell in a short time without hurting the market. A common practice: Sell enough to get back the original investment at the issue price, and hold onto the rest for a free ride.

☐ The best profit opportunities are in a

down market. Companies that do go public then are usually stronger and will probably outperform, on average, companies brought out in a frothy market.

Source: Patrick Rooney, president of Rooney Pace, Inc., New York.

Safe haven for investors

Top-quality municipal bonds have traditionally been a favorite safe, non-taxable berth for investors whose chief investment goal is the preservation of capital. The willingness to accept somewhat more risk for somewhat higher yield, in municipal bond investing, means selecting a portfolio of issues by:

Maturity

☐ Generally, the longer the maturity, the higher the risk.

☐ Lowest risk: Turning over short-term municipal notes or investing in a variety of money-market funds.

☐ Better: Devising a portfolio of municipals that reflects your ability to tolerate risk—say, nothing longer than three years for great safety, or not more than 20% in 20-year maturities to increase the yield at the cost of some safety.

Credit Standing

☐ The most conservative investors will not accept a rating that is lower than AA.

☐ Alternative: Bonds backed by letters of credit or insurance—though you should not give up more than five basis points (.05 of a percentage point) in yield for such guarantees.

Two Safe Bets

The municipal market gives an opportunity to increase yield without experiencing much reduction in safety through two factors:

☐ First is the inefficiency of the municipal market. All trading is done by phone, with no central electronic exchange such as NASDAQ. Thus, brokers who do not have depth in the municipals business call only two or three dealers (checking with 15 is a great deal better) for a price or simply sell issues in the firm's inventory.

☐ Second is the variety. An investor who understands the intricacies of outs and calls, sinking funds insurance, etc., and rigorously researches both the issues and the financial status of the

issuing bodies can uncover special situations in which higher yields can be achieved with very little increase in risk.

Source: Arthur L. Schwarz, president, Ehrlich Bober Advisors, Inc., a subsidiary of Ehrlich Bober & Co., Inc., 80 Pine St., New York 10005.

Dividend reinvestment plans

Some 1,000 corporations now offer stockholders special inducements to reinvest their dividends. Important: Dividend reinvestment plans should only be considered by an investor with a high degree of confidence in the future outlook of the issuing company.

What an investor should know about such offers:

☐ Some companies offer a 5% price discount. Buying additional stock this way eliminates brokerage commissions, although a few plans have a small service charge.

☐ Stockholders may be able to invest additional cash, saving more on commissions and price discounts.

☐ Reinvestment plans provide investment discipline for those who would otherwise fritter away small amounts.

☐ The agent for the plan will hold original shares for safekeeping and send a regular statement to the stockholder.

☐ One slight drawback is tax treatment. A private ruling* by the IRS states that any administrative service charges and brokerage fees that are subsidized by company reinvestment plans may be treated as additional dividend income to the investor.

☐ Reinvested dividends are still subject to income tax ($100 dividend exclusion could partially offset income tax consequences. If some shares are put in a spouse's name, the exclusion is boosted to $200.)

*7830104, July 24, 1978.

Source: Robert Ferris, Georgeson & Co., New York.

Misperceived companies: An opportunity to make money

☐ Companies with excess assets against which an acquiring company can borrow. These are generally the most attractive companies for potential buyers or raiders. And that buying effort could raise the price of the stock.

☐ Firms with very little debt and very good borrowable assets. Ideal: A company with a lot of cash, inventory and salable real estate but very little bank debt. Make an estimate of how much an investor could borrow against these assets. If the borrowing power less the bank debt divided by the number of shares works out to be less than the price of the stock, look more closely at the company.

☐ Firms with undervalued real estate. One clue is the date real estate was purchased. Sometimes the book value of the real estate will appear in a financial footnote.

☐ Company assets that could be sold or spun off for substantial values.

☐ Companies with overfunded pension funds—i.e., funds with more assets than their liabilities to employees and retirees. An overfunded pension fund makes the company a more attractive buyout candidate.

Source: Norman Weiner, Oppenheimer & Co., Inc., New York.

Merger failures are opportunities too

Although some well-publicized mergers and tenders have profited shareholders, the majority of merger rumors prove unfounded, and shares fall when denials are issued. Even when takeovers occur, delays often cause high price volatility, both upward and downward.

Trading strategies using options can be useful when an issue appears to have risen too far too fast on the basis of takeover rumors:

☐ Sell the stock short in anticipation of a price decline should the rumor prove false. This high-risk strategy is rarely used because, if the takeover does take place, losses can be heavy.

☐ Buy a put on the stock, limiting risk to the option premium. This is safer, but tends to be expensive. Investors can lose all they put into the play if the stock merely stands still in price and an at-the-money put has been bought.

☐ Sell the stock short, while simultaneously purchasing an in-the-money call. If XYZ Corp., selling at 50, for example, is a merger candidate, an investor might sell 100 shares short at 50 while purchasing a four-month call option with a strike price of 45 for $750 per call. There will be a substantial profit if the stock declines sharply in price. The risk in this case is limited to $250, no matter how high the stock rises. Example: If the common falls to 30, an investor makes $2,000 on the short sale (50 — 30 x 100 shares), but the call premium of $750 is lost. Profit: $1,250 less commissions. If the common rises to 80, the investor will lose $3,000 on the short sale (80 — 50 x 100 shares), but the call purchased at $750 will be worth $3,500. The total loss: No more than $250 plus commissions. This strategy of buying a call ties up more capital than buying a put, but the advantage is that the risk is less.

Source: *Value Line Options & Convertibles,* New York.

Basics for successful option trading

Most investors who deal in puts and calls have their own pet strategies, but the most successful generally follow these basic rules as well:

☐ They trade in high-priced active issues. (Stocks in the $40 to $100 range are favored by professional traders.)

☐ They stay in the market only when they feel certain about its direction.

☐ They trade in stocks that have shown a predictable price pattern.

☐ They treat options as short-term speculative vehicles. If a trade does not go their way within five days, they usually close it out.

☐ They place limit orders on buy positions. They don't let enthusiasm overrule reason.

☐ They watch the underlying stock closely if good news is released. The best prices are often available the morning after the news is released.

☐ They never feel so certain about any one situation that 100% of cash and confidence go into it. Instead, they diversify, and evaluate the action of the stock unemotionally.

☐ If an option has gone up by 100% but is expected to go higher, they sell at least 50% of the position and let the rest ride.

Source: Joseph T. Stewart, Jr., author of *Dynamic Option Trading*, John Wiley & Sons, New York.

Stock options as an alternative to buying on margin

Aggressive investors who think the market will advance often buy options instead of buying stock on margin.

Advantages:

☐ The choice of options avoids margin interest charges, which can be very high when the prime rate is high.

☐ There's a much smaller loss if the stock drops sharply.

☐ If the stock goes up as expected, the profit will be almost as big as with buying on margin.

Disadvantages:

☐ Loss to the investor is larger if the stock doesn't move at all.

☐ Profits will be taxed as a short-term gain rather than long-term.

Wise tactics for picking a mutual fund

☐ Analyze the advertising the mutual fund runs in the financial press. Usually it gives an excellent performance record to lure new investors.

☐ Consider the time frame of the fund's performance. It may be a very select period, when the fund's performance was exceptional, or a time when everyone did well in the market. During a longer period the fund may have had just a so-so performance.

☐ Find out what happened to the fund in down markets.

☐ Avoid fad funds. You can learn about new funds from many financial periodicals, from reference books such as Wiesenberger's handbook on mutual funds, or from the no-load fund directories put out by a number of organizations. Too often, when a particular industry such as gold, high technology, or international stocks gets hot, the funds jump in to grab a piece of the action. But they don't have the ultimate ability to use the money they raise, because they have bought at the top of the elevator.

☐ Study the discipline of the funds that interest you. This is stated in the prospectus. Some funds have a mandate to be fully invested at all times. Trap: In a major market slide, such as the one from 1968 through 1974, full investment (even with the strictest discipline) will not bring about good performance. It is better to find a fund that can get in and out of cash instruments. Alternative: Switch in and out of various funds yourself, based on the signals of a competent timer.

☐ Identify the risk profile of the fund. Read the prospectus to learn the price/earnings ratio and dividend yield of the average stock the fund holds. Is the average stock selling at 27 times earnings (the high end of the spectrum)? Or is it at an average or below-market multiple, as usually befit a more conservative fund? Does the firm buy volatile stocks? Find out if the fund manager is a trader or a long-term investor. And then decide whether the profile conforms to your own investment style and needs.

☐ Don't sign up for a family of funds with the belief that, if the stock market sinks immediately, you can switch into a money-market fund. Most funds require that money be at the institution at least 30 days before a switch is allowed.

☐ Mutual funds aren't banks. Although many people are used to check-writing privileges on money-market funds, they should not view equity mutual funds the same way.

☐ Distinguish between an investment portfolio and transactions portfolio. Don't put rent money into an equity fund. Mutual funds fall in value at times. You don't want to be forced to liquidate at a loss.

How to read a mutual fund prospectus

A mutual fund prospectus is not easy reading. The way to pry out the information needed to make a good investment decision is to focus on the following questions:

☐ Does the fund's portfolio mesh with your investment goals? Some funds have highly volatile portfolios and employ leverage or margin selling to enhance return, but at greater risk.

] What's the fund's performance record? Select a fund that has matched or surpassed *Standard & Poor's 500* during periods of both rising and falling markets. Most prospectuses include several years' performance data. Best performers are usually funds with less than $50 million in assets.

] What are the minimum initial and subsequent investments? The lower the better.

] Is there a switch privilege? It is highly desirable to pick a fund that allows investors to switch back and forth between a firm's equity and money-market funds by phone. (Some funds charge for switching, but the charges usually don't amount to much, except for the frequent trader.)

] Are there fees for opening and closing an account? There is no reason to pay such fees.

] Is it a load (i.e., sales commission) fund or a no-load? As a group, no-load funds, those without sales commissions, perform pretty much as well as those with fees.

] What are the limitations on how the fund can invest money? Some funds must diversify their portfolios, while others allow management to concentrate highly on one or more industry groups. As a general rule, diversification reduces risk.

] Does the fund have a policy of moving into cash during bear markets? While a fund can cut losses this way, it may also delay reinvestment in equities when the market starts to rise. Long-term holders often adopt the strategy of investing in funds that have a record of increasing cash positions by selling equities before bear markets or at least at their earliest stages.

Source: *Switch Fund Advisory*, MD.

Evaluating a mutual fund

Before taking a position in a mutual fund, answer these questions:

] Does the fund suit your tolerance for risk? Certain funds are extremely volatile in price action. They suit investors with risk capital better than those who cannot afford to run the risk of a sharp decline in their capital. Secure a price history on the fund, either from the fund itself or by visiting the public library of a financial publication. Analyze the fund's historical ups and downs.

□ Does the fund have a good track record during declining markets? Does the management make an attempt to reduce portfolio exposure during down markets or does the fund generally stay fully invested? Don't expect helpful answers to questions like these from a commissioned salesperson for the fund.

□ Has the fund's management altered policies in the past counter to your own investment objectives? Certain funds are steadily increasing redemption charges to discourage trading. Or they're imposing restrictions that may not suit your purposes. Verify the facts in the current prospectus. Inquire if any changes are contemplated.

Fitting your psychology to a mutual fund

Techniques useful to investors for evaluating performances:

For aggressive investors:

□ Each week that the market rises, divide the closing price of the mutual fund at the end of the week by the closing level of either the *Standard & Poor's 500* Stock Index or the N.Y.S.E. Index. Plot the results on a graph for comparison. If the fund is indeed stronger than the average during a rising market, it will show up clearly, indicating that it is suitable for an aggressive investor.

□ Remember that since such funds also frequently decline more sharply than the averages during falling market periods, they may be suitable only for investors with an accurate sense of market timing.

For safety-oriented investors:

□ Each week the market declines, divide the closing price of the mutual fund at the end of the week by the closing level of one of the averages. If your fund resists the downtrend more than the average stock during a falling market, the plotted results will show the fund's line declining less than that of the average.

□ Don't be disappointed when mutual funds advance less than more aggressive funds during rising market periods.

For investors who want to try to beat the averages:

☐ At the end of each week divide the price of the mutual fund (rising or falling) by the price of one of the broad market averages, and plot the results. The result will demonstrate the relative strength curve of the fund, indicating whether it is outperforming the broad market, regardless of the price trend.

☐ To protect yourself, as soon as your fund's relative strength curve begins to show weakness, consider switching your holdings to a better-performing vehicle.

Guidelines for investing in closed-end funds

A closed-end fund is like a mutual fund, in that it invests in a number of other securities. But unlike mutual (or open-end) funds, it doesn't constantly sell new shares and redeem shares at net asset values. Rather, the shares of a closed-end fund trade in the open market, just like stocks of individual corporations.

Most closed-end funds sell at a 15% to 30% discount from their net asset value. In a rising market closed-end funds generally outperform other securities. And in a declining market, if shares were purchased at a heavy discount from net asset value, a decline in the portfolio should have relatively little, if any, effect on the price of the fund's shares.

Criteria for selecting the right closed-end funds:

☐ Find out the fund's discount from net asset value over the last year. Shares that sell at 5% below their normal value are a good buy, although 10% below the normal discount would be even better.

☐ Be selective. Some funds are selling at a heavy discount for a good reason. The assets in the portfolio may be illiquid or unmarketable.

☐ Don't buy a fund "at the market." These funds can be fairly volatile. Instead, put in the order to buy at a specific price.

☐ Avoid funds with bylaws that require a supermajority of shareholders (usually two-thirds) to change the fund's status from a closed-end fund to an open-end fund. Reason: If a fund becomes open-end, the shareholders get an immediate step-up in the value

of some 20% to 30%, depending on the actual discount of the fund from net asset value.

How to hedge with closed-end funds: Buy a stock fund and then sell naked (uncovered) options against the large holdings in the fund.

☐ If the stock market declines: Option will make a lot of money, while the closed-end fund may not decline at all because it is already selling at a large discount from net asset value.

☐ If the stock market rallies: Gain in the price of the fund should more than offset losses in the options.

Source: Thomas J. Herzfeld, executive vice president, Bishop, Rosen & Co., Inc., South Miami, FL.

Ten laws of venture-capital investments

Many people are intrigued by the prospect of investing in start-up companies especially those on the leading edge of technological development.

But before plunging into the brave new world of venture capital, be sure you understand these "laws":

☐ The probability that a company will succeed is inversely proportional to the amount of publicity received before it began to manufacture its first product.

☐ An investor's ability to talk about winners is an order of magnitude greater than the ability to remember the losers.

☐ If a venture-capital investor does not think he has a problem, he has a big problem.

☐ Happiness is a positive cash flow. Everything else will come later.

☐ The probability of a small firm's success is inversely proportional to the president's office size.

☐ Would-be entrepreneurs who pick up the check after luncheon discussions are usually losers.

☐ The longer the investment proposal, the shorter the odds of success.

☐ There is no such thing as an overfinanced company.

☐ Managers who worry a lot about voting control usually have nothing worth controlling.

☐ There is no limit on what a person can do or where he can go if he does not mind who gets the credit.

Source: Frederick R. Adler, senior partner, Adler & Shaykin, New York.

Selecting a full-service stockbroker

Be sure that you do the interviewing. Don't let the prospective broker turn the tables and interview you. If you are reluctant to ask all these questions, select at least some of them and have the answers supplemented with a resume.

☐ Where did he study? What?

☐ How long has he been with the brokerage firm? How long has he been in the securities industry?

☐ What was his prior employment? Why did he leave his last place of employment?

☐ From where does he get his investment recommendations? His firm's research department? Company contacts? Friends in the business? His own research? A combination?

☐ Can he supply a certified history of his firm's and his own research recommendations?

☐ Does he have any client references?

☐ What is his theory on giving sell advice and profit taking?

☐ How many clients does the account executive service? (You want your telephone calls to be answered promptly.)

☐ How diversified is the brokerage firm? Does it have, for example, a bond department? How about an economist? An in-house market technician (essential for timing)? Money-market experts? Commodity department? Option department? Tax shelter experts?

☐ How many industries does his firm's research department follow? How many companies? How many senior analysts does the firm have?

☐ Will you get weekly, monthly or only occasional printed research reports?

☐ What fees, if any, will be charged for such services as securities safekeeping?

☐ What is the firm's commission structure? What discounts is it willing to offer?

☐ Can the investor talk directly to the investment-research analyst to get firsthand clarifications and updates on research reports? Must everything be funneled through the account executive?

☐ What is the financial condition of the brokerage firm? (You want the latest annual and quarterly financial statements.)

☐ How many floor brokers does the firm have at the various stock exchanges? (You want prompt order execution.)

☐ Is the potential broker willing to meet personally on a regular basis (monthly or quarterly, depending on portfolio size and activity) to discuss progress?

☐ What kind of monthly customer statements are prepared? (More and more firms now offer tabulation of monthly dividend income, portfolio valuation and annual portfolio yield estimate.)

Using discount brokers

Discount brokers generally charge 35% to 85% less in commissions than full-service houses. Savings are particularly good on trades involving large numbers of shares, but discounters generally don't give investment advise. Otherwise, confirmations, monthly statements, and account insurance are generally the same for discounters as they are for full-service brokerage firms.

Investors who can benefit by using discounters:

☐ Investors liquidating market holdings.

☐ Investors buying on margin. Margin rates are generally better, but this matters only if you're borrowing a substantial amount.

☐ Beneficiaries of estates who are moving inheritance from stocks and bonds to other kinds of investments.

☐ Employees whose only holdings are stocks in the companies they work for, who sell these stocks occasionally.

☐ Lawyers, accountants, and other professionals who believe their personal contacts and own market analyses make for better guidance than what brokers are offering.

☐ Retired persons or other investors with free time to do their own market research.

Who should not use discounters?

☐ Investors interested in commodity trading. Discount houses handle stocks, bonds, and options only.

☐ Investors who need mortgages, tax shelters, special bonds.

☐ Those with less than $2,000 to invest. Savings on discount commissions at this level do not outweigh the plus of free advice from full-service houses.

☐ Individuals without stock market experience.

Source: J. Bud Feuchtwanger, financial consultant, New York.

How to place orders with a stockbroker

Most investors are familiar with the basic forms of execution orders which they may give to their stockbrokers. The most common are limit orders (orders to buy and/or sell at the best available price), and stop loss orders (orders to buy and/or sell at the best available price if specified price levels are crossed).

Far fewer investors are familiar with other instructions:

☐ Fill or kill orders. These are either executed immediately or canceled. The investor wants to buy and/or sell immediately in light of current market conditions.

☐ Clean-up basis. Buy an amount of stock at the asked price only if the purchase "cleans up" all available stock at that price. If the order is executed, the investor has reasonable assurance that no other heavy seller exists at the price range at which he purchased the shares. So price is unlikely to drop rapidly.

☐ Not held. The investor provides the floor broker with full authority to use his judgment in the execution of the order, which may mean a more advantageous price. But if the floor broker makes an error in judgment, the investor has no recourse.

☐ All or none. When buying or selling multiple lots, the investor requests that his entire position or none be sold at a limit price. He can often save on commissions by trading in large lots.

☐ Short, short exempt. If the investor holds securities or bonds which may be converted into common stock, he can sell short the amount of stock into which these convertible issues may be converted without waiting for an uptick. To do this, he places a "short, short exempt" order. Advantages: The market for many convertible securities is thinner than the market for the underlying common. He will often get superior executions by selling the common short and then turning the convertible security into common, which is then employed to cover the short sale.

Source: Irving Waxman, R.F. Lafferty & Co., New York.

When not to listen to your broker

The few words the average investor finds hardest to say to his broker are, "Thanks for calling, but no thanks." There are times when it is in your own best interest to be able to reject a broker's blandishments.

☐ When the broker's hot tip is that a certain stock is supposed to go up because of impending good news. Ask yourself: If the "news" is so superspecial, how come you (and/or your broker) have been able to learn about it in the nick of time? Often insiders have been buying long before you get the hot tip. After you buy, when the news does become "public," who'll be left to buy?

☐ When the market is sliding. When your broker asks, "How much lower can they go?" the temptation can be very great to try to snag a bargain. But before you do, consider: If the stock, at that price, is such a bargain, wouldn't some big mutual funds or pension funds be trying to buy up all they could? If that's the case, how come the stock has been going down?

☐ Don't fall for the notion that a stock is "averaging down." It's a mistake for the broker (or investor) to calculate that if he buys more "way down there," he can get out even. Stock market professionals average up, not down. They buy stocks that are proving themselves strong, not ones that are clearly weak.

How to protect yourself in disputes with stockbrokers

☐ Keep a diary of all conversations with stockbrokers that involve placing of orders, purchase recommendations, and other important matters. A detailed record adds credibilty if the dispute oes to court, arbitration, or the broker's boss.

❏ Note the exact time of conversation, as well as the date. The brokerage firm is liable if it fails to place an order promptly and you lose money as a result of the delay.

❏ If necessary, complain to the head of the brokerage firm. That's sure to get attention.

❏ If that doesn't get results, write a complaint letter to the SEC, which regularly examines such letters.

❏ If none of these work, get a new broker.

Source: Nicholas Kelne, attorney, American Association of Individual Investors, Chicago.

When not to pay a stockbroker's commission

It's not necessary to use a broker and pay a commission to make a gift of stock. Or if a sale of stock is negotiated privately.

How to transfer stock ownership to another person:

❏ Enter the other person's name, address and Social Security number on the back of the certificate.

❏ Sign the back of the certificate and have the signature guaranteed by a commercial bank.

❏ Send it by registered mail to the transfer agent, whose name is on the certificate.

❏ Allow two to six weeks for the other person to receive the new certificate. There will be no charge, although in some states the seller, or donor, has to pay a small transfer tax.

Investing in gold

Almost all the advisers who pushed gold several years ago continue to believe every portfolio should contain some gold as a protection against inflation or economic collapse. Here are some shrewd ways to invest:

❏ Stay away from the gold futures market. Diversify holdings among gold coins, bullion, and stocks of South African gold mines.

❏ Pick the mines with the most marginal, high-cost production. These companies are traded internationally, and their reserves are known. As the price of gold goes up, their production becomes economic and they offer very high yields.

❏ Keep in mind that, as a rule, the price of mining shares moves with the price of gold, although the swings are more exaggerated. Calling the turn in the gold market is difficult because gold is a very emotional investment. The political stability of gold-mining countries is a factor to consider.

❏ When buying or selling, remember that gold prices are generally strong on Fridays and lower on Mondays. This is because investors are reluctant to carry short positions over weekends, when central banks sometimes make announcements that affect prices.

❏ Prices are also stronger toward the end of the year and weaker in summer. The supply decreases toward the end of the year because laborers on short-term contracts to South African gold mines return home to harvest crops. Demand decreases in summer, when the European gold-jewelry industry closes.

Guidelines for investing in diamonds

Diamonds are complex—no field for tyros looking for a safe investment. Diamond prices fluctuate as supply and demand conditions change, and the swings can be sharp. Invest only funds not needed for three to five years. That's how long it takes for the wholesale price (at which you can sell) to catch up with the retail price (at which you buy). Thus, even if prices continue steadily upward, it may take three years or more to break even.

❏ If liquidity is your most important consideration, buy the same grades that jewelers do. That is, diamonds worth less than $2,000 (roughly the maximum amount most people are willing to pay for an engagement ring).

❏ Look for a GIA (Gemological Institute of America) color grade not lower than J (K and lower grades have traces of yellow visible to the naked eye). The GIA clarity grade should be no lower than VS (very slight imperfection) or SI (slight imperfection).

□ For maximum appreciation, buy high-quality diamonds, which are the rarest. Top grade is D (pure white) Flawless (no imperfections). Also accepted as high quality are diamonds with color grades down to about F and clarity grades down to VVS (very very slight imperfection).

□ Buy the finest diamonds at major jewelers, diamond investment firms, and auction houses as well as through private investors.

□ Check the reputation of a firm carefully before doing business. Talk to the firm's banker, and get the latest Dun & Bradstreet report. Ask the local Better Business Bureau if it has received any complaints about the company.

□ Shop around before choosing your firm. Markups range from 20% to 100%. Ask diamond investment firms, jewelers, and diamond brokers (who sell to jewelers) what they would charge for a diamond of a specific weight, cut, color and clarity.

□ Insist on a grading certificate from a major independent laboratory. Don't rely solely on a certificate from the seller. Diamonds graded by the Gemological Institute of America are the most salable and can command a 15% to 20% premium. Other laboratories whose certificates are widely accepted: American Gemological Laboratories, United States Gemological Services.

□ Avoid buying on margin plans. Some firms have misappropriated investor funds.

□ Insist on prompt delivery. If diamonds are ordered by phone or mail, the contract should specify that the diamonds will be sent within ten days after the firm receives good funds.

□ Make sure you get a satisfaction guarantee. Thirty days is a reasonable guarantee period, although not every firm offers that much. Use the guarantee period to check whether the diamond that was ordered matches the diamond that was received. Note: The guarantee should remain in force even though a laboratory report is received after the guarantee period has expired.

□ Have the diamonds reappraised every six months. The longer the delay, the greater the uninsured risk. Use an appraisal firm linked via computer to diamond cutters and dealers across the country. Two such firms:

International Gemological Institute, New York; United States Gemological Services, Santa Ana, California.

□ Follow news affecting diamond investments by reading *Diamond Registry Bulletin*, New York, or *Precious Stones Newsletter*, Thousand Oaks, CA.

Why rubies, emeralds and sapphires are a safer investment than diamonds

When prices of investment-grade diamonds plunged as much as 30%, colored gemstones magically held on to heady price gains. Reason: Scarcity. Only some $200 million in rubies, emeralds, and sapphires were sold in the US in a recent year, a fraction of the amount of diamonds sold.

The areas where the finest stones come from: Cambodia, Thailand, Ceylon, Burma and parts of Africa. Scarcity factor: These areas are politically unstable and, therefore, are not reliable sources.

□ Grading. Although techniques in grading colored stones are less advanced than those for diamonds, tests under microscopes and refractometers allow gemologists to distinguish synthetic stones from real ones. They can often tell you the origin of the stone. Certain countries of origin command higher prices. Example: Burma rubies.

□ Flaws. Although all stones have flaws, gross flaws ruin the stone.

□ Setting. Determine whether the setting does justice to the stone. Does it overwhelm the stone?

□ Color. It is the most important determinant of price once the stone is adjudged authentic. Never view a single stone. Compare it with several others. Why: The clarity of the redness of a ruby, and the absence of orange, pink, purple or brown, is what makes it most valuable. The variation is best seen by looking at several stones.

□ A family-owned jewelry retailer with an excellent reputation is the best place to buy. Leaders: VanCleef & Arpels or Harry Winston. They are willing to risk their own money investing in fine gems from around the world. Larger chains of jewelers can't afford to invest. They custom-order.

❑ In small towns without direct access to a large selection of colored gemstones, go to reputable retail jewelers and commission them to find the kind of stone you like and can afford. Many fine jewelers have connections with the American Gem Society, which will send them a selection of stones for conditional purchase. The jewelers receive a commission for their advice and service.

❑ The best gems to buy are stones over one carat that are free of externally visible flaws. Buy one that will look good mounted in jewelry. That way, if the investment does not gain in value, at least you will have a remarkable piece of jewelry, not just a stone in a glass case.

❑ Expect to keep a colored gem for at least five years, when buying for investment. Then evaluate what the stone would go for on the dealers' (wholesale) market. Alternative: Put stones up for auction at Sotheby Parke Bernet or Christie's. Although you cannot be sure of a definite sales price, you can put a minimum price on your item.

Penny stock traps

❑ Avoid a company that is not generating unit growth, that has high debt or whose management doesn't have a good track record.

❑ Stay away from companies in very competitive situations.

❑ Don't get caught up in other investors' stories.

❑ Be leery of companies with 20 million shares outstanding of a penny stock.

Source: Stephen Leeb, president of Money Growth Institute, Jersey City, NJ. The company publishes *Penny Stock Ventures, The Speculator,* and *The Investment Strategist.*

Stockbroker traps

Watch out for:

❑ Recommendations for a stock you've never heard of.

❑ An investment strategy that depends on exceptionally heavy trading.

❑ Transactions involving investments such as low-activity, over-the-counter stocks or Ginnie Mae securities, for

which up-to-the-minute prices are rather difficult to obtain.

❑ Pressure to use the company's cash-management account.

Source: *Fortune.*

How to choose a prime growth stock

Prime growth stocks should meet all or most of the following characteristics:

❑ A dominant position in a growth industry.

❑ A long record of rising earnings and high profit margins.

❑ Superb management.

❑ A commitment to innovation and a good research program.

❑ The ability to pass on cost increases to the consumer.

❑ A strong financial position.

❑ Ready marketability of the stock.

❑ Relative immunity to consumerism and government regulation.

Source: *Preserving Capital* by John Train, Clarkson N. Potter Publishers, New York.

What to ask a financial planner

The probing questions to ask:

❑ *What's your specialty?* If the planner lists specialties—say, hard assets or insurance or stocks or tax shelters—scratch him/her from your list. What you should be looking for: A generalist with a professional staff.

❑ *What percentage of your income comes from fees and how much from commissions?* If much of the income is generated by commissions, also scratch him.

❑ *What are your educational background and professional experience?* If he passes the background test, call his references.

❑ *Are you affiliated with any other firm?* Some planners are affiliated with an insurance company, a stockbroker, or even a marketer of tax shelters. You should eliminate them.

❑ *Can you quantify what you can do for me?* Eliminate planners who jump to that bait and start reeling off numbers.

❑ *How much will it cost?* If he immediately quotes you a package price, go on the next candidate.

Source: Connie S.P. Chen, a former financial consultant at Merrill Lynch's Personal Financial Planning Group and for the last seven years head of Chen Planning Consultants, New York.

What to look for in good-quality stock...

☐ A price/earnings ratio that's lower than the market average. Right now the S&P 500 index has a p/e ratio of 18. I'm buying stocks with p/e's of no more than 14—and preferably no more than 12. When their p/e's rise to market levels, it's usually time to sell.

☐ A solid track record. The growth of its earnings and dividends over the past five to 10 years should have outpaced the S&P 500.

☐ Above-average return on equity compared with the S&P 500 for the past five to 10 years. This shows that the company really knows how to use capital intelligently to create higher profits.

☐ A strong balance sheet. A good company can have long-term debt, but it should not exceed the company's equity. In recent years we've seen far too many companies struggling to get out from under debt that has prevented them from growing and prospering as they otherwise would have done.

Source: David Dreman, chairman, Dreman Value Management, which manages 2.7 billion in stocks, bonds and mutual funds for individual and institutional clients, 10 Exchange Place, Jersey City, New Jersey 07302.

Raising money on property

Selling property and leasing it back may be a better way to raise money than taking out a mortgage loan.

The biggest advantage is immediate cash amounting to 100% of current value of the property. A mortgage loan would probably produce only 75%.

The seller (lessee):

☐ Continues to use the property for term of lease, including renewal options.

☐ Pays rent which is fully deductible.

☐ Realizes taxable gain or loss on sale.

The buyer (lessor):

☐ Puts up the cash, maybe borrowing some of the amount needed.

☐ Receives taxable rental income.

☐ Takes depreciation deductions.

When the lease runs out:

☐ There is usually an option to repurchase the property. Generally, this must provide for purchase at fair market value at the time.

☐ IRS will look very carefully at sale-leasebacks. It's sure trouble if there's an option to repurchase for $1. In that case, IRS may claim it isn't really a sale, but a sham with no real change of ownership, really a disguised mortgage loan. Then the "rent" will not be deductible, only the part of it considered to be "interest" on the "loan."

What you should know about real estate agents

Knowing your legal rights and responsibilities when selling your home yourself or through a real estate broker can save you thousands of dollars.

☐ Shop around to find a broker who is knowledgeable about your community and with whom you feel comfortable.

☐ Be sure to read the legal documents pertaining to brokers' contracts to avoid misunderstandings.

☐ Be aware that commissions paid by the seller to the broker are no longer established by any state agency or private trade association (by federal law). Individual brokers set fees for their own offices.

☐ Try to negotiate the commission rate. Some brokers will; others will not. The law does not require them to.

☐ Understand the listing agreement before you sign it. It is a legal document that outlines the understanding between you and the broker about how your home will be listed for sale. It includes your name, the broker's name, the address of the property, the asking price and other details about the home, as well as the amount of time you are giving the broker to find a buyer (30, 60 or 90 days is usual).

☐ The most common type of listing offered by a broker is the exclusive right to sell. This means that you will pay full commission to the listing broker, regardless of which real estate office brings in the buyer—even if the seller brings in the buyer.

☐ Signing a contract and accepting a buyer's "earnest" money commit you to the sale—unless the buyer reneges and therefore forfeits the money, or some contingency to the sale negates the contract.

☐ If you've signed a contract and then refuse to follow through, you could face a lawsuit should the buyer want to initiate one. In any event you may still be responsible for the broker's commission.

Source: John R. Linton, vice president, legal affairs, National Association of Realtors.

Getting a higher price for an old house

An old house (built between 1920 and 1950) can be sold as easily as a new one. The right strategy and a few improvements can raise the selling price significantly.

☐ Invest in a complete cleaning, repainting, or wallpapering. Recarpet or have the rugs and carpets professionally cleaned.

☐ Get rid of cat and dog odors that you may be used to but potential buyers will notice.

☐ With the trend to smaller families and working couples, it may be desirable to convert and advertise a four-bedroom house as two bedrooms, library and den.

☐ The exterior of the house is crucial. It's the first thing a buyer sees. Clean and repair porch and remove clutter.

Repaint porch furniture.

☐ Landscaping makes a great difference and can sell (or unsell) a house. Get expert advice on improving it.

☐ Good real estate agents are vital to a quick sale. There are one or two top people in every agency who will work hard to show houses and even arrange financing. Multiple listings lets these super salespeople from different agencies work for the seller.

Tax-saving tactics for home sellers

A person who purchases a new primary residence but can't sell the old one can be in the expensive position of carrying two homes at once. To rent out the old home until it can be sold:

☐ Give the tenant of the old house a month-to-month lease requiring him to move when the house is sold. It's also possible to lease the house to a prospective purchaser before a sale agreement is finalized.

☐ Use the cash earned to offset the cost of carrying two houses.

☐ Deduct expenses related to the old home (such as insurance, utilities and repairs) up to the amount of rental income received. (Rents collected are sheltered from tax.)

☐ When the old home is sold, the sale proceeds will still qualify for tax-deferred treatment when applied against the cost of the new home (as long as the old home is sold within two years after the new home was bought).

☐ Rule: The homeowner's primary goal must always be to sell the old home, rather than rent it.

Source: Stephen Bolaris, 81 TC No. 52.

Selling an expensive house

Improvements that do the most to increase the resale value of houses in high price ranges (ranked in order):

☐ Separate family room.

☐ Fireplace.

☐ Separate dining room.

☐ Linen storage closet.

☐ Garbage disposal system.

☐ Wall-to-wall carpeting.

☐ Smoke and fire detector.

☐ Two-bowl vanity in bathroom.

☐ Double-glass windows.

☐ Hood (with fan) over range.

☐ Bathroom dressing area.

☐ Patio.

☐ Heavy-duty locks.

☐ Central air conditioning.

☐ Bathroom exhaust fan.

☐ Den/guest room.

Source: *Professional Builder* magazine, New York.

Refinancing a mortgage

Rule of thumb: If the difference between the old rate on a 30-year fixed mortgage and the current rate is three percentage points, it usually pays to refinance.

But there can be some big costs associated with refinancing:

☐ Prepayment penalties (for paying off the old mortgage before it's due) can cost up to 3% to 5% of the outstanding balance on the loan. In some states, the penalty may be based on time, say, six months. (FHA and VA mortgages don't have penalties. Some states have laws that restrict or ban penalties.)

☐ Legal fees. Another closing will inevitably mean that you'll have to pay additional legal fees.

☐ Title insurance. This will require a new search to determine whether there are liens against the property or title problems. Even if you use the same lender, there will be new title insurance and the burden of paying for a new search.

☐ Credit check. Whatever bank you use, even your original one, will want an up-to-the-minute review of your credit rating.

☐ Points. All banks charge an origination fee of one to three percentage points (and sometimes more) of the face amount of the mortgage. This fee is tax deductible as interest. But to get the deduction, you must pay the fee up front rather than simply tack it on to the mortgage. If you don't pay up front, the IRS will insist that the deduction be spread over the life of the mortgage.

☐ Appraisal fees.

❏ Inspections.

❏ Mortgage recording tax. This varies from state to state.

❏ Tax consequences can be huge. Payback question: How soon will the savings in monthly mortgage payments equal the additional costs of refinancing?

❏ Guidelines: If the drop in interest rates equals the points you have to pay the bank, refinancing will pay off in about a year. During the second year, and sometimes a third, the other costs will be recovered. Then the savings will be gravy.

❏ It generally doesn't pay to refinance if you'll be moving within a year or if your mortgage is nearly paid off.

❏ If you must pay a prepayment penalty, it will take longer to recoup. But even then, refinancing usually shows a saving in five years or less.

Source: PHH Group, Inc., which for 30 years has been counseling business on employee relocation, Hunt Valley, MD.

Mortgage refinancing trap

❏ "Points," or finance charges that are paid to obtain a mortgage loan, are generally tax deductible in the year in which they are paid—provided the mortgage is taken out for the "purchase or improvement" of a taxpayer's principal residence.

❏ Trap: The IRS has now ruled, however, that points paid in order to *refinance* a mortgage loan are *not* currently deductible, because the new mortgage is *not* used for purchase of a residence, but for repayment of an existing debt. As a result, the usual rule on prepaid interest applies—the points must be amortized and deducted at an even rate over the entire period of the loan.

❏ Example: Jones pays $3,000 in points to refinance a $100,000 mortgage over 20 years. He cannot deduct the $3,000 this year. Jones can deduct only $150 a year over the 20-year period.

New rules on mortgage interest deductions

Under the 1986 Tax Reform Act, you could deduct the interest on mortgage debt up to the cost of the house and improvements, plus any additional amounts borrowed for medical or educational expenses up to the current market value of the house. *Note:* Additional amounts might be deducted if the mortgage was taken out on or before August 16, 1986.

New law: You can deduct the interest on up to $1 million of *acquisition debt,* used to purchase, construct, or improve the residence, *plus* an additional $100,000 of *home-equity debt,* used for any purpose whatsoever.

Important saving: Interest on mortgages taken out before October 14, 1987, is *fully deductible without regard to the dollar limits.* The amount of the old mortgage must be subtracted from the amount of new *acquisition debt* still available but does not affect home-equity debt.

Getting personal tax benefits from depreciated business property

A taxpayer who owns property (a building or medical equipment, for instance) that is used for a business but which has used up most or all of its depreciation, can arrange, with expert advice, to get personal tax benefits by arranging a gift-leaseback with lower-income family members.

☐ The business owner makes a gift of the property to a family member and immediately leases it back.

☐ The rental payments are treated as expenses to the business.

☐ The rental payments are income to the lower-income family members who now own the building.

☐ The donor must not retain the same control over the physical property that he had before the gift-leaseback arrangement.

☐ The lease must be in writing and the leaseback rental must be reasonable.

☐ The donor may not continue to own

substantial equity in the property after the gift-leaseback arrangement.

☐ Expert tax and law advice is essential in setting up this tax-saving arrangement. If the gift-leaseback is successfully challenged by the IRS, the business owner will be denied the rental deduction and the person or persons who received the rental payments may be required to pay income tax on those distributions.

Winning with large loss real estate tax shelters

The major impact the Tax Reform Act of 1986 has had on real estate investing is the restriction placed on the use of passive-activity losses and passive-activity income.*

Losses from passive activities, such as most rental-property investments and limited partnerships are now deductible only if taken against income from other passive activities. (Unused losses can be carried forward, however, to offset future income in the activity or partnership.) Losses cannot be used as deductions against ordinary income—wages or portfolio income (interest and dividends).

These changes have made for some interesting opportunities.

Opportunities

☐ Real estate losses not taken in one year as a result of restrictions on passive-activity income can be carried forward indefinitely.

☐ Benefit: Losses can be used to offset passive-activity income in future years.

☐ …or even taken against gains made on sale of the properties from which the losses originated.

☐ Find investments that generate passive-activity income to be sheltered by your passive-activity losses.

☐ Best bet: Real estate purchased for all cash or with very little debt that has a large annual cash flow.

☐ Look for properties (or partnerships buying properties) with established occupancy levels and attractive locations to guarantee adequate rental income after operating expenses. A reasonable rate of return: 7%-8%.

☐ Some investors in rental real estate will be able to deduct up to $25,000 in losses each year. Such an investor must have an adjusted gross income o below $100,000 (because of the phaseout between $100,000 and $150,000)…must "actively participate" in the property's management…and must have more than a 10% direct interest in the investment.

*Passive activity is any business or trade in which the investor does not materially participate. The investment could take the form of a sole proprietorship, a limited or general partnership, or an S operation.

Source: Robert A. Stanger, chairman, Robert A Stanger & Co., publisher of *The Stanger Report: A Guide to Partnership Investing,* 1129 Broad St., Shrewsbury, NJ 07701.

Traps in real estate tax shelters

The key to a valid tax shelter is economic substance, the shelter's value as an investment. If you don't understand how the deal works, you can't judge its investment merit.

Test the assumptions:

☐ If the cash flow projections are based on an apartment house being rented 100% of the time, watch out. How likely is this to happen? A 95% occupancy rate in a low-vacancy area is optimistic. That leaves a 5% difference between the assumption and reality. That 5% comes off the projected cash flow, diminishing the return on your investment.

☐ Rental income projections may also be inflated. To find out a reasonable rent projection for a given area, check with real estate brokers.

Check management fees:

☐ In addition to fees for continuing to manage the property, does the shelter management company get fees for selling the project to the group and for selling the property at the end?

☐ Does the shelter management get a piece of the profit on final sale?

☐ Are the managing partners getting

so big a share of the profit on sale? Has too large a fee been built into the selling price?

☐ Are the fees reasonable? Continuing management fees should not be more than 5% to 6% of the gross rents.

☐ Does the total amount that the managers get from the project seem "fair"? This is something you must decide for yourself—at what point does the managers' return affect your opinion of the whole deal?

☐ Do the managers get most of their fees up front? Better: Managers ride along with the investors and get their fees as they go along. That gives them a continuing stake in the property.

Source: Herbert C. Speiser, partner, Deloitte & Touche, New York.

What to investigate in a real estate investment

☐ Find out who the high-paying tenants are. One may be the building owner, and the others may be affiliated with the seller. Or the owner may have offered the tenants a free month's rent or a delayed increase to sign a lease at the higher rates. It may be hard to raise rents any higher.

☐ Low operating expenses. Sellers may be operating the building themselves to avoid a management fee. If buyers cannot take care of the building personally, this fee must be added to real operating expenses.

☐ Reasonable property tax. If the building has not been assessed for several years, the buyer may have a substantial tax bite on the next reassessment.

☐ Assessments: Ask the local assessment office for the tax card or listing sheet. It will show the building's assessment and when it was assessed. If it was assessed a year and a half ago and there has been no significant addition to the building, reassessment may not hurt the buyer. But if it has not been assessed for eight years, there could be a significant tax boost.

☐ Check the owner's property description against the one listed on the card. If the owner says that 20,000 square feet are being sold, but the tax card says 15,000 square feet, there has been some addition to the structure that has not been recorded and, therefore, has not been assessed. Or there may be an assessment error

that, when corrected, will raise costs.

☐ Low insurance premiums. Is coverage in line with the structure's current value? What does the policy cover? Ask to see the policy. If coverage is insufficient, how much more will proper coverage cost?

☐ Energy efficient. Verify the owner's claim with the local utility to determine actual energy costs. Also: Check with regulatory commissions to see whether utility companies are scheduled to increase their tariffs.

Source: Thomas L. O'Dea, O'Dea & Co., Inc., investment real estate consultants, Winston-Salem, NC, and senior editor *Rental House and Condo Investor.*

Before investing in condos or co-ops

Despite the recent drop in housing starts, many investors are turning again to condominium and cooperative apartment houses, especially in big cities. Smart investors today can profit from errors made in the last decade. Now they know that:

☐ It's best to avoid investing in the development of condos or co-ops that are surrounded by rental apartments. Best investment: Co-ops and condos that are next to single-family housing.

☐ People who buy individual apartment units like buildings where apartments cost less than comparable single-family housing nearby. Rule of thumb: Apartments should sell for 25% less than the lowest-priced houses in the area.

☐ Apartment buyers also avoid units in outlying areas. For psychological reasons, people don't mind commuting 20 to 30 miles to work from a suburban house, but many dislike an apartment in a remote area.

☐ It's easier to overbuild the apartment market than standard housing because the cost per unit is cheaper for apartments. When there's a housing glut, a co-op or condo can have high vacancy rates for many months or even years.

☐ Factors that make houses cheaper will almost always make apartments difficult to sell. Examples: Lower interest rates. Oversupply. Changes in zoning or building codes that favor house construction.

Source: Vincent Mooney, real estate consultant on condominium building and conversion and president of Condominium Home Realtors, Tulsa, OK, and author of *Condoeconomics.*

Investing in a single-family house

☐ Make sure there is an active rental market for homes in the area you choose. Know the odds of finding a good tenant, keeping the tenant and getting the price you need on rent.

☐ Leverage for a single-family home is more expensive than financing for other real estate investments. Home mortgages may be several percentage points higher than financing for commercial properties.

☐ Single-family homes bought as rental properties are usually either 100% rented or 100% vacant. That means significant risk and a cash drain if the house goes empty for months.

☐ Don't discount mortgage payments because they are tax deductible. Tax benefits should always be looked at as incidental to the investment. The investment should make economic sense without tax benefits.

Investing in multi-family buildings or condos

☐ Multi-family apartment houses are less risky than single-family homes if the location is satisfactory. If one of four apartments is vacant, the property is still 75% leased.

☐ This type of property is management intensive. Floors must be swept and lightbulbs changed. There are emergency repairs. Either the owner must be handy and have free time, or he should hire a professional manager—which means less profit.

☐ Condos are less management intensive than straight rentals, since the condo association cares for day-to-day maintenance.

☐ Resort condos are more risky than condos in a well-populated area within a driving radius of your own home. If the property can't be rented in season, the investor is in serious trouble. Another minus: Resort properties typically are remote, far from the investor's area, so he can't inspect or manage them. He must depend on the condo operator.

Investing in a shopping center

☐ Shopping centers are for wealthy investors.

☐ They can be an easy real estate operation. Outside contractors are hired for management duties, and tenants have responsibility for most of the maintenance.

☐ For an existing property with all space leased on a three- to five-year basis, the key question is: How are the tenants doing? If well, they will renew their leases and rents will go up. The increase in rent increases the property's income and value.

☐ Ask what existing leases are going for and what new leases can go for in that area.

☐ Quantify the difference. That is what you can capture when the current leases expire.

The smart way to buy a condominium

Experience in buying and selling several single-family homes doesn't alert you to all the things to look for in good condo deal. Basic guidelines:

☐ Don't buy on impulse.

☐ Make sure your lawyer reads the covenant of condominium (also called the master deed or declaration of condominium).

☐ Be aware that clauses in a covenant are non-negotiable: All participants must have the same wording.

If you spot any of these traps, consider walking away from the whole deal:

☐ Resale restrictions. The condo association may have a 30-, 60-, or 90-day right of first refusal. That delay could cost you a sale. Be advised that FHA, VA and other government-insured mortgages are not available when there are certain resale restrictions. Your resale market could be cut significantly.

☐ Use restrictions. Does the covenant permit owners to rent their units? If you are buying the condo as an investment you must be able to rent. But, if you are planning to live in a unit, you may want this restriction. Other use restrictions may concern children, pets, window decorations, even the type of mailbox you can put up.

☐ Sweetheart deals. The most common one is when the developer owns the common areas and leases them back to the association. Such leases are usually long term and include escalator clauses and pass-alongs that could cause big jumps in your monthly association fees. In other cases, the developer does not own the common areas, but has a long-term contract to manage them.

The best deal for the buyer is when the condo association owns all the common areas. All management agreements with the condo association should strictly control costs and contain termination provisions.

Potential problems that won't show up in the covenant:

☐ Subsidized fees. Developers of newly-built condos often manage common areas for a fee until most of the new units are sold. To speed sales, the developer may keep the management fee below cost. Then, when the condo association assumes management, the owners' monthly costs soar. Compare fees charged by similar condo associations in the same area.

☐ Construction problems. Before you buy, have an engineer inspect the entire property, if feasible, not just your unit. If the condo association has to make repairs, you will be assessed for the cost.

If you are buying a unit in a converted building, ask the condo salesperson for the engineer's report. Most converted buildings need one to obtain financing.

☐ Other tips: The best times to buy are when prices are lowest during the pre-construction sale of new units, or early in the conversion of a building.

☐ But if you buy too soon, you could end up as one of the few owners. As long as units remain unsold, your investment will not appreciate. Check the price and demand for similar units in the area.

Source: Thomas L. O'Dea, O'Dea and Co., Inc., Winston-Salem, NC.

How to avoid condominium (and co-op) unhappiness

Investment differences between apartments and houses are far greater than most individual buyers realize.

What the experts know:

☐ Apartments are more volatile in price than houses are. Apartments can easily be overbuilt, and that's when it's best to buy them.

☐ Anything that makes houses easier to buy hurts apartment sales. Examples: Lower interest rates, lower inflation, an oversupply of houses and changes in building codes or in zoning laws that make houses less expensive to build.

☐ For the best chance at resale, buy an apartment priced 25% lower than the starting prices on houses in the same area. Apartments that cost the same or more than the average one-family house will appeal only to prospects who prefer an apartment over a house. These people are only 30% of all condominium/co-op buyers.

☐ Ideally, neighboring houses should cost an average of twice what an apartment costs. It's a matter of psychology. Apartment buyers are often looking for an inexpensive way to live in an expensive neighborhood.

☐ Prices of condos and co-ops are very sensitive to rental vacancies. They're difficult to sell when rental units are cheap. Advice: Buy when vacancy rates are high, sell when they're low. Ironically, most investors do just the opposite because they want to buy an apartment only when it's hard for them to find one to rent.

☐ Don't buy an apartment in an area where there are many rental apartments. Buy in neighborhoods of single-family houses.

☐ Try to get an assumable loan. If you're forced to sell in a down market, the only way you may be able to attract buyers is by letting them take over the payments on your loan.

Source: Vince Mooney, real estate consultant and president of Condominium Home Realtors, Tulsa, and author of *Condoeconomics*.

When you rent out your vacation house or resort apartment

☐ Use a comprehensive lease. The Blumberg form available at most stationery stores is a fine starting point.

☐ Check the standard lease and take out all sections that are not acceptable to you.

☐ Have the lease witnessed or notarized, preferably by a lawyer or real estate agent.

☐ Add to the lease a list of all household property and the condition of each.

☐ Tell the renter about any recurrent problems, such as summer floods, insect or rodent infestations or anything else that affects the habitability of the house or apartment. Failure to do so is grounds for the renter to break the lease and get his money back.

☐ Ask for business and personal references and check them out thoroughly. Don't rely only on the appearance of the renters.

☐ Make clear, in writing, if the renter is to be responsible for care and watering of plants and lawn, for raking the beach, or for any other regular maintenance.

☐ Make sure your insurance will cover any burglary, accident, or damage to the house and grounds while renters occupy it.

How to buy property with little...or no money down

As hard as it is to believe, it's not only possible to buy property with no money down, it's not even that hard to do—provided you have the right fundamental information.

Note: No money down means the seller receives no down payment. It means the down payment doesn't come from your pocket.

Success strategies

☐ Paying the real estate agent. If a seller uses a real estate agent on the sale, he's obligated to pay the agent's commission. Strategy: You, the buyer, pay the commission, but not up front. You approach the agent and offer a deal. Instead of immediate payment, suggest that the agent lend you part of the commission. In return, you offer a personal note guaranteeing to pay the money at some future date, with interest. If you make it clear that the sale depends on such an arrangement, the agent will probably go along with the plan. If he balks, be flexible. Negotiate a small monthly amount, perhaps with a balloon payment at the end. You then subtract the agent's commission from the expected down payment.

☐ Assuming the seller's debts. Let's say, as so often happens, that the seller is under financial pressure. Strategy: With the seller's cooperation, contact all his creditors and explain that you, not the seller, are going to make good on the outstanding debts. In some cases, the relieved creditors will either extend the due dates, or, if you can come up with some cash, they'll likely agree to a discount. Deduct the face amount of the debts you'll be assuming, pocketing any discounts, from the down payment.

☐ Prepaid rent. Sometimes you, the buyer, are in no rush to move in and the seller would like more time to find a new place to live—but you'd both like to close as soon as possible. Strategy: Offer to let the seller remain in the house or apartment, setting a fixed date for vacating. Then, instead of the seller paying the buyer a monthly rent, you subtract from the down payment the full amount of the rent for the entire time the seller will be living there.

☐ Satisfying the seller's needs. During conversations with the seller, you learn that he must buy some appliances and furniture for a home he's moving into. Strategy: Offer to buy those things—using credit cards or store credit to delay payment—and deduct the lump sum from the down payment.

Source: Robert G. Allen, a real estate insider and author of the bestseller *Nothing Down*. He's also publisher of the monthly newsletter *The Real Estate Advisor*, Provo, UT.

How to make your money work

☐ Earn up to 21% risk-free by paying off charge-card balances early. You may not realize that carrying a $500 balance on a bank card can cost as much as $105 per year.

☐ Make contributions to your IRA or Keogh Plan as early in the year as possible.

☐ Borrow money from your corporate profit-sharing or pension plan rather than from a bank. You may still claim the interest expense as a deduction.

☐ Shift income to your children with trusts or custodial accounts. The money will be taxed at their low rate.

☐ Increase your insurance deductibles.

☐ Don't rely on your accountant to find the best possible tax deductions for you. Invest in a good self-help manual.

☐ Prepay your mortgage. An extra $100 a month will dramatically shorten your term and total interest expenses.

Source: Dr. Paul A. Randle, professor of finance, Utah State University, writing in *Physicians Management*, New York.

Quick and easy ways to save money

☐ Comparison shop by phone, not by car.

☐ Make your own gift wrap and greeting cards.

☐ Use heavy-duty brown bags from the supermarket for garbage.

☐ Make your own liquid dishwashing soap out of leftover soap slivers (put them in a jar, cover with water and stir occasionally).

☐ Use toll-free numbers (call the toll-free information operator at 800-555-1212).

☐ Rent a room in your home to a local college student.

Source: *Parents* magazine, New York.

Stretching due dates on bills

Due dates on bills can be stretched—but not far—without risk. Typical grace periods: Telephone companies, eight days. Gas and electric utilities, 10 days. Banks and finance companies, 10 days. Even after a late charge is imposed on an unpaid bill your credit rating should be safe for 30 days.

Source: Terry Blaney, president of Consumer Credit Counseling Service of Houston and the Gulf Coast Area.

Maximum privacy and your financial affairs

There are a number of incentives for keeping your financial affairs secret besides personal whim: From dodging a hostile ex-spouse or business partner to protecting your assets from liability suits to make yourself "judgment proof."

Whatever the reason, with money and footwork, there are many ways to insure your financial privacy to the maximum:

☐ Set up a nominee corporation to rent a safe-deposit box. It doesn't help to rent a box in your own name; for less than $100, a company can make a search of every bank in the country to see if you are a safe-deposit box customer. The IRS, if it's looking for assets of yours, will also perform a search. (This is especially easy for the IRS if you pay for one with a personal check…it simply goes through your cancelled checks.)

To conceal the existence of a safe-deposit box:

☐ Ask your lawyer to set up a nominee corporation—a corporation that has no other function but to stand in your place for the purposes you designate, such as to rent a safe-deposit box.

☐ Rent a box in the name of the corporation and pay for it in cash. Your name and signature will be on the bank signature card, but the corporation, not you, will be listed as the box's owner on the bank's records. Because you paid cash, there will be nothing in your records to connect the box with you.

☐ Name another person as signatory in addition to yourself. Then, if something happens to you, that person will be able to get into the box.

☐ Open a post office box to receive sensitive mail. To avoid giving your own name or current address: Open the post office box in the name of the nominee corporation. Give the address of the lawyer who set up the corporation. This creates a barrier between you and the box. You're not the owner on record of the box, and the post office does not have your current address. Of course, your lawyer has your name and address, but unless you, the lawyer or both are breaking the law, he will not disclose either your name or your address—that's information protected by attorney-client privilege.

☐ Put all of your assets into a revocable living trust. This is a trust that you set up during your lifetime, and it provides a high level of privacy. The assets transferred to the trust are no longer in your name, but you retain control of them because the trust is revocable. When you die, the trust property is kept out of the probate court and is immediately transferred to the trust beneficiaries.

How to find money you didn't know you had

Few people take full advantage of the capital at their disposal. There are a myriad of simple ways to optimize your personal financial resources:

☐ Convert passbook savings accounts, savings bonds, etc. into better investments. American still have $300 billion sitting in low-interest passbook savings accounts when they could be so easily transferred to CDs at nearly double the yield! Review your portfolio now, particularly bonds that have recently registered nice gains. Should you still be owning what you do? People often hold investments long after they've forgotten why they originally made them.

☐ Borrow on life insurance (such low interest rates aren't being offered today). Many folks who bought life insurance back in the 1960s and 1970s (term insurance is more prevalent today) could borrow back the money at 3% to 6% and reinvest it in insured CDs at a higher rate.

☐ Pay real estate taxes directly instead of through the bank. Most banks withhold an amount on monthly mortgage payments for paying the homeowner's real estate taxes. Yet, in most towns, real estate tax bills are sent annually. The bank is earning interest on your money. Caution: You must make the payments on time. Banks can call in your mortgage if the taxes are delinquent, and they'd just love to do it if you are fortunate enough

to have a low-interest mortgage.

☐ Prepay mortgage principal. Making a monthly $25 prepayment of principal from day one on a $75,000, 30-year, 13% mortgage would save $59,372, and the mortgage would be paid off in 23 years and four months. (Most mortgages allow prepayment.)

☐ Conduct a garage sale. Turn unwanted items into cash. (Sotheby's or another auction house will appraise a possible collectible free.)

If you are self-employed:

☐ Keep good records of travel and entertainment expenses and of the business use of cars, computers and other property used for both business and personal purposes. Taxpayers who can't back up their deductions with good records will lose the deductions and may be charged negligence penalties.

☐ Reward yourself first. Plan for your future by putting money into your tax-deferred retirement plan now. Too many entrepreneurs wait until they're successful before taking money out of the business and risk receiving nothing.

☐ Park company cash in the highest yielding CDs. It's easy to compare CDs. Look at the table called Highest Money-Market Yields, now published in 23 major newspapers. The highest-yielding CDs in the country are paying 2% to 3% above the average yield. That translates into $200 to $300 a year with a $10,000 CD.

Source: William E. Donoghue, publisher of several investment newsletters, including *Donoghue's Moneyletter*, Holliston, MA.

Smart borrowing

Even many super-successful business people find themselves short of cash at times, whether in paying a child's college tuition or in taking advantage of an irresistible investment.

Once you have decided on a sound reason and a sound plan for borrowing, you naturally want to find the best possible interest rate. There are a variety of ways to avoid the high unsecured loan rates being offered at most banks and thrifts across the country:

☐ Insurance policy loan: Particularly attractive if you have an old policy that provides for low interest rate loans. It is especially good if the policy has been in effect for more than seven years. Reason: There is a legal provision that policyholders must have paid four out of the first seven payments to get a tax-deductible loan. If the policy has been in effect for seven years, there is no question about tax deductibility. Safety valve: Many people fear borrowing on their life insurance policies because this reduces the coverage in case of death. Solution: You can use the dividends on the policy to buy additional term insurance to keep the insurance level at face value. That permits you to borrow and to maintain the death value.

☐ Qualified savings plan: Many corporate savings plans, including 401(k) plans, permit employees to borrow the savings that they (and their employer) have put into the plan. Typically, the borrowing rate on savings plans is lower than bank rates, although each company has its own rules. Ask your personnel office about your company's policies. Caution: Do not confuse this with IRAs or Keoghs. You cannot borrow against them. And although some firms permit employees to borrow against their pension funds, it isn't advisable.

☐ Brokerage house loan: The current big thing in the brokerage houses is cash management accounts (in their various guises)—and home equity accounts. Cash management accounts let you borrow against stocks and bonds. Home equity accounts include the value of your home as collateral against loans. Brokerage houses have the resources to appraise your home, and they permit you to borrow at a fairly good rate—the broker loan rate. Problem: Margin loans against stock can be called if the stock market goes down sharply and the collateral loses value.

☐ Second mortgage: Exercise extreme caution when using this technique. You are giving someone a lien on your home. You might lose your job, or your business might falter. It is a dangerous way to get into a bind—and you could end up losing your home.

Source: Thomas Lynch, senior vice president, Ayco/American Express, a financial consulting group that advises corporate personnel about financial and tax matters.

The best places to borrow money

There are now more ways to borrow money than ever before. By carefully shopping around, you may be able to save big dollars while establishing valuable new credit lines.

☐ Interest-free loans from the company have been a favored perk for key executives for years. The bookkeeping is now more complicated, but both the company and the executive may be left in the same position they were in before the new tax laws went into effect, owing little or no tax as a result of the loan.

☐ Preferred financing terms are often provided by banks to the employees of major commercial accounts. Typical benefit: Home mortgages at a half point to a full point lower than the standard mortgage rate.

☐ Company pension plans frequently contain provisions that allow employees to borrow against their plan accounts. Many plans allow loans to be made at a reasonable interest rate in order to help finance the purchase of a new primary residence or to meet specified emergencies. Employees can typically borrow as much as half the value of their non-forfeitable retirement benefits, up to a maximum of $50,000.

☐ Credit unions are usually a cheap source of funds for their members. Because they have less overhead than banks and are looking to break even rather than to make a profit, they lend at rates lower than commercial rates. Typical: Personal loans of up to half your salary. Many credit unions also have insurance programs.

☐ Home equity loans. When the original mortgage on a house has been largely paid off, and the house has gone up in value, a borrower may be able to get a loan at about two points over the prime rate. Caution: There are drawbacks to using your house as collateral. First, you're establishing a lien against your home. Second, there are charges involved—often a one-time fee of 2% on the credit line, plus an annual maintenance fee of $25 to $100, and perhaps a mortgage recording tax.

☐ Bank loans. It's important to shop around for the best terms. Remember that as a borrower you don't have to worry about the bank's solvency. You can safely take advantage of unusual terms offered by a bank that's desperate for business.

☐ Credit and debit cards may be the most expensive form of financing (typically charging interests rate of 18% to 20%), but they also offer the most convenient source of cash around. Danger: Letting charges pile up. Rule of thumb: Monthly loan payments, exclusive of the home mortgage, should total no more than 10% to 15% of net income.

☐ Merchant financing may represent a better deal than the average bank loan. Typical case: An auto purchase. While a local bank may offer auto loans at 12% to 13%, many auto dealers, helped out by funds from the major manufacturers, can extend credit at 8% to 9%.

Source: David S. Rhine, partner, BDO Seidman, New York, and Israel A. Press, partner and director of personal financial management, Touche Ross Financial Services Center, New York.

How to beat the banks before they beat you

Since deregulation, banks vary widely in their services and in the costs of those services. In order to turn the best profit, banks depend on the fact that customers don't know what to ask for. How you can get the most for your banking dollar:

☐ Deal with the smallest bank you can find. After deregulation, most large banks decided to get rid of smaller depositors. They find it cheaper to serve one corporate account than 10 individual accounts. Smaller banks, on the other hand, are more responsive to individual depositors because they need this business.

Ask about checking accounts:

☐ What is the minimum-balance requirement? How does the bank calculate it? Watch out for a minimum-balance calculation that uses the lowest balance for the month. A figure based on the average daily balance is best.

☐ Does the balance on other accounts count toward the checking-account minimum balance?

☐ What is the clearing policy for deposits? This is especially important if you have a NOW account.

☐ What is the overdraft charge? Often it is outrageous. In parts of the Midwest, for example, most banks charge $20.

☐ Don't buy loan insurance from the bank. Credit life or disability insurance is often routinely included on loan forms and added to the cost of your loan. Don't sign any such policy when you take out a loan. This insurance benefits the bank—not you. It covers the bank for the balance of your loan should you die or become disabled. You can get more coverage from an insurance agent for half (or even less) of what the bank charges.

☐ Avoid installment loans. These loans are front-end loaded: Even though your balance is declining, you're still paying interest on the original balance throughout the term of the loan. Ask for a single-payment note with simple interest and monthly payments. If you do have an installment loan, don't pay it off early—this actually adds to its real cost.

☐ Pay attention to interest computations. Most people compare rates and assume higher is better. Look for interest figured on a day-of-deposit-to-day-of-withdrawal basis, compounded daily.

☐ Avoid cash machines. The farther bankers can keep you from their tellers and loan officers, the more money they'll make and the less responsive they'll be to your needs. Bankers like machines because people can't argue with them.

☐ Negotiate interest rates. This sounds simple, but it means combating banks' tendencies to lump loans in categories—commercial, mortgage, retail, etc. For example, banks offer a long-time depositor the same interest rate on a car loan as they do a complete newcomer. But often all it takes to get a better rate is to say, "I think my car loan should be 2% lower. I've been banking here for 15 years and I have $10,000 in my savings account."

☐ Forget FDIC security. Given the option of a higher interest rate investment with a secure major corporation that probably has more reserves than the FDIC, many people will still automatically opt for the bank investment because of FDIC insurance. But the FDIC has only $16 billion in reserves. That's a miniscule portion of the money it's insuring. Now that more and more banks are closing every year, the FDIC may soon find itself in big trouble.

☐ Ignore the banks amortization schedule for mortgages. When you make your monthly payment, especially in the early part of your mortgage, very little goes toward the principal. However, if you choose to pay a small amount extra every month, this will go toward the principal and save you an enormous amount of money.

☐ Don't put all your money in one certificate of deposit. Now that you can deposit as little as $1,000 for the money-market rate, split your deposits so that you get the same interest rate and more liquidity. If you put your money into a $10,000 or $20,000 CD and then find you need to take out $1,000 or $2,000, you will have to pay a horrendous penalty. Instead buy 10 or 20 $1,000 CDs.

Source: Edward F. Mrkvicka, Jr., a former bank president and author of *The Bank Book: How To Revoke Your Bank's License To Steal*, HarperCollins, New York.

Bank ad deception

The high-yield certificates of deposit advertised by many banks are often not what the ads say they are. Trap: The annual yield is meaningless when you buy a three-month CD. And— "effective annual yield" doesn't mean compounded annual yield. Many advertised CDs are so-called simple interest securities that aren't compounded. Advice: Don't buy CDs from a bank. Buy shares in money market mutual funds. They shop for the best CDs.

Source: William E. Donoghue, publisher, *Donoghue's Moneyletter*, Box 6640, Holliston, MA 01746.

Prime rate secret

Banks calculate their lending rate in arbitrary ways that differ from institution to institution. Your rate may be based on the prime rate set by large money center banks, but it will be calculated and applied by the bank's own formula, which will almost always be higher. Self-protection: Before taking out any loan, read and be sure you understand the fine print that spells out the interest rate adjustment formula. Then make comparisons from bank to bank.

Source: Edward F. Mrkvicka, Jr., president of Reliance Enterprises, a financial consulting company, Box 413, Marengo, IL 60152 and editor of *Money Insider*, a monthly newsletter.

Offshore banking

An offshore bank is any bank that operates outside the jurisdiction of US regulators. Major Swiss banks in Switzerland or elsewhere around the world are offshore banks. So are the Bank of Montreal in Canada, Barclay's Bank in London and the vast world of well-capitalized foreign banks. Those banks may also have branches in the US where they follow US regulations in every way—here. But overseas and in their own countries, they follow the regulations of their host country. And— at times they pay rates to depositors that are better than those obtainable in the US.

Offshore banks are not illegal. There are even facilities of major US banks within the US called International Banking Facilities (IBFs) that are restricted to taking deposits only from overseas customers and making overseas loans. They may not deal with domestic customers. Many major US banks have IBFs. It is really an accounting system in which foreign accounts stay segregated.

☐ Offshore banks offer more privacy to depositors. The privacy feature is useful for law-abiding citizens who would like to keep their assets and records away from a snooping ex-spouse, a business colleague or some other prying investigator.

☐ Only if the money deposited in an offshore bank is *undeclared income* is there any criminal activity. For the average person who has reported his income and already paid his taxes, it is not illegal to put that money in an offshore bank either for secrecy reasons or to get a higher return than is obtainable in the US.

☐ Don't do business with a private offshore bank that's trying to lure you with tax avoidance schemes. Check out the institutions in *Polk's Directory of International Banks* (found in most libraries). Each bank listed must submit its financial statement and the names of its officers and explain its operating procedures.

☐ Report any interest that accrues on an overseas account. Offshore banks report your interest earnings directly to you only. They do not report them to the IRS. It is your responsibility to report that income on your tax return. Although it is tempting not to report the interest, since it would be difficult for US authorities to find small bits of interest earnings overseas, it is illegal.

☐ Mailing your deposits overseas and writing checks on overseas accounts are not dissimilar to using a money-market account. When you want to make a withdrawal, just write a check to a local domestic bank on your foreign account. Deposits work similarly. The transfer of funds overseas between banks is very rapid.

☐ Hold an offshore account in dollars unless you are a very sophisticated currency trader. You need professional intelligence in the currency markets to try to guess which currencies will appreciate.

Source: J. F. Straw, publisher and editor of *Off Shore Banking News*, Dalton, GA.

Safe-deposit boxes

Guarantee that you will be able to locate all important documents quickly by renting a bank safe-deposit box. Fees are reasonable. Only two keys are made to fit the box, and you keep both of them. The box cannot be opened without your permission unless you die or you don't pay your rental fee for a whole year. In a nonpayment situation, you will receive a certified or registered letter to give you one last chance to pay up. If you don't, the contents of the box will be removed in the presence of a bank official, inventoried, verified, and then stored in a safe place until you eventually claim them.

Keep in your safe-deposit box:

☐ Birth, marriage, and death certificates.

☐ Divorce or separation agreements.

☐ Adoption or custody papers.

☐ Title papers to real estate, car, etc.

☐ Mortgage papers.

☐ Contracts and legal agreements.

☐ Stock certificates.

☐ Military discharge papers.

☐ Copies of credit cards.

☐ Copies of passport (or the original and keep copies at home).

☐ Photographs of the inside and outside of a home to support insurance claims.

Do not put in a safe-deposit box:

☐ Your will. Keep it at your attorney's office, with only a copy in the safe-deposit box. Reason: Safe-deposit boxes are sealed at death until the IRS sees what's inside. This could prevent relatives from getting into the box right away to see if a will even exists.

☐ Money or other valuables on which income tax has not been paid. This is illegal and your heirs might be taxed on

the money at your death anyway.

Source: Safe Deposit Department, Marine Midland Bank, NA, New York.

Choosing between private and bank deposit boxes

You can rent a safe-deposit box at either a bank or a private corporation that specializes in safety boxes. Weigh the advantages of both types before making a final decision. What to look for:

☐ Business hours: Private safe-deposit corporations have a much longer business day than banks. Some are open 365 days a year. You also can make an appointment to get into your box after business hours.

☐ Insurance: Some private corporations automatically insure the contents of your box for $10,000, with more insurance available at nominal prices. Banks provide a minimum amount of insurance, but the customer is free to insure the box with his own insurance company.

☐ Cost: Private safe-deposit boxes are generally more expensive than those at banks.

☐ Confidentiality. Your access to a private safe-deposit box is a numbered code, not your bank account number (as with bank boxes). This insures the confidentiality of both your safe-deposit box and your bank account.

☐ Security rating: Private companies are often rated higher than banks by the Insurance Institute.

☐ Sealing: Bank safe-deposit boxes are automatically sealed at your death. To seal a private-company box, a court order, usually from the IRS, is necessary. And since in a private company, your box is not tagged with your bank account number, it is much harder to trace.

Source: Michael Butcher, general manager, Universal Safe Deposit Corp., New York.

Protecting your credit cards

☐ Don't be fooled by a "Good

Samaritan" phone call that your stolen or lost cards have been found. It may be from a thief seeking time to run up charges. Carry cards separately from your wallet. Leave infrequently used cards at home. Make photo copies of each card you own, and keep these at home and at the office with a list of the issuers' toll-free numbers.

Source: Peter Herrick, president of the Bank of New York.

❏ When you check your statements each month, be on the lookout for hotels and restaurants that throw away the ticket you sign, substitute another one with inflated tips or other charges, and then forge your name on the inflated ticket. Where it happens frequently: Las Vegas.

Source: John Kaiser, marketing director, Summa Four Co., Merrimack, NH, quoted in *Teleconnect*, 205 W. 19 St., New York 10011.

Withholding credit-card payments

You may be able to withhold payments on a credit card used to purchase goods or services that proved substandard. This is the result of a little-known provision of the Fair Credit Billing Act, which enables the credit card companies to reclaim disputed amounts from merchants after credit-card slips are signed.

You must meet four conditions to be entitled to withhold credit-card payments:

❏ The amount of the charge must be more than $50.

❏ The charge must be made within the customer's home state, or within 100 miles of the customer's home.

❏ The customer must first attempt to settle the dispute with the merchant directly.

❏ The customer must give the bank that issued the card written notice that the attempt to settle has failed.

When the bank receives your notice, it credits your account with the amount of the charge. It then charges this amount back to the bank that serves the merchant. That bank then charges the merchant.

Prevent credit-card rip-offs

Here's a simple trick: Pick a number and if possible—make sure that all your credit card charges end in that number. For example: Say you choose the number 8 and your dinner bill comes to $20.00. Instead of adding a $3.00 tip, add $3.08. When your bill comes at the end of the month, check to see if all the charges have 8 as the last digit. If they don't, compare them against your receipts and report discrepancies to the card issuer.

Beware of low credit-card rates

In many cases, bank cards with the lowest rates (11%-14%) can cost much more than cards with traditional 18%-21% charges. Reason: A growing number of banks begin tacking on interest charges the minute a transaction is posted to their books. This interest charge accrues until the charge amount and the interest are paid in full. Even if you pay your charges off as soon as you receive the bill each month, you'll still have to pay an interest charge. Solution: If you pay in full whenever you use a credit card, choose a bank that charges interest only on balances that are still outstanding following the payment due date on the bill.

Source: *Money*.

Deciding who should own the family home

From a tax-saving point of view, the decision as to who owns the family home depends on:

❏ State laws. Many state laws require that a personal residence belongs to a surviving spouse, either outright or as a life interest. Special rules also govern the management, control and disposition of community property in community property estates.

❏ Size of the estate involved.

❏ Provision for children.

❏ How much control over the property the actual purchaser or owner of the home feels is necessary.

Types of joint home ownership

❏ *Joint ownership with right of survivorship* (JTROS) means the home is owned by two or more persons and the entire property passes to the survivor(s) on the death of one of the owners. This type of ownership is common between married couples, but it can be used by any individuals—parent and child, brothers and sisters or any two or more people. A JTROS can be terminated unilaterally by selling the property, dividing it, exchanging it for other property or transferring one's interest to the other owner. Advantage: Property passes to the survivors without going through probate. Warning: Except in the case of husband and wife, there are gift tax consequences to consider in a JTROS. If one individual contributes the entire amount or an amount more than his or her proportionate ownership of the property, a gift is considered to have been made to the other owner(s).

□ *Joint tenancy by the entireties* (JTE) is similar to JTROS in that the property passes to one owner automatically at the death of the other. A JTE can be created only between spouses and is not recognized in all states. A JTE cannot be ended unilaterally. Both parties must consent or the JTE can be terminated when the marital relationship is terminated.

□ *Tenancy in common* means that title to the home is held by two or more persons, each of whom owns a fractional interest in the undivided property. Upon the death of one of the tenants in common, the fractional interest becomes part of the person's estate and is distributed according to the individual's will. This is a typical form of ownership for individuals who are not married and who want to have more control over their property than is possible with a JTROS.

□ *Shared equity* is a useful arrangement when one of the owners uses the home as a personal residence. Typically, the higher-tax-bracket individuals (say, parents) become co-owners of the home with a son or daughter. Usually, the co-owners share in the down payment and may also share in the mortgage. They also share in the proceeds if the home is sold. The individual(s) who live in the home pay rent for the portion of the house owned by the co-owner. Both the resident and non-resident are treated as homeowners for tax purposes and so can take income tax deductions for interest and property taxes paid. The non-residents are treated as owners of rental property for their proportionate share of the home. They, therefore, report the rent paid as income and can deduct expenses, such as depreciation, on their tax returns.

Source: *Family, The Best Tax Shelter and Tax Savings Opportunity of Them All*, the Deloitte & Touche *Book of Family Tax Planning*, Boardroom Books, New York.

Financing the sale of your home

It's often difficult for homeowners to sell without giving the buyer help with the financing. However, many sellers have been hurt by incautious secondary financing arrangements. When the buyer can't come up with the payments, the seller must go through costly foreclosure proceedings and may end up with nothing—the bank holding the first mortgage takes all proceeds from the forced sale.

To minimize the risk before agreeing to any secondary financing:

□ Think carefully about lowering your price rather than accepting secondary financing.

□ See a lawyer. Don't sign papers without first getting sound legal advice. No reputable broker will urge a seller to get involved in secondary financing unless the seller has relied on an attorney for advice.

□ Get a credit check on the prospective buyer. A strong, creditworthy buyer is the best protection an owner-financer can have. If you're working with a real estate broker, the broker will run the check for you. If not, you can tell a credit company and have the company run the check. Or, the bank holding the first mortgage might help.

□ Give a second mortgage only if the purchaser is putting at least 25% to 30% of his own money into the property. The more of his own equity the buyer has tied up in the deal, the less chance he'll walk away from it.

□ Avoid very short-term balloon mortgages.* The balance of the second mortgage should not be due for at least three to five years. If you give only a one-year balloon and interest rates are worse in a year, you'll have put the buyer—and yourself—in an impossible position. If he can't come up with the money or refinancing, you'll have to force a foreclosure.

☐ Have someone in the area watch the property to make sure the buyer is maintaining it properly. Rundown property can hurt you badly.

☐ Prepare to take steps should the buyer fall behind in his payments. Banks, for a service charge, will collect mortgage payments for you. Alternative: Sell the second mortgage. You'll take a loss, but you might be better off in the long run.

*The buyer makes small monthly payments for a limited time, then makes one large ("balloon") payment for the full amount due.

Source: Margot Robinson, G.R.I., C.R.S., John Garrison Real Estate, Stamford, CT.

Reducing taxable gains when you sell your house

If you sell your home and then do not use the proceeds to buy another one, you are taxed on any gain realized from the deal (unless you're over 55 and gain is less than $125,000—and you can only do this once). Gain, in general, is the difference between your cost basis and the selling price, less selling expenses.

It's important then to understand: (1) How your cost basis is computed, and (2) what selling expenses are deductible. It's essential to keep an accurate record of those items which will help to reduce your tax liability.

Cost basis includes:

☐ Price paid in cash or property and by mortgage obligation assumed or mortgage to which property is subject.

☐ Attorney's fees and expenses in connection with the purchase contract and its closing or settlement; also the cost of searching, defending, or perfecting title.

☐ Costs of appraisal, recording of deed and mortgage, survey.

☐ Title search and title insurance.

☐ Cost of getting cash for purchase (mortgage broker's fees, lender's origination fee, title search and/or title insurance legal fees for drafting bond and mortgage), but not "points."

☐ Architectural and engineering fees, plus termite inspection.

☐ Restoration of building or improvements prolonging its useful life or increasing its value which are in the nature of capital investment and long-term improvements. Example: Owner replaces the roof when house is sold.

☐ The cost of improvements outside the building(s), such as landscaping, grading, driveways, wells, kitchens, walks, patio.

☐ Real estate taxes of the seller assumed by the buyer as part of the purchase price.

☐ Purchasing commissions.

☐ Insurance during construction.

☐ "Rent" paid while occupying under option to purchase and applied to purchase price on exercise of option.

Deductible selling expenses include:

☐ Broker's commission.

☐ Legal expenses and attorney's fees.

☐ Advertising.

☐ Sales tax, if applicable.

☐ Title abstract.

☐ "Points" paid by the seller to enable buyer to obtain financing.

☐ Fixing-up expenses if incurred within 90 days of the sale contract and paid within 30 days after sale.

Float can work both ways

The textbook definition of float is "converting a negotiable instrument into cash or the transit period required to turn a contingency into an asset." This means, on the one hand, the time lapse between your deposit and the date the bank allows you to use those funds or, on the other hand, the time lapse between when you make a payment by check or other draft and the date that debit is charged to your account.

Assuming that the money in question is "working," using float is a way of "creating money."

Perhaps the first step in dealing with float is to minimize its use against you. Find a bank with a reasonable "hold" policy (the delay in crediting deposits to customer accounts).

Once you have arranged to make your deposits work as long and hard as possible, you might give some attention to making float work to positive financial advantage. If you have a NOW account or a money-market account, by making payment by mail on the last possible day, you may keep that money earning as much as a week longer than otherwise, given mail delivery time and time for the draft to clear through the system. (A postmarked mailing is the legal equivalent of making payment in person on the same date.)

There are ways to use float in your savings program, too. There are still banks that offer an in-by-the-tenth, earning-from-the-first policy. You can routinely turn this to your advantage by the simple expedient of opening a second account in a day-of-deposit-to-day-of-withdrawal bank (we'll call it Bank 2) and playing one bank against the other: withdraw funds from Bank 2 on the tenth of the month, depositing them in Bank 1, thus earning an extra 10 days' interest on the sum every month. On the last day of the month, simply transfer funds back to Bank 2 and begin again. (Note: Some in-by-the-tenth banks offer this privilege only on a quarterly basis. Still, that's 40 days' double interest per year.)

Source: Edward F. Mrkvicka, Jr., founder and president of Reliance Enterprises, Inc., P.O. Box 413, Marengo, IL 60152.

Cashing CDs before maturity

☐ Many investors don't realize that they can also buy bank CDs through Merrill Lynch and other brokers. Benefit: Merrill Lynch maintains a market in CDs, so it's possible to sell them back before maturity.

Your pension payout: The partial distribution option

When it comes time to collect your company pension benefits, there are a bewildering range of payout options. An option that is less used, but could have benefits to you under certain circumstances, is to take some of the money out of the pension plan in a lump sum and leave the rest in. Make sure to get good tax advice before electing a partial distribution, however.

☐ If you have big tax deductions, it may be to your advantage to take some of the distribution as income and roll over the balance into an IRA or another company plan. The deductions will offset the distribution, so you may wind up with some tax-free income.

☐ You may also want to take a partial distribution if you have to pay the alternative minimum tax (AMT). Reason: The most tax you can pay on the extra income is 24%—the flat AMT tax rate.

☐ You can roll over any qualifying portion of a lump-sum distribution into an IRA or into another qualified company pension plan. But you cannot roll over any nondeductible voluntary contributions you may have made to the plan over the years.

Source: *Tax Hotline,* Boardroom Reports, Inc., New York.

Tax loopholes to finance your retirement nest egg

The tax laws are peppered with loopholes designed to help us live comfortably in retirement. Eight to spice up your retirement financial plan:

☐ Tax-free home sales. If you or your spouse is 55 or older when you sell your house, and you've lived in it for three of the last five years, you have an optional tax break on the first $125,000 of profit on the sale.

If you're about to remarry and one partner has already used the home sales exclusion, the one who hasn't should sell his house *prior* to the marriage to take the exclusion. The right will be revoked after the marriage.

☐ Gifts to grandchildren. Before selling appreciated assets, such as securities, to give cash gifts to your descendants, give the actual securities and let the kids sell them. A gift of the property will save tax (and create a bigger gift) if the recipient is in a lower tax bracket than you. The recipient will pay less tax on the gain than you would.

Reverse the strategy if the recipient intends to retain the property. In this case, give cash now and let the intended recipient inherit the appreciated property. *Reason:* The recipient will inherit the property at a stepped-up basis, that is, its value at the date of your death. He or she won't have to pay capital gains tax on the property's increase in value.

☐ Rent a condominium from your children. Get Uncle Sam to subsidize the cost of supporting an elderly parent by getting the children to buy the parent's retirement condominium and rent it to the parent. At the very least, the children will get tax deductions for mortgage interest and property taxes. These deductions will produce a greater tax benefit to high-income children than they would to a low-bracket retired parent. And if the children charge the parent fair market rent, they will also be able to take depreciation deductions on the condo.

You can deduct up to $25,000 of losses if your adjusted gross income is less than $100,000. This loss allowance is phased out between $100,000 and $150,000 of the adjusted gross income.

☐ Plan in advance for nursing home care. Before the government will pay your nursing home bills, you have to use up the money that's in your name. *Strategy:* Put your money into a trust that pays you income but which doesn't allow you to touch the principal. Then only the income would be lost to nursing home care—you won't lose the principal. *Caution:* In most states, a trust that is set up within two years of a person's entering a nursing home *won't* be effective. Check with an attorney about your state's laws.

☐ IRS vs. remarriage. A married couple, both age 65 or over, will pay more tax on a joint return than the combined tax they would pay if they were single. *Another consideration:* If income (including tax-exempt income) plus one-half Social Security benefits exceeds certain levels, half the Social Security benefits are taxable. *The levels are:* $25,000 for a single person, or $32,000 for a married couple. Combining incomes on a joint return may force taxation of Social Security benefits that would completely escape taxation if the couple did not marry.

☐ IRA strategy. Now, arrange for IRA certificates of deposit (CDs) to mature at the same time, so you can then reinvest the accumulated funds *together* in a single, higher-yielding investment. *Example:* Put this year's IRA in a five-year CD, next year's in a four-year CD, and so on. *General rule:* The larger your IRA, the better your return.

Then, as you approach age 70½, don't lock up all accounts in certificates of deposit that won't be accessible at that age. *Reason:* You are required by law to begin taking distributions from your IRA by April 1 of the year following the taxable year in which you become 70½…even if that entails paying an early withdrawal penalty.

☐ Collecting Social Security early can pay off. Even though benefits are reduced, they'll usually add up to more in the long run. *Example:* If full benefits are $750 per month for retiring at age 65, you can get reduced benefits of $600 a month by retiring at age 62. You'd have to collect full benefits for 12 years to make up the $21,600 you'd receive during the three years of early payments.

☐ Retirement plan distributions. You must start taking money out of your Individual Retirement Account by April 1 following the year in which you reach age 70½. *Loophole:* You may be able to slow the distribution down (take less in the early years) by using actuarial tables. Check with the IRA trustee to see if a slower distribution schedule can be used for your payouts.

Source: Edward Mendlowitz, partner, Mendlowitz Weitsen, 2 Pennsylvania Plaza, New York 10121.

What it takes

Comfortable retirement requires about 50%-75% of the final working year's income.

Source: *CPA Digest,* Milwaukee.

Which Keogh is best for you?

☐ The defined-benefit type works best if you are within, say, 20 years of retirement. This type can produce a larger Keogh fund, from bigger tax-deductible contributions, than the other types. Also, inflation and mediocre investment performance matter less with this type.

☐ The money-purchase type is favored if you have a Midas touch with your investments, or if you start your Keogh relatively early in life.

☐ Profit-sharing plans are much like money-purchase plans, though easier to set up and operate. But since 1984 law changes that liberalized defined-benefit and money-purchase Keoghs, profit-sharing plans now lag behind in tax benefits. The top deduction in a profit-sharing Keogh is only 60% of what's possible with a money-purchase Keogh, and only 15% of what's possible (though not typical) with defined-benefit Keoghs.

For economic reasons, you might have to settle for a plan that's less than the best for you, if you have employees who must be included in your plan.

Source: *Tax Hotline,* Boardroom Reports, Inc., New York.

IRA vs. deferred annuities: A checklist

One of the most attractive investment products around is the insurance industry's deferred annuities.

☐ Deferred annuities are an alternative for individuals whose incentive to continue to make IRA contributions was devastated by tax reform.

Although contributions to a deferred annuity are not tax deductible, earnings accumulate tax deferred. Advantage over an IRA: There is no limit to the amount of money you can invest in an annuity.

☐ Variable annuities are the ideal replacement for investments that used to receive the benefit of favorable long-term capital-gains treatment. *Reason:* Long-term gains from investments in stocks, which are now taxed as ordinary income, can be sheltered in a variable annuity. That income is not taxed until you withdraw your money.

☐ When you buy an annuity from an insurance company you pay in a lump sum or a series of payments over time. In return, the insurance company guarantees that the funds will grow at a certain tax-free rate. On a specified date you begin to receive regular income payments for the rest of your life.

☐ Payments depend on the amount of money contributed to the account, the length of time the funds are left in it, and the rate of return earned on the funds.

☐ Another factor in determining the size of the payments is whether you include your spouse and other heirs as beneficiaries.

☐ Different options enable you to have payments continue to your wife, or to your children, or for a minimum of, say, 20 years, regardless of who is there to receive them after you die.

☐ Deferred annuities are part insurance and part investment. If you are willing to part with at least $5,000 (the minimum amount can differ from company to company) for five years or longer, you can be guaranteed a competitive, tax-free return on your funds. Because the earned income is not taxed until you begin withdrawing the money (presumably at a much lower tax rate), your funds accumulate much faster than they would if they were taxed. The insurance component, of course, is guaranteed regular monthly income payments for the rest of your life—taking the worry and risk out of budgeting for your retirement income.

☐ Should you die before you begin receiving payments, your heirs are guaranteed to receive the full amount of your original principal.

Source: Alexandra Armstrong, Armstrong, Welch & MacIntyre, Washington, DC.

Making voluntary contributions to a company pension plan

Making voluntary payments to your company's pension plan, in addition to the contributions your employer already makes for you, makes tax sense.

☐ The voluntary contribution isn't deductible but the interest it earns accumulates tax free.

☐ You won't be taxed on what the contribution earns until you take it out at retirement.

☐ When you make a withdrawal from the plan, that part of the withdrawal that is attributable to your voluntary contributions is tax-free. (The percentage is figured by a complex formula set by law. Check with your tax advisor before making a withdrawal.)

☐ Voluntary contribution limit: 10% of your salary.

How safe is your pension?

Whether you are examining pension information of public or private firms, you are seeking the same sort of basic information.

How to check on the safety of your retirement income:

☐ For employees of public companies: Basic information is included in the firm's annual report. Usually the size of a firm's unfunded pension liability and the size of its past service liability are disclosed in footnotes. More detailed information is available in the financial section of the firm's 10K report, filed with the Securities and Exchange Commission.

☐ For employees of private companies: Everyone who is in a qualified plan (one approved by the IRS under the Code) has the right to obtain information about his pension from the trustees of the plan. They may be either internal or external trustees. The average person may not be able to decipher the information. If you can't, then take it to a pension expert, actuary, lawyer or accountant for an analysis.

☐ The size of a company's liability for retirement payouts is not as important as the assumptions about funding these liabilities. Like a mortgage, these obligations don't exist 100% in the present. Concern yourself with how the company expects to fund its liabilities.

Types of liabilities:

☐ Unfunded pension liabilities. The amount a firm expects to need over the next 20 to 30 years to supply vested workers with promised pension benefits. These figures are derived from various actuarial assumptions.

☐ Past service liabilities. Created when a company raises its pension compensation. For instance, a company may have been planning to provide 40% of compensation as a pension. One year, they may raise that to 45% and treat it retroactively.

Trouble signs:

☐ A poor record on investing. Compare the market value of the assets in the pension with their book value. If book value is more than market value, the trustees have not been investing wisely. Point: If the fund had to sell those assets today, there would be a loss. Another bad sign: The fund is still holding some obscure bonds or other fixed-income obligations issued at low rates years ago.

☐ Funding assumptions are overstated. Actuaries have a myriad of estimates on how long it takes to fund pension plans and what rate of return a company will get.

What to look at:

☐ Time frame: This should not be too long. If the firm is funding over 40 years, find out why and how; 10 to 20 years is more customary. Assumptions made on 40 years may not hold up at all.

☐ Rate of return: If a company assumes a conservative 6% to 7% or less right now, you can be comfortable. If the assumed rate is 10% or more, question how they are going to meet that expectation for the entire fund over the long run.

☐ Salary and wage scales: The company should be assuming an increase in compensation over years. Most plans have such provisions.

☐ Assumptions about the employee turnover rate: These should be consistent with the historically documented turnover of the company. If a firm has a very high turnover rate and assumes a 4% turnover, the company will be underfunded at some time. Estimates should be conservative.

☐ To assess your own status in a corporate pension plan, see how many years you have been vested. Many people have the illusion that they are fully vested for maximum pensions after a few years. In truth, companies couldn't afford to vest people fully with such short service. With so much job-hopping in the past two decades, an individual's pension-fund status may be much less than imagined.

☐ Employees of troubled or even bankrupt companies need not panic. Trustees of the plan have an obligation to the vested employees. The assets of the plan are segregated, and no creditor can reach them. In fact, as a creditor, the corporate pension plan can grab some corporate assets under certain circumstances. And if there has been gross mismanagement of pension funds, stockholders of a closely held company can be held personally liable.

Source: James E. Conway, president of The Ayco Corporation, Albany, NY.

Home equity trap

Young professionals planning to retire on the appreciated value of their house or condominium—like their parents—are being unrealistic. The surge in population that has caused housing prices to skyrocket since 1960 is "a movie that won't be rerun."

Source: Robert Gough, senior vice president, Data Resources, Inc.

Retire early without spouse's consent

Now you aren't required to get your spouse's approval if you want to retire early and take your pension benefits, according to a regulation of the Retirement Equity Act of 1984. But: You still must consult your spouse about how to take retirement benefits payments.

Source: Tax Hotline, Boardroom Reports, Inc., New York.

Better than an IRA

Cash or deferred profit-sharing plans, technically called 401(k) plans, offer retirement-minded employees much bigger tax benefits than Individual Retirement Accounts (IRAs). Key to the potential tax windfall: A cut in pay. These plans also provide tax savings for the employer.

How they work:

☐ The company sets up a qualified profit-sharing plan or conforms its present plan to the tax law's 401(k) requirements.

☐ The plan permits employees to defer taking a portion of their salary—let's say 5%. The deferred salary is contributed directly into the plan by the company.

☐ The employee pays no tax on the contribution. The income earned builds up tax-free in the plan.

☐ There is an $8,994 (for 1993) annual limit on contributions indexed for inflation annually.

☐ Retirement distributions from a deferred-salary plan may qualify for 5-year-forward income tax averaging. This can result in substantial savings.

How to get the most out of your IRA

Your IRA may be your most important source of retirement income. You can contribute up to $2,000 a year, as long as you're working (until the year you reach age 70½). In addition, if you leave a job, you might be able to roll over your pension or profit-sharing distributions into your IRA. As the years go by, an IRA can grow into big money.

The pros and cons of the most common ways to invest IRA money:

Banks or Savings & Loans

☐ Usually don't charge any fees.

☐ Your money is insured by the federal government up to $100,000. If your IRA grows larger than this, just open a second account at a different bank.

☐ A psychological advantage: Most people are familiar with local banks and trust them. But many taxpayers feel nervous about stocks, bonds and similar investments.

☐ Banks offer IRAs the same accounts (except checking) as any other depositors, including passbook savings accounts, money-market accounts and CDs of varying rates and lengths.

☐ Penalties are charged for early withdrawal of CDs (though some banks will waive the penalty for depositors at retirement age).

☐ Essential: Keep a detailed record of maturity dates of all CDs or time deposits, so you'll know when you can withdraw the funds or switch investments.

Insurance Companies

☐ Insurance companies sell retirement annuities. Most common: traditional fixed-rate annuity, at a specified interest rate, which guarantees a specific amount at retirement for each $1,000 contributed.

☐ Advantage of fixed annuity: You know in advance how much you'll get. And you're guaranteed an income for your lifetime (and your spouse's, if the annuity is set up that way). You can't outlive your investment.

☐ Big disadvantage of fixed annuity: No protection against inflation.

☐ In recent years, many insurance companies have begun offering variable annuities, invested in money markets, stocks or other investments that rise and fall with the economy and the rate of inflation.

☐ Advantage of variable annuity: They've generally worked out much better in inflationary times.

☐ Disadvantages of a variable annuity: Less certain than fixed-rate annuities and involve some risk.

☐ Generally, insurance companies charge fees for setting up and maintaining an IRA. There also may be a charge on contributions and withdrawals.

☐ These fees are tax deductible to the extent allowed by law. Pay them separately from your IRA contributions…and deduct the amount as "IRA fees" as a miscellaneous deduction on your income tax return.

Mutual Funds

☐ Advantages of mutual fund IRAs: flexibility and diversification. Most mutual fund companies operate several funds—money market, common stock, bond funds, etc. Important: You can usually move your money from one fund in the family of funds to another at will, usually for little or no charge.

☐ Caution: Some funds are more speculative than others. Some are growth funds and some are income funds. (And some funds charge sales commissions.)

Brokerage Houses

☐ The main attraction of a brokerage house as a trustee for an IRA account is for the taxpayer who wants to manage his own IRA by setting up a self-directed account. The brokerage house is still the trustee, but you make all investment decisions—what to buy, what to sell, etc.

☐ Caution: This kind of account is for the experienced investor, who is willing to take the responsibility—and the risk.

☐ Brokerage houses normally charge a fee for setting up and maintaining an IRA, as well as their normal commissions on any transactions.

☐ The fees (but not the commissions) are deductible if separately billed and paid.

Source: Peter I. Elinsky, tax partner, KPMG Peat Marwick, CPAs, Washington, DC.

Early IRA withdrawals

Although the Tax Reform Act clobbered the IRA deduction for many taxpayers, it created a penalty-free way to withdraw money from the account before you reach age 59 1/2.

☐ Old law: You had to pay an additional 10% penalty tax on distributions from IRA accounts before age 59 1/2.

☐ New Law: You won't pay the extra 10% penalty tax if you convert the account to an annuity and receive the money in a scheduled series of substantially equal payments over your life or your life expectancy.

Managing your own IRA account

With a brokerage house account or a no-load family of mutual funds for an IRA, the investor can change his mind about an investment without penalty.

At a bank or S&L, the investor who changes his mind about a five-year certificate of deposit pays an early-withdrawal penalty. But the only penalty for changing an IRA investment at a brokerage house is commission.

☐ Investors should not take chances with their IRA money. They should buy high-yielding instruments or equities with the ability to pay a dividend (whether they actually do or not) and the potential for high growth.

☐ The big mistake made in self-directed IRAs is overtrading. Some people think there is a magical way for them to double their money in a very short time, especially in an IRA, and they buy highly speculative securities. In volatile, aggressive stocks, investors can lose money at least as easily as they can make it. And any dollar in an IRA is worth even more to the investor than a regular dollar, since the money it earns is tax free. The account can turn into a sizable amount without risk.

☐ If you lose money in an IRA account, you get no tax help from the government—it gives you no tax deduction for such a loss.

☐ There is usually a custodial fee ($30 or so a year) for self-directed IRAs. Although the custodial fee is tax deductible, it is difficult for an investor with only a $2,000 account to justify it. It is easier to justify the custodial fee when there is $5,000 or more in an account. And when the account reaches a significant size, the investor can buy a greater number of instruments and increase diversification.

☐ Favorite investments for IRAs in recent years: Zero-coupon bonds, Ginnie Mae bonds, convertible bonds and common stocks (particularly oil companies and utility issues).

Source: Robert L. Thomas, executive vice president, Advest, Hartford, CT.

IRA investment traps

The April 15 tax deadline for personal income taxes is also the deadline for making IRA contributions. Everyone who is eligible to should make the maximum contribution the law allows. But before you invest:

☐ Read the fine print. Watch for set-up

charges, management fees, and early withdrawal penalties that institutions charge (over and above the tax-law penalties). The penalties can be steep and fees vary widely. Shop around.

☐ Make IRA contributions in cash or check only. That's the law. You won't get a deduction for a transfer of stock from your investment account into an IRA.

☐ Stay within the contribution limits. If you exceed the limit, you're liable for a nondeductible excise tax (6% of the excess amount) for each year the excess remains in your account. To avoid the penalty, you must withdraw the excess along with the earnings attributable to such excess, before your return is due (including extensions).

☐ Don't put your IRA in an investment that already provides tax-exempt income, such as municipal bonds or a municipal investment trust. Reason: Tax-exempt bonds typically yield less than taxable bonds because the tax exemption is of value to investors. By law, the income earned in an IRA builds up tax free until withdrawn. Thus, tax-free interest on municipal bonds is of no value to an IRA.

☐ Don't invest your IRA in the federal government's Individual Retirement Bonds. Problem: With other IRA investments you can take your money out over a period of years, starting when you're 59½. But you must take the whole Individual Retirement Bond out in one piece. (You can't redeem just a part of the bond.)

Source: Brett D. Yacker, tax partner, and Leonard J. Senzon, tax manager, Price Waterhouse, New York.

Better retirement benefits for the self-employed

Businesses no longer have to be incorporated for the owners to obtain maximum benefits from a tax-favored retirement plan. Keogh-type plans for self-employed persons and unincorporated businesses have been liberalized to provide larger benefits:

☐ The maximum deductible contribution has been increased to $30,000 or 25% of income—whichever is less.

Working after retirement

Many retirees would like to keep working after retirement, at least part-time. But those who want to work for financial reasons should be aware of the drawbacks and some alternatives.

☐ You can earn up to $10,560 a year (for 1993) if you're age 65 to 69 and still collect full Social Security benefits. But for every $3 earned above that amount, you lose $1 in benefits. When you add your commuting costs, job-related expenses and payroll deductions, you may find part-time work doesn't pay off.

☐ If you continue working part-time for the same company, you may not be eligible to collect your pension. One way around this, if the company will go along, is to retire as an employee and return as a consultant or freelancer. Since you're now self-employed, your pension won't be affected.

☐ Although most employees can't legally be compelled to retire before age 70, companies still set up retirement ages of 65 or under. You can work past that age, but you won't necessarily earn further pension credits. And you lose Social Security and pension benefits while you continue to work.

☐ A very attractive alternative to working part-time is to start your own business. Professionals such as lawyers can often set up a practice, setting their own hours. Or you might turn a hobby into a business.

Source: William W. Parrott, a chartered financial consultant at Merrill Lynch, Pierce, Fenner & Smith, Inc., New York.

Five kinds of pay that are exempt from social security taxes

☐ Wages paid to your child under 18, when the business is a proprietorship. Wages paid by a corporation are subject to tax.

☐ Loans taken out from the company by an employee or shareholder. But be sure the loan is fully documented, so that there is no doubt about its legitimacy. If the IRS concludes that the loan will not be paid back, tax will be imposed. The loan must carry an interest rate equal to 110% of the applicable federal rate at the time of the loan. IRS will announce this rate twice each year.

☐ Health-insurance payments made into an employee accident, health or medical reimbursement plan.

☐ Educational benefits which add to employee's on-the-job skills.

☐ Moving-expense reimbursements when a move is job-related, covers more than 35 miles, and the worker stays at the new job site at least 39 weeks during the next year.

Tax considerations for expatriate retirees

Before you retire abroad, be prepared for many more complex variables than there are in US retirement communities.

☐ All American citizens are subject to US income tax, regardless of where they live. But they get US tax credit for income taxes paid to the other government. However, they won't get a refund from the US if local tax rates are higher than US rates, and that's often the case. In fact, some foreign countries tax US Social Security income as well.

☐ Only by renouncing US citizenship can an individual escape US income taxes. Dividends and other passive income are taxed at their source. However, if the IRS can prove that US citizenship has been renounced within the last 10 years with the principal reason being to escape income taxes, the individual will be taxed as a US citizen.

☐ Test of foreign residency for US

income tax: Living abroad for a full calendar year or having a physical presence outside the US for 12 of 13 consecutive months. Foreign residents are, however, exempt from state and local taxes in the US.

☐ Good idea: Americans who can arrange to earn income while residing abroad (through a personal company, for example) qualify for a US tax exemption on the first $70,000 of earned income plus a living allowance exclusion, provided they meet the residency or presence test above. For someone locating in a country without an income tax, that can amount to quite a windfall.

☐ Some retirees prefer to maintain their US home either as a place to stay while visiting or as an investment that can be rented and depreciated to tax advantage while they live abroad. The US government won't consider it a principal place of residence if it's used as a permanent abode for fewer than 183 days a year.

☐ The once-in-a-lifetime tax-free gain of $125,000 on the sale of a principal residence can be applied to a foreign home, provided it's been used as a principal residence for three out of the last five years.

☐ A person moving abroad has four years, not just two as in the US, to buy a home of equivalent value after the sale of the principal residence and qualify for the tax deferral on the gain.

☐ Reason to rent rather than buy a home: Currency restrictions and capital gains rules vary from country to country. As a general rule, it's easier to invest abroad than it is to repatriate dollars after a sale.

Source: Israel Press, partner, and Alan Brad, manager, tax department, Financial Services Center, Deloitte & Touche, New York.

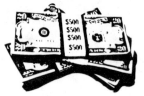

Economic indicators to watch

By simply following the indicators reported in the financial press and watching for the same signals as the economists do, any investor can spot the signals that mean that the caution flag should go up.

The five indicators to watch:

☐ Total employment. Released on the first or second Friday of the month. The number of people employed reflects labor demand. Thus, it's more meaningful as a recession indicator than the rate of unemployment (which reflects the labor supply), which usually gets more attention in the media.

☐ Monthly retail sales. This indicator is published about the tenth of the following month. It takes a sales increase of 0.6%–0.7% month-to-month just to stay even with inflation. If the increase in dollar sales is less than that, it means that unit sales have actually declined. And if retail sales in dollar figures actually decrease from month to month, consider that to be a strong negative indicator.

☐ Industrial production index. Issued about the 15th of the following month. If this index declines, that's a negative signal. But it may be a negative signal if it rises, too. Here's why: Suppose industrial production rises while retail sales for a month are up less than 0.5% in dollars, which means no real change in unit sales. That shows that factories are producing more goods than stores are selling and means inventories are building up. Sooner or later, production will have to be cut back in order to bring inventories into line.

☐ Personal income. This figure is released about the 18th of the following month. It should go up by at least 0.6% per month just to stay even with inflation. Any smaller increase is a negative signal, which shows that the buying power of consumers is falling.

☐ Consumer price index. This is the principal fever chart of inflation. Compare it with retail sales and personal income for the same month to determine whether those indicators are staying even with the inflation rate or falling behind it.

These five are what economists call coincident indicators. They do not forecast the future, rather they tell what is happening in the present. Why not use the highly publicized leading indicators? Because they just are not dependable.

Source: Dr. Irwin Kellner, senior economist, Chemical Banking, New York, NY.

Insurance traps and opportunities

☐ Don't buy travel insurance at airports. Coverage is much more expensive and rates vary from city to city. Instead, buy directly from insurance company.

☐ A fire or burglar alarm should entitle you to a reduction in insurance premiums. The saving on homeowners premiums is about 2% to 10% a year. Addition of a smoke detector should lower premiums another 3%.

☐ Bargain policy picks up when major medical runs out. The cost of really complicated illness today can exceed major medical coverage. To protect yourself, buy an "excess" major medical policy with deductible equal to maximum benefit under your current plan. Features to shop around for: Guaranteed renewability; five-year benefit period; coverage of children from birth to age 18 or 21; payment of "reasonable" or "usual" hospital costs rather than specified daily rate.

☐ Don't buy insurance that pays off a loan or installment debt if you die or are disabled. Instead, buy decreasing term life insurance for the duration of the installments. Saves up to 44%.

How much insurance is enough

It's conventional wisdom that you need life insurance equal to five or seven times your annual income. That's OK as a general rule, but following it too closely can be costly. The danger of over- or underinsuring is especially great as your asset base changes.

Before deciding how much life insurance to carry, look at:

☐ Cash needs for settling the estate and paying uninsured medical costs and funeral expenses.

☐ Outstanding debts. It's nice to give the family greater financial freedom by paying off the mortgage, car loans, outstanding installment debt and credit-card balances.

☐ Educational goals for children.

☐ Surviving family income fund. The amount of insurance needed is the difference between expenses and income, including Social Security. Always include a cushion for emergencies.

☐ Inflation protection. Figure 9% inflation a year to protect current purchasing power. Be prepared to alter your coverage as inflation expectations change.

☐ Accumulated assets. The same assets that can provide income for your heirs can be wiped out unless you have adequate liability coverage. Never settle for $1 million—because you can get $5 million for very little more. Here, the sky is almost the limit.

☐ Present age. Insurance is most essential for people who haven't yet accumulated substantial assets. It's important to start young, even if you can afford only term insurance. The danger with term insurance is that as it becomes more expensive with age, it's increasingly tempting to drop it.

☐ Instead of a raise, ask the company for more disability insurance. It's deductible for the company, and the premiums aren't considered income to you for tax purposes. But unless the company plan is adequate, be prepared to buy substantially more disability coverage.

☐ Set a definite time each year—preferably twice a year—to review your financial plan and insurance coverage. For business owners, these reviews are especially useful because the business will be growing and changing, too. Then act. Change your financial plan and insurance coverage to reflect the current situation.

Source: J. Gary Sheets, chairman, CFS Financial Corp., financial planners, Salt Lake City, UT.

How not to buy insurance coverage that you don't need

While so many people worry about being under-insured, we should all be concerned instead about having too much insurance.

The most common insurance mistakes are wasting money on the wrong kind of insurance…and on insurance that duplicates coverage already provided by another policy.

Myth: By purchasing all of your insurance from the same agent, you'll get co-ordinated at the best value.

Reality: For personal insurance, you'll very often pay more by using an agent. According to one authoritive study, the best price and service was delivered by Amica Mutual Insurance and United Services Auto Association, both of which sell direct. Some of the biggest and best-known companies were the worst buys.

Best: Carefully determine your own needs, then shop around. Get quotes both from agents and from direct insurance writers. Compare the rates and coverages and pick the best value.

Coverage You Don't Need

The biggest insurance trap is being sold insurance you don't need. If you're single and have no dependents, for example, you really have no need for life insurance. And there's no financial reason to buy life insurance on a child who does not contribute to the family's income. Other insurance you don't need:

☐ Flight insurance. Many people buy flight insurance as a kind of good-luck charm, but it is grossly over-priced. Take the money you would spend to buy insurance on a two-hour flight and use it, instead, to buy more term life insurance that covers you 365 days a year, around the clock, wherever you are.

☐ Cancer insurance. This is very expensive and protects you against only that one disease. You're much better off buying good comprehensive health insurance that covers all illnesses.

☐ Mortgage insurance. In a recent study, we found that bank mortgage insurance was more than twice as expensive as plain term life insurance. And if you die, your family might be better off not repaying the mortgage—if, for example, they can invest their money to earn a rate of return that exceeds the after-tax cost of deductible mortgage interest. Best strategy: Buy enough life insurance from one company to cover all your family needs. Don't be talked into buying extra insurance that is for the benefit of the bank, not you.

☐ Credit-card life insurance. If you are being charged premiums for life insurance to cover your unpaid credit-card balance, ask that it be eliminated or switch to a credit-card company that doesn't burden you with insurance that is only for the benefit of the credit-card company.

☐ Liability duplication. If you have an umbrella liability policy, be sure not to duplicate liability coverage with your auto insurance.

Example: If your automobile insurance policy includes $300,000 of liability, and the umbrella liability policy kicks in after the first $100,000, you don't need the extra $200,000 of coverage on your auto policy.

You may also find there's duplication under your homeowner's policy.

Also…if you have good comprehensive health insurance, you don't need to buy additional coverage in your auto insurance.

Buying Smart

☐ Generally speaking, with liability and health insurance it's smart to take the largest possible deductibles to hold premiums down.

Put aside the money you save in a family savings account that earns interest. You can use it to pay whatever deductibles do arise under your policies, and in the end you—not the insurance company—will probably have a nice nest egg.

With homeowners insurance, you should get coverage for the full replacement cost of your property. Even then, the biggest mistake many people make is not keeping an adequate inventory of what they have and how much it is all worth. You can have the finest insurance in the world, but if you don't have any proof of loss to show the insurance company, you will not get a fair settlement. Most of us could never remember everything that's in our homes, especially after the trauma of a fire.

Solution: Take time now to make a room-by-room inventory on paper. Back this up with photos and receipts or appraisals. Keep all of this material in your safe deposit box or with a friend—but not in your house.

Source: J. Robert Hunter, president of the National Insurance Consumer Organization, 121 N. Payne St., Alexandria, Virginia 22314.

How much life insurance you need

After the death of its principal income-producer, a family requires 75% of its former after-tax income to maintain its standard of living, and at least 60% to get along at all.

Here is the amount of life insurance (in terms of annual earnings multiples) needed at different ages to provide this income (taking into account Social Security benefits and assuming the insurance proceeds were invested to produce an after-inflation return of 5% a year, with the entire principal consumed over survivor's life expectancy).

Your age	Current Income				
	$15M	$23.5M	$30M	$40M	$65M
☐ 25 years					
75%	4.5	6.5	7.5	7.5	7.5
60%	3.0	4.5	5.0	5.0	5.5>
☐ 35 years					
75%	6.5	8.0	8.0	8.0	7.5
60%	6.0	6.5	6.5	6.0	6.0
☐ 45 years					
75%	8.0	8.5	8.5	8.0	7.5
60%	6.0	6.5	6.5	6.0	6.0
☐ 55 years					
75%	7.0	7.5	7.0	7.0	6.5
60%	5.5	5.5	5.5	5.5	5.0

The chart implicitly shows capital requirements. These requirements can be met by life insurance or through savings and investments, employee benefits, or inheritance. Thus, to the extent that the independent capital resources are built up, insurance needs diminish.

Shopping for life insurance bargains

☐ Over the past five to 10 years, life insurance rates have plummeted 50%–75%. So it's quite likely that you can now cash in your life insurance policy and buy a new one for the same amount of coverage—maybe even more—at a significantly lower cost.

☐ Benchmark: A nonsmoking male, 45 years old or younger, able to pass a simple physical (that usually doesn't even include a blood test or X-ray), can buy $1 million in coverage now for an annual premium one quarter the price ten years ago. Rates for women are even lower.

☐ It's quite possible that an individual life insurance policy purchased right now could cost less than the group rate available to your company.

□ The biggest bargains are in jumbo policies—$1 million or more in coverage—for individuals who can pay the annual premium up front (often worth a 25% discount).

□ It can benefit executives with insurance needs to overinsure. Under the tax law, companies can provide only up to $50,000 in insurance coverage for a single individual. Premiums paid for any coverage above that amount are treated as taxable income to the executive. Make sure those premiums are as low as possible, even if the company pays.

□ Look for preferential rates for nonsmokers and the physically fit.

□ In their eagerness to write new policies against stiffer and stiffer competitive pressures and also to reduce their costs in acquiring new business, many insurers have dropped the requirement for physicals, even for quite substantial policies.

□ Look for back-end loads. Typically, insurance companies take the sales charge (often 125% of the first year's premium) out of the premiums paid during the first five years the policy is in force. This so-called front-end load cuts down the amount of money the insurance buyer actually puts away in the savings portion of whole-life insurance, annuities and even the popular universal-life policies (universal life offers competitive interest rates on the savings portions). Far better: The new back-end load current interest rate products (called BELCIR) that put all the premiums directly into the purchase of insurance and interest-earning savings…until the policy is terminated.

□ Vanishing premiums. *High-interest earnings*, if they continue in the future, permit a policy to become paid up after five years or so.

Source: Frederick S. Townsend, chief of investment research, Conning & Co., specialists in insurance stocks, Hartford, CT.

Preparing for your insurance physical

□ Have the test done at your convenience. Do it when you feel best.

□ If it suits you, arrange for an early morning exam. Most people are relaxed then, you don't lose too much time out from a busy workday, and it's easier to fast if blood tests are required.

□ If you have to be tested in the afternoon, avoid caffeine and don't eat heavily during the day. If you must have coffee, make it decaffeinated.

□ Limit your intake of salt for several days before the physical. Avoid alcohol for at least 24 hours. Both can raise your blood pressure.

□ If you're a nonsmoker, make sure the examining physician knows it, because premiums are lower for nonsmokers who meet a specific height and weight standard. (If you do smoke, go "cold turkey" for two hours or more before the exam.)

□ See your personal doctor before the exam to make sure there'll be no surprises. If there is any sensitive medical or physical information in your records, ask your doctor exactly what you should tell the insurance company.

□ If you feel tired or ill before the physical, cancel it. Don't worry about delaying the process. The most important thing is to feel relaxed and healthy when you take the physical exam.

Source: Benjamin Lipson, Benjamin Lipson Insurance Agency, Boston, MA.

When to surrender or change your life insurance policy

A change might be in order if:

□ You have an old life insurance policy with a cash value that is 30% or more of its face value, and you are in good health (meaning you will have no trouble getting a standard life insurance policy).

□ You have an old policy that you have borrowed against fully at the guaranteed low rates. You have no intention of paying back the loan and you are not in a high tax bracket. (Replacing your policy in this case probably has attractive tax advantages for you.)

□ Your present policy is "rated" for health reasons (you are paying higher premiums because of the risks of your illness), but your health has improved. You may be eligible for a less expensive policy or the "rate" (higher premium) may be removed from the policy.

□ Your insurance needs have changed…your income has increased or decreased dramatically, your mortgage is paid off or your children are through college.

☐ You are paying on several small policies. Consolidation may be cost-effective.

☐ Caution: Because new life insurance products are coming on the market at a rapid pace, there are many high-pressure salespeople at work to persuade you to turn in your old policy without reason. Many of the new policies are better. But sometimes the old policy may be upgraded internally through company changes. Most are offering upgrades without commission.

Source: Arthur Schechner, president, Schechner Corp., insurance consultants, Millburn, NJ.

Saving on house insurance

☐ Fire or burglar alarms should entitle the owner to a reduction in insurance premiums. The saving on homeowner's premiums is about 2% to 10% a year. Addition of a smoke detector should lower premiums another 3%.

☐ Save on title insurance. Many title insurers have a special reissue rate for property on which they're written a policy within the past five years. Advantage: A full title search is not necessary. Savings can be considerable. Companies usually don't mention the special rate unless a customer asks for it.

☐ Poor lock can lose insurance claim. Most insurers won't pay if lock was opened by key (even if it was a stolen key).

☐ Collecting when insurance company says no. Even insurance agents and claims investigators are sometimes unaware of the policy's full coverage. Claimant who's told he's not covered should always ask to speak to the disclaimer's manager. If the answer is still no, there is plenty of time to check with a lawyer.

Boat insurance guidelines

☐ The policy should cover ice, freezing, and racing damage.

☐ It should include protection and indemnity coverage. A boat can be sued much like a corporation ashore. Personal homeowners insurance won't

protect it from confiscation to satisfy an award against it.

☐ The policy should cover use of the boat in all planned geographic areas.

☐ Ask about discounts based on owner experience, Power Squadron courses, automatic fire extinguishing systems, diesel engine, etc.

Insurance you may not know you own

☐ Homeowners policy usually covers stolen purses and wallets, lost luggage, and property taken in a car break-in. It also covers many offbeat accidents, such as: damage to power mower borrowed from neighbor; trees, shrubs, fences or tombstones; damages by vandals or motor vehicles; and property lost or damaged while moving.

☐ $25,000 travel life insurance if the ticket is bought on American Express, Diners Club, or Carte Blanche card.

☐ American Automobile Association (AAA) members have automatic hospital and death benefits if hurt in a car accident.

☐ Many clubs and fraternal organizations have life and health benefits.

☐ It's possible to collect twice on car accident injuries, once through health insurance and again through medical payments provision of auto insurance.

☐ Family health policies usually cover children away at college. Check before buying separate policies for them.

Getting a fair settlement from an insurance company

Some insurance companies process settlements fairly and quickly. Others are notoriously difficult and slow. Ask your insurance agent or a negligence attorney about the company you are dealing with. You may need legal help to negotiate a favorable settlement with a difficult company.

☐ Pain and suffering. When multiples of

out-of-pocket expenses are involved due to pain and suffering, it is best to hire a lawyer. Lawyers can point out losses you have not even thought of. Also, the insurance company will take into account what you are saying by not hiring a lawyer and offer you less.

☐ Find out what your claim is worth. Ask your insurance agent or a negligence lawyer what a reasonable offer would be in your situation.

☐ Be prepared to take a discount. There has to be a motivation for the insurer to settle a claim. One advantage of negotiating without a lawyer is that a quick settlement may be offered to avoid legal expenses. So decide what amount you are willing to settle for.

☐ The settlement offer will depend on various factors, including clarity, proof of coverage, damages, documentation, how likely you are to prevail at trial and the caseload of the court you would have to sue in. (Some insurers offer nothing until the trial date.)

☐ If you feel that the company is either unreasonably delaying your claim or acting in bad faith, make a complaint to your state insurance regulatory agency. In most cases, the agency will write a letter to the company.

☐ If your time is being wasted by the insurance company's bureaucracy, the small claims court may be appropriate. Such action will pressure the company to settle with you more quickly on your terms.

☐ Many states have laws penalizing an insurer for bad faith. If you feel the company has been acting in bad faith, you can initiate a lawsuit and possibly collect a multiple of your claim in punitive damages.

Source: Dan Brecher, a New York attorney.

Collecting for disability

Who Can Collect—and How Much

There are two disability programs under Social Security.

☐ Supplemental Security Income Program is basically a nationalization of welfare benefits for the unemployable.

☐ Old Age and Survivors Disability Insurance (OASDI) applies to working people and is the basic insurance program that you pay into as the FICA tax.

☐ Disability criteria for acceptance are the same under both programs.

☐ You don't have to prove financial need for OASDI. You're eligible if you've worked and paid into the system for 20 quarters out of the last 40 (5 years out of the last 10) and have the necessary years of work credit, depending upon your age.

☐ If your last day in the system was 10 years ago or more, you're not eligible for disability benefits now, though you may be eligible eventually for retirement benefits.

☐ Benefits are based on what you've paid into the system, since dependents are taken into account.

How the System Works

☐ The first step: File an application with your local Social Security office. You'll be interviewed by a claims representative, who will ask you basic questions about your disability. The interviewer will also note any evidence of your disability that he observed.

☐ This material is sent to a trained disability examiner at a state agency, who will contact your medical sources.

☐ If the medical information you have submitted isn't sufficient, the agency will send you to a consulting specialist, at the government's expense. This information becomes part of your file.

☐ If you've met the medical disability requirements (which are extremely stringent), you'll be granted benefits.

☐ You can still be found disabled even if you don't meet the medical requirements. Age, past work experience and education are also taken into account. The approach is individualized throughout the process.

☐ The final eligibility decision is made and signed by the disability examiner, together with a physician who works for the state (not the consulting physician).

☐ If benefits are denied, you can appeal the decision or reapply.

Proving Your Disability

☐ Social Security's definition of medical disability: The inability to do any substantial, gainful activity by reason of any medically determinable physical or mental impairment which can be expected to result in death, or which has lasted, or can be expected to last, for a continuous period of not less than 12 months. To meet the definition you must have a severe impairment that makes you unable to do your previous work or any other gainful work that exists in the national economy.

☐ It's crucial that your doctor submit very precise medical information, including all test results—the same kind of information a doctor would use in coming up with a diagnosis and treatment plan. Social Security won't accept your doctor's conclusions. It wants the medical evidence that led to the conclusion.

☐ Social Security has a long list of impairments under which your disability should fall. The listing, broken down into 13 body systems, covers about 99% of the disabilities that people apply for. Recommended: You and your doctor should take a look at the listings before you apply. If your doctor answers in enough detail, you might avoid a visit to the agency's consulting physician.

Filing an Appeal

☐ When benefits are denied, a notice is sent. A brief paragraph explains the reason in general terms. At that point you can go back to the Social Security office and file for a reconsideration, which is simply a review of your case.

☐ If the reconsideration is denied, you can take your case to an administrative law judge within Social Security's Office of Hearings and Appeals. You don't need a lawyer for this hearing, but many people do have one. At the hearing you present your case, review the evidence in your file, add other relevant evidence and personally impress the judge. The reversal rate at this level is fairly high (40% to 60%).

☐ If denied at this hearing, you can go to the Appeals Council and then up through the courts. The chances of reversal improve at each level. Most people just go up to the administrative law judge level. If they're turned down there, they file a new claim and start all over.

Source: Dan Wilcox, Disability Program Specialist, Social Security Administration, Disability Programs Branch, New York.

Photographic proof

To speed up an insurance claim in case of fire, flood, or other damage to your home, a photographic record of your possessions is the best means of establishing proof of loss.

Check your policy. Furnishings (for example, sofas and silverware) are usually covered under the heading of actual cash value (ACV).

Guidelines for photographic household possessions:

☐ Use an instant-copy camera, to get the job done to your satisfaction in a day.

☐ Photograph everything you own. Open cupboards to show contents. Even objects that appear to be inexpensive and ordinary may be costly to replace.

☐ Don't forget the boiler, water heater, and pump.

☐ Mark the backs of the photos with model and serial numbers and other pertinent information.

☐ Unstack pots and pans and group small appliances when shooting kitchen appliances.

☐ Put silver and bric-a-brac on black velvet material to make them look as valuable as they are. Shoot them with color film.

☐ Don't neglect the bicycles, tools, and barbecues in the garage.

☐ Get exterior shots of shrubbery and other landscaping, which are generally covered by insurance.

☐ File the pictures, along with receipts and related documents, categorizing them by room.

Reducing home and auto insurance

Do you qualify for any of these insurance discounts?

Home

☐ No smokers.

☐ Personal articles (jewelry, etc.) are kept in a vault.

☐ Protective devices (burglar alarms, fire alarms, smoke alarms, deadlock bolts and other locking devices).

☐ Near a fire department or a source of water.

Some companies give discounts to retirees, and in some states co-op owners are entitled to homeowner's insurance. Or consider taking a higher deductible to keep premiums down.

Auto

☐ Equipped with antitheft locks and alarms.

☐ One of the drivers insured on the

policy is away from home (at college, for instance).

☐ "No fault" insurance laws reduce payments in some states.

How to cut auto insurance

Cut auto insurance costs by:

☐ Raising deductibles from $100 to $500 or even $1,000. That saves 35%–60% on premiums.

☐ Dropping collision coverage on cars over five years old.

☐ Finding out whether the car qualifies for discounts on autos less likely to be stolen or less costly to repair.

☐ Discontinuing medical coverage if it's duplicated by your employer's health plan.

☐ Reconsidering extras such as coverage for towing or car rentals during repair.

Source: National Consumer Insurance Organization, as reported in *Money*.

Buying disability insurance

What to aim for when you buy disability insurance:

☐ The policy is noncancelable. That means the company cannot cancel the policy for medical condition or number of claims or change the premium before the individual's 65th birthday.

Not as good: A guaranteed renewable policy. Premiums on such a policy may be increased.

☐ Benefits are payable over a long period. The first choice is a lifetime policy. Second choice: One that covers you until you reach the age of 65. Anything less than that leaves a major gap.

☐ The policy will pay benefits as long as you cannot practice your "own occupation." Policies that use the phrase "own occupation" will pay you a benefit as long as you cannot work full time at the type of work you did full time before the disability. With such a policy you can "double dip" by working at a position that pays less than you earned before and collect full benefits. Less attractive policies will stop paying benefits if you can do any work, even if that work brings far less income. Compromise: A residual policy. This is true income-replacement insurance, and it is satisfactory for many people. How it works: If the disability results in your being able to work, but in a position that brings in, for example, only 50% of your former income, you will receive 50% of your total benefit.

☐ The insuring company has a good reputation for paying claims. Your broker's knowledge and sophistication are critical in choosing a company that you won't have trouble with.

☐ The benefits are subject to cost-of-living adjustments. This feature is worth the extra cost in premiums.

How to get what you need from your accountant

The biggest mistake people make in dealing with the professionals they hire to work on their tax returns is to drop everything in the professional's lap and walk away. To get the most from your accountant, you must take an active role in the preparation of your returns...even if you pay hundreds of dollars in preparation fees to the most prestigious firm in town. Not only must you help your accountant find everything that will save you tax dollars, but you must also understand how every figure that's reported on the return was arrived at.

☐ Organize the information. This saves his time and your money.

☐ Bring to his attention any out-of-the-ordinary deductions...job-hunting expenses, child care or dependent care, unreimbursed business travel, etc.

☐ Be complete. The more last-minute changes you call in after your return has been prepared, the bigger your bill will be.

☐ Mention changes in essential personal and financial data. If, for example, you don't tell your accountant that you're supporting aged parents, he isn't likely to know about the dependency exemptions or possible medical deductions for them, or to recommend a multiple-support agreement with your brothers and sisters.

☐ Discuss your audit tolerance. If you want a return that will save you top tax dollars, you must take aggressive positions on your various financial dealings. The more aggressive you are, the more likely your return will be audited. If you want to cut your audit risk, you must take a more conservative approach to the way you handle your return. You can't have it both ways.

☐ Assume that your return will be audited. Using a tax professional doesn't lessen that likelihood. Your accountant isn't responsible to the IRS for your return. You are. The IRS auditor will ask you how your charitable contributions were calculated, how your interest was calculated, or when depreciable assets were purchased.

☐ Keep worksheets detailing the calculations for each figure on your tax return.

Source: Paul N. Strassels, a former IRS tax-law specialist.

Prudent accountant-client communications

Be careful of what you say to your accountant...if you have something to hide. Suppose that for years you consistently neglected to tell your accountant about a certain source of income. If you now tell the accountant about it, he can be called on by the government to testify against you in court, since accountant-client communications aren't privileged. But conversations you have with an attorney are privileged. An attorney can't be compelled to testify against a client who has admitted that he committed a crime. Best advice for someone in this position: Hire an attorney, who can then hire the accountant and include him under his umbrella of privilege.

Source: Ms. X, Esq., a former IRS agent, who is still well-connected.

Should you file a joint or separate tax return?

The effect of a joint tax return is to treat a married couple as one taxpayer, no matter which spouse realized the income. Filing a joint return will usually result in tax savings because the joint return rates are generally more favorable than the rates for married persons filing separately.

☐ Credit for child care expenses is only available on a joint return.

☐ Keep in mind that when a couple files a joint return, both parties are liable for the full amount of tax due, regardless of who earned the income.

But there are some advantages to filing separately:

☐ In community property states, all community income and deductions are reported one-half on each return. This can result in lower tax-bracket filings.

Some married couples file separate returns so they won't have to disclose to their spouse the source and extent of their earnings.

Filing separate returns may make sense if one of the spouses has extraordinary medical expenses. These expenses are deductible only to the extent that they exceed 7½% of the combined income of both spouses. Therefore, the smaller income on a separate return might result in a deduction that would be reduced or eliminated on a joint return because of the larger combined income.

In certain states, the income tax saving from filing separate returns can be greater than the federal tax saving from filing a joint return.

Source: *Family: The Best Tax Shelter.* Boardroom Books, New York.

Before mailing in a tax return

Getting the details right the first time can save the time and trouble of dealing with the IRS later. Checklist:

☐ Sign the return.

☐ Did your preparer sign?

☐ Did you answer every question on the return?

☐ Put your Social Security number on every page and every attachment, including your check.

☐ Put your tax-shelter registration number on the return.

☐ Make copies of your return.

☐ Compare your return with last year's to make sure you didn't overlook anything.

☐ Put the return away for a few days or a week so that you can look at it with a fresh eye before mailing it.

☐ Send it by certified mail so there will be no question that your return was filed on time. Mailed on time is considered to be filed on time by the IRS.

☐ Use a separate envelope for each return.

☐ Put your children's returns or estimated payments in separate envelopes.

☐ Attach your W-2.

☐ Include your check if you owe money to the IRS.

☐ Include any receipts and forms required to prove your charitable contributions.

☐ Include a check for the tax you owe if you are filing an extension request.

Top filing mistakes... according to the IRS

☐ Miscalculating medical and dental expenses. This deduction is based on your adjusted gross income—AGI. Carefully complete up to the AGI line on your 1040 before attempting to figure your medical expenses.

☐ Taking the wrong amount of earned income credit. Use the worksheet in the instruction booklet to avoid mistakes.

☐ Entering the wrong amount of tax. Use the right tax tables.

☐ Confusion about income tax withheld. Don't confuse this with the Social Security tax that was withheld from your pay.

☐ Unemployment compensation errors. Use the special formula in the IRS instruction booklet to calculate the amount of taxable unemployment.

☐ Mistakes in calculating child and dependent care expenses. Use Form 2441 and double-check your math.

☐ Errors in tax due. Believe it or not, taxpayers often err in determining the bottom line of their tax return—are they entitled to a refund or do they owe the IRS? Carefully compare the tax you owe with the amount you have paid through withholding or estimated tax payments.

☐ Overlooking credits. Read all IRS instructions carefully.

☐ Adding income incorrectly. Mistakes are frequently made by taxpayers when adding the income section of Form 1040.

Source: *IRS Publication No. 910.*

Filing late

Reasons for getting an extension:

☐ You don't have all the information you need to fill out the return.

☐ You need time to find the cash to make a contribution to your Keogh account. (Unlike IRAs, which must be made by April 15, Keogh contributions can be made up to the extended due date of your return—as late as October 15.)

☐ You have a complicated transaction that you need time to ponder.

Timetable:

☐ First extension. April 15 is the due date for tax returns. But you can get an automatic four-month extension by filing Form 4868 by April 15. If you pay late you'll owe late-payment penalties, plus interest on the tax paid late. *Trap:* You must make estimated tax payments on Form 1040-ES by April 15. You can't get an extension of time to make quarterly estimated payments.

☐ Second extension. It's possible to get a second filing extension of two months. But the second extension isn't automatic; you must have a valid reason for requesting it, such as a death in the family or loss of your records. Loophole: It has been my experience that the closer you file to October 15 (after August 15) the less chance there is that you'll be audited. A second extension may be the way to get off the audit treadmill if you've been audited every year for the last few years.

Source: Edward L. Mendlowitz, partner, Mendlowitz Weitsen, New York.

To avoid late-filing penalties

A person who files a late tax return without getting a prior extension faces stiff penalties. It's possible to avoid these penalties, but you must convince the IRS that you had a good excuse for filing late.

Situations in which the IRS has said it may accept a late return without penalty:

☐ The return was postmarked on time, even if it had insufficient postage.

☐ The return was filed on time but in the wrong IRS district or office.

☐ The return was filed late because of inaccurate information received from an IRS employee.

☐ A filing delay was caused by the destruction of the taxpayer's records in a fire, flood or other casualty.

☐ An individual couldn't get proper tax forms from the IRS, in spite of asking for them at a reasonable time.

☐ The filer was not able to get

necessary information from an IRS official, despite a personal visit to an IRS office.

☐ The taxpayer died, was seriously injured or was forced to be away from home for a reason that was unexpected and beyond his or her control.

☐ The taxpayer was ignorant of the law, in that he or she never had to file a particular kind of form or return before.

☐ The death or illness of an immediate family member.

☐ Incapacitating illness of the taxpayer himself.

☐ A competent and informed tax adviser told the taxpayer that a tax return was not necessary.

How to proceed: Make your request for abatement of the penalty in writing to your local IRS Service Center. Give a detailed explanation of your reason for filing late. Use the term "reasonable cause" both at the beginning and the end of the letter. To speed up the process, attach your letter to the return you are filing late. Don't wait until you get a penalty notice—that could take months.

Not-so-safe amendments

Filing an amended return to take a deduction for the following may result in an audit because of the high susceptibility of these items to audit:

☐ Travel and entertainment expenses.

☐ Unreimbursed business expenses.

☐ Casualty losses.

☐ Transactions with relatives.

☐ Charitable donations of property.

☐ Home office deductions.

Audit triggers

Red flags most likely to bring on an audit.

☐ Deductions that are excessively high in relation to your income. A return that shows $50,000 of income and $40,000 of itemized deductions is almost certain to be pulled for an audit. Keep your deductions reasonable. But don't cheat yourself just because you're afraid of an audit. Attach an explanation to your return for an item that you believe the IRS may question. When your return gets kicked out of the computer that screens all returns for possible audit, an IRS official will read your explanation. If he's satisfied, he will probably put the return back into the processing system without sending it on to be audited.

☐ Undocumented charitable gifts. Attach a statement to your return showing the date of all property contributions, the fair market value, and the name of the charity. If you don't automatically supply this statement, the IRS will pull your return to look for it—increasing your chance of audit. You must now attach an independent appraisal for charitable gifts of property worth more than $5,000.

☐ Overstated casualty losses. Many audits are triggered because taxpayers exceeded the legal limits on casualty-loss deductions. Use the IRS worksheet, Form 4684. You can deduct only the part of your loss that exceeds 10% of your adjusted gross income. And then you deduct only the lesser of what you paid for the item or the decrease in its value as a result of the casualty.

☐ Overstated medical deductions. To be deductible, medical expenses must exceed 7½% of your adjusted gross income.

☐ Tax shelters with very large losses. These almost always trigger an audit. Avoid tax shelters unless you get professional advice. Make sure it's a legitimate shelter.

☐ Inclusion of Schedule C. Self-employed individuals must file a Schedule C with their tax returns. It shows all business-related income and deductions. Warning: It is also a red flag for an audit. Prepare it carefully, and have the records to back it up.

☐ Home-office deductions. These must meet stringent IRS guidelines. The office must be used regularly and exclusively for business purposes. If your family watches television there when it's not in use as an office, you lose the deduction. The office must be your principal place of business. If you have an office at the company where you are employed, you can't deduct the home office. But if you freelance in a different business at night, the office is deductible.

☐ Overstated business expenses. The IRS will scrutinize these deductions. Keep your travel and entertainment deductions reasonable. (And be very careful to stay within the tax law's limits for deducting your business car and computer.)

☐ Sloppy returns. Simple errors cause many tax returns to be kicked out of the IRS computers This means the chances for audit are greater because the return is now in human hands. Don't make these mistakes on your return:

☐ Errors in simple mathematics.

☐ Failure to transfer totals correctly from one page to the next.

☐ Use of the wrong rate tables for your filing status (single, joint, head of household, etc.).

☐ Failure to follow IRS instructions.

☐ Failure to answer all questions. A blank space where there should be an answer will wake up the computer.

☐ Failure to attach W-2s or other required statements.

Source: Michael L. Borsuk, tax partner and managing partner of the Long Island office of Coopers & Lybrand, Melville, NY.

When it pays to ask for an audit

☐ When someone dies, the heirs can count only on sharing in the after-tax proceeds of the estate. So the sooner the IRS examines matters to settle things the better.

☐ When you close down a business, its records and the key personnel who can explain its tax strategies may soon disappear. An IRS examination at a much later date could prove awkward and costly.

☐ When you ask for a prompt assessment of taxes that are due, the IRS must act within 18 months. Otherwise it has up to three years to conduct an examination of the year's return.

☐ Use Form 4810 to ask for the prompt assessment. You don't have to use this form, but if you don't use it, be sure to eliminate any possible confusion by mentioning in your letter to the IRS that your request for an examination is made under Code Section 6501(d).

Most frequently overlooked job-related deductions

☐ Moving expenses incurred to get a new job, including the cost of selling your residence and getting out of your lease.

☐ Job-hunting expenses, including the cost of typing or printing a resume, employment agency fees, etc.

☐ Professional magazines related to your job.

☐ Work- or business-related educational expenses that don't qualify you for a new trade or business.

☐ Transportation necessary for medical care. You can deduct your actual expenses or a standard mileage rate of 9¢ per mile, plus parking fees and tolls in either case.

☐ Traveling expenses to a second job, if you go directly from the first job to the second.

☐ Business gifts up to $25.

How to avoid the 2% floor for miscellaneous deductions

Miscellaneous itemized deductions include expenses directly connected with the production of investment income, such as…

1. Fees for managing investment property.

2. Legal and professional fees.

3. Fees for tax preparation and advice, investment advice and financial planning.

Problem: Most taxpayers are unable to deduct any investment expenses on Schedule A because their total miscellaneous expenses don't exceed 2% of their adjusted gross income.

Solution: Put as many expenses as possible out of reach of the 2% floor by accounting for them elsewhere on your return. Possibilities:

☐ Schedule C. Report non-wage miscellaneous income such as that earned from consulting, lecturing, or speaking engagements, on Schedule C as business income, rather than as "other income" on the 1040. The expenses you incur in producing that income are deductible on Schedule C, where they are not subject to the 2% floor.

☐ Schedule E. Expenses of earning rent, royalties, or other income that is reportable on Schedule E are deductible on Schedule E, where they are not subject to the 2% floor.

☐ Adjust the cost of assets. Add the expenses of acquiring a capital asset to the asset's cost. This will reduce the amount of capital gain you must report when you eventually sell. While this approach doesn't give you a current deduction for the expense, it does reduce the tax you pay on the gain.

☐ Bunch payment of expenses so that you get two years' worth into one year and exceed the 2% floor in at least one year.

Source: Richard Lager, national director of tax practice, Grant Thornton, CPAs 1850 M St. NW, Washington, DC 20036.

Most frequently overlooked real estate deductions

☐ Points, also called loan origination fees, paid for obtaining a mortgage on your principal residence. They must be a customary practice in your area.

☐ Mortgage prepayment penalties.

☐ Real estate taxes. If you sold your home during the year, don't forget the portion you paid while you still owned the house.

☐ Your proportion of co-op or condo real estate taxes.

Deduction for home computer used for business

You must know the new record-keeping rules and comply with them, or risk losing deductions for perfectly legitimate business expenses, including a home computer used for business.

The record-keeping requirements are tied to new rules on listed property that generally limit deductions on property placed in service after June 18, 1984. That is property used partly for business and partly for personal reasons, including home computers.

Tax breaks for listed property depend on the percentage of business use. New rules:

☐ The computer must be required for

the convenience of the employer and as a condition of employment. A statement from your employer isn't enough. (It can be helpful, though.) You must also show the property is required for your job.

☐ The computer must be used more than 50% for business, or you will not be entitled to first-year expensing or to the ACRS method of depreciation.

☐ If business use is 50% or less, you may still deduct depreciation, but you must figure it on a straight-line basis.

☐ If business use drops to below 50% in later years, you may have to give back part of your deductions.

☐ You must record all use of the computer. Just recording business use isn't enough, as it won't enable you to calculate the percentage of business use.

☐ Write down the time you spend at the computer, the program you run and the purpose of the use.

☐ Maintain documentation for all expenses, including repair bills, purchase of software, diskettes, other supplies and any other costs.

☐ Home computers are comparatively new, and record-keeping rules aren't well established yet. But the more extensive your records, the easier it will be to substantiate the deductions you claim.

Source: Dean Schuckman, partner, executive financial services, Price Waterhouse, Stamford, CT.

Deducting your hobby

For your personal bottom line, it can make a huge difference whether you operate a hobby as a hobby or as a sideline business.

☐ As a hobbyist, your tax deductions are pretty much limited to the amount of income the activity generates.

☐ If you run the hobby as a business, all your expenses are deductible, even if they exceed business income.

Hobby or Business

The distinction between a hobby and a business is very fine. When you deduct losses from a business that the IRS could label as a hobby, you must be able to prove that you intended to make a profit.

☐ If you show a profit in three of any five consecutive years (two out of seven for breeding, showing, training or racing horses), it is presumed you

are engaged in an activity for profit. Although the IRS can challenge the presumption, normally it will not.

☐ You can elect to delay any IRS determination until the first five years are up by filing a special form. But in making this election, you sign a waiver of the three-year statute of limitations for the tax years involved.

☐ If you don't meet the presumption, the IRS may challenge your deductions as hobby losses. It will be necessary for you to prove your good intentions.

☐ Operate your hobby in a businesslike manner. Keep accurate books and records.

☐ Institute new operating procedures to correct past business practices that resulted in losses.

☐ Act professionally. Show that you hired or consulted with recognized experts in the field, and that you followed their advice.

☐ Hire qualified people to run your day-to-day operation or hire part-time help. Remember, no rule says you must devote 40 hours a week to your sideline business.

☐ Even if your business continually produces losses, you can still prove a profit motive by showing that assets you have acquired are expected to appreciate.

☐ It may help establish a profit motive if you can show that in the past you were successfully involved in your current activity.

☐ Register your business name by filing a "doing business as" statement with your local county clerk.

☐ Use business cards and stationery.

☐ Take out a company listing in the *Yellow Pages*.

☐ Keep a log of the business contacts you've seen during the year.

☐ Advertise in local papers.

☐ Send promotional mailings to prospective customers.

☐ Set up a business bank account.

☐ Get a business telephone.

☐ Buy a postage meter and a copying machine.

Source: Randy Bruce Blaustein, Esq., a former IRS agent now with Blaustein Greenberg & Co., 155 E. 31 St., New York 10016.

Deducting travel luxuries

Here are some high-roller travel expenses that, with a bit of luck, your employer will consider ordinary and necessary. As long as the expenses are business related, they are deductible by the company and are not included in your income.

☐ A limousine to take you to the airport and drop you off at your hotel. If you're traveling with an entourage, you may need a separate limo just for the luggage.

☐ First class transportation on luxury airlines, to work and relax in comfort.

☐ Suites in the best hotels, with flowers and a well-stocked bar.

☐ Dry cleaning, laundry, pressing.

☐ Alterations to clothes for a business meeting.

☐ Repairs to shoes you have to wear with a business suit.

☐ A new shirt or tie to replace one that was stained on the plane.

Source: Ms. X, Esq., a former IRS agent who is still well-connected, is the author of *How to Beat the IRS: Insider Tactics,* Boardroom Books, Springfield, NJ 07081.

Justifying a deduction for lost jewelry

Jewelry is missing from your luggage when you get back from vacation. How do you prove that there was a theft? How do you prove the cost of the items stolen?

☐ Hopefully you reported the theft to the airport security office. Get a copy of its report. Otherwise be prepared to explain why nothing was done.

☐ You must prove to the IRS agent the original cost of the jewelry. A casualty loss is limited to the lesser of the cost or fair market value. It will be presumed that the jewelry was bought years ago and has since gone up in value. If you don't have receipts to verify the original cost:

☐ Best approach: Write down the approximate year each piece of jewelry was acquired, the store's location and an estimate of the cost.

☐ Next to each item, write a detailed description, including the kind of stone, cut, weight, and any other distinguishing qualities.

☐ Get a statement from a qualified jeweler who can attest to the fact that your estimates of original cost are reasonable.

If you can't document business deductions

The trick to surviving an audit when your records are not in perfect order is to reconstruct the amounts you spent and prove they were spent on tax-deductible items. Although the IRS doesn't advertise the fact, it often allows deductions in full or in part when the taxpayer's documentation is less complete than is officially required.

To reconstruct means to come up with reasonable evidence to corroborate expenses. It does not mean fabricating or otherwise falsifying documents. That is a crime.

Records can be legitimately reconstructed by:

☐ Providing affidavits from relevant third parties.

☐ Proving your expenditures by indirect methods.

☐ Assembling enough facts to substantiate your deductions even though you can't prove every dollar that you claimed.

The key to establishing credibility: Go into the audit organized and well-prepared. Before you meet with the agent:

☐ Find out which items on your return will be examined. The agent may want to look at only one or two deductions. Tell him, without admitting that your records are incomplete, that you want to have all the necessary information for your first meeting.

☐ Make a list of all the individual items that you lumped together and claimed as a deduction. Prepare this worksheet list on a plain piece of paper. Make sure the figures add up to the deduction you claimed.

☐ Attach to the worksheet the receipts that you do have in your possession.

☐ Try to get copies of missing receipts. If you can't, try to find canceled checks that prove you made the payment.

☐ Estimate expenses for which you have no record whatsoever. Write down as many details about the expenses as you can remember. For a business meal, for example, write down whom you entertained, the date, the restaurant, and the business purpose of the meeting.

☐ Out of town trips. You must prove that you had a business purpose for taking the trip. Establish this by showing the agent a list of the people you met and their business affiliation. If you have had any subsequent correspondence with these people, show these letters to the agent. The correspondence establishes a business purpose for the trip and also proves you were in the city when you said you were.

Source: Randy Bruce Blaustein, Esq., Blaustein Greenberg & Co., 155 E. 31 St., New York 10016.

If you can't document a charitable deduction

When you donate old clothing, appliances or furniture to a charity, get a receipt and hold on to it. It's the best evidence if your deduction is challenged. But if you cannot produce the receipt:

☐ Show the agent bills for purchase of the merchandise.

☐ List each item you gave.

☐ Describe each item, including quality, fabric it was made of, brand name, the store from which it was purchased, and when the purchase was made.

☐ Add up your estimate of the original costs of the items.

☐ Discount this amount by 50% to 75% to take into account wear and tear.

☐ The more detailed your support, the better the chance that your deduction will be allowed.

Putting family members on the payroll of a family-owned business

There are numerous ways business income can be shifted to family members. One of the easiest methods is putting family members who perform services for the business on the payroll. Some of the advantages, however, are not immediately obvious. Some things to consider:

☐ Putting family members on the payroll of an incorporated company may incur the cost of Social Security, unemployment, and self-employment taxes, but the income tax savings from income splitting will usually more than offset this cost.

☐ Family members on the payroll must perform services and their compensation must be reasonable in relation to the services performed. If the payments are considered excessive by the IRS, the amounts could be reclassified as earnings of the parent and a gift to the child.

☐ A spouse on the payroll may not reduce tax on income for the business owner since a joint return is usually filed.

☐ If a child or other family relative performs services for the business, the income can be effectively split and shifted to lower tax brackets.

☐ A child in college who works during the summer for his or her parents can use the earnings for college and, essentially, fund the cost with pre-tax dollars.

☐ In order to split business income among family members who do not actually perform services for the business, an interest in the business must be shifted to that family member. The transfer of a business interest is often accomplished through the use of a family partnership or a corporation. There are exceptions to this rule, so check with your tax lawyer.

How Social Security is taxed

Social Security benefits are taxable if the individual's total income for the year exceeds these dollar limits...

☐ $25,000 if you are single.

☐ $32,000 if you are married and file a joint return.

☐ $25,000 if you are married, do not file a joint return, and do not live with your spouse.

☐ Zero if you are married, do not file a joint return, and did live with your spouse at any time during the year.

Trap: Total income includes adjusted gross income (AGI), tax-exempt interest and half of your Social Security benefits.

If you are likely to exceed the limit, consider these strategies...

☐ Invest in assets that appreciate in value without producing current income, such as Series EE savings bonds or growth stocks.

☐ Time the recognition of income (IRA withdrawals, etc.) so that you receive it for instance, in alternate years, or when you have deductions that reduce your adjusted gross income.

☐ Divorce...while a married couple filing jointly will have a $32,000 income limit, two single people can take $25,000 each, or $50,000 together.
Source: *Ernst & Young's Arthur Young Tax Guide.*

Windfall loopholes

The sudden receipt of a big amount of money can make any taxpayer nervous about tax consequences. Loopholes to consider:

☐ The only estimated tax you have to pay is an amount equal to the tax shown on your last year's return. You must pay 90% of this year's tax if your adjusted gross income is $75,000 or more, increased by $40,000 over last year, and you paid estimated taxes in any of the three prior years.

☐ If you sell your business or have any other large boost to your income, double-check your total withholdings for the year. If you continue working, the amount that's withheld from your paycheck will probably be enough to cover your taxes...for that year.

☐ If you quit your job, send the IRS enough tax, in addition to what was withheld, to equal last year's tax bill.

☐ If you win big money from gambling or the lottery, and find yourself in the top tax bracket, take part of your new fortune and gamble with it. If you win, you'll end up with even more money. If you lose, your tax bill is lower because you can offset the gambling losses against the winnings.
Source: Edward Mendlowitz, Mendlowitz Weitsen, 2 Pennsylvania Plaza, New York 10121.

Delaying income until next year

To postpone income:

☐ Delay collecting rent on investment property until after the first of the year.

☐ Ask your employer to delay paying your year-end bonus until January.

☐ Postpone billing clients so that the money doesn't come in until early in the next year.

☐ Sell property under an installment sale agreement.

☐ Don't cash in US savings bonds until next year.

☐ Wait until next year to exercise employee stock options that will be taxed as ordinary income.

☐ Take money from your money-market account and buy Treasury bills that come due next year.

How to avoid penalties for underpaying estimated taxes

The tax law now requires that your estimated tax payments include any alternative minimum tax (AMT) you might owe for the year. Problem: Most taxpayers don't know in advance whether they'll be subject to the AMT or how much it will come to.

To avoid penalties:

☐ Pay estimated taxes that are at least equal to last year's tax bill. You must pay 90% of this year's tax if your adjusted gross income is $75,000 or more, increased by $40,000 over last year, and you paid estimated taxes in any of the three prior years.

☐ Alternative: Make estimated tax

payments that equal 90% of the current year's tax.

☐ These two "safe harbors" are the only ones remaining in the law.

Dependent status according to the IRS

Federal tax laws allow one exemption (adjusted for inflation) for each dependent who satisfies the following five tests: (1) relationship, (2) citizenship, (3) joint return, (4) gross income, and (5) support.

A person related in any of the following ways does not have to be a member of the taxpayer's household:

☐ Son, daughter, grandchild or great-grandchild.

☐ Stepchild.

☐ Sibling, half-sibling, step-sibling.

☐ Parent, grandparent or great-grandparent.

☐ Stepmother or stepfather.

☐ Niece or nephew.

☐ Aunt or uncle.

☐ In-law.

A person not related in the above ways must be a member of the taxpayer's household for the entire year. If a joint return is filed, the dependent does not have to be related to both spouses.

☐ The dependent must be a US citizen, or a resident of the US, Canada, or Mexico for some part of the year.

☐ The dependent must not file a joint return. This test does not apply if the dependent and the dependent's spouse are not required to file a return, but they file a joint return in order to claim a refund of tax withheld. If a dependent is eligible to file a joint return, the tax benefit of the joint return should be compared with the tax benefit of the dependency exemption to determine the greatest tax benefit for the entire family unit.

☐ Generally, a dependent must not have gross income in excess of the amount of the allowed personal exemption. Nontaxable income, such as Social Security benefits, is not included in the determination of gross income for this purpose. Gross income for the dependent includes all rental receipts not reduced by payment of rental expenses. Therefore, a dependent may receive very little

economic benefit from his or her rental income and it may result in disallowance of the dependency exemption. In this situation, consideration should be given to transferring all or part of the rental property to the person providing the support.

☐ If a child is under 19 at the end of the year, the gross income test does not apply. A child under 19 may have any amount of income and still be a dependent, if the tests of relationship, citizenship, joint-return and support are met.

☐ If a child is a student, the gross income test does not apply. The child must be a full-time student during some part of each of five calendar months of the year. Attendance at most, but not all, schools will qualify for this test.

☐ The dependent generally must receive more than one-half of his or her total support from the taxpayer. Total support includes expenditures for food, shelter, clothing, education, medical and dental care, recreation, transportation, and similar necessities. The dependent's own funds, including Social Security benefits, are counted in determining the total amount spent for support, unless it can be demonstrated that these funds were not used for support. (If the dependent puts some of his or her income in the bank or other investment and doesn't use it for his or her own support, the taxpayer may be able to meet the 50-percent support test.)

☐ If several family members share the cost of supporting a dependent relative and no one person contributes more than one-half of the support, the members of the group may decide among themselves who is to receive the dependency exemption by executing a multiple-support agreement. To be eligible to claim the exemption, the taxpayer must have contributed more than 10 percent of the dependent's support, and the group must have furnished over 50 percent. Each year a different qualifying family member may claim the exemption by changing the agreement.

☐ When parents are separated or divorced, the custodial parent is entitled to the dependency exemption in all cases unless he or she expressly waives the right to claim it. This rule does not apply in cases where the noncustodial parent has been awarded the exemption under a divorce decree or separate mainte- nance agreement executed before January 1, 1985, provided that such parent furnished at least $600 of the child's support.

How to protect yourself with a private IRS ruling

Before risking a large amount of money on a transaction that has questionable tax consequences, find out first how the IRS will treat the transaction. Ask for a private letter ruling, which is a written statement from the IRS National Office on the tax effect of the proposed transaction.

Under the Revenue Act of 1987, the IRS is required to charge a fee for all rulings. Fees range from $50 to $1,000 de- pending on the complexity of the issue.

When to Ask

You should get a ruling when you believe the law is favorable and a major transaction hinges on favorable treatment.

☐ You must get a ruling when certain tax-free transactions involving foreign corporations are made.

Ask for a ruling if:

☐ You are considering an exchange of property, but only if the exchange is ruled tax free.

☐ Your child has a reading disability. You've found an expensive special school, but you must know whether the tuition will be deductible as a medical expense.

☐ You want to retire from the family business, passing control to your chil- dren via a complicated stock redemp- tion. But will the redemption be given favorable capital-gains treatment?

☐ You want to give the government a right-of-way over your land, to be used as a hiking trail, but only if you get a charitable deduction for the gift.

☐ It's important that you know whether to withhold Social Security tax for employees who work for you in an unusual capacity.

When Not to Ask for a Ruling

☐ It's dangerous to ask for a ruling when you're sure it will go against you. In such a situation it's better to proceed without a ruling. If your return isn't audited, the transaction may not be challenged. But a private ruling acts as a red flag. It should be attached to your tax return. An adverse ruling is certain to catch the examiner's eye, resulting in disallowance of the questionable item.

☐ If you have other tax problems, you may be alerting the IRS to them.

How to Ask for a Private Ruling

☐ There is no prescribed form...and no charge. Send a letter to the Internal Revenue Service, Associate Chief Counsel (Technical), Attention: CC:IND:S, Room 6545, 1111 Constitution Ave. NW, Washington, DC 20224.

☐ To speed things up: Call the IRS in advance (202-622-5000) and state the general area of the ruling request. You'll be given a code number to add to the address. That will direct the request to the individual in charge of rulings in that area.

☐ Write the names, addresses and taxpayer identification numbers of all the people involved.

☐ Give a complete statement of all the facts concerning the proposed transaction.

☐ Make a precise statement of the business reasons for the transaction.

☐ Make clear which type of ruling you are asking for.

☐ Give arguments supporting your position, with citations of authorities such as court decisions.

☐ Request a conference to discuss the matter if an adverse ruling is expected.

☐ Make clear that the issue is not being litigated.

☐ Declare that the facts are true and that you sign the request under penalty of perjury.

Important: Include in the letter a request that all confidential information be deleted from the published ruling. This ensures that IRS personnel don't slip up when making the deletions that are required by law.

☐ Attach copies of all relevant documents to your letter.

What to Expect

☐ Within 21 calendar days, an IRS agent will call to discuss the issues involved.

☐ If the agent says he is inclined to

approve the request, a favorable letter will follow. Depending on the complexity of the transaction and the issues involved, this can take from 60 days to six months.

☐ If the agent says the IRS will rule unfavorably, you can withdraw the request and proceed with the transaction. There is no obligation to inform the IRS of the withdrawn request when your tax return is filed. However, the information the IRS has collected on your specific issues may be sent to your district IRS office.

☐ If the agent is uncertain, you may be able to amend your ruling request so as to come up with a favorable ruling.

☐ If matters aren't resolved in this first conversation with the agent, you can exercise your right to a conference with the IRS. Here you will have a chance to discuss your position and to negotiate changes in the proposed transaction. If the IRS position is still negative, you may withdraw your request. No ruling is better than a negative ruling.

Where the IRS Will Not Rule

☐ Purely hypothetical questions.

☐ Questions of fact—for instance, What is the value of this piece of property?

☐ How the estate tax will apply to the property of a living person.

☐ Issues on which there are court decisions the IRS may be planning to appeal.

☐ Issues involving tax laws for which regulations have not yet been written.

☐ A long list of specific questions and problems that the IRS won't rule on in advance is published regularly in the *Internal Revenue Bulletin.*

Tax traps in divorce

Divorcing couples often fall into tax traps that prove costly for both spouses. Family-law attorneys and judges often don't understand the tax law, and in many states judges aren't required even to consider taxes when rendering decisions.

Divorcing couples are likely to do much better, taxwise, by reaching a voluntary agreement that benefits both of them. Planning points:

☐ Dependency exemptions: The exemption goes to the parent with custody, unless that parent agrees in writing to give up the exemption. If there are several children, the parents can agree to divvy up the exemptions. Normally, an exemption is most valuable to the parent in the higher tax bracket.

☐ Lower tax rates are available to a parent who qualifies for head-of-household tax status. To get this, a parent must have at least one child living with him or her. Otherwise, the divorced parent must file as a single person and pay higher tax rates, even if that parent is making large support payments and claims the dependency exemption.

☐ Alimony is deductible by the spouse who pays and taxed to the spouse who receives it, while child support isn't deductible by or taxable to either spouse. But if a divorce decree requires regular payments covering both, without making an allocation between them, all the payments are treated as alimony unless there's a clear indication to the contrary. For example, if a monthly payment of $1,000 for a mother and child is to be reduced to $700 when the child reaches age 18, it's clear that $300 of the monthly payment is intended as child support. This can produce net savings if the paying spouse is in a much higher tax bracket than the receiving one.

☐ Year-end divorces should be timed to have favorable tax impact. One's marital status on December 31 determines his or her filing status.

New-job loophole

Roll a pension-plan distribution from your old company over into the qualified plan at your new firm.

☐ You won't pay any tax on the distribution now. Taxes are deferred until you receive a distribution from your new company's pension plan.

☐ Even better: You'll preserve the right to use five-year averaging on the distribution, a very special tax-saving method used to figure the tax on retirement distributions.

☐ Danger: Don't make the mistake of rolling your pension-plan distribution over into your IRA. That makes it ineligible for five-year averaging.

☐ There are many different tax strategies available when you receive a distribution from a retirement plan. Examine them all to see which one is best for you.

Advantage: Ownership

Excellent tax saving opportunities occur when people own real estate or equipment used by their own company or business, even if that business is only a sideline. Advantages of personal ownership:

☐ Tax shelter. Personal ownership lets depreciation deductions be claimed on the owner's personal tax return. Further, the investor controls the investment. Deductions aren't acquired by investing in an unfamiliar tax-shelter business that is managed by someone else.

☐ Liquidity. The owner may be able to use the property to obtain cash in a tax-favored way. Examples: If the value of real estate goes up, it can be refinanced to obtain a tax-free cash inflow. When property is no longer needed by the company, it can be sold for the owner's personal account. If property is leased to a family-owned company, the owner gets cash flow from the rental payments.

☐ Estate-planning flexibility. More options are available for the disposal of your property. For example, a building can be given to a spouse or child to insure their financial well-being, without giving up a controlling interest in the business.

Working for yourself tax loopholes

Very few of the millions of Americans who are self-employed either in full-time businesses or part-time take advantage of all the special tax benefits they're entitled to. Not to be missed:

☐ As a self-employed person you can have a Keogh plan into which you can put up to $30,000 a year. And if you set up a defined-benefit Keogh, you can put away far more than $30,000 a year.

☐ Lump-sum withdrawals from Keoghs qualify for special five-year averaging—a benefit that can substantially cut the tax you'll ultimately owe on your Keogh.

☐ Instead of giving your children allowances, find them real jobs to do in your business. Pay them reasonable salaries for the work, and deduct the salaries as a business expense. Youth is no barrier. The IRS recently agreed with a Tax Court ruling that a seven-year-old could earn deductible wages for genuine work done in his father's business.

☐ As a sole proprietor you don't have to pay Social Security tax on wages paid to a child who is under 18.

☐ Home office. If you work out of your house and that is your main place of business, you can deduct a portion of your expenses—rent, insurance, utilities, etc. You can also deduct depreciation, but it's probably not wise to do that unless it's a substantial amount. Reason: You're converting part of your house into business property. When you sell, you lose the right to defer tax on your gain on that portion.

☐ Commuting loophole. What constitutes commuting if you work out of your house? IRS position: The first trip from your house and the last trip back are nondeductible commuting. Loophole: Rent a post office box near your house for business mail. Make your first car trip of the day to the post office and back home. Then stop off at the post office on the last trip back home. Impact: All trips *except* the first and last are deductible.

☐ Estimated taxes. If you're self-employed you're not considered an employee for payroll tax purposes. You don't have to report yourself on the IRS' quarterly payroll tax return. Nor do you have to pay monthly withholding tax. You do, however, have to pay estimated tax. Advantage: Estimated tax is payable in quarterly installments at the end of the period in which the income was earned. Being self-employed gives you the use of that tax money through the quarter until you have to pay the installment.

☐ Deductible losses. A business can deduct all its expenses whether it operates at a profit or at a loss. If your business is unincorporated, any losses you incur when you're starting out are fully deductible against other income on your personal income tax return. You can carry your losses forward for up to 15 years.

☐ Under Section 1231 of the Tax Code, gains on the sale of certain business assets can be treated as capital gains while losses can be taken as ordinary losses. (These losses are not subject to the $3,000 capital loss deduction limit.) Section 1231 property is generally depreciable property and real estate used in your business and held for the long-term holding period. Note: In calculating your gain when you sell this property at a profit, you have to recapture and give back depreciation you've taken.

☐ Start-up costs. If you're considering going into a new business, it's better to actually start up (on a small scale) than to spend nondeductible dollars on feasibility studies and financial and legal advice. That money becomes deductible once you're in business, not before.

Source: Edward Mendlowitz, partner, Mendlowitz Weitsen, 2 Pennsylvania Plaza, New York 10121.

About home offices

☐ Homework: A home office is normally deductible only if it is your primary place of business. Three landmark cases:

The Court of Appeals has ruled that orchestra musicians could claim home-office deductions for their practice studios, in spite of the IRS' claim that their primary place of business was the concert hall. Key: The musicians spent more time at home practicing than they did performing. Impact: Salespersons, professors, writers and others who in fact spend most of their time working at home can use this case to try to justify deductions for themselves.

Source: Ernest Drucker, 715 F2d 67.

☐ Proportion: Sally Meiers owned and managed a laundromat. Each day she spent an hour at the laundry and two hours in her home office, where she did necessary administrative work. The Tax Court denied Sally's home-office deduction, because the laundromat, not her home, was her principal place of business. Sally appealed. Court of Appeals: Sally spent more time working at home than anywhere else. Thus, the home office was her principal place of business and the deduction was allowed.

Source: John and Sally Meiers, CA-7, No. 85-1209.

☐ Kind of work: A college professor spent 80% of the work week doing research and writing in an office at home. The IRS ruled the home office was not his "principal place of business" (he had an office at the college), nor was it used "for the convenience of the employer." Court of Appeals: The home office was the professor's principal place of business, as his college office wasn't private enough for the scholarly work required by his job. Moreover, the use of the professor's home was for the employer's convenience, as it relieved the college of the necessity of providing a suitable office. Home office deductions allowed.

Source: David J. Weissman, CA-2, 751-F2d 512.

Drive the company car tax free—almost

Business owners can drive the company car until it has fully depreciated and then switch to keep it for personal use without tax liability.

☐ The car will not become taxable until it is sold. At that time, there will be a taxable gain to the extent that the sale price exceeds the depreciated basis in the car—that is, the original cost of the car reduced by the depreciation deductions that were claimed.

Home-office ground rules

An employee must meet these tests before deducting a home office:

☐ The office must be for the convenience of the employer.

☐ It must be used exclusively for business on a regular basis.

☐ It must be the employee's principal place of business...or it must be used by patients, clients or customers to meet or deal with the employee in the normal course of trade or business...or if it is a separate structure not attached to the employee's residence, it must be used in the employee's trade or business.

After filing your income tax

Don't relax too quickly after filing your income tax return. Post–April 15 problems and what to do about them:

☐ If you haven't received your refund, and it's 12 weeks since you filed your return, contact the taxpayer service representative at the Internal Revenue Office where you filed your return. If you write, include your name, address and Social Security number. (As a general rule, the closer to the April 15 deadline you filed, the longer it will take you to get your refund.)

☐ If your refund check is bigger or smaller than you expected, request a transcript of your account from the IRS. A computer printout shows all payments you've made to the IRS for the past few years and how much of your tax liability has been paid. The transcript will help you determine where the extra refund came from or why the refund wasn't as large as you thought it would be.

☐ If you receive a refund that's too big, get it straightened out with the IRS. Reason: You are responsible for interest on the extra amount, even if it is the IRS' fault. So don't spend the portion that you aren't entitled to. Strategy: Deposit the check in your own account rather than return it to the IRS uncashed. There's less chance of a mixup, and you won't be stuck waiting for the portion of the money that you are entitled to have now. Contact the IRS for the correct amount and then send a check for the difference.

☐ If your refund check is too small, you can safely cash the check without giving up any of your rights to contest the amount.

☐ You are entitled to interest from the IRS if you filed on time but didn't receive your refund until after May 30.

☐ If you didn't file your return on time, file as quickly as possible to limit the interest you will owe the IRS on the amount that's overdue. Escape hatch: You won't owe a penalty for late filing if you filed a valid extension application and submitted a check by April 15 for at least 90% of the tax you owe. However, you will owe interest for any additional tax due with the return when it is filed.

☐ If the IRS sends you a notice stating that you didn't report all your income, don't automatically assume that the IRS is right and pay the extra tax. Make sure you understand the notice itself, and carefully go over your records and your return.

☐ If you made a mistake on your return that you didn't realize until after you filed: The general rule is that you have three years from the original due date of the return to file an amended return. It's not wise to wait this long, however, especially if you *owe* tax. Interest and penalties just keep adding up. If the income that you forgot to report was reported to the IRS on a 1099 form, it will be just a matter of time until the IRS catches up with you anyway. Better: Amend your return as soon as possible to avoid the extra payment or claim your refund.

☐ If a financial institution reported your tax-exempt interest as taxable income to the IRS, contact the institution and have the correct amount reported to the IRS.

Source: Arnold H. Koonan, tax partner in charge, Coopers & Lybrand, CPAs, Washington, DC.

What the IRS double checks

You will receive a W-2 wage and tax statement and 1099 statements from the sources listed below, showing the amount of income you received from each. Make sure you include every dollar of this income on your return. The IRS matches all 1099s with your return…by computer. If the figures don't agree, you will be contacted by the IRS.

☐ Interest and dividends. The 1099-INT and 1099-DIV statements show income from bank accounts, certificates of deposit and credit unions and dividends from securities.

☐ State tax refunds. The 1099-G shows the amount you received as a state tax refund last year. If you took an itemized deduction for state and local taxes in the previous year and obtained a full tax benefit, report the amount of any refund as income in your current tax return.

☐ Stock sales income. Your 1099-B shows the sales price of stock you sold last year. Part of the amount shown on 1099-B may be attributable to transfer taxes and brokers' commissions rather than to income from the sale itself. Exclude these nonincome items and show the IRS why you aren't including the whole 1099-B amount in your income by reconciling it carefully on Schedule D.

☐ Social Security income. Your SSA 1099 shows all Social Security income you received last year. Depending on your income from other sources and the amount of Social Security you receive, it could be taxable. Use the worksheet in the IRS instructions to calculate your tax.

☐ IRS interest refund. The 1099-C shows the amount of interest income you must report from an IRS refund.

☐ W-2 wage and tax statements. These statements show your salary and amounts withheld for the year. Make sure you know the reason for every entry on your W-2, and be sure the information agrees with the amounts shown on your December 31 pay stub.

☐ All of the above statements should be correct and in agreement with your records. If they aren't, contact the source immediately and have a new statement issued. If there isn't enough time to get a new statement, attach a note to your return showing why there is a discrepancy between the information return and the amounts you actually report. You alone are responsible for making sure all these statements are correct.

☐ If you didn't receive a 1099 from a source who paid you money last year, be sure to arrange to get one. Chances are the income is being reported to the federal government whether you received the statement or not.

Source: Lester A. Marks, partner, Ernst & Young, New York.

IRS bellringers

Discuss the proper handling of any of the following immediately with your tax adviser:

☐ Any out-of-the-blue request, penalty or demand;

☐ Any notice containing errors, even "little" mistakes;

☐ All IRS correspondence relating to tax shelters.

Source: *Tax Hotline,* Boardroom, Inc., New York.

IRS communications

☐ Audit notices. Normally, no written response is required for notices of office or field audits. Information Document Requests (IDRs), for field audits, simply list what records the agent wants to examine. You may need to prepare schedules, etc. to respond to an IDR. You do need to reply to a so-called correspondence audit. What's needed is clearly spelled out.

☐ Agreement forms received following an audit generally require you to sign only if you agree with the specified changes on your return. However, a no-change letter requires no action on your part.

☐ Tax bill. Termed "Notice and Demand," is to be treated like any bill. Pay it on time, or accept the consequences.

☐ Penalty notice. Related to a specific penalty (e.g., Form 2210 for underpayment of estimated taxes). The reason for it, amount due and what's required of you are noted. Many penalties can be abated by proper action.

☐ 30-day letter. Gives you 30 days to submit a written protest against the IRS adjustments specified in the letter or pay the amount noted. Protest-filing instructions and details regarding an appeals hearing accompany the letter. (If your tax involves $2,500 or less, a written protest is not required.)

☐ 90-day letter. This statutory notice of deficiency gives you 90 days to file a petition with the Tax Court, or else you must pay the amount specified.

☐ Request to extend the statute of limitations. Sign only if you agree. Pitfall: If you don't agree, you'll probably receive a 90-day letter.

☐ Tax shelter notices. A prefiling notification states that a shelter's benefits are nondeductible and, if claimed, will subject you to penalties. No response is required. And you may receive a shelter questionnaire (sometimes conducted during an audit) requesting various information.

☐ Important: Consult your tax adviser before acting on any IRS document that you receive.

Handling mail from the IRS

The types of written IRS communications that most taxpayers receive are generally cut-and-dried.

Never ignore any IRS communication. If you're not certain about what to do, consult your tax adviser…the sooner, the better.

When documents are requested (as in a correspondence audit), send only copies, never originals.

Send all replies and payments by certified mail, "return receipt requested." Certification provides legal proof of time of mailing. The return-receipt procedure gives you an early warning of possible nondelivery, alerting you to follow up.

Tag every piece of paper with your name and Social Security number to speed IRS processing and help guard against misfiling.

For multipage documents, provide internal numbering (e.g., "page 1 of 10"). For multidocument replies, number each item and supply a finding list. This checklisting helps you organize and ensures that you omitted nothing.

Strictly observe time limits for your reply. Even if your adviser is handling the reply, verify that all was mailed on time (check the receipt). It's always your responsibility to meet IRS deadlines.

When the IRS claims you didn't report income

One of the most troubling IRS communications a taxpayer can get these days is a "matching notice"—a long, confusing computer printout summarizing income that you failed to report and recalculating your tax. In the IRS matching program, a computer matches the 1099 information forms that report income from various sources with the income taxpayers declare on their returns. Although it's good, the program isn't sophisticated enough to deal with some fairly common situations. Here are a few examples:

☐ Custodial accounts. You have a custodial account for your child. But your Social Security number, not the child's, is on the account. You get a matching notice saying that you failed to report the interest on the account. What to do: Send a copy of the bank passbook to the IRS, together with a letter explaining that the money in the account is your child's and that you will see to it that your child gets a Social Security number.

☐ Hidden items: When you prepared your return you may have included some income on a schedule. For example, you may have reported some self-employment income on Schedule C. The computer may not find that income, in which case it will generate a notice saying you failed to report it. Defense: Write back to the IRS, showing how the 1099 income is included in the gross receipts on Schedule C.

☐ Incorrect 1099s. The IRS assumes that income reported on a 1099 is correct and that you are wrong if you declare some other figure. But your broker may have made a mistake. The broker's computer may have incorrectly listed nontaxable income as taxable income. Defense: Send copies of bank or brokerage statements explaining the discrepancy. Show which part of the 1099 income was not taxable.

Contesting IRS penalties: Problems to watch out for

Always check penalty notices from the IRS carefully to make sure you really are liable for the penalty. You may not be. But it's up to you to get yourself off the hook.

Possible problems:

☐ Estimated tax. When withholding estimated-tax payments don't total at least 90% of the tax owed, the IRS automatically assesses a penalty on the underpayments. You may, however, qualify for one of the tax law's exceptions to the penalty. (For example, you may be able to base your payments on "annualized income" if you earned most of your income late in the year.) To avoid the penalty: Fill out Form 2210 (Underpayment of Estimated Tax by Individuals), indicating which of the exceptions applies. Send the form back to the IRS, together with a copy of the penalty notice.

☐ Late filing. Penalties are assessed automatically when you file a tax return late. But you may have a legitimate excuse for late filing. Send the IRS a letter, explaining why you had "reasonable cause" for filing late and should, therefore, be excused from the penalty. Send a copy of the notice along with your letter.

☐ If you didn't file a return, it is possible to get a letter from the IRS asking why a return wasn't filed, even though none was required. This often happens when a trust or a company becomes inactive. Send the IRS a statement saying that the company or trust had insufficient income to warrant filing a return.

☐ If the IRS slips up and sends you a refund check even though you asked that over-payment be applied to next year's tax, this can be a problem if your accountant intended the overpayment to cover your first estimated-tax installment. If you keep the refund check, you'll be short on your estimated payments and liable for a penalty. Always confirm refunds with your accountant.

☐ If you can't get action from the IRS Service Center or District Office, take the matter to the IRS's Problems Resolution Office. This special section of the IRS is staffed by people whose job is to cut through IRS red tape. Call the Problems Resolution Office directly. Each IRS district has one. You can get the number by calling your local Taxpayer Service office. Suggestion: Call early in the morning. All lines are busy by noon.

If you can't pay your taxes

Most creditors must have a court order before they can seize your property. All that's required of the IRS is that it present you with a bill for unpaid tax and wait 10 days. After that, if you still haven't paid, it can seize your bank accounts, garnish your wages, and even sell your house. Fortunately, the IRS seizes property only as a last resort in the collection process. Before invoking its enforcement powers, the IRS generally gives financially strapped taxpayers a chance to try to work out a payment agreement.

Here's how to proceed when there's no cash to pay the bill:

☐ File a tax return. The worst thing you can do when you owe the IRS money is not file a tax return. Owing money to the IRS that you simply can't pay is not a crime. The IRS can't put you in jail for not having the money. But it is a crime not to file a tax return—a crime for which you can go to jail. By filing, you also avoid the big penalties for late filing. If you don't get your return in on time (or don't have a valid extension), you'll incur a late-filing penalty of 5% a month (or any fraction of a month), up to a maximum of 25% of the tax you owe.

☐ Pay what you can when you file your return. Keep to a minimum your penalties for late payment and interest on the tax you owe. Trap: If you file for an extension, you must send the IRS 90% of the tax you expect to owe or they'll charge you late-payment penalties. And if you lie on the extension form and say you expect to owe no tax, you can be charged with perjury.

☐ Six to eight weeks after you've filed, you'll get a bill for the unpaid balance. The bill will include interest and penalties. Don't ignore it. If you're still short of money, arrange a meeting at your local IRS office to work out an installment-payment arrangement.

☐ Be prepared to submit a financial statement showing that you don't have assets that can be liquidated to pay your tax. Don't expect the IRS to give you extra time to pay if you have certificates of deposit in the bank that you simply don't want to cash in early.

☐ Go easy on the hard-luck stories when asking for an installment arrangement. The IRS has heard them all. Concentrate on negotiating, in a businesslike manner, a series of monthly payments that you'll be able to manage.

☐ When you give the IRS an analysis of your monthly income and expenses, show that there's money left over for tax payments. If you come up broke each month, the IRS will be less inclined to agree to installment payments. Where will you find the money to make the payments?

☐ The IRS likes to see a tax bill paid up in a year or less. If you can figure out a way to pay the debt in less than a year, you have a better shot at getting an installment agreement than if you say you need five years to pay.

☐ File all your delinquent tax returns before you negotiate an installment agreement. Establish all your tax liabilities, and have them all covered by the agreement. Trap: If you agree to a payment plan for one year and then get a bill for other years' back taxes, you'll be in default on the agreement. The IRS will then demand payment in full.

☐ Never miss a payment without first talking to a revenue officer. You're technically in default of the agreement when you miss just one payment. And when you're in default, you have to start over again, trying to negotiate a new agreement.

☐ If you can't make a payment: Meet with a revenue officer. Explain the unusual circumstances that make it impossible for you to pay and hope that the officer will alter the terms of your agreement.

Source: Randy Bruce Blaustein, Esq., partner, Blaustein & Greenberg, New York, and author of *How to Do Business With the IRS.*, Prentice-Hall, Inc., Englewood Cliffs, NJ.

What the IRS cannot seize if you fail to pay your taxes

The IRS is vested with the power to seize your property without a court order. The only requirement is that it have a valid assessment, give notice with a demand for payment (which has to be sent to your last known address), and give notice of intent to seize.

In addition to seizing your property, the IRS can also place a levy on your bank accounts and on your salary. This means that both your bank and your employer must turn over to the IRS all funds being held for you, to the extent of the levy. (Note: Special rules apply to salary.)

Property exempt by law from levy:

☐ Apparel and schoolbooks. (Expensive items of apparel such as furs are luxuries and are not exempt from levy.)

☐ Fuel, provisions, furniture, and personal effects, not to exceed $1,650 in value (for the head of a household).

☐ Books and tools used in your trade, business or profession, not to exceed $1,100 in value.

☐ Unemployment benefits.

☐ Undelivered mail.

☐ Certain annuity and pension payments (including Social Security benefits).

☐ Workers compensation.

☐ Salary, wages or other income subject to a prior judgment for court-ordered child-support payments.

☐ A minimum amount of wages, salary and other income—$75 per week—plus an additional $25 for each legal dependent.

The IRS is now seizing personal residences more frequently. After a Notice of Seizure is placed on the front door of your house, you have 10 days to come up with the money you owe, or there is an excellent chance that it will be sold at auction to satisfy the tax bill. The house may be redeemed at any time within 180 days after the sale by paying the purchaser the amount paid for the property, plus interest. By law, the purchaser must sell.

Excuses that work with the IRS

Suppose you filed your tax return late and did not obtain an extension. Worse still, you also owe the IRS money. The IRS has sent you a bill for the tax you owe plus interest and penalties. You know that the tax and interest must be paid but feel that you have "reasonable cause" for filing your return late. If one of the following situations honestly applied to you, you may be able to persuade the IRS to drop the penalties:

☐ You were seriously ill or there was a death or serious illness in your immediate family. In the case of failure to pay a previous penalty, the death or serious illness must be of an individual having the sole authority to make payment.

☐ Your place of business or business records were destroyed by fire or other disaster.

☐ You were unavoidably absent from home or business.

☐ You were unable to obtain records necessary to determine the amount of tax due, for reasons beyond your control.

☐ Your ability to pay was materially impaired by civil disturbances.

☐ You were in a combat zone.

☐ You have exercised ordinary business care and prudence in providing for payment of taxes and have posted a bond or acceptable security, coupled with a collateral agreement showing that paying the tax when due would have caused undue hardship.

☐ Any other reason showing that you exercised ordinary care and prudence but still were unable to pay the tax when due.

☐ Seasonal changes resulted in sudden increases in your tax liability, even though you are not ordinarily required to make deposits. (This excuse applies to penalties for late payment or nonpayment of payroll taxes.)

☐ Failure to file a tax return upon the advice of a reputable accountant or attorney whom you selected with reasonable and ordinary prudence and whom you furnished in good faith with information you reasonably believed was sufficient.

☐ Late filing by tax preparer. When a taxpayer has relied on an accountant or attorney to prepare a tax return, which was then not filed on a timely basis, the IRS usually allows this as an acceptable excuse. Technically, such an excuse is not reasonable cause, but it usually works, particularly when the accountant or attorney admits blame to the IRS in writing.

☐ Absence of key employees. When a business has had heavy employee turnover or when an important financial executive such as a vice-president or controller is no longer employed by the business, it can be considered reasonable cause for late filing and late payment.

☐ Change of CPA firm. If you recently fired a CPA firm because it was not taking care of things properly and on time and the problem wasn't discovered until new accountants were retained, it may be reasonable cause to abate a penalty.

☐ Lost or misplaced records. This usually works if the information needed to prepare the tax return in question was misfiled or lost and had to be reconstructed.

Excuses that don't work with the IRS...

Excuses probably won't work if:

☐ You made the same mistake on a previous return.

☐ You filed a negligent return and you are an accountant or lawyer.

☐ You didn't keep proper records and you are a CPA. (Professionals are less likely to escape a penalty because the IRS thinks they should know better than nonprofessionals.)

Source: Peter A. Weitsen, partner, Mendlowitz Weitsen, New York.

Negotiation tactics

☐ Provide only the information requested. For an office audit: Take with you only the documentation relating to the requested items.

☐ If the agent requests support for other items, suggest, diplomatically, that since this would require yet another meeting, perhaps such information could be mailed in.

☐ Involve a supervisor only if necessary. If you've reached an impasse—because of an honest disagreement or a personality conflict—enlist the agent's help by asking, "Would you discuss this with your supervisor?" Communicate through—not around—the agent.

☐ Avoid a change of agents, if possible. You'll avoid the double audit that results from starting afresh.

☐ Know your appeal rights, and let the agent know that you do. Use this knowledge to achieve agreements. Agents like to close cases "agreed."

☐ Sign an agreement form only if you truly agree with all the proposed adjustments. Never allow yourself to cave in to pressure. If unsure, ask for time to consider and to consult your tax adviser.

Dealing personally with the IRS

Taxpayers sometimes choose to deal personally with the IRS on routine matters. Here are some pointers to help you deal productively with the Service.

Be prepared. It's to your advantage to organize and summarize all requested information. Have an adding machine tape to show how you calculated each questioned deduction. This will expedite the review and let the reviewer know you're in control.

☐ Be honest. Don't try to disguise a problem area, such as lack of certain types of documentation. Never risk arousing IRS suspicion. Best: Explain the problem in terms of what proof you have. If that's not sufficient, then ask if you can gather additional proof to satisfy the IRS.

☐ Be businesslike. Use good-sense rules of courtesy and tact in all your dealings with the IRS.

☐ Be prudent. Limit your involvement to nontechnical, routine matters. Don't get in over your head. Do only what, and as much as, you feel comfortable doing. Alarm bells: Uncertainty, anxiety, frustration and anger are the signs that professional help is needed.

☐ Office audits held at a local IRS office—are typically used to determine if income and deductions claimed are properly supported by documentation. They are usually limited to several items, and are not likely to involve technical or legal issues.

☐ Field audits—held at the taxpayer's business and/or residence are generally used to scrutinize a variety of IRS concerns—in many cases related to business returns—often involving technical or legal issues. Discuss how best to handle such an audit with your tax adviser. In most cases, it's wise to have your adviser represent you at the audit.

Source: Roy B. Harrill, tax partner in charge of firmwide practice for IRS procedures and administration, Arthur Andersen & Co., Chicago.

How to handle an IRS audit

An audit need not be an ordeal…if you are prepared.

☐ Respond promptly to the audit notification letter. You have 10 days from the date of the letter either to contact the IRS or send in the proof requested in the letter.

☐ If you can't get your records together in time, call the IRS phone number that is on the audit notice. It's important that you respond in some way. Trap: If you don't respond within 10 days, the IRS can automatically adjust your tax bill.

☐ Call your accountant if the IRS is proposing a sizable adjustment of the sum that you owe. Ask your accountant to call the IRS and handle the audit for you. Strategy: By insulating yourself from the auditor in this way, you can't say the wrong things. Also, your accountant will gain more time to think about answers to complex questions, since he will have to get more information from you and then get back to the auditor. Point: Weigh the cost of bringing in your accountant against the amount of any potential tax assessment. If the tax is relatively small, it may not be worth it to pay for an accountant.

☐ Don't volunteer anything. You are likely to get yourself in even more trouble by saying too much. Answer only the questions that are asked…nothing more. For example, if you are asked to substantiate only your medical deductions, don't bring records pertaining to any other type of deduction to the audit. Otherwise, the auditor might start asking you questions about deductions that he didn't originally intend to question.

☐ Do your homework. Gather the records that relate to the questioned item. Be able to explain what each canceled check, bill or other related document is about. Arrange this information in the order that the deductions appear on your return. Also prepare an explanatory worksheet with an adding machine tape attached.

☐ If you've lost records, get a copy or a statement from the original source verifying them.

☐ Credibility counts. If you can't substantiate expenses with documents or other evidence, the IRS may accept your "credible oral testimony." The examiner must believe that you have an otherwise substantially correct return.

☐ Don't antagonize the auditor. Be reasonable. If you attack the IRS or the auditor, he is likely to rule against you whenever he has to make a decision.

☐ Request a conference with the auditor's supervisor if you are uncomfortable with the way an audit is being conducted or can't agree on proposed disallowances. The supervisor can persuade the auditor to rule in your favor. Because the IRS tries to settle cases at the lowest level, the supervisor may be more likely to concede one issue if you agree to another.

□ If you have been questioned in the two previous years about the same issue, you can get the audit canceled if it's the only item being examined. The previous audits must have resulted in no change in tax on that item. What to do: Call the IRS office and ask to have repetitive-audit procedures applied. You then must send copies of the IRS letters stating that there was no change to the item in the previous years.

Which court to appeal a tax case to

A taxpayer who wants to appeal an IRS decision has the choice of three courts:

□ Tax Court. A proceeding in Tax Court (of which the Small Case Division is part) is a direct appeal from the IRS' decision. The taxpayer need not pay the disputed tax until the case is decided. If he loses, however, he has to pay interest on any judgment. To prevent interest from piling up, he can pay the disputed amount to the court in advance. Then, if he wins or compromises the case, he gets all or part of the money back.

□ Claims Court or District Court: The taxpayer must pay the disputed amount and sue for a refund. In effect, though not in form, he is appealing the IRS' decision.

□ Which court to use is a matter of legal strategy to be discussed with your lawyer or tax adviser. Disputed or unsettled legal issues have often been decided differently by different courts, so there can be a distinct advantage in picking the right one.

Dealing with special agents

The primary purpose of the active IRS role in the area of criminal investigations is to promote voluntary compliance by all taxpayers. If a Special Agent of the IRS makes contact, bear in mind:

□ The typical Special Agent presents himself or herself in a low-key, even friendly, manner. The goal, after all, is to collect evidence to support the government's contention that a tax crime has been committed.

The time to involve an experienced lawyer is right at the beginning of an investigation, not when the IRS has already developed its case against you.

□ Avoid the trap of believing that if you answer all of the Special Agent's questions honestly and even volunteer information, the agent will either go easy on you or just go away. Nothing could be further from the truth. A self-incriminating statement does not leave the Special Agent with much more to do than wrap up the case and recommend prosecution.

□ Don't lie during the investigation. Lying is a separate crime! The Special Agent typically will not challenge misleading statements you make at the interview. But these statements will be introduced by the government at your trial (if there is one) to help prove that you intended to break the law and/or that any defense you raise at the trial is not credible because you lied during the investigation.

□ Beware of undercover snares. One successful criminal investigation project is called "BOP" for Business Opportunities Project. This undercover operation might involve a Special Agent responding to an advertisement in the business section of the local newspaper soliciting a buyer for a business. Usually two Special Agents will approach the targeted owner for the purpose of negotiating a price for the business. Inevitably, the conversation turns to the fact that cash is skimmed and that there is a second set of books. Now the Special Agents know how much money is not being reported and have all the evidence they need to close the case.

Source: *How to Beat the IRS*, Boardroom Books, Springfield, NJ.

Taking your own case to tax court

Taxpayers who want to challenge an IRS decision can save time, trouble and legal fees by using the Small Case Division of the Tax Court

☐ The Division's streamlined procedures are now available in all disputes of up to $10,000 (formerly $5,000). The Division handles estate and gift-tax cases, as well as income tax ones.

Advantages

☐ Paperwork is simplified and kept to a minimum. Trials are informal. The strict rules of evidence are relaxed.

☐ You can have a lawyer if you want, but you don't need one. Most taxpayers appear for themselves.

☐ Cases are reached and disposed of much faster than cases in the regular Tax Court. In addition, over half the cases are settled before trial, by agreement between the IRS and the taxpayer.

☐ The Division's judges travel to over 100 cities around the country, including cities where the regular Tax Court does not hold sessions. You can pick whichever city is most convenient.

Rules

☐ Decisions of the Small Case Division are final. Neither party may appeal. Furthermore, no decision may be used as a precedent in deciding any other case, even one involving the same taxpayer.

☐ In rare instances, a case may be transferred from the Small Case Division to the regular Tax Court. This might happen if the case presented a new or unusual legal issue and it was desirable to get a decision that could be used as precedent for future cases.

☐ Get all the forms you need by writing the Clerk of the Court, US Tax Court, 400 Second St. NW, Washington, DC 20217. You'll receive a simplified petition (Form 2), a form for designating the place of trial, and a booklet explaining how the Division works and including a list of cities it visits.

☐ You must file your petition along with a $60 filing fee, within 90 days of the date the IRS mails you a notice of deficiency. (The date is shown at the top of the notice.) The time limit is absolute. Caution: 90 days does not mean three months. If, for example, a notice of deficiency is mailed to you on October 10, you must file your petition by January 8—not January 10.

☐ Use registered or certified mail. That way, you'll have proof of the date of mailing.

Procedure

☐ In your petition, state your disagreement with the IRS as clearly as possible, including your reasons for disagreeing. You don't have to use legal language and you won't be penalized, even if you forget something. But the clearer your statement, the faster the case can be handled and the greater the possibility of a settlement.

☐ A copy of your petition will be sent to the IRS, and the Service will probably contact you soon afterward. Be prepared to discuss a settlement arrangement. Most cases are settled at this stage of the proceedings.

☐ If no settlement is reached, you will receive notice of trial about 60 days in advance. Depending on the Division's workload and its schedule of cities to be visited, you can expect to receive notice about seven to ten months after filing your petition.

☐ At the trial, you can testify, call witnesses, argue your case orally or in writing, and submit any evidence you have to support your case. Documentary evidence is particularly important; bring everything you can. Some legal questions depend entirely on documentary evidence. The tax status of payments to an ex-spouse, for example, may depend on the wording of the divorce decree.

☐ The more documents and records that you have to support the accuracy of your tax return, the more likely it is that court will believe your testimony on disputed or undocumented matters. Caution: Documents already submitted to the IRS are not automatically a part of the record. Be sure to request the Service, in writing, to bring them to the trial. Play safe and spell out exactly what documents you want.

Source: Charles Casazza, Clerk of the Court, US Tax Court, Washington, DC.

Lending money to a friend

☐ No matter how friendly a loan, draw up a note stating terms and conditions.

☐ Be businesslike. Include a provision for reasonable interest.

☐ Be prepared to document the loan, so that you can take a tax deduction on any loss.

Collecting on a judgment

After getting a judgment, many people find that they have spent much time and money and gone to a lot of trouble to get a worthless piece of paper. According to one lawyer, less than 25% of all judgments are collected. To make winning a judgment worthwhile, it is important to know what to do and what to avoid.

☐ Don't sue a firm just because its name is on a sign outside a place of business, and don't sue the person you assume owns the business. Check with the local county clerk's office, business-licensing bureau, department of consumer affairs or police department to find out the real name in which the business is registered.

☐ Sue where the assets are. The service person who did the damage, the franchise owner, the corporate owner or the parent corporation may all be liable if you can prove wrongful involvement. Sue whichever entity or entities have enough assets to pay your judgments. You can sue more than one.

☐ If you have ever received a check from or given a check to the debtor, you may have a clue to the whereabouts of the debtor's bank account.

☐ If you have a judgment against someone who owns a home, check the county's homeownership records in that area of residence.

☐ If you have won a judgment against a business, go personally to the business location to see what equipment and machinery are on the site.

☐ If the judgment is large enough, hire an agency to do an asset search. Before paying for a professional search, find out what the agency is actually going to do to uncover assets and what results you can realistically expect.

☐ To avoid creditors, an unscrupulous company will often go out of business in one name and start up the same business the next day with a different name—on the same location and with the same equipment. To collect on your judgments, you will need a lawyer to prove that the transfer of assets took place for the purposes of fraud.

☐ Judgments can be forcibly collected only by an enforcement officer (a local marshal, sheriff or constable) or sometimes the court clerk. You are responsible for informing the officer where to find the debtor's assets.

☐ The enforcement officer may seize any property that is not exempt and sell it at auction to pay the debt.

☐ The enforcement officer may garnishee a debtor's salary. You can collect 10%-25% of take-home pay, depending on state law. (You must tell the officer where the debtor works.)

☐ Generally exempt from collection*: Household and personal items, including furniture, stove, refrigerator, stereo, TV, sewing machine, clothing, cooking utensils, tools of a person's trade.

☐ Generally collectible items*: Motor vehicles, valuable jewelry, antiques, real estate, bank accounts, business equipment, stocks, bonds and the like.

☐ A home lived in by the debtor is exempt up to a certain amount (which varies from state to state). The major problem in collecting on a home: If a judgment is obtained against only the wife, for instance, the house can't be touched if it's also in her husband's name. But if only the debtor owns it, you can have it seized, sell it and return the exempt amount.

☐ Legal help is recommended if you are suing for an amount over the small-claims-court limit. After you win the judgment, your lawyer may arrange an asset search for you or recommend an agency to do one.

☐ Collection agencies are not recommended. They deal mostly with large accounts and not with one-shot cases. Also: A collection agency can only dun a debtor in a formal, legalistic way to convince him to pay voluntarily. After assets have been uncovered, only an enforcement officer can actually collect.

*These are general guidelines. Details vary from state to state. Check with the local marshal or other enforcement officer for more information.

Source: Kenneth D. Litwach, director, bureau of city marshals, New York City Department of Investigation.

Liability lawsuits: Beware

You may be even more vulnerable to personal liability lawsuits than you fear. In some states, for example, you can be held liable for injuries sustained by firefighters battling a blaze in your house…or by a pedestrian who falls on a public sidewalk abutting your property.

☐ Your first line of defense is homeowner's insurance with liability coverage. Most people get adequate protection from standard policies.

☐ If you have a large income or sizable assets, an additional "umbrella" policy may be necessary. Umbrella policies provide extra liability coverage for virtually any litigious incident (including libel and slander). They are surprisingly inexpensive.

☐ By the time a liability suit reaches court, there is seldom any question over the occurrence of the alleged wrong. What is under dispute is where the blame should fall.

☐ Most juries today are instructed by the judge to use a single criterion in deciding liability cases: Did the defendant (property owner) exercise "reasonable care" in guarding against injury and property damage? Although this may sound straightforward, the ways juries interpret "reasonable care" vary widely.

☐ In some states, the identity of the wronged person helps determine the meaning of "reasonable care." A person who is invited onto your property, for example, is entitled to more care than a trespasser. And someone hired to work for you is entitled to more consideration than a friend.

☐ Increasingly, states are adopting a so-called "single standard of care," which means that every person who ventures onto your property is entitled to the same level of protection. Impact: Homeowners must be careful to protect not only guests but anyone who happens onto their property. This includes children who cut through your yard on the way home from school, neighbors soliciting for charity, or door-to-door salespeople.

The increasing reliance on the single standard of care doctrine makes it significantly more difficult for homeowners to fight lawsuits. It is more and more important to maintain your home in such a way that you will not be sued in the first place. Some suggestions:

☐ Hire cautiously. Hire only fully bonded, insured contractors. Keep an eye out for potentially hazardous work conditions.

☐ Cover your chimney. Homeowners have been held liable for fires and smoke damage caused by sparks that escaped from uncovered chimneys. A chimney cover can prevent sparks from flying. Don't burn anything that might produce noxious fumes or dense soot, other potential sources of litigation.

☐ Get rid of vicious pets. Many pet owners assume they can limit their liability for dog bites by posting a *Beware of dog* sign in plain view. Not true. In fact, posting such a sign indicates to authorities that you are aware of your pet's "vicious propensities."

☐ Eliminate potential hazards. Swimming pools, trampolines, uncovered ditches and "attractive nuisances" that are likely to draw children must be made safe. Fence them in—well. Make and enforce strict rules as to their use: No diving in the pool…No jumping on the trampoline without "spotters" or adult supervision.

☐ Keep trees healthy and trimmed. If a bolt of lightning knocks a well-cared for tree on your property onto a neighbor's house or car, you probably will not be liable. (There is no way to protect against such an event.) However, if the tree that falls is obviously diseased, or if it was leaning precariously, that's another matter.

☐ Clear snow and ice carefully. If you clear a public sidewalk of snow and someone falls and is injured there, you could be held liable. And what if a local ordinance requires you to clear the sidewalk in front of your house and you don't? In most cases, if someone does fall, the worst that can happen is that you would be fined for failing to clear the sidewalk. Chances are you would not be held liable for any injuries suffered in the fall. Rule of thumb: If there's a public sidewalk in front of your property, clear it very, very carefully—or don't clear it at all.

☐ Perform routine maintenance. Any loose brick on a staircase or pothole in your driveway can mean trouble.

Source: Melvin M. Belli, Sr., and Barry G. Saretsky. Belli, the well-known "king of torts" and father of "demonstrative evidence" (dramatic visual aids in the courtroom), heads the law firm Belli & Belli, San Francisco. Saretsky is a partner with Bower & Gardner, a firm that specializes in defending negligence cases, New York.

How liable are you for your child's mischief?

The issue of who is to blame when your child damages someone else's property or endangers another person is complicated. The growing number of homes where both parents work and depend on day-care centers or makeshift supervision of their children after school contributes to the problem. The legal issue is clouded by joint custody of divorced parents and by children's rights concepts that are concerned with stemming child abuse and neglect.

☐ No federal law directly holds a parent responsible for a child's actions simply because he is the child's parent. However, if it can be proved that a child was acting as the agent of a parent when he committed his crime, the parent is tried as though he had committed the crime himself. (This would apply, for example, to the burglar who used his small child to get through a tiny opening into a house.)

☐ Although statutes differ, case law decisions seem to have established the age of 12 as the point at which a child can be tried in juvenile court. Younger children usually cannot be tried. At 17 or 18, a young person is considered to be an adult and is therefore tried as an adult.

☐ A parent can be held responsible for a child's mischief if it can be proved that the parent neglected to exercise reasonable control over his child's behavior. This concept comes from state laws called *vicarious liability statutes.* Almost every state has some form of vicarious liability law that requires a parent to pay for damages to property up to certain maximum ($200 to $10,000, depending on the state) if it can be proved that the parent neglected to control the child's behavior. About half the states hold parents liable for personal injuries their child may have inflicted on others.

☐ Several states with large urban populations have implemented laws to deal specifically with the vandalization of public buildings and transit systems. New Jersey law: If it can be shown that the parents failed to supervise the child, they are liable for up to $1,000 worth of damage done by that child to a public utility, plus court costs. The penalty is levied in lieu of charging juvenile delinquency. Many parents pay just to keep their children from having a police record.

Bottom line: If your child gets into trouble by vandalizing property, your best bet is to pay the damages yourself. That keeps the problem out of court and in the family. For more serious crimes, you need a lawyer.

Source: David Schechner, partner, Schechner and Targan, lawyers, West Orange, NJ.

The business side of divorce

Divorce law has entered a new era. The new laws on divorce say, in effect, that no one is at fault when a marriage breaks up and that there is no victor to whom the spoils should belong. State legislatures now view marriage as an economic partnership and divorce as the dissolution of that partnership. Details to be aware of for negotiations:

Equitable Distribution Versus Community Property

☐ Community property, a system that has been around since the turn of the century, simply means that all property acquired during a marriage is split 50-50 upon divorce, no matter who holds title. There are less than a dozen community-property states that retain this system.

☐ The new game in divorce law is equitable distribution. Unlike community property, which is fairly clear cut, equitable distribution means that all property acquired during a marriage must be distributed equitably (fairly). Enormous problems have arisen with equitable distribution because nobody knows exactly what fairness is. Fairness, it seems, is in the eye of the beholder. Case law is coming down from day to day, defining the parameters of equitable distribution, but no clearcut guidelines have yet emerged.

☐ The only thing that is crystal clear about equitable distribution is that negotiation between the parties is crucial. The cost of a full-blown equitable distribution trial can be enormous.

Men Versus Women

The women's movement opposed equitable distribution because it foresaw that women would get the short end.

☐ The split in equitable distribution has been running about 70-30 in favor of the men.

☐ Since under equitable distribution a woman gets property, she can get alimony only for a fixed time, whereas previously she often got it for life. She can come back to court to ask for an extension, but this puts her in the supplicant position.

☐ The working wife comes out behind in many equitable distribution cases because she usually doesn't get alimony. She can wind up being penalized for having worked, even though she might have earned only a fraction of what her husband made.

☐ The man who suffers under equitable distribution is usually not the one with a six-figure income. It's the one who makes $32,000 a year and has a wife, four kids and a house. His wife, who usually stays home with the kids, gets their only asset—the house. He often winds up with nothing but support payments.

New Trends

☐ Equitable distribution has encouraged a whole new movement toward *mediation* of divorce. Mediation can be particularly good for the average middle-class divorce, where huge sums of money aren't involved. Problem: A lot of unqualified people have set themselves up as mediators. Recommended: A large mediation service with access to business experts, psychiatrists and other support staff. Mediation works only if both sides are equally informed. If one side is financially sophisticated and the other is not, the agreement will not be fairly mediated. It might not stand up in court.

☐ Custody. There's a national trend toward *joint custody* of the children, but most judges will order it only if there's an amicable agreement between the spouses. Another recent trend: Many fathers seek custody of the children.

☐ Blue-chip involvement. Divorce used to be considered a slightly seedy legal area, better left to single practitioners.

But now, many major law firms that previously wouldn't touch a divorce action are actively involved. Reason: Their clients are getting divorced, and in community property or equitable distribution states, the outcome of a divorce can seriously affect the continuation of a business or the ownership of stock. Also: Big firms can provide the team approach, with tax, estate and other relevant services available "in-house."

Negotiating Effectively

☐ Detach yourself from the emotional issues. Under equitable distribution, the party who tries to get revenge can do himself in financially. Strongly recommended: Psychotherapy, at least on a short-term basis, to resolve the emotional problems.

☐ Develop a business support system. Hire an accountant and bring in real estate appraisers and other experts if necessary, especially if the valuation of a business is involved.

☐ Make them an offer they can't refuse. For the person with substantial assets (usually the husband) who doesn't want both the IRS and the spouse's lawyer snooping through business records, it pays to be generous. Remember, there's a third partner to every divorce of people with substance: The IRS. There's no reason to make the IRS a full partner if it can be avoided. Example: The man who says, "I won't give her a dime in alimony," should keep in mind that alimony is tax-deductible. Also: People who fail to take a businesslike approach to divorce frequently find themselves getting reported to the IRS a year or two later by an "innocent" spouse.

☐ Separate the financial issues from the custody issue. Divorce is hard enough for children. Don't make it worse.

Source: Marilyn S. Lashin, an attorney specializing in divorce law, New York.

Dealing with divorce lawyers

☐ Never ask your company's lawyer to handle a divorce. There is one question that you should ask him, however (and, even then, check out his answer independently): Who's the best divorce lawyer around?

☐ Don't use a general-purpose lawyer. The corporate lawyer knows he doesn't know divorce law. The general lawyer thinks he does. And you will pay for that mistake.

☐ To find a good divorce lawyer, just ask around. The best names in the area will come up automatically.

☐ As good as the recommendation is, check the lawyer out personally. Interview him. See if you two can communicate. Do you understand him? Does he swamp you with details?

☐ Discuss fee arrangements. Tell him you'd like the arrangement in writing. Don't feel that the fee isn't negotiable; it frequently is.

☐ Make sure the lawyer understands that you want to be kept abreast of everything he does (every document and every conference on your case). It's not that you'll necessarily be able to make any legal contributions (although you may). It's just that you must deal with your peace of mind. Divorce is so mind-shattering that you don't want to make it even more disconcerting by feeling you don't know what is going on—a common complaint.

☐ Expect to be emotionally upset much of the time when dealing with the divorce proceeding. It's important, however, that your lawyer doesn't make you feel worse. (If he does, consider someone else.)

☐ Don't waste time (and money) putting a notice in the newspapers saying you're not responsible for your spouse's debts. Instead, send a certified letter to every creditor your spouse has dealings with. (Prepare a list of those credit cards before the divorce proceedings get under way.)

☐ Never let your spouse become a party to any agreement without his or her own lawyer providing advice. In many states, weakness becomes strength; the law holds that any disagreement over interpretation must be construed in favor of the party who entered the agreement without any legal advice.

Writing a will that works

☐ Include a simultaneous-death clause that dictates how property will be disposed of in the event both you and your spouse die simultaneously in a common disaster. This prevents acrimony among the beneficiaries as well as potential litigation.

☐ Consider a no-contest clause to prevent a disappointed beneficiary from suing to have your will overturned. Such a clause says that any beneficiary who challenges the will must forfeit his share under the will.

☐ Tailor bequests to the beneficiary. Leave property to each beneficiary in the form he can best handle it. This may mean outright transfers. But depending on the beneficiary's age, experience, financial sophistication and personal inclinations, a trust or a custodianship, or some other form of management may be more appropriate.

☐ Avoid giving complicated or risky investments, such as tax shelters, to financially unsophisticated beneficiaries who may not have your desire to fight the IRS.

☐ Don't leave property in joint ownership when one of the co-owners is likely to be dominated by the other.

☐ Don't give undivided fractional interests in property to beneficiaries who have very different ideas about the management or selling price of the property. Instead, transfer the property to a corporation and give the beneficiaries voting shares.

☐ Consider percentage bequests to favored beneficiaries, rather than absolute dollar amounts. In inflationary times, an estate can turn out to be worth far more than anticipated. A bequest of a dollar amount, no matter how generous it seemed at the time you made it, may be embarrassingly small in relation to the size of the inflated estate.

Source: Dr. Robert S. Holzman, professor emeritus of taxation at New York University and author of *Estate Planning: The New Golden Opportunities,* Boardroom Books, Springfield, NJ.

Limits on estate planning

Any will or estate plan must take into account the legal limits that govern the allocation of inherited property. The principal ones:

☐ Under varying state laws, a spouse has the right to a minimum portion of the partner's estate. A particular state's law may specify, for example, 35%. If the survivor is left a smaller amount, he or she can sue. In a few states, minor children are allowed specified percentages of a parent's estate.

☐ If a person dies without a will, his property will be distributed according to the intestacy laws of his state. These apportion his assets to the next of kin (spouse, children, siblings, etc.), according to definitions that vary from state to state. Even when a person has a will, if it is legally flawed, the laws of intestacy override the stated wishes of the deceased. Most common flaw: The will lacks the minimum number of witnesses specified by state law.

☐ An individual may have left property to persons who die before he does. Unless the decedent makes provisions for contingent or successor beneficiaries, the property will go to the "remainderman" (the person named to get what is left after all specific bequests have been honored). This could leave the remainderman with far more than had been intended.

☐ A person may write a will with the intention of leaving the bulk of the property to favored beneficiaries and very little to the remainderman. But inflation could raise the value of the person's properties far above his expectations. Specific dollar bequests to favored beneficiaries account for a small part of the estate, and the remainderman becomes the chief beneficiary. To avoid this, make bequests in percentages rather than in dollar amounts to self-adjust for inflation.

☐ The laws of some states place restrictions upon certain bequests. A state may provide, for example, that bequests to tax-exempt organizations, such as hospitals or churches, are void if made within 30 days of death. The laws are intended to discourage "bequests under pressure." But they can prevent a person's intentions from being carried out.

☐ Joint or mutual wills (usually by husband and wife) can ensure that upon the death of the second spouse, property that had been owned by the first spouse to die will go, under a prearranged plan, to relatives or friends of each spouse. Result: The second spouse to die must leave property according to the terms of the joint or mutual wills. But check with your tax adviser first. There can be heavy tax penalties for restrictions on property left to a surviving spouse.

☐ Many corporations purchase group insurance for employees in which the policy specifies that proceeds have to go to the surviving spouse (or to the children if there is no surviving spouse, or to the parents if there should be no children, and the like). This limits the ability of the employee to designate who will benefit financially from his death.

☐ The Internal Revenue Service can make a prior claim against an estate. For example, if the deceased owed back taxes, the IRS can attach the cash-surrender value of any insurance policies on the decedent's life which he owned or in which he had a significant incident of ownership.

Source: Dr. Robert S. Holzman, author, *Estate Planning: The New Golden Opportunities,* Boardroom Books, Springfield, NJ.

Revoking a will

It sounds fairly simple to do, but many individuals who try to revoke their wills don't succeed, and others have discovered that their wills have been revoked—by law—against their wishes. How these unwanted consequences can occur:

☐ In the aftermath of a death, no one is sure that the will was revoked. Testator (person making the will) may have destroyed it alone or in the presence of a witness who has also died. Much time and effort can be wasted looking for a document that no longer exists. Worse yet, a serious mistake may be made. In some states, a copy of a will may be accepted when the original can't be found and there's no indication it was revoked.

☐ In many states, a will is automatically revoked—wholly or partly—whenever certain events occur in the lifetime of a testator, such as marriage, divorce, birth of a child, or death of a major beneficiary:

What to do:

☐ Write a separate document spelling out revocation. Keep it where the will would have been.

☐ Check with a lawyer whenever a family event could trigger automatic revocation.

Source: Paul P. Ashley, author of *You & Your Will,* McGraw-Hill, New York.

Living will legislation and the right to die

Doctors are ambivalent about terminally ill patients. The Hippocratic oath tells them to preserve life, but it also directs them to relieve suffering. These two goals too often conflict.

American courts and legislatures are still in the process of confronting the legal issues of the right to die, but guidelines are emerging.

☐ Twenty-three states have what's called *living-will legislation*. It recognizes the right of an individual to have honored a written statement that he doesn't wish his life to be artificially prolonged if there is no expectation of recovery.* Living wills have been tested and upheld in three courts. *Informed consent* provides the legal basis for living-will legislation. No doctor in the US should now be able to perform a procedure without the patient's or a family member's express permission. Problem: Such laws are written in varying ways, providing different degrees of protection.

☐ If there is a living will, make sure it's been shown to the doctor and is on the patient's medical chart.

☐ Ask the doctor if there is any chance the relative will ever return to his or her former condition. If not, ask why the hospital is maintaining the patient. The doctor has to answer this question.

☐ Try for interim measures. Try to get a do-not-resuscitate order put on the chart. If you're trying to get a dying person off tubes, the last thing you want is the cardiovascular rescue team running in to start the patient's heart when it fails.

☐ If the doctor refuses to do what you want, find out why. Then talk to the hospital's patient representative or ombudsman, if there is one. This person often is the interface between patients and staff and can be helpful.

☐ If the doctor is uncooperative, try to get a more cooperative doctor assigned to the case. Failing that, try to get the person transferred to another hospital.

☐ Finally, you can ask to see the hospital attorney and say, "This is assault and battery. My relative did not give consent for this procedure." If that's the case, you can sue the hospital if its staff doesn't take the patient off the equipment.

☐ As a last resort, you can take the person home to die. It's been done. A hospital can't hold a patient against his or her will.

☐ No matter how desperate you feel, don't pull the plugs yourself. That's murder. Although mercy killers are generally found not guilty in this country, such a trial is a terrible ordeal.

☐ Call Choice for Dying for advice.

Source: Choice for Dying, an educational council, New York.

How to choose a guardian for your children

Whom do you want to take care of your children in the event you and your spouse die in the same accident? If you don't appoint a guardian, a probate judge will. And you are likely to make a better choice than the judge.

To do the job right, follow these guidelines:

☐ Prepare a list of possible guardians. Rate each individual or couple according to their degree of responsibility, accessibility, lifestyle, moral tenets, opinions on child raising, personal compatibility with your children, the candidates' ages, whether they have children and the ages of their children.

☐ Have meetings with the candidates. Assess their willingness to become your children's guardians.

☐ Select only individuals who satisfy all your criteria. And remember to provide for alternates in case your first choices become unable or unwilling to be your children's guardians.

☐ Keep in touch with the guardians you have appointed. Meet with them from time to time to fill them in on the current needs and plans for your children. These meetings will also give the guardians a chance to voice changes in their own lives that might have a dramatic impact on your children. You might use these sessions to let your children and other guardians get to know each other.

*For a copy of a living will, advice, or more information, call Choice for Dying (212) 246-6962. States with living-will legislation: AL, AR, CA, DE, FL, GA, ID, IL, KS, LA, MS, NV, NM, NC, OR, TX, VA, VT, WA, WI, WV, WY, and Washington, DC.

☐ Prepare a memorandum of instructions for the guardians, and keep it up to date. Include a list of things important to your children's well-being, such as their allergies, medical requirements, family medical history, personality traits and behavior responses. State your personal opinions about allowances, dating, schooling, driving, drinking and other areas of parental discretion.

☐ Provide direction about spending funds to achieve short-range and long-range goals. Indicate which goals have priority, such as a college education, and which are secondary, such as a car or a vacation in Europe.

☐ Set a minimum monthly allowance to be paid to the guardians for the children's day-to-day spending needs. Review this amount from time to time for reasonableness. Give your trustee the power to increase the allowance if necessary.

☐ Project your estate's future cash flow.

Source: Alan Gold, CPA, senior tax associate, Siegel, Mendlowitz & Rich, CPAs, New York.

When you rent a holiday home...

It's important to be clear about the respective responsibilities of landlords and renters. As a rule:

☐ Be prepared to give business and personal references when you rent a summer place. References commonly requested: Your place of business and length of time employed. A current or former landlord as a personal reference. Your phone and utility account numbers (to check your payment record). A credit reference (some owners are now subscribing to services that check the credit rating of prospective tenants).

☐ Expect to pay all the rent plus the security (which is as much as half the rent) in advance. Installment payments are generally unacceptable. Your security will be returned when the outstanding bills have been paid. The best way to insure that you will get your security back in full is to check the house thoroughly before the lease is signed. Make sure everything is listed so you can't be accused of taking something that wasn't there.

☐ Improvements you plan to make must be noted in the lease, along with the owner's approval and any reimbursement agreement.

☐ Expect to pay for heat, hot water, electricity and telephone for the rental period. You may be asked to install a phone in your own name.

☐ The renter is generally responsible for the care and watering of the plants and lawn, raking the beach, keeping the place reasonably clean and other standard household maintenance. Responsibility for expensive or highly technical maintenance, such as pool cleaning or skilled gardening, should be discussed and outlined in the lease. (Owners often include items such as pool maintenance as part of the rental price.)

☐ The house must be left in the same condition you found it in. If you damage something, you must replace it with a similar item. Recommended: Attempt to work things out amicably with the owner. Offer to pay for anything you have broken before the owner discovers the problem.

☐ The owner must repair any essential items that break down in midseason (such as the refrigerator or the plumbing). If he is unavailable, you can pay for repairs and bill him.

☐ The owner must tell the renter about climatic changes (such as summer floods), insect or rodent infestation or anything else that affects the house's habitability. Failure to do so is grounds for breaking the lease and getting your money back.

☐ Your summer house should be covered by your landlord's homeowners policy for burglary, accident, damage to the house and grounds, fire and flood. However, if you caused the damage, you can be held responsible.

☐ Insure your own property. Your jewelry and other valuables will not be covered by your landlord's homeowners policy.

Source: Jacqueline Kyle Kall, City Island, NY, realtor specializing in resort properties in the US and worldwide.

Forming a tenants' organization

The most effective method of confronting a landlord about problems with rented apartments is through a tenant organization. If you are having problems with your landlord, the other tenants in your building probably are, too. If you approach the problem as a group, your chances of success improve immeasurably.

How to go about it:

☐ Speak with the tenants in your building and distribute flyers calling a meeting. At the meeting, elect a committee of tenants to lead the group.

☐ Pass out questionnaires to all tenants, asking them to list needed repairs in their apartments.

☐ After the questionnaires have been collected and reviewed, call the landlord and suggest a meeting with him to negotiate complaints. Many landlords will comply with this request, since the specter of all their tenants withholding rent can be a frightening prospect. Negotiation is always preferable to litigation.

☐ If negotiation fails, organize a rent strike. That's a procedure whereby tenants withhold rent collectively, depositing the money each month in an escrow fund or with the court until repairs are made. If your tenant organization is forced to go this route, you will need a good lawyer. Be prepared for a long court battle.

Tenant vs. tenant

If a tenant in your building is involved in a crime or drugs or is excessively noisy, you have a number of ways to deal with the problem.

☐ Take out a summons, claiming harassment or assault. Probable result: The court will admonish the tenant to stop causing a disturbance (which may or may not have any effect).

☐ Sue for damages in civil court. You may win (although collecting the judgment is another story).

☐ Try to persuade your landlord to evict the undesirable tenant. Best way: Put pressure on him through your tenant organization. A landlord can't be forced to evict anyone. He has the right to rent to whomever he chooses. But if your association has a decent relationship with the landlord, he might comply, especially if the tenant is causing a dangerous condition or destroying property.

☐ You have the right to break your lease if you're being harassed by another tenant, but this may not be much comfort if apartments are scarce in your area.

If you become disabled

Delegate power of attorney to someone with financial expertise to handle your business and financial affairs. But be aware of the drawbacks:

☐ The power ends in some states if you become legally incompetent.

☐ It ends in all states when you die.

☐ You are personally liable for any acts the proxy commits in your name.

☐ Some third parties may be reluctant to deal with the proxy for fear he may be exceeding his mandate.

Additional hints:

☐ Set up a standby trust triggered by a specific event, like an illness. The trust ends when the disability ceases. This avoids probate.

☐ Declare yourself a trustee of all or part of your property. If you become incapacitated, a substitute trustee automatically steps in. This type of trust also avoids probate. (But the trust can be overridden in some cases, so discuss this with your lawyer.)

☐ Avoid a judicial guardianship. It's complex and expensive because the courts require a periodic accounting from the trustee.

Filing a claim for bodily injury

Claims against insurance companies for bodily injury can be the most complicated and negotiable type of claim, especially when based upon pain and suffering. Be aware:

☐ In a no-fault state, you are limited to out-of-pocket expenses in a nonserious injury. This includes lost wages. In a fault-governed state, you can negotiate for more.

☐ Don't miss damages. Start at the top of your head and go down to your toes, to include every part that's been hurt.

☐ Photograph your injury. In addition to medical reports, photos are the best documentation of suffering.

☐ Consider every aspect of your life affected by your injury. Include your career, sports, hobbies, future interests and family relationships.

☐ Ask the insurance company what a lawyer would ask—at least twice the actual expenses when there has been no permanent disability. Where liability is clear, the insurance company will be likely to give you what you ask, if it believes that you really had difficulties and were out of work for a few weeks. However, where there has been permanent disability, multiples of expenses do not apply. Example: Your medical bills for a lost eye might have been only $3,000, but a jury might award you 50 times that amount.

Source: Dan Brecher, a New York City attorney.

Financial aid for the mugging victim

Financial compensation programs for mugging victims exist in more than 30 states. Compensation can cover both medical expenses and lost earnings. However, most of these programs utilize a means test that effectively eliminates all but lower-income victims. Additionally, the victim's own medical and unemployment insurance must be fully depleted before state compensation is granted.

If you are mugged, check the following:

☐ Workers compensation may cover you if you were mugged on the job or on your way to or from company business during your workday. It will not cover you while commuting.

☐ Homeowners' policies may cover financial losses suffered during a mugging.

☐ Federal crime insurance insures up to $10,000 against financial losses from a mugging. This program is for people who have had difficulty purchasing homeowners' insurance privately.

☐ Mugging insurance is now available in New York. It covers property loss, medical care and mental anguish. If successful, it may spread rapidly to other states.

☐ A lawsuit may be successful if you can prove that the mugging was the result of negligence.

Source: Lucy N. Friedman, executive director, Victim Services Agency, New York.

Before you sign a contract with a health club

☐ Inspect the club at the time of day you'd be most likely to attend. Check on how crowded the pool, sauna, and exercise rooms are.

☐ Make certain all facilities that are promised are available.

☐ Avoid clubs that require long-term contracts.

☐ Once you sign a contract, if you wish to terminate, it's usually possible to avoid liability for the full term of the contract by notifying the club by registered mail, paying for services already rendered and a small cancellation fee. Check your local consumer protection agency for rules.

☐ Most important: Don't be pushed into a hasty decision by a low-price offer. Specials are usually repeated.

If the dry cleaner loses or ruins a garment

☐ You should be reimbursed or given a credit. Most dry cleaners are neighborhood businesses where reputation is vital. You can hurt a cleaner's reputation by giving the cleaner bad word-of-mouth. You might remind the store of this fact if there is resistance to satisfying your complaint.

☐ If your cleaner fails to remove a stain you were told could be removed, you still have to pay for the cleaning job.

☐ If your cleaner dry cleans a garment with a "do not dry clean" label, the store is responsible for ruining the garment.

☐ If your cleaner ruins a garment that should not be dry cleaned but lacks the "do not dry clean" label, responsibility is a matter of opinion. The cleaner may reimburse you to keep your goodwill, or you may have to complain to an outside agency.

☐ The amount you will be reimbursed is always up for bargaining. You will have to consider original value and depreciation, and whether you have a receipt.

☐ If you cannot get satisfaction from your cleaner voluntarily, most states have dry cleaners associations to arbitrate complaints. These associations go under various names in different states, so check with your local Department of Consumer Affairs. Make sure to keep all dry cleaning receipts and other relevant information to substantiate your complaint.

When to use small claims court

Suing in small claims court can bring both spiritual and material satisfaction when you feel that you have been wronged. Although the monetary stakes are low—most states limit small claims settlements to no more than $1,000—the rewards can be high.

Take a case to small claims court when you:

☐ Have the time. Usually it takes a month for a case to be called and you'll have to spend at least a few hours in court during the hearing.

☐ Value justice over a monetary settlement.

☐ Want a public hearing of your grievance.

☐ Feel the money involved represents a significant sum to you.

Social Security number secret

Few people know it, but the first three digits of a Social Security number are a code for the state in which the card was issued. This code, which can be used to confirm a place of birth or an employment history, is not public knowledge. However, many private detectives have the key to the code and will crack the Social Security number for a fee.

Source: Milo Speriglio, director and chief of Nick Harris Detectives, Inc., Van Nuys, CA, the second-oldest private detective agency in the US, and administrator of Nick Harris' Detective Academy.

Hiring a private detective

Times have changed for private detectives. They're no longer breaking down hotel doors to snap incriminating photos for divorce cases.

The modern private eye's bread and butter lies in serving the business world, in both security and personnel matters.

☐ Consider hiring a private detective to track down runaway children. A missing persons bureau may have to worry about 30 cases at a time; a private eye can focus and coordinate the leads for a single client, giving the matter undivided attention. Be cautious, however. If the detective can't find a hard lead within three days but is eager to continue, he may be "milking" you.

☐ Use a detective to devise a home security plan that will satisfy any insurance company, including itemized lists, photographs, locks and alarms. This should take three hours.

☐ Before hiring a detective, get a resume. After reviewing it, interview the person for at least 20 minutes to discuss your needs and how they'll be met.

☐ Be sure the detective is licensed and bonded. A bond larger than the minimum bond might be advisable for a broad investigation covering several states or even a foreign country.

☐ To make certain the private eye's record is clean, check with the appropriate state division on licensing (usually the Department of State). Ask the detective for the names of previous clients. Check with them. The best gauge is frequently word of mouth—reputations are hard won in the private-eye business.

Source: James Casey, private investigator and former New York City police detective, East Northport, NY.